AN INTRODUCTION TO FINANCIAL ACCOUNTING

2nd Edition

Margaret D'Arcy

CHARTERED
ACCOUNTANTS
IRELAND

Published in 2019 by
Chartered Accountants Ireland
Chartered Accountants House
47–49 Pearse Street
Dublin 2
www.charteredaccountants.ie

ISBN: 978-1-912350-28-5

Typeset by Datapage
Printed by Grafo S.A.

Contents

PART II   SOLE TRADERS

PART III   SPECIALISED FINANCIAL STATEMENTS

PART IV   PARTNERSHIPS

Acknowledgements

This book would not have been possible without the help and support of a number of people. Michael Diviney, Director of Publishing at Chartered Accountants Ireland, for giving me the opportunity and for trusting me to write this book; and Becky McIndoe and Liam Boyle who patiently guided me through the process of writing and updating the text. I would also like to thank my colleague Ruth Hamilton who readily took my calls when I needed a second opinion or advice.

Finally, thank you to all those who have provided their valued and much appreciated feedback.

1

Financial Accounting: Key Terms and Concepts

LEARNING OBJECTIVES

Having studied this chapter, readers should be able to identify/understand:
1. the main financial statements and outline the information they provide;
2. the elements of financial statements;
3. the users of financial statements and explain their information requirements; and
4. the accounting equation.

1.1 INTRODUCTION

The purpose of this textbook is to provide the reader with an ability to record financial transactions and prepare financial statements using both fundamental accounting concepts and the specific accounting rules as set out in generally accepted accounting standards, and in accordance with company law (this will be dealt with in more detail in **Chapter 18, The Regulatory and Conceptual Frameworks for Financial Reporting**).

One of the most fundamental accounting concepts is **double-entry bookkeeping**, which recognises the fact that every financial transaction has a two-fold effect upon each 'entity' involved in that transaction.

Financial information is recorded in the accounting records to provide information to assist in the day-to-day management of organisations and the preparation of financial statements for entities. Financial statements are prepared periodically and show an entity's profitability for a period of time and its financial position at a particular point in time.

This textbook is divided into a number of parts:
- Part I explains how to record financial transactions using double-entry bookkeeping. The accounting treatment for the most common items any entity has to deal with, such as accruing for expenses and dealing with bad debts, is explained in this part.
- Part II deals with the preparation of financial statements for sole traders.
- Part III demonstrates the preparation of financial statements for clubs and societies.
- Part IV explains how to account for partnerships, dealing with the sharing of profits and changes in ownership of the partnership.
- Part V sets out the format of financial statements for a company and deals with a number of accounting standards. Accounting standards detail the rules in relation to a number of specific issues, such as current tax and leases. The regulatory framework is made up of company law, accounting frameworks and the regulations of relevant stock exchanges. The accounting frameworks that can

be applied to the preparation and presentation of financial statements in Ireland and the UK are international accounting standards (by which is meant those standards issued by the International Accounting Standards Board (IASB), and includes International Financial Reporting Standards (IFRSs) and International Accounting Standards (IASs)); or UK and Irish GAAP, i.e. FRS 100–105 (issued by the Financial Reporting Council (FRC)). The financial reporting frameworks are dealt with in **Chapter 18**.

- Part VI, Interpretation of Financial Statements, sets out the ratios to use to assess the financial performance, liquidity, level of debt and return on capital employed of an entity.

Section 1.2 introduces some of the key terms and concepts underlying financial accounting, and the recording of individual financial transactions.

1.2 RECORDING FINANCIAL TRANSACTIONS

Entities

Throughout this text reference is made to '**entities**', a term used to refer to a variety of organisations that prepare financial statements. 'Entities' include sole traders, partnerships, companies, not-for-profit organisations and government organisations. All of these different types of entities have been established for different purposes and they all need to be managed efficiently and effectively; to do this, those entrusted with running the entity must understand both its financial performance and its financial position.

Financial Transactions

The financial statements reflect the underlying **financial transactions** that have occurred. A 'financial transaction' (referred to below simply as a 'transaction') is any event that impacts the profitability and/or the financial position of an entity. Examples of financial transactions that affect profitability include: the sale of goods and the purchase of goods for resale. Examples of transactions that affect the financial position of an entity include: the purchase of production machinery; the repayment of a loan; and the additional investment of funds by the owner(s) into the business.

Transactions are recorded in the accounting records of an entity from documents giving details of the financial transactions, including the amounts involved. The most common documents are invoices and credit notes. **Invoices** are issued by the entity to its customers for sales made; invoices are also received by an entity from its suppliers providing details of goods purchased or services consumed. (The term '**suppliers**' is often used to describe providers of goods or services.) The information provided by an invoice includes:
- a brief description of the goods or services provided;
- the quantity of goods provided;
- the unit price of goods or unit price of a service, for example, cost of kilowatt hour of electricity;
- the date of the transaction;
- the VAT rate applicable to the transaction;
- the trade name and address of the provider of the goods or services;
- the methods of payment, for example, a credit transfer slip to facilitate payment by the customer direct to the seller's bank account; and
- if payment is to be made by direct debit or standing order, the date the customer's bank account will be debited by the amount of the invoice.

A **credit note** is issued by the seller of goods when the goods are returned by the customer or the amount for which a customer has been invoiced needs to be reduced. A credit note may be required if, for example, the seller and the purchaser had agreed a particular price for the goods but the invoice was issued for a higher amount. The impact of a credit note upon the seller's accounting records and the purchaser's accounting records is as follows:
- when the selling entity issues a credit note to its customer it means that the amount owed by the customer to the entity is reduced by the amount of the credit note; and
- when the purchasing entity receives a credit note from its supplier it means that the amount owed by the entity to its supplier is reduced by the amount of the credit note.

It is important to understand that these source documents are maintained by the business for inspection by internal auditors, external auditors and to help resolve any queries that may arise in relation to individual transactions.

Books of Prime Entry

Every transaction must be recorded in an entity's accounting records, i.e. its **ledger accounts**, but due to the volume of transactions it may not be practicable to enter every transaction individually (ledger accounts are explained in detail in **Chapter 2, Recording Financial Transactions and Preparing Financial Statements**). Instead, use is made of the '**books of prime entry**' to record similar types of transactions. The books of prime entry record details of transactions according to their type, e.g. sales, purchases, sales returns and purchases returns. While the individual transactions recorded in the books of prime entry are **not** part of the double-entry system, the entries in the books of prime entry as totalled periodically and '**posted**' to the financial records are part of the double-entry system. ('Posted' means that a figure is recorded in the ledger accounts.)

The books of prime entry include:
- the sales day book (SDB) – used to record each credit sale transaction;
- the purchases day book (PDB) – used to record each credit purchase transaction;
- the sales return day book (SRDB) – used to record each sales return transaction made by a customer;
- the purchases return day book (PRDB) – used to record each purchases return transaction made by the entity to a supplier; and
- the cash book (CB) – used to record each cash receipt and cash payment made by the entity.

(Books of prime entry are dealt with in more detail in **Chapter 9, Control Accounts**.)

Ledger Accounts

The '**general ledger**' (also known as the 'nominal ledger') contains all the 'ledger accounts', which are the accounting records that **are** part of the double-entry bookkeeping system. While the details of the transactions are in the books of prime entry, the ledger accounts of the general ledger summarise and classify these transactions. As mentioned above, the totals of the books of prime entry are periodically recorded in, or posted to, the general ledger accounts.

Controls

Two examples of ledger accounts, as contained in the general ledger, are the:
- **trade receivables** (what is owed by customers) control account; and
- **trade payables** (what is owed to suppliers) control account.

When an entity is preparing its financial statements it needs to know the **total** amount due from its customers and the **total** amount owed to its suppliers – the balances on the **control accounts** provide this information.

Of course, in order to operate a business efficiently its managers need more information than just the balances provided by such control accounts; they need to know to whom the entity owes money and who owes money to it. The details of each transaction relating to individual customers and suppliers are recorded in a business's receivables and payables management systems. These accounts are monitored to ensure that customers pay on time and suppliers are paid promptly.

Another element of 'control' comes in when ensuring that the total amounts owed to and owed by the business as per its control accounts **equal** the totals as per its receivables and payables management systems (see **Chapter 9, Control Accounts**).

Information recorded in the financial records is needed to prepare the financial statements and to control the business. Information presented in the financial statements must be accurate and verifiable – accounting systems will include controls to ensure that this is achieved.

Some of the control systems within the accounting system include:
- Comparing and, if necessary, 'reconciling' the total of the trade receivables ledger listing of balances (part of the receivables management system and **not** part of the double-entry system) and the trade receivables control account balance (part of the double-entry system). **Reconciliation** is the process of examining the financial records to find the reasons for the differences, in this case to explain the difference between the total of the trade receivables ledger listing of balances and the trade receivables control account balance. As stated above, only the totals from the books of prime entry are posted to the financial records but the entity will have information in its receivables management system in relation to each customer to ensure that appropriate credit collection procedures are in place to ensure prompt collection of amounts due. By comparing the total of the trade receivables ledger listing of balances and the balance on the trade receivables control account, the business can have some confidence that all the relevant transactions have been properly recorded.
- Similarly, comparing and, if necessary, reconciling the total of the trade payables ledger listing of balances (part of the payables management system and **not** part of the double-entry system) and the trade payables control account (part of the double-entry system). Again, only the totals from the books of prime entry are posted to the financial records but the entity will have information in its payables management system in relation to each supplier to ensure that payments are made on time and discounts availed of whenever it is desirable to do so. By comparing the total payables ledger listing of balances and the balance on the trade payables control account, the entity can have some confidence that all the relevant transactions have been properly recorded.
- Reconciling the bank account balance per the entity's records and the bank account balance per the bank statement provided by the bank. There may be entries on the bank statement that the entity is not aware of, e.g. interest charges, bank fees, direct debits and standing orders processed by the bank (see **Chapter 10, Bank Reconciliations**).
- Stock-counting to verify the amount and value of stock on hand at a particular date. Stock (or **inventory**) includes (but is not limited to) goods purchased for resale and goods manufactured and available for sale. The value based on the physical stock count is compared with the stock records maintained by the entity and any differences are investigated.

Having seen how the financial transactions of an entity are recorded and summarised, the next section introduces how this information is reported in an entity's financial statements, specifically in relation to its profitability, financial position and cash position.

1.3 FINANCIAL STATEMENTS

The Statement of Profit or Loss

The financial performance of an entity indicates whether it has made a profit or a loss for a particular period of time. The profit or loss is presented in a financial statement known as the '**statement of profit or loss**' (**SOPL**) (also known as the statement of trading, profit or loss).

A SOPL is prepared for a particular period of time, which is referred to as the '**reporting period**'. The reporting period should be clearly identified in the title of this financial statement. **Figure 1.1** below sets out an example of how to title a SOPL.

FIGURE 1.1: HOW TO TITLE A STATEMENT OF PROFIT OR LOSS

Swag Ltd

STATEMENT OF PROFIT OR LOSS

for the year ended 31 December 2019

'Swag Ltd' is the name of the entity for which the financial statement is prepared. 'Ltd' (an abbreviation of the word 'limited') indicates that the entity is a company whose owners have limited liability for the company's obligations. (Limited liability is explained in more detail in **Section 1.4**.)

The second line of this heading identifies the financial statement as the 'statement of profit or loss'.

The period of time to which the information contained in this example relates is the year ended 31 December 2019. This means the income earned and expenses incurred between 1 January 2019 and 31 December 2019 have been included in the SOPL to determine the profit or loss for the period.

The '**reporting date**' is the last day of the reporting period, in this case, 31 December 2019.

The profit or loss is calculated by deducting the expenses incurred for the period from the income earned for that same period as shown in **Figure 1.2**.

FIGURE 1.2: PROFIT/LOSS CALCULATION

PROFIT (OR LOSS) = INCOME EARNED – EXPENSES INCURRED

The terms '**income**', 'income accounts', '**expense**' and 'expense accounts' are explained below.

Income Accounts

Income earned by an entity is recorded in its income accounts. Typically income includes such items as:

- **revenue** – amounts invoiced by a business for goods or services that it has provided to its customers, e.g. sales of goods by a supermarket, and fee income of a firm of accountants;
- **gains** arise when assets appreciate in value or where an asset is sold for an amount greater than the amount at which it was presented in the statement of financial position, e.g. an investment sold for a higher amount than that for which it was originally purchased;
- interest income, e.g. interest earned from placing funds on deposit with a financial institution, such as a bank;
- investment income, e.g. rental income earned from renting a building; and
- other income, e.g. a settlement **discount received** from a supplier by the entity for paying the amount outstanding within a particular period of time. A discount received from a supplier means that the amount the entity has to pay is less than the amount at which the transaction was originally recorded.

'**Income earned**' means that the amount of income presented in the SOPL relates to a particular reporting period, irrespective of when the income is received. The income earned includes:
- amounts invoiced to customers for goods or services provided during the reporting period for which payment has been received in full from the customer;
- amounts invoiced to customers for goods or services provided during the reporting period for which payment has not been received from the customer by the reporting date;
- income earned during the reporting period for which an invoice has not been issued to the customer by the reporting date; and
- income received in an earlier reporting period but earned in the current period.

Expense Accounts

The expenses incurred by an entity are recorded in expense accounts. Typically expenses include a wide range of costs, such as:
- purchases of goods for resale or for use in production;
- cost of salaries and wages;
- motor expenses related to delivery of goods to customers;
- electricity and heating costs;
- insurance;
- interest on loans (also known as finance cost); and
- discounts allowed, e.g. a settlement discount where an entity allows a discount to those customers paying within a certain credit period. A **discount allowed** to a customer means that the amount the entity will receive is less than the amount at which the transaction is originally recorded.

It is very important to note that 'expenses incurred' is not the same as 'actual payments made to suppliers of goods and services' during the period and 'income earned' is not the same as 'cash received'. The SOPL is prepared on an '**accrual basis**'. This means that when the profit or loss for a certain period of time is calculated, the calculation is based on expenses incurred and income earned.

'**Expenses incurred**' means that costs related to a particular reporting period are included in the calculation of profit, irrespective of when the payment is made. Expenses incurred include:

- costs of goods or services consumed during the reporting period for which an invoice has been received and the provider of the goods/services was paid in full during the reporting period;
- costs of goods or services consumed during the reporting period for which an invoice has been received but the supplier has not been paid by the reporting date;
- costs of goods or services consumed during the reporting period but for which an invoice has not been received from the supplier by the reporting date; and
- expenses paid in an earlier reporting period but incurred in the current period.

Example 1.1 illustrates the impact of the accrual concept.

EXAMPLE 1.1: CALCULATION OF PROFIT BASED ON THE ACCRUAL CONCEPT

An entity is trying to find out if it made a profit or loss for a given period. The following information has been provided:

	€
Sales invoiced to customers	240,000
Cash received from customers	234,000
Goods and services used during the period	180,000
Payments made for these goods and services	132,000

Profit calculated on an accrual basis = Income earned − Expenses incurred
$$= €240,000 - €180,000$$
$$= €60,000$$

The profit figure reported in the financial statements would be €60,000 and not €102,000 [€234,000 – €132,000] as would be calculated on a cash basis. The €102,000 represents the net receipts for the period and not the profit.

The Statement of Financial Position

The financial position of an entity is set out in the **statement of financial position (SOFP)** (also known as the **balance sheet**). The SOFP is a list of ledger account balances presented in a particular format and order (this is explained in more detail in **Chapter 2**). Formats of the SOPL and the SOFP vary depending on the type of entity – the specific formats of these financial statements will be dealt with in the respective parts and chapters of this textbook dealing with each type of entity.

The SOFP is prepared at a particular date, called the 'reporting date', which is the last day of the reporting period. The reporting date is clearly identified in the heading to this financial statement. **Figure 1.3** below sets out an example of how to title a SOFP.

FIGURE 1.3: HOW TO TITLE A STATEMENT OF FINANCIAL POSITION

Swag Plc
STATEMENT OF FINANCIAL POSITION
as at 31 December 2019

'Swag Plc' is the name of the entity for which the financial statement is prepared. 'Plc' is the abbreviation of the words 'public limited company' and indicates that the entity is a publicly quoted company.

The second line of this heading identifies the financial statement as the 'statement of financial position'.

The financial statement relates to a particular date, in this case 31 December 2019. The date at which the SOFP is prepared is known as the reporting date.

The SOFP provides information in relation to the following:
• amounts owed to the entity by its customers;
• amounts owed by the entity to suppliers and lenders;
• investment of funds in the entity made by the owners of the entity known as '**capital**'; and
• property used by the entity to run the business, e.g. buildings and motor vehicles.

Information in the SOFP is presented within the following categories:
• assets,
• liabilities, and
• capital/equity.

These categories are dealt with in more detail below in **Section 1.5**.

The Statement of Cash Flows

In addition to the financial statements discussed above, a **statement of cash flows** (**SOCF**) is also prepared. The SOCF identifies the cash received and paid by an entity during a reporting period. The information provided in this financial statement is very important as it allows users of the statement to understand where and how cash is being generated and spent by the entity. It presents the cash received and paid during the reporting period (net cash inflows/outflows) in relation to three specific areas of activity: **operating activities**, **investing activities** and **financing activities**.
• Operating activities – cash utilised for and generated from the day-to-day business operations. (The operating activities section of the SOCF shows whether the entity has collected sufficient cash from its customers to cover the cash paid for the expenses it incurred to run the business.)
• Investing activities – cash utilised or generated from buying and selling items of property, plant and equipment, and for investments made or proceeds from the sale of investments.
• Financing activities – cash utilised to repay loans, or generated by issuing shares or taking out new loans.

Figure 1.4 sets out an example of how to title a SOCF.

FIGURE I.4: HOW TO TITLE A STATEMENT OF CASH FLOWS

Swag Plc

STATEMENT OF CASH FLOWS
for the year ended 31 December 2019

'Swag Plc' is the name of the entity for which the financial statement is prepared. 'Plc' is the abbreviation of the words 'public limited company' and indicates that the entity is a publicly quoted company.

The second line of this heading identifies the financial statement as the 'statement of cash flows' (SOCF).

The period of time to which the information contained in this financial statement relates is the year ended 31 December 2019. This means the cash received and expenses paid between 1 January 2019 and 31 December 2019 have been included in the SOCF for the period.

1.4 ENTITIES

An entity, as mentioned in **Section 1.2**, is any organisation that records financial transactions. The '**business entity concept**' is an underlying assumption of accounting. It means that, for accounting purposes, the business is separate and distinct from its owners, for example, if Mr Ryan, a sole trader, bought a car for his son, the vehicle is not an asset of his business and would not be included in the accounting records of his business. This concept applies to all entities regardless of their form (sole trader, partnership or company) – only transactions relating to the entity should be recorded in that entity's accounting records.

A company, unlike a sole trader and a partnership, has a separate legal identity from its owners; this means that the company has many of the same rights in law as a person, e.g. a company can own property and enter into contracts. A company can therefore enter into contracts in the company's name and it can sue others and be sued. As a result of being a separate legal entity, the owners of a limited company are not liable for its debts.

Entities may be classified according to their primary activity: manufacturers, retailers, service providers, not-for-profits (e.g. charities), etc.

Another way in which entities can be classified is according to the structure of their ownership, for example sole traders, partnership, companies, etc. The features of each of these business entity types will be dealt with in turn.

Sole trader – a business owned by a single individual and operated to generate a profit. The business is run by the owner. The owner is liable for the debts of the business.

Partnership – a business owned by a number of people and operated to generate a profit. Many accounting firms and firms of solicitors are partnerships. Partners may choose to be involved in the day-to-day operations of the business (known as active partners) or just invest in the business (known as silent partners).

A partnership may have a partnership agreement in place that sets out rules in relation to the individual partners' roles and responsibilities. It may also set out other details, e.g. in relation to the amount to be invested in the entity by each partner (i.e. each partner's capital contribution), partners' salaries and the interest rate to be paid on capital balances. In the absence of a partnership agreement the provisions of the Partnership Act 1890 will apply. Partners are liable for the debts of the partnership. Partnerships are dealt with in more detail in **Chapters 15, 16** and **17**.

Company – a business set up to generate a profit may be set up with **limited liability** or a not-for-profit company may be limited by guarantee. When a company is set up it is said to have been '**incorporated**'. As part of the incorporation process the company must prepare and file certain documents with the relevant state authority.

As a result of the benefit to its owners of limited liability there are many requirements on limited liability companies to file documents with the relevant state authority. As the owners of a company with limited liability can avoid having to make good on any liabilities of the business it is important to ensure that those dealing with the company have access to more information than that available about other entities that do not have limited liability; this information enables them to evaluate their decisions regarding trading with the company. These documents are available for public inspection. Legislation sets out filing requirements for companies, which vary according to the size of the entity.

1.5 ELEMENTS OF FINANCIAL STATEMENTS

Each type of financial statement presents different financial information in a particular format. There are different formats required for different sized companies and other types of entity; these requirements will be dealt with in later chapters when dealing with specific types of entity. Irrespective of the type of entity, they all have to present information relating to each of the '**elements of financial statements**', which are: income, expenses, assets, liabilities and capital. As presented in **Figure 1.5** below, income and expenses are presented in the SOPL assets, liabilities and capital are presented in the SOFP.

FIGURE 1.5: ELEMENTS OF THE SOPL AND THE SOFP

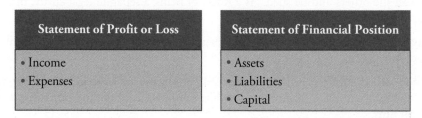

Statement of Profit or Loss	Statement of Financial Position
• Income • Expenses	• Assets • Liabilities • Capital

With regard to the SOCF, the third type of financial statement introduced above, this explains the changes (increases/decreases) in the elements presented in the SOFP from the previous reporting date to the latest reporting date. In other words, changes in the three elements presented in the SOFP that occur during the reporting period are presented in the SOCF. The figures presented in the SOCF are either cash inflows or cash outflows. For example, if an entity purchased a motor vehicle during the reporting period and paid cash for the asset, the payment made would be presented as a cash outflow in the SOCF. The SOCF will be explained in more detail in **Chapter 20, Statement of Cash Flows**.

Income and expenses have already been discussed in **Section 1.3**. The other elements of financial statements – assets, liabilities and capital – are explained below.

Assets are resources used in the entity to generate economic benefits for the entity, for example:
- buildings in which administrative tasks are carried out;
- factory buildings used for producing goods;
- motor vehicles used by sales staff and for the delivery of goods to customers;
- inventory (also known as stock) on hand at the reporting date. Inventory can include: goods purchased for resale, e.g. in the case of a supermarket, all its inventory would be goods purchased for resale; raw materials to be used in a manufacturer's production process; work in progress, i.e. raw materials in the process of being converted into finished goods by a manufacturer; and consumables, i.e. items used in the ordinary course operating the business, such as printer cartridges and other stationery items;
- amounts due from customers to whom goods were sold on credit (known as '**trade receivables**');
- investments;
- cash on hand; and
- bank balances.

Liabilities are amounts owed by the entity at the reporting date, the settlement of which is expected to result in an outflow of economic resources from the entity. Liabilities include:
- bank loans;
- amounts due to suppliers in relation to goods bought on credit with the intention of resale (known as '**trade payables**'); and
- overdrawn bank balances.

Capital represents the owner's(s') residual interest in the assets of an entity after deducting all the entity's liabilities – it is the net investment contributed by the owner(s) of the business; it is also referred to as '**equity**'. The capital invested is increased by profits made by the entity or, conversely, reduced by losses made. The way in which capital can be taken out of a business is dependent on the business's legal status.
- The business of a sole trader or partnership has no legal identity separate from its owners so a sole trader or partner can remove cash or other assets from the business and the amounts withdrawn are known as '**drawings**'.
- A company's identity is legally separate from those of its owners so a company can make distributions to its owners. These distributions are known as '**dividends**'.

1.6 THE ACCOUNTING EQUATION

The elements of financial statements have been explained above; now these elements will be used in the accounting equation to illustrate the basis of recording financial transactions. Before presenting the accounting equation, however, the basis of recording financial transactions must be understood. This basis could be summarised by stating that there are two sides to each transaction. To understand this two-sided impact a number of examples will be considered and their impact on the elements of financial statements identified.

Transaction 1 A business is set up with an investment by the owner of €20,000 in cash.

The dual effect of this transaction is to increase the capital of the business and to increase the cash (an asset) available to the business. Thus, this transaction affects two of the elements presented in the SOFP – assets and capital. After this transaction is recorded in the financial records of the business, the impact can be summarised as:

TABLE 1: IMPACT OF TRANSACTION 1 ON THE ELEMENTS OF THE SOFP

Assets	Liabilities	Capital
Cash €20,000	Nil	Capital investment by owner €20,000

Transaction 2 The owner of the business subsequently buys a van to use in making deliveries to its customers. The van costs €10,000 and it is paid for by taking out a loan from a local bank. The effect of this transaction is to increase the assets of the business (specifically the asset named 'delivery vehicle') and increase the liabilities of the business (specifically the liability named 'bank loan'). After this transaction is recorded in the financial records of the business, the **cumulative** effect of the transactions to date can be summarised as:

TABLE 2: IMPACT OF TRANSACTION 2 ON THE ELEMENTS OF THE SOFP

Assets	Liabilities	Capital
Cash + Delivery van €30,000	Loan €10,000	Capital investment by owner €20,000

From the above tables it can be seen that each of the transactions affected **two** of the following: assets, liabilities and capital. As each transaction has a dual effect, this means that the SOFP will only balance if both sides of the transactions are recorded.

In **Table 1** only one transaction has occurred and it has impacted both the assets and the capital of the entity. In **Table 2** the assets and liabilities of the business have both increased as a result of the second transaction.

In both **Table 1** and **Table 2** the total of the assets minus the value of liabilities equals the value of the capital of the business; this will **always** apply when both sides of the transaction are recorded correctly and is known as the **accounting equation**, which is presented in **Figure 1.6** below.

FIGURE 1.6: THE ACCOUNTING EQUATION

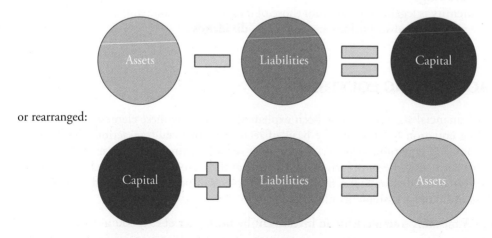

or rearranged:

Example 1.2 below shows how to use the accounting equation to determine the value of a missing element of a SOFP.

EXAMPLE 1.2: CALCULATE THE VALUE OF CAPITAL USING THE ACCOUNTING EQUATION

Assets	–	Liabilities	=	Capital
€200,000		€105,000		?

What is the value of capital in this entity?

Solution

Assets	–	Liabilities	=	Capital
€200,000		€105,000		€95,000

To balance the accounting equation, the value of capital must be €95,000 (assets of €200,000 minus liabilities of €105,000).

In **Section 1.5** attention was drawn to the link between the profit or loss (calculated in the SOPL) and the capital balance of an entity (reported in the SOFP): "The capital invested is increased by profits made by the entity or, conversely, reduced by losses made." (See **Chapter 2**, **Example 2.24**.) **Example 1.3** below demonstrates the impact of profit on the SOFP.

EXAMPLE 1.3: IMPACT OF PROFIT EARNED ON THE STATEMENT OF FINANCIAL POSITION

A business was set up on 1 January 2019 with an investment by the owner of €30,000 cash lodged to the business's bank account. On 1 January the summary of the SOFP information would be:

For the year ended 31 December 2019 the business had bought goods worth €18,000 and paid for them in full by issuing a cheque. All of the goods purchased were sold for €34,000 on a cash basis. The sales proceeds were lodged to the bank account. The net effect on the assets of the entity of these purchases and sales is to increase cash by €16,000, i.e. increased by €34,000 cash received and reduced by €18,000 paid for purchases.

As shown in **Figure 1.2**, profit is calculated in the SOPL. Owners of an entity take a risk by investing in a business; profit is the reward they earn by making that investment and losses are the downside of that investment. The profit earned is attributable to the owners of the entity and thereby increases the capital attributable to them. Based on the equation in **Figure 1.2** the profit earned for the reporting period ended 31 December 2019 was €16,000, as shown below:

Profit = Income earned − Expenses incurred
€16,000 = €34,000 − €18,000

The effect of the sales and purchase transactions during the reporting period is to increase the assets and increase the capital of the business.

Figure 1.7 below sets out how the amount of capital attributed to an entity can change from one reporting period to another and thus how to calculate the capital at the end of a reporting period.

FIGURE 1.7: CALCULATION OF CAPITAL AT THE END OF THE REPORTING PERIOD

'Profit made during the period' can be replaced with 'the difference between the income earned and expenses incurred during the reporting period'. The profit or loss earned in the reporting period has an impact on the capital figure presented in the SOFP.

Using **Figure 1.7** to calculate the capital balance as at 31 December 2019:

The elements of the SOFP as at 31 December 2019 will reflect the profit earned during the period. On 31 December the summary of the SOFP information would be as follows:

Example 1.4 demonstrates the calculation of the capital balance at the end of the reporting period (at the reporting date), i.e. the closing capital balance.

Example 1.4: Calculation of Capital at the Reporting Date

In the SOFP as at 31 December 2018 of J Smith, a sole trader, the capital amounted to €43,000. During the year the following transactions occurred:

Transaction Description	Amount Involved
Profit reported in SOPL for year ended 31 December 2019	€28,500
Drawings by owner (see **Section 1.5**)	€6,500

Requirement Using the equation from **Figure 1.7**, calculate the capital as at 31 December 2019.

Solution

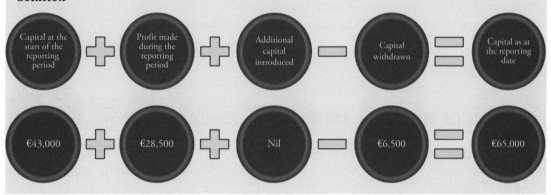

As we have seen, the capital attributable to the owners of an entity is affected by the profit earned/loss made during the reporting period. Profit earned increases the capital of the owners, while a loss made will reduce the capital. Other items that affect the capital attributable to owners include:

- the investment of additional funds by the owners – this will increase the capital available;
- drawings made by owners of certain types of entities, that is, sole traders and partnerships. Drawings are the withdrawal of cash, goods or other assets by the owners from the business for their own personal use. Drawings will reduce the capital available; and
- owners of companies are known as **shareholders**. Shareholders cannot make drawings from a company. A company may make dividend payments to shareholders and these payments will reduce the capital available to a company. These movements in the equity of a company are presented in a financial statement known as the **statement of changes in equity** and will be discussed further in **Chapter 19, Presentation of Financial Statements**.

Capital is presented differently in the ledger accounts and financial statements of different entities; the presentation depends on the type of entity, as follows.

- Sole trader – a single figure is presented in the SOFP in relation to capital. The capital figure in a sole trader represents the funds invested by the owner plus the profit retained by the business. Profit retained is the amount of profit made in the reporting period less any drawings made by the owner.
- Partnership – the capital attributable to each partner is identified. The capital balance of each partner is the funds invested by them individually plus their share of profit made less any drawings made. Partnerships make use of two accounts to record amounts due to and from each partner. These accounts are known as capital accounts and current accounts. The uses of these accounts will be explained in **Chapters 15–17**.
- Company – the capital invested by the owners is referred to as **ordinary share capital**. The ordinary share capital is recorded in the SOFP at its **nominal value**. The market price of a share (that is, the price the share can be purchased for on a stock exchange market) may be higher than the nominal value; when shares are issued at a price above their nominal value (explained in further detail in **Chapter 19**) the excess is **recognised** in the **share premium account**. The profit retained by the company is presented as a separate item, known as '**retained earnings**', in the SOFP. Retained earnings represent the accumulated profits made by the entity net of the amount of dividends paid. Capital of a company consists of ordinary share capital, retained earnings and other reserves (other reserves will be dealt with in later chapters).

The key point to remember is that profit/loss impacts the capital balance of the entity, which is presented in the SOFP.

1.7 USERS OF FINANCIAL STATEMENTS

Financial statements are prepared to provide information to a number of different parties. The users of published financial statements prepared by companies are shareholders/investors (existing and potential), lenders, customers, suppliers, competitors, government bodies and the general public. In this section, each of these groups will be dealt with in turn and their information needs explained.

Shareholders

'Shareholders' is the term used to describe those who own shares in companies – they are also referred to as 'investors'. Shareholders purchase shares to make a return on their investment – by receiving dividend income or by selling their shares at a profit at a later date.

Shareholders will make an investment in a company if it is likely to generate profits, thereby increasing the value of the company and enabling it to pay dividends. The shareholders will look at the SOPL to see how the company is performing and use that information to help them assess the company's future performance.

Potential investors will also look at past profitability and the strength of the company's financial position to help them make their investment decision. To assess the strength of the financial position the investor, or potential investor, will look at how the company is financed (through investments by owners or debt finance, which is financing provided by lenders) and how additional funds have been invested, i.e. utilised by the entity.

Lenders

Lenders are those who provide finance to entities, usually banks and other financial institutions. Lenders provide loans in order to earn interest income. Lenders will look at an entity's financial statements to assess whether the entity can make its interest and loan repayments as they fall due. Information provided in the SOPL helps lenders assess an entity's ability to generate a profit and the SOCF provides information about an entity's ability to generate cash.

If the lender has concerns about the entity's ability to repay the debt, it will look at the SOFP to assess the quality of the assets owned that could be sold to repay the debt and how much debt the entity already has.

Customers

Customers who purchase an entity's goods or services want to ensure that they have a reliable future supply. As users of the entity's financial statements for this purpose, they will interpret past profits as an indication of the future continuity of the business. Customers will be more interested in an entity's future where the goods/services it supplies have limited availability or there is a very restricted supply of raw materials.

Suppliers

It is normal business practice for suppliers to provide goods/services 'on credit', which means that payment is not made at the time the goods are delivered or the services provided but at a later date. Suppliers will be interested to see that their customer is doing well and will continue in business and that they will therefore be likely to receive payment.

Competitors

Other entities operating the same type of business are interested to see how their competitors are performing: whether the competitor's sales levels and profit margins are increasing or decreasing, competitors' levels of debt, and changes in competitors' investment in assets, such as machinery and property.

Government Bodies

Government bodies, such as the taxation revenue authorities, are interested in how an entity is performing – the greater the profit, the greater the government's tax revenue. Other government bodies will be interested in the entity to ensure that it is acting in compliance with legislation. Different industries will be subject to different types of regulation, and specific regulations may be set out in legislation to establish compliance areas for entities operating in these industries, e.g. banks will have to maintain certain liquidity ratios to ensure that sufficient funds are available to repay customers of the bank. Government agencies will be interested to ensure that entities comply with all relevant legislative requirements.

General Public

The general public may be interested in how an entity is performing, particularly if there is a link between the entity's performance and the well-being of the local community. An improved performance by the entity usually means more business for local businesses and employment for the local community in the form of community initiatives, such as providing support to local schools and charities. Some entities may attract more public attention due to consumer or environmental issues.

1.8 CONCLUSION

In this chapter, some of the most frequently used terminology and the basic concepts of financial accounting have been introduced and explained. In **Part I** these concepts will be developed to show how transactions are recorded using double-entry bookkeeping. In **Chapter 2**, the stages of the accounting cycle will be demonstrated, i.e. the step-by-step process from undertaking and recording transactions to the preparation of financial statements.

SUMMARY OF LEARNING OBJECTIVES

Learning Objective 1 Identify/understand the main financial statements and outline the information they provide.

The main financial statements and the information each provides are set out below.

Financial Statement	Information provided
Statement of Profit or Loss	Financial performance of the entity. Details of the profit earned or loss incurred in the reporting period by comparing the income earned and the expenses incurred. *Note:* prepared on the accrual basis.
Statement of Financial Position	Financial position of the entity. Provides the following information in relation to the entity at a particular date, known as the reporting date: • assets, • liabilities, and • capital. *Note:* prepared on the accrual basis.
Statement of Cash Flows	Details the cash receipts and payments during the reporting period classified according to the type of activity: • operating, • investing, and • financing. *Note:* prepared on the cash basis.

Learning Objective 2 Identify/understand the elements of financial statements.

The elements of the financial statements are as follows.

- 'Income' is the term used to refer to revenue, gains and other income. Revenue arises from the sale of goods and/or the provision of services. Gains arise when assets appreciate in value or where an asset is sold for an amount greater than the amount at which it was presented in the SOFP. Other income includes such items as interest income earned on investments.
- 'Expenses' refers to costs incurred by an entity to run the organisation. Examples include wages, cost of goods purchased for resale, electricity costs, etc.
- 'Assets' are resources used by the entity to generate future economic benefit. Assets can be cash or resources that enable the entity to generate future profits.
- 'Liabilities' are amounts owed by the entity to suppliers and providers of finance other than the owners.
- 'Capital' is the investment made by owner(s) of the entity.

Learning Objective 3 Identify/understand the users of financial statements and explain their information requirements.

The users of financial statements together with their information requirements:

- shareholders, existing and potential – profitability of the business and its ability to generate future profits;
- employees – the company's past performance as an indication of its future performance and therefore of job security;
- lenders – ability of the entity to repay its debts as they fall due or the value of any assets that can be sold to pay the amounts due;
- customers – continuation of the supply of goods in the future;
- suppliers – the company's profitability and therefore its probable continued demand for products;
- government bodies – compliance with tax and other legal requirements; and
- general public – impact of the company's operations on the local economy and environment.

Learning Objective 4 Identify/understand the accounting equation.

The accounting equation is:

The basis of accounting for transactions is that there are two sides to each transaction.

It is important to remember that the profit earned (or loss incurred) in the reporting period increases (or reduces) the capital and that the capital is presented in the SOFP.

Furthermore, it is important to remember all the constituent elements of the capital balance – this is set out in the following diagram:

Note: a loss made in the reporting period will reduce the capital balance.

QUESTIONS

Review Questions

(See **Appendix A** for Solutions to Review Questions.)

Question 1.1
Solve each of the following equations:

(a)

Assets	–	Liabilities	=	Capital
€150,000		€120,000		

What is the capital balance?

(b)

Assets	–	Liabilities	=	Capital
€80,000				€25,000

What is the value of the liabilities?

(c)

Assets	–	Liabilities	=	Capital
		€90,000		€45,000

What is the value of the assets?

Question 1.2
You are provided with the following information in relation to the activities of a sole trader's business in a recent reporting period.

	€
Capital as at 1 January 2019	45,000
Profit for year ended 31 December 2019	25,600
Drawings made by owner during the year ended 31 December 2019	4,500

Requirement What is the capital attributable to the owner as at 31 December 2019?

Question 1.3
Alan Jones has been trading for a number of years; he has provided you with the following information in relation to his business in a recent reporting period.

	€
Capital as at 1 January 2019	63,000
Profit for year ended 31 December 2019	48,900
Withdrawal of cash by owner during the year ended 31 December 2019	26,500
Withdrawal of goods by the owner during the year ended 31 December 2019	1,200

Requirement What is the capital attributable to the owner as at 31 December 2019?

PART I

DOUBLE-ENTRY BOOKKEEPING

CHAPTERS

Recording Financial Transactions and Preparing Financial Statements

Having studied this chapter, readers should:
1. understand what double-entry bookkeeping is, and know its terminology;
2. know how to prepare the journal entries to recognise (i.e. record) transactions;
3. understand how journal entries impact ledger accounts;
4. know what a trial balance is and how to prepare one; and
5. know how to use a trial balance to prepare a statement of profit or loss (SOPL) and a statement of financial position (SOFP).

2.1 INTRODUCTION

This chapter will explain how to record the most frequently occurring transactions and their impact on the financial statements will be shown. The terms '**financial transaction**' and '**entity**' were explained in **Chapter 1, Financial Accounting: Key Terms and Concepts**.

Figure 2.1 shows how any transaction undertaken by an entity works through the financial accounting system, from being initially recorded to inclusion in the financial statements – this is often referred to as the **accounting cycle**.

FIGURE 2.1: FINANCIAL TRANSACTIONS THROUGH TO FINANCIAL STATEMENTS

Transactions undertaken → Journal entries created to record transactions in financial records → Ledger accounts updated by posting journal entries → Trial balance lists the balances on the ledger accounts of the entity → Financial statements prepared from the trial balance

Double-entry bookkeeping was developed as a means of recording the financial transactions entered into by an entity. The basic concept behind this method is that there are **always** two sides to each transaction. For example, if an entity makes a cash repayment on a car loan, it owes the bank less money on that loan **and** the amount of cash the entity has is reduced by the amount of the loan repayment.

Typically we would use the words 'increase' and 'decrease' to describe the impact of such transactions on the balance of the account. In the above example, the impact of the repayment is to **decrease** the balance on the loan account and **decrease** the amount of cash the entity has on hand. However, this is not the only possible impact – there are three possible effects or impacts of a transaction:

- both sides of the transaction can cause the balance on each account impacted by the transaction to be decreased (as above); or
- both sides of the transaction can cause the balance on each account impacted by the transaction to be increased; or
- one side of the transaction can cause an increase in the account balance of one account and a decrease in the account balance of the other account.

Figure 2.2 below shows an example of each possibility.

FIGURE 2.2: THE IMPACT OF TRANSACTIONS

Transaction Example	Impact	Impact
A business sells goods for cash	Cash is increased	Sales are increased
An entity repays part of a loan by cash	Amount owed on loan is decreased	Cash is decreased
A business buys a motor vehicle for cash	Value of motor vehicles owned is increased	Cash is decreased

Journal Entries

An entity records its transactions for a number of reasons: for internal control of the business; to comply with regulatory requirements; and to provide information to the various users of its financial statements, which are based on the information recorded.

Each transaction is recorded as a **journal entry**. A journal entry is prepared in order to make a note of the transaction that is to be input to the accounting system. When the information noted in the journal entry is input to the accounting system, the journal entry is said to be '**posted**' to the relevant ledger accounts. The format of a journal entry is as follows (where X represents the amount of the transaction):

FIGURE 2.3: FORMAT FOR A JOURNAL ENTRY

	Debit €	Credit €
Account name	X	
Account name		X
Narrative – providing a brief summary of the transaction being recorded.		

The 'account name' is simply the name of the account affected by the debit or credit side of the transaction. (The abbreviation 'dr' is frequently used for debit and the abbreviation 'cr' is frequently used for credit.) In our example above, when a business entity sells goods for cash the transaction impacts both its cash and sales. When the transaction is recorded as a journal entry, the two accounts to which data will be input are referred to as the 'cash account' and the 'sales account' respectively.

It is important to ensure that for each journal entry prepared a brief explanation (or 'narrative') of the transaction is included. This explanation is particularly important if the transaction is being reviewed at a later date. For example, if the journal entry is to record cash sales, the explanation would read: '*To record cash sales.*'

In the examples above, we looked at transactions, identified each transaction's dual effect and its impact – increase or decrease. Now, we are going to take these transactions and deal with them using accounting terminology.

Accountants use their own terminology to explain the effect of financial transactions. Instead of saying 'increase' or 'decrease', they refer to '**debit**' and '**credit**'. An account balance may be increased by either a debit or credit entry to the ledger account – the impact of a debit or credit entry depends on the type of account involved. Taking our above examples, using the terminology of debits and credits and identifying the types of accounts involved, we look at these transactions again. The steps involved are:

1. identify the accounts affected by the transaction;
2. identify the element of the financial statements involved, that is, asset, liability, income, expense or capital (see **Chapter 1**);
3. understand the impact of the transaction on each account identified in step 1 (does the balance on the account increase or decrease as a result of the transaction?); and
4. apply accounting terminology of 'debit' and 'credit'.

Figure 2.4 below uses the previous examples to apply the steps detailed above.

FIGURE 2.4: APPLYING ACCOUNTING TERMINOLOGY TO TRANSACTIONS

Transaction I: A business sells goods for cash

Account Name	Element	Impact	Accounting action
Cash	Asset	Increase	Debit
Sales	Income	Increase	Credit

Transaction II: An entity repays part of a loan by cash

Account Name	Element	Impact	Accounting action
Loan	Liability	Decrease	Debit
Cash	Asset	Decrease	Credit

Transaction III: A business buys a motor vehicle for cash

Account Name	Element	Impact	Accounting action
Motor vehicle	Asset	Increase	Debit
Cash	Asset	Decrease	Credit

You will note from the above figure that assets are **increased** by a 'debit' (the cash received in Transaction I above), but that liabilities are **decreased** by a 'debit' (the loan balance reduced when payment is made in Transaction II above). **Not all account types are affected by debits and credits in the same way**.

As shown in the format of a journal entry in **Figure 2.3** above, transactions are recorded by debiting and crediting accounts. For each transaction, one or more accounts are debited and one or more accounts are credited; the total of the amounts debited always equals the total of the amounts credited. (In this chapter, we will start by considering transactions that only affect two accounts – one account being debited and one account being credited.) **Figure 2.5A** below shows the impact of the debit and credit side of a transaction on each type of account.

FIGURE 2.5A: IMPACT OF DEBITING AND CREDITING EACH TYPE OF ACCOUNT

Element (Type of Account)	Impact of Debiting	Impact of Crediting
Income	Decrease	Increase
Expense	Increase	Decrease
Asset	Increase	Decrease
Liability	Decrease	Increase
Capital (or Equity)	Decrease	Increase

Figure 2.5B shows whether an increase or decrease in an account will be recorded as a debit or a credit, depending on the element or type of account.

FIGURE 2.5B: RECORDING AN INCREASE OR DECREASE IN EACH TYPE OF ACCOUNT

Element (Type of Account)	Increase	Decrease
Income	Credit	Debit
Expense	Debit	Credit
Asset	Debit	Credit
Liability	Credit	Debit
Capital (or Equity)	Credit	Debit

Elements of Financial Statements

The elements of financial statements (see **Chapter 1**) are often referred to as types of accounts. There are only five types of account:
• income;
• expense;
• asset;
• liability; and
• capital (also referred to as equity).

For each account **type**, there is often more than one account in the accounting records. For example, an entity could have a number of:
• income accounts, such as 'revenue' or 'interest income';
• expense accounts, such as 'electricity', 'purchases' or 'wages and salaries';
• asset accounts, such as 'property', 'motor vehicles' or 'equipment';
• liability accounts, such as 'trade payables' or 'loans'; and
• capital accounts, such as 'drawings' or 'capital introduced'.

Ledger Accounts

Ledger accounts are used to record **similar** transactions, for example, a sales account would be set up in the accounting system to record the value of all **sales** transactions for a particular period of time, rather than an account being opened for each sales transaction. The format of a ledger account (a simple form of which is referred to as a 'T' account) is shown in **Figure 2.6**

FIGURE 2.6: FORMAT FOR A LEDGER ACCOUNT

ACCOUNT NAME					
Debit Side of Account			**Credit Side of Account**		
Date	Account Name	€	Date	Account Name	€

The 'date' referred to in the ledger account is the date that the transaction occurred.

When a debit entry is made in a ledger account, the debit is always entered on the left-hand side of the account and the name of account receiving the corresponding credit (i.e. the **other** side of the double entry) is given in the column headed 'account name'.

It then follows that when the corresponding credit entry is made in the relevant ledger account, the credit is always entered on the right-hand side of that account and the name of the account that receives the corresponding debit (i.e. the **other** side of the double entry) is given in the column headed 'account name'.

As we saw above, transactions are recorded by debiting and crediting accounts. For each transaction one or more accounts are debited and one or more accounts are credited; the total of the amounts debited **always** equals the total of the amounts credited.

Example 2.1 presents a journal entry to record a cash sale and shows its impact when it is posted to (i.e. recorded in) the cash and sales accounts.

EXAMPLE 2.1: RECORDING A JOURNAL ENTRY AND POSTING IT TO LEDGER ACCOUNTS

To take the example of a business selling goods for cash, there are two sides to the transaction – cash and sales. From **Figures 2.5A** and **2.5B**, the accounting impact can be identified as:

Account Name	Element	Impact	Accounting Action
Cash	Asset	Increase	Debit
Sales	Income	Increase	Credit

The table is helpful to understand the **process** of recording the transactions. The transactions are actually **recorded** as a journal entry. So if the business sells goods for €20,000 cash on 1 January, the journal entry would appear as follows:

	Debit €	Credit €
Cash account	20,000	
Sales account		20,000

To record a cash sale.

When the journal entry is posted, the ledger accounts would appear as follows (assuming no previous cash or sales transactions have occurred):

CASH ACCOUNT

Debit Side of Account			Credit Side of Account		
Date	**Account Name**	**€**	**Date**	**Account Name**	**€**
1 Jan	Sales	20,000			

SALES ACCOUNT

Debit Side of Account			Credit Side of Account		
Date	**Account Name**	**€**	**Date**	**Account Name**	**€**
			1 Jan	Cash	20,000

The next section explains how records of similar transactions are accumulated in ledger accounts, summarised in the trial balance and then presented in financial statements of an entity. This is, in effect, the '**accounting system**'.

The Accounting System

As discussed in **Chapter 1**, two purposes of financial statements are to set out the financial performance and the financial position of an entity. The financial statements are prepared from the balances on the ledger accounts at a particular point in time. A statement known as a **trial balance** is prepared that lists down, in no particular order, the balance on each account in the accounting system. The '**balance**' on an account is the difference between the totals of the debit and credit sides of that account. For example, if the total of all transactions recorded on the debit side of a ledger account is €300 and the total of all the transactions recorded on the credit side is €200, then the balance brought forward on the ledger account is €100 on the debit side (or a '€100 debit balance'). Balances carried forward and balances brought forward are illustrated below.

Example 2.2 presents a ledger account, specifically a 'trade receivables' account in relation to a credit customer, i.e. a customer to whom goods were sold on credit during the reporting period.

EXAMPLE 2.2: BALANCING A LEDGER ACCOUNT

TRADE RECEIVABLES ACCOUNT

Debit Side of Account			Credit Side of Account		
Date	**Account Name**	**€**	**Date**	**Account Name**	**€**
1 Jan	Sales	300	10 Jan	Cash	200

The transactions recorded in the above trade receivables account are:
- on 1 January the entity sold goods to a customer on credit (in the sales account, not shown, there will be a credit entry for €300 in relation to this sales transaction);
- on 10 January the customer has made a cash payment in relation to the balance on their account of €200 (in the cash account, again not shown, there will be a debit entry in relation to this cash receipt from the customer).

The payment is not sufficient to cover the full amount due so a balance remains on this account. The difference between the debit and credit sides of the ledger account is €100. A balancing figure of €100 is entered on the credit side of the ledger account to make the totals on the debit and credit sides of the ledger account equal; this **balancing figure** is referred to as the '**balance carried down**' (balance c/d) (also known as the balance carried forward (balance c/f)).

TRADE RECEIVABLES ACCOUNT

	Debit Side of Account			Credit Side of Account	
Date	**Account Name**	**€**	**Date**	**Account Name**	**€**
1 Jan	Sales	300	10 Jan	Cash	200
			10 Jan	Balance c/d	100
		300			300

After the balance c/d figure is entered in the ledger account the totals of all debit and credit entries are equal. The total amounts on the debit and credit sides of the account are double underlined.

To complete the double entry, the amount entered in the account as the balance carried down (before the totals) is also entered on the other side of the account (after the totals) and labelled '**balance brought down**' (balance b/d) (also known as 'balance brought forward' (balance b/f)).

TRADE RECEIVABLES ACCOUNT

	Debit Side of Account			Credit Side of Account	
Date	**Account Name**	**€**	**Date**	**Account Name**	**€**
1 Jan	Sales	300	10 Jan	Cash	200
			10 Jan	Balance c/d	100
		300			300
11 Jan	Balance b/d	100			

The balance on the trade receivables account is listed in the trial balance as a €100 debit; the side of the ledger account on which the balance b/d is entered indicates whether the balance listed in the trial balance is a debit balance or a credit balance. In this example the balance b/d of €100 is entered on the debit side of the ledger account, so the balance would be listed in the trial balance as a debit balance.

The reason for balancing accounts in this way is so that the balances on all ledger accounts can be listed in the **trial balance** (see **Section 2.3**). In **Example 2.2** above the balance on the trade receivables account is obvious. Often, however, there will be numerous entries on both sides of a ledger account and the balance carried down (and therefore brought down) will not be immediately apparent and will have to be calculated.

It is important to note that the balance c/d can be entered on either the debit or credit side of the ledger account. For example, if the total of the transactions recorded on the debit side of the account is less than the total of the transactions recorded on the credit side of the account, then the balance c/d will be on the debit side of the ledger account and the balance b/d will be on the credit side of the ledger account. The opposite is also the case, i.e. if the total of the debit side of the account is more than the total of the credit side the balance c/d will be on the credit side and the balance b/d will be on the debit side.

2.2 PREPARATION OF JOURNAL ENTRIES AND LEDGER ACCOUNTS

In this section we will set out the journal entries and prepare the ledger accounts for a number of different but frequently occurring transactions of a typical business. In doing so, the following issues will be dealt with:
- recording transactions;
- balancing ledger accounts; and
- preparing a trial balance from ledger accounts.

For each transaction we will follow the process we used earlier in **Section 2.1**:
1. identify the accounts affected by the transaction;
2. identify the element of the financial statements involved, that is, asset, liability, income, expense or capital;
3. understand the impact of the transaction on each account identified in step 1 (does the balance increase or decrease as a result of the transaction?); and
4. apply accounting terminology of 'debit' and 'credit'.

With practice this will become automatic for you and the progression through the steps will become quicker and easier.

(*Note:* it is worth noting at this stage that in the real world most transactions are automatically posted to an entity's ledger accounts when the information is input to its computerised accounting system. It is only unusual transactions that need to be recorded and posted individually, e.g. transactions prepared to correct errors or that are infrequently occurring transactions, e.g. purchases of non-current assets.)

Sales-related Transactions

As explained in **Chapter 1**, sales of goods are income of the business and are presented in the SOPL. **Income earned** is reduced by the **expenses incurred** by the business to determine the profit or loss for the period. **Section 1.3** explains the terms 'income earned' and 'expenses incurred'.

Transaction 1 – A Cash Sale

An entity sells goods for cash. The ledger accounts that are affected by this transaction are the sales account and the cash account. The sales account is an **income** account and the cash account is an **asset** account. The effect of this transaction to increase the total amount of the sales made by the entity and to increase the amount of cash held by the entity. Therefore, as shown in **Figure 2.5**, in order to record this transaction the sales account should be credited and the cash account debited as shown below:

Step 1 Accounts affected by the Transaction	Step 2 Account Type	Step 3 Increase/Decrease the Account Balance	Step 4 Debit/Credit Account
Sales	Income	Increase	Credit
Cash	Asset	Increase	Debit

As stated earlier in this section, the journal entry to record and therefore recognise the sale of the goods for cash, and the record from which the data is input into the entity's accounts, i.e. posted to the ledger accounts, is:

	Debit €	Credit €
Cash account	X	
Sales account		X

To record a cash sale transaction.

Thus, the cash account will be debited and the sales account credited.

Example 2.3 illustrates the recording of a cash sale transaction.

EXAMPLE 2.3: RECORDING A CASH SALE TRANSACTION

M. Smyth sold €20,000 worth of goods to A. Walsh for cash on 10 March.

To record this transaction in M. Smyth's accounts, prepare the journal entry and post it to the ledger accounts as follows.

Journal entry:

	Debit €	Credit €
Cash account	20,000	
Sales account		20,000

To record a cash sale transaction.

Ledger accounts:

CASH ACCOUNT

Debit Side of Account			Credit Side of Account		
Date	Account Name	€	Date	Account Name	€
10 Mar	Sales	20,000			

SALES ACCOUNT

Debit Side of Account			Credit Side of Account		
Date	Account Name	€	Date	Account Name	€
			10 Mar	Cash	20,000

Example 2.3 dealt with a cash sales transaction; the next few examples deal with credit sales transactions.

Transaction 2 – A Sale on Credit

An entity sells goods to a customer on the understanding that the customer will pay for the goods after an agreed length of time. In other words, the entity has sold goods to a customer 'on credit'.

The accounts that are affected by this transaction are the sales account and the trade receivables account. The sales account is an **income** account and the trade receivables account is an **asset** account. The effect of this transaction is to increase the total amount of sales made by the entity (i.e. the balance on its sales account) and increase the amount owed to the entity by its customers (i.e. the balance on its trade receivables account). Therefore, as shown in **Figure 2.5**, in order to record this transaction the sales account should be credited and the trade receivables account should be debited as shown below:

Step 1 Accounts affected by the Transaction	Step 2 Account Type	Step 3 Increase/Decrease the Account Balance	Step 4 Debit/Credit Account
Trade receivables	Asset	Increase	Debit
Sales	Income	Increase	Credit

The journal entry to record and therefore recognise the sale of the goods on credit, and the record from which the data is input into the entity's accounts, i.e. posted to the ledger accounts, is:

	Debit €	Credit €
Trade receivables account	X	
Sales account		X

To record a credit sale transaction.

Note: as we saw in **Example 2.2** above, when a customer is provided with credit, they become a 'credit customer' or in accounting terminology are known as a 'trade debtor' or a 'trade receivable'. The balance due to the entity is presented in the **trade receivables** account.

Example 2.4 demonstrates the recording of a credit sale transaction.

EXAMPLE 2.4: RECORDING A CREDIT SALE TRANSACTION

R. Tyrell sold €10,500 worth of goods on credit to B. Meyler on 4 May.

To record the transaction in R. Tyrell's accounts, prepare the journal entry and post it to the ledger accounts as follows.

Journal entry:

	Debit €	Credit €
Trade receivables account	10,500	
Sales account		10,500

To record a credit sale transaction.

Ledger accounts:

TRADE RECEIVABLES ACCOUNT: B. MEYLER

	Debit Side of Account				Credit Side of Account	
Date	Account Name	€		Date	Account Name	€
4 May	Sales	10,500				

SALES ACCOUNT

	Debit Side of Account				Credit Side of Account	
Date	Account Name	€		Date	Account Name	€
				4 May	Trade receivables	10,500

Transaction 3 – Cash Received from a Credit Customer

An entity receives cash from a customer to whom it sold goods on credit. The accounts that are affected by this transaction are the cash account and the trade receivables account. The cash account is an **asset** account and the trade receivables account is also an **asset** account. The effect of this transaction is to increase the amount of cash held by the entity and decrease the amount owed by trade receivables to the entity. Therefore, as shown in **Figure 2.5**, in order to record this transaction the cash account should be debited and the trade receivables account credited, as shown below:

Step 1 Accounts Affected by the Transaction	Step 2 Account Type	Step 3 Increase/Decrease the Account Balance	Step 4 Debit/Credit Account
Cash	Asset	Increase	Debit
Trade receivables	Asset	Decrease	Credit

The journal entry to record and therefore recognise a cash receipt from a credit customer, and the record from which the data is input into the entity's accounts, i.e. posted to the ledger accounts, is as follows:

	Debit €	Credit €
Cash account	X	
Trade receivables account		X

To record a cash payment made by a customer to whom goods were sold on credit.

Example 2.4 above deals with recording a sale of goods on credit. **Example 2.5** below deals with the recording of two transactions involving a trade receivable: a sale of goods on credit (see **Transaction 2**) **and** a cash payment received from a credit customer (see **Transaction 3**).

EXAMPLE 2.5: CREDIT SALE AND CASH RECEIVED SUBSEQUENTLY FROM CUSTOMER

R. Jones sold goods worth €8,000 to a credit customer, B. Lyons, on 12 June. On 30 June B. Lyons paid cash of €8,000 to R. Jones.

To record these transactions in the accounts of R. Jones, prepare the journal entries and the ledger accounts as follows.

Journal entries:

	Debit €	Credit €
Trade receivables account	8,000	
Sales account		8,000
To record a credit sale transaction.		
Cash account	8,000	
Trade receivables account		8,000
To record cash received from a credit customer.		

Ledger accounts:

TRADE RECEIVABLES ACCOUNT: B. LYONS

Debit Side of Account			Credit Side of Account		
Date	**Account Name**	**€**	**Date**	**Account Name**	**€**
12 June	Sales	8,000	30 June	Cash	8,000

SALES ACCOUNT

Debit Side of Account			Credit Side of Account		
Date	**Account Name**	**€**	**Date**	**Account Name**	**€**
			12 June	Trade receivables	8,000

CASH ACCOUNT

Debit Side of Account			Credit Side of Account		
Date	**Account Name**	**€**	**Date**	**Account Name**	**€**
30 June	Trade receivables	8,000			

Transaction 4 – Cheque Received from Credit Customer

An entity receives a cheque from a customer in respect of a credit sale previously made by the entity to the customer. The cheque is lodged to the entity's bank account. The accounts that are affected by this transaction are the trade receivables account and the bank account. The trade receivables account is an **asset** account and the bank account is also an **asset** account. (However, if the bank account is overdrawn it is a liability, not an asset.) The effect of this transaction is to decrease the amount owed by trade receivables to the entity and to increase the amount held by the entity in its bank account. Therefore, as shown in **Figure 2.5**, in order to record this transaction the trade receivables account should be credited and the bank account should be debited as shown below.

Step 1 Accounts Affected by the Transaction	Step 2 Account Type	Step 3 Increase/Decrease the Account Balance	Step 4 Debit/Credit Account
Bank	Asset	Increase	Debit
Trade receivables	Asset	Decrease	Credit

The journal entry to record and therefore recognise the receipt of a cheque from a credit customer, and the record from which the data is input into the entity's accounts, i.e. posted to the ledger accounts, is:

	Debit €	Credit €
Bank account	X	
Trade receivables account		X

To record a cheque received from a customer to whom goods were sold on credit.

Example 2.6 demonstrates the recording of a credit sale transaction (see **Transaction 2**) and a cheque received in payment from a credit customer (see **Transaction 4**).

EXAMPLE 2.6: CREDIT SALE TRANSACTION AND CHEQUE RECEIVED FROM CUSTOMER

L. Toomey sold goods worth €5,000 to a credit customer, C. Wilson, on 5 July. On 30 July C. Wilson paid a cheque of €5,000 to L. Toomey.

To record these transactions in the accounts of L. Toomey, prepare the journal entries and the ledger accounts as follows.

Journal entries:

	Debit €	Credit €
Trade receivables account	5,000	
Sales account		5,000

To record a credit sale transaction.

	Debit €	Credit €
Bank account	5,000	
Trade receivables account		5,000

To record a cheque received from a customer to whom goods were sold on credit.

Ledger accounts:

TRADE RECEIVABLES ACCOUNT: C. WILSON

Debit Side of Account			Credit Side of Account		
Date	Account Name	€	Date	Account Name	€
5 July	Sales	5,000	30 July	Bank	5,000

SALES ACCOUNT

	Debit Side of Account			Credit Side of Account	
Date	Account Name	€	Date	Account Name	€
			5 July	Trade receivables	5,000

BANK ACCOUNT

	Debit Side of Account			Credit Side of Account	
Date	Account Name	€	Date	Account Name	€
30 July	Trade receivables	5,000			

(Try **Review Questions 2.1–2.3** at the end of this chapter.)

Purchases-related Transactions

In this section we will deal with the typical transactions related to the purchase of goods for use in a business. As explained in **Chapter 1**, purchases of goods are an expense of the entity and are presented in the SOPL. Income earned is reduced by the expenses incurred to determine the profit or loss for the period.

Transaction 5 – A Cash Purchase

An entity purchases goods from a supplier for cash. The accounts that are affected by this transaction are the purchases account and the cash account. The purchases account is an **expense** account and the cash account is an **asset** account. The effect of this transaction is to increase the total amount of purchases made by the entity and decrease the amount of cash it holds. Therefore, as shown in **Figure 2.5**, in order to record this transaction the purchases account should be debited and the cash account should be credited as shown below:

Step 1 Accounts Affected by the Transaction	Step 2 Account Type	Step 3 Increase/Decrease the Account Balance	Step 4 Debit/Credit Account
Purchases	Expense	Increase	Debit
Cash	Asset	Decrease	Credit

The journal entry to record and therefore recognise the purchase of goods for cash, and the record from which the data is input into the entity's accounts, i.e. posted to the ledger accounts, is:

	Debit €	Credit €
Purchases account	X	
Cash account		X

To record the purchase of goods for cash.

Example 2.7 demonstrates the recording of a cash purchase transaction.

EXAMPLE 2.7: CASH PURCHASE TRANSACTION

C. Williams purchased €2,300 worth of goods for cash on 15 April.

To record the transaction in C. Williams' accounts, prepare the journal entry and the ledger accounts as follows.

Journal entry:

	Debit €	Credit €
Purchases account	2,300	
Cash account		2,300

To record a cash purchase transaction.

Ledger accounts:

PURCHASES ACCOUNT

Debit Side of Account			Credit Side of Account		
Date	Account Name	€	Date	Account Name	€
15 Apr	Cash	2,300			

CASH ACCOUNT

Debit Side of Account			Credit Side of Account		
Date	Account Name	€	Date	Account Name	€
			15 Apr	Purchases	2,300

Transaction 6 – A Credit Purchase

An entity purchases goods on credit from a supplier. The accounts that are affected by this transaction are the purchases account and the trade payables account (a 'trade payable' is an amount due to a supplier in relation to goods bought on credit). The purchases account is an **expense** account and the trade payables account is a **liability** account. The effect of this transaction is to increase the total amount of purchases made by the entity and increase the amount owed by the entity to its suppliers. Therefore, as shown in **Figure 2.5** above, in order to record this transaction the purchases account should be debited and the trade payables account should be credited as shown below:

Step 1 Accounts Affected by the Transaction	Step 2 Account Type	Step 3 Increase/Decrease the Account Balance	Step 4 Debit/Credit Account
Purchases	Expense	Increase	Debit
Trade payables	Liability	Increase	Credit

The journal entry to record and recognise the purchase of goods on credit, and the record from which the data is input into the entity's accounts, i.e. posted to the ledger accounts, is as follows:

	Debit €	Credit €
Purchases account	X	
Trade payables account		X

To record the purchase of goods on credit.

Example 2.8 demonstrates the recording of a credit purchase transaction.

EXAMPLE 2.8: CREDIT PURCHASE TRANSACTION

T. Brown purchases €1,750 worth of goods on credit from S. Connors on 20 August.

To record this transaction in T. Brown's books, prepare the journal entry and the ledger accounts as follows.

Journal entry:

	Debit €	Credit €
Purchases account	1,750	
Trade payables account		1,750
To record a credit purchase transaction.		

Ledger accounts:

PURCHASES ACCOUNT

Debit Side of Account			Credit Side of Account		
Date	**Account Name**	**€**	**Date**	**Account Name**	**€**
20 Aug	Trade payables	1,750			

TRADE PAYABLES ACCOUNT: S. CONNORS

Debit Side of Account			Credit Side of Account		
Date	**Account Name**	**€**	**Date**	**Account Name**	**€**
			20 Aug	Purchases	1,750

Transaction 7 – Cash Paid to a Supplier From Whom Goods Were Purchased on Credit

An entity pays a credit supplier by cash. The accounts that are affected by this transaction are the trade payables account and the cash account. The trade payables account is a **liability** account and the cash account is an **asset** account. The effect of this transaction is to decrease the total amount owed by the entity to its suppliers and decrease the amount of cash held by the entity. Therefore, as shown in **Figure 2.5**, in order to record this transaction the trade payables account should be debited and the cash account should be credited as shown below:

Step 1 Accounts Affected by the Transaction	Step 2 Account Type	Step 3 Increase/Decrease the Account Balance	Step 4 Debit/Credit Account
Trade payables	Liability	Decrease	Debit
Cash	Asset	Decrease	Credit

The journal entry to record and therefore recognise the cash payment to a credit supplier, and the record from which the data is input into the entity's accounts, i.e. posted to the ledger accounts, is:

	Debit €	Credit €
Trade payables account	X	
Cash account		X
To record a cash payment to a supplier who provided goods on credit.		

Example 2.9 demonstrates the recording of a credit purchase transaction (see **Transaction 6**) and its subsequent payment in cash (see **Transaction 7**).

EXAMPLE 2.9: CREDIT PURCHASE TRANSACTION AND PAYMENT IN CASH

On 14 March B. Jones purchased goods on credit from L. Ryan for €800. On 8 April B. Jones paid L. Ryan by cash in full.

To record the transactions in B. Jones' accounts, prepare the journal entries and the ledger accounts as follows.

Journal entries:

	Debit €	Credit €
Purchases account	800	
Trade payables account		800
To record a credit purchase transaction.		
Trade payables account	800	
Cash account		800
To record cash paid to a supplier from whom goods were purchased on credit.		

Ledger accounts:

PURCHASES ACCOUNT

Debit Side of Account			Credit Side of Account		
Date	**Account Name**	**€**	**Date**	**Account Name**	**€**
14 Mar	Trade payables	800			

TRADE PAYABLES ACCOUNT: L. RYAN

Debit Side of Account			Credit Side of Account		
Date	**Account Name**	**€**	**Date**	**Account Name**	**€**
8 Apr	Cash	800	14 Mar	Purchases	800

CASH ACCOUNT

Debit Side of Account			Credit Side of Account		
Date	**Account Name**	**€**	**Date**	**Account Name**	**€**
			8 Apr	Trade payables	800

Transaction 8 – Cheque Payment to a Supplier who Provided Credit

An entity pays a credit supplier by cheque. The accounts that are affected by this transaction are the trade payables account and the bank account. The trade payables account is a **liability** account and the bank account is an **asset** account. The effect of this transaction is to decrease the amount owed by the entity to its suppliers and decrease the amount held by the entity in its bank account. Therefore, as shown in **Figure 2.5**, in order to record this transaction the trade payables account should be debited and the bank account should be credited as follows.

Step 1 Accounts Affected by the Transaction	Step 2 Account Type	Step 3 Increase/Decrease the Account Balance	Step 4 Debit/Credit Account
Trade payables	Liability	Decrease	Debit
Bank	Asset	Decrease	Credit

The journal entry to record and therefore recognise the payment by cheque to a credit supplier, and the record from which the data is input into the entity's accounts, i.e. posted to the ledger accounts, is:

	Debit €	Credit €
Trade payables account	X	
Bank account		X

To record a cheque payment to a supplier who provided goods on credit.

Example 2.10 demonstrates the recording of a credit purchase transaction (see **Transaction 6**) and its subsequent payment by cheque (see **Transaction 8**).

EXAMPLE 2.10: CREDIT PURCHASE TRANSACTION AND PAYMENT BY CHEQUE

On 10 April T. Fahy purchased €500 worth of goods on credit. On 30 April, T. Fahy paid for the goods in full by cheque.

To record the transactions in T. Fahy's accounts, prepare the journal entry and the ledger accounts as follows.

Journal entries:

	Debit €	Credit €
Purchases account	500	
Trade payables account		500

To record a credit purchase transaction.

	Debit €	Credit €
Trade payables account	500	
Bank account		500

To record a cheque payment to a credit supplier.

Ledger accounts:

PURCHASES ACCOUNT

Debit Side of Account			Credit Side of Account		
Date	Account Name	€	Date	Account Name	€
10 Apr	Trade payables	500			

TRADE PAYABLES ACCOUNT

Debit Side of Account			Credit Side of Account		
Date	Account Name	€	Date	Account Name	€
30 Apr	Bank	500	10 Apr	Purchases	500

BANK ACCOUNT					
Debit Side of Account			**Credit Side of Account**		
Date	**Account Name**	**€**	**Date**	**Account Name**	**€**
			30 Apr	Trade payables	500

(Try **Review Questions 2.4–2.6** at the end of this chapter.)

Expense Transactions

The **recognition** of expenses other than purchases of goods is dealt with next. Typical expenses include rent, rates, electricity, insurance and wages. Expenses may be paid for in cash or by cheque at the time the expense is incurred, or the supplier may provide the entity with a credit period. When credit is provided by suppliers in relation to expenses the amount due is presented in '**other payables**'; only credit provided by suppliers of goods (that is purchases) is presented in 'trade payables'.

When an entity incurs an expense and a cash payment is made at the time the expense is incurred, the relevant expense account is debited and the credit entry is to the cash account (an asset account).

When an entity incurs an expense and makes a cheque payment at the time the expense is incurred, the relevant expense account is debited and the credit entry is to the bank account (an asset account).

When an entity incurs an expense and a credit period is provided by the supplier, the relevant expense account is debited and the credit entry is to the other payables account (a liability account).

Transaction 9 – Cash Payment for an Expense

An entity pays an expense by cash. The accounts that are affected by this transaction are an expense account and the cash account. The expense account is, of course, an **expense** account and the cash account is an **asset** account. The effect of this transaction is to increase the total amount of expenses incurred by the entity and decrease the amount of cash held by the entity. Therefore, as shown in **Figure 2.5**, in order to record this transaction an expense account should be debited and the cash account should be credited as follows.

Step 1 Accounts Affected by the Transaction	Step 2 Account Type	Step 3 Increase/Decrease the Account Balance	Step 4 Debit/Credit Account
Expense	Expense	Increase	Debit
Cash	Asset	Decrease	Credit

The journal entry to record and therefore recognise expenses paid by cash, and the record from which the data is input into the entity's accounts, i.e. posted to the ledger accounts, is:

	Debit €	Credit €
Expense account	X	
Cash account		X

To recognise an expense incurred in the reporting period paid for in cash.

Example 2.11 demonstrates the recording of a transaction in relation to the cash payment of an expense.

EXAMPLE 2.11: EXPENSE PAID BY CASH

W. Jones pays cash for rent on a retail property of €1,200 on 12 June.

To record this transaction in the accounts of W. Jones, prepare the journal entry and the ledger accounts as follows.

Journal entry:

	Debit €	Credit €
Rent expense account	1,200	
Cash account		1,200

To record a cash purchase transaction.

Ledger accounts:

RENT ACCOUNT

	Debit Side of Account			Credit Side of Account	
Date	**Account Name**	**€**	**Date**	**Account Name**	**€**
12 June	Cash	1,200			

CASH ACCOUNT

	Debit Side of Account			Credit Side of Account	
Date	**Account Name**	**€**	**Date**	**Account Name**	**€**
			12 June	Rent	1,200

Transaction 10 – Expense Incurred by an Entity on Credit

An entity has incurred an expense (other than purchase of goods) **on credit**. The accounts that are affected by this transaction are an expense account and the 'other payables' account. Amounts owing to providers of goods and services, other than suppliers of goods for resale, are recorded in the 'other payables' account as distinct from the 'trade payables' account. The expense account is an **expense** account and the other payables account is a **liability** account. The effect of this transaction to increase the total amount of expenses incurred by the entity and increase the amount owed by the entity to its suppliers of goods and services other than goods for resale. Therefore, as shown in **Figure 2.5**, in order to record this transaction an expenses account should be debited and the other payables account should be credited:

Step 1 Accounts Affected by the Transaction	Step 2 Account Type	Step 3 Increase/Decrease the Account Balance	Step 4 Debit/Credit Account
Expense	Expense	Increase	Debit
Other payables	Liabilities	Increase	Credit

The journal entry to record and therefore recognise expenses on credit, and the record from which the data is input into the entity's accounts, i.e. posted to the ledger accounts, is:

	Debit €	Credit €
Expense account	X	
Other payables account		X

To recognise an expense incurred in the reporting period on credit.

Example 2.12 demonstrates the recording of an expense incurred on credit terms and the subsequent payment.

EXAMPLE 2.12: EXPENSE INCURRED ON CREDIT TERMS AND SUBSEQUENT PAYMENT BY CHEQUE

P. Corrigan receives an invoice on 1 March for €2,100 from the local council in relation to a rates expense. The local council allows 30 days' credit. P. Corrigan pays the rates by cheque on 31 March.

To record these transactions in P. Corrigan's business records, prepare the journal entries and the ledger accounts as follows.

Journal entries:

	Debit €	Credit €
Rates expense account	2,100	
Other payables account		2,100

To record an expense on credit terms.

	Debit €	Credit €
Other payables account	2,100	
Bank account		2,100

To record the payment by cheque of the rates expense.

Ledger accounts:

RATES ACCOUNT

Debit Side of Account			Credit Side of Account		
Date	Account Name	€	Date	Account Name	€
1 Mar	Other payables	2,100			

OTHER PAYABLES ACCOUNT

Debit Side of Account			Credit Side of Account		
Date	Account Name	€	Date	Account Name	€
31 Mar	Bank	2,100	1 Mar	Rates	2,100

BANK ACCOUNT

Debit Side of Account			Credit Side of Account		
Date	Account Name	€	Date	Account Name	€
			31 Mar	Other payables	2,100

(Try **Review Questions 2.7 and 2.9** at the end of this chapter.)

Property, Plant and Equipment-related Transactions

Property, plant and equipment is defined by the international accounting standard IAS 16 *Property, Plant and Equipment* as "tangible items that:
(a) are held for use in the production or supply of goods or services, for rental to others, or for administrative purposes; and
(b) are expected to be used during more than one reporting period."

Items of property, plant and equipment are therefore tangible assets, i.e. they have a physical existence – they are assets that can be touched, felt and seen.

Property, plant and equipment is divided into different classes. A class of property, plant and equipment is a grouping of similar assets; they are either similar due to their nature (e.g. motor vehicles would include cars and delivery vans owned by the entity) or based on their use in the entity's operations. The most common classes of 'property, plant and equipment' are:
• land;
• ships;
• aircraft;
• property;
• plant;
• equipment;
• machinery;
• motor vehicles; and
• fixtures and fittings.

The recognition of an item of property, plant and equipment when it is first purchased is dealt with next. Other aspects of property, plant and equipment will be dealt with in greater detail in **Chapter 6, Property, Plant and Equipment, and Depreciation**.

Transaction 11 – Property, Plant and Equipment Acquired for Cash

An entity purchases property, plant and equipment by paying cash. The accounts that are affected by this transaction are the property, plant and equipment account and the cash account. The property, plant and equipment account is an **asset** account and the cash account is also an **asset** account. The effect of this transaction is to increase the total amount of property, plant and equipment held by the entity and decrease the amount of cash the entity holds. Therefore, as shown in **Figure 2.5**, in order to record this transaction the property, plant and equipment account should be debited and the cash account should be credited as follows.

Step 1 Accounts Affected by the Transaction	Step 2 Account Type	Step 3 Increase/Decrease the Account Balance	Step 4 Debit/Credit Account
Property, plant and equipment – cost	Asset	Increase	Debit
Cash	Asset	Decrease	Credit

The journal entry to record and therefore recognise the acquisition of property, plant and equipment for cash, and the record from which the data is input into the entity's accounts, i.e. posted to the ledger accounts, is:

	Debit €	Credit €
Property, plant and equipment – cost account	X	
Cash account		X

To recognise the purchase of an item of property, plant and equipment for cash.

Example 2.13 demonstrates the recording of an item of property, plant and equipment bought for cash.

EXAMPLE 2.13: PURCHASE OF AN ITEM OF PROPERTY, PLANT AND EQUIPMENT FOR CASH

R. Wiley buys a delivery van for cash on 15 July. The van costs €10,000.

To record the transaction in R. Wiley's accounts, prepare the journal entry and the ledger accounts as follows.

Journal entry:

	Debit €	Credit €
Motor vehicle – cost account	10,000	
Cash account		10,000
To record the purchase of a van for cash		

Ledger accounts:

MOTOR VEHICLE – COST ACCOUNT

Debit Side of Account			Credit Side of Account		
Date	**Account Name**	**€**	**Date**	**Account Name**	**€**
15 July	Cash	10,000			

CASH ACCOUNT

Debit Side of Account			Credit Side of Account		
Date	**Account Name**	**€**	**Date**	**Account Name**	**€**
			15 July	Motor vehicle	10,000

Transaction 12 – Property, Plant and Equipment Acquired and Paid for by Cheque

An entity purchases property, plant and equipment by cheque payment. The accounts that are affected by this transaction are the property, plant and equipment – cost account and the bank account. The property, plant and equipment – cost account is an **asset** account and the bank account is also an **asset** account. The effect of this transaction is to increase the total amount of property, plant and equipment held by the entity and decrease the amount held by the entity in its bank account. Therefore, as shown in **Figure 2.5**, in order to record this transaction the property, plant and equipment – cost account should be debited and the bank account should be credited as follows.

Step 1 Accounts Affected by the Transaction	Step 2 Account Type	Step 3 Increase/Decrease the Account Balance	Step 4 Debit/Credit Account
Property, plant and equipment – cost	Asset	Increase	Debit
Bank	Asset	Decrease	Credit

The journal entry to record and therefore recognise the acquisition of property, plant and equipment by cheque, and the record from which the data is input into the entity's accounts, i.e. posted to the ledger accounts, is:

	Debit €	Credit €
Property, plant and equipment – cost account	X	
Bank account		X

To recognise the purchase of an item of property, plant and equipment by cheque.

Example 2.14 below demonstrates the recognition of an item of property, plant and equipment acquired by cheque.

EXAMPLE 2.14: PURCHASE OF AN ITEM OF PROPERTY, PLANT AND EQUIPMENT BY CHEQUE

T. Armstrong buys a new machine on 13 June for €25,000 and pays for the machine by cheque.

To recognise this transaction in T. Armstrong's books, prepare the required journal entry and post it to the relevant ledger accounts as follows.

Journal entry:

	Debit €	Credit €
Machine – cost account	25,000	
Bank account		25,000

To record the purchase of a machine by cheque.

Ledger accounts:

MACHINE – COST ACCOUNT

Debit Side of Account			Credit Side of Account		
Date	**Account Name**	**€**	**Date**	**Account Name**	**€**
13 June	Bank	25,000			

BANK ACCOUNT

Debit Side of Account			Credit Side of Account		
Date	**Account Name**	**€**	**Date**	**Account Name**	**€**
			13 June	Machine	25,000

Transaction 13 – Acquisition of Property, Plant and Equipment Financed by a Loan

An entity purchases property, plant and equipment by taking out a loan. The accounts that are affected by this transaction are the property, plant and equipment – cost account and a loan account. The property, plant and equipment – cost account is an **asset** account and the loan account is a **liability** account. The effect of this transaction is to increase the total amount of property, plant and equipment held by the entity and increase the amount owed by the entity to the provider of the loan. Therefore, as shown in **Figure 2.5**, in order to record this transaction the property, plant and equipment – cost account should be debited and the loan account should be credited as follows.

Step 1 Accounts Affected by the Transaction	Step 2 Account Type	Step 3 Increase/Decrease the Account Balance	Step 4 Debit/Credit Account
Property, plant and equipment – cost	Asset	Increase	Debit
Loan	Liability	Increase	Credit

The journal entry to record and therefore recognise the acquisition of property, plant and equipment funded by a loan, and the record from which the data is input into the entity's accounts, i.e. posted to the ledger accounts, is:

	Debit €	Credit €
Property, plant and equipment – cost account	X	
Loan account		X

To recognise the purchase of an item of property, plant and equipment using a loan facility.

Example 2.15 demonstrates the recording of an item of property, plant and equipment financed by a loan.

EXAMPLE 2.15: PURCHASE OF AN ITEM OF PROPERTY, PLANT AND EQUIPMENT FINANCED BY A LOAN

P. Sweeney buys a property on 8 January for €240,000. The property is financed by a loan from a local bank.

To record the transaction in the books of P. Sweeney, prepare the journal entry and the ledger accounts as follows.

Journal entry:

	Debit €	Credit €
Property – cost account	240,000	
Loan account		240,000

To record the purchase of a property by loan.

Ledger accounts:

PROPERTY – COST ACCOUNT

Debit Side of Account			Credit Side of Account		
Date	**Account Name**	**€**	**Date**	**Account Name**	**€**
8 Jan	Loan	240,000			

LOAN ACCOUNT

Debit Side of Account			Credit Side of Account		
Date	**Account Name**	**€**	**Date**	**Account Name**	**€**
			8 Jan	Property – cost	240,000

(Try **Review Questions 2.10** and **2.11** at the end of this chapter.)

Capital-related Transactions

Every business requires funds to be invested by the owners; these funds are referred to as 'capital'. The concept of capital was introduced in **Chapter 1**; it represents the funds introduced by the owners of the business and the profit retained in the business less any losses incurred and any withdrawals of funds by the owners. '**Profit retained**' is the profit made by the entity reduced by any losses and any payments made to the owners. Payments made to the owners are either '**drawings**' in the case of a sole trader or partnership or '**dividends**' in the case of a company.

Transaction 14 – The Owner(s) of an Entity Invest Cash in the Entity

An entity's owner introduces cash into the business as a capital contribution. The accounts that are affected by this transaction are the cash account and the capital account. The **capital account** is the account in which all the owner's transactions with the entity are recorded. The cash account is an **asset** account and the capital account is a **capital** or **equity** account. The effect of this transaction is to increase the amount of cash held by the entity and the total amount of capital owed by the entity to its owner. Therefore, as in **Figure 2.5**, in order to record this transaction the cash account should be debited and the capital account should be credited as follows.

Step 1 Accounts Affected by the Transaction	Step 2 Account Type	Step 3 Increase/Decrease the Account Balance	Step 4 Debit/Credit Account
Cash	Asset	Increase	Debit
Capital/Equity	Capital/Equity	Increase	Credit

The journal entry to record and therefore recognise the introduction of cash to the business as a capital contribution, and the record from which the data is input into the entity's accounts, i.e. posted to the ledger accounts, is:

	Debit €	Credit €
Cash account	X	
Capital account		X

To recognise capital introduced to the business by the owner, capital is in the form of cash.

Example 2.16 demonstrates the recording of capital introduced into a business.

EXAMPLE 2.16: CAPITAL INTRODUCED IN THE FORM OF CASH

On 12 March, A. Higgins set up his new business with €10,000 cash. On 14 March, A. Higgins lodged €9,500 of the business cash to the business bank account.

To record the transactions in A. Higgins' books, prepare the journal entries and the ledger accounts as follows.

Journal entries:

	Debit €	Credit €
Cash account	10,000	
Capital account		10,000

To record the capital introduced into the business.

	Debit €	Credit €
Bank account	9,500	
Cash account		9,500

To record the cash lodgement to the bank account.

Ledger accounts:

CASH ACCOUNT

Debit Side of Account			Credit Side of Account		
Date	**Account Name**	**€**	**Date**	**Account Name**	**€**
12 Mar	Capital	10,000	14 Mar	Bank	9,500

CAPITAL ACCOUNT

Debit Side of Account			Credit Side of Account		
Date	**Account Name**	**€**	**Date**	**Account Name**	**€**
			12 Mar	Cash	10,000

BANK ACCOUNT

Debit Side of Account			Credit Side of Account		
Date	**Account Name**	**€**	**Date**	**Account Name**	**€**
14 Mar	Cash	9,500			

Transaction 15 – The Owner(s) of an Entity Invests in it by Paying a Cheque into the Entity's Bank Account

The owner of an entity introduces additional capital into the business by cheque. The accounts that are affected by this transaction are the capital account and the bank account. The capital account is a **capital** or **equity** account and the bank account is an **asset** account. The effect of this transaction is to increase the total amount of capital owed by the entity to its owner and increase the funds held by the entity in its bank account. Therefore, as shown in **Figure 2.5**, in order to record this transaction the capital account should be credited and the bank account should be debited as follows.

Step 1 Accounts Affected by the Transaction	Step 2 Account Type	Step 3 Increase/Decrease the Account Balance	Step 4 Debit/Credit Account
Bank	Asset	Increase	Debit
Capital	Capital/Equity	Increase	Credit

The journal entry to record and therefore recognise the introduction of a cheque to the business as a capital contribution, and the record from which the data is input into the entity's accounts, i.e. posted to the ledger accounts, is:

	Debit €	Credit €
Bank account	X	
Capital account		X

To recognise capital introduced into the business by the owner – capital is in the form of a cheque.

Example 2.17 demonstrates the recording of capital introduced into a business by cheque.

EXAMPLE 2.17: CAPITAL INTRODUCED BY CHEQUE

On 18 January, D. Watkins sets up his new business with a €8,500 cheque.

To record the transaction in D. Watkins' business records, prepare the journal entry and the ledger accounts as follows.

Journal entry:

	Debit €	Credit €
Bank account	8,500	
Capital account		8,500

To record the capital introduced into the business.

Ledger accounts:

BANK ACCOUNT

Debit Side of Account			Credit Side of Account		
Date	**Account Name**	**€**	**Date**	**Account Name**	**€**
18 Jan	Capital	8,500			

CAPITAL ACCOUNT

Debit Side of Account			Credit Side of Account		
Date	**Account Name**	**€**	**Date**	**Account Name**	**€**
			18 Jan	Bank	8,500

Transaction 16 – The Owner(s) of an Entity Invests Property, Plant and Equipment in the Entity

An owner introduces an asset, such as a motor vehicle, into the business. The accounts that are affected by this transaction are the property, plant and equipment account and the capital account. The property, plant and equipment account is an **asset** account and the capital account is a **capital** or **equity** account. The effect of this transaction is to increase the amount of property, plant and equipment held by the entity and increase the total amount of capital owed by the entity to its owner. Therefore, as shown in **Figure 2.5**, in order to record this transaction the property, plant and equipment account should be debited and the capital account should be credited as follows.

Step 1 Accounts Affected by the Transaction	Step 2 Account Type	Step 3 Increase/Decrease the Account Balance	Step 4 Debit/Credit Account
Motor vehicle – cost	Asset	Increase	Debit
Capital	Capital	Increase	Credit

The journal entry to record and therefore recognise the introduction of a motor vehicle to the business as a capital contribution, and the record from which the data is input into the entity's accounts, i.e. posted to the ledger accounts, is:

	Debit €	Credit €
Motor vehicle – cost account	X	
Capital account		X

To recognise capital introduced to the business by the owner, capital is in the form of an asset such as a motor vehicle.

Example 2.18 demonstrates the recording of capital introduced into a business in the form of a motor vehicle.

EXAMPLE 2.18: CAPITAL INTRODUCED IN THE FORM OF A MOTOR VEHICLE

On 20 January, G. Tompkins introduces a motor vehicle into the business for use by the business sales staff. The vehicle is worth €16,400.

To record this transaction in the books of G. Tompkins, prepare the journal entry and the ledger accounts as follows.

Journal entry:

	Debit €	Credit €
Motor vehicle – cost account	16,400	
Capital account		16,400

To record the capital introduced into the business.

Ledger accounts:

MOTOR VEHICLE – COST ACCOUNT

Debit Side of Account			Credit Side of Account		
Date	**Account Name**	**€**	**Date**	**Account Name**	**€**
20 Jan	Capital	16,400			

CAPITAL ACCOUNT

Debit Side of Account			Credit Side of Account		
Date	**Account Name**	**€**	**Date**	**Account Name**	**€**
			20 Jan	Motor vehicle	16,400

Transaction 17 – The Owner(s) of an Entity take Cash out of the Entity

The owner of an entity withdraws cash from the business for their personal use. The accounts that are affected by this transaction are the cash account and the drawings account (see **Chapter 1**). The drawings account is the account in which all the owner's withdrawals of assets from the entity are recorded. The drawings account is a **capital** or **equity** account and the cash account is an **asset** account. The effect of this transaction is to decrease the capital owed by the entity to its owner and decrease the amount of cash held by the entity. Therefore, as shown in **Figure 2.5**, in order to record this transaction the cash account should be credited and the drawings account should be debited:

Step 1 Accounts Affected by the Transaction	Step 2 Account Type	Step 3 Increase/Decrease the Account Balance	Step 4 Debit/Credit Account
Drawings	Capital	Decrease	Debit
Cash	Asset	Decrease	Credit

The journal entry to record and therefore recognise the withdrawal of cash from the business by the owner, and the record from which the data is input into the entity's accounts, i.e. posted to the ledger accounts, is:

	Debit €	Credit €
Drawings account	X	
Cash account		X

To recognise the withdrawal of cash from the business by the owner.

Example 2.19 demonstrates the recording of cash withdrawals from a business by the owner.

EXAMPLE 2.19: CASH DRAWINGS

On 19 May, M. Willis, the owner, withdrew €2,800 cash from the business.

To record this transaction, prepare the journal entry and the ledger accounts as follows.

Journal entry:

	Debit €	Credit €
Drawings account	2,800	
Cash account		2,800

To record the cash withdrawal from the business by the owner.

Ledger accounts:

DRAWINGS ACCOUNT

Debit Side of Account			Credit Side of Account		
Date	Account Name	€	Date	Account Name	€
19 May	Cash	2,800			

CASH ACCOUNT					
Debit Side of Account			**Credit Side of Account**		
Date	**Account Name**	**€**	**Date**	**Account Name**	**€**
			19 May	Drawings	2,800

Transaction 18 – The Owner/s of an Entity Take Goods for Their Own Use That Were Previously Bought/Manufactured by the Entity for Resale/Sale

The owner of an entity withdraws inventory/goods from the business for personal use. The accounts that are affected by this transaction are the purchases account and the drawings account. The purchases account is an **expense** account and the drawings account is a **capital** or **equity** account. The effect of this transaction is to decrease the capital owed by the entity to its owner and decrease the amount of purchases made by the entity. Therefore, as shown in **Figure 2.5**, in order to record this transaction the purchases account should be credited and the drawings account should be debited as follows.

Step 1 Accounts Affected by the Transaction	Step 2 Account Type	Step 3 Increase/Decrease the Account Balance	Step 4 Debit/Credit Account
Drawings	Capital	Decrease	Debit
Purchases	Expense	Decrease	Credit

The journal entry to record and therefore recognise the withdrawal of inventory/goods from the business by the owner for personal use, and the record from which the data is input into the entity's accounts, i.e. posted to the ledger accounts, is:

	Debit €	Credit €
Drawings account	X	
Purchases account		X

To recognise the withdrawal of inventory/goods from the business by the owner.

Example 2.20 demonstrates the recording of a purchase of goods on credit (see **Transaction 6**) followed by the withdrawal of goods from a business by the owner.

EXAMPLE 2.20: PURCHASE OF GOODS ON CREDIT AND DRAWINGS OF INVENTORY/GOODS

P. Doyle is a sole trader who started his business on 1 May. On 10 May P. Doyle purchased €10,000 worth of goods on credit. On 25 May P. Doyle withdrew €3,950 worth of goods from the business for his personal use.

To record these transactions in the books of P. Doyle, prepare the journal entries and the ledger accounts as follows.

The first journal entry is to recognise the purchase of goods on credit (see **Transaction 6**).

The second journal entry is to recognise the withdrawal of goods from the business that will be for the owner's own personal use rather than a sale of goods.

Journal entries:

	Debit €	Credit €
Purchases account	10,000	
Trade payables account		10,000
To record the purchase of goods on credit.		
Drawings account	3,950	
Purchases account		3,950
To record the withdrawal of goods from the business by the owner.		

Ledger accounts:

PURCHASES ACCOUNT

Debit Side of Account			Credit Side of Account		
Date	**Account Name**	**€**	**Date**	**Account Name**	**€**
10 May	Trade payables	10,000	25 May	Drawings	3,950

DRAWINGS ACCOUNT

Debit Side of Account			Credit Side of Account		
Date	**Account Name**	**€**	**Date**	**Account Name**	**€**
25 May	Purchases	3,950			

TRADE PAYABLES ACCOUNT

Debit Side of Account			Credit Side of Account		
Date	**Account Name**	**€**	**Date**	**Account Name**	**€**
			10 May	Purchases	10,000

(Try **Review Questions 2.12–2.15** at the end of this chapter.)

Up until this point individual, or small numbers of, transactions have been considered in each example. In the next example a number of transactions will be looked at together to reflect more accurately the real business world.

Example 2.21 demonstrates the recording of a series of transactions of the types we have examined above.

EXAMPLE 2.21: A SERIES OF TRANSACTIONS

You are provided with the following information in relation to transactions undertaken by Mr Powell's business in the month of July 2019:

On 1 July 2019, Mr Powell starts a business with €10,000 cash from his own personal funds.

On 2 July 2019 Mr Powell purchases goods for resale worth €2,000 for cash.

On 5 July 2019 Mr Powell sold all of the goods purchased on 2 July for cash of €3,000.

Requirement Prepare the journal entries and ledger accounts for each of these transactions.

Solution

Transaction on 1 July 2019: Mr Powell starts a business with €10,000 cash from his own personal funds. The accounts that are affected are the cash account and the capital account. The cash account is an **asset** account and the capital account is a **capital** or **equity** account. The effect of this transaction is to increase the amount of cash held by the entity and increase the amount of capital owed by the entity to its owner. Therefore, in order to record this transaction the cash account should be debited and the capital account should be credited as follows.

Step 1 Accounts Affected by the Transaction	Step 2 Account Type	Step 3 Increase/Decrease the Account Balance	Step 4 Debit/Credit Account
Cash	Asset	Increase	Debit
Capital	Capital	Increase	Credit

Therefore the journal entry is:

	Debit €	Credit €
Cash account	10,000	
Capital account		10,000

To recognise the capital introduced into the business.

The ledger accounts are:

CASH ACCOUNT

Debit Side of Account			Credit Side of Account		
Date	**Account Name**	**€**	**Date**	**Account Name**	**€**
1 July	Capital	10,000			

CAPITAL ACCOUNT

Debit Side of Account			Credit Side of Account		
Date	**Account Name**	**€**	**Date**	**Account Name**	**€**
			1 July	Cash	10,000

Transaction on 2 July 2019: Mr Powell purchases goods worth €2,000 for cash. The accounts that are affected are the purchases account and the cash account. The purchases account is an **expense** account and the cash account is an **asset** account. The effect of this transaction is to increase the amount of purchases made by the entity and decrease the amount of cash held by the entity. Therefore, in order to record this transaction the purchases account should be debited and the cash account should be credited as follows.

Step 1 Accounts Affected by the Transaction	Step 2 Account Type	Step 3 Increase/Decrease the Account Balance	Step 4 Debit/Credit Account
Purchases	Expense	Increase	Debit
Cash	Asset	Decrease	Credit

Therefore the journal entry is:

	Debit €	Credit €
Purchases account	2,000	
Cash account		2,000

To recognise cash purchases.

The ledger accounts are:

CASH ACCOUNT

Debit Side of Account			Credit Side of Account		
Date	**Account Name**	**€**	**Date**	**Account Name**	**€**
1 July	Capital	10,000	2 July	Purchases	2,000

PURCHASES ACCOUNT

Debit Side of Account			Credit Side of Account		
Date	**Account Name**	**€**	**Date**	**Account Name**	**€**
2 July	Cash	2,000			

Transaction on 5 July 2019: Mr Powell sold all of the goods purchased on 2 July for cash of €3,000.

The accounts that are affected are the sales account and the cash account. The sales account is an **income** account and the cash account is an **asset** account. The effect of this transaction is to increase the amount of sales made by the entity and increase the amount of cash held by the entity. Therefore, in order to record this transaction the sales account should be credited and the cash account should be debited as follows.

Step 1 Accounts Affected by the Transaction	Step 2 Account Type	Step 3 Increase/Decrease the Account Balance	Step 4 Debit/Credit Account
Sales	Income	Increase	Credit
Cash	Asset	Increase	Debit

Therefore the journal entry is:

	Debit €	Credit €
Cash account	3,000	
Sales account		3,000

To recognise the sales transaction.

The ledger accounts are:

Cash Account

Debit Side of Account			Credit Side of Account		
Date	Account Name	€	Date	Account Name	€
1 July	Capital	10,000	2 July	Purchases	2,000
5 July	Sales	3,000			

Sales Account

Debit Side of Account			Credit Side of Account		
Date	Account Name	€	Date	Account Name	€
			5 July	Cash	3,000

More Unusual Sales-related Transactions

Discounts Allowed and Sales Returns

The recording of sales transactions on both a cash and credit basis was dealt with above in this section under the heading, 'Sales-related Transactions'. Two less common sales-related transactions are dealt with in this section, namely allowing discounts to customers and goods returned by customers (also referred to as sales returns/**returns inwards**).

Examples 2.2–2.5 dealt with the recording of payments received in relation to sales, but only where full payment is received. Situations where sales are recognised but the full amounts are not received arise when customers avail of discounts offered or because they have returned some or all of the goods provided to them by the entity. These situations are dealt with below.

Discounts Allowed to Customers   Entities can sell goods on a cash basis or allow their customers a certain period of time to pay for the goods – this period of time is known as the '**credit period**'. The usual credit period is 30 days but can vary from industry to industry. Discounts are allowed by an entity to encourage customers to behave in a certain way. A number of different types of discount can be offered by an entity.

- **Trade discount:** offered to customers who operate certain types of business – for example, a hardware provider may offer discounts to builders, plumbers and electricians. This discount would not be available to any other customers.
- **Cash discount:** offered to customers to encourage them to pay on receipt of goods rather than taking advantage of the credit period offered.
- **Discount for payment within a specified period:** while a business may offer a credit period to its customers, it may encourage earlier payment by offering a discount. For example, an entity may provide its customers with a 30-day credit period and offer a 2% discount on the amount due if payment is made within, say, 10 days instead of at the end of the credit period.

Transaction 19 – Settlement Discount Allowed

When entities sell goods on credit, customers may be incentivised to pay within a certain credit period by being offered a settlement discount. The accounts that are affected by this discount are the discounts allowed account and the trade receivables account. The discounts allowed account is an **expense** account and the trade receivables account is an **asset** account. The effect of the granting of this discount is to decrease the amount owed by trade receivables and increase the amount of the entity's expenses. Therefore, as shown in **Figure 2.5**, in order to record this transaction the trade receivables account should be credited and the discounts allowed account debited as follows.

Accounts Affected by the Transaction	Account Type	Increase/Decrease the Account Balance	Debit/Credit Account
Discounts allowed	Expense	Increase	Debit
Trade receivables	Asset	Decrease	Credit

The journal entry to record and therefore recognise a settlement discount given to a customer, and the record from which the data is input into the entity's accounts, i.e. posted to the ledger accounts, is:

	Debit €	Credit €
Discounts allowed account	X	
Trade receivables account		X
To recognise the discount allowed.		

Example 2.22 demonstrates the journal entries and ledger accounts to record a credit sale followed by the receipt of the payment from the credit customer and the giving of a settlement discount to that customer.

EXAMPLE 2.22: RECORDING A CREDIT SALE FOLLOWED BY FULL SETTLEMENT NET OF DISCOUNT ALLOWED

On 12 June 2019 Algernon Ltd sold goods to Swift Ltd on credit. The terms of the sale were that 30 days' credit was allowed to Swift Ltd, but if they paid the balance in full within 20 days they would receive an early settlement discount of 1%. The credit sales transaction amounted to €3,600. A cheque was received from Swift Ltd on 22 June 2019 in full settlement of the amount due, net of the early settlement discount.

The transactions in relation to the initial credit sale, the provision of the discount and the payment received from the customer net of the discount are recorded as follows.

Journal entries:

	Debit €	Credit €
Trade receivables account	3,600	
Sales account		3,600
To recognise a credit sale.		
Discounts allowed account (€3,600 × 1%)	36	
Trade receivables account		36
To recognise the discount allowed.		
Bank account	3,564	
Trade receivables account		3,564
To recognise the payment received from the customer (€3,600 – €36).		

The ledger accounts recording the above transactions are as follows.

SALES ACCOUNT

	Debit Side of Account			Credit Side of Account	
Date	**Account Name**	**€**	**Date**	**Account Name**	**€**
			12 June	Trade receivables	3,600

TRADE RECEIVABLES ACCOUNT

	Debit Side of Account			Credit Side of Account	
Date	**Account Name**	**€**	**Date**	**Account Name**	**€**
12 June	Sales account	3,600	22 June	Discounts allowed	36
			22 June	Bank	3,564

DISCOUNTS ALLOWED ACCOUNT

	Debit Side of Account			Credit Side of Account	
Date	**Account Name**	**€**	**Date**	**Account Name**	**€**
22 June	Trade receivables	36			

BANK ACCOUNT

	Debit Side of Account			Credit Side of Account	
Date	**Account Name**	**€**	**Date**	**Account Name**	**€**
22 June	Trade receivables	3,564			

Sales Returns/Returns Inwards   Goods may be returned by a customer for a number of reasons, including:
- goods received by a customer from the entity were faulty; or
- incorrect goods were delivered by the entity to a customer; or
- incorrect quantity of goods was delivered by the entity to a customer.

The journal entries required to record the return of goods by a customer are now explained.

Transactions involving the returns of goods by customers to the entity are recorded in the **sales returns account** rather than in the sales account. The reason for maintaining a separate account for returned goods is a business one – it is important for an entity to be able to monitor the frequency and volume of returned goods. In this section we will look at a number of different situations in relation to the return of goods.

Transaction 20 – Customer Returns Goods Originally Paid for in Cash and Receives a Cash Refund

When goods are returned that were sold for cash originally and the entity provides a cash refund, the accounts that are affected are the sales returns account and the cash account. The sales returns account is an **expense** account and the cash account is an **asset** account. The effect of making this refund is to decrease the amount of cash the entity holds and increase the amount of sales returns accepted by the entity. Therefore, as shown in **Figure 2.5**, in order to record this transaction the sales returns account should be debited and the cash account should be credited as follows.

Step 1 Accounts Affected by the Transaction	Step 2 Account Type	Step 3 Increase/Decrease the Account Balance	Step 4 Debit/Credit Account
Sales returns	Expense	Increase	Debit
Cash	Asset	Decrease	Credit

The journal entry to record and therefore recognise a cash refund on goods returned by a customer, and the record from which the data is input into the entity's accounts, i.e. posted to the ledger accounts, is:

	Debit €	Credit €
Sales returns account	X	
Cash account		X

To recognise goods returned by customer for a cash refund.

Transaction 21 – Customer Returns Goods Originally Paid for in Cash and Receives a Credit Note

When goods are returned that were sold for cash originally and the entity provides a credit note the accounts that are affected are the sales returns account and the other payables account. The sales returns account is an **expense** account and the other payables account is a **liability** account. The effect of providing the credit note is to increase the other payables and increase the amount of sales returns accepted by the entity. Therefore, as shown in **Figure 2.5**, in order to record this transaction, the sales returns account should be debited and the other payables account credited as follows.

Accounts Affected by the Transaction	Account Type	Increase/Decrease the Account Balance	Debit/Credit Account
Sales returns	Expense	Increase	Debit
Other payables	Liability	Increase	Credit

The journal entry to record this transaction is:

	Debit €	Credit €
Sales returns account	X	
Other payables account – credit notes		X

To recognise goods returned by a customer and a credit note issued to the customer.

Transaction 22 – Credit Customer Returns Goods

When goods are returned that were sold on credit originally the accounts that are affected are the sales returns account and the trade receivables account. The sales returns account is an **expense** account and the trade receivables account is an **asset** account. The effect of accepting the returned goods is to decrease the amount owed by the customer and increase the amount of sales returns accepted by the entity. Therefore, in order to record this transaction the sales returns account should be debited and the trade receivables account credited as follows.

Step 1 Accounts Affected by the Transaction	Step 2 Account Type	Step 3 Increase/Decrease the Account Balance	Step 4 Debit/Credit Account
Sales returns	Expense	Increase	Debit
Trade receivables	Asset	Decrease	Credit

The journal entry to record and therefore recognise a refund on goods returned by a credit customer, and the record from which the data is input into the entity's accounts, i.e. posted to the ledger accounts, is:

	Debit €	Credit €
Sales returns account	X	
Trade receivables account		X

To recognise goods returned by customer.

(Try **Review Questions 2.16–2.18** at the end of this chapter.)

More Unusual Purchases-related Transactions

Discounts Received and Purchases Returns

The recording of purchases transactions made by an entity on both a cash and credit basis is dealt with above under the heading, 'Purchases-related Transactions'. Two related items are now dealt with in this section, namely receiving discounts from suppliers and goods returned to suppliers (also referred to as purchases returns/**returns outwards**).

Examples 2.6–2.9 dealt with the recording of payments made to suppliers but only in the situations where full payment is made in relation to goods purchased. Situations arise where purchases are recognised but the full amounts are not to be paid because the entity avails of discounts offered or the entity has returned some or all of the goods to its suppliers. These situations are dealt with below.

Discounts from Suppliers   Entities can either purchase goods on a cash or credit basis. Discounts received by an entity reduce the amount the entity has to pay for the goods it uses and the services it consumes. A number of different types of discount can be offered to an entity:

• **Trade discount:** offered by suppliers to entities that operate certain types of business – for example, builders, plumbers and electricians may be offered discounts by a hardware provider.
• **Cash discount:** offered to an entity when it pays for goods or services upon receipt.
• **Discount for payment within a specified period:** a business may have been offered a credit period by its supplier, but to encourage earlier payment its supplier may offer a discount. For example, an entity may have been provided by its supplier with a 30-day credit period and offer a 2% discount on the amount due if payment is made within, say, 10 days instead of at the end of the 30-day credit period.

Transaction 23 – Settlement Discounts Received from a Credit Supplier

When entities purchase goods on credit, the supplier may offer them a discount to encourage payment to be made within a specified time period. The accounts that are affected by this discount are the discounts received account and the trade payables account. The discounts received account is an **income** account and the trade payables account is a **liability** account. The effect of receiving this discount is to decrease the amount owed by the entity to trade payables and increase the amount of the entity's income. Therefore, as shown in **Figure 2.5**, in order to record this transaction the trade payables account should be debited and the discounts received account credited as follows.

Accounts Affected by the Transaction	Account Type	Increase/Decrease the Account Balance	Debit/Credit Account
Discounts received	Income	Increase	Credit
Trade payables	Liability	Decrease	Debit

The journal entry to record and therefore recognise a discount received from a credit supplier, and the record from which the data is input into the entity's accounts, i.e. posted to the ledger accounts, is:

	Debit €	Credit €
Trade payables account	X	
Discounts received account		X
To recognise the discount received.		

Example 2.23 below demonstrates the journal entries and the ledger accounts to record a credit purchase followed by the payment to the supplier net of the settlement discount.

EXAMPLE 2.23: RECORDING A CREDIT PURCHASE FOLLOWED BY PAYMENT NET OF SETTLEMENT DISCOUNT RECEIVED

On 29 September 2019 Sonnet Ltd purchased goods from Crunch Ltd on credit. The terms of the transaction are that 30 days' credit was allowed to Sonnet Ltd, but if it paid the balance in full within 20 days it would receive an early settlement discount of 1%. The purchase transaction amounted to €5,300. A cheque was issued by Sonnet Ltd to Crunch Ltd on 15 October 2019 in full settlement of the amount due, net of the early settlement discount.

To record these transactions in Sonnet Ltd's accounting records, prepare the journal entries and ledger accounts in relation to these transactions as follows.

Journal entries:

	Debit €	Credit €
Purchases account	5,300	
Trade payables account		5,300
To recognise the credit purchase transaction.		
Trade payables account (€5,300 × 1%)	53	
Discounts received account		53
To recognise the discount received.		

	Debit €	Credit €
Trade payables account	5,247	
Bank account		5,247

To recognise the payment made to the supplier (€5,300 – €53).

The ledger accounts recording the above transactions are as follows.

Purchases Account

Debit Side of Account			Credit Side of Account		
Date	**Account Name**	**€**	**Date**	**Account Name**	**€**
29 Sep	Trade payables	5,300			

Trade Payables Account

Debit Side of Account			Credit Side of Account		
Date	**Account Name**	**€**	**Date**	**Account Name**	**€**
15 Oct	Discounts received	53	29 Sep	Purchases	5,300
15 Oct	Bank	5,247			

Discounts Received Account

Debit Side of Account			Credit Side of Account		
Date	**Account Name**	**€**	**Date**	**Account Name**	**€**
			15 Oct	Trade payables	53

Purchases Returns/Returns Outwards Goods may be returned for a number of reasons, including:
* goods received by the entity were faulty;
* incorrect goods were delivered by the supplier to the entity; or
* incorrect quantity of goods was delivered by the supplier to the entity.

Transaction 24 – Goods Returned to a Supplier in Exchange for Cash

Where goods are returned that were purchased for cash originally and the supplier provides a cash refund, the accounts affected are the purchases returned account and the cash account. The **purchases returned account** is an **income** account and the cash account is an **asset** account. The effect of returning the goods is to increase the amount of the entity's income and to increase the amount of cash the entity holds. Therefore, as shown in **Figure 2.5**, in order to record this transaction the purchases returns account should be credited and the cash account debited as follows.

Accounts Affected by the Transaction	Account Type	Increase/Decrease the Account Balance	Debit/Credit Account
Purchases returns	Income	Increase	Credit
Cash	Asset	Increase	Debit

The journal entry to record and therefore recognise a cash refund for goods returned to a supplier, and the record from which the data is input into the entity's accounts, i.e. posted to the ledger accounts, is:

	Debit €	Credit €
Cash account	X	
Purchases returns account		X

To recognise goods returned to supplier.

Transaction 25 – Goods That had been Paid for in Cash Returned to a Supplier in Exchange for a Credit Note

Where goods are returned that were purchased for cash originally and the supplier provides a credit note, the accounts affected are the purchases returned account and the other receivables account. The purchases returned account is an **income** account and the other receivables account is an **asset** account. The effect of returning the goods is to increase the amount of the entity's income and to increase the amount due from other receivables to the entity. Therefore, as shown in **Figure 2.5**, in order to record this transaction the purchases returns account should be credited and the other receivables account debited as follows.

Accounts Affected by the Transaction	Account Type	Increase/Decrease the Account Balance	Debit/Credit Account
Purchases returns	Income	Increase	Credit
Other receivables	Asset	Increase	Debit

The journal entry to record and therefore recognise a credit note on goods returned to a supplier, and the record from which the data is input into the entity's accounts, i.e. posted to the ledger accounts, is:

	Debit €	Credit €
Other receivables account – credit notes	X	
Purchase returns account		X

To recognise goods returned to the supplier.

Transaction 26 – Goods That had Been Purchased on Credit Returned to a Supplier

Where goods are returned that were purchased on credit originally, the accounts affected are the purchases returns account and the trade payables account. The purchases returns account is an **income** account and the trade payables account is a **liability** account. The effect of returning the goods is to increase the amount of the entity's income and to decrease the amount owed by the entity to trade payables. Therefore, in order to record this transaction the purchases returns account should be credited and the trade payables account should be debited as follows.

Accounts Affected by the Transaction	Account Type	Increase/Decrease the Account Balance	Debit/Credit Account
Purchases returns	Income	Increase	Credit
Trade payables	Liability	Decrease	Debit

Therefore the journal entry to record and therefore recognise the return of goods to a supplier, and the record from which the data is input into the entity's accounts, i.e. posted to the ledger accounts, is:

	Debit €	Credit €
Trade payables account	X	
Purchases returns account		X

To recognise goods returned to the supplier.

(Try **Review Questions 2.19–2.21** at the end of this chapter.)

2.3 THE TRIAL BALANCE

So far the recording of some of the most frequently occurring transactions in the financial records of an entity has been considered. The next step is to understand how transactions, recorded as journal entries that update ledger accounts, result in the figures presented in the financial statements (i.e. the SOPL and the SOFP). The steps involved are as follows.

1. Each ledger account is 'balanced' (see **Section 2.1**), showing the balance carried down (balance c/d), also referred to as the balance carried forward (balance c/f), and the balance brought down (balance b/d), also referred to as the balance brought forward (balance b/f).
2. The balance brought down (or brought forward) is listed in a financial statement known as a '**trial balance**'.
3. Using the information listed in the trial balance, the SOPL and SOFP are prepared.

A 'trial balance' is the basis upon which the financial statements are prepared. The trial balance lists the balance in each of the ledger accounts in an entity's accounting records, listing the figures for the accounts with debit balances in the debit column and the figures for the accounts with credit balances in the credit column. Due to the fact that every financial transaction results in debit entries in the ledger accounts that are perfectly equal to their corresponding credit entries in the ledger accounts, the total of the figures in the debit column should always be equal to the total of the figures in the credit column. If these two totals differ, this means that mistakes have been made in the posting of journal entries. Indeed, one of the purposes of the trial balance is to identify at least some errors in the accounting records before the financial statements are prepared.

Example 2.24 demonstrates the journal entries and ledger accounts for a number of transactions and shows their impact on the trial balance.

Note: it is important to point out that while, in **Example 2.24**, there is only one transaction per day, each day is treated as a reporting period and a trial balance is prepared at the end of each day; this is purely to illustrate how ledger accounts are balanced off. Normally, ledger accounts are only balanced off after **all** transactions for a reporting period of more than one day have been recorded; only then the trial balance would be prepared.

Example 2.24: Preparation of a Trial Balance

Transaction (a) Ms R. Reilly set up a business on 1 August 2019. She introduced €20,000 of her own funds into the business, which she immediately lodged to the business bank account.

As explained above (see **Transaction 15**), the journal entry is:

	Debit €	Credit €
Bank account	20,000	
Capital account		20,000

To recognise the introduction of capital into the business by the owner.

The ledger accounts are:

Bank Account

Debit Side of Account			Credit Side of Account		
Date	Account Name	€	Date	Account Name	€
1 Aug	Capital account	20,000			

Capital Account

Debit Side of Account			Credit Side of Account		
Date	Account Name	€	Date	Account Name	€
			1 Aug	Bank account	20,000

Before the list of balances on the ledger accounts can be prepared (i.e. the trial balance is extracted from the ledger accounts), each account must be balanced (see **Section 2.1**). Each of the above accounts will now be balanced.

Balancing the Ledger Accounts

Bank account – the bank account has €20,000 on the debit side of the account and there are no entries on the credit side. A balancing entry is required on the credit side of the account to make the debit and credit sides equal:

Bank Account

Debit Side of Account			Credit Side of Account		
Date	Account Name	€	Date	Account Name	€
1 Aug	Capital	20,000	1 Aug	Balance c/d	20,000
2 Aug	Balance b/d	20,000			

The balancing figure entered on the credit side is labelled 'balance carried down' or 'balance c/d'. The balance is carried down on the last day of the reporting period, in this case one day, i.e. 1 August, and brought down ('balance b/d') on the opposite side of the account (the debit side in this case) as the opening figure for the next reporting period. The date on which the balance is brought down is the first day of the next reporting period, i.e. 2 August.

Capital account – the capital account has €20,000 on the credit side of the account and there are no entries on the debit side. A balancing entry is required on the debit side of the account to make the debit and credit sides equal:

CAPITAL ACCOUNT					
Debit Side of Account			**Credit Side of Account**		
Date	**Account Name**	**€**	**Date**	**Account Name**	**€**
1 Aug	Balance c/d	20,000	1 Aug	Bank	20,000
			2 Aug	Balance b/d	20,000

The balancing figure entered on the debit side is labelled 'balance carried down' or 'balance c/d' on the last day of a reporting period. This figure is brought down on the opposite side of the account (the credit side in this case) as the opening figure for the first day of the next reporting period; it is referred to as 'balance brought down' or 'balance b/d'. When a balance is carried down, an entry is made on one side of an account; when the same amount is brought down on the opposite side of the account, the double entry for that amount is completed, i.e. when a balance is carried down and also brought down, double entry is preserved.

After this transaction has been recorded in the two relevant ledger accounts, the trial balance would be presented as follows:

Ms R. Reilly
TRIAL BALANCE
at 1 August 2019 (being the last day of the reporting period)

	Debit €	Credit €
Bank	20,000	
Capital		20,000
	20,000	20,000

(*Note*: remember, a trial balance lists the **balances** in each of the accounts in an entity's accounting records, listing the figures for the accounts with debit balances in the debit column and the figures for the accounts with credit balances in the credit column.)

Transaction (b) On 2 August 2019 Ms R. Reilly's business purchased goods worth €2,500 and paid for them by cheque. (*Note*: in introducing Transaction (b), we are assuming that Transactions (a) and (b) occur within the same reporting period, i.e. 1–2 August, and that the ledger accounts are balanced and the balances carried down on 2 August and brought down on 3 August.)

As explained in a similar transaction above (see **Transaction 5**), the journal entry is:

	Debit €	Credit €
Purchases account	2,500	
Bank account		2,500
To recognise the purchase of goods.		

The ledger accounts showing both the transactions to date (**Transaction (a)** and **Transaction (b)**) are as follows.

BANK ACCOUNT

Debit Side of Account			Credit Side of Account		
Date	**Account Name**	**€**	**Date**	**Account Name**	**€**
1 Aug	Capital	20,000	2 Aug	Purchases	2,500

CAPITAL ACCOUNT

Debit Side of Account			Credit Side of Account		
Date	**Account Name**	**€**	**Date**	**Account Name**	**€**
			1 Aug	Bank	20,000

PURCHASES ACCOUNT

Debit Side of Account			Credit Side of Account		
Date	**Account Name**	**€**	**Date**	**Account Name**	**€**
2 Aug	Bank	2,500			

Balancing the Ledger Accounts

Bank account – there are entries on both the debit and credit sides of the bank account. The difference between the amounts on the debit and credit sides is the balance carried down. In this example the balance carried down is €17,500 (i.e. €20,000 – €2,500).

Both sides of the account are totalled and should agree to the same figure, in this case €20,000. On the debit side the total is made up of a single entry, the €20,000 capital introduced to the business, and on the credit side it is made up of the purchases transaction for €2,500 and the balancing figure of €17,500. *Note:* the total figures are double underlined.

BANK ACCOUNT

Debit Side of Account			Credit Side of Account		
Date	**Account Name**	**€**	**Date**	**Account Name**	**€**
1 Aug	Capital account	20,000	2 Aug	Purchases	2,500
			2 Aug	Balance c/d	17,500
		20,000			20,000
3 Aug	Balance b/d	17,500			

The balancing figure, which is before the totals, is brought down for the start of the next reporting period on the opposite side of the account after the totals. The balance b/d is presented in the ledger account above as the entry on 3 August 2019, i.e. the first day of the next reporting period. An entity's ledger accounts are normally balanced at the end of a reporting period during which numerous transactions would have been recorded. For the purpose of this example, in order to show the impact upon the ledger accounts of individual transactions as they accumulate over a short period of time, the ledger accounts are balanced after only a few transactions have been recorded.

Capital account – the capital account has €20,000 on the credit side of the account and there are no entries on the debit side. The double entry required as a result of **Transaction**

(b) did not impact the capital account, so the balancing of the capital account is as illustrated above except for the date on which the balance is carried down and brought down, i.e. 2 and 3 August.

CAPITAL ACCOUNT

Debit Side of Account			Credit Side of Account		
Date	**Account Name**	**€**	**Date**	**Account Name**	**€**
2 Aug	Balance c/d	20,000	1 Aug	Bank	20,000
			3 Aug	Balance b/d	20,000

Purchases account – the purchases account has €2,500 on the debit side of the account and there are no entries on the credit side. A balancing entry is required on the credit side of the account to make the debit and credit sides equal:

PURCHASES ACCOUNT

Debit Side of Account			Credit Side of Account		
Date	**Account Name**	**€**	**Date**	**Account Name**	**€**
2 Aug	Bank	2,500	2 Aug	Balance c/d	2,500
3 Aug	Balance b/d	2,500			

After **Transactions (a)** and **(b)** have been recorded in the relevant ledger accounts, the trial balance would be presented as follows:

Ms R. Reilly
TRIAL BALANCE
at 2 August 2019

	Debit €	Credit €
Bank	17,500	
Capital		20,000
Purchases	2,500	
	20,000	20,000

Transaction (c) On 3 August 2019 the business sold goods worth €2,900 for cash. (**Note:** again, in introducing Transaction (c) we are assuming that Transactions (a), (b) and (c) occur within the same reporting period, i.e. 1–3 August, and that the ledger accounts are balanced and the balances carried down on 3 August and brought down on 4 August.)

As explained above (see **Transaction 1**), the journal entry is:

	Debit €	Credit €
Cash account	2,900	
Sales account		2,900

To recognise the cash sale.

The ledger accounts showing all the transactions to date (**Transactions (a), (b)** and **(c)**), after they have been balanced on 3 August (for the first time), are as follows:

BANK ACCOUNT

	Debit Side of Account			Credit Side of Account	
Date	Account Name	€	Date	Account Name	€
1 Aug	Capital	20,000	2 Aug	Purchases	2,500
			3 Aug	Balance c/d	17,500
		20,000			20,000
4 Aug	Balance b/d	17,500			

CAPITAL ACCOUNT

	Debit Side of Account			Credit Side of Account	
Date	Account Name	€	Date	Account Name	€
3 Aug	Balance c/d	20,000	1 Aug	Bank	20,000
			4 Aug	Balance b/d	20,000

PURCHASES ACCOUNT

	Debit Side of Account			Credit Side of Account	
Date	Account Name	€	Date	Account Name	€
2 Aug	Bank	2,500	3 Aug	Balance c/d	2,500
4 Aug	Balance b/d	2,500			

CASH ACCOUNT

	Debit Side of Account			Credit Side of Account	
Date	Account Name	€	Date	Account Name	€
3 Aug	Sales	2,900	3 Aug	Balance c/d	2,900
4 Aug	Balance b/d	2,900			

SALES ACCOUNT

	Debit Side of Account			Credit Side of Account	
Date	Account Name	€	Date	Account Name	€
3 Aug	Balance c/d	2,900	3 Aug	Cash	2,900
			4 Aug	Balance b/d	2,900

After **Transactions (a), (b)** and **(c)** have been recorded in the relevant ledger accounts, the trial balance would be presented as follows:

Ms R. Reilly
TRIAL BALANCE
at 3 August 2019

	Debit €	Credit €
Bank	17,500	
Capital		20,000
Purchases	2,500	
Cash	2,900	
Sales		2,900
	22,900	22,900

Transaction (d) On 10 August 2019 the business bought goods on credit worth €3,200. (**Note**: again, in introducing Transaction (d) we are assuming that Transactions (a), (b), (c) and (d) occur within the same reporting period, i.e. 1–10 August, and that the ledger accounts are balanced and the balances carried down on 10 August and brought down on 11 August.)

As explained above (see **Transaction 6**), the journal entry is:

	Debit €	Credit €
Purchases account	3,200	
Trade payables account		3,200

To recognise the purchase of goods on credit.

The ledger accounts showing all the transactions to date (**Transactions (a), (b), (c)** and **(d)**), after they have been balanced on 10 August are as follows:

BANK ACCOUNT

Debit Side of Account			Credit Side of Account		
Date	Account Name	€	Date	Account Name	€
1 Aug	Capital	20,000	2 Aug	Purchases	2,500
			10 Aug	Balance c/d	17,500
		20,000			20,000
11 Aug	Balance b/d	17,500			

CAPITAL ACCOUNT

Debit Side of Account			Credit Side of Account		
Date	Account Name	€	Date	Account Name	€
10 Aug	Balance c/d	20,000	1 Aug	Bank	20,000
			11 Aug	Balance b/d	20,000

PURCHASES ACCOUNT

Debit Side of Account			Credit Side of Account		
Date	Account Name	€	Date	Account Name	€
2 Aug	Bank	2,500	10 Aug	Balance c/d	5,700
10 Aug	Trade payables	3,200			
		5,700			5,700
11 Aug	Balance b/d	5,700			

CASH ACCOUNT

Debit Side of Account			Credit Side of Account		
Date	Account Name	€	Date	Account Name	€
3 Aug	Sales	2,900	10 Aug	Balance c/d	2,900
11 Aug	Balance b/d	2,900			

SALES ACCOUNT

Debit Side of Account			Credit Side of Account		
Date	Account Name	€	Date	Account Name	€
10 Aug	Balance c/d	2,900	3 Aug	Cash	2,900
			11 Aug	Balance b/d	2,900

TRADE PAYABLES ACCOUNT

Debit Side of Account			Credit Side of Account		
Date	Account Name	€	Date	Account Name	€
10 Aug	Balance c/d	3,200	10 Aug	Purchases	3,200
			11 Aug	Balance b/d	3,200

After **Transactions (a), (b), (c)** and **(d)** have been recorded in the relevant ledger accounts, the trial balance would be presented as follows:

Ms R. Reilly
TRIAL BALANCE
at 10 August 2019

	Debit €	Credit €
Bank	17,500	
Capital		20,000
Purchases	5,700	
Sales		2,900
Cash	2,900	
Trade payables		3,200
	26,100	26,100

Transaction (e) On 15 August 2019 Ms R. Reilly's business sold goods worth €4,000 on credit. (**Note:** again, in introducing Transaction (e) we are assuming that Transactions (a), (b), (c), (d) and (e) occur within the same reporting period, i.e. 1–15 August, and that the ledger accounts are balanced and the balances carried down on 15 August and brought down on 16 August.)

As explained above (see **Transaction 2**), the journal entry is:

	Debit €	Credit €
Trade receivables account	4,000	
Sales account		4,000
To recognise the credit sales.		

The ledger accounts showing all the transactions to date (**Transactions (a), (b), (c), (d) and (e)**) after they have been balanced on 15 August are as follows:

BANK ACCOUNT

Debit Side of Account			Credit Side of Account		
Date	Account Name	€	Date	Account Name	€
1 Aug	Capital	20,000	2 Aug	Purchases	2,500
			10 Aug	Balance c/d	17,500
		20,000			20,000
11 Aug	Balance b/d	17,500			

CAPITAL ACCOUNT

Debit Side of Account			Credit Side of Account		
Date	**Account Name**	**€**	**Date**	**Account Name**	**€**
10 Aug	Balance c/d	20,000	1 Aug	Bank	20,000
			11 Aug	Balance b/d	20,000

PURCHASES ACCOUNT

Debit Side of Account			Credit Side of Account		
Date	**Account Name**	**€**	**Date**	**Account Name**	**€**
2 Aug	Bank	2,500	10 Aug	Balance c/d	5,700
10 Aug	Trade payables	3,200			
		5,700			5,700
11 Aug	Balance b/d	5,700			

CASH ACCOUNT

Debit Side of Account			Credit Side of Account		
Date	**Account Name**	**€**	**Date**	**Account Name**	**€**
3 Aug	Sales	2,900	10 Aug	Balance c/d	2,900
11 Aug	Balance b/d	2,900			

TRADE RECEIVABLES ACCOUNT

Debit Side of Account			Credit Side of Account		
Date	**Account Name**	**€**	**Date**	**Account Name**	**€**
15 Aug	Sales	4,000	15 Aug	Balance c/d	4,000
16 Aug	Balance b/d	4,000			

SALES ACCOUNT

Debit Side of Account			Credit Side of Account		
Date	**Account Name**	**€**	**Date**	**Account Name**	**€**
15 Aug	Balance c/d	6,900	3 Aug	Cash	2,900
			15 Aug	Trade receivables	4,000
		6,900			6,900
			16 Aug	Balance b/d	6,900

TRADE PAYABLES ACCOUNT

Debit Side of Account			Credit Side of Account		
Date	**Account Name**	**€**	**Date**	**Account Name**	**€**
10 Aug	Balance c/d	3,200	10 Aug	Purchases	3,200
			11 Aug	Balance b/d	3,200

After **Transactions (a)**, **(b)**, **(c)**, **(d)** and **(e)** have been recorded in the relevant ledger accounts, the trial balance would be presented as follows:

Ms R. Reilly
TRIAL BALANCE
at 15 August 2019

	Debit €	Credit €
Bank	17,500	
Capital		20,000
Purchases	5,700	
Sales		6,900
Cash	2,900	
Trade payables		3,200
Trade receivables	4,000	
	30,100	30,100

(Try **Review Questions 2.22** and **2.23** at the end of this chapter.)

2.4 FINANCIAL STATEMENTS

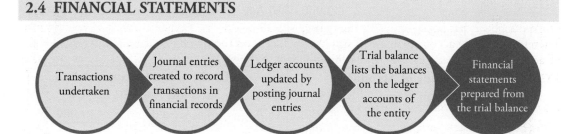

The purpose of financial statements is to provide users of those statements with information that is relevant to them, such as the performance of the entity in a particular reporting period, e.g. whether a business entity has generated a profit or incurred a loss. The SOPL provides this information (see **Chapter 1**).

An entity will prepare a number of financial statements for each reporting period. In this chapter we will examine in more detail two of the financial statements that are normally prepared by business entities:
• the statement of profit or loss; and
• the statement of financial position.

The Statement of Profit or Loss (SOPL)

The SOPL, which we introduced in **Chapter 1**, is a ledger account – in fact, one of the very few ledger accounts that do not have the word 'account' included in their names. There are two reasons for preparing the SOPL: first, to calculate the profit made, or the loss incurred, by the business for the reporting period (also referred to as the accounting period); secondly, to clear the balances off the income and expense accounts in preparation for the next reporting period. Each income account and each expense account only records income/expenses for one reporting period – their balances need to be transferred at the end of each reporting period so as to start each new reporting period with a zero balance. These two objectives are met by transferring the balances on all the income accounts and expense accounts to the SOPL (or, in some cases, to the cost of sales account – see below). The resultant balance on the SOPL (the profit or loss for the period) is then posted to the capital account (in the case of sole traders and partnerships) or the retained earnings account (in the case of companies).

The balance on an income account is recorded in the SOPL by posting the following journal entry:

	Debit €	Credit €
Income account	X	
SOPL		X

Transfer of the balance on an income account to the SOPL.

The balance on an expense account is transferred to the SOPL by posting the following journal entry:

	Debit €	Credit €
SOPL	X	
Expense account		X

Transfer of the balance on an expense account to the SOPL.

Once the SOPL has been prepared, the balance on all income and expense accounts will be zero. Therefore the only accounts that will still have balances on them will be the remaining three types of accounts, i.e. asset, liability and capital/equity accounts, which we will discuss in the next section on the SOFP.

Cost of Sales Accounts: Retailers and Manufacturers

If the SOPL is that of either a retailer or a manufacturer, before it can be prepared, a **cost of sales account** (also referred to as the cost of goods sold account) must be prepared.

Retailers   In the case of a retailer, the cost of sales account is the account to which all the balances on the accounts that are directly attributable to the acquisition of the goods sold by an entity are transferred at the end of a reporting period. Items that are directly attributable to the acquisition of goods sold by an entity include: purchases of goods for resale, returns of purchases of goods for resale, transportation costs relating to goods purchased for resale (also known as **carriage inwards**), customs duty on goods purchased for resale, and opening and closing inventories of goods purchased for resale. (*Note*: items that are **indirectly** attributable to the acquisition of goods sold by an entity are **excluded** from the cost of sales account, i.e. selling and distribution expenses and administration expenses.)

Manufacturers   In the case of a manufacturer, the cost of sales account is the account to which all the balances on the accounts that are directly attributable to the acquisition of the raw materials purchased **and** the conversion of the raw materials into finished goods by an entity are transferred at the end of a reporting period. Items that are directly attributable to the acquisition of raw materials include: purchases of raw materials to be used in the production process, returns of purchases of raw materials, transportation costs relating to raw materials purchased for resale, customs duty on raw materials purchased, and opening and closing inventory/(ies). Costs of converting the raw materials into finished goods include: manufacturing workers' wages, production supervisor's salary and expenses incurred in repairing and maintaining the production machinery. (Again, items that are **indirectly** attributable to the acquisition and conversion of raw materials into goods sold by an entity are **excluded** from the cost of sales account, i.e. selling and distribution expenses and administration expenses.)

Transferring Relevant Balances to the Cost of Sales Account   Once those accounts that need to be transferred to the cost of sales account have been identified, the transfers are made as follows. If an account for an item directly attributable to the cost of sales has a debit balance on it, such as carriage inwards and purchases, the debit balance on this account is transferred to the cost of sales account. The following journal entry shows the posting in relation to the cost of sales:

	Debit €	Credit €
Cost of sales account	X	
Carriage inwards account		X

Transfer of the debit balance on an account directly attributable to the cost of sales.

If an account for an item directly attributable to the cost of sales has a credit balance on it, such as purchases returns, this credit balance is transferred to the cost of sales account by posting the following journal entry:

	Debit €	Credit €
Purchases returns account	X	
Cost of sales account		X

Transfer of the credit balance on an account directly attributable to the cost of sales.

Transferring the Debit Balance from the Cost of Sales Account to the SOPL   When the balances on all the relevant accounts have been transferred to the cost of sales account, the balance on the cost of sales account, which is an expense account, is itself transferred to the SOPL in the same way as all other expense account balances are transferred to the SOPL, as shown above. (We will look at this in greater detail in **Chapter 3, Inventory and Cost of Sales**.)

Format of the Statement of Profit or Loss

The layout or format of the statement of profit or loss in the ledger, i.e. as a ledger account, is often not easily understood by many users of the financial statements. As a result, the information recorded in the SOPL ledger account is redrafted and presented in the financial statements in a format that is more easily comprehensible by non-accountants.

Generally, financial statements are prepared annually and the SOPL would be headed up as follows:

Business Name
STATEMENT OF PROFIT OR LOSS
for the period of time (e.g. year ended), date (e.g. 31 December 2019)

The date given in the heading of the SOPL is the final date of the period covered by the statement. In this instance, the SOPL relates to the year ended 31 December 2019, which means that the income earned and expenses incurred in the period 1 January 2019 to 31 December 2019 are included in the calculation of the profit or loss for the period. Income and expenses outside of this period are not reflected in the SOPL for this period.

The format of the SOPL of a retail business would be as follows:

Business Name
STATEMENT OF PROFIT OR LOSS
for the year ended 31 December 2019

	€
Sales	X
Cost of sales	(X)
Gross profit	X
Rent	(X)
Insurance	(X)
Light and heat	(X)
Net profit	X

The gross profit figure should be clearly identified and is calculated as the difference between the sales and the cost of sales figures.

(***Note***: the list of expenses (rent, insurance, light and heat) provided in the above SOPL is not a definitive list – it is merely to provide a few examples of typical expenses incurred by any entity.)

The Statement of Financial Position (SOFP)

As introduced in **Chapter 1**, the SOFP is an organised list of the balances that remain on the ledger accounts after the SOPL has been prepared. It details the balances on the following types of ledger account:
- assets,
- liabilities, and
- capital (also known as equity).

The SOFP is prepared at a particular **point** in time (unlike the SOPL, which relates to a specific **period** of time – usually one year). The date at which the SOFP is prepared is known as the **reporting date**, or the accounting date.

On a SOFP the total of the asset figures should always be equal to the total of all the capital (or equity) and the liabilities figures. If these two totals differ, it means that mistakes have been made in the posting of the journal entries relating to the preparation of the SOPL (see above) or the addition of the figures in the SOFP.

Presentation of Assets and Liabilities   Assets are classified in the SOFP as either non-current assets or current assets:
- **Non-current assets** are assets intended to be used continuously by the entity for more than 12 months.
- **Current assets** are cash and other assets reasonably expected to be converted to cash in the normal course of the entity's activities (usually within 12 months), including inventories and receivables. (There is an exception to this 12-month rule, which will be dealt with in **Chapter 19, Presentation of Financial Statements**.) Current assets are listed in order of the least liquid to the most liquid. The more '**liquid**' an asset is, the more readily it is convertible to known amounts of cash. Normally, the least liquid current asset held by an entity will be inventory, and the most liquid will be cash. Therefore, the first current asset listed will normally be inventory, then trade receivables as, for the most part, payment will be received from them within the credit period allowed by the entity. Bank and cash are always listed last as they are liquid resources available to the company.

Liabilities are classified in the SOFP as either non-current liabilities or current liabilities.
- **Non-current liabilities** are amounts owed by the entity that will take longer than 12 months from the reporting date to be paid.
- **Current liabilities** are the amounts owed by the entity that will be paid within 12 months of the reporting date.

Format of the Statement of Financial Position

The format of a typical SOFP is shown below. Note that totals are double underlined.

Business Name
STATEMENT OF FINANCIAL POSITION
as at (the reporting date) 31 December 2019

	€	€
Non-current Assets		
Property		X
Equipment		X
Motor vehicles		X
		X
Current Assets		
Inventory	X	
Trade receivables	X	
Cash and cash equivalents	X	X
TOTAL ASSETS		X
Equity		
Capital		X
Retained earnings		X
		X
Non-current Liabilities		
Loans		X
Current Liabilities		
Bank overdraft	X	
Trade payables	X	X
TOTAL EQUITY AND LIABILITIES		X

(**Note:** the list of assets, liabilities and capital provided in the above SOFP is not a definitive list – it is merely to provide a few examples of typical items that appear in this financial statement.)

Preparing Financial Statements from a Trial Balance

Once a trial balance has been prepared that balances, it can be used as the basis on which to draft financial statements.

Example 2.25 demonstrates the preparation of a SOPL and a SOFP from a trial balance.

EXAMPLE 2.25: PREPARATION OF FINANCIAL STATEMENTS FROM A TRIAL BALANCE

You have been provided with the following trial balance of B. Newton as at 31 December 2019 and are asked to prepare the following financial statements:

(a) the SOPL of B. Newton for the year ended 31 December 2019; and
(b) the SOFP of B. Newton as at 31 December 2019.

B. Newton
TRIAL BALANCE
as at 31 December 2019

	Debit €	Credit €
Sales		800,000
Purchases	483,500	
Rent	48,000	
Insurance	15,000	
Light and heat	42,000	
Motor expenses	26,000	
Manufacturing wages	90,000	
Administration salaries	51,000	
Equipment	220,000	
Motor vehicles	80,000	
Trade receivables	37,000	
Bank	12,500	
Capital		157,000
Loan		120,000
Trade payables		28,000
	1,105,000	1,105,000

(**Note:** to simplify the example, we are assuming that B. Newton did not have any inventory at either the start or the end of the reporting period. This would not typically be the case. See **Chapter 3, Inventory and Cost of Sales**.)

Solution

As this is the first time that we are preparing financial statements in this textbook, let us look through the trial balance and identify the account type of each line item and in which financial statement the item will be presented: the SOPL or the SOFP.

	Account Type	Financial Statement	Debit €	Credit €
Sales	Income	SOPL		800,000
Purchases	Expense	SOPL	483,500	
Rent	Expense	SOPL	48,000	
Insurance	Expense	SOPL	15,000	
Light and heat	Expense	SOPL	42,000	
Motor expenses	Expense	SOPL	26,000	
Manufacturing wages	Expense	SOPL	90,000	

Administration salaries	Expense	SOPL	51,000	
Equipment	Asset	SOFP	220,000	
Motor vehicles	Asset	SOFP	80,000	
Trade Receivables	Asset	SOFP	37,000	
Bank	Asset	SOFP	12,500	
Capital	Capital	SOFP		157,000
Loan	Liability	SOFP		120,000
Trade payables	Liability	SOFP		28,000
			1,105,000	1,105,000

In now preparing the SOPL it is important to remember that the SOPL is part of the double-entry system, i.e. it is a ledger account (see **Section 2.2**). Therefore, journal entries are required in order to transfer the balances from only the income and expense ledger accounts to the SOPL. (As we have seen, for retailers and manufacturers the balances or relevant accounts are first gathered together in a cost of sales account, the balance of which is then transferred to the SOPL.) To prepare the SOPL, the balance on each income and expense account must be posted from its respective account to the SOPL.

After the journal entry is posted the sales account will appear as follows:

SALES ACCOUNT

Debit Side of Account			Credit Side of Account		
Date	Account Name	€	Date	Account Name	€
31 Dec	SOPL	800,000	31 Dec	Balance b/d	800,000

The balance on the sales account is now zero for the new reporting period commencing on 1 January 2020.

For each of the expense accounts relating to the calculation of the cost of sales figure (in this case purchases and manufacturing wages), a journal entry will be posted in the accounts of the entity:

	Debit €	Credit €
Cost of sales account	483,500	
Purchases account		483,500

To recognise the purchases incurred for the period in the cost of sales account.

After the journal entry is posted the purchases account will appear as follows:

PURCHASES ACCOUNT

Debit Side of Account			Credit Side of Account		
Date	Account Name	€	Date	Account Name	€
31 Dec	Balance b/d	483,500	31 Dec	Cost of sales	483,500

	Debit €	Credit €
Cost of sales account	90,000	
Manufacturing wages account		90,000

To recognise the manufacturing wages incurred for the period in the cost of sales account.

After the journal entry is posted the manufacturing wages account will appear as follows:

Manufacturing Wages Account

	Debit Side of Account			Credit Side of Account	
Date	**Account Name**	**€**	**Date**	**Account Name**	**€**
31 Dec	Balance b/d	90,000	31 Dec	Cost of sales	90,000

Once all the relevant entries have been made in the cost of sales account, its balance is transferred to the SOPL. The journal entry to make the transfer is:

	Debit €	Credit €
SOPL	573,500	
Cost of sales account		573,500

To record the cost of sales in the SOPL.

In this example, the cost of sales account would appear as follows:

Cost of Sales Account

	Debit Side of Account			Credit Side of Account	
Date	**Account Name**	**€**	**Date**	**Account Name**	**€**
31 Dec	Purchases	483,500	31 Dec	SOPL	573,500
31 Dec	Manufacturing wages	90,000			
		573,500			573,500

The remaining balances on the expense accounts will be transferred to the SOPL by creating and posting journal entries. The journal entry to transfer the balance on the rent account is:

	Debit €	Credit €
SOPL	48,000	
Rent account		48,000

To recognise the rent cost incurred for the period in the SOPL.

After the journal entry is posted the rent account appears as follows:

Rent Account

	Debit Side of Account			Credit Side of Account	
Date	**Account Name**	**€**	**Date**	**Account Name**	**€**
31 Dec	Balance b/d	48,000	31 Dec	SOPL	48,000

The journal entry to transfer the balance on the insurance account to the SOPL is:

	Debit €	Credit €
SOPL	15,000	
Insurance account		15,000

To recognise the insurance cost incurred for the period in the SOPL.

After the journal entry is posted, the insurance account appears as follows:

INSURANCE ACCOUNT

Debit Side of Account			Credit Side of Account		
Date	**Account Name**	**€**	**Date**	**Account Name**	**€**
31 Dec	Balance b/d	15,000	31 Dec	SOPL	15,000

The journal entry to transfer the balance on the light and heat account to the SOPL is:

	Debit €	Credit €
SOPL	42,000	
Light and heat account		42,000

To recognise the light and heat cost incurred for the period in the SOPL.

After the journal entry is posted, the light and heat account appears as follows:

LIGHT AND HEAT ACCOUNT

Debit Side of Account			Credit Side of Account		
Date	**Account Name**	**€**	**Date**	**Account Name**	**€**
31 Dec	Balance b/d	42,000	31 Dec	SOPL	42,000

The journal entry to transfer the balance on the motor expenses account to the SOPL is:

	Debit €	Credit €
SOPL	26,000	
Motor expenses account		26,000

To recognise the motor expenses incurred for the period in the SOPL.

After the journal entry is posted, the motor expenses account appears as follows:

MOTOR EXPENSES ACCOUNT

Debit Side of Account			Credit Side of Account		
Date	**Account Name**	**€**	**Date**	**Account Name**	**€**
31 Dec	Balance b/d	26,000	31 Dec	SOPL	26,000

The journal entry to transfer the balance on the administration salaries account to the SOPL is:

	Debit €	Credit €
SOPL	51,000	
Administration salaries account		51,000

To recognise the administration salaries incurred for the period in the SOPL.

ADMINISTRATION ACCOUNT

Debit Side of Account			Credit Side of Account		
Date	**Account Name**	**€**	**Date**	**Account Name**	**€**
31 Dec	Balance b/d	51,000	31 Dec	SOPL	51,000

The layout of the SOPL in the ledger, i.e. as a ledger account, is as follows:

STATEMENT OF PROFIT OR LOSS

Debit Side of Account			Credit Side of Account		
Date	Account Name	€	Date	Account Name	€
31 Dec	Cost of sales	573,500	31 Dec	Sales	800,000
	Rent	48,000			
	Insurance	15,000			
	Light and heat	42,000			
	Motor expenses	26,000			
	Admin. salaries	51,000			
	Capital	44,500			
		800,000			800,000

As explained in **Chapter 1**, the profit or loss is then transferred to the capital account:

CAPITAL ACCOUNT

Debit Side of Account			Credit Side of Account		
Date	Account Name	€	Date	Account Name	€
31 Dec	Balance c/d	201,500	31 Dec	Balance b/d (see trial balance)	157,000
			31 Dec	SOPL	44,500
		201,500			201,500
			1 Jan	Balance b/d	201,500

The SOPL ledger account is redrafted and presented in the financial statements in a format that is more easily comprehensible by non-accountants as follows:

B. Newton
STATEMENT OF PROFIT OR LOSS
for the year ended 31 December 2019

	€
Sales	800,000
Cost of sales	(573,500)
Gross profit	226,500
Rent	(48,000)
Insurance	(15,000)
Light and heat	(42,000)
Motor expenses	(26,000)
Administration salaries	(51,000)
Net profit	44,500

Now that the SOPL has been prepared, the SOFP can be drafted. Remember, the SOFP is an organised list of the balances left on the assets, liabilities and capital ledger accounts as summarised by the trial balance, after the SOPL has been prepared by transferring the balances on the income and expenses accounts:

B. Newton
STATEMENT OF FINANCIAL POSITION
as at 31 December 2019

	€	€
Non-current Assets		
Equipment		220,000
Motor vehicles		80,000
		300,000
Current Assets		
Trade receivables	37,000	
Cash and cash equivalents	12,500	49,500
TOTAL ASSETS		349,500
Capital		201,500
Non-current Liabilities		
Loans		120,000
Current Liabilities		
Trade payables		28,000
TOTAL EQUITY AND LIABILITIES		349,500

EXAM TIPS

- Double-entry is a key skill – it is critically important to get sufficient practice at preparing journal entries and T accounts.
- Read the details of the question carefully.
- Common mistakes include:
  - recording payment transactions through the bank account when the question indicates it was a cash transaction; and
  - heading up the financial statements incorrectly:
    - for example, stating 'Statement of Profit or Loss as at 31 December 2019' – the statement of profit or loss does not relate to a single date but to a reporting period ended at a certain date. The correct heading in this instance is 'Statement of Profit or Loss for the year ended 31 December 2019'.
    - for example, stating 'Statement of Financial Position for the year ended 31 December 2019' – the statement of financial position relates to a single date and not a reporting period ended at a certain date. The correct heading in this instance is 'Statement of Financial Position as at 31 December 2019'.
- Follow the formats for the financial statements and use the correct terminology.
- Remember: the SOPL is part of the double-entry bookkeeping system.

2.5 CONCLUSION

There are two sides to each transaction – a debit and credit. The impact of debiting or crediting an account depends on the type of account in which the debit or credit is being recorded. Details of transactions are recorded in journal entries, which are posted to individual ledger accounts so as to update them. At the end of each reporting period the balances on ledger accounts are listed in the trial balance, which forms the basis for the preparation of the financial statements.

This chapter has dealt with the fundamentals of recording transactions. In the following chapters we will look at specific accounting rules and concepts and their impact on the information recorded in ledger accounts and presented in financial statements.

SUMMARY OF LEARNING OBJECTIVES

Having studied this chapter you should:

Learning Objective 1 Understand what double-entry bookkeeping is, and know its terminology.

Double-entry bookkeeping is the system used to record financial transactions. It is based on the concept that there are two sides to each transaction. To record a transaction, both sides of the transaction and the elements of the financial statements affected must be identified.

Learning Objective 2 Know how to prepare the journal entries to recognise (i.e. record) transactions.

There are two sides to every transaction: an account/(s) must be debited and another account/(s) must be credited. A summary of how to increase and decrease the balances on different types of accounts is set out below:

Element (Type of Account)	Increase	Decrease
Income	Credit	Debit
Expense	Debit	Credit
Asset	Debit	Credit
Liability	Credit	Debit
Capital (or Equity)	Credit	Debit

(**Note:** a useful cornerstone to remember is that in order to account for an increase in an asset and an expense the account is **debited**, i.e. the entry is made on the left-hand side.)

Learning Objective 3 Understand how journal entries impact ledger accounts.

Journal entries update the balances on individual ledger accounts containing information in relation to particular elements of the financial statements, e.g. particular expense accounts.

Learning Objective 4 Know what a trial balance is and how to prepare one.

Periodically throughout the reporting period a trial balance is prepared that lists the balance on each account at a particular point in time. The total of all debit balances should equal the total of the credit balances; if there is a difference, this would indicate an error has been made in the posting of journal entries.

Learning Objective 5 Know how to use a trial balance to prepare a statement of profit or loss (SOPL) and a statement of financial position (SOFP).

The trial balance lists the balances in each of the accounts in an entity's accounting records, listing the figures for the accounts with debit balances in the debit column and the figures for the accounts with credit balances in the credit column. It is the basis for the preparation of the financial statements. The financial statements indicate how the entity has performed during the reporting period (reported in the SOPL) and the financial position at the reporting date (reported in the SOFP).

QUESTIONS

Review Questions

(See **Appendix A** for Solutions to Review Questions.)

Question 2.1

A. Smith sells goods on credit on 12 July 2019 to the value of €8,000.

Requirement Prepare the journal entry and ledger accounts to record this transaction.

Question 2.2

A. Malone sells €2,500 worth of goods for cash on 3 January 2019.

Requirement Prepare the journal entry and ledger accounts to record this transaction.

Question 2.3

J. Wilson sells goods to A. Bright on credit for €6,150 on 10 January 2019 and receives a cheque for payment in full of the amount outstanding on 8 February 2019.

Requirement Prepare the journal entries and ledger accounts to record these transactions in J. Wilson's accounts.

Question 2.4

N. Jones purchased goods on credit on 20 June 2019 to the value of €11,000.

Requirement Prepare the journal entry and ledger accounts to record this transaction.

Question 2.5

S. Wilkins purchases €3,750 worth of goods for cash on 5 March 2019.

Requirement Prepare the journal entry and ledger accounts to record this transaction.

Question 2.6

On 8 August 2019 M. Coleman purchased goods from B. Crawford on credit for €10,300. On 25 August 2019 M. Coleman paid for the goods in full by cheque.

Requirement Prepare the journal entries and ledger accounts to record these transactions in M. Coleman's accounts.

Question 2.7

L. Smith paid by cheque an insurance expense on 13 November 2019 to the value of €1,200.

Requirement Prepare the journal entry and ledger accounts to record this transaction.

Question 2.8

Arctic Biz Ltd received an invoice from its electricity supplier on 10 November 2019 for €1,209. The company issued a cheque on 30 November to pay the invoice in full.

Requirement Prepare the journal entries and ledger accounts to record these transactions.

Question 2.9

Pat's Stores Ltd received an invoice from its insurance company on 4 September 2019 for €1,098. The company has a direct debit set up to make the payment in relation to this supplier. The direct debit is processed by the bank on 25 September 2019.

Requirement Prepare the journal entries and ledger accounts to record these transactions.

Question 2.10

On 15 July 2019 a company purchases two new motor vehicles that cost €20,000 and €34,000 respectively. The company has taken out a loan to finance the purchase.

Requirement Prepare the journal entry and ledger accounts to record this transaction.

Question 2.11

On 31 October 2019 Barter Ltd moved into new premises that it is renting at a cost of €2,500 per month. Under the terms of the rental agreement, Barter Ltd must make rental payments quarterly in advance, which means that the first payment is due on 31 October covering the rental period 31 October to 31 January 2020. The rent was paid by cheque on 31 October 2019.

Requirement Prepare the journal entry and ledger accounts to record the transaction of the 31 October 2019.

Question 2.12

Cash is introduced to a business by the owner on 1 April 2019 of €40,000.

Requirement Prepare the journal entry and ledger accounts to record this transaction.

Question 2.13

J. Duggan runs a business as a sole trader. He withdrew cash from the business on 10 April 2019 of €2,300.

Requirement Prepare the journal entry and ledger accounts to record this transaction.

Question 2.14

M.J. Wright runs a business as a sole trader. On 20 May 2019, she takes goods out of the business for her own personal use that had originally cost €1,500 and could be sold for €2,250.

Requirement Prepare the journal entry and ledger accounts to record this transaction.

Question 2.15

O. Warren runs his own business – a small retail outlet in the main shopping area in Carlow. He receives his telephone bill for his home and used the business cheque book to make payment. The bill was for €230 and he paid it in full on 12 December 2019.

Requirement Prepare the journal entries and ledger accounts to record these transactions.

Question 2.16

You have been provided with the following information in relation to Trident Ltd:
- 3 March 2019   Sold goods on credit to A. Bainbridge for €7,200.
- 10 March 2019   A. Bainbridge returned €500 worth of the goods to Trident Ltd.
- 20 March 2019   A. Bainbridge paid their account in full by cash: €6,700.

Requirement Prepare the journal entries and ledger accounts to record these transactions in the accounts of Trident Ltd.

Question 2.17

You have been provided with the following information in relation to Mulligan Ltd:
- 8 January 2019   Goods sold on credit to T. Wilson for €5,000 – the terms of the sale are that a 2% discount is allowed if payment is received within 30 days.
- 30 January 2019   T. Wilson paid their account by cheque net of the discount allowed by Mulligan Ltd.

Requirement Prepare the journal entries and ledger accounts to record these transactions in the accounts of Mulligan Ltd.

Question 2.18

You have been provided with the following information in relation to Twinkle Ltd:
- 3 April 2019   Goods sold on credit to H. Sweeton for €6,800 – the terms of the sale are that a 3% discount is allowed if payment is received within 30 days.
- 6 April 2019   H. Sweeton returned €1,000 worth of the goods.
- 30 April 2019   H. Sweeton paid the balance due on their account by cash, net of the discount allowed by Twinkle.

Requirement Prepare the journal entries and ledger accounts of Twinkle Ltd to record these transactions.

Question 2.19

You have been provided with the following information in relation to Super Ltd:
- 12 May 2019   Purchased goods on credit from B. Albert for €6,100.
- 15 May 2019   Super Ltd returned €800 worth of the goods to B. Albert.
- 20 May 2019   Super Ltd paid its account in full by cash – €5,300.

Requirement Prepare the journal entries and ledger accounts of Super Ltd to record these transactions.

Question 2.20

You have been provided with the following information in relation to Trimble Ltd:
- 2 September 2019   Purchased goods on credit from A. Wall for €6,300 – the terms of the sale are that a 2% discount is allowed if payment is received within 30 days.
- 20 September 2019 Trimble Ltd paid A. Wall by cheque net of the discount allowed by A. Wall.

Requirement Prepare the journal entries and ledger accounts of Trimble Ltd to record these transactions.

Question 2.21

You have been provided with the following information in relation to Lonestar Ltd:
- 9 June 2019   Purchased goods on credit from M. Hewson for €9,500 – the terms of the sale are that a 2% discount is allowed if payment is received within 30 days.
- 11 June 2019   Lonestar Ltd returned €2,000 worth of the goods as they were faulty.
- 26 June 2019   Lonestar Ltd paid the balance due on its account by cash, net of the discount allowed by M. Hewson.

Requirement Prepare the journal entries and ledger accounts of Lonestar Ltd to record these transactions.

Question 2.22

Adam began business on 1 January 2019, introducing cash of €20,000:
- On 2 January Adam buys goods for resale on a cash basis for €3,400.
- On 5 January Adam buys a car for use in the business for €5,000 cash.
- On 8 January Adam pays €1,000 cash for rent of premises.
- On 20 January Adam withdraws €900 cash for his personal living expenses.
- On 25 January Adam sells goods for cash of €6,300.

Requirement Prepare the ledger accounts to record the above transactions and prepare the trial balance as at 31 January 2019.

Question 2.23

Joyce began business on 1 January 2019, introducing cash of €24,000:
- On 3 January Joyce buys goods for resale on a cash basis for €4,900.
- On 7 January Joyce buys a car for use in the business for €4,500 cash.
- On 8 January Joyce pays €1,200 cash for rent of premises.
- On 10 January Joyce withdraws €1,100 cash for his personal living expenses.
- On 15 January Joyce sells goods for cash of €6,600.

Requirement Prepare the ledger accounts to record the above transactions and the trial balance as at 31 January 2019.

Challenging Questions

(Suggested Solutions to Challenging Questions are available through your lecturer.)

Question 2.1

The following information has been extracted from the books of Alan for the month of January 2019:

1 January	Alan introduced €40,000 to start his business. He lodged €26,000 to his bank account and kept the balance as cash in the business.
3 January	Bought goods for resale on credit for €28,000.
4 January	Paid rent for the premises by cheque for one year, €12,000.
6 January	Alan arranged a bank overdraft of €25,000.
9 January	Alan provided a loan to the business of €60,000. The money was from his personal savings and was lodged to the company bank account.
10 January	Bought stationery for cash – €490.
12 January	Paid electricity bill of €340 by cheque.
15 January	Bought computer equipment for the business at a cost of €10,000. This was paid for by cheque.
18 January	Paid €21,000 to trade payables by cheque.
20 January	Sold goods for cash – €8,900.
21 January	Sold goods on credit for €18,650.
22 January	Paid wages by cheque – €4,690.
23 January	Repaid €3,000 of the loan to Alan by cheque.
25 January	Sold goods for cash – €6,800.
26 January	Bought goods for resale on credit – €2,700.

| 27 January | Paid for advertising in local newspaper – €1,500 by cheque. |
| 28 January | Paid trade payables by cheque – €5,000. |

Requirement:
(a) Enter the above transactions in the relevant ledger accounts.
(b) Extract the trial balance as at 31 January from the ledger accounts above.

Question 2.2

The following information has been extracted from the books of Bernard Hogan for the month of January 2019:

1 January	William introduced €50,000 to start his business. He lodged €40,000 to his bank account and kept the balance as cash in the business.
3 January	Bought goods for resale on credit for €25,000.
4 January	Paid rent for the premises for one year – €10,000 by cheque.
6 January	William arranged a bank overdraft of €10,000.
9 January	William provided a loan to the business of €35,000. The money was from his personal savings and was lodged to the company bank account.
10 January	Bought stationery for cash, €890.
12 January	Paid electricity bill of €810 by cheque.
15 January	Bought a motor vehicle for the business at a cost of €15,000. This was paid for by cheque.
18 January	Paid €12,000 to trade payables by cheque.
20 January	Sold goods for cash – €19,700.
21 January	Sold goods on credit for €23,500.
22 January	Paid wages by cheque – €5,950.
23 January	Repaid €4,000 of the loan to William in cash.
24 January	Bought goods for resale on credit for €8,500.
25 January	Sold goods for cash – €10,200.
26 January	Sold goods on credit for €4,600.
27 January	Paid for advertising in a trade magazine – €950 by cheque.
28 January	Paid trade payables by cheque – €5,000.

Requirement:
(a) Enter the above transactions in the relevant ledger accounts.
(b) Extract the trial balance as at 31 January from the ledger accounts above.

Question 2.3

The following information has been extracted from the books of Jan Smith for the month of January 2019:

| 1 January | Jan introduced €60,000 to start his business. He lodged €50,000 to his bank account and kept the balance as cash in the business. |
| 2 January | Bought goods for resale on credit for €25,000. |

5 January	Paid rent for the premises for one year – €18,000 by cheque.
8 January	Jan arranged a bank overdraft of €12,000.
9 January	Jan provided a loan to the business of €20,000. The money was from his personal savings and was lodged to the business bank account.
10 January	Bought stationery for cash – €340.
14 January	Paid heating bill of €530 by cheque.
16 January	Bought motor vehicle for the business at a cost of €18,000. This was paid for by cheque.
19 January	Paid €19,000 to trade payables by cheque.
20 January	Sold goods for cash – €12,400.
21 January	Sold goods on credit for €20,300.
22 January	Paid wages by cheque – €10,780.
23 January	Repaid €6,000 of the loan to Jan in cash.
24 January	Bought goods for resale on credit for €5,100.
25 January	Sold goods for cash – €6,500.
26 January	Received cash from a customer of €12,700 and lodged it to the bank account.
27 January	Paid for advertising in a trade magazine – €1,230 by cheque.
28 January	Paid trade payables by cheque – €8,200.

Requirement:
(a) Enter the above transactions in the relevant ledger accounts.
(b) Extract the trial balance as at 31 January from the ledger accounts above.

Inventory and Cost of Sales

LEARNING OBJECTIVES

Having studied this chapter, readers should be able to:
1. identify the different types of inventory;
2. account for both opening and closing inventory; and
3. calculate the cost of sales.

3.1 INTRODUCTION

As mentioned in **Chapter 1, Financial Accounting: Key Terms and Concepts**, the statement of profit or loss (SOPL) is prepared on an accrual basis, which means that **income earned** and **expenses incurred** (see **Chapter 1, Section 1.3**) are presented in this financial statement. The difference between the income earned and expenses incurred is the profit or loss made in the reporting period.

At the end of the reporting period, after the trial balance has been prepared, various adjustments are normally required to be made to the ledger accounts so as to account for all the financial transactions the entity has entered into during the reporting period. Two of the most common adjustments that must be made to the ledger accounts are adjustments to account for inventory on hand at the beginning and end of the reporting period. These adjustments affect the inventory account and the cost of sales account. For purposes of internal control, the inventory on hand is counted at least annually and compared to the stock records to ensure correct accounting for all inventory. Entities hold inventory for a number of reasons which include:
- demand for products may not be constant and the entity wants to make sure that there is sufficient inventory on hand to meet sales requests from customers; and
- to ensure that there is sufficient inventory to meet any future shortage of supply.

The cost of goods **purchased** during the period does not necessarily represent the cost of goods **sold** during the period; applying the accrual basis of accounting means the revenue earned must be matched with the cost of the goods actually sold in the period. Goods sold in the period may have been purchased in an earlier reporting period (i.e. opening inventory) or in the current reporting period (i.e. purchases). Some of the goods purchased in the current reporting period may not have been sold – they may still be owned by the entity (i.e. closing inventory).

There are different types of inventory, including:
- raw materials – goods purchased to be used in the production process that will be converted into finished goods, for example, fabric for a company involved in the manufacture of clothing;
- work in progress – goods currently in the production process but not yet fully converted into finished goods;
- goods for resale – goods purchased that will be sold on to customers without any alteration being made to them, for example, a supermarket buys groceries and then sells them to its customers; and

- finished goods – goods that have completed the production process and are available for sale to customers. For example, for a business that manufactures games consoles, when the products are fully assembled and in a saleable condition they are referred to as finished goods.

It is important to remember that the SOPL is part of the double-entry system (see **Chapter 2, Recording Financial Transactions and Preparing Financial Statements**); at the end of each reporting period the following journal entries have to be posted:

	Debit €	Credit €
SOPL	X	
Expense account		X
To transfer the expense to the SOPL.		
Income account	X	
SOPL		X
To transfer the revenue or income to the SOPL.		

3.2 ACCOUNTING FOR OPENING AND CLOSING INVENTORY

Opening Inventory

Opening inventory is the inventory on hand at the end of the previous reporting period – it represents goods that were purchased or produced in an earlier reporting period that were still on hand at the end of the previous reporting period. Opening inventory is presented in the SOPL as an expense in the cost of sales figure. The SOPL matches the revenue earned with the costs incurred to achieve those sales.

The opening inventory for the reporting period is an expense for the current period. The journal entry to recognise the inventory cost in the cost of sales account is:

	Debit €	Credit €
Cost of sales account	X	
Inventory account		X
To transfer the opening inventory cost to the cost of sales account.		

Closing Inventory

Closing inventory is the figure derived from the annual stock count and the reconciliation of a physical count to the inventory records of the business.

Closing inventory is presented in the financial statements:
- in the cost of sales figure in the SOPL – the value of closing inventory reduces the cost of sales expense for the reporting period; and
- under current assets in the statement of financial position (SOFP).

The journal entry to recognise the value of the closing inventory in the cost of sales account is:

	Debit €	Credit €
Inventory account	X	
Cost of sales account		X
To recognise the closing inventory in the cost of sales account.		

Example 3.1 demonstrates the journal entry to recognise the cost of sales in the SOPL at the reporting date. Recognition in the context of the cost of sales expense means that the expense is incorporated in the SOPL because the cost has been incurred in the period in generating the income earned for the period.

As stated previously, at the end of the reporting period the balance on an expense account is transferred to the SOPL by way of a journal entry; the effect of this transaction in relation to the cost of sales account is to reduce the balance on the cost of sales account to zero and recognise the cost of sales in the SOPL as an expense of the reporting period. The journal entry is as follows:

	Debit €	Credit €
SOPL – cost of sales	X	
Cost of sales account		X

To recognise the cost of sales, an expense, in the SOPL.

EXAMPLE 3.1: COST OF SALES

You have been provided with the following extract from the trial balance of Wilf Ltd as at 31 December 2019:

	Debit €	Credit €
Inventory as at 1 January 2019	14,300	
Purchases	189,200	

The value of the closing inventory as at 31 December 2019 is €20,600.

Requirement Prepare the journal entry to recognise the cost of sales expense in the SOPL for the year ended 31 December 2019.

Solution

The individual journal entries to recognise the cost of sales in the SOPL are:

	Debit €	Credit €
Cost of sales account	14,300	
Inventory account		14,300

To transfer the cost of the opening inventory to the cost of sales account.

	Debit €	Credit €
Cost of sales account	189,200	
Purchases account		189,200

To transfer the expense to the cost of sales account.

	Debit €	Credit €
Inventory account	20,600	
Cost of sales account		20,600

To recognise the closing inventory in the cost of sales account.

At the end of the reporting period the balance on the cost of sales account is posted to the cost of sales expense line in the SOPL. The impact of this transaction is to reduce the balance on the cost of sales account to zero and to reduce the profit reported for the period.

The journal entry is as follows:

	Debit €	Credit €
SOPL – cost of sales	182,900	
Cost of sales account		182,900

To recognise the cost of sales expense in the SOPL.

The above journal entries can be combined as follows:

	Debit €	Credit €
Inventory account – Note 1	6,300	
Cost of sales account	182,900	
Purchases account		189,200

To recognise the cost of sales.

(Note 1: in some examinations students will be asked to prepare journal entries on a net basis. This means that, in this example, rather than showing a debit entry in relation to inventory of €20,600 and a credit entry of €14,300, a net debit amount of €6,300 would be presented in the combined journal entry. This net figure is the difference between the debit and credit amounts.)

The cost of sales figure is calculated as:

	€
Opening inventory	14,300
Purchases	189,200
	203,500
Less closing inventory	(20,600)
	182,900

(Try **Review Questions 3.1** and **3.2** at the end of this chapter.)

3.3 COST OF SALES

The cost of sales figure in the SOPL represents the cost of purchasing goods and converting them to finished goods.

The cost of sales typically includes the following costs:
• opening inventory,
• purchases,
• carriage inwards (which is a cost incurred in respect of the transport costs in relation to goods purchased),
• manufacturing wages, and
• manufacturing costs.

The following items reduce the cost of sales charge in the SOPL:
• closing inventory, and
• purchases returns, also referred to as 'returns outwards'. (See **Chapter 2** for the accounting entries and some of the reasons for the return of goods to a supplier.)

Note: students often get confused between carriage inwards and **carriage outwards**; both are expenses of an entity. The carriage inwards expense is included in cost of sales while carriage outwards is included in the SOPL after the gross profit figure has been calculated.

(Try **Review Questions 3.3** and **3.4** at the end of this chapter.)

EXAM TIPS

- Make sure that all appropriate costs are included in the cost of sales.
- Know the journal entries required to account for cost of sales.

3.4 CONCLUSION

In **Chapter 2** an explanation of the cost of sales figure was provided without taking into consideration the impact of opening and closing inventory. In this chapter the impact on the cost of sales figure of opening and closing inventory was explained. The opening inventory (i.e. the amount of inventory on hand at the start of the reporting period) is expensed to the SOPL through the cost of sales figure and thereby reduces the profit for the period. Closing inventory reduces the cost of sales expense because the items are still on hand and therefore the costs related to them cannot be matched to the income earned in the period.

It is important to understand that the costs included in the cost of sales figure vary depending on the type of entity, for example:
- for a manufacturing entity cost of sales includes the costs of purchasing goods and production costs incurred in converting raw materials to finished goods; and
- for a retail entity cost of sales includes the costs of goods purchased for resale.

SUMMARY OF LEARNING OBJECTIVES

After having studied this chapter, readers should be able to:

Learning Objective 1 Identify the different types of inventory.

There are a number of different categories of inventory and they include:
- raw materials (e.g. of a manufacturing business);
- work in progress (e.g. of a manufacturing business);
- finished goods (e.g. of a manufacturing business); and
- goods for resale (e.g. of a retail business).

Learning Objective 2 Account for both opening and closing inventory.

Opening inventory is the value of goods on hand at the end of the previous reporting period. It is charged as an expense, as part of cost of sales, in the period that the goods were sold. The journal entry to recognise the opening inventory in cost of sales is:

	Debit €	Credit €
SOPL – cost of sales	X	
Inventory account		X

Closing inventory is the value of goods on hand at the reporting date; it reduces the cost of sales charge recognised in the SOPL. The journal entry to recognise the closing inventory in cost of sales is:

	Debit €	Credit €
Inventory account	X	
SOPL – cost of sales		X

Learning Objective 3 Calculate the cost of sales.

The cost of sales figure in the SOPL includes (but is not limited to) the following costs:
- opening inventory;
- purchases;
- manufacturing expenses; and
- carriage inwards.

The cost of sales figure in the SOPL is reduced by:
- the value of goods returned by the entity to its suppliers; and
- any inventory still on hand at the reporting date.

QUESTIONS

Review Questions

(See **Appendix A** for Solutions to Review Questions.)

Question 3.1

Adder Ltd has just completed its annual stocktake and valued its inventory on hand (closing inventory) at €14,600.

Requirement Prepare the journal entry to recognise the closing inventory in the financial statements.

Question 3.2

You have been provided with the following extract from the trial balance of Bright Ltd as at 31 December 2019:

	Debit €	Credit €
Inventory as at 1 January 2019	35,100	
Purchases	289,700	

The value of the closing inventory as at 31 December 2019 is €44,900.

Requirement Prepare the journal entry to recognise the cost of sales expense in the statement of profit or loss for the year ended 31 December 2019.

Question 3.3

You have been provided with the following extract from the trial balance of Carton Ltd as at 31 December 2019:

	Debit €	Credit €
Inventory as at 1 January 2019	34,200	
Purchases	512,500	
Purchases returns		10,500

The value of the closing inventory as at 31 December 2019 is €38,700.

Requirement Prepare the journal entry to recognise the cost of sales expense in the statement of profit or loss for the year ended 31 December 2019.

Question 3.4

The inventory as at 31 December 2018 was €121,960. The following costs were incurred in the reporting period ended 31 December 2019:

	€
Purchases	1,238,100
Purchases returns	33,670
Carriage inwards	25,900
Manufacturing wages	362,400

The annual stock-take took place on 31 December 2019 and valued inventory on hand at €105,850.

Requirement Prepare the journal entry to recognise the cost of sales expense in the statement of profit or loss for the year ended 31 December 2019.

Challenging Questions

(Suggested Solutions to Challenging Questions are available through your lecturer.)

Question 3.1

	€
Sales	32,800
Opening inventory	5,200
Closing inventory	3,600
Purchases	25,600
Carriage inwards	800
Carriage outwards	600
Returns in	156
Returns out	345

Requirement What is the cost of sales figure?
    (Based on Chartered Accountants Ireland, CAP 1 Financial Accounting, Autumn 2010, Question 1.1)

Question 3.2

Sophie Ltd has the following transactions during 2019:

	€
Sales	39,600
Inventory 1 January 2019	3,750
Inventory 31 December 2019	4,270
Purchases	28,900
Carriage inwards	650
Carriage outwards	760
Returns in	576
Returns out	895
Discounts allowed	265

Requirement What is the cost of sales during 2019?
    (Based on Chartered Accountants Ireland, CAP 1 Financial Accounting, Summer 2011, Question 1.10)

4

Accruals and Prepayments

LEARNING OBJECTIVES

Having studied this chapter, readers should be able to:
1. account for the accrual of expenses at the beginning and end of each reporting period;
2. account for the prepayment of expenses at the beginning and end of each reporting period;
3. account for the income due at the beginning and end of each reporting period; and
4. account for the income received in advance at the beginning and end of each reporting period.

4.1 INTRODUCTION

To determine the profit or loss for the reporting period, the revenue earned in the period needs to be compared with the expenses incurred in the period.

Revenue 'earned' means that all the sales made in the reporting period must be recognised, even if payment from customers has not yet been received.

Expenses 'incurred' means any costs that relate to the reporting period are included in the determination of the profit or loss for the reporting period irrespective of whether or not the amounts have actually been paid or invoices received from suppliers. (See **Chapter 1, Section 1.3.**)

4.2 ACCRUALS

In the reporting period expenses are incurred and are recognised when the invoice is received from the supplier/service provider. However, expenses may have been incurred in the period but the invoices for these expenses may not have been received by the business at the reporting date, for example, electricity bills are paid in arrears. At the end of the reporting period an estimate of the amount due in relation to the expenses incurred for which an invoice has not yet been received is made; this estimate is known as an accrual.

An accrual increases the expense. As explained in **Chapter 2, Recording Financial Transactions and Preparing Financial Statements**, to recognise an expense for which an invoice **has** been received the journal entry is:

	Debit €	Credit €
Expense account	X	
Trade payables/other payables/bank account		X

To recognise an expense.

The purpose of **Example 4.1** is to reiterate the recognition of expenses.

EXAMPLE 4.1: EXPENSE RECOGNITION

On 20 March 2019 Howard Ltd received an invoice for €2,340 in relation to stationery costs. The supplier provides 30 days' credit. On 15 April 2019 Howard Ltd paid the invoice in full by cash.

The balance on the cash account at 15 April 2019 was €12,650.

Howard prepares its financial statements to 30 June each year.

Requirement Prepare the journal entries and ledger accounts for the above transactions.

Solution

	Debit €	Credit €
Stationery expenses account	2,340	
Other payables account		2,340
To recognise the stationery cost.		
Other payables account	2,340	
Cash account		2,340
To recognise cash payment made to supplier.		

At the end of the reporting period the expense is transferred to the statement of profit or loss (SOPL):

	Debit €	Credit €
SOPL – stationery expenses	2,340	
Stationery expenses account		2,340
To transfer the stationery cost to profit or loss.		

STATIONERY EXPENSES ACCOUNT

Date	Account Name	€	Date	Account Name	€
20/03/2019	Other payables	2,340	30/06/2019	SOPL	2,340

OTHER PAYABLES ACCOUNT

Date	Account Name	€	Date	Account Name	€
15/04/2019	Cash	2,340	20/03/2019	Stationery	2,340

CASH ACCOUNT

Date	Account Name	€	Date	Account Name	€
15/04/2019	Balance b/d	12,650	15/04/2019	Other payables	2,340
			30/06/2019	Balance c/d	10,310
		12,650			12,650
01/07/2019	Balance b/d	10,310			

It is important to make a distinction between an accrual and a liability. A liability is an amount owed for which an obligation has arisen; the obligation and the amount are known with certainty. The amount of a liability can be verified by looking at either the invoice or any other supporting documentation. An accrual is an estimate of an amount owed by the entity for which an invoice has not yet been received.

At the reporting date, an entity may not have received invoices for all goods purchased and services consumed during the reporting period. At the reporting date the entity will review its costs and raise an accrual for (i.e. account for) any amount owed by the entity for which an invoice has not been received (see **Chapter 1, Financial Accounting: Key Terms and Concepts**).

The accounts that are affected by an accrual are the expense account and the accruals account. The expense account is, of course, an **expense** account and the accruals account is a **liability** account. The effect of the transaction is to increase the total amount of both the expense and the accrual. Therefore, in order to record this transaction the expense account should be debited and the accruals account should be credited as follows.

	Debit €	Credit €
Expense account	X	
Accruals account		X

To recognise an accrual of an expense.

Example 4.2 demonstrates the accounting entries required in relation to the accrual of expenses.

EXAMPLE 4.2: ACCRUAL OF EXPENSES AT THE END OF THE REPORTING PERIOD

During the reporting period ended 31 December 2019, the following invoices were received and paid:

Date Invoice received	Invoice No.	Period covered	Amount
31/05/2019	12463	01/01/2019–31/05/2019	€5,000
31/10/2019	12936	01/06/2019–31/10/2019	€5,000

The above invoices were paid by cheque on the same day that the invoices were received.

The invoices relate to energy costs that are paid in arrears. Management estimates the cost from 1 November to 31 December 2019 for energy costs at €2,000.

Requirement Prepare the journal entries and ledger accounts to account for these transactions.

Solution

	Debit €	Credit €
Energy expense account	5,000	
Bank account		5,000

To recognise the payment of energy expense on 31 May 2019.

	Debit €	Credit €
Energy expense account	5,000	
Bank account		5,000

To recognise the payment of energy expense on 31 October 2019.

A journal entry is posted to recognise the energy expenses incurred during the reporting period for which an invoice had not been received by the reporting date. The management of the entity estimates the cost of energy consumed during the period 1 November 2019 to 31 December 2019 as €2,000. An accrual increases the expenses for the period and increases the amount that the company owes in relation to this expense. The journal entry is as follows:

	Debit €	Credit €
Energy expense account	2,000	
Accruals account		2,000

To recognise the accrual of energy expense.

Expenses and income accounts are cleared out to the SOPL at the end of the reporting period. It is important to remember that the SOPL is part of the double-entry system.

	Debit €	Credit €
SOPL – energy expense	12,000	
Energy expense account		12,000

To recognise the total cost in relation to energy expense in SOPL.

ENERGY EXPENSE ACCOUNT

Date	Account Name	€	Date	Account Name	€
31/05/2019	Bank	5,000	31/12/2019	SOPL – energy cost	12,000
31/10/2019	Bank	5,000			
31/12/2019	Accruals	2,000			
		12,000			12,000

BANK ACCOUNT

Date	Account Name	€	Date	Account Name	€
31/12/2019	Balance c/d	10,000	31/05/2019	Energy expense	5,000
			31/10/2019	Energy expense	5,000
		10,000			10,000
			01/01/2020	Balance b/d	10,000

ACCRUALS ACCOUNT

Date	Account Name	€	Date	Account Name	€
31/12/2019	Balance c/d	2,000	31/12/2019	Energy expense	2,000
			01/01/2020	Balance b/d	2,000

The balance on the accruals account is carried forward into the next reporting period. The balance on the accruals account is presented in the statement of financial position (SOFP) under current liabilities.

(Try **Review Questions 4.1** and **4.2** at the end of this chapter.)

In **Example 4.2** the recognition of an accrual at the end of the reporting period was dealt with; this becomes an opening accrual at the start of the next reporting period. As stated in **Chapter 1**, the expense charged to the SOPL is the expense **incurred** in the reporting period, not the expense **paid** in the reporting period.

An opening accrual means that an invoice in relation to this expense will be received and paid in the current reporting period but the invoice relates, either in part or in full, to an expense incurred in the previous reporting period (and therefore is included in the expenses in the SOPL for the previous reporting period). When the invoice is received in relation to the opening accrual amount, the journal entry posted is to debit the expense account and credit the bank account (assuming the expense is paid immediately the invoice is received). However, as stated above, the expense does not relate to the current reporting period; a journal entry must be posted to reduce the expense account by the amount of the opening accrual and reduce the balance on the opening accruals account to zero. Therefore, as explained above, to recognise the opening accrual in the current reporting period the accruals account is debited and the expense account is credited, as shown in the following journal entry.

	Debit €	Credit €
Accruals account	X	
Expense account		X

To transfer the opening accrual to the related expense account.

Example 4.3 demonstrates the situation where an entity has an accrual in its financial statements at the start of the reporting period.

EXAMPLE 4.3: OPENING ACCRUAL

At the start of the reporting period, i.e. on 1 January 2019, Bennett Ltd had an accrual of €1,200 in relation to electricity expenses. The accrual related to the period 1 December 2018 to 31 December 2018.

The following transactions occurred in relation to electricity in the reporting period ended 31 December 2019:

Date Invoice Received	Invoice No.	Period Covered	Amount
31/01/2019	520	01/12/2018–31/01/2019	€2,500
31/07/2019	1034	01/02/2019–31/07/2019	€7,500
31/12/2019	1720	01/08/2019–31/12/2019	€5,600

Each invoice was paid by cheque on the same date that the invoice was received.

Requirement Prepare the journal entries and the ledger accounts in relation to the electricity expense for the reporting period ended 31 December 2019.

Solution

Step 1 Open up the accruals account.

ACCRUALS ACCOUNT

Date	Account Name	€	Date	Account Name	€
			01/01/2019	Balance b/d	1,200

Step 2 Transfer the balance on the accruals account to the related expense account at the start of the new reporting period. The journal entry to do this is:

	Debit €	Credit €
Accruals account	1,200	
Electricity expense account		1,200

To transfer the accrual at the start of the reporting period to the related expense account.

The ledger accounts after this transaction are:

ACCRUALS ACCOUNT

Date	Account Name	€	Date	Account Name	€
01/01/2019	Electricity expense	1,200	01/01/2019	Balance b/d	1,200

ELECTRICITY EXPENSE ACCOUNT

Date	Account Name	€	Date	Account Name	€
			01/01/2019	Accruals	1,200

The credit entry on the electricity expense account will reduce the electricity expense charged to the SOPL for the year ended 31 December 2019. This is correct as part of the payment made in relation to the invoice received on 31 January 2019 relates to the previous reporting period. The invoice received on 31 January relates to electricity charges for the period 1 December 2018 to 31 January 2019, i.e. the invoice relates to electricity costs for two accounting periods:

Period Covered by Invoice No. 520	Reporting Period to which Expense Relates
1 December 2018 to 31 December 2018	1 January 2018 to 31 December 2018
1 January 2019 to 31 January 2019	1 January 2019 to 31 December 2019

The expense related to December 2018 was estimated and included as an accrual (under current liabilities) in the SOFP as at 31 December 2018 and the expense was recognised in that SOPL for the year ended 31 December 2018.

Step 3 Recognise the electricity expenses.

The journal entries are:

	Debit €	Credit €
Electricity expense account	2,500	
Bank account		2,500

To recognise the payment of electricity expense on 31 January 2019.

	Debit €	Credit €
Electricity expense account	7,500	
Bank account		7,500

To recognise the payment of electricity expense on 31 July 2019.

	Debit €	Credit €
Electricity expense account	5,600	
Bank account		5,600

To recognise the payment of electricity expense on 31 December 2019.

	Debit €	Credit €
SOPL – electricity expense	14,400	
Electricity expense account		14,400

To recognise the total cost in relation to electricity expense in the SOPL.

The electricity expense recognised in the SOPL is made up as follows:

	€
January invoice (€2,500 – €1,200 accrual for 2018)	1,300
July invoice	7,500
December invoice	5,600
SOPL charge for 1 January 2019 to 31 December 2019	14,400

ACCRUALS ACCOUNT

Date	Account Name	€	Date	Account Name	€
01/01/2019	Electricity expense	1,200	01/01/2019	Balance b/d	1,200

There is no accrual at the end of the reporting period so there is no balance carried forward on the accruals account.

ELECTRICITY EXPENSE ACCOUNT

Date	Account Name	€	Date	Account Name	€
31/01/2019	Bank	2,500	01/01/2019	Accruals	1,200
31/07/2019	Bank	7,500	31/12/2019	SOPL	14,400
31/12/2019	Bank	5,600			
		15,600			15,600

(Try **Review Questions 4.3** and **4.4** at the end of this chapter.)

The next stage is to understand the impact of opening and closing accruals on the expense charged to the SOPL, which will have an impact on the profit for the year. The expense charged to the SOPL must represent the expense **incurred** in the reporting period. The expense incurred is the amount paid reduced by the accrual at the start of the year and increased by the accrual at the end of the reporting period. The accrual at the start of the year is the expense incurred in the previous reporting period but the relevant invoice was received and paid in the current reporting period. The accrual at the end of the year is the expense incurred in the current reporting period but the relevant invoice was not received by the reporting date.

Example 4.4 demonstrates the situation where the entity has an accrual in its financial statements at both the start and the end of the reporting period.

EXAMPLE 4.4: OPENING AND CLOSING ACCRUALS

At the start of the reporting period, i.e. 1 January 2019, Simpson Ltd had an accrual balance of €900 in relation to its rates expense. The accrual related to the period 1 October 2018 to 31 December 2018.

The following transaction occurred in relation to the rates expense in the reporting period ended 31 December 2019:

Date Invoice Received	Invoice No.	Period Covered	Amount	Payment Date
30 September 2019	5,688	01/10/2018–30/09/2019	€3,600	30/09/2019

At the reporting date, 31 December 2019, management estimate an accrual is required in relation to the rates expense of €1,000.

Requirement Prepare the journal entries and the ledger accounts in relation to the rates expense for the reporting period ended 31 December 2019.

Solution

Step 1 Open up the accruals account.

ACCRUALS ACCOUNT

Date	Account Name	€	Date	Account Name	€
			01/01/2019	Balance b/d	900

Step 2 Transfer the balance on the accruals account to the related expense account at the start of the next reporting period. The journal entry to do this is:

	Debit €	Credit €
Accruals account	900	
Rates expense account		900

To transfer the accrual at the start of the reporting period to the related expense account.

The ledger accounts after this transaction are:

ACCRUALS ACCOUNT

Date	Account Name	€	Date	Account Name	€
01/01/2019	Rates expense	900	01/01/2019	Balance b/d	900

RATES EXPENSE ACCOUNT

Date	Account Name	€	Date	Account Name	€
			01/01/2019	Accruals	900

The expense related to December 2018 was estimated and included as an accrual (under current liabilities) in the SOFP as at 31 December 2018 and the expense was recognised in the SOPL for the year ended 31 December 2018.

Step 3 Recognise the rates expenses.

The journal entries are:

	Debit €	Credit €
Rates expense account	3,600	
Bank account		3,600

To recognise the payment of rates expense on 30 September 2019.

	Debit €	Credit €
Rates expense account	1,000	
Accruals account		1,000

To recognise the accrual required in relation to rates expense as at 31 December 2019.

	Debit €	Credit €
SOPL – rates expense	3,700	
Rates expense account		3,700

To recognise the total cost in relation to rates expense in SOPL.

The rates expense recognised in the SOPL is made up as follows:

	€
September invoice (€3,600 – €900 accrual as at 31/12/2018)	2,700
Accrual as at 31/12/2019	1,000
SOPL charge for 01/01/2019 to 31/12/2019	3,700

ACCRUALS ACCOUNT

Date	Account Name	€	Date	Account Name	€
01/01/2019	Rates expense	900	01/01/2019	Balance b/d	900
31/12/2019	Balance c/d	1,000	31/12/2019	Rates	1,000
		1,900			1,900
			01/01/2020	Balance b/d	1,000

There is an accrual at the end of the reporting period, so there is a balance of €1,000 on the account that is carried forward into the next reporting period. The closing balance on the accruals account of €1,000 is presented under current liabilities in the SOFP as at 31 December 2019.

RATES EXPENSE ACCOUNT

Date	Account Name	€	Date	Account Name	€
30/09/2019	Bank	3,600	01/01/2019	Accruals	900
31/12/2019	Accruals	1,000	31/12/2019	SOPL – rates	3,700
		4,600			4,600

(Try **Review Questions 4.5–4.7** at the end of this chapter.)

4.3 PREPAID EXPENSES

Some expenses are billed on a time basis that is not the same as the reporting period. For example, an insurance policy is renewed on 30 April 2018 (so each premium covers the period 1 May to the following 30 April), but the reporting period is the year to 31 December each year (i.e. the reporting period is 1 January to 31 December each year). The insurance premium paid in April 2018 relates to two reporting periods:

Insurance Charge	Reporting Period in which Included
1 May 2018 to 31 December 2018 (8 months)	1 January 2018 to 31 December 2018
1 January 2019 to 30 April 2019 (4 months)	1 January 2019 to 31 December 2019

When an expense is paid that relates to both the current period and the next reporting period, the payment in relation to the expense is recorded as normal (i.e. Debit Expense account; Credit Bank account). The full amount of the expense paid is not charged to the SOPL for the current period as it does not solely relate to this reporting period; the expense account is decreased by the amount of the expense that relates to the next reporting period.

The accounts that are affected by this transaction are the expense account and the **prepayments** account. The prepayments account is an **asset** account. The effect of accounting for a prepayment is to decrease the balance on the expense account and increase the balance on the prepayments account. Therefore, as explained above, in order to record this transaction the prepayments account should be debited and the expense account should be credited as follows.

	Debit €	Credit €
Prepayments account	X	
Expense account		X

To recognise the prepayment of an expense.

The prepayment is presented in the SOFP under current assets.

Example 4.5 demonstrates the situation where costs paid during the current year relate to the next reporting period.

EXAMPLE 4.5: PREPAYMENT AT THE END OF THE REPORTING PERIOD

Kent Ltd prepares its financial statements to 31 December each year. Rent on its new retail property is paid quarterly in advance. The following payments were made in the financial reporting period ended 31 December 2018.

Date	Period Covered	Amount
1 June 2018	1 June 2018 to 31 August 2018	€15,000
1 September 2018	1 September 2018 to 30 November 2018	€15,000
1 December 2018	1 December 2018 to 28 February 2019	€15,000

Requirement Prepare the journal entries and ledger accounts in relation to rental cost for reporting period ended 31 December 2018.

Solution

Prepare the journal entries to recognise the expenses paid during the reporting period:

	Debit €	Credit €
Rent expense account	15,000	
Bank account		15,000

To recognise the rent expense paid on 1 June 2018.

	Debit €	Credit €
Rent expense account	15,000	
Bank account		15,000

To recognise the rent expense paid on 1 September 2018.

	Debit €	Credit €
Rent expense account	15,000	
Bank account		15,000

To recognise the rent expense paid on 1 December 2018.

RENT EXPENSE ACCOUNT

Date	Account Name	€	Date	Account Name	€
01/06/2018	Bank	15,000			
01/09/2018	Bank	15,000			
01/12/2018	Bank	15,000			

BANK ACCOUNT

Date	Account Name	€	Date	Account Name	€
			01/06/2018	Rent expense	15,000
			01/09/2018	Rent expense	15,000
			01/12/2018	Rent expense	15,000

The amount of the prepayment must be calculated first. The prepayment relates to the period 1 January 2019 to 28 February 2019. The rent expense is €15,000 for a three-month period therefore the prepayment required is €10,000 [€15,000 × 2/3]. The prepayment is recognised as follows:

	Debit €	Credit €
Prepayments account	10,000	
Rent expense account		10,000

To recognise the prepayment of rent expense relating to the next reporting period.

RENT EXPENSE ACCOUNT

Date	Account Name	€	Date	Account Name	€
01/06/2018	Bank	15,000	31/12/2018	Prepayments	10,000
01/09/2018	Bank	15,000	31/12/2018	SOPL	35,000
01/12/2018	Bank	15,000			
		45,000			45,000

The rates expense recognised in the SOPL is made up as follows:

	€
Invoice June 2018	15,000
Invoice September 2018	15,000
Invoice December 2018 (€15,000 – €10,000 prepayment in relation to 2019)	5,000
	35,000

PREPAYMENTS ACCOUNT					
Date	**Account Name**	**€**	**Date**	**Account Name**	**€**
31/12/2018	Rent expense	10,000	31/12/2018	Balance c/d	10,000
01/01/2019	Balance b/d	10,000			

The balance on the prepayment account is presented under current assets in the SOFP.

(Try **Review Questions 4.8** and **4.9** at the end of this chapter.)

In **Example 4.5** the recognition of a prepayment at the end of the reporting period was dealt with; this becomes an opening prepayment at the start of the next reporting date. As stated in **Chapter 1**, the expense charged to the SOPL is the expense **incurred** in the reporting period, not the expense **paid** in the reporting period.

An opening prepayment means that an invoice in relation to the relevant expense was received and paid in the previous reporting period but the invoice relates to an expense incurred in the current reporting period (and therefore included in the expenses in the SOPL for the current and not the previous reporting period when the invoice was received and paid). An invoice will not be received in the current reporting period in relation to this opening prepayment, but the expense has to be recognised in the SOPL to which the expense relates (i.e. the current reporting period). To recognise the prepaid expense in the current reporting period the expense account has to be increased and the balance on the prepayments account (an **asset** account) decreased.

A journal entry must be posted to increase the expense account by the amount of the opening prepayment and reduce the balance on the prepayments account to zero. Therefore, as explained above, to recognise the effect of the opening prepayment in the current reporting period the expense account is debited and the prepayments account credited, as shown in the following journal entry.

	Debit €	**Credit €**
Expense account	X	
Prepayments account		X

To transfer the opening prepayment to the related expense account.

Example 4.6 demonstrates the situation where the entity has an opening prepayment in relation to an expense.

EXAMPLE 4.6: OPENING PREPAYMENT

As at 1 January 2019 Hilda Ltd had a prepayment in relation to its insurance expense of €600, which relates to the period 1 January 2019 to 31 March 2019.

The insurance premium for the year ended 31 March 2020 was €2,700. The management of Hilda decided to set up a quarterly direct debit to pay the insurance premium; the first payment was taken from the bank account on 1 April 2019.

Requirement Prepare the journal entries and ledger accounts in relation to the insurance expense for the year ended 31 December 2019.

Solution

Step 1 Open up the prepayments account.

PREPAYMENTS ACCOUNT

Date	Account Name	€	Date	Account Name	€
01/01/2019	Balance b/d	600			

Step 2 Transfer the balance on the prepayments account to the related expense account at the start of the next reporting period. The journal entry to do this is:

	Debit €	Credit €
Insurance expense account	600	
Prepayments account		600

To transfer the prepayment at the start of the reporting period to the related expense account.

The ledger accounts after this transaction are:

PREPAYMENTS ACCOUNT

Date	Account Name	€	Date	Account Name	€
01/01/2019	Balance b/d	600	01/01/2019	Insurance	600

INSURANCE EXPENSE ACCOUNT

Date	Account Name	€	Date	Account Name	€
01/01/2019	Insurance	600			

The debit entry on the insurance expense account will increase the insurance expense charged to the SOPL for the year ended 31 December 2019. This is correct, as part of the expense for the reporting period ended 31 December 2019 was paid in the previous reporting period (ended 31 December 2018).

The insurance invoice paid in the reporting period ended 31 December 2018 relates to insurance charges for the period 1 April 2018 to 31 March 2019; the invoice relates to costs for two reporting periods:

Period Covered by Insurance	**Reporting Period to which Expense Relates**
1 April 2019 to 31 December 2019	1 January 2019 to 31 December 2019
1 January 2020 to 31 March 2020	1 January 2020 to 31 December 2020

The expense relating to the period 1 January to 31 March 2019 was presented as a prepayment (under current assets) in the SOPL as at 31 December 2018 and the expense will be recognised in the SOPL for the year ended 31 December 2019.

Step 3 Recognise the insurance expenses.

The journal entries are:

	Debit €	Credit €
Insurance expense account	675	
Bank account		675

To recognise the payment of insurance expense on 1 April 2019 (i.e. €2,700 × 3/12).

	Debit €	Credit €
Insurance expense account	675	
Bank account		675

To recognise the payment of insurance expense on 1 July 2019.

	Debit €	Credit €
Insurance expense account	675	
Bank account		675

To recognise the payment of insurance expense on 1 October 2019.

	Debit €	Credit €
SOPL – insurance expense	2,625	
Insurance expense account		2,625

To recognise the total cost in relation to insurance expense in SOPL.

The insurance expense recognised in the SOPL is made up as follows:

	€
Prepayment as at 1 January 2019	600
April direct debit	675
July direct debit	675
October direct debit	675
SOPL charge for 1 January 2019 to 31 December 2019	2,625

PREPAYMENTS ACCOUNT

Date	Account Name	€	Date	Account Name	€
01/01/2019	Balance b/d	600	01/01/2019	Insurance	600

There is no prepayment at the end of the reporting of the period so there is no balance carried forward on the account.

INSURANCE EXPENSE ACCOUNT

Date	Account Name	€	Date	Account Name	€
01/01/2019	Prepayments	600	31/12/2019	SOPL – Insurance	2,625
01/04/2019	Bank	675			
01/07/2019	Bank	675			
01/10/2019	Bank	675			
		2,625			2,625

(Try **Review Question 4.10** at the end of this chapter.)

The next stage is to understand the impact of opening and closing prepayments on the expense charged to the SOPL and therefore used to calculate the profit for the year. The expense charged to the SOPL must represent the costs incurred in the reporting period. The amount incurred is the amount paid increased by the prepayment at the start of the reporting period and decreased by the prepayment at the end of the reporting period. The prepayment at the start of the reporting period would be in respect of the invoice received and paid in the previous reporting period but for an expense relating to the current reporting period. The prepayment at the end of the reporting period would be the invoice received and paid by the reporting date but for an expense relating to the next reporting period.

Example 4.7 demonstrates the situation where the entity has both an opening and a closing prepayment in relation to an expense.

EXAMPLE 4.7: OPENING AND CLOSING PREPAYMENTS

Stanley Ltd prepares its financial statements to 31 December annually. Its insurance premium is due for renewal on 1 October annually.

Insurance Premium for Year Ended	Premium Amount	Paid by Cheque on
30 September 2019	€32,000	27 September 2018
30 September 2020	€35,200	28 September 2019

Requirement:
(a) Prepare the journal entries for the year ended 31 December 2019.
(b) Prepare the ledger accounts for the year ended 31 December 2019.
(c) Prepare the extracts from the financial statements for the year ended 31 December 2019.

Solution

(a)

As at 1 January 2019 Stanley Ltd had an opening prepayment of €24,000, representing the insurance premium paid on 27 September 2018 that related to the reporting period ended 31 December 2019. The insurance premium prepaid is calculated as €32,000 × 9/12; this relates to the period from 1 January 2019 to 30 September 2019.

	Debit €	Credit €
Insurance account	24,000	
Prepayments account		24,000

To transfer the prepayment to the insurance expense account at the start of the reporting period.

Insurance account	35,200	
Bank account		35,200

To recognise the insurance expense paid.

The insurance expense paid in September 2019 relates to two reporting periods:

Period covered by Insurance	Reporting Period to which Expense Relates	Amount
1 October 2019 to 31 December 2019	1 January 2019 to 31 December 2019	€8,800 (i.e. €35,200 × 3/12)
1 January 2020 to 30 September 2020	1 January 2020 to 31 December 2020	€26,400 (i.e. €35,200 × 9/12)

	Debit €	Credit €
Prepayments account	26,400	
Insurance account		26,400

To recognise the prepaid insurance expense as at 31 December 2019.

SOPL – insurance	32,800	
Insurance account		32,800

To recognise the insurance expense for the reporting year ended 31 December 2019.

Insurance expense in profit or loss is made up as follows:

	€
Prepayment at start of year (covers 1 January 2019 to 30 September 2019)	24,000
Payment made September 2019 (1 October 2019 to 31 December 2019)	8,800
SOPL charge	32,800

(b)

PREPAYMENTS ACCOUNT

Date	Account Name	€	Date	Account Name	€
01/01/2019	Balance b/d	24,000	01/01/2019	Insurance	24,000
31/12/2019	Insurance	26,400	31/12/2019	Balance c/d	26,400
		50,400			50,400
01/01/2020	Balance b/d	26,400			

There is a prepayment at the end of the reporting period, so there is a balance carried forward on the account into the next reporting period. The prepayment is presented under current assets in the SOFP as at 31 December 2019.

INSURANCE EXPENSE ACCOUNT

Date	Account Name	€	Date	Account Name	€
01/01/2019	Prepayments	24,000	31/12/2019	Prepayments	26,400
28/09/2019	Bank	35,200	31/12/2019	SOPL	32,800
		59,200			59,200

(c)

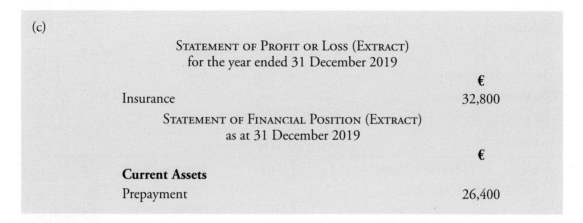

STATEMENT OF PROFIT OR LOSS (EXTRACT)
for the year ended 31 December 2019

	€
Insurance	32,800

STATEMENT OF FINANCIAL POSITION (EXTRACT)
as at 31 December 2019

	€
Current Assets	
Prepayment	26,400

(Try **Review Question 4.11** at the end of this chapter.)

4.4 INCOME DUE

In the preparation of the SOPL for a particular reporting period the income earned is recognised even if it has not yet been invoiced or received. Income earned for which an invoice has not been issued to the customer by the reporting date is recognised in the financial statements as follows:
- as income in the SOPL in the period to which it relates; and
- as income due in the SOFP under current assets.

A jonrnal entry must be posted to record the income earned in the current period even though an invoice has not been issued and the amount is owed by the customer. The income earned is an income account and the amount owed by the customer is an asset account. The balance on both the income and asset account are increased as a result of this transaction.

The journal entry to recognise income due is:

	Debit €	Credit €
Income due account – SOFP	X	
Income/revenue account		X

To recognise the income due at the reporting date.

Example 4.8 demonstrates the situation where income has been earned but for which an invoice has not been issued by the end of the reporting period.

EXAMPLE 4.8: INCOME DUE AT THE END OF THE REPORTING PERIOD

A health and fitness club charges members an annual fee of €800. Up to the reporting date, 31 December 2019, €115,800 was received but €2,600 was outstanding. The subscriptions received have been recorded in the financial records but no journal entries have been made in relation to the subscriptions outstanding at the reporting date.

Requirement Prepare the journal entries and ledger accounts.

Solution

	Debit €	Credit €
Income due account – SOFP	2,600	
Subscriptions income account		2,600

To recognise the subscription income outstanding at the reporting date.

SUBSCRIPTION INCOME ACCOUNT

Date	Account Name	€	Date	Account Name	€
31/12/2019	SOPL – subscription income	118,400	31/12/2019	Bank	115,800
			31/12/2019	Income due	2,600
		118,400			118,400

INCOME DUE ACCOUNT

Date	Account Name	€	Date	Account Name	€
31/12/2019	Subscription income	2,600	31/12/2019	Balance c/d	2,600
		2,600			2,600
01/01/2020	Balance b/d	2,600			

(Try **Review Questions 4.12** and **4.13** at the end of this chapter.)

4.5 INCOME RECEIVED IN ADVANCE

Income recognised in the SOPL only relates to the reporting period for which the financial statement is being presented.

Income received in the reporting period relating to the next reporting period is not included in the SOPL but is recognised as income paid in advance and presented in the SOFP under current liabilities. Income received in advance is a liability in the SOFP as the goods/services have not yet been provided by the entity. The effect of the transaction is to increase the bank balance (which is an asset), and to increase the liability (income in advance). Therefore, as explained above, in order to record this transaction the bank account should be debited and the income in advance account credited as follows.

	Debit €	Credit €
Bank account	X	
Income in advance account		X

To recognise income received in advance.

Example 4.9 demonstrates accounting for income received in advance, some of which relates to the next reporting period.

EXAMPLE 4.9: INCOME IN ADVANCE

Walker Ltd sublets part of its office building. Under the rental agreement, quarterly rental payments of €6,000 are required to be paid in advance.

The following rental income was received in the reporting period ended 31 December 2018:

Date Rent Received	Period Covered	Amount
1 February 2019	1 February 2019 to 30 April 2019	€6,000
1 May 2019	1 May 2019 to 31 July 2019	€6,000
1 August 2019	1 August 2019 to 31 October 2019	€6,000
1 November 2019	1 November 2019 to 31 January 2020	€6,000

Requirement Prepare the journal entries and ledger accounts in relation to the rental income for the reporting period ended 31 December 2019.

Solution

	Debit €	Credit €
Bank account	6,000	
Rental income account		6,000

To recognise the rental income received on 1 February 2019.

	Debit €	Credit €
Bank account	6,000	
Rental income account		6,000

To recognise the rental income received on 1 May 2019.

	Debit €	Credit €
Bank account	6,000	
Rental income account		6,000

To recognise the rental income received on 1 August 2019.

	Debit €	Credit €
Bank account	6,000	
Rental income account		6,000

To recognise the rental income received on 1 November 2019.

The rent received on 1 November 2019 relates to both the current and the next reporting period.

Period Covered by Rent	Reporting Period to which Income Relates	Amount
1 November 2019 to 31 December 2019	1 January 2019 to 31 December 2019	€4,000 (i.e. €6,000 × 2/3)
1 January 2020 to 31 January 2020	1 January 2020 to 31 December 2020	€2,000 (i.e. €6,000 × 1/3)

The journal entry to recognise the rental income related to the reporting period ended 31 December 2020, that is income in advance, is:

	Debit €	Credit €
Rental income account	2,000	
Income in advance account		2,000

To recognise the rental income in advance.

The rental income has to be posted to the SOPL at the end of the reporting period. Rental income presented in the SOPL relates to the income earned during the reporting period ended 31 December 2019. The rental income was earned for the period 1 February 2019 to 31 December 2019. The journal entry to recognise the rental income in the SOPL is set out below.

	Debit €	Credit €
Rental income account	22,000	
SOPL – rental income		22,000

To recognise the rental income for reporting period ended 31 December 2019.

RENTAL INCOME ACCOUNT

Date	Account Name	€	Date	Account Name	€
31/12/2019	Income in advance	2,000	01/02/2019	Bank	6,000
31/12/2019	SOPL – rental income	22,000	01/05/2019	Bank	6,000
			01/08/2019	Bank	6,000
			01/11/2019	Bank	6,000
		24,000			24,000

INCOME RECEIVED IN ADVANCE ACCOUNT

Date	Account Name	€	Date	Account Name	€
31/01/2019	Balance c/d	2,000	31/12/2019	Rental income	2,000
		2,000			2,000
			01/01/2020	Balance b/d	2,000

(Try **Review Question 4.14** at the end of this chapter.)

EXAM TIPS

- Read the question carefully and note the reporting date and the period the invoice/payment covers.
- Know the journal entries relevant to the recording of income and expenses and accruals and prepayments.

4.6 CONCLUSION

The expenses charged to the SOPL are the expenses incurred in the period; these are not simply the expenses paid in the reporting period. To determine the expenses charged to the SOPL the expenses paid are reduced by opening accruals and closing prepayments and increased by opening prepayments and closing accruals.

The income presented in the SOPL represents the income earned in the period; this is not simply the income received in the reporting period. To determine the income earned to be presented in the SOPL the income received is reduced by opening income due and closing income in advance, and increased by opening income in advance and closing income due.

SUMMARY OF LEARNING OBJECTIVES

After having studied this chapter, readers should be able to:

Learning Objective 1 Account for the accrual of expenses at the beginning and end of each reporting period.

Financial statements are prepared on the accrual basis, so when an expense has been incurred in the current reporting period but an invoice has not been received by the reporting date, an estimate of the amount owing must be made. This estimate is referred to as an accrual. The effect of the accrual is to increase the expense charged to the SOPL. Therefore, as explained above, in order to record this transaction the accruals account should be credited and the expense account should be debited as shown below:

	Debit €	Credit €
Expense account	X	
Accruals account		X

To recognise the expense.

At the end of the reporting period in which the accrual is recognised it is presented under current liabilities in the SOFP.

The accrual at the end of the reporting period is known as the closing accrual; at the start of the next reporting period it is referred to as the opening accrual. The effect of the opening accrual is to decrease the expense charged to the SOPL. In order to record this transaction, thereby eliminating the opening accrual and reducing the current year's expense, the accruals account should be debited and the expense account should be credited as shown below:

	Debit €	Credit €
Accruals account	X	
Expense account		X

To transfer the accrual to the related expense account.

Learning Objective 2 Account for the prepayment of expenses at the beginning and end of each reporting period.

When a payment is made during the current reporting period that relates to an expense that will be incurred in the next reporting period, a prepayment has to be recognised in the financial statements. The effect of a prepayment is to decrease the expense charged to the SOPL and increase the balance on the prepayments account (an asset account). Therefore, as explained above, in order to record this transaction the prepayments account should be debited and the expense account should be credited, as shown below:

	Debit €	Credit €
Prepayments account – SOFP	X	
Expense account		X

To recognise the prepayment of an expense.

The prepayment at the end of the reporting period is known as the closing prepayment; at the start of the next reporting period it is referred to the opening prepayment. The effect of the opening prepayment is to increase the expense charged to the SOPL. In order to record this transaction, thereby eliminating the opening prepayment and increasing the current year's expense, the expense account should be debited and the prepayments account should be credited, as shown below:

	Debit €	Credit €
Expense account	X	
Prepayments account – SOFP		X

To transfer the prepayment to the related expense account.

Learning Objective 3 Account for income due at the beginning and end of each reporting period.

The income figure presented in the SOPL represents the amount of income earned in the reporting period. If an invoice was not issued in the reporting period but the income was earned in that period, then a journal entry must be recorded to recognise the income. In order to record the transaction the income due account must be debited and the income account credited, as shown below:

	Debit €	Credit €
Income due account – SOFP	X	
Income account		X

To recognise the income due.

In the reporting period in which the income due is recognised, it is presented under current assets in the SOFP.

The income due at the end of the reporting period is known as closing income due; at the start of the next reporting period it is referred to as opening income due. The effect of the opening income due is to decrease the income recognised in the SOPL. In order to record this transaction, thereby eliminating the closing income due and reducing the current year's income, the income due account should be credited and the income account should be debited, as shown below:

	Debit €	Credit €
Income account	X	
Income due account – SOFP		X

To transfer the income due to the related income account.

Learning Objective 4 Account for income received in advance at the beginning and end of each reporting period.

The income figure presented in the SOPL represents the amount of income earned in the reporting period. If an entity receives payment from a customer in the current reporting period that relates to income that will be earned in a later reporting period, then a journal entry must be recorded to defer the income. In order to record the transaction, the income in advance account must be credited and the income account debited, as shown below:

	Debit €	Credit €
Income account	X	
Income in advance account – SOFP		X

To recognise the income in advance.

In the reporting period in which the income in advance has been received it is presented under current liabilities in the SOFP.

The income in advance at the end of the reporting period is known as the closing balance on the income in advance account; at the start of the next reporting period it is referred to as the opening balance on the income in advance account. The effect of the opening balance on the income in advance account is to increase the income recognised in the SOPL. In order to record this transaction, thereby eliminating the opening balance on the income in advance account and increasing the current year's income, the income in advance account should be debited and the income account should be credited, as shown below:

	Debit €	Credit €
Income in advance account – SOFP	X	
Income account		X

To transfer the income received in advance to the related income account.

QUESTIONS – CHAPTER 4

QUESTIONS

Review Questions

(See **Appendix A** for Solutions to Review Questions.)

Question 4.1

Nolan Ltd wants to raise an accrual in relation to electricity costs at the reporting date, 31 December 2019, of €830.

Requirement Prepare the journal entry to recognise the accrual at the reporting date.

Question 4.2

Morton Ltd has paid €13,600 in relation to heat and lighting expenses during the reporting period. An invoice has not been received in relation to heat and lighting expenses for December 2019. Management estimates the heat and lighting cost for December 2019 at €1,150.

Financial statements are prepared to 31 December each year.

Requirement Prepare the journal entries and ledger accounts in relation to the above transactions.

Question 4.3

As at 1 January 2019 Mint Ltd had an opening accrual of €450 in relation to its rates expense. Mint paid €2,120 by cheque on 2 February 2019 in relation to the rates for the period 1 October 2018 to 31 December 2019.

Requirement Prepare the journal entries and ledger accounts in relation to the rates expense for the year ended 31 December 2019.

Question 4.4

Basil Ltd made the following payments in relation to its light and heating costs:

Invoice Number	Amount	Period Covered	Date Cheque Issued and Invoice Received
1425	€630	1 November 2019 to 31 January 2020	3 February 2020
1987	€490	1 February 2020 to 30 April 2020	4 May 2020

At 31 December 2019 management of Basil Ltd estimates the light and heating costs for the period 1 November 2019 to 31 December 2019 at €420.

Requirement Prepare the journal entries in relation to the light and heating expenses as at 31 December 2019 and 1 January 2020.

Question 4.5

Wootton Ltd rented premises on 1 November 2019. Under the terms of the rent agreement the rent is payable quarterly in arrears. The quarterly rental charge is €600. The first rental payment will be made on 31 January 2020.

Wootton prepares its financial statements to 31 December 2019.

Requirement Prepare the journal entries and ledger accounts in relation to the rent expense for the year ended 31 December 2019.

Question 4.6

Fable Ltd has an opening accrual on its electricity expense account of €230. During the year Fable made the following payments in relation to the electricity costs:

Invoice Number	Amount	Period Covered	Date Cheque Issued
5415	€870	1 December 2018 to 31 March 2019	5 April 2019
6007	€810	1 April 2019 to 31 July 2019	6 August 2019
8104	€780	1 August 2019 to 30 November 2019	1 December 2019

Management estimate the electricity cost for December 2019 at €290.

Fable prepares its financial statements to 31 December each year.

Requirement Prepare the journal entries and ledger accounts in relation to the electricity expense for the year ended 31 December 2019.

Question 4.7

Lindon Ltd is billed annually in arrears for its rates charges. The bill for rates is received on 1 April each year and is paid by direct debit on 30 April each year.

Period to which Payment Relates	Invoice Number	Amount	Paid
1 April 2016 to 31 March 2017	2344	€1,080	30 April 2017
1 April 2017 to 31 March 2018	4429	€1,240	30 April 2018
		€1,320	Estimate for April 2019

Lindon prepares its financial statements to 31 December each year.

Requirement Prepare the journal entries and ledger accounts in relation to the rates expense for the year ended 31 December 2018.

Question 4.8

On 1 July 2019 Abbott Ltd paid its insurance bill by cheque: €3,300. The insurance payment relates to the period 1 July 2019 to 30 June 2020.

Abbott prepares its financial statements to 31 December each year.

Requirement Prepare the journal entries and ledger accounts in relation to the insurance expense for the year ended 31 December 2019.

Question 4.9

Benson Ltd rented new premises from 1 May 2019. Under the terms of the rental agreement, rental payments are to be made quarterly in advance at a rate of €2,700 per quarter. The first payment under the rental agreement was made on 1 May 2019.

Benson prepares its financial statements to 31 December each year.

Requirement Prepare the journal entries and ledger accounts in relation to the rent expense for the year ended 31 December 2019.

Question 4.10

Haddington Ltd had an opening prepayment in relation to its electricity expenses. The prepayment amounted to €440 and related to the period January and February 2019. The amount paid in 2019 in relation to electricity expenses was €2,300.

Haddington prepares its financial statements to 31 December each year.

Requirement Prepare the journal entries and ledger accounts in relation to the electricity charges for the year ended 31 December 2019.

Question 4.11

As at 1 January 2019 Sword Ltd had a prepayment of €480 in relation to heating costs. During the year ended 31 December 2019 Sword paid €2,520, €425 of which relates to January 2020.

Sword prepares its financial statements to 31 December each year.

Requirement Prepare the journal entries and ledger accounts in relation to the heating expense for the year ended 31 December 2019.

Question 4.12

Halibut Ltd sublets one of the floors of its head office to Smithson Ltd. The rental agreement began on 1 August 2019 and is paid by Smithson quarterly in arrears at a rate of €8,400 per quarter. A cheque was received from Smithson on 31 October 2019 and it was lodged to the bank account on 4 November 2019.

Requirement Prepare the journal entries and ledger accounts of Halibut in relation to the rental income for the year ended 31 December 2019.

Question 4.13

Swindon Ltd has provided you with the following information in relation to income receipts from one of its customers – Swinford Ltd:

Date of Receipt	Amount	Period to which Income Relates
1 February 2019	€4,500	1 November 2018 to 31 January 2019
1 May 2019	€4,500	1 February 2019 to 30 April 2019
1 August 2019	€4,500	1 May 2019 to 31 July 2019
1 November 2019	€4,500	1 August 2019 to 31 October 2019

The service agreement between Swindon and Swinford was renegotiated and with effect from 1 November 2019 the annual charge will be €18,720, paid quarterly in arrears.

Requirement Prepare the journal entries and ledger accounts of Swindon in relation to the rental income for the year ended 31 December 2019.

Question 4.14

Hazel Ltd sublets part of its premises to Harold Ltd at an annual rent of €21,000. Under the terms of the rental agreement it begins on 1 June 2019 for a period of three years. Rental payments are to be made quarterly in advance, beginning on 1 June 2019.

Requirement Prepare the journal entries and ledger accounts of Hazel in relation to the rental income for the year ended 31 December 2019.

Challenging Questions

(Suggested Solutions to Challenging Questions are available through your lecturer.)

Question 4.1

Aidan is a sole trader and has just realised that he has not received his electricity bill for the period 1 November 2019 to 31 December 2019. He estimates the bill at €360. Electricity costs related to 1 January 2019 to 31 October 2019 have been dealt with correctly.

Aidan prepares his financial statements for the reporting period ended 31 December annually.

Requirement Explain to Aidan the accounting requirements, if any, in relation to the electricity expense for the period 1 November 2019 to 31 December 2019.

Question 4.2

At 1 January 2019, Rachel had an opening accrual for rent of €350 and a prepayment for rates of €260. During 2019 she paid rent and rates of €4,750, including rates for the year to 31 March 2020 of €1,200. There was no accrual for rent at 31 December 2019.

Requirement What is the rent and rates expense in Rachel's statement of profit or loss for the year ended 31 December 2019?

(Based on Chartered Accountants Ireland, CAP 1 Financial Accounting, Autumn 2009, Question 1.10)

Question 4.3

K. Daly signed a property agreement with a landlord in 2016, renting a building at €57,000 per annum. He utilises the ground floor himself as retail premises. He sublets the first floor to E. Reilly for €19,000 per annum and the second floor to M. Flaherty for €9,000 per annum.

The following was the position on 1 January 2019:

	€
Rent paid in advance by K. Daly to landlord	14,500
Rent owed to K. Daly by E. Reilly	4,750
Rent paid in advance to K. Daly by M. Flaherty	2,500

During the year ended 31 December 2019, the following transactions took place:

	€
Rent paid by K. Daly to landlord	28,500
Rent received by K. Daly from E. Reilly	23,000
Rent received by K. Daly from M. Flaherty	5,000

K. Daly also pays rates on these premises. Rates are payable in advance on 1 April each year.

At 1 January 2019 K. Daly had paid rates in advance of €6,000.

K. Daly paid €24,000 for rates on 6 April 2019. No other payments were made in the year ended 31 December 2019. K. Daly has been informed by the rates office that the rates on the premises will be €36,000 per annum from 1 April 2019 due to improvements made to the premises.

Requirement:
(a) Show, in T account format, the entries in the rent payable account, rates payable account and the rent receivable account for the year ended 31 December 2019.

18 Minutes

(b) Show the relevant entries in the statement of profit and loss and the statement of profit and loss of K. Daly for the year ended 31 December 2019.

4 Minutes

(Based on Chartered Accountants Ireland, CAP 1 Financial Accounting, Summer 2009, Question 6)

5

Bad Debts and Allowances for Bad Debts

LEARNING OBJECTIVES

Having studied this chapter, readers should understand how to:
1. account for bad debts;
2. account for a general provision for bad debts;
3. account for a specific provision for bad debts; and
4. account for bad debts recovered.

5.1 INTRODUCTION

Any business that provides credit to its customers runs the risk that some of the amounts due will not be paid in full – this is a risk of operating a business. Businesses must be competitive and therefore offer credit terms. In order to minimise their credit risk, entities will have a number of procedures in place as follows.
1. Performance of credit assessment on new customers and making credit references a requirement.
2. On acceptance of a new credit customer, the setting of a credit limit. The credit limit represents the maximum amount of credit to be provided to that customer.
3. Only allowing credit sales to customers whose payments are up to date and balances are within agreed credit limits.
4. Follow-up procedures that set out the actions to be taken when customers do not pay on time or exceed their credit limit.

To recap from **Chapter 2, Recording Financial Transactions and Preparing Financial Statements**, to recognise the sale of goods on credit, the following journal entry is required:

	Debit €	Credit €
Trade receivables account	X	
Revenue account		X

To recognise the revenue in relation to a credit sale.

At the end of the reporting period the balance on the revenue account is transferred to the statement of profit or loss (SOPL).

	Debit €	Credit €
Revenue account	X	
SOPL – revenue		X

To recognise the revenue in SOPL.

The sale transaction is recognised when it takes place, but how does an entity deal with the situation where a customer is unable to make payment for the goods sold on credit? The most common reason for a customer being unable to pay the amounts that it owes is that it is in financial difficulty. The seller in these circumstances cannot continue to recognise the amount as owing to them – they must write-off the balance due from the customer. In **Section 5.2** the accounting entries will be explained in relation to the write-off of the balance due, which is also referred to as 'the write-off of a bad debt'.

5.2 BAD DEBTS WRITE-OFF

The risk associated with providing goods or services on credit to customers is that the entity will not be paid for those goods or services. An entity may write-off the balance due from a customer when it is informed that the customer is unable to pay its debt and has gone into liquidation or in accordance with its credit management policies. An entity will have procedures in place that, based on its past experience, indicate that when payments are outstanding for a certain period of time, the entity is unlikely to get paid. For example, an entity provides its customers with a credit period of 30 days based on its past experience; if a customer has not paid by 90 days from the date of the invoice, the customer is not likely to make payment, so the amount due from the customer will be written off.

The impact of a debt being written off (also referred to as a bad debt) is to increase the **bad debts expense** in the SOPL and decrease the trade receivables asset. Therefore, as shown in **Figure 2.5**, in order to record this transaction the bad debts expense account should be debited and the trade receivables account should be credited as shown below:

	Debit €	Credit €
Bad debts expense account	X	
Trade receivables account		X

To recognise the write-off of amounts due from credit customers.

Always remember that at the end of the reporting period expense accounts are posted to the SOPL as follows:

	Debit €	Credit €
SOPL – bad debts	X	
Bad debts expense account		X

To transfer the bad debt expense to the SOPL.

Example 5.1 shows the accounting treatment and the impact on the financial statements of a bad debt write-off.

EXAMPLE 5.1: BAD DEBT WRITE-OFF

Winter Ltd has a balance on its trade receivables account of €86,300 on 31 December 2019. Winter Ltd is in the process of finalising its financial statements for the year and wants to write-off the balance due from A. Jones, who went into liquidation on 28 December 2019 owing €1,480.

Requirement Prepare the journal entries and ledger accounts in relation to the bad debt write-off.

Solution

	Debit €	Credit €
Bad debts expense	1,480	
Trade receivables		1,480

To recognise the write-off of a bad debt.

TRADE RECEIVABLES ACCOUNT

Date	Account Name	€	Date	Account Name	€
31/12/2019	Balance b/d	86,300	31/12/2019	Bad debts expense	1,480
			31/12/2019	Balance c/d	84,820
		86,300			86,300
01/01/2020	Balance b/d	84,820			

	Debit €	Credit €
SOPL – bad debts expense	1,480	
Bad debts expense account		1,480

To transfer bad debt to SOPL.

BAD DEBTS EXPENSE ACCOUNT

Date	Account Name	€	Date	Account Name	€
			31/12/2019	SOPL – bad debts expense	1,480
31/12/2019	Trade receivables	1,480			

The trade receivables balance of €84,820 will be presented under current assets in the statement of financial position (SOFP).

(Try **Review Questions 5.1** and **5.2** at the end of this chapter.)

In **Example 5.1** above the entity knows that the customer will not be able to pay its debts in full. In the next example the situation in which an entity intends to create a provision for bad debts will be dealt with. A provision is used when the entity considers, based on its past experience, that some customers may not be able to pay their debts but at the reporting date the entity knows neither the extent nor the timing of any future default.

5.3 PROVISION FOR BAD DEBTS

There are two types of provisions (also known as 'allowances') in relation to bad debts:
• A **general provision** relating to the total receivables balance of the entity and the possibility that some of its customers may not pay the balances due.
• A **specific provision** relating to a particular receivable account. A provision is required as there is some uncertainty about the ability of the customer to pay the amounts outstanding.

The balance on a provision for bad debts account (this applies to both specific and general provision accounts) is presented in the SOFP. The balances on the trade receivables and the provision for bad debts accounts are 'netted off' against one another; this means they are presented as a single figure under current assets. Netting off does not involve any journal entries; it simply means reducing the debit balance on receivables by the credit balance on the provision account.

Example 5.2 demonstrates the presentation of provisions in the SOFP.

EXAMPLE 5.2: NETTING OFF OF A PROVISION AGAINST TRADE RECEIVABLES

You have been provided with the following extract from the trial balance of G. Swan, a sole trader, as at 31 December 2019.

	Debit €	Credit €
Trade receivables account	81,230	
Provision for bad debts account		1,980

Requirement How are these figures presented in the SOFP as at 31 December 2019?

Solution

The balances on the two accounts are 'netted off' against each other and presented as a single line item.

G. Swan
STATEMENT OF FINANCIAL POSITION AS AT 31 DECEMBER 2019

Current Assets

Trade receivables (€81,230 – €1,980)	€79,250

General Provision for Bad Debts

When an entity cannot identify particular debts that will be in default, it will raise a general provision/allowance for bad debts. In this section references to 'provision' can be taken to refer to 'general provision'.

The provision/allowance for bad debts is based on management's past experience and expectations that a certain number of customers will not pay the balances due on their accounts.

The expectations of management are based on:
• knowledge about customers,
• general economic conditions, and
• past patterns of default and any changes noted.

There are three scenarios to be considered:
1. a provision/allowance set up for the first time;
2. an increase in an existing provision/allowance is required; and
3. a decrease in the existing provision/allowance is required.

The movement in the provision is charged to the bad debts expense account. In the reporting period in which the provision for bad debts is first set up, the charge to the bad debts expense is for the full amount of the provision. This is because the movement in the provision is from zero (as there was no provision at the start of the reporting period) to the amount of the provision required.

Therefore, in the reporting period in which the provision for bad debts is set up, in order to record the transaction the bad debts expense account should be debited and the provision for bad debts account should be credited, as shown below:

	Debit €	Credit €
Bad debts expense account	X	
Provision for bad debts account		X

To recognise an increase in the provision for bad debts.

The purpose of **Example 5.3** is to illustrate the initial recognition of a provision for bad debts.

EXAMPLE 5.3: INITIAL PROVISION

Alpha Ltd has been in business for the past five years, in which time it has experienced a significant increase in its revenue from both credit and cash customers.

Due to economic conditions, Alpha has, for the first time, had to write-off balances due from a number of credit customers in the most recent financial period. The amount of these write-offs is €2,500 and it has not yet been recognised in the accounting records.

Management has given careful consideration to the situation and, due to competitive pressures, believes it must continue to offer credit facilities. Management considers it prudent to start to recognise a provision for future bad debts; the provision level required is estimated at 0.5% of the balance on the trade receivables account as at 31 December 2019 which was €152,500.

Requirement Prepare the journal entries and the ledger accounts to recognise the accounting transactions above.

Solution

	Debit €	Credit €
Bad debts expense account	2,500	
Trade receivables account		2,500

To write-off bad debts.

The provision for bad debts is calculated by reference to the balance on the trade receivables account after any bad debts have been written off.

	€
Trade receivables	152,500
Bad debts to be written off	(2,500)
	150,000
Provision (€150,000 × 0.5%)	750

The journal entry would therefore be:

	Debit €	Credit €
Bad debts expense account	750	
Provision for bad debts account		750

To create a provision for bad debts.

(*Note:* the provision is calculated with reference to the trade receivables balance after bad debts have been written off.)

	Debit €	Credit €
SOPL – bad debts expense	3,250	
Bad debts expense account		3,250

To recognise the expense in the SOPL.

TRADE RECEIVABLES ACCOUNT

Date	Account Name	€	Date	Account Name	€
31/12/2019	Balance b/d	152,500	31/12/2019	Bad debts expense	2,500
			31/12/2019	Balance c/d	150,000
		152,500			152,500
01/01/2020	Balance b/d	150,000			

Note: there is no impact on the trade receivables account as a result of the provision for bad debts being set up.

BAD DEBTS EXPENSE ACCOUNT

Date	Account Name	€	Date	Account Name	€
31/12/2019	Trade receivables	2,500	31/12/2019	SOPL – bad debts expense	3,250
31/12/2019	Provision	750			
		3,250			3,250

PROVISION FOR BAD DEBTS ACCOUNT

Date	Account Name	€	Date	Account Name	€
31/12/2019	Balance c/d	750	31/12/2019	Bad debts expense	750
			01/01/2020	Balance b/d	750

Alpha Ltd
STATEMENT OF PROFIT OR LOSS (EXTRACT)
for the year ended 31 December 2019

	€
Gross profit	X
Bad debts expense	(3,250)

Alpha Ltd
STATEMENT OF FINANCIAL POSITION (EXTRACT)
as at 31 December 2019

	€
Current assets	
Inventory	X
Trade receivables (€150,000 – €750)	149,250
Cash and cash equivalents	X

The bad debts expense account is cleared out at the end of a financial period by double entry to the SOPL. It is important to always remember that the SOPL is part of the double-entry system but that the SOFP is a list of balances at a particular point in time, for example, 'as at 31 December 2019'. The accounts listed in the SOFP are assets, liabilities and equity of the entity.

Subsequent Reporting Period – Increase in the Provision for Bad Debts

The balance on the provision for bad debts account at the end of a reporting period is carried forward to the next reporting period. At each reporting date the entity's management must consider the level of the provision required, in light of the information available. If a change in the amount of the provision is required, this can result in the amount of the provision being either increased or decreased. If management's new estimate of the provision for bad debts is higher than the existing provision level, this results in an increase in the bad debts expense and an increase in the provision for bad debts, and vice versa. Therefore, as explained above, in order to record this transaction, the bad debts expense account should be debited and the provision for bad debts account should be credited, as shown below:

	Debit €	Credit €
Bad debts expense account	X	
Provision for bad debts account		X

To recognise an increase in the bad debt provision.

Example 5.4 demonstrates the accounting entries and presentation in the SOFP of a provision for bad debts at the reporting date when it has increased from the previous reporting date.

EXAMPLE 5.4: INCREASE IN PROVISION FOR BAD DEBTS

Olive Ltd has balances on its trade receivables and provision for bad debts of €115,000 debit (dr) and €2,400 credit (cr) respectively.

The following adjustments need to be posted to the financial records as at 31 December 2019:
- bad debts to be written off of €800; and
- the balance on the provision needs to be increased to €3,000.

Requirement
(a) Prepare the journal entries and the ledger accounts to recognise the above accounting transactions.
(b) Identify the amount to be presented in the SOFP with respect to these transactions.

Solution

(a)

	Debit €	Credit €
Bad debts expense account	800	
Trade receivables account		800

To recognise the write-off of bad debts.

	Debit €	Credit €
Bad debts expense account	600	
Provision for bad debts account		600

To recognise the increase in the bad debts provision (€3,000 – €2,400).

	Debit €	Credit €
SOPL – bad debts expense	1,400	
Bad debts expense account		1,400

To recognise the expense in the SOPL.

TRADE RECEIVABLES ACCOUNT

Date	Account Name	€	Date	Account Name	€
31/12/2019	Balance b/d	115,000	31/12/2019	Bad debts expense	800
			31/12/2019	Balance c/d	114,200
		115,000			115,000
01/01/2020	Balance b/d	114,200			

BAD DEBTS EXPENSE ACCOUNT

Date	Account Name	€	Date	Account Name	€
31/12/2019	Trade receivables	800	31/12/2019	SOPL – bad	
31/12/2019	Provision	600		debts expense	1,400
		1,400			1,400

PROVISION FOR BAD DEBTS ACCOUNT

Date	Account Name	€	Date	Account Name	€
31/12/2019	Balance c/d	3,000	31/12/2019	Balance b/d	2,400
			31/12/2019	Bad debt expense	600
		3,000			3,000
			01/01/2020	Balance b/d	3,000

(b)

Olive Ltd
STATEMENT OF FINANCIAL POSITION (EXTRACT)

€

Current assets

Inventory	X
Trade receivables (€114,200 – €3,000)	111,200

The trade receivables figure presented in the SOFP is reduced by the full amount of the provision (€114,200 – €3,000).

Subsequent Reporting Period – Decrease in the Provision for Bad Debts

When the entity's management requires the provision at the end of the reporting period to be less than the provision at the start of the reporting period, the result is a decrease in the bad debts expense and a decrease in the provision for bad debts. Therefore, as shown in **Figure 2.5**, in order to record this transaction the bad debts expense account should be credited and the provision for bad debts account should be debited, as shown below:

	Debit €	Credit €
Provision for bad debts account	X	
Bad debts expense account		X

In the SOFP the trade receivables figure is reduced by the new balance on the provision for bad debts account.

Example 5.5 demonstrates the journal entries and presentation of a provision for bad debts at the reporting date when it has decreased from the previous reporting date.

EXAMPLE 5.5: DECREASE IN THE PROVISION FOR BAD DEBTS

Flipper Ltd has the following balances extracted from its trial balance as at 31 December 2019:

	Debit €	Credit €
Trade receivables	192,000	
Provision for bad debts as at 01/01/2019		3,600

The following adjustments need to be posted to the accounting records:
- bad debts of €750 have to be written off; and
- management believes a more appropriate balance on the provision for bad debts is €3,200.

Requirement:
(a) Prepare the journal entries and the ledger accounts to recognise the above accounting transactions.
(b) Identify the amounts to be presented in the financial statements with respect to these transactions.

Solution

	Debit €	Credit €
Bad debts expense account	750	
Trade receivables account		750

To recognise the bad debts expense.

	Debit €	Credit €
Provision for bad debts account	400	
Bad debts expense account		400

To recognise decrease in provision for bad debts (€3,600 – €3,200).

	Debit €	Credit €
SOPL – bad debts expense	350	
Bad debts expense account		350

To recognise the expense in the SOPL.

TRADE RECEIVABLES ACCOUNT

Date	Account Name	€	Date	Account Name	€
31/12/2019	Balance b/d	192,000	31/12/2019	Bad debts expense	750
			31/12/2019	Balance c/d	191,250
		192,000			192,000
01/01/2020	Balance b/d	191,250			

BAD DEBTS EXPENSE ACCOUNT

Date	Account Name	€	Date	Account Name	€
31/12/2019	Trade receivable	750	31/12/2019	Provision for bad debts	400
			31/12/2019	SOPL – bad debts expense	350
		750			750

PROVISION FOR BAD DEBTS ACCOUNT

Date	Account Name	€	Date	Account Name	€
31/12/2019	Bad debts expense	400	01/01/2019	Balance b/d	3,600
31/12/2019	Balance c/d	3,200			
		3,600			3,600
			01/01/2020	Balance b/d	3,200

Flipper Ltd
STATEMENT OF PROFIT OR LOSS (EXTRACT)
for the year ended 31 December 2019

	€
Gross profit	X
Bad debts expense	(350)

Flipper Ltd
STATEMENT OF FINANCIAL POSITION (EXTRACT)
as at 31 December 2019

	€
Current assets	
Inventory	X
Trade receivables (€191,250 – €3,200)	188,050

The trade receivables figure presented in the SOFP is €188,050. The balance on the trade receivables account, €191,250, is reduced by the balance on the provision for bad debts account of €3,200.

(Try **Review Questions 5.3–5.5** at the end of this chapter.)

Specific Provision for Bad Debts

A provision can be set up in relation to a particular customer rather than the general provisions dealt with above. A specific provision is set up when the entity has concerns about a particular customer but does not know that the customer is going into liquidation, or when the level of default is not sufficient to write-off the debt in full by the reporting date. The effect of making a specific provision is to increase the bad debts expense and increase the specific provision. Therefore, to record the transaction the bad debts expense has to be debited and the specific provision has to be credited, as shown below:

	Debit €	Credit €
Bad debts expense account	X	
Specific provision for bad debts account		X
To recognise the specific provision for bad debts.		
SOPL – bad debts expense	X	
Bad debts expense account		X
To recognise the expense in the SOPL.		

Example 5.6 will set out the accounting entries for the recognition of a specific provision.

EXAMPLE 5.6: SPECIFIC PROVISION

Spring Ltd is preparing its financial statements as at 31 December 2019. Spring has a balance of €24,800 on its trade receivables account.

The management of Spring is concerned that one of its customers, Abigail Ltd, which is now 60 days in arrears, may not be able to pay the amount outstanding on its account of €540. Management believes a specific provision should be raised in relation to the balance on Abigail's account.

Requirement:
(a) Prepare journal entries to recognise the specific provision.
(b) What amounts are presented in the financial statements?

Solution

(a)

	Debit €	Credit €
Bad debts expense account	540	
Specific provision for bad debts account		540
To recognise the specific provision for bad debts.		
SOPL – bad debts expense	540	
Bad debts expense account		540
To recognise the expense in the SOPL.		

(b)

Spring Ltd
STATEMENT OF PROFIT OR LOSS (EXTRACT)
for the year ended 31 December 2019

	€
Gross profit	X
Bad debts expense	(540)

Spring Ltd
STATEMENT OF FINANCIAL POSITION (EXTRACT)
as at 31 December 2019

	€
Current Assets	
Trade receivables (€24,800 – €540)	24,260

Note: no journal entry in relation to the provision is posted to the trade receivables account at this stage. When a specific provision is raised it will remain in the financial statements until additional information becomes available.

A specific provision may be recognised in a reporting period, but then at a later date (possibly a subsequent reporting period) further information becomes available which either:
• confirms that the customer is unable to pay the amount due; or
• confirms that the customer is able to pay the amount due and the specific provision in no longer required.
Each of these situations will be dealt with separately.

Specific Provision Realised

When future information confirms that a customer cannot pay the amounts outstanding on their receivable account the provision is no longer required and the amount must be written off. The journal entry is:

	Debit €	Credit €
Specific provision for bad debts account	X	
Trade receivables account		X

To apply the specific provision to the trade receivables.

When the specific provision is realised (that is, written off to trade receivables), there is no impact on the SOPL. This is because the SOPL was impacted when the provision was originally set up.

Example 5.7 demonstrates the situation where more information becomes available and the business realises that the customer is unable to pay the amount due. A specific provision has been previously raised in relation to the amount due.

EXAMPLE 5.7: SPECIFIC PROVISION REALISED

In the reporting period ended 31 December 2018, Martin Ltd recognised a specific provision in relation to the amount due from one of its customers – Heidi Ltd. As at 31 December 2018, Heidi owed Martin €975; a specific provision was raised for the full amount.

On 15 April 2019, Martin was informed that Heidi had gone into liquidation and would be unable to pay any of the amount due to Martin. The balance on Heidi's receivable account is unchanged from 31 December 2018.

The balance on the trade receivables account in the SOFP of Martin as at 31 December 2018 was €64,800. Martin prepares its financial statements to 31 December each year.

Requirement:
(a) Prepare the journal entries in relation to the above transaction for the reporting periods ended 31 December 2018 and 2019.
(b) What is the impact on the SOPL for the years ended 31 December 2018 and 2019?

Solution

(a)

	Debit €	Credit €
Bad debts expense account	975	
Specific provision for bad debts account		975

To recognise the specific provision in the reporting period ended 31 December 2018.

	Debit €	Credit €
SOPL – bad debts expense	975	
Bad debts expense account		975

To recognise the bad debts expense in the SOPL in the reporting period ended 31 December 2018.

	Debit €	Credit €
Specific provision for bad debts account	975	
Trade receivables account		975

To apply the specific provision to the trade receivables in the reporting period ended 31 December 2019.

(b) The impact on the SOPL in each year is as follows:
- year ended 31/12/2018 – a charge of €975 is made in the calculation of the profit; and
- year ended 31/12/2019 – there is no impact on the SOPL.

If future information confirms that the specific provision was not required, the provision is removed from the financial statements and the trade receivables account is unaffected. The journal entry to remove the provision is:

	Debit €	Credit €
Specific provision for bad debts account	X	
Bad debts expense account		X

To remove the specific provision from the financial records.

Specific Provision no longer Required

When the specific provision is reversed, there is an impact on the statement of profit or loss. This is because the charge to the statement of profit or loss when the specific provision was originally set up has to be reversed as the provision is no longer required.

Example 5.8 demonstrates the situation where more information becomes available and the business realises that the customer is able to pay the amount due – a specific provision had been previously raised in relation to the amount due.

EXAMPLE 5.8: SPECIFIC PROVISION NO LONGER REQUIRED

In the reporting period ended 31 December 2018, Ringo Ltd recognised a specific provision in relation to the amount due from one of its customers – Bingo Ltd. As at 31 December 2018, Bingo owed Ringo €336; a specific provision was raised for the full amount.

On 8 March 2019, Ringo was informed that Bingo had fully resolved all of its financial difficulties and would be able to pay the amount due to Ringo in full. The balance on Bingo's receivable account in the financial records of Ringo is unchanged from 31 December 2018.

Ringo prepares its financial statements to 31 December each year.

Requirement Prepare the journal entries and ledger accounts in relation to the above transaction for:
(a) year ended 31 December 2018; and
(b) year ended 31 December 2019.

Solution
(a) Year ended 31 December 2018

	Debit €	Credit €
Bad debts expense account	336	
Specific provision for bad debts account		336
To recognise the specific provision.		
SOPL – bad debts expense	336	
Bad debts expense account		336
To recognise the specific provision in the SOPL.		

BAD DEBTS EXPENSE ACCOUNT

Date	Account Name	€	Date	Account Name	€
31/12/2018	Specific provision	336	31/12/2018	SOPL – bad debts expense	336

SPECIFIC PROVISION FOR BAD DEBTS ACCOUNT

Date	Account Name	€	Date	Account Name	€
31/12/2018	Balance c/d	336	31/12/2018	Bad debts expense	336
			01/01/2019	Balance b/d	336

(b) Year ended 31 December 2019

	Debit €	Credit €
Specific provision for bad debts account	336	
Bad debts expense account		336
To derecognise the specific provision.		

	Debit €	Credit €
Bad debts expense	336	
SOPL – bad debts expense account		336

To recognise reversal of specific provision in SOPL.

BAD DEBTS EXPENSE ACCOUNT

Date	Account Name	€	Date	Account Name	€
31/12/2019	SOPL – bad debts expense	336	08/03/2019	Specific provision	336

SPECIFIC PROVISION FOR BAD DEBTS ACCOUNT

Date	Account Name	€	Date	Account Name	€
08/03/2019	Bad debts expense	336	01/01/2019	Balance b/d	336

Note: in this situation the specific provision impacts the SOPL twice:
- in the reporting period ended 31 December 2018, when the specific provision is created, it reduces the reported profit for the period; and
- in the reporting period ended 31 December 2019, when the specific provision is reversed, it increases the reported profit for the period.

So far the write-off of bad debts has been explained. Some customers whose debts have been written off may make payments in the future in relation to the amounts owed by them, which is known as a 'bad debt recovery'. Such a payment may be for some or all of the balance due. In the next section the accounting entries in relation to bad debt recoveries will be explained.

(Try **Review Question 5.6** at the end of this chapter.)

5.4 BAD DEBTS RECOVERED

The situation in which an entity writes-off the balance due on a customer account as it considers it unlikely that it will be paid was dealt with previously. The situation when a customer whose balance due had been written off previously in an earlier reporting period then makes a payment will be dealt with now. The receipt of cash or cheque from the customer is known as a bad debt recovery. The effect of the transaction in the period the payment is received is to decrease the bad debts expense and increase the cash or bank account (an asset account).

Entities may approach the accounting for **bad debts recovered** by either:
- opening a separate bad debt recovery account to record the amounts received from a customer whose balance had been written off previously; or
- taking the bad debt recovery through the bad debts expense account.

Both approaches are acceptable.

Each of these two possible methods of accounting for a bad debt recovered will be dealt with separately below.

Bad Debts Recovered: Method 1

First, reinstate the trade receivable written off in the earlier reporting period using the following journal entry:

	Debit €	Credit €
Trade receivables account	X	
Bad debts expense/bad debt recovered account		X

To recognise the bad debt recovered.

Then, when the money is received, the journal entry is:

	Debit €	Credit €
Bank account	X	
Trade receivables account		X

To recognise receipt of payment.

	Debit €	Credit €
Bad debts expense/bad debt recovered account	X	
SOPL – bad debts expense		X

To recognise the bad debt recovered in profit or loss.

Bad Debts Recovered: Method 2

Alternatively, the following journal entries can be processed instead of the two above:

	Debit €	Credit €
Bank account	X	
Bad debts expense/bad debt recovered account		X

To recognise the bad debt recovered.

	Debit €	Credit €
Bad debts expense/bad debt recovered account	X	
SOPL – bad debts expense		X

To recognise the bad debt recovered in profit or loss.

Example 5.9 demonstrates the journal entries to recognise a bad debt recovered.

EXAMPLE 5.9: BAD DEBT RECOVERED

Archie Ltd has a balance on its trade receivables account of €75,600 at its reporting date – 31 December 2019. On 28 December 2019 the accounts clerk did not know how to account for a cheque for €285 received from Blunt Ltd in full and final settlement of the amount it owes. No accounting entry has been made in relation to the cheque.

Archie had written off the amount due from Blunt Ltd in the previous reporting period.

Requirement Prepare the journal entries and ledger accounts to reflect the transactions for the reporting period ended 31 December 2019.

Solution

There are two different methods that can be used.

Method One

	Debit €	Credit €
Trade receivables account	285	
Bad debts expense/bad debt recovered account		285

To recognise the bad debt recovered.

Upon receipt of the money the journal entries are:

	Debit €	Credit €
Bank account	285	
Trade receivables account		285

To recognise payment.

Bad debts expense/bad debt recovered account	285	
SOPL – bad debts expense		285

To recognise the bad debt recovered in profit or loss.

TRADE RECEIVABLES ACCOUNT

Date	Account Name	€	Date	Account Name	€
31/12/2019	Balance b/d	75,600	31/12/2019	Bank	285
31/12/2019	Bad debts expense	285	31/12/2019	Balance c/d	75,600
		75,885			75,885
01/01/2020	Balance b/d	75,600			

BAD DEBTS EXPENSE ACCOUNT

Date	Account Name	€	Date	Account Name	€
31/12/2019	SOPL – bad debts expense	285	31/12/2019	Trade receivables	285

Method Two

	Debit €	Credit €
Bank account	285	
Bad debts expense/bad debt recovered account		285

To recognise the bad debt recovered.

Bad debts expense/bad debt recovered account	285	
SOPL – bad debts expense		285

To recognise the bad debt recovered in profit or loss.

TRADE RECEIVABLES ACCOUNT

Date	Account Name	€	Date	Account Name	€
31/12/2019	Balance b/d	75,600	31/12/2019	Balance c/d	75,600
01/01/2020	Balance b/d	75,600			

BAD DEBTS EXPENSE ACCOUNT

Date	Account Name	€	Date	Account Name	€
31/12/2019	SOPL – bad debts expense	285	31/12/2019	Bank	285

A number of different issues in relation to bad debts and provisions have now been dealt with individually; the following example deals with some of these issues collectively.

Example 5.10 is a comprehensive example dealing with bad debt write-offs and provisions for bad debts.

EXAMPLE 5.10: COMPREHENSIVE EXAMPLE

On 31 December 2019, Murphy Ltd had a trade receivables balance of €184,000. Bad debts were written off during the year of €2,000. The provision for doubtful debts as at 1 January 2019 was €2,500. Management considers a provision of 2% is required at the reporting date.

B. Crawley was a customer of Murphy who went into liquidation during 2017 owing €2,800. A cheque was received from the liquidator for €500; this was in full and final settlement of the debt. The full debt of €2,800 was written off in 2017 and the trainee accountant was unsure how to treat the cheque received from the liquidator.

Requirement:
(a) Prepare the journal entries in relation to the above transactions that took place in the reporting period ended 31 December 2019.
(b) Prepare the ledger accounts in relation to the above transactions that took place in the reporting period ended 31 December 2019.
(c) Prepare the relevant extracts from the financial statements for the reporting period ended 31 December 2019.

Solution

(a)

	Debit €	Credit €
Bad debts expense account	2,000	
Trade receivables account		2,000
To recognise the bad debt expense.		
Bad debts expense account*	1,180	
Provision for bad debts account		1,180
To recognise the increase in the bad debts provision.		

* Calculation of change in provision for bad debts:

	€
Balance on trade receivables	184,000
Provision required (€184,000 × 2%)	3,680
Current provision	(2,500)
Increase in provision	1,180

Note: the balance used in this calculation is €184,000; the question states that the bad debts were written off during the year, so the balance on the trade receivables account already reflects the bad debt of €2,000 written off during the reporting period.

	Debit €	Credit €
Bank account	500	
Bad debts expense account		500

To recognise the bad debt recovered.

(b)

TRADE RECEIVABLES ACCOUNT

Date	Account Name	€	Date	Account Name	€
31/12/2019	Balance b/d	184,000	31/12/2019	Balance c/d	184,000

The bad debt has already been written off, so the balance is after the bad debt of €2,000 has been taken into account.

BAD DEBTS EXPENSE ACCOUNT

Date	Account Name	€	Date	Account Name	€
31/12/2019	Trade receivable	2,000	31/12/2019	Bank	500
31/12/2019	Provision	1,180	31/12/2019	SOPL – bad debts expense	2,680
		3,180			3,180

PROVISION FOR BAD DEBTS ACCOUNT

Date	Account Name	€	Date	Account Name	€
31/12/2019	Balance c/d	3,680	31/12/2019	Balance b/d	2,500
			31/12/2019	Bad debts expense	1,180
		3,680			3,680
			01/01/2020	Balance b/d	3,680

(c)

Murphy Ltd
STATEMENT OF PROFIT OR LOSS (EXTRACT)
for the year ended 31 December 2019

	€
Bad debts expense	(2,680)

Murphy Ltd
STATEMENT OF FINANCIAL POSITION (EXTRACT)
as at 31 December 2019

	€
Current Assets	
Trade receivables (€184,000 – €3,680)	180,320

EXAM TIPS

- Know the journal entries to account for the write-off of bad debts, changes in the allowance for bad debts and bad debt recoveries.
- Be careful to note whether or not the bad debts have already been written off.
- Remember: the change in provision can be either an increase or a decrease.
- Bad debt write-offs must be posted before the provision required at the reporting date is calculated.

5.5 CONCLUSION

When an entity sells goods on credit it runs the risk that a number of its customers will be unable to pay their debts as they fall due. When an entity knows with certainty that a customer is unable to pay its debts, the balance due to the entity has to be written off as an expense to the SOPL.

Entities may maintain a provision for bad debts when they know, based on past experience, that not all customers will be able to pay their debts in full. The provision is an estimate and is reassessed at each reporting date. The changes in the provision for bad debts are taken to the SOPL – an increase in the provision reduces the reported profit and a decrease in the provision increases the reported profit.

A bad debt written off in one reporting period may be subsequently recovered in part or in full. The amount of the bad debt recovery increases the profit in the reporting period in which the amount is received.

SUMMARY OF LEARNING OBJECTIVES

After having studied this chapter, readers should be able to:

Learning Objective 1 Account for bad debts.

When a customer of an entity gets into financial difficulty and is unable to pay its debts, the entity must write-off part or all of the balance on its account. To write-off part or all of the balance on a receivable account, the following journal entry must be posted in the accounting records of the entity:

	Debit €	Credit €
Bad debts expense account	X	
Trade receivables account		X
To recognise the write-off of amounts due from credit customers.		
SOPL – bad debts expense	X	
Bad debts expense account		X
To transfer the bad debts expense to the SOPL.		

Learning Objective 2 Account for a general provision for bad debts.

When a provision is set up initially or there is an increase required in an existing provision for bad debts, the following journal entries are required:

	Debit €	Credit €
Bad debts expense account	X	
Provision for bad debts account		X
To recognise/increase the provision for bad debts.		
SOPL – bad debts expense	X	
Bad debts expense account		X
To recognise the expense in the SOPL.		

When a reduction in the level of the provision is required the following journal entries are required:

	Debit €	Credit €
Provision for bad debts account	X	
Bad debts expense account		X
To recognise the reduction in the provision for bad debts.		
Bad debts expense account	X	
SOPL – bad debts expense		X
To recognise the expense in the SOPL.		

Learning Objective 3 Account for a specific provision for bad debts.

When a specific provision is set up the following journal entry is recorded:

	Debit €	Credit €
Bad debts expense account	X	
Specific provision for bad debts account		X
To initially recognise a specific provision in relation to a customer.		

When a specific provision recognised in an earlier reporting period for an amount owed by a particular customer is no longer required as the amount is to be written off, it is derecognised by posting the following journal entry:

	Debit €	Credit €
Specific provision for bad debts account	X	
Trade receivables account		X
To remove the specific provision for bad debts and write-off the debt as irrecoverable.		

When the specific provision recognised in an earlier reporting period is no longer required because the customer has resolved their financial difficulties, the following journal entry is required:

	Debit €	Credit €
Specific provision for bad debts account	X	
Bad debts expense account		X

To reverse the specific provision for bad debts.

Learning Objective 4 Account for bad debts recovered.

There are two methods of dealing with a bad debt recovered:

Method One

Reinstate the trade receivable balance written off in the earlier reporting period:

	Debit €	Credit €
Trade receivables account	X	
Bad debts expense/bad debts recovered account		X

To recognise the bad debt recovered.

Upon receipt of the money from the customer the journal entries are:

	Debit €	Credit €
Bank account	X	
Trade receivables account		X

To recognise payment received.

Bad debts expense/bad debts recovered account	X	
SOPL – bad debts expense		X

To recognise the bad debt recovered in profit or loss.

Method Two

	Debit €	Credit €
Bank account	X	
Bad debts expense/bad debts recovered account		X

To recognise the bad debt recovered.

Bad debts expense/bad debts recovered account	X	
SOPL – bad debts expense		X

To recognise the bad debt recovered in profit or loss.

QUESTIONS

Review Questions

(See **Appendix A** for Suggested Solutions to Review Questions.)

Question 5.1

Chicago Ltd is owed €1,440 by its customer, Baltimore Ltd. Baltimore has got into financial difficulty and a liquidator has been appointed. Baltimore will be unable to pay any of the amount outstanding.

Requirement Prepare the journal entries to recognise the bad debt write-off.

Question 5.2

The following is an extract from the trial balance of Thompson as at 31 December 2019:

	Debit €	Credit €
Trade receivables	105,200	

Included in the trade receivables balance is an amount due from Reed Ltd of €950. Reed Ltd is unable to pay its debts, so Thompson has decided to write-off the amount due from Reed in full.

Requirement Prepare the journal entries, ledger accounts and extracts from the financial statements for the reporting period 31 December 2019.

Question 5.3

Warrick Ltd has a balance on its trade receivables account of €94,500. Management has decided that, due to the poor economic conditions in which it is currently operating, it may be appropriate to set up a provision for bad debts of 2%.

Requirement Prepare the journal entries and the ledger accounts in relation to the above transaction.

Question 5.4

Morton Ltd has a balance on its trade receivables account of €75,280 as at 31 December 2019.

At the start of the current reporting period the balance on the general provision for bad debts account was €1,220. Management has reviewed all accounting estimates and believes a provision is required of 2.5%.

Requirement Prepare the journal entries and the ledger accounts in relation to the above transaction.

Question 5.5

The following has been extracted from the trial balance of Neptune Ltd as at 31 December 2019:

	Debit €	Credit €
Trade receivables	123,600	
Provision for bad debts as at 1 January 2019		3,260

On 31 December 2019, the management of Neptune received a letter from the receiver appointed to one of its customers, Ocean Ltd. The letter set out the current difficulties that are being experienced by Ocean and that it is able to pay only 25% of the amounts due to its creditors. A cheque for €700 was enclosed. Ocean owed Neptune €2,800 as at 31 December 2019.

Management estimates that the provision for bad debts should be 2%.

Requirement Prepare the journal entries and the ledger accounts in relation to the above transactions as at reporting date 31 December 2019.

Question 5.6

At 31 December 2019 management of Pluto Ltd has heard a number of rumours about the financial condition of one of its main customers, Mercury Ltd. Mercury owes Pluto €6,580 and management has decided to raise a specific provision in relation to this account.

Requirement Prepare the journal entries and the ledger accounts in relation to the above transaction.

Challenging Questions

(Suggested Solutions to Challenging Questions are available through your lecturer.)

Question 5.1

Reid Ltd supplies catering services to businesses and private individuals.

At the year-end, 31 December 2018, the bookkeeper extracted the following information:
• Total amount owed by customers is €18,950.
• Included in the list of balances due is €3,360, owed by Mr Uppity, which is considered a bad debt.
• Other customers' balances considered to be doubtful debts amount to 10% of receivables.
• At 1 January 2018, Reid had an opening balance on its doubtful debt provision account of €4,200.

The bookkeeper extracted the following information at 31 December 2019:
• The total amount owed by customers is €28,200.
• Included in the list of balances due is €960 owed by Mrs Lord, which is considered a bad debt.
• Other customers considered to be doubtful debts amount to 10% of receivables.
• In July 2019 Mr Uppity paid €2,500 in final settlement of his balance of €3,360 at 31 December 2018. This payment was credited to sundries.

Requirement:
(a) Prepare the T accounts for:
   (i)   bad debts account, and
   (ii) doubtful debts provision account for the year ended 31 December 2006 and the year ended 31 December 2019.

9 Minutes

(b) Show the income statement extracts in respect of bad and doubtful debts for the year ended 31 December 2006 and the year ended 31 December 2019.

7 Minutes

(c) Show the balance sheet extracts for receivables as at 31 December 2018 and 31 December 2019.

7 Minutes

(Based on Chartered Accountants Ireland, CAP 1 Financial Accounting, Summer 2008, Question 2)

Question 5.2

You have been provided with the following information in relation to a number of customers who currently owe Finster Ltd money in relation to services provided as at 31 December 2019:

Customer	Amount outstanding on receivables account	Comment
A. Lake	€890	A specific provision was raised in the reporting period ended 31 December 2018. This customer has gone into liquidation and will be unable to pay any of the balance outstanding on their account. Balance to be written off in full.
B. Poole	€935	Customer is in arrears and there are general concerns about their ability to repay so a specific provision needs to be created in relation to the amount due.

C. River	€1,245	A specific provision was raised in the reporting period ended 31 December 2018.
		The customer has restructured their business and at a recent creditors' meeting it was agreed to accept 60% in full and final settlement. The cheque has been received from the customer, but no journal entry has been made in the financial records.

Requirement Prepare the journal entries and the ledger accounts in relation to the above transactions.

Question 5.3

During the reporting period ended 31 December 2018 management of Star Ltd wrote off the balance due from Twinkle Ltd in full. The amount written off was €1,360.

The following transactions occurred during the reporting period ended 31 December 2019 but have not been dealt with in the financial statements:
• Bad debts to be written off of €1,100
• A general provision to be set up representing 2% of the balance on trade receivables
• Twinkle paid the amount of €1,360 in full

The balance on the trade receivables prior to the above transactions was €174,300.

Requirement Prepare the journal entries and the ledger accounts in relation to the above transactions.

Question 5.4

You have been provided with the following information in relation to Mammooth Ltd:

	As at 31/12/2018 Debit €	As at 31/12/2018 Credit €	As at 31/12/2019 Debit €	As at 31/12/2019 Credit €
Trade receivables	89,750		91,605	
Bad debts	2,380		1,050	
Provision for bad debts		2,100		2,100

You are preparing the financial statements for the reporting period ended 31 December 2019 and have been provided with the following information and asked to prepare the necessary journal entries:
• Bad debts to be written off of €1,805.
• Provision for bad debts to represent 2.5% of trade receivables balance.
• Included in the write-off of bad debts of €2,380 was an amount of €510 due from Tiny Ltd. Tiny Ltd has sent in a cheque for 80% of the amount it owes in full and final settlement of the debt.

Requirement Prepare the journal entries and the ledger accounts in relation to the above transactions for the reporting period ended 31 December 2019.

6

Property, Plant and Equipment, and Depreciation

LEARNING OBJECTIVES

Having studied this chapter, readers should be able to:
1. explain the accounting treatment of property, plant and equipment;
2. explain the accounting concept of depreciation; and
3. account for the sale of an item of property, plant and equipment.

6.1 INTRODUCTION

Property, plant and equipment are assets that are acquired for use in a business. They are expected to generate benefits for the entity for longer than just the reporting period in which the asset is acquired.

'Property, plant and equipment' includes the following:
- buildings,
- machinery,
- plant and equipment, and
- motor vehicles.

This chapter deals with the recording of an item of property, plant and equipment in the financial records at the date it was acquired; this is known as initial recognition. The journal entry in relation to the purchase of an item of property, plant and equipment was explained in **Chapter 2, Recording Financial Transactions and Preparing Financial Statements**.

The item of property, plant and equipment acquired will be used over a number of reporting periods and various accounting methods are used to charge some of the cost to the entity of the item of property, plant and equipment over the period of ownership to the statement of profit or loss (SOPL) in each reporting period in which the item of property, plant and equipment is used by the entity to generate revenue. The charging of a share of the cost to the entity of the item of property, plant and equipment to the SOPL is consistent with the matching concept. The accounting charge to the SOPL that reflects the share of the asset's cost used during the reporting period is known as **depreciation**.

When the item of property, plant and equipment is sold at the end of its **useful life**, the asset is no longer presented in the statement of financial position (SOFP); the accounting term for this is '**derecognition**'. The journal entries and calculations involved at the date that the item of property, plant and equipment is sold will be dealt with later in this chapter.

The first issue to be dealt with is the initial recognition of an item of property, plant and equipment.

6.2 COST OF ASSET

The purpose of this chapter is to explain the basic accounting concepts with respect to property, plant and equipment. **Chapter 25, Property, Plant and Equipment** will deal with these issues in more detail.

When an asset is purchased the journal entry is:

	Debit €	Credit €
Property, plant and equipment – cost account	X	
Bank/cash/loan/other payables account		X

To recognise the asset at cost when it is purchased.

The asset is presented in the SOFP under 'non-current assets'.

Example 6.1 demonstrates the journal entries to recognise an item of property, plant and equipment.

EXAMPLE 6.1: RECOGNITION OF AN ITEM OF PROPERTY, PLANT AND EQUIPMENT

Bob Smith is a sole trader who has been trading for a number of years. On 12 May 2019 he purchased a new van to be used to deliver goods directly to his customers. The van cost €37,400 and he paid for it by taking out a loan from his local bank for the full amount.

Requirement Prepare the journal entries to recognise the motor vehicle.

Solution

	Debit €	Credit €
Motor vehicles – cost account	37,400	
Loan account		37,400

To recognise the asset at cost when it is purchased by loan.

In **Example 6.1** the recognition of an item of property, plant and equipment was accounted for; that item, a motor vehicle, will be used by the entity over a number of reporting periods in the ordinary course of running the business. It would not be appropriate to charge the full cost of the motor vehicle to the SOPL in the period in which it was incurred as this would result in costs relating to the asset only being charged against the profit for one reporting period, rather than over the period of time that the asset is in use. The fundamental concept, explained in **Chapter 1, Financial Accounting: Key Terms and Concepts**, was to match the income earned in the period with the costs incurred in achieving that income. Applying that concept to the motor vehicle, a portion of the cost that reflects the benefit derived by the entity from the use of the asset should be charged to the SOPL in each reporting period in which the motor vehicle is used. This charge to SOPL, which represents a portion of the cost of the asset, is known as depreciation.

(Try **Review Question 6.1** at the end of this chapter.)

6.3 DEPRECIATION

Depreciation is the measure of the use of the asset over its useful life. The useful life of the asset is the period of time over which the entity intends to use the asset.

The maximum amount of depreciation that an entity can charge over the period of ownership of the asset is the **depreciable amount**. The depreciable amount is the difference between the cost of the asset and the amount it is estimated to be sold for at the end of its useful life. 'Residual value' is the term used for the estimated sales proceeds of the asset at the end of its useful life.

There are two methods most commonly used to calculate depreciation:
- **straight-line method**; and
- **reducing-balance method**.

The method chosen to depreciate an item of property, plant and equipment should reflect the pattern of usage of the asset over its useful life.

Depreciation is an expense; the impact of the depreciation charge in the reporting period is to increase the balance on the expense account and decrease the value of the asset. The depreciation charged on the asset from its acquisition date to its disposal date is recorded in an accumulated depreciation account rather than decreasing the asset cost account itself. Therefore, based on the above explanation, to record this transaction the depreciation expense account is debited and the accumulated depreciation account is credited as follows.

	Debit €	Credit €
Depreciation expense account	X	
Accumulated depreciation account		X

To recognise the depreciation expense.

The accumulated depreciation account records all depreciation charged in relation to the asset from the date of purchase to the date the asset is sold.

	Debit €	Credit €
SOPL – depreciation expense	X	
Depreciation expense account		X

To transfer the depreciation expense to the SOPL.

In the SOFP, assets are presented at their **carrying amount**. The carrying amount is the balance on the asset cost account less the balance on the accumulated depreciation account.

In **Chapter 2** the SOPL was presented with expenses simply listed one after another. This is acceptable when the number of items is small in number. However, as businesses grow the number of different expenses can be quite significant and this approach of simply listing them would result in a very long SOPL, which would be difficult for a user of the financial statements to follow. Instead of simply listing all the individual expenses, similar items are grouped together under the following headings (also known as line items in the SOPL):
- **Cost of sales**, which relates to the cost of purchase and conversion of raw materials to finished goods (i.e. production costs).
- **Selling and distribution**, which relates to the costs associated with the sale of goods and delivery to customers, e.g. petrol, insurance of vehicles, bad debts, carriage outwards, etc.
- **Administration**, which relates to the cost of running the business, e.g. administration salaries, directors' fees and auditors' fees.

The depreciation expense is presented in the SOPL. Some questions may specify the line item in which depreciation is to be presented for each class of property, plant and equipment, in which case follow the instructions provided in the question. If no indication is provided in the question of where to present the depreciation charge, apply the following rules:
- depreciation on assets used in production – present within cost of sales;
- depreciation on motor vehicles – present within selling and distribution expenses; and
- depreciation on buildings used for administrative purposes – present within administration expenses.

The property, plant and equipment figure presented in the SOFP is its carrying value, i.e. its cost less the balance in the accumulated depreciation account at the reporting date.

Straight-line Method

Under the straight-line method of charging depreciation, the depreciation charge is the same each year. The only exception to this is when the asset is not owned for the full year and the entity time apportions the depreciation charge. Time apportionment of the depreciation expense occurs when the entity does not own the asset for the full reporting period; this can occur in the year of purchase and the year of disposal. The entity will make a policy choice to either time apportion depreciation in the year of purchase and disposal **or** to charge a full year's depreciation in the year of purchase and none in the year of disposal. Depreciation under the straight-line method is calculated as follows:

Step 1 Calculate the depreciable amount.

$$\text{Cost} - \text{Residual value} = \text{Depreciable amount}$$

Step 2 Calculate the depreciation charge.

$$\text{Depreciation charge per annum} = \text{Depreciable amount} \div \text{useful life}$$

or

$$\text{Depreciation charge per annum} = \text{Depreciable amount} \times \text{Depreciation rate}$$

Example 6.2 applies the calculation given above to a practical example.

EXAMPLE 6.2: STRAIGHT-LINE DEPRECIATION

Otis Ltd purchased a machine on 1 July 2018 for €110,000. Otis expects to use the machine for five years, at the end of which it expects to sell the machine for €10,000.

Requirement Calculate the depreciation charge for the year ended 30 June 2019 and the journal entries in relation to depreciation. Prepare the machine cost account and the accumulated depreciation account.

Solution

Step 1 Calculate the depreciable amount.
Cost – Residual value = Depreciable amount
 €110,000 – €10,000 = €100,000

Step 2 Calculate the depreciation charge.
Depreciation charge per annum = Depreciable amount ÷ useful life
　　　　€100,000 ÷ 5 years = €20,000 per annum

The journal entries are:

	Debit €	Credit €
Depreciation expense account	20,000	
Accumulated depreciation account		20,000
To recognise the depreciation expense.		

	Debit €	Credit €
SOPL – depreciation expense	20,000	
Depreciation expense account		20,000

To recognise the depreciation expense in profit or loss.

MACHINE – COST ACCOUNT

Date	Account Name	€	Date	Account Name	€
01/07/2018	Bank	110,000	30/06/2019	Balance c/d	110,000
01/07/2019	Balance b/d	110,000			

MACHINE – ACCUMULATED DEPRECIATION ACCOUNT

Date	Account Name	€	Date	Account Name	€
			30/06/2019	Depreciation expense	20,000
30/06/2019	Balance c/d	20,000	01/07/2019	Balance b/d	20,000

DEPRECIATION EXPENSE ACCOUNT

Date	Account Name	€	Date	Account Name	€
30/06/2019	Accumulated depreciation	20,000	30/06/2019	SOPL – depreciation	20,000

It is important to note that the balance on the accumulated depreciation account is carried down at the end of the reporting period and brought down at the beginning of the next reporting period. The balance on the accumulated depreciation account represents the total depreciation charged to SOPL from the purchase date to the current date.

The machine is presented in the SOFP as follows:

Non-current Asset	Cost €	Accumulated Depreciation €	Carrying Value €
Machine	110,000	20,000	90,000

In the above example the asset was acquired on the first day of the reporting period; in reality, assets can be acquired at any time during the year. An entity will adopt one of the following policies in relation to assets owned for part of the reporting period:
- depreciation is charged for a full year in the year of acquisition and there is no charge in the year that the asset is sold; or
- the depreciation charge is time apportioned in both the year of purchase and in the year that the asset is sold. For example, if the asset is only owned for three months of the reporting period, then the annual charge is time apportioned, that is, multiplied by 3/12. This reduced amount is charged to the SOPL in the reporting period.

Example 6.3 demonstrates the impact of an entity's policy on the depreciation charge in the year of purchase and the year of sale.

EXAMPLE 6.3: STRAIGHT-LINE METHOD DEPRECIATION RATE EXPRESSED AS A PERCENTAGE

On 1 April 2019, Albert Ltd purchased a piece of equipment for €130,000. Management estimates that depreciation should be charged at a rate of 10% per annum. Management expects that the equipment will have a residual value of €5,000.

Albert prepares its financial statements to 31 December each year.

Requirement For the reporting period ended 31 December 2019:
(a) Calculate the depreciation charge if Albert's policy is to charge a full year's depreciation in the year of purchase.
(b) Calculate the depreciation charge if Albert's policy is to time apportion the depreciation charge in the year of purchase.

Solution

(a) A full year's depreciation charged in the year of purchase:

Step 1 Calculate the depreciable amount.
Cost – Residual value = Depreciable amount
  €130,000 – €5,000 = €125,000

Step 2 Calculate the depreciation charge.
Depreciation charge per annum = Depreciable amount × Depreciation rate
= €125,000 × 10%
= €12,500 per annum

(b) Depreciation is time apportioned in the year of purchase:

Step 1 Calculate the depreciable amount.
Cost – Residual value = Depreciable amount
  €130,000 – €5,000 = €125,000

Step 2 Calculate the depreciation charge.
Depreciation charge per annum = Depreciable amount ÷ useful life
= €125,000 ÷ 10 years
= €12,500 per annum

The asset was held for nine months of the current year, so the depreciation charge in the SOPL for the year ended 31 December 2019 is €9,375 (i.e. €12,500 × 9/12).

(Try **Review Questions 6.2** and **6.3** at the end of this chapter.)

Reducing-balance Method

Under this method the depreciation charge is different each year. The depreciation charge reduces progressively over the useful life of the asset. This method is typically used for the depreciation of motor vehicles.

The depreciation charge is calculated as:

In Year 1: Cost × Depreciation rate

In subsequent years: Carrying amount × Depreciation rate

Example 6.4 shows how depreciation is calculated using the reducing-balance method. The carrying amount is as at the previous reporting date and is calculated as cost less accumulated depreciation.

EXAMPLE 6.4: REDUCING-BALANCE METHOD

On 1 January 2017, Herbert Ltd purchased a motor vehicle for €48,000.

Management estimates that the most appropriate way to charge depreciation is to use the reducing-balance method at a rate of 20% per annum.

Herbert's reporting date is 31 December annually.

Requirement Calculate the depreciation charge and carrying amount as at the following reporting dates:
(a) 31 December 2017,
(b) 31 December 2018, and
(c) 31 December 2019.

Solution
(a) Reporting date 31 December 2017:

In Year 1 the depreciation charge is based on the cost of the asset:
Cost × Depreciation rate = €48,000 × 20%
$$= €9,600$$

	€
Cost as at 01/01/2017	48,000
Depreciation year ended 31/12/2017	(9,600)
Carrying amount as at 31/12/2017	38,400

(b) Reporting date 31 December 2018:

In subsequent years the depreciation charge is based on the carrying amount of the asset:
Carrying amount × Depreciation rate = €38,400 × 20%
$$= €7,680$$

	€
Carrying amount as at 01/01/2018	38,400
Depreciation year ended 31/12/2018	(7,680)
Carrying amount as at 31/12/2018	30,720

(c) Reporting date 31 December 2019:

In subsequent years the depreciation charge is based on the carrying amount of the asset:
Carrying amount × Depreciation rate = €30,720 × 20%
$$= €6,144$$

	€
Carrying amount as at 01/01/2019	30,720
Depreciation year ended 31/12/2019	(6,144)
Carrying amount as at 31/12/2019	24,576

In the previous example the asset was purchased on the first day of the reporting period, but in reality assets may be acquired at any time during the reporting period. Management must decide on a policy in relation to the calculation of the depreciation charges in the year in which the asset is first purchased and the year it will be disposed of. The policy options are to either time-apportion in the years of purchase and disposal; or to charge a full year's depreciation in the year of purchase (irrespective of the purchase date) and none in the year of disposal (irrespective of the disposal date).

Example 6.5 demonstrates how an entity's policy with regard to the treatment of depreciation in the years of purchase and sale impact the depreciation charge.

EXAMPLE 6.5: REDUCING-BALANCE METHOD

On 1 July 2018 Montgomery Ltd purchased a truck for €80,000. Montgomery depreciates its truck on a reducing-balance basis at a rate of 15% per annum.

Montgomery prepares its financial statements to 31 December each year.

Requirement Calculate the depreciation charge and carrying amount for the reporting periods ended 31 December 2018 and 2019 using each of the following policies:
(a) Montgomery's policy is to charge a full year's depreciation in the year of purchase and none in the year of sale.
(b) Montgomery's policy is to time apportion depreciation in the year of purchase and the year of sale.

Solution
(a) Year 1: Depreciation charge = Cost × Depreciation rate
$$= €80,000 × 15\%$$
$$= €12,000$$

	€
Cost as at 01/07/2018	80,000
Depreciation year ended 31/12/2018	(12,000)
Carrying amount as at 31/12/2018	68,000

Subsequent year: Depreciation charge = Carrying amount × Depreciation rate
$$= €68,000 × 15\%$$
$$= €10,200$$

	€
Carrying amount as at 01/01/2019	68,000
Depreciation year ended 31/12/2019	(10,200)
Carrying amount as at 31/12/2019	57,800

(b) Year 1: Depreciation charge = Cost × Depreciation rate
$$= €80,000 × 15\%$$
$$= €12,000$$

The effect of the time apportionment is as follows:

The asset was in use for only six months, so the charge for the reporting period ended 31 December 2018 is €6,000 (i.e. €12,000 × 6/12)

	€
Cost as at 01/07/2018	80,000
Depreciation year ended 31/12/2018	(6,000)
Carrying amount as at 31/12/2018	74,000

Subsequent years: Depreciation charge = Carrying amount × Depreciation rate

$$= €74,000 \times 15\%$$
$$= €11,100$$

	€
Carrying amount as at 01/01/2019	74,000
Depreciation year ended 31/12/2019	(11,100)
Carrying amount as at 31/12/2019	62,900

(Try **Review Questions 6.4** and **6.5** at the end of this chapter.)

In this chapter so far the accounting at initial recognition and depreciation have been explained. Next, the accounting entries in relation to the disposal of the asset will be reviewed.

6.4 SALE OF PROPERTY, PLANT AND EQUIPMENT

When an asset is no longer required by the entity, it is sold; this is also referred to as a disposal of an asset. An asset sold must be removed from the financial records of the entity; the term used to describe this is 'derecognition'.

For each asset there are two accounts, which are netted off against one another to determine the carrying amount reflected in the SOFP in relation to an item of property, plant and equipment:
• cost account, and
• accumulated depreciation account.

On disposal the asset is removed from the financial records of the entity and a profit or loss on disposal is calculated. To account for the disposal of an item of property, plant and equipment, a ledger account named 'disposal account' is opened. The balances on the accounts relating to the asset (i.e. the cost and accumulated depreciation) are posted to the disposal account as well as the proceeds/trade in value of the asset. To determine if the entity has made a profit or loss on the disposal, the sales proceeds or trade-in value of the asset is compared to the carrying amount of the asset at the date of disposal.

	Debit €	Credit €
Disposal account	X	
Property, plant and equipment – cost account		X

To transfer the cost of the asset to the disposal account on derecognition.

	Debit €	Credit €
Property, plant and equipment – accumulated depreciation account	X	
Disposal account		X

To transfer the accumulated depreciation of the asset to the disposal account on derecognition.

When the asset is sold for cash the following journal entry is posted to the financial records:

	Debit €	Credit €
Cash account	X	
Disposal account		X

To recognise the proceeds from sale of asset.

When an asset is traded in for another asset, the new asset is recognised at its full cost – that is, the amount paid by the entity plus the trade-in value allowed for the old asset. The amount credited to the disposal account is the trade-in allowance provided by the retailer. The journal entry is as follows:

	Debit €	Credit €
Property, plant and equipment – cost account	X	
Bank account		X
Disposal account		X

To recognise the trade-in of an item of property, plant and equipment for a new asset.

Over the period of ownership the entity has estimated the proportion of the asset's cost that has been used. The carrying amount of the asset may not be equal to the sales proceeds/trade-in value achieved on disposal:
• when the sales proceeds/trade-in value of the asset is higher than the carrying amount of the asset, a profit on disposal is recognised;
• when the sales proceeds/trade-in value of the asset is lower than the carrying amount of the asset, a loss on disposal is recognised.

The journal entry to recognise a profit on disposal is:

	Debit €	Credit €
Disposal account	X	
SOPL – profit on disposal		X

To recognise the profit on disposal of the asset.

The journal entry to recognise a loss on disposal is:

	Debit €	Credit €
SOPL – loss on disposal	X	
Disposal account		X

To recognise the loss on disposal of the asset.

Example 6.6 demonstrates the journal entries necessary to recognise the disposal of a motor vehicle where the carrying amount is less than the sales proceeds.

EXAMPLE 6.6: PROFIT ON DISPOSAL OF PROPERTY, PLANT AND EQUIPMENT

On 31 December 2019, Grampley Ltd sold a motor vehicle for €6,350 cash. At the disposal date the asset had accumulated depreciation of €24,300 – it had originally cost €28,700.

Requirement Prepare the journal entries and ledger accounts for the disposal of the asset.

Solution

	Debit €	Credit €
Disposal account	28,700	
Motor vehicle – cost account		28,700

To transfer the cost of the asset to the disposal account on derecognition.

	Debit €	Credit €
Motor vehicle – accumulated depreciation account	24,300	
Disposal account		24,300

To transfer the accumulated depreciation of the asset to the disposal account on derecognition.

	Debit €	Credit €
Cash account	6,350	
Disposal account		6,350

To recognise the proceeds from the sale of the asset.

Calculation of profit/loss on disposal

	€
Proceeds	6,350
Carrying amount (€28,700 – €24,300)	(4,400)
Profit/(loss) on disposal	1,950

	Debit €	Credit €
Disposal account	1,950	
SOPL – profit on disposal		1,950

To recognise the profit on disposal of the asset.

MOTOR VEHICLE – COST ACCOUNT

Date	Account Name	€	Date	Account Name	€
31/12/2019	Balance b/d	28,700	31/12/2019	Disposal account	28,700

MOTOR VEHICLE – ACCUMULATED DEPRECIATION

Date	Account Name	€	Date	Account Name	€
31/12/2019	Disposal account	24,300	31/12/2019	Balance b/d	24,300

DISPOSAL ACCOUNT

Date	Account Name	€	Date	Account Name	€
31/12/2019	Motor vehicle – cost	28,700	31/12/2019	Accumulated depreciation	24,300
31/12/2019	SOPL – profit	1,950	31/12/2019	Cash	6,350
		30,650			30,650

Example 6.7 demonstrates the journal entries to recognise the disposal of a motor vehicle where the carrying amount is greater than the sales proceeds.

EXAMPLE 6.7: LOSS ON DISPOSAL OF PROPERTY, PLANT AND EQUIPMENT

On 31 December 2019 Wonder Ltd sold a piece of equipment for €3,750 for cash. The equipment had originally cost €40,000 and the balance on the accumulated depreciation account at the date of disposal was €31,400.

Requirement Prepare the journal entries and the ledger accounts to recognise the disposal of the item of equipment.

Solution

	Debit €	Credit €
Disposal account	40,000	
Equipment – cost account		40,000

To transfer the cost of the asset to the disposal account on derecognition.

	Debit €	Credit €
Equipment – accumulated depreciation account	31,400	
Disposal account		31,400

To transfer the accumulated depreciation of the asset to the disposal account on derecognition.

	Debit €	Credit €
Cash account	3,750	
Disposal account		3,750

To recognise the proceeds from the sale of the asset.

Calculation of profit/loss on disposal:

	€
Proceeds	3,750
Carrying amount (€40,000 – €31,400)	(8,600)
Profit/(loss) on disposal	(4,850)

	Debit €	Credit €
SOPL – loss on disposal	4,850	
Disposal account		4,850

To recognise the loss on disposal of the asset.

EQUIPMENT – COST ACCOUNT

Date	Account Name	€	Date	Account Name	€
31/12/2019	Balance b/d	40,000	31/12/2019	Disposal account	40,000

EQUIPMENT – ACCUMULATED DEPRECIATION ACCOUNT

Date	Account Name	€	Date	Account Name	€
31/12/2019	Disposal account	31,400	31/12/2019	Balance b/d	31,400

DISPOSAL ACCOUNT

Date	Account Name	€	Date	Account Name	€
31/12/2019	Equipment – cost	40,000	31/12/2019	Accumulated depreciation	31,400
			31/12/2019	Cash	3,750
			31/12/2019	SOPL – loss	4,850
		40,000			40,000

Examples **6.6** and **6.7** above are quite straightforward and focus purely on the journal entries. **Example 6.8** demonstrates both the depreciation calculations and the disposal of an asset.

EXAMPLE 6.8: DISPOSAL OF AN ASSET

On 1 October 2016 Sherman Ltd purchased a machine for €150,000. At the purchase date the management of Sherman estimates that the useful life of the asset is eight years and the residual value is €30,000.

Management's policy is to time apportion depreciation in the year of purchase and the year of disposal.

On 30 June 2019 the machine was sold for €98,500.

The company prepares its accounts to 31 December each year.

Requirement Prepare the ledger accounts and journal entries to recognise the disposal of the asset.

Solution

Step 1 Calculate the depreciable amount.
Cost – Residual value = Depreciable amount
€150,000 – €30,000 = €120,000

Step 2 Calculate the depreciation charge.
Depreciable amount ÷ Useful life = Depreciation charge
€120,000 ÷ 8 years = €15,000 per annum

	€	€
Cost		150,000
Depreciation		
Year ended 31/12/2016 (W1)	(3,750)	
Year ended 31/12/2017	(15,000)	
Year ended 31/12/2018	(15,000)	
Year ended 31/12/2019 (W2)	(7,500)	
Accumulated depreciation as at 30/06/2019		(41,250)
Carrying amount as at 30/06/2019		108,750

W1: Depreciation charge in 2016: €15,000 × 3/12 = €3,750.

W2: Depreciation charge in 2019: €15,000 × 6/12 = €7,500.

	Debit €	Credit €
Disposal account	150,000	
Equipment – cost account		150,000

To transfer the cost of the asset to the disposal account on derecognition.

	Debit €	Credit €
Equipment – accumulated depreciation account	41,250	
Disposal account		41,250

To transfer the accumulated depreciation of the asset to the disposal account on derecognition.

	Debit €	Credit €
Cash account	98,500	
Disposal account		98,500

To recognise the proceeds from the sale of the asset.

Calculation of profit/loss on disposal:

	€
Proceeds	98,500
Carrying amount (€150,000 – €41,250)	(108,750)
Loss on disposal	(10,250)

	Debit €	Credit €
SOPL – loss on disposal	10,250	
Disposal account		10,250

To recognise the loss on disposal of the asset.

EQUIPMENT – COST ACCOUNT

Date	Account Name	€	Date	Account Name	€
01/10/2016	Bank	150,000	31/12/2016	Balance c/d	150,000
01/01/2017	Balance b/d	150,000	31/12/2017	Balance c/d	150,000
01/01/2018	Balance b/d	150,000	31/12/2018	Balance c/d	150,000
01/01/2019	Balance b/d	150,000	30/06/2019	Disposal	150,000

EQUIPMENT – ACCUMULATED DEPRECIATION ACCOUNT

Date	Account Name	€	Date	Account Name	€
31/12/2016	Balance c/d	3,750	31/12/2016	Depreciation expense	3,750
			01/01/2017	Balance b/d	3,750
31/12/2017	Balance c/d	18,750	31/12/2017	Depreciation expense	15,000
		18,750			18,750
31/12/2018	Balance c/d	33,750	01/01/2018	Balance b/d	18,750
			31/12/2018	Depreciation expense	15,000
		33,750			33,750
30/06/2019	Disposal	41,250	01/01/2019	Balance b/d	33,750
			30/06/2019	Depreciation expense	7,500
		41,250			41,250

DEPRECIATION EXPENSE ACCOUNT

Date	Account Name	€	Date	Account Name	€
31/12/2016	Accumulated depreciation	3,750	31/12/2016	SOPL	3,750
31/12/2017	Accumulated depreciation	15,000	31/12/2017	SOPL	15,000
31/12/2018	Accumulated depreciation	15,000	31/12/2018	SOPL	15,000
31/12/2019	Accumulated depreciation	7,500	31/12/2019	SOPL	7,500

DISPOSAL ACCOUNT

Date	Account Name	€	Date	Account Name	€
30/6/2019	Equipment – cost	150,000	30/6/2019	Accumulated depreciation	41,250
			30/6/2019	Bank	98,500
			30/6/2019	SOPL – loss on disposal	10,250
		150,000			150,000

(Try **Review Questions 6.6** and **6.7** at the end of this chapter.)

EXAM TIPS

- Use the depreciation method indicated in the question, i.e. straight-line method or reducing-balance method.
- When assets are not held for the entire reporting period, note the policy, i.e. whether it is to time apportion depreciation in the years of purchase and disposal **or** to charge a full year's depreciation in the year of purchase and none in the year of disposal.

- Questions will generally indicate where the depreciation expense is to be presented in the SOPL; if no indication is provided, the following is a general guide:

Class of Property, Plant and Equipment	SOPL Line Item in which to be Presented
Production machinery or equipment	Cost of sales
Motor vehicles	Selling and distribution
Buildings	Administration
Factory buildings	Cost of sales

6.5 CONCLUSION

An item of property, plant and equipment is initially recognised at the acquisition date at cost and presented in the SOFP under non-current assets.

Depreciation is an expense charged to the SOPL over the useful life of an item of property, plant and equipment. The total depreciation charged over the useful life is equal to the depreciable amount of the asset, i.e. the cost less the residual value of the asset. The method chosen to calculate depreciation (straight-line or reducing-balance) should reflect the way in which the entity benefits from the use of the asset. At each reporting date property, plant and equipment is presented in the SOFP at its carrying amount, that is, its cost less its accumulated depreciation.

An item of property, plant and equipment is derecognised on disposal or at the end of its useful life and a profit or loss on disposal is calculated. The profit or loss is determined by comparing the sales proceeds/trade-in value with the carrying amount of the asset at the disposal date.

SUMMARY OF LEARNING OBJECTIVES

After having studied this chapter, readers should be able to:

Learning Objective 1 Explain the accounting treatment of property, plant and equipment.

Items of property, plant and equipment are purchased for use within the entity for more than one reporting period. As the entity will benefit from the asset for a number of years, it is appropriate to use a method that allocates the cost to the entity of the asset to the reporting periods in a manner that reflects the benefit that the entity has obtained from the use of the asset.

The journal entry to recognise an asset is:

	Debit €	Credit €
Property, plant and equipment – cost account	X	
Bank/cash/loan/other payables account		X

To recognise the asset at cost when it is purchased.

Learning Objective 2 Explain the accounting concept of depreciation.

Depreciation is the measure of the use of the asset over its useful life. The total depreciation charge over the useful life is the depreciable amount (i.e. cost less residual value).

Two of the methods used to calculate depreciation are the:
* straight-line method, and
* reducing-balance method.

Year	Straight-line Method	Reducing-balance Method
First year of ownership	Depreciable amount ÷ Useful life **or** Depreciable amount × Depreciation rate	Cost × Depreciation rate
Subsequent years	Depreciable amount ÷ Useful life **or** Depreciable amount × Depreciation rate	Carrying amount × Depreciation rate

The journal entries to recognise and charge depreciation in the financial records are:

	Debit €	Credit €
Depreciation expense account	X	
Accumulated depreciation account		X

To recognise the depreciation expense.

	Debit €	Credit €
SOPL – depreciation expense	X	
Depreciation expense account		X

To transfer the depreciation expense to the SOPL.

Learning Objective 3 Account for the sale of an item of property, plant and equipment.

When a non-current asset is sold, it must be derecognised from the financial records and a profit or loss on disposal calculated. The profit or loss arises because the amount the non-current asset is sold for or the trade-in value is different from the carrying amount of the asset.

The journal entries to derecognise a non-current asset are as follows:

	Debit €	Credit €
Disposal account	X	
Property, plant and equipment – cost account		X

To transfer the cost of the asset to the disposal account on derecognition.

	Debit €	Credit €
Property, plant and equipment – accumulated depreciation account	X	
Disposal account		X

To transfer the accumulated depreciation of the asset to the disposal account on derecognition.

	Debit €	Credit €
Cash/Bank/Property, plant and equipment – cost account	X	
Disposal account		X
To recognise proceeds on disposal.		

	Debit €	Credit €
Disposal account	X	
SOPL – profit on disposal		X
To recognise the profit on disposal of the asset.		

The journal entry to recognise a loss on disposal is:

	Debit €	Credit €
SOPL – loss on disposal	X	
Disposal account		X
To recognise the loss on disposal of the asset.		

QUESTIONS

Review Questions

(See **Appendix A** for Solutions to Review Questions.)

Question 6.1

On 8 May 2019 Wilson Ltd purchased a machine for €800,000. The purchase was made by cheque payment to the supplier.

Requirement Prepare the journal entry to recognise the purchase of the machine.

Question 6.2

Matthews Ltd purchased a piece of equipment on 1 April 2018 for €60,000 cash. At the purchase date management estimate the useful life of the asset at 10 years and the residual value at €5,000. The equipment is used in the production of Matthews' best-selling product.

Matthews uses the straight-line method of depreciation. The company's policy is to charge a full year's depreciation in the year of purchase and none in the year of sale.

Matthews prepares its financial statements to 31 December each year.

Requirement:
(a) Calculate the depreciation charge for the years ended 31 December 2018 and 2019.
(b) Prepare the journal entries for 2018 and 2019.
(c) What is the carrying amount of the equipment for the reporting years ended 31 December 2018 and 2019?

Question 6.3

Wilko Ltd purchased a property on 1 September 2018 for use as its new administrative headquarters. The useful life and residual value of the property were estimated at 40 years and €nil, respectively.

Wilko prepares its financial statements to 31 December each year. The company's policy is to time apportion the depreciation charge in both the year of purchase and the year of sale. Wilko depreciates its properties on a straight-line basis. The property purchase was financed by a loan; the asset cost €2 million.

Requirement:
(a) Calculate the depreciation charge for the years ended 31 December 2018 and 2019.
(b) Prepare the journal entries for 2018 and 2019.
(c) What is the carrying amount of the equipment for the reporting years ended 31 December 2018 and 2019?

Question 6.4

On 1 January 2018 Mercury Ltd purchased a new truck for €85,000. The asset is expected to have a residual value of €22,000.

Depreciation is charged on a reducing-balance basis at a rate of 15% per annum in the financial statements. Depreciation is time apportioned in the year of purchase and in the year of sale.

Mercury prepares its financial statements to 31 December.

Requirement Calculate the depreciation charge for the reporting periods ended 31 December 2018 and 2019.

Question 6.5

On 30 April 2018 Brent Ltd purchased a motor vehicle for €32,000 for cash. Brent depreciates its motor vehicles on a reducing-balance basis at a rate of 20% per annum. The depreciation charge is time apportioned in the year of purchase and the year of sale.

Brent prepares its financial statements to 31 October each year.

Requirement Calculate the depreciation charge and prepare the journal entries for the reporting periods ended 31 October 2018 and 2019.

Question 6.6

On 31 December 2019 Anderson Ltd sold one of its properties for €2,085,000. The asset had originally cost €2,400,000 and the balance on the accumulated depreciation account was €410,000 at the date the asset was sold.

Requirement Prepare the journal entries to record the disposal of the property and the disposal account.

Question 6.7

On 1 April 2017 Montgomery Ltd purchased a machine for €680,000; the asset was paid for in cash. Montgomery depreciates the machine on a reducing-balance basis at a rate of 10% per annum; a full year's depreciation is charged in the year of purchase and none in the year of disposal.

The residual value of the asset is estimated at €60,000.

Montgomery prepares its financial statements to 31 December each year.

Montgomery sold the machine on 31 August 2019 for €525,000.

Requirement Prepare the journal entries to record the disposal of the machine and the disposal account.

Challenging Questions

(Suggested Solutions to Challenging Questions are available through your lecturer.)

Question 6.1

Pitt Ltd paid €57,500 for a piece of equipment on 1 January 2017. The equipment was expected to have a useful life of five years and a residual value at the end of 2021 of €6,500.

Requirement What would be the carrying amount of the equipment at 31 December 2019 if the asset is depreciated on a straight-line basis?

(Based on Chartered Accountants Ireland, CAP 1 Financial Accounting, Summer 2008, Question 1.2)

Question 6.2

Lime Ltd acquired a non-current asset on 1 July 2017 for €10 000. The asset had an expected useful economic life of five years and an estimated residual value of €2,000. On 1 January 2019 the entity sold the asset for €9,100. Lime Ltd uses the straight-line depreciation method. Depreciation is time apportioned in both the years of purchase and disposal.

Requirement At the date of sale, what is the accumulated depreciation on this asset?

(Based on Chartered Accountants Ireland, CAP 1 Financial Accounting, Summer 2009, Question 1.8)

Question 6.3

Pepper Ltd depreciates its vehicles at a rate of 20% per annum on a reducing-balance basis. It had purchased a vehicle at a cost of €12,000 on 1 January 2017 and sold this same vehicle for €6,000 on 31 December 2019.

Requirement Prepare the disposal account on the sale of the vehicle.

(Based on Chartered Accountants Ireland, CAP 1 Financial Accounting, Summer 2013, Question 1.3)

Accounting for Value-added Tax

7

LEARNING OBJECTIVES

Having studied this chapter, readers should be able to:
1. explain the concept of value-added tax (VAT);
2. explain and account for expenses and costs when the VAT is irrecoverable;
3. explain and account for expenses and costs when the VAT is recoverable;
4. understand what is meant by the terms used in questions: 'exclusive', 'inclusive', 'net' and 'gross';
5. account for a return of goods when the original transaction involved VAT; and
6. account for a bad debt write-off when the original transaction was recorded with VAT.

7.1 INTRODUCTION

Value-added tax (VAT) is charged at each point in the production and distribution cycle until the final sale is made. Examples of the stages at which VAT may be charged are as follows.

Stage 1   Goods are manufactured and sold for €1,000 (exclusive of VAT). VAT is charged at a rate of 21%. The VAT on the sales proceeds is collected by the seller and they pay €210 to the revenue authorities. VAT returns are submitted at regular intervals throughout the year to revenue authorities.

Stage 2   The above goods are used in the purchaser's production process. Additional costs are incurred in the production process and the goods are sold for €2,300 (exclusive of VAT), on which VAT is charged at a rate of 21%.

	€
VAT collected on sales proceeds (€2,300 × 21%)	483
VAT paid on purchase of goods (€1,000 × 21%)	(210)
VAT paid over to revenue authorities	273

Stage 3   The goods are bought by the final consumer for €2,783 [€2,300 + €483 VAT]. The VAT is borne by the final consumer.

7.2 ACCOUNTING TREATMENT WHEN VAT IS NOT RECOVERABLE

When VAT is not recoverable, the total cost of the goods or services, that is, the amount inclusive of VAT, is treated as an expense of the entity. VAT is not recoverable when an entity is not registered for VAT.

Example 7.1 illustrates the accounting treatment of costs where the VAT is not recoverable.

Example 7.1: VAT Not Recoverable

Gregory Ltd purchased a machine for cash that has a list price before VAT of €45,000. VAT is charged on the cost of the asset at a rate of 21%. VAT on the purchase of the asset is not recoverable.

Requirement Prepare the journal entry to recognise the purchase of the machine.

Solution

Rates of VAT can vary (rates will be supplied in exam questions). VAT is charged on the cost of the goods, thereby increasing the total cost:

	€
Cost	45,000
VAT @ 21%	9,450
Total cost	54,450

	Debit €	Credit €
Machine – cost account	54,450	
Cash account		54,450
To recognise the asset at cost.		

The cost that the asset is recognised at is the cost inclusive of VAT as the VAT is not recoverable.

(Try **Review Question 7.1** at the end of this chapter.)

The accounting treatment of transactions when VAT is recoverable is different from that outlined in this section. By 'recoverable' it is meant that the VAT incurred in relation to purchases can be offset against the VAT collected by an entity on the sale of goods/provision of services to its customers. The accounting in relation to transactions when VAT is recoverable will be considered next.

7.3 ACCOUNTING TREATMENT WHEN VAT IS RECOVERABLE

Before explaining the accounting treatment in relation to VAT, an explanation of the calculations is required. A common issue for students in relation to accounting for VAT is to understand the terminology used to explain whether the amount provided is reflective of the total transaction amount with VAT or the transaction amount before VAT. The terms used in questions tend to refer to the amount provided being 'inclusive', 'exclusive', 'gross' or 'net' of VAT. Each of these situations is explained in **Figure 7.1** below.

FIGURE 7.1: VAT TERMINOLOGY

Term used	Explanation	Calculation
The electricity cost incurred was €2,420, **inclusive** of VAT at a rate of 21%	The cost of €2,420 includes the VAT charge. To record the transaction in the financial records the amount of VAT attributable to the transaction needs to be quantified.	VAT amount = Transaction amount $\times \dfrac{\text{VAT rate}}{100 + \text{VAT rate}}$ $€2,420 \times \dfrac{21}{100 + 21} = €420$ The amount of the transaction before VAT was added is €2,000 (i.e. €2,420 – €420)
The purchase expense incurred was €2,500, **exclusive** of VAT at a rate of 21%	The expense of €2,500 is before the VAT charge. To record the transaction in the financial records the amount of VAT attributable to the transaction needs to be quantified.	VAT amount = Amount $\times \dfrac{\text{VAT rate}}{100}$ $€2,500 \times \dfrac{21}{100} = €525$ The total value of the transaction is €3,025 (i.e. €2,500 + €525)
The credit sales amount is €3,000, **net** of VAT at 10%	The amount of €3,000 is before the VAT charge. To record the transaction in the financial records the amount of VAT attributable to the transaction needs to be quantified.	VAT amount = Amount $\times \dfrac{\text{VAT rate}}{100}$ $€3,000 \times \dfrac{10}{100} = €300$ The total value of the transaction is €3,300 (i.e. €3,000 + €300)
The cash sales amount is €4,500, **gross** of VAT at 20%	The amount of €4,500 includes the VAT charge. To record the transaction in the financial records the amount of VAT attributable to the transaction needs to be quantified.	VAT amount = Transaction amount $\times \dfrac{\text{VAT rate}}{100 + \text{VAT rate}}$ $€4,500 \times \dfrac{20}{100 + 20} = €750$ The amount of the transaction before VAT was added is €3,750 (i.e. €4,500 – €750)

To summarise, for each transaction the amount attributable to the following must either be known or calculated:
• VAT amount;
• total transaction amount; and
• transaction amount before VAT was added.

Figure 7.2 outlines for each of the VAT terms used when an amount needs to be calculated (or if it is known).

FIGURE 7.2: VAT – AMOUNTS TO BE CALCULATED

	VAT Amount	Total Transaction Amount	Transaction Amount before VAT
Inclusive of VAT	To be calculated	Known	To be calculated
Exclusive of VAT	To be calculated	To be calculated	Known
Net of VAT	To be calculated	To be calculated	Known
Gross of VAT	To be calculated	Known	To be calculated

Once the terminology is understood, the application of the journal entries should be easier to understand.

It is important to remember that the balance on the VAT account may be either a debit or credit one:
• When the balance on the VAT account is a **debit** one, this means that the entity is owed money by the revenue authorities, i.e. it has collected a lesser amount of VAT from its customers than the amount of VAT incurred on its purchases and/or expenses for the period.
• When the balance on the VAT account is a **credit** one, this means that the entity owes money to the revenue authorities, i.e. it has collected more VAT from its customers than the amount of VAT the entity has incurred on its purchases and/or expenses for the period.

Chapter 2, Recording Financial Transactions and Preparing Financial Statements explained the recording of sales transactions without any VAT implications. When VAT is charged on a sale, the transaction impacts the income account, VAT account and appropriate asset account (bank or trade receivables). Therefore, the effect of the transaction is to debit the trade receivables account (or bank account), credit the sales account (with the sales value net, or exclusive, of VAT) and credit the VAT account, as explained below.

VAT on Sales Transactions

When an entity is registered for VAT it will charge VAT on sales transactions. The entity merely collects the VAT on behalf of the revenue authorities and submits VAT returns on a regular basis.

When VAT is 'recoverable' this means that expenses and income in the statement of profit or loss (SOPL) are recognised net of the VAT amounts. The journal entries in relation to transactions when VAT is recoverable will now be explained.

Cash Sales

	Debit €	Credit €
Cash account	X	
Revenue account		X
VAT account		X

To recognise the cash sales subject to VAT.

Credit Sales

	Debit €	Credit €
Trade receivables account	X	
Revenue account		X
VAT account		X

To recognise the credit sales subject to VAT.

The amount of revenue recognised in the SOPL is **before** VAT.

Example 7.2 demonstrates a practical example of credit sales transaction subject to VAT.

EXAMPLE 7.2: VAT ON CREDIT SALE

Zorba Ltd sold goods on credit for €18,000 before VAT. VAT is charged on sales at a rate of 21%.

Requirement Prepare the journal entry to recognise the sale of the goods.

Solution

Irrespective of whether or not VAT is recoverable, the total amount inclusive of VAT must be calculated:

	€
Cost	18,000
VAT @ 21%	3,780
Total cost	21,780

	Debit €	Credit €
Trade receivables account	21,780	
Revenue account		18,000
VAT account		3,780

To recognise the credit sales subject to VAT.

(Try **Review Questions 7.2** and **7.3** at the end of this chapter.)

VAT on Purchases

Chapter 2 explained the recording of: purchases of goods, expenses incurred and acquisition of property, plant and equipment transactions without any VAT implications. When VAT is charged on these transactions it impacts the purchase/expense/asset – cost account, VAT account and either a liability or an asset account. The effect of the transaction is as shown below.

Cash Expense/Purchase of Goods

	Debit €	Credit €
Purchases/expense asset – cost account	X	
VAT account	X	
Cash account		X

To recognise the cash purchase subject to VAT.

Credit Purchases

	Debit €	Credit €
Purchases/expense account	X	
VAT account	X	
Trade payables account		X

To recognise the credit purchases subject to VAT.

Credit Expenses

	Debit €	Credit €
Expenses account	X	
VAT account	X	
Other payables account		X

To recognise the credit expenses subject to VAT.

Example 7.3 demonstrates the journal entries to recognise the purchase of goods that are subject to VAT.

EXAMPLE 7.3: VAT ON PURCHASES

Omega Ltd purchased goods on credit at a cost of €12,000, before VAT. VAT is charged at 20%.

Requirement Prepare the journal entries to recognise the purchase transaction.

Solution

In this example, the cost is provided before VAT. VAT must be added to determine the amount that is to be paid for the goods:

	€
Cost	12,000
VAT @ 20%	2,400
Total cost	14,400

	Debit €	Credit €
Purchases account	12,000	
VAT account	2,400	
Trade payables account		14,400

To recognise the credit purchases subject to VAT.

(Try **Review Questions 7.4** and **7.5** at the end of this chapter.)

Having detailed individual sale and purchase transactions, **Example 7.4** below demonstrates the VAT impact on a series of sale and purchase transactions.

EXAMPLE 7.4: VAT ON PURCHASES AND SALES

On 20 March 2019 Walton Ltd purchased raw materials on credit for €2,900 before VAT at 21%. Walton paid for the goods on 15 April 2019.

Walton Ltd incurred additional costs to convert raw materials to finished goods.

On 8 April 2019 the goods were sold on credit for €6,000 before VAT at a rate of 21%. Payment was received on 28 April 2019.

On 30 April 2019 Walton has to submit its VAT return and any amount due to/from the revenue authorities is settled 10 days later.

Requirement Prepare the journal entries and the ledger accounts to recognise the above transactions.

Solution

Journal entries:

	Debit €	Credit €
Purchases account	2,900	
VAT account	609	
Trade payables account		3,509
To recognise the credit purchases subject to VAT.		
Trade payables account	3,509	
Bank account		3,509
To recognise the payment to trade payables.		
Trade receivables account	7,260	
Revenue account		6,000
VAT account		1,260
To recognise the credit sales subject to VAT.		
Bank account	7,260	
Trade receivables account		7,260
To recognise the receipt from customers.		
VAT account	651	
Bank account		651
To recognise the payment of VAT to revenue authorities (€1,260 − €609).		

Ledger accounts:

TRADE RECEIVABLES

Date	Account Name	€	Date	Account Name	€
08/04/2019	Sales	7,260	28/04/2019	Bank	7,260

VAT

Date	Account Name	€	Date	Account Name	€
20/03/2019	Trade payables	609	08/04/2019	Trade receivables	1,260
10/05/2019	Bank	651			
		1,260			1,260

TRADE PAYABLES

Date	Account Name	€	Date	Account Name	€
15/04/2019	Bank	3,509	20/03/2019	Purchases	3,509

PURCHASES

Date	Account Name	€	Date	Account Name	€
20/04/2019	Trade payables	2,900			

SALES

Date	Account Name	€	Date	Account Name	€
			08/04/2019	Trade receivables	6,000

(Try **Review Question 7.6** at the end of this chapter.)

Previous examples demonstrated the recording of transactions with VAT implications, but what if goods are returned by a customer, or goods are returned to a supplier, or a customer's balance is written off as a bad debt? There are VAT implications in relation to these transactions that will now be explained.

Goods Sold on Credit Returned by a Customer

If a customer returns goods to an entity, sales returns are increased, trade receivables decreased and either the VAT liability is decreased or the VAT asset is increased (remember the VAT account may have either a debit balance (asset) or credit balance (liability)). Therefore, based on the above, to record the transaction: debit the sales returns account, debit the VAT account and credit the trade receivables account. The relevant journal entry is:

	Debit €	Credit €
Sales returns account	X	
VAT account	X	
Trade receivables account		X

To record goods returned by a customer that were originally sold on credit.

Example 7.5 illustrates the journal entries required to recognise goods returned by a customer.

EXAMPLE 7.5: GOODS RETURNED BY A CUSTOMER

Acorn Ltd sold goods on credit to Oak Ltd on 3 February 2019 for €12,000, exclusive of VAT. The goods are subject to VAT at a rate of 20%. On 10 February, Oak Ltd returned €2,400 (inclusive of VAT) to Acorn Ltd.

Requirement: Prepare the journal entries in relation to the above transactions.

Solution

Transaction 1 – Acorn Ltd sold goods on credit; the journal entry to be posted to the financial records is:

	Debit €	Credit €
Trade receivables account	14,400	
Sales account		12,000
VAT account		2,400

To record goods sold on credit.

Note: the sales figure provided is exclusive of VAT; this means that the €12,000 is before the VAT is applied to the transaction. To calculate the total amount owed by the customer, the VAT-inclusive amount must be calculated, i.e. the sales figure plus VAT.

	€
Sales figure before VAT, i.e. exclusive of VAT	12,000
VAT [€12,000 × 20%]	2,400
Sales figure (i.e. inclusive of VAT)	14,400

Transaction 2 – Oak Ltd, a customer, returned goods; the journal entry to be posted to the financial records would be as follows:

	Debit €	Credit €
Sales returns account	2,000	
VAT account	400	
Trade receivables account		2,400

To record goods returned by a customer that were originally sold on credit.

Note: the sales value of the goods returned is provided inclusive of VAT. The sales returns figure is exclusive of VAT and needs to be calculated as follows:

$$\text{Amount inclusive of VAT} \times \frac{\text{VAT rate}}{100 \text{ plus the VAT rate}}$$

$$= €2,400 \times \frac{20}{(100 + 20)}$$

$$= €400$$

Goods Purchased on Credit and Returned to a Supplier

If an entity returns goods to its suppliers, purchases returns are increased, trade payables are decreased and VAT liability is increased or VAT asset is decreased. Therefore, based on the above, to record the transaction: credit the purchases returns account, credit the VAT account and debit the trade payables account. The relevant journal entry is:

	Debit €	Credit €
Trade payables account	X	
Purchases returns account		X
VAT account		X

To record goods returned to a supplier that were originally bought on credit.

Example 7.6 illustrates the journal entries required to recognise goods returned to a supplier.

EXAMPLE 7.6: GOODS RETURNED TO A SUPPLIER

Alder Ltd purchased €15,000 worth of goods on credit, inclusive of VAT, on 10 February. On 15 February Alder Ltd returned €1,400 (exclusive of VAT) worth of goods to its supplier.

VAT is charged at a rate of 20%.

Requirement Prepare the journal entries in relation to the above transactions.

Solution

Transaction 1 – Alder Ltd purchased goods on credit; the journal entry to be posted to the financial records is:

	Debit €	Credit €
Purchases account	12,500	
VAT account	2,500	
Trade payables account		15,000

To record goods purchased on credit.

Note: the purchases figure provided is inclusive of VAT; this means that the €15,000 is after the VAT is applied to the transaction. To calculate the amount attributable to purchases, calculate the VAT-exclusive amount:

$$\text{Amount inclusive of VAT} \times \frac{100}{100 \text{ plus the VAT rate}}$$

$$= €15,000 \times \frac{100}{(100 + 20)}$$

$$= €12,500$$

Transaction 2 – Alder Ltd returned goods previously bought on credit; the journal entry to be posted to the financial records is:

	Debit €	Credit €
Trade payables account	1,680	
VAT account		280
Purchases returns account		1,400

To record goods returned to a supplier that were originally purchased on credit.

Note: the trade payables figure is the purchases value of the goods returned inclusive of VAT. The purchases returns figure is exclusive of VAT. The value of returns provided is exclusive of VAT so the VAT-inclusive amount needs to be calculated as follows:

$$\text{Amount inclusive of VAT} \times \frac{100 + \text{VAT rate}}{100}$$

$$= €1,400 \times \frac{100 + 20}{100}$$

$$= €1,400 \times \frac{120}{100}$$

$$= €1,680$$

Writing-off of an Amount Due from a Customer

When goods are sold on credit to customers there is a risk that not all of those customers to whom credit was provided will be able to pay their debts in full. **Chapter 5, Bad Debts and Allowances for Bad Debts** dealt with the accounting entries in relation to the writing-off of bad debts without considering the VAT implications. The write-off of bad debts when the original sale transaction was subject to VAT is explained below.

When a customer is unable to pay what is owed, the entity will not receive payment and will not have to pay over the VAT on the transaction to the revenue authorities. The impact of the write-off of the bad debt is to decrease the trade receivable, increase the expense and increase the VAT asset or reduce the VAT liability. Therefore, based on the above, to record the transaction: debit the bad debts expense account, debit the VAT account and credit the trade receivables account, as shown in the journal entry below:

	Debit €	Credit €
Bad debts expense account	X	
VAT account	X	
Trade receivables account		X
To write-off a bad debt.		

Example 7.7 illustrates the journal entries required to recognise the write-off of a customer's balance.

EXAMPLE 7.7: BAD DEBT WRITE-OFF WITH VAT

A customer owes €6,900 to Elm Ltd on 20 January. The original sales transaction that made up the balance was subject to VAT at a rate of 15%.

On 25 June Elm receives a notice informing it that the customer has gone into liquidation and will be unable to make any payment in relation to the amount outstanding on its account. Elm must write-off the debt in full.

Requirement Prepare the journal entry to record the write-off of the bad debt.

Solution

The balance on the customer's account is **always** VAT-inclusive. The following figures need to be calculated:

1. amount due exclusive of VAT; and
2. amount of VAT included in the customer's balance due.

Calculation 1 Amount due exclusive of VAT:

$$\text{Amount inclusive of VAT} \times \frac{100}{100 \text{ plus the VAT rate}}$$

$$= \text{€}6{,}900 \times \frac{100}{(100 + 15)}$$

$$= \text{€}6{,}000$$

Calculation 2 VAT Amount

$$\text{Amount inclusive of VAT} \times \frac{\text{VAT rate}}{100 \text{ plus the VAT rate}}$$

$$= \text{€}6{,}900 \times \frac{15}{(100 + 15)}$$

$$= \text{€}900$$

The journal entry to write-off the bad debt is:

	Debit €	Credit €
Bad debts expense account	6,000	
VAT account	900	
Trade receivables account		6,900
To write-off a bad debt.		

7.4 VAT-EXEMPT AND ZERO-RATED GOODS AND SERVICES

When products or services are 'VAT exempt' they are not subject to VAT. Examples of exempt services are:

- hospital and medical care or treatment provided by a hospital, nursing home, clinic or similar establishment; and
- public postal services.

A person who supplies VAT-exempt services may have to register for VAT if other services provided by them are taxable supplies.

Some goods and services are subject to tax at a zero rating, an example would be footwear for children under the age of 11. (More examples are available on the websites of the revenue authorities.)

EXAM TIPS

- Be careful when reading questions and make sure to note whether the amounts provided are inclusive or exclusive of VAT.
- When VAT is recoverable, sales, purchases and expenses are presented in the SOPL net of VAT.

7.5 CONCLUSION

The impact of VAT on transactions needs to be understood. When VAT is not recoverable, income and expense figures presented in the SOPL are inclusive of VAT. When VAT is recoverable, income and expenses are presented in the SOPL exclusive of VAT.

SUMMARY OF LEARNING OBJECTIVES

After having studied this chapter, readers should be able to:

Learning Objective 1 Explain the concept of value-added tax (VAT).

VAT is charged on the cost of goods and services provided. The business acts as a collector on behalf of the revenue authorities. An entity can offset the VAT it incurs on its expenses against the VAT it collects on its sales. VAT is borne by the final consumer.

Learning Objective 2 Explain and account for expenses and costs when the VAT is irrecoverable.

When VAT is not recoverable, expenses are recognised in the SOPL inclusive of VAT.

Learning Objective 3 Explain and account for expenses and costs when the VAT is recoverable.

Expenses and revenue are recognised in the SOPL net of VAT. VAT is collected on sales. The VAT incurred on expenses in the period reduces the amount to be paid over to the revenue authorities.

Regular returns must be prepared and submitted to the revenue authorities; this may involve the entity making a payment to the revenue authorities or receiving a refund from the revenue authorities. The VAT account may represent either an asset (if a refund is due from the revenue authorities) or a liability (if a payment is to be made to the revenue authorities). A refund is due from the revenue authorities when a greater amount of VAT has been incurred on purchases in the period than VAT collected on revenue. A payment is required to revenue authorities in a period when the VAT collected on sales is higher than the VAT on expenses and purchases.

Learning Objective 4 Understand what is meant by the terms used in questions: 'exclusive', 'inclusive', 'net' and 'gross'.

If the amount provided is 'exclusive of VAT' or the 'net' amount, this means that the VAT has not been added to the transaction amount. To record the transaction fully, the VAT amount and the total transaction amount have to be calculated.

To calculate the VAT amount:

$$\text{Amount exclusive, or net, of VAT} \times \frac{\text{VAT rate}}{100} = \text{VAT amount.}$$

The total amount = Amount exclusive of VAT + VAT amount, as calculated above.

If the amount provided in the question is 'inclusive of VAT' or the 'gross' amount, this means that the VAT amount attaching to the transaction has been included, i.e. it is the total transaction amount. In this case the VAT amount and the transaction amount before VAT have to be calculated.

To calculate the VAT amount:

$$\text{Transaction amount} \times \frac{\text{VAT rate}}{100 + \text{VAT rate}} = \text{VAT amount}$$

The transaction amount before VAT = VAT-inclusive amount − VAT amount.

Learning Objective 5 Account for a return of goods when the original transaction involved VAT.

When a sales transaction involving VAT was recorded and the goods are subsequently returned by the customer, the following journal entry is recorded:

	Debit €	Credit €
Sales returns account	X	
VAT account	X	
Trade receivables/cash account		X
To record goods returned by a customer.		

When a purchase transaction was recorded with VAT and the goods are subsequently returned by the entity, the following journal entry is recorded:

	Debit €	Credit €
Trade payables/cash account	X	
VAT account		X
Purchases returns account		X
To record goods returned by the entity.		

Learning Objective 6 Account for a bad debt write-off when the original transaction was recorded with VAT.

When a credit sale transaction is recorded, the amount due from the customer is recorded inclusive of the VAT. If a customer cannot subsequently pay the amount due on the account, the VAT on the transaction can be recovered. To write-off a bad debt when the original sales transaction had VAT charged in relation to the sale:

	Debit €	Credit €
Bad debts expense account	X	
VAT account	X	
Trade receivables account		X
To write-off a bad debt.		

QUESTIONS

Review Questions

(See **Appendix A** for Solutions to Review Questions.)

Question 7.1

Vincent Ltd purchased goods on credit for €10,000, net of VAT at 21%, on 11 March. Vincent is not registered for VAT.

Requirement Prepare the journal entries to recognise this transaction.

Question 7.2

Sorahan Ltd sold goods for cash, €2,600, net of VAT, on 10 December. Sorahan is registered for VAT. VAT is charged at a rate of 21%.

Requirement Prepare the journal entries to recognise this transaction.

Question 7.3

Wiggins Ltd sold goods, for cash, valued at €30,250, gross of VAT. Wiggins is registered for VAT. VAT is charged at a rate of 21%.

Requirement Prepare the journal entries to recognise this transaction.

Question 7.4

Long Ltd purchased goods for cash, €5,100, net of VAT at a rate of 21%. Long is registered for VAT.

Requirement Prepare the journal entries to recognise this transaction.

Question 7.5

Watkins Ltd purchased goods on credit of €14,600, exclusive of VAT at a rate of 21%. Watkins is registered for VAT.

Requirement Prepare the journal entries to recognise this transaction.

Question 7.6

You have been provided with the following information in relation to sales and purchase transactions for January:

Transaction Type	Transaction Date	Amount net of VAT €	VAT rate
Purchase	8 January	28,000	21%
Sale	10 January	14,100	21%
Sale	15 January	3,600	13%
Sale	20 January	9,300	21%

Requirement Prepare the VAT account.

Challenging Questions

(Suggested Solutions to Challenging Questions are available through your lecturer.)

Question 7.1

Mr McGowan accepts VIVA credit cards as payment for goods in his chemist shop. VIVA Credit Card Company deducts a commission of 3% of the retail value of credit card transactions when it pays the shop at the end of each month.

For December, the total VIVA credit card sales had a retail value of €18,000, inclusive of VAT at 20%. Mr McGowan is registered for VAT. There is no VAT on VIVA's commission.

Requirement What journal entries are required at 31 December to correctly record this transaction?
(Based on Chartered Accountants Ireland, CAP 1 Financial Accounting, Autumn 2008, Question 1.9)

Question 7.2

Stewart Ltd is registered for VAT. During December it purchased a piece of machinery on credit with a list price of €105,000 (excluding VAT). The invoice also included delivery costs of €3,000 (excluding VAT) and a one-year maintenance contract at a cost of €6,000 (excluding VAT). If VAT is charged at 15%:

Requirement Write a journal entry for this transaction.
(Based on Chartered Accountants Ireland, CAP 1 Financial Accounting, Summer 2010, Question 1.6)

Question 7.3

Mr Brown, who is registered for VAT, has reviewed his receivables ledger. He has decided that the balance outstanding from Mr Short is unrecoverable and therefore should be written off. The balance on Mr Short's account is €11,500. This includes VAT at 15%.

Requirement Prepare the journal entries to write-off Mr Short's balance.
(Based on Chartered Accountants Ireland, CAP 1 Financial Accounting, Autumn 2011, Question 1.1)

Question 7.4

During the year ended 31 December 2019 the following details were extracted from Mr Nelson's accounting records:

	€
VAT liability 1 January 2019	17,800
Sales (inclusive of VAT)	248,400
Purchases (inclusive of VAT)	104,400
Purchase of motor vehicle (includes non-deductible VAT)	24,800
Payments to VAT authorities	34,600

VAT is charged at 20%.

Requirement Prepare the VAT control account for the year to 31 December 2019.
(Based on Chartered Accountants Ireland, CAP 1 Financial Accounting, Autumn 2012, Question 1.3)

8

Accounting for Wages and Salaries

Learning Objectives

Having studied this chapter, readers should be able to:
1. explain and account for wages and salaries expenses.

8.1 INTRODUCTION

Wages and salary expenses incurred in the reporting period are charged to the statement of profit or loss (SOPL).

When someone is offered a job, their contract states their **gross pay**. The gross pay is the employee's income before deductions. An employee's **net pay** is their gross pay after deductions. The typical deductions from an employee's salary are:
- pay as you earn (PAYE) (also known as income tax);
- employees' pay-related social insurance (PRSI) contributions or National Insurance contributions (NICs); and
- Universal Service Charge (USC) (applies to RoI only).

These deductions reduce the amount received by the employee and are paid over to the revenue authorities by the employer at regular intervals throughout the year.

Employers must pay PRSI/NIC for each employee – this is an additional cost of employing staff. All of the deductions and the employer's PRSI/NIC are listed on the employees' payslips.

Other deductions may be made from employees' salaries on their behalf, such as:
- health insurance,
- pension contributions,
- savings schemes, and
- share purchase plans.

The **total wages** expense charged to the SOPL is made up of the employees' gross salaries and the employer's PRSI/NIC.

As stated previously, the impact of the transaction is to increase the wages expense, increase liabilities and decrease the amount of cash or the balance in the bank, which are assets. Therefore, to record the transaction: debit the wages expense account, credit the wages-related liabilities accounts (PAYE, PRSI and other deductions from employees' salaries accounts) and credit the relevant asset account (cash account or bank account), as shown below:

	Debit €	Credit €
Wages expense account	X	
Net wages payable/bank account		X
PAYE liability/bank account		X

Employees' PRSI/NIC liability/bank account		X
Employer's PRSI/NIC liability/bank account		X
USC liability/bank account		X

To recognise the wage cost.

Example 8.1 demonstrates the journal entries to recognise the wages cost.

EXAMPLE 8.1: WAGES COST

On 20 December 2018, the wages cost was calculated and recognised for the month of December. On 31 December 2018 the employees were paid their net salaries. Payments to the revenue authorities were made on 15 January 2019.

The following information was provided in relation to December's salary costs:

	€
Net wages	218,350
PAYE deducted	45,200
Employees' PRSI/NIC	18,160
Employer's PRSI/NIC	15,090
USC	10,830

Requirement Prepare the journal entries in relation to the December wages cost.

Solution

	Debit €	Credit €
Wages expense account	307,630	
Net wages payable account		218,350
PAYE liability account		45,200
Employees' PRSI/NIC liability account		18,160
Employer's PRSI/NIC liability account		15,090
USC liability account		10,830

To recognise the wage cost on 20 December 2018.

Net wages payable account	218,350	
Bank account		218,350

To recognise the payment of net wages to employees on 31 December 2018.

PAYE liability account	45,200	
Employees' PRSI/NIC liability account	18,160	
Employer's PRSI/NIC liability account	15,090	
USC liability account	10,830	
Bank account		89,280

To recognise the payment of taxes to revenue authorities on 15 January 2019.

The employees' gross wages are €292,540 [€218,350 + €45,200 + €18,160 + €10,830].

Total wages cost, as presented in the SOPL, is the gross wages plus employer's PRSI: €292,540 + €15,090 = €307,630.

Example 8.2 demonstrates the accounting for payroll costs when there are additional deductions made on behalf of employees.

EXAMPLE 8.2: PAYROLL DEDUCTIONS

On 25 March 2019 the wages cost was calculated and recognised for the month of March. On 31 March 2019 the employees were paid their net salaries.

Payments to the revenue authorities were made on 15 April 2019.

The company makes deductions from employees' salaries on their behalf to a health insurance provider. The payments to the health insurance provider are made quarterly; the next payment will be made on 10 June 2019.

The following information was provided in relation to March's salary costs:

	€
Net wages	257,210
PAYE deducted	48,170
Employees' PRSI/NIC	19,220
Employer's PRSI/NIC	14,930
USC	11,910
Health insurance	8,600

Requirement Prepare the journal entries in relation to the March 2019 wages costs.

Solution

	Debit €	Credit €
Wages expense account	360,040	
Net wages payable account		257,210
PAYE liability account		48,170
Employees' PRSI/NIC liability account		19,220
Employer's PRSI/NIC liability account		14,930
USC liability account		11,910
Health insurance provider liability account		8,600

To recognise the wage cost on 25 March 2019.

	Debit €	Credit €
Net wages payable account	257,210	
Bank account		257,210

To recognise the payment of net wages to employees on 31 March 2019.

	Debit €	Credit €
PAYE liability account	48,170	
Employees' PRSI/NIC liability account	19,220	
Employer's PRSI/NIC liability account	14,930	
USC liability account	11,910	
Bank account		94,230

To recognise the payment of taxes to revenue authorities on 15 April 2019.

The employees' gross wages is €345,110 [€257,210 + €48,170 + €19,220 + €8,600 + €11,910].

Total wages cost is the gross wages plus employer's PRSI/NIC: €345,110 + €14,930 = €360,040.

	Debit €	Credit €
Health insurance liability account	8,600	
Bank account		8,600

To recognise the payment to health insurance provider.

EXAM TIPS

- Read questions carefully.
- Make sure you note whether the payments have been made or liabilities are to be recognised.
- You need to know your journal entries relating to salaries and wages.
- The expense charge for wages presented in the SOPL is the total of gross pay and employer's PRSI/NIC.

8.2 CONCLUSION

Wages and salaries are an expense of the business, to be recognised in the financial statements on an accrual basis. The wages and salaries expense presented in the SOPL is the gross employee pay plus the employer's PRSI/NIC.

SUMMARY OF LEARNING OBJECTIVES

After having studied this chapter, readers should be able to:

Learning Objective 1 Explain and account for wages and salaries expenses.

The total wages cost is the employees' gross pay plus the employer's PRSI/NIC.

The following are the journal entries to recognise the wage cost:

	Debit €	Credit €
Wages expense account	X	
Net wages payable/bank account		X
PAYE liability/bank account		X

	Debit €	Credit €
Employees' PRSI/NIC liability/bank account		X
Employer's PRSI/NIC liability/bank account		X
USC liability/bank account		X
To recognise the wage cost.		

At the end of the reporting period the wages expense is posted to the SOPL.

QUESTIONS

Review Questions

(See **Appendix A** for Solutions to Review Questions.)

Question 8.1

Employees' gross pay for the period was €110,240. The company has to pay employer's PRSI/NIC at a rate of 8% of gross pay.

Requirement What is the total wages cost for the company?

Question 8.2

You have been provided with the following information:

	€
Amount paid to employees	82,105
PAYE deductions	38,903
PRSI/NIC deductions – employees'	15,570
PRSI/NIC – employer's	17,540

Requirement What is the gross wage cost for the company?

Challenging Questions

(Suggested Solutions to Challenging Questions are available through your lecturer.)

Question 8.1

Mrs Crawford is paid monthly, earning €2,000 gross per month. Her tax-free pay is €590 per month. She pays tax at 20% on the first €1,000 per month, and at 30% on the balance. Employee's PRSI/NIC is payable at 10% of the gross earnings, as is employer's PRSI/NIC.

Requirement:
(a) What is Mrs Crawford's net pay each month?
(b) What is the cost to Mrs Crawford's employer each month?

   (Based on Chartered Accountants Ireland, CAP 1 Financial Accounting, Autumn 2008, Question 1(d))

Question 8.2

Mr Franklin is paid monthly, earning €3,200 gross per month. His tax-free allowance is €650 per month. He pays tax at 10% on the first €500 per month and at 20% on the balance. Employee's PRSI/NIC is payable at 10%, as is employer's PRSI/NIC.

Requirement:
(a) What is Mr Franklin's net pay each month?
(b) What is the total cost to Mr Franklin's employer each month?

   (Based on Chartered Accountants Ireland, CAP 1 Financial Accounting, Autumn 2009, Question 1(c))

9

Control Accounts

LEARNING OBJECTIVES

Having studied this chapter, readers should be able to:
1. reconcile the balance on the trade receivables control account with the total of the customer ledger listing; and
2. reconcile the balance on the trade payables control account with the total of the supplier ledger listing.

9.1 INTRODUCTION

When double-entry bookkeeping was first introduced in **Chapter 2, Recording Financial Transactions and Preparing Financial Statements**, every transaction was recorded as it happened. This approach is only practicable when the volume of transactions is relatively small; as a business grows, similar types of transactions are grouped together and accumulated in day books. At regular intervals, the day books are totalled and journal entries posted with these totals (the individual transactions are not part of the double-entry system) to the financial records of the company. The day books are as follows:
* sales day book (SDB) – which records credit sales transactions;
* purchases day book (PDB) – which records credit purchase transactions;
* sales returns day book (SRDB) – which records sales returns transactions;
* purchases returns day book (PRDB) – which records purchase returns transactions; and
* cash book (CB) – which records cash receipts and payments.

At the end of each reporting period a set of financial statements is produced by the entity. The financial information contained in the financial records is subject to a number of checks and controls to ensure that the financial information is correct. Examples of these checks and controls include:
* stock counts to verify that the physical stock is the same as the information contained in the financial system;
* reconciliation of the balance on the trade receivables control account to the total amount due from all of the entity's credit customers; and
* reconciliation of the balance on the trade payables control account to the total amount due to all of the entity's suppliers.

The totals of the transactions from the day books are posted to the control accounts. Control accounts were discussed briefly in **Chapter 1, Financial Accounting: Key Terms and Concepts**. The balances on control accounts are used in the preparation of the financial statements, but they do not provide sufficient information to manage the business. Trade receivables and payables control accounts will be discussed in this chapter.

This chapter will look at the reconciliation process for trade receivables and trade payables separately. In some instances reference might be made to 'the total of the individual ledger balances of customers/ suppliers' as 'the sales/purchases ledger listing'. Before the control accounts can be reconciled with the supporting ledger listings, it is necessary to have an understanding of why it is desirable to have control accounts in addition to individual ledger accounts.

To prepare financial statements at the reporting date, it is necessary to know the total amount:
- due from customers to whom goods have been sold on credit but who have not paid by the reporting date; and
- the amount the entity owes for goods purchased on credit that have not been paid for at the reporting date.

In the financial statements, single figures are presented for trade receivables and trade payables but to manage a business efficiently, the following need to be known at any given point in time:
- how much each customer owes the entity;
- whether there are customers whose payments are overdue;
- how much is owed by the entity to its suppliers; and
- when payments are due to be made.

To be able to meet these requirements individual records for each customer and supplier need to be maintained.

It is important to understand the difference between the trade receivables/trade payables control account and the trade receivables/trade payables subsidiary ledger. The trade receivables/trade payables subsidiary ledger listing is the total of the balances on all the accounts in the trade receivables/trade payables subsidiary ledger. **Figures 9.1** and **9.2** provide a summary of the information and use of the information contained in the control accounts and the subsidiary ledgers.

FIGURE 9.1: TRADE RECEIVABLES CONTROL ACCOUNT AND RECEIVABLES LEDGER

	Trade Receivables Control Account	**Receivables Ledger**
Purpose	Provides the total owed to the entity by all of its credit customers at a particular date.	Provides detailed information about each credit customer in terms of sales transactions, payments, discounts, etc.
Use	Balancing figure on the trade receivables control account is presented in the statement of financial position (SOFP) under current assets as the trade receivables amount.	Provides information to help in the effective management of the business to ensure that customers pay on time and do not exceed their pre-determined credit limits.
Source of Information	Total figures from relevant day books.	Individual transactions recorded in relevant day books.
Double-entry system	Part of double-entry system (within the general ledger).	Not part of the double-entry system (subsidiary ledger).

The reconciliation of the control accounts to the ledger listing assists management in ensuring the integrity of the financial information presented in the financial statements. The entity will receive statements from its suppliers detailing transactions that have taken place in the period; upon receipt of these statements the entity will compare the information they provide with their own records for that supplier contained in the payables ledger; any differences are investigated. Similarly, statements are provided to customers on a regular basis who will reconcile the information contained therein with their own financial records.

FIGURE 9.2: TRADE PAYABLES CONTROL ACCOUNT AND PAYABLES LEDGER

	Trade Payables Control Account	Payables Ledger
Purpose	Provides the total owed by the entity to its credit suppliers at a particular date.	Provides detailed information about each credit supplier in terms of purchases transactions, payments, discounts, etc.
Use	Balancing figure on the trade payables control account is presented in the SOFP under current liabilities as the trade payables amount.	Provides information to help in the effective management of the business to ensure that suppliers are paid on time and the entity does not exceed its predetermined credit limits with the supplier.
Source of Information	Total figures from relevant day books.	Individual transactions recorded in relevant day books.
Double-entry system	Part of double-entry system (within the general ledger).	Not part of the double-entry system (subsidiary ledger).

Each of the day books will now be considered in turn illustrating their impact on the control accounts and individual ledger accounts. The most important point to remember is that **the control account is part of the double-entry system** but the individual customer/supplier ledger accounts are not.

9.2 TRADE RECEIVABLES CONTROL ACCOUNT RECONCILIATION

Sales Day Book

The sales day book contains a record of each credit sales transaction for a particular period of time. At regular intervals the day book is totalled and a journal entry is posted to the financial records. When the journal entry to record the total of the sales day book is posted, it will increase the asset account and increase the income account. Therefore, the asset account 'trade receivables' is debited and the income account 'sales' is credited. The journal entry posted is as follows:

	Debit €	Credit €
Trade receivables control account	X	
Sales account		X

To recognise credit sales.

Example 9.1 demonstrates the recording of a number of sales transactions.

EXAMPLE 9.1: THE SALES DAY BOOK AND ITS IMPACT ON THE TRADE RECEIVABLES CONTROL ACCOUNT

On 10 February 2019 Murphy had the following credit sales transactions:

Customer	Transaction amount	Invoice Number
A. Jones	€500	114
B. Willis	€720	115
C. Dempsey	€240	116

Requirement:
(a) Record the sales transactions in the sales day book.
(b) Show the journal entry in relation to the sales day book.
(c) Prepare the trade receivables control account.
(d) Prepare the ledger listing.
(e) Prepare the reconciliation of the trade receivables control account to the ledger listing.

Solution

(a)

SALES DAY BOOK

Date	Customer	Amount €	Invoice
10/02/2019	A. Jones	500	114
10/02/2019	B. Willis	720	115
10/02/2019	C. Dempsey	240	116
		1,460	

(b)

JOURNAL ENTRY

	Debit €	Credit €
Trade receivables control account	1,460	
Sales account		1,460

To recognise the credit sales transactions for 10 February 2019.

The total of the sales day book is posted to the trade receivables control account. The individual transactions are recorded in the receivables (also known as debtors) management system, but this recording is **not** part of the double-entry system.

(c)

TRADE RECEIVABLES CONTROL ACCOUNT

Date	Account Name	€	Date	Account Name	€
10/02/2019	Sales	1,460			

(d) For each customer an account will be set up in the receivables ledger, which is a subsidiary ledger, also known as the receivables (debtors) management system:

TRADE RECEIVABLES ACCOUNT – A. JONES

Date	Account Name	€	Date	Account Name	€
10/02/2019	Sales	500			

TRADE RECEIVABLES ACCOUNT – B. WILLIS

Date	Account Name	€	Date	Account Name	€
10/02/2019	Sales	720			

TRADE RECEIVABLES ACCOUNT – C. DEMPSEY

Date	Account Name	€	Date	Account Name	€
10/02/2019	Sales	240			

The ledger listing will typically be a print-out from the computer system that could appear as follows:

Debtors Management System   10 February 2019

LEDGER LISTING

Customer Name	Balance €
A. Jones	500
B. Willis	720
C. Dempsey	240
Total	1,460

The total of the ledger listing should agree with the balance on the trade receivables control account.

(e)

TRADE RECEIVABLES RECONCILIATION
as at 10 February 2019

	€
Balance per trade receivables control account	1,460
Total per ledger listing	1,460

The balance on the trade receivables control account agrees with the total per the ledger listing, therefore there are no reconciling items.

In exam questions there are frequently references to '**overcasting**' and '**undercasting**' of the day books; at their simplest, these terms mean that when a group of figures was totalled an error was made.

When the total is 'overcast' it means the total calculated was higher than the correct figure. For example, three sales invoices for €200, €180 and €250 are totalled as €650, but the correct figure is €630. In an exam question you may be told that the total was overcast by €20, i.e. the difference between the figure calculated of €650 and the actual total of the sales invoices of €630.

When the total is 'undercast' it means the total calculated was lower than the correct figure. For example, three purchases invoices for €60, €190 and €510 are totalled as €670, but the correct figure is €760. In an exam question you may be told that the total was undercast by €90, i.e. the difference between the figure calculated of €670 and the actual total of the purchases invoices of €760.

When the sales day book has been overcast, the error must be corrected. To correct the error made the income account must be decreased and the asset account must be decreased. Therefore, the income account 'sales' is debited and the asset account 'trade receivables' is credited. The journal entry to be posted is as follows:

	Debit €	Credit €
Sales account	X	
Trade receivables control account		X

To correct the overcasting of the sales day book.

Example 9.2 demonstrates the situation where an error is made in the totalling of the sales day book.

EXAMPLE 9.2: OVERCASTING OF SALES DAY BOOK

You have been provided with the following information from the sales day book:

Date	Customer	Amount €	Invoice Number
03/01/2019	A. Boyd	1,800	204
03/01/2019	C. Dunne	1,950	205
03/01/2019	E. Flynn	2,500	206
03/01/2019	G. Hayes	800	207

An error was made in the totalling of the sales day book and as a result the journal entry posted was for the incorrect amount. The total of the sales day book is €7,050 [€1,800 + €1,950 + €2,500 + €800], but an error was made and the journal entry was posted as €7,150.

The trade receivables control account will have a balance of €7,150 due to the error, i.e. the journal entry posted was for the incorrect amount:

	Debit €	Credit €
Trade receivables control account	7,150	
Sales account		7,150

To recognise the credit sales transactions for 1 January 2019.

For each customer an account will be set up in the receivables ledger, which is a subsidiary ledger, also known as the receivables (debtors) management system:

TRADE RECEIVABLES CONTROL ACCOUNT

Date	Account Name	€	Date	Account Name	€
03/01/2019	Sales	7,150			

For each customer an account will be set up in the receivables (debtors) management system:

TRADE RECEIVABLES ACCOUNT – A. BOYD

Date	Account Name	€	Date	Account Name	€
03/01/2019	Sales	1,800			

TRADE RECEIVABLES ACCOUNT – C. DUNNE

Date	Account Name	€	Date	Account Name	€
03/01/2019	Sales	1,950			

TRADE RECEIVABLES ACCOUNT – E. FLYNN

Date	Account Name	€	Date	Account Name	€
03/01/2019	Sales	2,500			

TRADE RECEIVABLES ACCOUNT – G. HAYES

Date	Account Name	€	Date	Account Name	€
03/01/2019	Sales	800			

The ledger listing will typically be a print-out from the computer system that could appear as follows:

Debtors Management System   3 January 2019

LEDGER LISTING

Customer Name	Balance €
A. Boyd	1,800
C. Dunne	1,950
E. Flynn	2,500
G. Hayes	800
Total	7,050

The total of the ledger listing does not agree with the balance on the trade receivables control account. A review would be undertaken to discover the reason for the difference. To correct the error the balance on the trade receivables control account would need to be reduced by €100, the difference between the amount posted, in error, of €7,150 and the correct total of €7,050. To correct the error the following journal entry would have to be posted:

	Debit €	Credit €
Sales account	100	
Trade receivables control account		100

To correct error in relation to the credit sales transactions for 31 January 2019.

The trade receivables control account should appear as follows after the error correcting the journal entry is posted:

TRADE RECEIVABLES CONTROL ACCOUNT

Date	Account Name	€	Date	Account Name	€
03/01/2019	Sales	7,150	31/01/2019	SDB overcast error	100
			31/01/2019	Balance c/d	7,050
		7,150			7,150
01/02/2019	Balance b/d	7,050			

TRADE RECEIVABLES RECONCILIATION
as at 31 January 2019

	€
Balance per trade receivables control account	7,050
Balance per ledger listing	7,050

Corrections are made to the control account and then the balances are reconciled. In an exam situation there would be reconciling items.

When the sales day book has been undercast the error must be corrected. To correct the error made the income account must be increased and the asset account must be increased. Therefore, the asset account 'trade receivables' is debited and the income account 'sales' is credited. The journal entry to be posted is as follows:

	Debit €	Credit €
Trade receivables control account	X	
Sales account		X

To correct the undercasting of the sales day book.

Example 9.3 will look at the situation in which the sales day book total is undercast.

EXAMPLE 9.3: UNDERCASTING OF THE SALES DAY BOOK

You have been provided with the following information from the sales day book:

Date	Customer	Amount €	Invoice Number
28/12/2018	T. Walsh	2,750	986
28/12/2018	R. Knight	3,600	987
		6,150	

An error was made in the totalling of the sales day book and as a result the journal entry posted was for the incorrect amount. The correct total of the sales day book is €6,350 [€2,750 + €3,600], but an error was made and the journal entry was posted as €6,150.

Requirement Prepare the journal entry to correct this error on 3 January 2019 and the trade receivables control account.

Solution

	Debit €	Credit €
Trade receivables control account	200	
Sales account		200

To correct the undercasting of the sales day book on 28 December 2018.

TRADE RECEIVABLES CONTROL ACCOUNT

Date	Account Name	€	Date	Account Name	€
28/12/2018	Sales	6,150	03/01/2019	Balance c/d	6,350
03/01/2019	SDB undercast error	200			
		6,350			6,350
03/01/2019	Balance b/d	6,350			

Sales Returns Day Book

The sales returns day book will reduce the balance on the trade receivables control account. The journal entry to post the total from the sales returns day book is:

	Debit €	Credit €
Sales returns account	X	
Trade receivables control account		X

To recognise the sales returned by credit customers.

When the sales return day book has been overcast the error must be corrected. To correct the error the expense account must be decreased and the asset account must be increased. Therefore, the expense account 'sales returns' is credited and the asset account 'trade receivables' is debited. The journal entry to be posted is as follows:

	Debit €	Credit €
Trade receivables control account	X	
Sales returns account		X

To correct the overcasting of the sales returns day book.

Example 9.4 demonstrates the situation where the total on the sales returns day book has been totalled incorrectly.

EXAMPLE 9.4: OVERCASTING OF THE SALES RETURNS DAY BOOK

You are provided with the details in relation to the sales day book and the sales returns day book:

SALES DAY BOOK

Date	Customer	Amount €	Invoice Number
05/03/2019	R. Walsh	1,150	2650
05/03/2019	P. Knight	1,600	2651
05/03/2019	S. King	400	2652
05/03/2019	R. Temple	1,230	2653

SALES RETURNS DAY BOOK

Date	Customer	Amount €	Sales Return Note
06/03/2019	R. Walsh	250	26
06/03/2019	R. Temple	80	27

The following journal entries were posted on the respective dates:

	Debit €	Credit €
Trade receivables control account	4,380	
Sales account		4,380

To recognise credit sales transactions on 5 March 2019.

	Debit €	Credit €
Sales returns account	430	
Trade receivables control account		430

To recognise the sales returned by credit customers on 6 March 2019.

Requirement:
(a) Prepare the trade receivables ledger control account based on the journal entries posted above.
(b) Prepare the ledger listing after the journal entries detailed in the question have been posted.
(c) Correct the error made in the journal entries.

Solution

(a)

TRADE RECEIVABLES CONTROL ACCOUNT

Date	Account Name	€	Date	Account Name	€
05/03/2019	Sales	4,380	06/03/2019	Sales returns	430
			06/03/2019	Balance c/d	3,950
		4,380			4,380
07/03/2019	Balance b/d	3,950			

(b) For each customer an account will be set up in the receivables ledger, which is a subsidiary ledger, also known as the receivables (debtors) management system:

TRADE RECEIVABLES ACCOUNT – R. WALSH

Date	Account Name	€	Date	Account Name	€
05/03/2019	Sales	1,150	06/03/2019	Sales returns	250
			06/03/2019	Balance c/d	900
		1,150			1,150
06/03/2019	Balance b/d	900			

TRADE RECEIVABLES ACCOUNT – P. KNIGHT

Date	Account Name	€	Date	Account Name	€
05/03/2019	Sales	1,600	06/03/2019	Balance c/d	1,600
06/03/2019	Balance b/d	1,600			

TRADE RECEIVABLES ACCOUNT – S. KING

Date	Account Name	€	Date	Account Name	€
05/03/2019	Sales	400	06/03/2019	Balance c/d	400
06/03/2019	Balance b/d	400			

TRADE RECEIVABLES ACCOUNT – R. TEMPLE

Date	Account Name	€	Date	Account Name	€
05/03/2019	Sales	1,230	06/03/2019	Sales returns	80
				Balance c/d	1,150
		1,230			1,230
06/03/2019	Balance b/d	1,150			

Debtors Management System   6 March 2019

LEDGER LISTING

Customer Name	Balance €
R. Walsh (€1,150 – €250)	900
P. Knight	1,600
S. King	400
R. Temple (€1,230 – €80)	1,150
Total	4,050

(c) The balance on the control account does not agree with the total of the ledger listing:
  - The total of the sales transactions was calculated and posted correctly.
  - The total of the sales returns transactions was posted as an amount €430. The correct total for sales returns is €330 [€250 + €80].

The sales returns day book was 'overcast', which means the amount credited to the trade receivables control account was too much. To correct the error, the trade receivables control account needs to be debited and the sales return account credited with €100.

	Debit €	Credit €
Trade receivables control account	100	
Sales returns account		100

To correct the error made in relation to the sales day returns book of 6 March 2019.

The trade receivables control account after the above journal entry has been posted is:

TRADE RECEIVABLES CONTROL ACCOUNT

Date	Account Name	€	Date	Account Name	€
06/03/2019	Balance b/d	3,950	06/03/2019	Balance c/d	4,050
06/03/2019	SRDB overcast error	100			
		4,050			4,050
07/03/2019	Balance b/d	4,050			

When the sales returns day book has been undercast the error must be corrected. To correct the error made the expense account must be increased and the asset account must be decreased. Therefore, the expense account 'sales returns' is debited and the asset account 'trade receivables' is credited. The journal entry to be posted is as follows:

	Debit €	Credit €
Sales returns account	X	
Trade receivables control account		X

To correct the undercasting of the sales returns day book.

Example 9.5 demonstrates how to account for the situation where there is an undercasting of the sales returns day book.

EXAMPLE 9.5: UNDERCASTING OF THE SALES RETURNS DAY BOOK

You are provided with the details in relation to the sales day book and the sales returns day book:

SALES DAY BOOK

Date	Customer	€	Invoice Number
12/01/2019	F. Long	820	8120
12/01/2019	P. Short	750	8121
12/01/2019	D. Quinn	390	8122
12/01/2019	M. Fortune	510	8123

Sales Returns Day Book

Date	Customer	€	Sales Return Note
12/01/2019	P. Short	140	31
12/01/2019	M. Fortune	220	32

The following journal entries were posted on the respective dates:

	Debit €	Credit €
Trade receivables control account	2,470	
Sales account		2,470

To recognise sales transactions on 12 January 2019.

	Debit €	Credit €
Sales returns account	310	
Trade receivables control account		310

To recognise the sales returns by customers on 12 January 2019.

Requirement:
(a) Prepare the trade receivables ledger control account based on the journal entries posted above.
(b) Prepare the ledger listing after the journal entries detailed in the question have been posted.
(c) Correct the error made in the journal entries.

Solution

(a)

Trade Receivables Control Account

Date	Account Name	€	Date	Account Name	€
12/01/2019	Sales	2,470	12/01/2019	Sales returns	310
			12/01/2019	Balance c/d	2,160
		2,470			2,470
12/01/2019	Balance b/d	2,160			

(b) For each customer an account will be set up in the receivables ledger, which is a subsidiary ledger, also known as the receivables (debtors) management system:

Trade Receivables Account – F. Long

Date	Account Name	€	Date	Account Name	€
12/01/2019	Sales	820	12/01/2019	Balance c/d	820
12/01/2019	Balance b/d	820			

Trade Receivables Account – P. Short

Date	Account Name	€	Date	Account Name	€
12/01/2019	Sales	750	12/01/2019	Sales returns	140
			12/01/2019	Balance c/d	610
		750			750
12/01/2019	Balance b/d	610			

Trade Receivables Account – D. Quinn

Date	Account Name	€	Date	Account Name	€
12/01/2019	Sales	390	12/01/2019	Balance c/d	390
12/01/2019	Balance b/d	390			

TRADE RECEIVABLES ACCOUNT – M. FORTUNE

Date	Account Name	€	Date	Account Name	€
12/01/2019	Sales	510	12/01/2019	Sales returns	220
			12/01/2019	Balance c/d	290
		510			510
12/01/2019	Balance b/d	290			

Debtors Management System   12 January 2019

LEDGER LISTING

Customer Name	Balance €
F. Long	820
P. Short (€750 – €140)	610
D. Quinn	390
M. Fortune (€510 – €220)	290
Total	2,110

(c) The balance on the control account does not agree with the total of the ledger listing:
  • The total of the sales transactions was totalled and posted correctly.
  • The total of the sales returns transactions was posted as an amount €310. The correct total for sales returns is €360 [€140 + €220].

The sales returns day book was 'undercast', which means the amount credited to the trade receivables control account was too low. To correct this error the sales returns account needs to be debited and the trade receivables control account credited with €50.

	Debit €	Credit €
Sales returns account	50	
Trade receivables control account		50

To correct the error made in relation to the sales returns day book for 12 January 2019.

The trade receivables control account after the posting of the above journal entry is:

TRADE RECEIVABLES CONTROL ACCOUNT

Date	Account Name	€	Date	Account Name	€
12/01/2019	Balance b/d	2,160	12/01/2019	SRDB undercast error	50
			12/01/2019	Balance c/d	2,110
		2,160			2,160
13/01/2019	Balance b/d	2,110			

(Try **Review Questions 9.1** and **9.2** at the end of this chapter.)

Cash Book

The cash book will record payments received from customers. The total of the cash receipts from credit customers will result in the following journal entry being posted:

	Debit €	Credit €
Cash account	X	
Trade receivables control account		X

To recognise the cash receipts from customers in payment for goods sold on credit.

When the cash book has been overcast the error must be corrected. To correct the error one asset account is increased and another asset account must be decreased. Therefore, the asset account 'trade receivables' is debited and the asset account 'cash' is credited. The journal entry to be posted is as follows:

	Debit €	Credit €
Trade receivables control account	X	
Cash account		X

To correct the overcasting of the cash book.

Example 9.6 demonstrates the impact of the total from the cash book being overcast.

EXAMPLE 9.6: OVERCASTING OF CASH RECEIPTS FROM CREDIT CUSTOMERS

The balance on the trade receivables control account was €18,195 on 31 December 2019. At the same date, the total of the ledger listing was €18,395.

The difference has been investigated and it has been discovered that the cash receipts from credit customers on 15 December 2019 was €2,300, but was totalled and posted to the trade receivables control and cash accounts as €2,500.

Requirement Prepare the journal entry to correct the error made and the trade receivables control account as at 31 December 2019 after the error has been corrected.

Solution

The correcting journal entry is as follows:

	Debit €	Credit €
Trade receivables control account	200	
Cash account		200

To correct the error in the totalling of the cash receipts on 15 December 2019.

How the above journal entry was derived is now demonstrated.

The journal entry posted on 15 December was:

	Debit €	Credit €
Cash account	2,500	
Trade receivables control account		2,500

The journal entry that should have been posted on 15 December was:

	Debit €	Credit €
Cash account	2,300	
Trade receivables control account		2,300

So to correct it, we had to post the journal entry as above.

The trade receivables control account as at 31 December 2019 after the error has been corrected would appear as follows:

TRADE RECEIVABLES CONTROL ACCOUNT

Date	Account Name	€	Date	Account Name	€
31/12/2019	Balance b/d	18,195	31/12/2019	Balance c/d	18,395
31/12/2019	CB overcast error	200			
		18,395			18,395
01/01/2020	Balance b/d	18,395			

When the cash book has been undercast the error must be corrected. To correct the error one asset account is increased and another asset account must be decreased. Therefore, the asset account 'cash' is debited and the asset account 'trade receivables control' is credited. The journal entry to be posted is as follows:

	Debit €	Credit €
Cash account	X	
Trade receivables control account		X

To correct the undercasting of the cash book.

Example 9.7 demonstrates the impact of the total from the cash book being undercast.

EXAMPLE 9.7: UNDERCASTING OF CASH RECEIPTS FROM CREDIT CUSTOMERS

The balance on the trade receivables control account was €22,494 on 31 December 2019. At the same date the total of the ledger listing was €22,458.

The difference has been investigated and it has been discovered that the total of cash receipts from credit customers on 21 December 2019 was €1,195, but was totalled and posted to the trade receivables control and cash accounts as €1,159.

Requirement Prepare the journal entry to correct the error made and the trade receivables control account as at 31 December 2019 after the error has been corrected.

Solution

The correcting journal entry is:

	Debit €	Credit €
Cash account	36	
Trade receivables control account		36

To correct the error in the totalling of the cash receipts on 21 December 2019.

How this journal entry was derived is demonstrated below.

The journal entry posted on 21 December was:

	Debit €	Credit €
Cash account	1,159	
Trade receivables control account		1,159

The journal entry that should have been posted on 21 December:

	Debit €	Credit €
Cash account	1,195	
Trade receivables control account		1,195

So to correct it, we had to post the journal entry as above.

The trade receivables control account as at 31 December 2019 after the error has been corrected would be as follows:

TRADE RECEIVABLES CONTROL ACCOUNT

Date	Account Name	€	Date	Account Name	€
31/12/2019	Balance b/d	22,494	31/12/2019	CB undercast error	36
			31/12/2019	Balance c/d	22,458
		22,494			22,494
01/01/2020	Balance b/d	22,458			

Control Account

The typical debit and credit entries in a trade receivables control account are as follows:

TRADE RECEIVABLES CONTROL ACCOUNT

Account Name	€	Account Name	€
Balance b/d – Note 1	X	Sales returns	X
Sales	X	Bank/cash	X
Refunds to customers – Note 2	X	Discounts allowed	X
Contra – Note 3	X	Contra – Note 3	X
		Balance c/d	X
	X		X
Balance b/d	X		

Note 1 In general the opening balance on the trade receivables account is a debit one. However, sometimes a question gives information about a number of credit balances in relation to trade receivables. Students often find the idea of a credit balance on a customer's account (meaning the company owes money to one of its customers) confusing but the following simple example helps to explain how this could occur.

Example 9.8 demonstrates a situation in which a customer may have a credit balance on their account.

EXAMPLE 9.8: CREDIT BALANCE IN RELATION TO A RECEIVABLE

The following transactions occurred in relation to one of the entity's customers – B. Young:
- 1 March: sold goods to on credit to customer for €2,100.
- 10 March: customer paid the balance in full by cash, €2,100.
- 15 March: customer returned €250 worth of the goods as they were faulty.

Once the above transactions have been recorded, the customer's account would appear as follows:

TRADE RECEIVABLES – B. YOUNG

Date	Account Name	€	Date	Account Name	€
1 March	Sales	2,100	10 March	Cash	2,100
31 March	Balance c/d	250	15 March	Sales returns	250
		2,350			2,350
			1 April	Balance b/d	250

Note 2 A refund may have to be paid to a customer; examples of situations in which this may arise are: when a customer has made an overpayment on their account or, as demonstrated by **Example 9.8** above, a customer paid their account in full and then returned goods.

The concept of debiting a refund to a customer to their account is quite difficult to grasp, but if the transaction is considered from the point of view of the cash or bank payment it is easier to understand. When a cash or cheque payment is made, the cash or bank account is credited and, to record the other side of the transaction, the trade receivables account is debited.

Looking at the trade receivables account of B. Young in **Example 9.8**, it can be seen that there is a credit balance on the account of €250. If the entity agrees to make a cash refund to B. Young in relation to the faulty goods, the journal entry to reflect this payment is:

	Debit €	Credit €
Trade receivables control account	250	
Cash account		250

To recognise cash refund provided to customer.

Note 3 A contra entry arises when there is a customer who is also a supplier. Entities may offset the balance on the trade receivables and the trade payables accounts against one another. The use of contra entries is only allowed when there is agreement with the customer/supplier and a legal right of set off exists.

When the balances on the respective accounts are:

Trade receivables	Debit
Trade payables	Credit

The journal entry to offset the balances is:

	Debit €	Credit €
Trade payables control account	X	
Trade receivables control account		X

Contra entry.

Example **9.9** demonstrates the use of a contra adjustment between the trade receivables and trade payables accounts.

EXAMPLE 9.9: CONTRA ENTRIES

Ormsby Ltd buys and sells goods to Prentice Ltd. The balances, in Ormsby Ltd's records, on its trading accounts with Prentice, at its most recent reporting date, 31 December 2019, are as follows:

Trade receivables €250 debit balance   Trade payables €180 credit balance

Ormsby has agreed with Prentice that rather than both companies making payments to one another, they will net off the balance and Prentice will make a payment for the balance on the account.

Solution

	Debit €	Credit €
Trade payables control account	180	
Trade receivables control account		180

Contra entry.

The contra adjustment is for the lower of the two balances. After the journal entry has been posted the ledger accounts will appear as follows:

TRADE RECEIVABLES – PRENTICE LTD

Date	Account Name	€	Date	Account Name	€
31 Dec	Balance b/d	250	31 Dec	Contra	180
			31 Dec	Balance c/d	70
		250			250
1 Jan	Balance b/d	70			

TRADE PAYABLES – PRENTICE LTD

Date	Account Name	€	Date	Account Name	€
31 Dec	Contra	180	31 Dec	Balance b/d	180

Prentice will issue a payment for the balance on the trade receivables account.

Example **9.10** demonstrates the reconciliation of the trade receivables control account to the ledger listing where there are a number of items to be either corrected or adjusted.

EXAMPLE 9.10: RECONCILIATION OF THE TRADE RECEIVABLES CONTROL ACCOUNT
TO THE LEDGER LISTING

You have been informed that the balance on the trade receivables control account as at 1 January 2019 was €164,950 – debit. As at the same date the ledger listing total was €159,640.

Subsequent to a review, the following information is available.
1. The sales day book was overcast by €1,500.
2. A customer's account, with a credit balance of €180, has been omitted from the receivables ledger listing.

3. Discounts allowed of €840 were not posted to the control account.
4. The sales returns day book was undercast by €2,800.
5. A balance on a customer's account, of €175 debit, has been treated as a credit balance.

Requirement:
(a) Make the necessary adjustment to the trade receivables control account.
(b) Reconcile the revised balance on the trade receivables control account with the ledger listing.

Solution

The following approach should be taken to these questions:
1. consider each adjustment and determine whether it impacts the control account, ledger listing or both;
2. make any adjustment necessary to the control accounts; and
3. make any corrections necessary to the ledger listing balance.

Item	Adjustment Required
1.	The total of the sales day book impacts the trade receivables control account. There is no comment in relation to the other side to the transaction, so it is assumed that both the debit and credit side of the transaction were for the incorrect amount. The total of the sales day book has been **overcast**; as shown earlier, when this occurs it means the value of sales that has been recorded was too large. Therefore, to reduce the credit sales recorded by the amount of the overcasting error, the sales must be reduced and the trade receivables must be reduced as shown below:

	Debit €	Credit €
Sales account	1,500	
Trade receivables control account		1,500

The item does not make any reference to the ledger listing so it is assumed that it has been dealt with correctly in the individual ledger account of the customer.

Item	Adjustment Required
2.	The ledger listing is the total of all balances due from credit customers. This will not impact the trade receivables control account. This item will be in the reconciliation as the total from the ledger listing is incorrect; it should have been reduced by €180, i.e. the credit balance.
3.	The item clearly states that the discounts allowed have not been posted to the trade receivables control account, so the adjustment needs to be made:

	Debit €	Credit €
Discounts allowed account	840	
Trade receivables control account		840

The item does not make any reference to the ledger listing, so it is assumed that it has been dealt with correctly in the individual ledger account for the customer.

4. The total of the sales returns day book impacts the trade receivables control account. There is no comment in relation to the other side of the transaction, so it is assumed that both the debit and credit side of the transaction were for the incorrect amount. The total amount of the sales returns was **undercast**; this means that the total recorded was for a smaller amount than the actual sales returns. To correct this error a sales return journal entry has to be recorded for the undercast amount – the journal entry is shown below:

	Debit €	Credit €
Sales returns account	2,800	
Trade receivables control account		2,800

The item does not make any reference to the ledger listing, so it is assumed that it has been dealt with correctly in the individual ledger account for the customer.

5. The total of the ledger listing has been reduced by a balance that it should have been increased by instead. To correct this error, the total of the ledger listing needs to be increased.

(a)

TRADE RECEIVABLES CONTROL ACCOUNT

Date	Account Name	€	Date	Account Name	€
01/01/2019	Balance b/d	164,950	01/01/2019	SDB overcast (1)	1,500
			01/01/2019	Discounts allowed (3)	840
			01/01/2019	SRDB undercast (4)	2,800
			01/01/2019	Balance c/d	159,810
		164,950			164,950
02/01/2019	Balance b/d	159,810			

(b)

RECONCILIATION OF THE TRADE RECEIVABLES CONTROL ACCOUNT BALANCE TO THE LEDGER LISTING

	€
Total of balances per ledger listing	159,640
Credit balance omitted (2)	(180)
	159,460
Debit balance omitted (5)	350
Balance per trade receivables control account	159,810

9.3 TRADE PAYABLES CONTROL ACCOUNT RECONCILIATION

Purchases Day Book

The purchases day book contains a record of each credit purchase transaction for a particular period of time. Like the sales day book, at regular intervals the purchases day book is totalled and a journal entry is posted to the financial records.

The journal entry to post the total of the purchase day book will increase the expense account and increase the liability account. Therefore, the expense account is debited and the trade payables control account is credited. The journal entry posted is as follows:

	Debit €	Credit €
Purchases account	X	
Trade payables control account		X

To recognise the credit purchases.

Example 9.11 demonstrates the recording of a number of purchases transactions to show the process involved.

EXAMPLE 9.11: PURCHASES DAY BOOK AND ITS IMPACT ON THE
TRADE PAYABLES CONTROL ACCOUNT

On 15 January 2019 Green had the following credit purchases transactions:

Supplier	Transaction amount	Invoice Number
T. Smith	€480	198
M. Walker	€690	220
K. Hennessy	€150	460

Requirement:
(a) Record the purchases transactions in the purchases day book.
(b) Show the journal entry in relation to the purchases day book.
(c) Prepare the trade payable control account.
(d) Prepare the ledger listing.
(e) Prepare the reconciliation of the trade payables control account to the ledger listing.

Solution

(a)

PURCHASES DAY BOOK

Date	Supplier	€	Invoice Number
15/01/2019	T. Smith	480	198
15/01/2019	M. Walker	690	220
15/01/2019	K. Hennessy	150	460
		1,320	

(b) Journal entry:

	Debit €	Credit €
Purchases account	1,320	
Trade payables control account		1,320

To recognise the purchases transactions for 15 January 2019.

The total of the purchases day book is posted to the trade payables control account. The individual transactions are recorded in the payables (also known as creditors) management system, but this recording is not part of the double-entry system.

(c)

TRADE PAYABLES CONTROL ACCOUNT

Date	Account Name	€	Date	Account Name	€
			15/01/2019	Purchases	1,320

(d) For each supplier an account will be set up in the payables ledger, which is a subsidiary ledger, also known as the payables (creditors) management system:

TRADE PAYABLES ACCOUNT – T. SMITH

Date	Account Name	€	Date	Account Name	€
			15/01/2019	Purchases	480

TRADE PAYABLES ACCOUNT – M. WALKER

Date	Account Name	€	Date	Account Name	€
			15/01/2019	Purchases	690

TRADE PAYABLES ACCOUNT – K. HENNESSY

Date	Account Name	€	Date	Account Name	€
			15/01/2019	Purchases	150

The ledger listing will typically be a print-out from the computer system, which could appear as follows:

Creditors Management System   15 January 2019

LEDGER LISTING

Supplier Name	Balance €
T. Smith	480
M. Walker	690
K. Hennessy	150
Total	1,320

The total of the ledger listing should agree with the balance on the trade payables control account.

(e)

TRADE PAYABLES RECONCILIATION
as at 15 January 2019

	€
Balance per trade payables control account	1,320
Total of balances per ledger listing	1,320

The balance on the trade payables control account agrees with the total per the ledger listing, so there are no reconciling items.

When the purchases day book has been overcast the error must be corrected. To correct the error a liability account is decreased and an expense account is decreased. Therefore, the liability account 'trade payables control' is debited and the expense account 'purchases' is credited. The journal entry to be posted is as follows:

	Debit €	Credit €
Trade payables control account	X	
Purchases account		X

To correct the overcasting of the purchases day book.

Example 9.12 demonstrates the situation where an error is made in the totalling of the purchases day book.

EXAMPLE 9.12: OVERCASTING OF THE PURCHASES DAY BOOK

You have been provided with the following information from the purchases day book:

Date	Supplier	€	Invoice Number
05/01/2019	A. Frank	2,100	142
05/01/2019	C. Boyle	1,350	1006
05/01/2019	E. Gillen	2,800	320

An error was made in the totalling of the purchases day book and as a result the journal entry posted was for the incorrect amount. The total of the purchases day book is €6,250 [€2,100 + €1,350 + €2,800], but an error was made and the journal entry was posted as €6,520.

The trade payables control account will have a balance of €6,520 due to the error – the journal entry posted was for the incorrect amount:

	Debit €	Credit €
Purchases account	6,520	
Trade payables control account		6,520

To recognise the credit purchases transactions for 5 January 2019.

TRADE PAYABLES CONTROL ACCOUNT

Date	Account Name	€	Date	Account Name	€
			05/01/2019	Purchases	6,520

For each supplier an account will be set up in the payables ledger, which is a subsidiary ledger, also known as the payables (creditors) management system:

TRADE PAYABLES ACCOUNT – A. FRANK

Date	Account Name	€	Date	Account Name	€
			05/01/2019	Purchases	2,100

TRADE PAYABLES ACCOUNT – C. BOYLE

Date	Account Name	€	Date	Account Name	€
			05/01/2019	Purchases	1,350

TRADE PAYABLES ACCOUNT – E. GILLEN

Date	Account Name	€	Date	Account Name	€
			05/01/2019	Purchases	2,800

The ledger listing will typically be a print-out from the computer system, which could appear as follows.

Creditors Management System   5 January 2019

LEDGER LISTING

Customer Name	Balance €
A. Frank	2,100
C. Boyle	1,350
E. Gillen	2,800
Total	6,250

The total of the ledger listing does not agree with the balance on the trade payables control account. A review would be undertaken to discover the reason for the difference. To correct the error the balance on the trade payables control account needs to reduced by €270, i.e. the difference between the amount posted in error of €6,520 and the correct total of €6,250.

The journal entry to correct the error:

	Debit €	Credit €
Trade payables control account	270	
Purchases account		270

To correct an error in relation to the purchases transactions for 5 January 2019.

When the total of any of the day books is calculated incorrectly as a higher amount than the actual figure, this is referred to as 'overcasting'. The trade payables control account would appear as follows after the error correction journal entry is posted:

TRADE PAYABLES CONTROL ACCOUNT

Date	Account Name	€	Date	Account Name	€
05/01/2019	PDB – error	270	05/01/2019	Purchases	6,520
05/01/2019	Balance c/d	6,250			
		6,520			6,520
			06/01/2019	Balance b/d	6,250

Corrections are made to the control account and then the total of the ledger listing and the balance on the control account are reconciled. In an exam situation there would be reconciling items.

TRADE PAYABLES RECONCILIATION
as at 6 January 2019

	€
Balance per trade receivables control account	6,250
Balance per ledger listing	6,250

When the purchases day book has been undercast the error must be corrected. To correct the error an expense account is increased and a liability account is increased. Therefore, the expense account 'purchases' is debited and the liability account 'trade payables control' is credited. The journal entry to be posted is as follows:

	Debit €	Credit €
Purchases account	X	
Trade payables control account		X

To correct the undercasting of the purchases day book.

Example 9.13 demonstrates the situation in which the purchases day book total is undercast.

EXAMPLE 9.13: UNDERCASTING OF THE PURCHASES DAY BOOK

You have been provided with the following information from the purchases day book:

Date	Supplier	Amount €	Invoice Number
29/12/2019	T. Knight	2,980	1002
29/12/2019	R. Walsh	3,640	2694
		6,620	

An error was made in the totalling of the purchases day book and as a result the journal entry posted was for the incorrect amount. The correct total of the purchases day book is €6,620 [€2,980 + €3,640] but an error was made and the journal entry was posted as €6,470.

Requirement Prepare the journal entry to correct this error on 29 December 2019 and the trade payables control account.

Solution

	Debit €	Credit €
Purchases account	150	
Trade payables control account		150

To correct the undercasting of the purchases day book on 29 December 2019.

TRADE PAYABLES CONTROL ACCOUNT

Date	Account Name	€	Date	Account Name	€
29/12/2019	Balance c/d	6,620	29/12/2019	Purchases	6,470
			29/12/2019	PDB undercast	150
		6,620			6,620
			30/12/2019	Balance b/d	6,620

Purchases Returns Day Book

The purchases returns day book will reduce the balance on the trade payables control account. The journal entry to post the total from the purchases returns day book is:

	Debit €	Credit €
Trade payables control account	X	
Purchases returns account		X

To recognise the purchases returns by customers.

When the purchases returns day book has been overcast the error must be corrected. To correct the error an income account is decreased and a liability account is increased. Therefore, the income account 'purchases returns' is debited and the liability account 'trade payables control' is credited. The journal entry to be posted is as follows:

	Debit €	Credit €
Purchases returns account	X	
Trade payables control account		X

To correct the overcasting of the purchases returns day book.

Example 9.14 demonstrates the situation where the total on the purchases returns day book has been incorrectly calculated.

EXAMPLE 9.14: OVERCASTING OF THE PURCHASES RETURNS DAY BOOK

You are provided with the details in relation to the purchases day book and the purchases returns day book:

PURCHASES DAY BOOK

Date	Supplier	€	Invoice Number
05/02/2019	S. Wynn	2,150	2670
05/02/2019	W. Jones	1,830	512
05/02/2019	P. Carstairs	510	820
05/02/2019	B. Wilson	1,970	1207

PURCHASES RETURNS DAY BOOK

Date	Supplier	€	Purchases Return Note
06/02/2019	S. Wynn	350	10
06/02/2019	W. Jones	105	230

The following journal entries were posted on the respective dates:

	Debit €	Credit €
Purchases account	6,460	
Trade payables control account		6,460

To recognise purchases transactions on 5 February 2019.

	Debit €	Credit €
Trade payables control account	545	
Purchases returns account		545

To recognise the purchases returns by customers.

Requirement:
(a) Prepare the trade payables control account based on the journal entries posted above.
(b) Prepare the ledger listing after the journal entries detailed in the question have been posted.
(c) Correct the error made in the journal entry.

Solution

(a)

TRADE PAYABLES CONTROL ACCOUNT

Date	Account Name	€	Date	Account Name	€
06/02/2019	Purchases returns	545	05/02/2019	Purchases	6,460
06/02/2019	Balance c/d	5,915			
		6,460			6,460
			07/02/2019	Balance b/d	5,915

(b) For each supplier an account will be set up in the payables ledger, which is a subsidiary ledger, also known as the payables (creditors) management system:

TRADE PAYABLES ACCOUNT – S. WYNN

Date	Account Name	€	Date	Account Name	€
06/02/2019	Purchases returns	350	05/02/2019	Purchases	2,150
06/02/2019	Balance c/d	1,800			
		2,150			2,150
			07/02/2019	Balance b/d	1,800

TRADE PAYABLES ACCOUNT – W. JONES

Date	Account Name	€	Date	Account Name	€
06/02/2019	Purchases returns	105	05/02/2019	Purchases	1,830
06/02/2019	Balance c/d	1,725			
		1,830			1,830
			07/02/2019	Balance b/d	1,725

TRADE PAYABLES ACCOUNT – P. CARSTAIRS

Date	Account Name	€	Date	Account Name	€
06/02/2019	Balance c/d	510	05/02/2019	Purchases	510
			07/02/2019	Balance b/d	510

TRADE PAYABLES ACCOUNT – B. WILSON

Date	Account Name	€	Date	Account Name	€
06/02/2019	Balance c/d	1,970	05/02/2019	Purchases	1,970
			07/02/2019	Balance b/d	1,970

(c) For each supplier an account will be set up in the payables ledger, which is a subsidiary ledger, also known as the payables (creditors) management system:

Creditors Management System   5 January 2019

LEDGER LISTING

Customer Name	Balance €
S. Wynn (€2,150 – €350)	1,800
W. Jones (€1,830 – €105)	1,725
P. Carstairs	510
B. Wilson	1,970
Total	6,005

(c) The balance on the control account does not agree with the total of the ledger listing:
- The total of the purchases transactions was correct.
- The total of the purchases returns transactions was posted as an amount €545. The correct total for sales returns is €455 [€350 + €105].

The purchases return journal was 'overcast', which means the amount debited to the trade payables control account was too much, so to correct this error the trade payables control account needs to be credited and the purchases returns account needs to be debited with €90.

	Debit €	Credit €
Purchases returns account	90	
Trade payables control account		90

To correct the error made in relation to purchases returns day book of 6 February 2019.

The trade payables control account after the above journal entry is:

TRADE PAYABLES CONTROL ACCOUNT

Date	Account Name	€	Date	Account Name	€
06/02/2019	Balance c/d	6,005	05/02/2019	Purchases	5,915
			06/02/2019	PRDB overcast error	90
		6,005			6,005
			07/02/2019	Balance b/d	6,005

When the purchases returns day book has been undercast the error must be corrected. To correct the error the journal entry to be posted is as follows:

	Debit €	Credit €
Trade payables control account	X	
Purchases returns account		X

To correct the undercasting of the purchases returns day book.

Example 9.15 demonstrates the situation where there is an undercasting of the purchases returns day book.

EXAMPLE 9.15: UNDERCASTING OF THE PURCHASES RETURNS DAY BOOK

You are provided with the details in relation to the purchases day book and the purchases returns day book:

PURCHASES DAY BOOK

Date	Supplier	€	Invoice Number
12/01/2019	L. Smartt	180	830
12/01/2019	C. McGinley	250	1520
12/01/2019	D. Counihan	890	695
12/01/2019	A. Madigan	330	3240

PURCHASES RETURNS DAY BOOK

Date	Supplier	€	Purchases Return Note
12/01/2019	L. Smartt	30	41
12/01/2019	D. Counihan	100	42

The following journal entries were posted on the respective dates:

	Debit €	Credit €
Purchases account	1,650	
Trade payables control account		1,650

To recognise purchases transactions on 12 January 2019.

Trade payables control account	30	
Purchases returns account		30

To recognise the purchases returns by customers.

Requirement:
(a) Prepare the trade payables control account based on the journal entries posted above.
(b) Prepare the ledger listing based on the information contained in the purchases and purchases returns day books.
(c) Correct the error made in the journal entries.

Solution

(a)

TRADE PAYABLES CONTROL ACCOUNT

Date	Account Name	€	Date	Account Name	€
12/01/2019	Purchases returns	30	12/01/2019	Purchases	1,650
12/01/2019	Balance c/d	1,620			
		1,650			1,650
			13/01/2019	Balance b/d	1,620

(b) For each supplier an account will be set up in the payables ledger, which is a subsidiary ledger, also known as the payables (creditors) management system:

TRADE PAYABLES ACCOUNT – L. SMARTT

Date	Account Name	€	Date	Account Name	€
12/01/2019	Purchases returns	30	12/01/2019	Purchases	180
12/01/2019	Balance c/d	150			
		180			180
			13/01/2019	Balance b/d	150

TRADE PAYABLES ACCOUNT – C. McGINLEY

Date	Account Name	€	Date	Account Name	€
12/01/2019	Balance c/d	250	12/01/2019	Purchases	250
			13/01/2019	Balance b/d	250

TRADE PAYABLES ACCOUNT – D. COUNIHAN

Date	Account Name	€	Date	Account Name	€
12/01/2019	Purchases returns	100	12/01/2019	Purchases	890
12/01/2019	Balance c/d	790			
		890			890
			13/01/2019	Balance b/d	790

TRADE PAYABLES ACCOUNT – A. MADIGAN

Date	Account Name	€	Date	Account Name	€
12/01/2019	Balance c/d	330	12/01/2019	Purchases	330
			13/01/2019	Balance b/d	330

Creditors Management System   12 January 2019

LEDGER LISTING

Customer Name	Balance €
L. Smartt (€180 – €30)	150
C. McGinley	250
D. Counihan (€890 – €100)	790
A. Madigan	330
Total	1,520

(c) The balance on the control account does not agree with the total of the ledger listing:
   • The total of the purchases transactions was correct.
   • The total of the purchases returns transactions was posted as an amount €30. The correct total for sales returns is €130 [€100 + €30].

The purchases returns day book was 'undercast', which means the amount debited to the trade payables control account was too low, so to correct this error the purchases returns account needs to credited and the trade payables control account debited by €100.

	Debit €	Credit €
Trade payables control account	100	
Purchases returns account		100

To correct the error made in relation to the purchases returns day book 12 January 2019.

The trade payables control account after the above journal entry has been posted:

TRADE PAYABLES CONTROL ACCOUNT

Date	Account Name	€	Date	Account Name	€
13/01/2019	PRDB undercast	100	13/01/2019	Balance b/d	1,620
13/01/2019	Balance c/d	1,520			
		1,620			1,620
			14/01/2019	Balance b/d	1,520

Cash Book

The cash book will record payments made to customers. The total of the cash payments to credit suppliers will result in the following journal entry being posted:

	Debit €	Credit €
Trade payables control account	X	
Cash account		X

To recognise the cash payments to suppliers.

When the cash book has been overcast the error must be corrected. To correct the error the cash account must be increased and the trade payables control account must be increased. Therefore, the cash account is debited and the trade payables control account is credited. The journal entry to be posted is as follows:

	Debit €	Credit €
Cash account	X	
Trade payables control account		X

To correct the overcasting of the cash book.

Example 9.16 demonstrates the impact of the total from the cash book being overcast.

EXAMPLE 9.16: OVERCASTING OF CASH PAYMENTS TO CREDIT SUPPLIERS

The balance on the trade payables control account was €17,240 on 31 December 2019. At the same date the total of the ledger listing was €17,740.

The difference has been investigated and it has been discovered that the total of the cash payments to credit suppliers on 20 December 2019 was €3,650, but was totalled and posted to the trade payables control and cash accounts as €4,150.

Requirement Prepare the journal entry to correct the error made and the trade payables control account as at 31 December 2019 after the error has been corrected.

Solution

	Debit €	Credit €
Cash account	500	
Trade payables control account		500

To correct the error in the totalling of the cash payments to suppliers on 20 December 2019.

How the above journal entry was derived is now demonstrated.

The journal entry posted on 20 December was:

	Debit €	Credit €
Trade payables control account	4,150	
Cash account		4,150

The journal entry that should have been posted on 20 December was:

	Debit €	Credit €
Trade payables control account	3,650	
Cash account		3,650

The trade payables control account as at 31 December 2019, after the error has been corrected, would appear as follows:

TRADE PAYABLES CONTROL ACCOUNT

Date	Account Name	€	Date	Account Name	€
31/12/2019	Balance c/d	17,740	31/12/2019	Balance b/d	17,240
			31/12/2019	CB overcast	500
		17,740			17,740
			01/01/2020	Balance b/d	17,740

When the cash book has been undercast the error must be corrected. To correct the error the cash account must be decreased and the trade payables control account must be decreased. Therefore, the cash account is credited and the trade payables control account is debited. The journal entry to be posted is as follows:

	Debit €	Credit €
Trade payables control account	X	
Cash account		X

To correct the undercasting of the cash book.

Example 9.17 demonstrates the impact of the total from the cash book being undercast.

EXAMPLE 9.17: UNDERCASTING OF CASH PAYMENTS TO CREDIT CUSTOMERS

The balance on the trade payables control account was €22,575 on 31 December 2019. At the same date the total of the ledger listing was €22,425.

The difference has been investigated and it has been discovered that the total of cash payments to credit suppliers on 28 December 2019 was €3,245, but was totalled and posted to the trade payables control and cash accounts as €3,095.

Requirement Prepare the journal entry to correct the error made and the trade payables control account as at 31 December 2019 after the error has been corrected.

Solution

	Debit €	Credit €
Trade payables control account	150	
Cash account		150

To correct the error in the totalling of the cash payments on 28 December 2019.

How the above journal entry was derived is now demonstrated.

The journal entry posted on 28 December was:

	Debit €	Credit €
Trade payables control account	3,095	
Cash account		3,095

The journal entry that should have been posted on 28 December was:

	Debit €	Credit €
Trade payables control account	3,245	
Cash account		3,245

The trade payables control account as at 31 December 2019, after the error has been corrected, would appear as follows:

TRADE PAYABLES CONTROL ACCOUNT

Date	Account Name	€	Date	Account Name	€
31/12/2019	CB undercast	150	31/12/2019	Balance b/d	22,575
31/12/2019	Balance c/d	22,425			
		22,575			22,575
			01/01/2020	Balance b/d	22,425

Control Account

The typical debit and credit transactions to a trade payables control account are as follows.

TRADE PAYABLES CONTROL ACCOUNT

Account Name	€	Account Name	€
Purchases returns	X	Balance b/d	X
Discounts received	X	Purchases	X
Bank/cash	X	Cash refunds from suppliers – Note 1	X
Contra – Note 2	X	Contra – Note 2	X
Balance c/d	X		X
	X		X

Note 1 A refund may be received from a supplier. An example of a situation in which this may arise is when the supplier has been overpaid. The concept of a refund from a supplier is quite difficult to grasp but if the transaction is considered from the point of view of the cash or bank payment, it is easier to understand why the suppliers' account is credited with the refund. When cash or a cheque is received, the cash or bank account is debited and the credit side of the transaction is recorded in the appropriate account.

Note 2 A contra entry arises when there is a customer who is also a supplier. Entities may offset the balances on the trade receivables and the trade payables accounts against one another. The use of contra entries is only allowed when there is agreement with the customer – supplier and a legal right of set off exists.

Example 9.18 demonstrates the reconciliation of the trade payables control account to the ledger listing with a number of items to be either corrected or adjusted.

EXAMPLE 9.18: RECONCILIATION OF TRADE PAYABLES CONTROL ACCOUNT TO LEDGER LISTING

You have been informed that the balance on the trade payables control account as at 1 January 2019 was €193,100 credit. As at the same date the ledger listing total was €194,288.

Subsequent to a review, the following information is available.
1. The purchases day book was undercast by €750.
2. Discounts received of €190 were not posted to the control account.
3. The purchases returns day book was overcast by €1,040.
4. A balance on a supplier's account of €206 credit has been treated as a debit balance.

Requirement:
(a) Make the necessary adjustment to the trade payables control account.
(b) Reconcile the revised balance on the trade payables control account with the ledger listing.

Solution

Each item needs to be considered so as to identify whether it impacts the control account or the ledger listing or both.

Item	Adjustment Required
1	The total of the purchases day book impacts the trade payables control account. There is no comment in relation to the other side of the transaction, so it is assumed that both the debit and credit sides of the transaction were for the incorrect amount.

	Debit €	Credit €
Purchases account	750	
Trade payables control account		750

The item does not make any reference to the ledger listing, so it is assumed that it has been dealt with correctly in the individual ledger account for the supplier.

2	The item clearly states that the discounts received have not been posted to the trade payables control account so the adjustment needs to be made:

	Debit €	Credit €
Trade payables control account	190	
Discounts received account		190

The item does not make any reference to the ledger listing, so it is assumed that it has been dealt with correctly in the individual ledger account for the supplier.

3	The total of the purchases returns day book impacts the trade payables control account. There is no comment in relation to the other side to the transaction, so it is assumed that both the debit and credit sides of the transaction were for the incorrect amount.

	Debit €	Credit €
Purchases returns account	1,040	
Trade payables control account		1,040

The item does not make any reference to the ledger listing, so it is assumed that it has been dealt with correctly in the individual ledger account for the supplier.

4   The total of the ledger listing has been reduced by a balance that should have been added; it should have been increased by this balance. To correct this error the total of the ledger listing needs to be increased.

(a)

TRADE PAYABLES CONTROL ACCOUNT

Date	Account Name	€	Date	Account Name	€
01/01/2019	Discounts received	190	01/01/2019	Balance b/d	193,100
01/01/2019	Balance c/d	194,700	01/01/2019	PDB undercast	750
			01/01/2019	PRDB overcast	1,040
		194,890			194,890
			02/01/2019	Balance b/d	194,700

(b)

RECONCILIATION OF TRADE PAYABLES CONTROL TO LEDGER LISTING

	€
Balance per ledger listing	194,288
Debit balance taken as credit (€206 × 2)	412
Balance per trade payables control account	194,700

(Try **Review Questions 9.3** and **9.4** at the end of this chapter.)

EXAM TIP

When there is an undercasting/overcasting error in relation to the day books, it can be assumed, unless otherwise stated, that both sides of the transaction were posted for the incorrect amount.

9.4 CONCLUSION

Sales and purchases transactions are recorded in the relevant day books, which are totalled at regular intervals. These totals are posted to the trade receivables and payables accounts respectively; to ensure the accuracy of the accounting records, the balances on these control accounts are reconciled to the totals of the receivables/payables ledger listing. The ledger listings are lists of the amounts owed by/to each of the entity's customers/suppliers. A receivable and payments management system is maintained to ensure prompt collection of receipts from customers and payments to suppliers.

SUMMARY OF LEARNING OBJECTIVES

After having studied this chapter, readers should be able to:

Learning Objective 1 Reconcile the balance on the trade receivables control account with the total of the customer ledger listing.

Identify whether the information provided indicates that an adjustment is required to the trade receivables control account or to the receivables ledger listing. Arithmetic errors in the totalling of the day books indicate an error in the trade receivables control account.

Learning Objective 2 Reconcile the balance on the trade payables control account with the total of the supplier ledger listing.

Identify whether the information provided indicates that an adjustment is required to the trade payables control account or to the payables ledger listing. Arithmetic errors in the totalling of the day books indicate an error in the trade payables control account.

QUESTIONS

Review Questions

(See **Appendix A** for Solutions to Review Questions.)

Question 9.1
The sales day book has been undercast by €540.

Requirement Which of the following will this error impact?
(a) Trade receivables control account.
(b) Receivables ledger listing.

Question 9.2
The balance on the trade receivable control account is €45,600 as at 31 December 2019. At that date the total of the ledger listing for the individual receivables accounts amounted to €45,750. A review has been undertaken and the following items have been identified:
1. The sales day book was overcast by €40.
2. Discounts allowed of €90 were posted to the control account but have not been reflected in the individual accounts of customers.
3. The sales returns day book was overcast by €100.

Requirement Reconcile the balance on the trade receivables control account with the ledger listing.

Question 9.3
The balance on the trade payables control account is €98,600. It has been discovered that:
* The purchases day book was undercast during the year by €160.
* The purchases returns day book was undercast during the year by €55.

Requirement
(a) What is the correct balance on the trade payables control account?
(b) Prepare the journal entries to correct the above errors.

Question 9.4

The balance on the trade payables control account is €59,720 as at 31 December 2019. At that date the total of the ledger listing for the individual payables accounts amounted to €60,055. A review has been undertaken and the following items have been identified:
1. The purchases day book was undercast by €120.
2. Discounts received of €120 were posted to the control account but have not been reflected in the individual account of the supplier.
3. The purchases returns day book was overcast by €95.

Requirement Reconcile the balance on the trade payables control account with the ledger listing.

Challenging Questions

(Suggested Solutions to Challenging Questions are available through your lecturer.)

Question 9.1

Mr Carroll is reconciling his receivables balances at 31 December 2019. The list of receivables balances at 31 December 2019 totalled €45,192.

The following information is also available:

	€
Receivables balance at 1 January 2019	56,140
Provision for doubtful debts at 1 January 2019	2,807
Transactions during 2019	
Credit sales	426,179
Cash received from customers	430,624
Cash refunds to customers	1,430
Discounts allowed	2,705
Bad debts written off	360
Returns inwards	4,385

The doubtful debt provision is maintained at 5% of receivables. The list of balances does not agree with the control account balance. Upon investigation, Mr Carroll discovered the following.
1. Mr Scott's balance per the ledger of €679 was included in the listing as €796.
2. A credit note issued to Mrs Walker for €350 was treated correctly in the day book but entered as an invoice in her account.
3. Sales of €650 were entered on the wrong side of the customer's account in the receivables ledger.
4. During 2017 a balance owed by Mr Payne had been written off when he was declared bankrupt. On 3 October 2019 a payment of €240 was received from the administrator and credited to the sundries account in the nominal ledger.

Requirement:
(a) Prepare the receivables control account for the year ended 31 December 2019.
10 Minutes
(b) Show the corrections that should be made to the list of receivables balances at 31 December 2019.
7 Minutes

(c) Prepare the extracts from the income statement for the year ended 31 December 2019 in respect of bad and doubtful debts.

4 Minutes

(d) Prepare the balance sheet extracts for receivables at 31 December 2019.

5 Minutes

(Based on Chartered Accountants Ireland, CAP 1 Financial Accounting, Autumn 2009, Question 2)

Question 9.2

The following information relates to the purchases ledger and sales ledger of Fitz Ltd:

	€
1 January 2019:	
Receivables debit balances	14,040
Receivables credit balances	100
Payables debit balances	185
Payables credit balances	10,920
Balance on allowance for doubtful debts	702
Transactions for year ended 31 December 2019:	
Purchases day book total	70,180
Purchase returns day book total	938
Sales day book total	111,585
Sales returns daybook total	2,109
Discounts allowed	4,075
Discounts received	2,565
Cheques paid to suppliers	65,285
Bad debts written off	580
Amounts due from customers offset against due to the same business in purchase ledger	756
Cheques received from customers	96,630
Cheques received from customers dishonoured by the bank	850
At 31 December 2019:	
Receivables credit balances	160
Payables debit balances	210

The doubtful debts allowance at 31 December 2019 is to be maintained at 5% of outstanding balances.

Requirement:

(a) Prepare the receivables control account for the year to 31 December 2019.

10 Minutes

(b) Prepare the payables control account for the year to 31 December 2019.

10 Minutes

(c) Prepare the statement of financial position extracts for receivables and payables as at 31 December 2019.

3 Minutes

(Based on Chartered Accountants Ireland, CAP 1 Financial Accounting, Autumn 2010, Question 6)

10

Bank Reconciliations

LEARNING OBJECTIVES

Having studied this chapter, readers should be able to:
1. explain why a bank reconciliation is prepared; and
2. reconcile the balance on the bank statement with the balance on the entity's bank account.

10.1 INTRODUCTION

To prepare the financial statements, the correct balance attributable to the bank needs to be known. The bank statement needs to be compared with the entity's records to determine the correct amount.

This checking exercise will:
- identify items that have gone through the entity's bank account with the financial institution (such as a bank) that the entity did not know about, for example, direct debits; and
- errors made in the recording of transactions.

10.2 WHY WOULD THE BALANCE PER THE BANK STATEMENT NOT AGREE WITH THE ENTITY'S FIGURE?

There are a number of different reasons why the balance per the bank statement issued by the financial institution would not agree with an entity's own records. Some of these reasons are discussed below.

Cheques Issued by the Entity have not been Presented to the Bank

When a business issues cheques in payment for goods or services, the business records the payment in its financial records. A cheque is valid for six months from the date stated on the cheque, so the holder of the cheque may not lodge the cheque immediately. Therefore, there may be a timing difference between the cheque being recognised in the books of the company and it being presented for payment at the bank.

The most common items that are included in the reconciliation of the balance per the bank statement issued by the financial institution and the entity's own records are **unpresented cheques**, that is cheques issued by the entity that have not been presented for payment at the bank by the reconciliation date.

Example 10.1 demonstrates the reconciliation where cheques issued have not been presented for payment at the bank.

EXAMPLE 10.1: CHEQUES NOT PRESENTED

You have been provided with the following information from the accounting records of A. Jones:

BANK ACCOUNT

Date	Detail	€	Date	Detail	€
01/01/2019	Balance b/d	5,654.00	02/01/2019	Cheque no. 10	500.00
05/01/2019	Lodgement	4,365.90	05/01/2019	Cheque no. 11	150.00
25/01/2019	Lodgement	1,256.00	15/01/2019	Cheque no. 12	190.00
			22/01/2019	Cheque no. 13	178.22
			31/01/2019	Balance c/d	10,257.68
		11,275.90			11,275.90
01/02/2019	Balance b/d	10,257.68			

A. Jones has received his bank statement which details the following transactions:

Friendly Bank plc
52 Main Street
Market

Page no. 5

Date	Transaction Details	Debit €	Credit €	Balance €
1 January	Balance forward			5,654.00
5 January	Lodgement		4,365.90	10,019.90
	Cheque no. 10	500.00		9,519.90
18 January	Cheque no. 12	190.00		9,329.90
25 January	Lodgement		1,256.00	10,585.90
31 January	Cheque no. 13	178.22		10,407.68

BANK RECONCILIATION
as at 31 January 2019

	€
Balance per bank statement	10,407.68
Unpresented cheques:	
Cheque no. 11	(150.00)
Balance per bank account	10,257.68

The only item creating the difference in the balances reported in the entity's records and the bank statement was a cheque issued but not yet presented to the bank for payment. This item has been recorded in the financial records of the company, so no adjustment is required.

(Try **Review Question 10.1** at the end of this chapter.)

Lodgements

A customer may make a payment directly to the entity's bank account. The entity may only discover that the payment has been made upon receipt of their statement of account from the bank; the entity must post an entry in its financial records in relation to such a lodgement. The lodgement is not a reconciling item in the bank reconciliation.

Fees, Charges and Automated Transactions

When a bank charges fees and interest to a bank account, it issues a notification to the customer in advance. The entity may or may not put through an accounting entry in relation to the cost on the date it receives the notice – it may wait until it receives its bank statement.

Many businesses use direct debits, rather than cheques, to pay for regular bills; these automated items may not have been reflected in the entity's own records and, if they have not, adjustments will have to be made.

Example 10.2 demonstrates the reconciliation when there are items on the bank statement that have not been taken into account in the entity's own accounting records.

EXAMPLE 10.2: ITEMS IN THE BANK'S RECORDS NOT RECORDED IN THE ENTITY'S RECORDS

You have been provided with the following information from the accounting records of H. Wright:

BANK ACCOUNT

Date	Detail	€	Date	Detail	€
01/01/2019	Balance b/d	10,150.00	05/01/2019	Cheque no. 850	2,920.00
12/01/2019	Lodgement	8,622.00	22/01/2019	Cheque no. 851	1,863.00
28/01/2019	Lodgement	2,450.00	31/01/2019	Balance c/d	16,439.00
		21,222.00			21,222.00
01/02/2019	Balance b/d	16,439.00			

H. Wright has received his bank statement, which details the following transactions:

Friendly Bank plc
52 Main Street
Market

Statement date:
31 January 2019

Page no. 82

Date	Transaction Details	Debit €	Credit €	Balance €
1 January	Balance forward			10,150.00
10 January	Cheque no. 850	2,920.00		
	Fees and charges	82.15		7,147.85
12 January	Lodgement		8,622.00	15,769.85
18 January	DD electricity	654.39		15,115.46
28 January	Lodgement		2,450.00	17,565.46

Step 1 Compare the bank statement with H. Wright's records and, starting with the bank statement, mark off each item against H. Wright's bank records as follows:

Use 'A' to indicate that the item has been agreed to both the bank's statement and H. Wright's records.

Friendly Bank plc
52 Main Street
Market

Statement date:
31 January 2019

Page no. 82

Date	Transaction Details	Debit €		Credit €		Balance €	
1 January	Balance forward					10,150.00	A
10 January	Cheque no. 850	2,920.00	A				
12 January	Fees and charges	82.15				7,147.85	
18 January	Lodgement			8,622.00	A	15,769.85	
28 January	DD electricity	654.39				15,115.46	
	Lodgement			2,450.00	A	17,565.46	

BANK ACCOUNT

Date	Detail	€		Date	Detail	€	
01/01/2019	Balance b/d	10,150.00	A	05/01/2019	Cheque no. 850	2,920.00	A
12/01/2019	Lodgement	8,622.00	A	22/01/2019	Cheque no. 851	1,863.00	
28/01/2019	Lodgement	2,450.00	A	31/01/2019	Balance c/d	16,439.00	
		21,222.00				21,222.00	
01/02/2019	Balance b/d	16,439.00					

From the checking exercise the following items are noted:

Item	Action to Take
Fees and charges on bank statement	Fees and charges have been charged by the bank in relation to the services provided by it. The fees and charges have not been recorded in the entity's own records. The journal entry to recognise this transaction must be recorded in the entity's financial records as follows:

	Debit €	Credit €
Bank charges account	82.15	
Bank account		82.15

Direct debit for electricity on bank statement	The electricity expense has been charged to the bank as a result of a direct debit raised by the service provider. The electricity expense has not been recorded in the entity's own records. The journal entry to recognise this transaction must be recorded in the entity's financial records as follows:

	Debit €	Credit €
Electricity expense account	654.39	
Bank account		654.39

Cheque no. 851 is recorded in H. Wright's bank records but not on bank statement.

The cheque is in the financial records of H. Wright but has not yet been presented to the bank for payment. This item will form part of the bank reconciliation.

Step 2 Make adjustments, as necessary, to H. Wright's bank account:

BANK ACCOUNT

Date	Account Name	€	Date	Account Name	€
01/02/2019	Balance b/d	16,439.00	01/02/2019	Fees	82.15
			01/02/2019	Electricity	654.39
			01/02/2019	Balance c/d	15,702.46
		16,439.00			16,439.00
01/02/2019	Balance b/d	15,702.46			

Step 3 Prepare the bank reconciliation.

BANK RECONCILIATION
as at 1 February 2019

	€
Balance per bank statement	17,565.46
Unpresented cheques:	
Cheque no. 851	(1,863.00)
Balance per bank account	15,702.46

The adjusted balance of €15,702.46 is the figure presented in the statement of financial position (SOFP) of H. Wright as its bank balance.

(Try **Review Question 10.2** at the end of this chapter.)

Opening Balances on the Bank Statement and the Entity's Records do not Agree

In the previous examples the opening balances in the entity's records and the bank statement have agreed. If the balances are different, the difference will be explained in the reconciliation prepared at the previous reconciliation date.

Example 10.3 demonstrates the reconciliation when the opening balances do not agree.

EXAMPLE 10.3: RECONCILING ITEMS AT THE START OF THE PERIOD

You have been provided with the following information from the accounting records of W. Gunne:

BANK ACCOUNT

Date	Detail	€	Date	Detail	€
01/03/2019	Balance b/d	14,690	02/03/2019	Cheque no. 814	6,390
21/03/2019	Lodgement	8,370	10/03/2019	Cheque no. 815	4,215
31/03/2019	Lodgement	1,490	31/03/2019	Balance c/d	13,945
		24,550			24,550
01/04/2019	Balance b/d	13,945			

W. Gunne has received his bank statement, which details the following transactions:

Friendly Bank plc
52 Main Street
Market

Statement date:
31 March 2019

Page no. 56

Date	Transaction Details	Debit €	Credit €	Balance €
1 March	Balance forward			18,244
2 March	Cheque no. 801	2,000		16,244
12 March	Cheque no. 814	6,390		9,854
18 March	Cheque no. 804	1,554		8,300
21 March	Lodgement		8,370	16,670

Step 1 The first thing that should always be checked is that the opening balance on the bank statement agrees to the opening balance on the entity's records. In this case there is a difference of €3,554 [€18,244 − €14,690]. If the last reconciliation prepared were scrutinised, the details of the transactions that make up this difference could be discovered, but it has not been provided.

From a careful consideration of W. Gunne's records it can be seen that the first cheque issued this period was cheque number 814. In the bank statement provided by the financial institution it can be seen that there were two cheques presented to the bank for payment during the period with cheque numbers lower than 814. In an exam situation it could be assumed that cheques are issued sequentially and that these cheques (numbers 801 and 804) were recorded in W. Gunne's records in an earlier period and make up the difference in the opening balances.

	€
Balance per bank statement at start of period	18,244
Cheques unpresented at start of period:	
Cheque no. 801	(2,000) B
Cheque no. 804	(1,554) B
Balance per W. Gunne's records at the start of the period	14,690

Both of these cheques have been agreed to the bank statement so will no longer be part of the reconciliation.

Step 2 Compare the bank statement and W. Gunne's records and, starting with the bank statement, mark off each item against W. Gunne's bank records as follows:

Use an 'A' to indicate that the item has been agreed to both bank statement and our own records.

BANK ACCOUNT

Date	Detail	€	Date	Detail	€	
01/03/2019	Balance b/d	14,690	02/03/2019	Cheque no. 814	6,390	A
21/03/2019	Lodgement	8,370 A	10/03/2019	Cheque no. 815	4,215	
31/03/2019	Lodgement	1,490	31/03/2019	Balance c/d	13,945	
		24,550			24,550	
01/04/2019	Balance b/d	13,945				

W. Gunne has received his bank statement, which details the following transactions:

Friendly Bank plc
52 Main Street
Market

Statement date:
31 March 2019

Page no. 56

Date	Transaction Details	Debit €		Credit €		Balance €
1 March	Balance forward					18,244
2 March	Cheque no. 801	2,000	B			16,244
12 March	Cheque no. 814	6,390	A			9,854
18 March	Cheque no. 804	1,554	B			8,300
21 March	Lodgement			8,370	A	16,670

From the checking exercise, the following items will be noted:

Item	Action to Take
Lodgement recorded 31 March.	The lodgement has been recorded in W. Gunne's records but has not been recorded in the bank statement.
	No adjustment is required to W. Gunne's records, but the item will form part of the reconciliation to explain the difference between the balance per the bank statement and the balance in W. Gunne's financial records.
Cheque no. 815 issued.	The cheque has been recorded in W. Gunne's records but has not been presented for payment to the bank.
	No adjustment is required to W. Gunne's records, but the item will form part of the reconciliation to explain the difference between the balance per the bank statement and the balance in W. Gunne's financial records.

Step 3 Make the necessary adjustments to W. Gunne's bank account.

Based on the above issues no adjustment is required to be made to the business records.

Step 4 Prepare the bank reconciliation.

BANK RECONCILIATION
as at 1 April 2019

	€
Balance per bank statement	16,670
Unpresented cheques:	
Cheque no. 851	(4,215)
	12,455
Lodgement not in bank statement	1,490
Balance per bank account	13,945

The balance of €13,945 is the figure presented in the SOFP of W. Gunne as the bank balance.

(Try **Review Question 10.3** at the end of this chapter.)

EXAM TIPS

- Have an approach to questions and follow it.
- Always check if the opening balances on the bank statement and business's own records agree or not, a difference is easily missed in an exam situation.
- Be careful when the bank balances are overdrawn: unpresented cheques will increase the overdraft on the account.

10.3 CONCLUSION

It is important that the bank figure presented in the financial statements is accurate. To ensure the figure is correct the balance on the statement issued by the bank is reconciled to the entity's bank records.

Items that are not reflected in the entity's financial records must be recorded in the entity's ledger accounts.

SUMMARY OF LEARNING OBJECTIVES

After having studied this chapter, readers should be able to:

Learning Objective 1 Explain why a bank reconciliation is prepared.

A bank reconciliation highlights items that have not been recorded in the financial records of the entity, any errors made in the recording of transactions that affect the bank accounts, and transactions that have not been presented at the bank yet.

Learning Objective 2 Reconcile the balance on the bank statement with the balance on the entity's bank account.

The following approach should be adopted for reconciliation questions.
1. Check the opening balances agree – if not, determine why they are different.
2. Check off items on the bank statement against the entity's bank record.
3. Identify the unticked items and determine whether they impact the business's bank account or are part of the reconciliation.
4. Make any necessary adjustment(s) to the business's own records.
5. Prepare the bank reconciliation.

QUESTIONS

Review Questions

(See **Appendix A** for Solutions to Review Questions.)

Question 10.1

You have been provided the following information from the accounting records of B. Wing:

BANK ACCOUNT

Date	Detail	€	Date	Detail	€
01/01/2019	Balance b/d	12,615	04/01/2019	Cheque no. 108	809
06/01/2019	Lodgement	2,239	08/01/2019	Cheque no. 109	499
19/01/2019	Lodgement	5,600	12/01/2019	Cheque no. 110	3,280
			22/01/2019	Cheque no. 111	1,745
			31/01/2019	Balance c/d	14,121
		20,454			20,454
01/02/2019	Balance b/d	14,121			

B. Wing has received his bank statement, which details the following transactions:

All Bank plc
38 Main Street
Wilderness

B. Wing
Account Number: 82255771

Page no. 82

Date	Transaction Details	Debit €	Credit €	Balance €
1 January	Balance forward			12,615
7 January	Lodgement		2,239	
	Cheque no. 108	809		14,045
15 January	Cheque no. 110	3,280		10,765
20 January	Lodgement		5,600	16,365

Requirement Prepare the bank reconciliation as at 31 January 2019.

Question 10.2

You have been provided with the following information from the accounting records of L. Brown:

BANK ACCOUNT

Date	Detail	€	Date	Detail	€
01/01/2019	Balance b/d	8,222	06/01/2019	Cheque no. 704	911
06/01/2019	Lodgement	1,654	07/01/2019	Cheque no. 705	1,255
31/01/2019	Lodgement	10,940	13/01/2019	Cheque no. 706	1,970
			28/01/2019	Cheque no. 707	744
			31/01/2019	Balance c/d	15,936
		20,816			20,816
01/02/2019	Balance b/d	15,936			

L. Brown has received his bank statement, which details the following transactions:

All Bank plc
38 Main Street
Wilderness

B. Wing
Account Number: 82255771

Page no. 121

Date	Transaction Details	Debit €	Credit €	Balance €
1 January	Balance forward			8,222
7 January	Lodgement		1,654	9,876
9 January	Cheque no. 705	1,255		8,621
20 January	Fees and charges	95		8,526
29 January	Cheque no. 707	744		7,782

Requirement Prepare the bank reconciliation as at 31 January 2019.

Question 10.3

You have been provided with the following information from the accounting records of J. Stone:

BANK ACCOUNT

Date	Detail	€	Date	Detail	€
01/03/2019	Balance b/d	14,822.00	03/03/2019	Cheque no. 245	3,080.00
05/03/2019	Lodgement	5,695.00	08/03/2019	Cheque no. 246	2,546.00
15/03/2019	Lodgement	6,450.00	12/03/2019	Cheque no. 247	955.00
			21/03/2019	Cheque no. 248	2,812.00
			31/03/2019	Balance c/d	17,574.00
		26,967.00			26,967.00
01/04/2019	Balance b/d	17,574.00			

J. Stone has received his bank statement, which details the following transactions:

All Bank plc
38 Main Street
Wilderness

J. Stone
Account Number: 82965478

Page no. 91

Date	Transaction Details	Debit €	Credit €	Balance €
1 March	Balance forward			15,633.00
6 March	Lodgement		5,695.00	21,328.00
9 March	Cheque no. 242	766.00		
	Fees and charges	87.50		20,474.50
16 March	Cheque no. 245	3,080.00		
			6,450.00	23.844.50
20 March	DD electricity	560.00		23,284.50
26 March	Cheque no. 239	45.00		23,239.50
30 March	Cheque no. 247	955.00		22,284.50

Requirement Prepare the bank reconciliation as at 31 March 2019.

Challenging Questions

(Suggested Solutions to Challenging Questions are available through your lecturer.)

Question 10.1

Olive was made redundant in 2017 and decided to use her severance pay to set up her own jewellery business on 1 January 2018. On that date she opened a business bank account and lodged €50,000. Since then she has been busy establishing her business and has kept limited records. She has given you the summary below, together with her bank statements for the year:

	€
Loan received from local enterprise agency (interest-free)	20,000
Cash sales	67,200
Cheques paid: purchases for resale	42,240
Purchase of shop lease (20-year term)	10,000
Rent and rates	5,700
Insurance	2,400
Wages for Olive	24,000
Wages for assistants	13,500
Shop fittings, including installation	22,150
Purchase of computer for Olive's daughter	600
Other general expenses	2,650

1. All sales are for cash.
2. Trade payables at 31 December 2018 amounted to €1,330 and inventory at that date was valued at cost at €9,460.
3. 'Rent and rates' includes rent for the quarter ended 31 March 2019 of €1,000.

4. All cash sales were banked with the exception of:

	€
Stationery and marketing	1,430
Repairs and maintenance	560
A cash float	200

5. The bank statement at 31 December 2018 shows a balance in hand of €12,680. Upon investigation you discover that:
- Lodgements made by Olive on 31 December 2018 of €1,390 had not been reflected in the bank statement until 3 January 2019.
- Cheques totalling €2,550, written by Olive in December 2018, had not been cleared through the bank until January 2019.
- Bank charges of €250 have not been recorded by Olive.
- The lease is to be written off on a straight-line basis over its life. Shop fittings are to be depreciated at 20% on a reducing-balance basis.
- The loan is interest-free and repayable in 10 equal instalments commencing on 10 January 2019.
6. Ignore VAT.

Requirement
(a) Prepare T accounts for the year ended 31 December 2018 for:
  (i) Bank account;
  (ii) Cash account;
  (iii) Payables.

8 Minutes

(b) Prepare the bank reconciliation statement as at 31 December 2018.

3 Minutes

(c) Prepare an income statement for the year ended 31 December 2018.

10 Minutes

(d) Prepare the statement of financial position of Olive as at 31 December 2018.

8 Minutes

(Based on Chartered Accountants Ireland, CAP 1 Financial Accounting, Summer 2010, Question 3)

Question 10.2

Raymond's cash book and bank statement are given below:

BANK STATEMENT 2019

		€	€	€
Dec 1	Balance brought forward			1,490.95
Dec 2	Cheque no. 123	145.00		1,345.95
Dec 9	Cheque no. 127	698.00		647.95
Dec 11	Lodgement		4,987.00	5,634.95
Dec 14	Cheque no. 125	1,050.00		4,584.95
	Bank charges	295.67		4,289.28
Dec 18	SO lease payment	335.00		3,954.28
	Lodgement 102		3,680.00	7,634.28
Dec 20	Cheque no. 128	499.99		7,134.29
Dec 22	Electronic transfer of funds		1,320.00	8,454.29
	Dishonoured cheque	500.00		7.954.29
	Dishonoured cheque	25.00		7,929.29

CASH BOOK

2019		€	2019		€
Dec 1	Balance b/f	1,490.95	Dec 4	Cheque no. 123	145.00
Dec 8	Lodgement	4,987.00	Dec 5	Cheque no. 124	54.96
Dec 15	Lodgement	3,860.00	Dec 7	Cheque no. 125	1,050.00
Dec 27	Lodgement	105.50	Dec 7	Cheque no. 126	368.95
				Cheque no. 127	698.00
			Dec 10	Cheque no. 128	449.99
			Dec 20	Cheque no. 129	78.64
				Cheque no. 130	245.50
				Balance c/f	7,352.41
		10,443.45			10,443.45

Note: upon investigation, it has been confirmed that all cheque amounts written up by Raymond in the cash book are correct. Lodgements in the bank statement may be assumed to be correct.

Requirement

(a) Prepare the cash book of Raymond to 31 December 2019 and state the amount to be included in Raymond's statement of financial position as at 31 December 2019.

10 Minutes

(b) Prepare the bank reconciliation statement as at 31 December 2019.

10 Minutes

(c) Explain why it is important to prepare bank reconciliation statements on a regular basis.

3 Minutes

(Based on Chartered Accountants Ireland, CAP 1 Financial Accounting, Summer 2011, Question 6)

11

Suspense Accounts

Learning Objectives

Having studied this chapter, readers should be able to:
1. explain the different types of errors that may occur in the recording of transactions;
2. identify the circumstances when a suspense account may be used; and
3. correct errors made when transactions were originally recorded.

11.1 INTRODUCTION

In **Chapter 2, Recording Financial Transactions and Preparing Financial Statements** the concept of double-entry bookkeeping was explained and applied to the correct recording of transactions. In this chapter transactions that have been recorded **incorrectly** during the reporting period will be reviewed and the necessary journal entries to correct these errors explained.

In the preparation of a trial balance the total of all the accounts with debit balances should equal the total of all the accounts with credit balances. Errors may occur in the recording of transactions – these errors may result in the trial balance not balancing (that is, the totals of all the debit and credit balances do not equal). When the total of all accounts with debit balances is not equal to the total of all accounts with credit balances, a **suspense account** is presented in the trial balance. The suspense account can have either a debit or credit balance. If the total of all the accounts with debit balances is, say, €190,000 and the total of all the accounts with credit balances is, say, €188,700 then the suspense account will be presented in the trial balance with a €1,300 credit balance; the impact of the inclusion of the suspense account is that the total of all accounts with debit balances now equals the total of all accounts with credit balances. Conversely, if the total of all the accounts with debit balances is, say, €214,500 and the total of all the accounts with credit balances is, say, €220,600 then the suspense account will be presented in the trial balance with a €6,100 debit balance.

It is important to note that not all errors will result in the total of all accounts with debit balances not agreeing with the total of all accounts with credit balances.

11.2 ERRORS THAT DO NOT UPSET THE BALANCING OF THE TRIAL BALANCE

There are a number of different types of errors that do not result in the trial balance not balancing. These errors include:
- error of omission;
- error of commission;
- error of principle;

- error of original entry;
- complete reversal of entries;
- transposition error; and
- compensating errors.

Each of these errors will be dealt with in turn and the approach taken to correcting errors will be:

Step 1 identify the journal entry that should have been recorded to recognise the transaction correctly;

Step 2 set out the journal entry recorded by the entity; and

Step 3 prepare the journal entry required, if any, to correct the original transaction.

Error of Omission

An **error of omission** occurs when a transaction is not recorded in the financial records of the entity at all. For example, Sweeney Ltd paid an insurance invoice of €850 by cheque but did not post an accounting journal entry in relation to this payment. Both sides of the accounting entry have been omitted so the trial balance of Sweeney will still balance. The expense and its payment need to be recognised in the company's financial statements, so the following journal entry has to be posted:

	Debit €	Credit €
Insurance expense account	850	
Bank account		850

To recognise the insurance expense omitted from the financial records.

This error would be detected when the company's bank records were compared to the bank statement issued by the bank. In the bank statement issued by the bank there would be an entry on the date the cheque was presented for payment and when the entity prepared its bank reconciliation the error would be detected.

Error of Commission

An **error of commission** occurs when a transaction is recorded in the wrong account but the account is the correct type of account (that is, income, expense, asset, liability or capital). For example, a credit sale of €1,280 to D. Flynn is posted incorrectly to F. Flynn's receivables account. The incorrect entry needs to be corrected.

Step 1 The following journal entry should have been posted:

	Debit €	Credit €
Trade receivables account – D. Flynn	1,280	
Sales account		1,280

To recognise the credit sale.

Step 2 However, the following journal entry was posted in error:

	Debit €	Credit €
Trade receivables account – F. Flynn	1,280	
Sales account		1,280

To recognise the credit sale.

Step 3 The journal entry to correct the error would be:

	Debit €	Credit €
Trade receivables account – D. Flynn	1,280	
Trade receivables account – F. Flynn		1,280
Correction of incorrect journal entry posted.		

This error will be discovered when the company issues customer statements. Upon receipt of the statement the customer will reconcile the balance on the statement received with its own records; the reconciliation will show that an invoice has been recorded in error. The customer will contact the entity to resolve the issue.

Error of Principle

From **Chapter 2** we know that there are a number of different types of account: income, expense, asset, liability and capital. An **error of principle** occurs when the journal entry is posted not only to the wrong account but to the wrong account type. For example, a company incurs machine maintenance costs of €8,200, which it pays by cheque but it posts the debit side of the entry to the machine cost account. The machine maintenance account is an example of an expense account while the machine cost account is an asset account. The incorrect entry needs to be corrected.

Step 1 The journal entry that should have been posted:

	Debit €	Credit €
Machine maintenance expense account	8,200	
Bank account		8,200
To recognise the machine maintenance expense.		

Step 2 The journal entry that was posted:

	Debit €	Credit €
Machine – cost account	8,200	
Bank account		8,200
To recognise the machine maintenance expense.		

Step 3 The journal entry to correct the error would be:

	Debit €	Credit €
Machine maintenance expense account	8,200	
Machine – cost account		8,200
To correct journal entry.		

Error of Original Entry

An **error of original entry** is made when the correct accounts are debited and credited to record the transaction but the incorrect amounts have been posted. For example, Warner Ltd incurs rent expenses of €1,900 but when recording the journal entry in the financial records does so for an amount of €900 (the correct accounts were debited and credited when the journal entry was posted).

Step 1 The journal entry that should have been posted was:

	Debit €	Credit €
Rent expense account	1,900	
Bank account		1,900

To recognise the rent expense.

Step 2 The journal entry that was posted in error:

	Debit €	Credit €
Rent expense account	900	
Bank account		900

To recognise the rent expense.

Step 3 The only error made in the journal entry was that the rent expense for the period should have been for €1,900. The incorrect entry needs to be corrected:

	Debit €	Credit €
Rent expense account	1,000	
Bank account		1,000

To correct the rent expense recognised.

Complete Reversal of Entries

When an error involving the complete reversal of entries has been made, the transaction has been posted incorrectly: the accounts have been correctly identified but the journal entry has been completely reversed. For example, a cash sale for €650 has been recorded by debiting revenue and crediting cash.

Step 1 The journal entry that should have been posted was:

	Debit €	Credit €
Cash account	650	
Revenue account		650

To recognise the cash sale.

Step 2 The journal entry that was posted in error:

	Debit €	Credit €
Revenue account	650	
Cash account		650

To recognise the cash sale.

Step 3 The original journal entry needs to be corrected as follows:

	Debit €	Credit €
Cash account	1,300	
Revenue account		1,300

To correct the journal entry posted.

You will notice that to correct this error the amount of the journal entry is double the amount of the original transaction; this is necessary when a debit entry is posted as a credit entry in error or vice versa.

Transposition Error

When a transposition error is made the accounts debited and credited are correct but the amount is incorrect, that is, the figures in the amount of the transaction have been reversed. For example, Toomey Ltd purchased €140 worth of goods for cash but the transaction was recorded as €410.

Step 1 The journal entry that should have been posted:

	Debit €	Credit €
Purchases account	140	
Cash account		140
To recognise cash purchases.		

Step 2 The incorrect journal entry that was posted:

	Debit €	Credit €
Purchases account	410	
Cash account		410
To recognise cash purchases.		

Step 3 To correct the error:

	Debit €	Credit €
Cash account	270	
Purchases account		270
To recognise cash purchases previously incorrectly recorded.		

Compensating Errors

Compensating errors occur when a number of errors are made that cancel each other out. For example, the following transactions were recorded in the period:

A supplier has issued an invoice to the entity detailing maintenance costs and a new item of equipment. On the invoice the maintenance costs for the period were €2,800 and the equipment cost €4,500. The entity paid the invoice by cheque and posted the following journal entry to its accounting system:

	Debit €	Credit €
Equipment – cost account	4,800	
Maintenance costs account	2,500	
Bank account		7,300
To recognise payment of invoice.		

When the entity recorded the above transaction it made an error in the attribution of costs to both the maintenance costs and the new equipment. The error made resulted in the new equipment being recognised at €300 above the cost per the invoice and the maintenance costs being recognised at €300 below the invoice amount. The error made in relation to the cost of the asset cancelled out the impact in relation to the maintenance costs and vice versa.

This error will not impact the suspense account. To correct the errors made, the following journal entry must be posted:

	Debit €	Credit €
Maintenance costs account	300	
Equipment – cost account		300

To correct the error made.

When an error results in the total of all accounts with debit balances not equalling the total of all accounts with credit balances the difference is recognised in a suspense account. The balance on the suspense account may be either a debit or a credit balance; it is investigated and the reasons for the difference found and corrected.

11.3 WHEN A SUSPENSE ACCOUNT IS IMPACTED BY A TRANSACTION ERROR

A suspense account is used to ensure that the accounting system is balanced, i.e. the total of the debits and credits are equal. There are a number of circumstances in which a transaction will impact a suspense account:

- When recording a transaction, the debit and credit sides of the transaction must be equal (see **Chapter 2**). If the transaction does not balance, the computer system will automatically balance the accounting system by either debiting or crediting the suspense account as required.
- The person preparing the journal entry is unsure how to process the transaction fully so they post part of the transaction to the suspense account.
- The accounts affected by the transaction may not be set up on the computer system so the transaction may be posted temporarily to the suspense account until the correct account is set up.

Most computer systems will generate a daily report identifying any transactions posted to the suspense account. This report will be actioned by someone who is responsible for clearing the suspense account.

Example 11.1 demonstrates the situation where a transaction is not balanced, that is the total of the debit side of the transaction is not equal to the credit side of the transaction.

EXAMPLE 11.1: TRANSACTION NOT BALANCED

The junior accountant has recorded the receipt of cash from a credit customer as follows:

	Debit €	Credit €
Cash	804	
Trade receivables	804	

Requirement:
(a) Did this transaction, as processed by the junior accountant, impact the suspense account?
(b) What was the impact on the suspense account?
(c) How will the transaction be corrected?

Solution
(a) Yes, this transaction will impact the suspense account. The transaction as recorded by the junior accountant is not balanced – the total of the debit side of the transaction is €1,608 but the total of the credit side is €Nil. In these circumstances the computer system will

automatically generate a transaction to the suspense account to balance up the financial records of the entity.

(b) The impact on the suspense account is that a credit entry of €1,608 will be posted to the suspense account to balance up the accounting journal entry.

	Debit €	Credit €
Cash account	804	
Trade receivables account	804	
Suspense account (automatically generated by computer system)		1,608

(c) In order to work out how to correct an error, the following step-by-step approach is recommended:

Step 1 Detail the journal entry that should have been processed.

In this case the journal entry should have been:

	Debit €	Credit €
Cash account	804	
Trade receivables account		804
To recognise payment received from credit customer.		

Step 2 Detail how the transaction was processed.

In this case the journal entry processed was:

	Debit €	Credit €
Cash account	804	
Trade receivables account	804	
Suspense account (automatically generated by computer system)		1,608

Step 3 Correct the error.

In this case the cash side of the transaction has been correctly recorded but the trade receivables account has been debited instead of being credited. The journal entry to correct this error is:

	Debit €	Credit €
Suspense account	1,608	
Trade receivables account		1,608
To correct journal entry processed incorrectly.		

The next example involves a situation where there is both a debit and a credit element to the incorrectly recorded transaction but the amounts of the debit and credit sides of the transaction are not equal.

Example 11.2 demonstrates the situation where the journal entry is not balanced.

EXAMPLE 11.2: CORRECTION OF ERROR

The accounts assistant got distracted while processing the credit purchase of goods for €532 and made the following journal entry:

	Debit €	Credit €
Purchases account	532	
Trade payables account		52

Requirement:
(a) Did this transaction, as processed by the accounts assistant, impact the suspense account?
(b) What was the impact on the suspense account?
(c) How will the transaction be corrected?

Solution

(a) Yes, the suspense account will be impacted by this transaction. The transaction as recorded by the accounts assistant is not balanced – the total of the debit side of the transaction is €532, but the total of the credit side is only €52. In these circumstances the computer system will automatically generate a transaction to the suspense account to balance up the financial records of the entity.

(b) The impact on the suspense account is a credit entry of €480, i.e. the difference between the debit amount of €532 and the credit amount of €52. This will be processed to suspense account to balance up the journal entry.

	Debit €	Credit €
Purchases account	532	
Trade payables account		52
Suspense account (automatically generated by computer system)		480

(c)

Step 1 Detail the journal entry that should have been processed.

In this case the journal entry should have been:

	Debit €	Credit €
Purchases account	532	
Trade payables account		532

To recognise credit purchase of goods.

Step 2 Detail how the transaction was processed.

In this case the journal entry processed was:

	Debit €	Credit €
Purchases account	532	
Trade payables account		52
Suspense account (automatically generated by computer system)		480

Step 3 Correct the error.

In this case the purchases side of the transaction has been correctly recorded but the incorrect amount has been posted to the trade payables – €52 instead of €532. The journal entry to correct this error is:

	Debit €	Credit €
Suspense account	480	
Trade payables account		480
To correct journal entry processed incorrectly.		

Example 11.3 demonstrates an incorrectly processed transaction and discusses its impact on the suspense account.

EXAMPLE 11.3: CORRECTION OF ERROR

On 20 December a cash payment of €180 was received from A. Murphy, a credit customer. The transaction was processed as follows:

	Debit €	Credit €
Cash account	180	
Trade receivables account – M. Murphy		180
To recognise cash received from a credit customer.		

Requirement Explain the impact of the above transaction on the suspense account.

Solution

The totals of the debit and credit sides of the transaction processed are equal so there is no impact on the suspense account. This error will not be detected by a review of the suspense account as no entry will be recorded in the suspense account.

Other controls in place within the entity would highlight this error, such as issue of statements of account to customers. When the customer receives the statement issued they would compare it to their own records and inform the entity that a payment made has not been processed to their account.

The error still needs to be corrected so that the payment is recorded against the correct credit customer:

	Debit €	Credit €
Trade receivables account – M. Murphy	180	
Trade receivables account – A. Murphy		180
To correct the payment processed from a credit customer incorrectly.		

(Try **Review Questions 11.1–11.5** at the end of this chapter.)

11.4 SUSPENSE ACCOUNT

The purpose of this section is to work through a full question and identify whether or not a suspense account is impacted by various issues and quantify any impact on profit.

EXAMPLE 11.4: SUSPENSE ACCOUNT

You have been informed that there is a debit balance of €294 on the suspense account and asked to deal with the following issues.

Issue 1   The company has purchased a new computer for €3,200. The computer was paid for by cheque. The bookkeeper has charged the cost of the computer to the computer expense account. The useful life of the computer is estimated at five years and depreciation is charged on a straight-line basis. The company's policy is to charge a full year's depreciation in the year of purchase and none in the year of disposal.

Issue 2   The company received cash of €810 from one of its customers in relation to a cash sales transaction. The sales account has been credited with €810 and the cash account debited with €180.

Issue 3   A credit customer has returned goods with a retail value of €4,500. The goods were sold at a price to generate a mark-up of 25% on cost. No entry has been made in relation to this transaction.

Issue 4   The company owed one of its suppliers €8,400; the supplier offered a discount of 2% for early payment. The company availed of this discount and paid the amount net of the discount within the credit period. The cheque payment was correctly recorded, but the discount received has been debited to the discounts allowed account.

Requirement:
(a) Prepare any journal entries required to correct any errors made in the processing of the above transactions. Explain the impact on the reported profit of the correcting journal entry, if any.
(b) Prepare the suspense account.

Solution
(a)

Issue 1   The company has purchased a new computer for €3,200. The computer was paid for by cheque. The bookkeeper has charged the cost of the computer to the computer expense account. The useful life of the computer is estimated at five years and the company's policy is to charge a full year's depreciation in the year of purchase and none in the year of disposal.

Step 1 Detail of the journal entry that should have been processed.

	Debit €	Credit €
Computer asset – cost account	3,200	
Bank account		3,200

To recognise the purchase of a computer for use over five years.

Step 2 Detail of how the transaction was processed.

	Debit €	Credit €
Computer expense account	3,200	
Bank account		3,200

Step 3 Correction of the error.

There is no impact on the suspense account as the debit side of the transaction is equal to the credit side of the transaction.

	Debit €	Credit €
Computer asset – cost account	3,200	
Computer expenses account		3,200

To correct a journal entry that was processed incorrectly.

The original transaction resulted in an item of capital expenditure (the purchase of the computer) being treated as an expense. When the correcting journal entry is posted, this will impact the reported profit; the reversal of the computer expense will result in the reported profit increasing by €3,200.

Assets used over more than one reporting period are depreciated over their estimated useful life (see **Chapter 6, Property, Plant and Equipment, and Depreciation**). The correcting journal entry will result in an item of property, plant and equipment being recognised, so a depreciation charge will have to be included in the financial statements. The depreciation charge is €640 [€3,200 ÷ 5 years]. The journal entry to recognise the depreciation charge is:

	Debit €	Credit €
Depreciation expense account	640	
Accumulated depreciation account		640

To recognise the depreciation charge on the computer equipment.

The reported profit will be reduced by the depreciation charge of €640.

Issue 2   The company received cash of €810 from one of its customers in relation to a cash sales transaction. The sales account has been credited with €810 and the cash account debited with €180.

Step 1 Detail the journal entry that should have been processed.

	Debit €	Credit €
Cash account	810	
Sales account		810

To recognise cash sales.

Step 2 Detail how the transaction was processed.

	Debit €	Credit €
Cash account	180	
Suspense account	630	
Sales account		810

There is an impact on the suspense account as the debit and credit sides of the transaction are not equal.

Step 3 Correct the error.

	Debit €	Credit €
Cash account	630	
Suspense account		630

To correct journal entry processed incorrectly.

(b)

SUSPENSE ACCOUNT

Date	Account Name	€	Date	Account Name	€
	Opening balance	294		Cash	630

Issue 3 A credit customer has returned goods with a retail value of €4,500. The goods were sold at a price to generate a mark-up of 25% on cost. No entry has been made in relation to this transaction.

There is no impact on the suspense account as no journal entry has been recorded in the financial records.

When goods are returned by a customer there are two journal entries required:
1. recognise the sales returns;
2. recognise the goods returned at their cost (not sales value) in the financial statements.

	Debit €	Credit €
Sales returns account	4,500	
Trade receivables account		4,500

To recognise return of goods by credit customer.

	Debit €	Credit €
Inventory account	3,600	
Cost of sales		3,600

To recognise the inventory [€4,500 × 100/125].

Profit will be reduced by €900 as a result of the goods returned now being recognised in the financial statements.

Issue 4 The company owed one of its suppliers €8,400; the supplier offered a discount of 2% for early payment. The company availed of this discount and paid the amount net of the discount within the credit period. The cheque payment was correctly recorded, but the discount received has been debited to the discounts allowed account.

Discount received: €8,400 × 2% = €168.

Step 1 Detail the journal entry that should have been processed.

	Debit €	Credit €
Trade payables account	8,400	
Discounts received account		168
Bank account		8,232

To recognise payment net of discount received.

Step 2 Detail how the transaction was processed.

	Debit €	Credit €
Trade payables account	8,400	
Discounts allowed account	168	
Bank account		8,232
Suspense account		336

Step 3 Correct the error.

There is an impact on the suspense account as the debit side of the transaction is not equal to the credit side of the transaction.

	Debit €	Credit €
Suspense account	336	
Discounts allowed account		168
Discounts received account		168

To correct journal entry processed incorrectly.

The profit will be increased by €336 as a result of the correction of this error. An expense was erroneously recorded in relation to discount **allowed** when an income of discount **received** should have been recorded.

SUSPENSE ACCOUNT

Date	Account Name	€	Date	Account Name	€
	Opening balance	294		Cash	630
	Discounts allowed	168			
	Discounts received	168			
		630			630

EXAM TIPS

- Read the information carefully, note the nature of the transaction and prepare the journal entry that should have been processed.
- A good knowledge of the preparation of journal entries is necessary in order to be able to identify incorrect journal entries posted and to prepare the necessary correcting journal entries.
- Be able to quantify the impact on the entity's profit of the correction of each error.
- Issues that commonly cause problems are around the area of discounts allowed and discounts received – be clear on the accounting treatment of these.

11.5 CONCLUSION

Errors may occur in the recording of transactions; controls in place within the organisation will identify these errors, which will then have to be corrected. Errors may or may not impact a suspense account.

The suspense account is impacted when:
- the journal entry does not balance, i.e. the total of the debit entries in the journal does not equal the total of the credit entries in the journal; or
- the person preparing the journal entry is unsure of the appropriate accounting treatment and posted the entry to the suspense account as a temporary measure.

SUMMARY OF LEARNING OBJECTIVES

After having studied this chapter, readers should be able to:

Learning Objective 1 Explain the different types of errors that may occur in the recording of transactions.

There are errors that occur which do **not** result in the total of the accounts with debit balances and the total of the accounts with credit balances differing. These errors are:
- errors of omission;
- errors of commission;
- errors of principle;
- errors of original entry;
- transposition errors; and
- compensating errors.

Errors that will cause the trial balance totals to differ are as a result of transactions being recorded where the totals of the debits and credits do not agree. These errors impact the suspense account.

Learning Objective 2 Identify the circumstances when a suspense account may be used.

When transactions are being processed the suspense account will be impacted when:
- the total of the debit side of the transaction does not agree with the total of the credit side of the transaction; or
- the person who processed the transaction is unsure how to process the transaction so puts one side of it into the suspense account; or
- one of the accounts involved in the transaction has not been set up correctly and the transaction cannot be posted to it.

Learning Objective 3 Correct errors made when transactions were originally recorded.

Adopt the following approach until you are more confident with the correction of errors.
1. Write down how the transaction should have been recorded.
2. Write down how the transaction was recorded. Remember that if the transaction is not balanced, an entry is posted to the suspense account to balance the financial records.
3. Based on the comparison of the journal entries in (1) and (2) prepare the journal entry to correct the error.

QUESTIONS

Review Questions

(See **Appendix A** for Solutions to Review Questions.)

Question 11.1

The trainee accounts assistant has recorded the purchase of machinery as follows:

	Debit €	Credit €
Machine – cost account	80,000	
Loan account	80,000	

To record the purchase of machinery financed by a loan.

Requirement Prepare the correcting journal entry, if any, in relation to the above transaction.

Question 11.2

The following journal entry was posted in relation to a capital repayment of a loan:

	Debit €	Credit €
Bank account	5,000	
Loan account		5,000

To record the capital repayment of a loan.

Requirement Prepare the correcting journal entry, if any, in relation to the above transaction.

Question 11.3

Swan Ltd received a discount from one of its suppliers of €230, which the bookkeeper treated as a discount allowed. The entry to the trade payables account was correctly recorded.

Requirement Prepare the correcting journal entry, if any, in relation to the above transaction.

Question 11.4

Cash sales of €830 made to A. Jones have been recorded as credit sales to A. Jones.

Requirement Prepare the correcting journal entry, if any, in relation to the above transaction.

Question 11.5

Cooper Ltd purchased a motor vehicle for €35,000 on 1 January 2019 by cheque. The junior accountant recognised the transaction by debiting the motor expense account and crediting the bank account. Cooper depreciates motor vehicles at a rate of 20% per annum. Cooper's reported profit for the reporting period ended 31 December 2019 was €185,240.

Requirement Prepare the journal entries to correct the above entry and recalculate the reported profit.

Challenging Questions

(Suggested Solutions to Challenging Questions are available through your lecturer.)

Question 11.1

Mr Martin is a plumber who operates his business as a sole trader. He employs a number of plumbers, a bookkeeper and a receptionist. Mr Martin's bookkeeper has prepared the draft financial statements to 31 December 2019, which show a profit of €80,000.

The following errors have come to light following the preparation of the draft financial statements and you have been asked to correct these errors:

1. Mr Martin wrote a cheque for €8,700 to Mac Garage Ltd, which the bookkeeper entered in the motor expense account. This cheque was the balancing payment for the purchase of a new van. A vehicle that had originally cost €8,000 and that had a carrying amount at 1 January 2019 of €3,700, was traded in as part exchange. Assume no gain or loss arose on the trade in.
2. Mr Martin charges depreciation on motor vehicles at 25% per annum with a full year's depreciation charged in the year of acquisition, and none in the year of disposal. No account was taken of the error in 1 above when calculating depreciation for the year to 31 December 2019.
3. An invoice for €1,560 was entered in the purchases day book as €1,650.
4. Discounts allowed of €2,890 were debited to the discounts received account in error.
5. Mr Martin purchased goods for the business, costing €1,500 plus VAT at 20%, using his private credit card. No entry has been made in the business records for this transaction.
6. A cash refund of €1,600 to Mr M. Murphy, a customer, was recorded as a payment to a supplier of the same name.
7. Part of the office was sub let. Rent received of €2,400 for subletting was collected by Mr Martin's wife and used to pay domestic bills.
8. No adjustment has been made for rates prepaid at 31 December 2019 of €1,800.

Requirement:
(a) Prepare the journal entries to correct the errors listed in 1–8 above. Narratives for the journal entries are required.

18 Minutes

(b) Show the adjusted profit for the errors corrected in (a) above.

7 Minutes

(Based on Chartered Accountants Ireland, CAP 1 Financial Accounting, Summer 2008, Question 7)

Question 11.2

Mr White is a sole trader. He prepares his own draft financial statements. His draft profit for the year ended 31 December 2018 was €96,500. His trial balance has a difference of €1,180. He has opened a suspense account and credited it with €1,180.

He has provided you with the following additional information:
1. Bank interest received of €565 was debited to the bank interest expense account.
2. Mr White traded-in his old van on 31 March 2018 for €5,000. The new van had a list price of €11,000. The traded-in van had originally cost €10,000 when purchased in May 2016. Depreciation on the van is charged at 20% on cost, with a full year's depreciation being charged in the year of acquisition and none in the year of disposal. Mr White charged €2,000 depreciation in the year to 31 December 2018, as this was the figure provided by his accountant last year.

The motor vehicles account is as follows:

MOTOR VEHICLES ACCOUNT

Date (2018)	Account Name	€	Date (2018)	Account Name	€
Jan 1	Balance b/d	10,000	Dec 31	Balance c/d	18,700
Mar 31	Bank	6,000			
Mar 31	3-year extended warranty on van	1,500			
Mar 31	Sign writer re new van	1,200			
		18,700			18,700

3. No adjustment has been made for an electricity bill that was received in late January 2019. €650 of this bill related to December 2018.

4. A receipt from Mr Black, a customer, for €400 was correctly posted to his account, but was entered in the cash book as €450.

5. Office equipment includes €500 (net of VAT) paid for a laptop computer for Mr White's son. VAT on this purchase of €75 was posted to the VAT account. Depreciation was charged at 10% on cost of office equipment.

Requirement:

(a) Prepare the journal entries to correct 1–5 above.

15 Minutes

(b) Prepare the suspense account in 'T' account format.

3 Minutes

(c) Prepare a statement showing the corrections needed to arrive at the adjusted net profit for the year ended 31 December 2018.

5 Minutes

(Based on Chartered Accountants Ireland, CAP 1 Financial Accounting, Autumn 2011, Question 2)

PART II

SOLE TRADERS

CHAPTERS

12

Financial Statements of Sole Traders

LEARNING OBJECTIVES

Having studied this chapter, readers should be able to:
1. identify the advantages and disadvantages associated with operating a business as a sole trader;
2. prepare and present the financial statements of a sole trader.

12.1 INTRODUCTION

A business may have different forms – sole trader, partnership or a company. In this chapter we are looking at the preparation of financial statements of a sole trader. A sole trader is a business operated and owned by a single individual.

A sole trader is a business owned and operated by a single individual who is entitled to all the profit made by the business. To set up a business as a sole trader the only action that needs to be taken is to inform the revenue authorities of the intention to be self-employed.

The advantages associated with operating as a sole trader include:
- profit earned after tax is attributable to the owner only and does not have to be shared with others;
- decision-making can be quick as there is no need to consult others and, due to the high level of day-to-day involvement of the owner, the business can react quickly to any changes in the business environment; and
- there are less compliance costs due to reduced filing requirements for sole traders compared to other types of businesses.

The disadvantages associated with being a sole trader include:
- the owner is liable for the debts incurred by the business; and
- there is no one else to help in making decisions.

Chapter 2, Recording Financial Transactions and Preparing Financial Statements explained the recording of transactions and the preparation of the trial balance; this chapter deals with the preparation of the financial statements incorporating the adjustments dealt with in **Chapters 3–11**.

12.2 LAYOUT OF FINANCIAL STATEMENTS

The layout of the statement of profit or loss (SOPL) for a sole trader is set out below:

Sole Trader's Name
STATEMENT OF PROFIT OR LOSS
for the year ended 31 December XXXX

	€	€	€
Sales		X	
Less: sales returns		(X)	X
Less: Cost of Sales			
Opening inventory		X	
Purchases	X		
Less: purchases returns	(X)	X	
Carriage inwards (see **Chapter 3**)		X	
		X	
Less: closing inventory		(X)	
Cost of sales			(X)
Gross Profit			X
Less: Expenses			
Electricity		X	
Rent and rates		X	
Wages and salaries		X	
Total expenses			(X)
Net Profit/(Loss)			X/(X)

The layout of the statement of financial position (SOFP) is as follows:

Sole Trader's Name
STATEMENT OF FINANCIAL POSITION
as at 31 December XXXX

	€	€	€
Assets	**Cost**	**Accumulated Depreciation**	**Carrying Amount**
Non-current Assets			
Buildings	X	X	X
Plant and machinery	X	X	X
Motor vehicles	X	X	X
	X	X	X
Current Assets			
Inventory		X	
Trade receivables		X	
Bank		X	X
Total Assets			X

continued overleaf

Equity and Reserves

Capital	X
Net profit/loss	X/(X)
Drawings	(X)
	X

Non-current Liabilities

Bank loan	X

Current Liabilities

Trade payables	X	
Bank overdraft	X	X
Total Equity and Liabilities		X

The financial statements are prepared based on the trial balance information and additional information about transactions that were not recorded by the entity before the trial balance was prepared. **Example 12.1** demonstrates the preparation of the financial statements of a sole trader from the trial balance and additional information.

EXAMPLE 12.1: PREPARATION OF THE FINANCIAL STATEMENTS OF A SOLE TRADER

A. Porter has the following trial balance as at 31 December 2019:

	Debit €	Credit €
Bank	3,100	
Capital		48,000
Purchases	99,000	
Purchases returns		2,200
Motor vehicles	100,000	
Accumulated depreciation as at 01/01/2019		20,000
Inventory as at 01/01/2019	17,800	
Trade payables		5,900
Sales		204,000
4% loan		5,000
Sales returns	3,000	
Carriage inwards	1,600	
Trade receivables	6,200	
Rent	7,000	
Electricity	5,400	
Wages and salaries	29,000	
Drawings	13,000	
	285,100	285,100

Additional information
1. The value of inventory as at 31 December 2019 was €19,500.
2. Rent prepaid at the year-end amounted to €500.

3. Electricity of €200 is outstanding at the year end.
4. Depreciation on motor vehicles is charged at a rate of 20% per annum on a reducing-balance basis.
5. Loan taken out on 1 April 2019.

Requirement Prepare the SOPL of A. Porter for the year ended 31 December 2019 and the SOFP as at that date.

Solution

It is important to review the trial balance before preparing the financial statements. Two key points are worth making in relation to this particular example:
- The inventory figure listed in the trial balance is the opening figure, i.e. the figure as at the start of the current reporting period (which is the closing inventory of the previous reporting period). See **Chapter 3, Inventory and Cost of Sales** for the journal entries required to post the opening and closing inventories before the financial statements are prepared.
- The accumulated depreciation in the trial balance reflects the depreciation charged from the date the assets were purchased until the start of the reporting period. In the trial balance the accumulated depreciation is as at 01/01/2019, which means that depreciation has not been charged for the current reporting period.

A. Porter
STATEMENT OF PROFIT OR LOSS
for the year ended 31 December 2019

	€	€	€
Sales		204,000	
Less: sales returns		(3,000)	201,000
Less: Cost of Sales			
Opening inventory		17,800	
Purchases	99,000		
Less: returns	(2,200)	96,800	
Carriage inwards		1,600	
		116,200	
Less: closing inventory		(19,500)	
Cost of Sales			(96,700)
Gross Profit			104,300
Less: Expenses			
Depreciation (*W1*)		16,000	
Rent (*W2*)		6,500	
Electricity (*W3*)		5,600	
Interest (*W4*)		150	
Wages and salaries		29,000	(57,250)
Total expenses			47,050
Net Profit/(Loss)			

W1 Depreciation

Under the reducing-balance method the depreciation charge is based on the carrying amount of the asset at the start of the year.

	€
Cost	100,000
Accumulated depreciation	(20,000)
Carrying amount	80,000
Depreciation rate	20%
Depreciation charge (€80,000 × 20%)	16,000

W2 Prepayment

A prepayment reduces the expense paid in the period. A prepayment means that the expense relates to the next reporting period.

	€
Rent expense per trial balance	7,000
Less prepayment	(500)
Figure for SOPL	6,500

The journal entry to recognise the prepayment in the financial statements is:

	Debit €	Credit €
Prepayments account – SOFP	500	
Rent expense account		500

To recognise the rent prepayment at the reporting date.

W3 Accruals

An accrual increases the expense for the period. An accrual means that expenses have been incurred but an invoice has not yet been received by the reporting date. The expenses incurred in the period are reflected in the financial statements.

	€
Electricity expense per trial balance	5,400
Plus accrual	200
Figure for SOPL	5,600

The journal entry to recognise the accrual in the financial statements is:

	Debit €	Credit €
Electricity expense account	200	
Accruals account – SOFP		200

To recognise the accrual in relation to the electricity expense.

W4 Interest Accrual

There is no loan interest expense listed in the trial balance, so an accrual needs to be made for the interest expense:

Interest (€5,000 × 4%)   €200

The loan was only issued for nine months of the reporting period, thus the annual expense must be time apportioned. The SOPL expense is €150 (€200 × 9/12).

The journal entry to recognise the accrual in the financial statements is:

	Debit €	Credit €
Interest cost account	150	
Accruals account – SOFP		150

To recognise the accrual for interest cost.

A. Porter
STATEMENT OF FINANCIAL POSITION
as at 31 December 2019

	Cost €	Accumulated Depreciation €	Carrying Amount €
Assets			
Non-current Assets			
Motor vehicles	100,000	36,000	64,000
Current Assets			
Inventory		19,500	
Trade receivables		6,200	
Prepayments		500	
Bank		3,100	29,300
Total Assets			93,300
Equity and Liabilities			
Equity and Reserves			
Capital			48,000
Net profit			47,050
Drawings			(13,000)
			82,050
Non-current Liability			
Loan			5,000
Current Liabilities			
Trade payables		5,900	
Accruals (€150 interest + €200 electricity)		350	6,250
Total Equity and Liabilities			93,300

(Try **Review Question 12.1** at the end of this chapter.)

Exam Tips

- The common mistakes made in relation to the preparation of financial statements are:
  - not using the correct depreciation method as indicated in the question; and
  - not following instructions in relation to the policy for depreciation in the years of purchase and disposal of an asset.
- Make sure you note the reporting date so you correctly calculate the relevant accrual or prepayment.
- Drawings are not an expense but a reduction in the capital of the sole trader.
- Make sure you know how to adjust account balances for the more common adjustments:
  - depreciation charge in the reporting period;
  - accrual of expenses;
  - prepayment of expenses;
  - bad debts written off;
  - change in provision for bad debts.

12.3 CONCLUSION

A sole trader is a business owned and operated by a single individual. The profits or losses made by the business are all attributable to the owner and are subject to income tax rather than corporation tax. As a sole trader you are liable for the debts of the business. A sole trader may withdraw cash and goods from the business, which is referred to as 'drawings' and reduces the capital of the business.

Summary of Learning Objectives

After having studied this chapter, readers should be able to:

Learning Objective 1 Identify the advantages and disadvantages associated with operating a business as a sole trader.

Advantages:
- any proft earned after tax is only attributable to the sole trader;
- quick decision-making as there is no need for consultation; and
- fewer compliance issues than apply to companies.

Disadvantages:
- the owner of the business is liable for the debts of the business; and
- there is no one to help with decision-making.

Learning Objective 2 Prepare and present the financial statements of a sole trader.

It is important to know the layout of each of the financial statements. The financial statements are drawn up from the information provided in the trial balance; it is important to know where the items in the trial balance are presented in the SOPL and the SOFP.

QUESTIONS

Review Questions

(See **Appendix A** for Solutions to Review Questions.)

Question 12.1

R. Wilson has provided you with his trial balance as at 31 December 2019.

R. Wilson
TRIAL BALANCE
as at 31 December 2019

	Debit €	Credit €
Property – cost	1,050,000	
Motor vehicles – cost	55,000	
Accumulated depreciation as at 31 December 2018:		
Property		126,000
Motor Vehicles		19,800
Inventory as at 31 December 2018	78,200	
Sales		1,570,000
Purchases	1,152,600	
Returns in	15,000	
Returns out		12,500
Trade receivables	150,000	
Trade payables		121,500
Cash at bank	48,600	
Administration salaries	95,800	
Rent and rates	25,500	
Prepayment	500	
Insurance	18,900	
Capital		259,100
Drawings	16,000	
Bad debts	2,800	
4% Loan		600,000
	2,708,900	2,708,900

The following information is available:
1. Inventory as at 31 December 2019 is valued at €96,500.
2. Depreciation is charged at the following rates:

Property	2% per annum on a straight-line basis
Motor Vehicles	20% per annum on a reducing-balance basis

3. Mr Wilson withdrew €2,500 (at cost) worth of goods from the business during the year. No accounting entry has been posted in relation to this transaction.
4. The insurance paid during the year relates to the period 1 February 2019 to 31 January 2020. The prepayment figure relates to insurance at the start of the year.
5. The loan was taken out on 1 July 2019 and under the terms of the loan interest is paid annually in arrears.

Requirement:
(a) Prepare the statement of profit or loss of R. Wilson for the year ended 31 December 2019.
(b) Prepare the statement of financial position of R. Wilson as at 31 December 2019.

Challenging Questions

(Suggested Solutions to Challenging Questions are available through your lecturer.)

Question 12.1

Mr Dickens is a sole trader. His trial balance as at 31 December 2018 is as follows:

	€	€
Capital account at 1 January 2018		152,880
Drawings – cash	26,800	
Premises at cost	120,000	
Fixtures and fittings at cost	49,350	
Accumulated depreciation – fixtures and fittings at 1 January 2018		9,870
Inventory at 1 January 2018	18,490	
Accumulated depreciation – premises at 1 January 2018		5,000
Receivables	1,310	
Payables		3,950
Cash at banks	1,530	
Wages	17,600	
Rent and rates	5,780	
Light and heat	3,450	
Telephone	490	
Insurance	2,170	
Purchases	57,540	
Revenue		104,650
General expenses	6,840	
Five-year bank loan		35,000
	311,350	311,350

Additional information:
1. Inventory at 31 December 2018 was €19,600.
2. Rent and rates includes a payment for €1,500 for the quarter ended 28 February 2019.
3. Light and heat does not include electricity for the month of December 2018 estimated to be €400.
4. Light and heat includes the purchase of oil for heating. At 31 December 2018 the stock of oil in the oil tank amounted to 2,000 litres at a cost of €810.
5. In addition to cash drawings, Mr Dickens took goods for his own use that cost €1,500 and had a resale value of €3,000. This has not been reflected in the trial balance.
6. Premises comprise of land at a cost of €70,000 and buildings at a cost of €50,000.
7. Depreciation is to be charged as follows:
    • buildings at 2% on cost, and
    • fixtures and fittings at 20% reducing balance.
8. The bank loan was taken out in December 2018 and is repayable in five equal annual instalments starting on 1 December 2019. No interest is payable for the year ended 31 December 2018.

Requirement:
(a) Prepare the statement of profit or loss for Mr Dickens for the year ended 31 December 2018.
10 Minutes

(b) Prepare the balance sheet as at 31 December 2018.

12 Minutes

(Based on Chartered Accountants Ireland, CAP 1 Financial Accounting, Autumn 2009, Question 6)

Question 12.2

Mr Evans has traded for many years. His trial balance at 31 December 2018 is given below:

	€	€
Capital account at 1 January 2018		29,090
Trade receivables	7,680	
Trade payables		13,320
Inventory at 1 January 2018	8,640	
Bank		2,116
Drawings	25,600	
Shop fittings at cost	19,200	
Motor vehicles at cost		
(2 vans, purchased 1 April 2017 and costing €11,000 each)	22,000	
Accumulated depreciation at 1 January 2018:		
Shop fittings		13,440
Motor vehicles		5,500
Revenue		105,600
Returns in	1,460	
Purchases	51,720	
Motor expenses	2,540	
Returns out		2,630
Allowance for doubtful debts		144
Wages	16,820	
Cash	200	
Sundry expenses	380	
Rent and rates	9,600	
Bad debts	400	
Telephone	1,120	
Heat and light	4,480	
	171,840	171,840

1. Inventory at 31 December 2018 was €9,820. This includes items that cost €1,500. These items are now less fashionable and it is considered that the best option is to sell them to a discount warehouse for €1,600. However, the warehouse requires that the goods be repackaged as a multi-buy, which will cost €300.
2. Mr Evans took goods for his own use that had cost €6,500 and had a retail price of €10,900. No adjustment has been made for this in the trial balance.
3. Depreciation is to be charged as follows: (i) Shop fittings 10% straight-line; (ii) Motor vehicles 25% reducing-balance. A full year's depreciation is charged in the year of acquisition and none in the year of disposal. During the year ended 31 December 2018, one of the delivery vans was sold for €7,000. No entry has been made in the business accounts in respect of the disposal as Mr Evans lodged the proceeds in his private bank account.

4. The allowance for doubtful debts at 31 December 2018 should be equal to 5% of receivables.
5. Rent and rates analysis:

Date	Details	Period	€
02/01/2018	Rent	01/01/2018 to 31/03/2018	1,600
28/03/2018	Rates	01/04/2018 to 31/03/2019	1,100
01/04/2018	Rent	01/04/2018 to 30/06/2018	1,600
06/07/2018	Rent	01/07/2018 to 30/09/2018	1,600
29/09/2018	Rent	01/10/2018 to 31/12/2018	1,850
20/12/2018	Rent	01/01/2019 to 31/03/2019	1,850
			9,600

Requirement:
(a) Prepare the income statement of Mr Evans for the year ended 31 December 2018.

12 Minutes

(b) Prepare the statement of financial position as at 31 December 2018.

10 Minutes

(Based on Chartered Accountants, CAP 1 Financial Accounting, Autumn 2011, Question 7)

13

Incomplete Records

LEARNING OBJECTIVES

Having studied this chapter, readers should be able to:
1. explain why an entity might not maintain a full set of financial records;
2. explain the implications for an entity of not maintaining a full set of financial records;
3. understand the key calculations required to compile a set of financial statements from cash records; and
4. prepare a set of financial statements from an incomplete set of records.

13.1 INTRODUCTION

Some businesses do not use the double-entry bookkeeping system; they only record transactions from the cash or bank perspective; the reason for this is that the owners/managers of the entity may lack the knowledge necessary to record the transactions correctly. The owners/managers may focus on cash availability as a key indicator of business performance. This approach will cause the following problems:
1. Financial statements are prepared on an accrual basis, this means that the statement of profit or loss (SOPL) reflects the revenue earned and expenses incurred in the period. If only transactions involving cash or bank are recorded, then the financial statements will not reflect sales made for which payment has not been received or expenses for which payment has not been made. The reporting profit will therefore be incorrect.
2. Some transactions in a business do not involve cash or bank so they are not recorded in the system.

Before going further in this chapter it may be beneficial to review **Chapter 2, Recording Financial Transactions and Preparing Financial Statements**.

Typically, a number of figures need to be calculated before a set of financial statements can be prepared. The typical items are:
• sales figure;
• purchases figure;
• accruals and prepayments; and
• impact of drawings.

13.2 SALES FIGURE

The assets and liabilities at the start of the period are provided in most exam scenarios. In real life the opening balances would be available from the previous year's financial statements. The typical transactions that impact on the trade receivables account are:

TRADE RECEIVABLES ACCOUNT

Date	Account Name	€	Date	Account Name	€
	Opening balance	X		Sales returns	X
	Credit sales	X		Bad debts written off	X
				Discounts allowed	X
				Bank/cash	X
				Closing balance	X
		X			X

If an entity has only maintained records of its transactions from a cash perspective, the only figure available will be the cash received from its customers and lodged in the entity's bank account. In **Chapter 1, Financial Accounting: Key Terms and Concepts** it was explained what is meant by 'income earned'. In relation to the 'sales revenue' component of income earned, the figure presented in the SOPL is the sales made during the reporting period and includes:

- payments received from customers in relation to sales invoiced during the current reporting period;
- sales invoiced during the current reporting period for which no payment has been received; and
- sales made during the reporting period for which neither an invoice has been issued nor payment received.

Example 13.1 demonstrates the calculation of the revenue figure for the SOPL.

EXAMPLE 13.1: REVENUE FIGURE FOR SOPL

You are told by A. Walsh that the total of the trade receivables is:

	€
As at 31 December 2018	26,200
As at 31 December 2019	15,900

From A. Walsh's bank records it can be seen that the business received €315,300 from credit customers during the reporting period.

Requirement What is the figure for revenue to be presented in the SOPL for the year ended 31 December 2019?

Solution

TRADE RECEIVABLES ACCOUNT

Date	Account Name	€	Date	Account Name	€
01/01/2019	Balance b/d	26,200	31/12/2019	Bank	315,300
01/01/2019–31/12/2019	SOPL – revenue	?	31/12/2019	Balance c/d	15,900
		331,200			331,200

The account does not balance; based on the limited information available, it would be logical to assume that the revenue figure to be presented in the SOPL is the balancing figure.

TRADE RECEIVABLES ACCOUNT

Date	Account Name	€	Date	Account Name	€
01/01/2019	Balance b/d	26,200	31/12/2019	Bank	315,300
01/01/2019–			31/12/2019	Balance c/d	15,900
31/12/2019	SOPL – revenue				
	(balancing figure)	305,000			
		331,200			331,200

Example 13.1 demonstrated the situation where sales are made on credit terms only; in reality a business may have both cash and credit sales.

Example 13.2 will look at the situation where the business has both cash and credit sales.

EXAMPLE 13.2: CALCULATION OF TOTAL REVENUE

B. Fortune sells goods for cash and on credit. The following balances on the trade receivables account are available:

	€
As at 31 December 2019	16,820
As at 31 December 2018	12,450

Customers paid €419,100 in relation to credit sales during the reporting period. In addition, €61,500 was lodged to the bank as takings for cash sales – this figure was after a number of expenses were paid for:

	€
Drawings	12,000
Purchase of goods	4,900
Electricity expense	5,300

Requirement What is the revenue figure to be presented in the SOPL for the year ended 31 December 2019?

Solution

TRADE RECEIVABLES ACCOUNT

Date	Account Name	€	Date	Account Name	€
01/01/2019	Balance b/d	12,450	31/12/2019	Bank	419,100
01/01/2019–	SOPL – revenue		31/12/2019	Balance c/d	16,820
31/12/2019	(balancing figure)	423,470			
		435,920			435,920

The 'SOPL – revenue' figure is the sales figure relating to credit sales only.

The cash sales figure is the amount lodged plus the expenses paid out of the cash takings:

	€
Amount lodged	61,500
Drawings	12,000
Purchase of goods	4,900
Electricity expense	5,300
Cash sales	83,700

The revenue figure presented in the SOPL is €507,170, i.e. €423,470 credit sales plus €83,700 cash sales.

(Try **Review Question 13.1** at the end of this chapter.)

13.3 PURCHASES FIGURE

In the majority of exam situations the opening and closing balances on the trade payables account will be provided along with the cash/bank payments made to suppliers during the reporting period. A typical trade payables account has the following:

TRADE PAYABLES ACCOUNT

Date	Account Name	€	Date	Account Name	€
	Bank/cash	X		Opening balance	X
	Credit purchases returns	X		Credit purchases	X
	Discounts received	X			
	Closing balance	X			
		X			X

Example 13.3 demonstrates the calculation of the purchases figure using the trade payables information.

EXAMPLE 13.3: TRADE PAYABLES FIGURE

You are provided with the following information in relation to trade payables:

	€
As at 31 December 2018	45,600
As at 31 December 2019	51,950

The payments made by cheque to the credit suppliers amounted to €302,140 and cash payments to credit suppliers were €28,620.

Requirement What is the purchases figure to be expensed to the SOPL for the year ended 31 December 2019?

Solution

TRADE PAYABLES ACCOUNT

Date	Account Name	€	Date	Account Name	€
31/12/2019	Bank	302,140	01/01/2019	Balance b/d	45,600
31/12/2019	Cash	28,620	01/01/2019–	Purchases	?
31/12/2019	Balance c/d	51,950	31/12/2019		
		382,710			382,710
			01/01/2020	Balance b/d	51,950

The ledger account does not balance; based on the limited information available, it would be logical to assume that the purchases figure to be presented in the SOPL is the balancing figure.

TRADE PAYABLES ACCOUNT

Date	Account Name	€	Date	Account Name	€
31/12/2019	Bank	302,140	01/01/2019	Balance b/d	45,600
31/12/2019	Cash	28,620	01/01/2019–	Purchases	
31/12/2019	Balance c/d	51,950	31/12/2019	(balancing figure)	337,110
		382,710			382,710
			01/01/2020	Balance b/d	51,950

The cash payments are included here as they are payments in relation to credit suppliers.

The recording of purchases-related transactions, including such items as discounts received, was explained in **Chapter 2**. The impact on the entity of receiving a discount is that the amount the entity is required to pay for its purchases is less than the amount of the original invoice.

Example 13.4 demonstrates the impact on the purchases figure of a discount being received by the entity.

EXAMPLE 13.4: IMPACT OF DISCOUNTS ON PURCHASES FIGURE

As at 1 January 2019, the balance on the trade payables account was €28,290; this was €6,790 higher than the balance on the account at 31 December 2019. Payments made to suppliers of goods on credit were €284,600. Cash purchases of €10,200 were paid out of cash takings.

Discounts were received during the reporting period, for early payment to credit suppliers, of €2,100.

Requirement What is the purchases figure to be expensed to the SOPL for the year ended 31 December 2019?

Solution

TRADE PAYABLES ACCOUNT

Date	Account Name	€	Date	Account Name	€
31/12/2019	Bank	284,600	01/01/2019	Balance b/d	28,290
31/12/2019	Discounts received	2,100	01/01/2019–	Purchases	
31/12/2019	Balance c/d	21,500	31/12/2019	(balancing figure)	279,910
		308,200			308,200
			01/01/2020	Balance b/d	21,500

The purchases figure for the income statement is:

	€
Credit purchases	279,910
Cash purchases	10,200
Total purchases	290,110

(Try **Review Question 13.2** at the end of this chapter.)

Example 13.5 will provide more detail than our earlier examples and require you to calculate the sales and purchases figures.

EXAMPLE 13.5: SALES AND PURCHASES FIGURES

You are provided with the bank account:

BANK ACCOUNT

Account Name	€	Account Name	€
Balance b/d	8,600	Trade payables	205,400
Trade receivables	296,500	Balance c/d	115,500
Lodgements	15,800		
	320,900		320,900
Balance c/d	115,500		

(The bank account gives a summary of the transactions that have occurred throughout the year so transaction dates are not presented.)

The lodgements figure represents cash sales for the period net of:

	€
Wages	32,000
Cash drawings	5,000
Cash purchase of goods	6,200
Heating cost	3,900

There is no inventory on hand at either the start or the end of the reporting period.

The following balances were outstanding:

	As at 31 December 2018	As at 31 December 2019
Trade receivables	€ 18,260	€ 24,100
Trade payables	€ 12,610	€ 9,350

Requirement What is the profit figure for the year ended 31 December 2019?

Solution

TRADE RECEIVABLES ACCOUNT

Date	Account Name	€	Date	Account Name	€
01/01/2019	Balance b/d	18,260	31/12/2019	Bank	296,500
01/01/2019–			31/12/2019	Balance c/d	24,100
31/12/2019	SOPL – revenue	302,340			
		320,600			320,600

TRADE PAYABLES ACCOUNT

Date	Account Name	€	Date	Account Name	€
31/12/2019	Bank	205,400	01/01/2019	Balance b/d	12,610
31/12/2019	Balance c/d	9,350	01/01/2019–		
			31/12/2019	Purchases	202,140
		214,750			214,750
			01/01/2020	Balance b/d	9,350

Cash sales

	€
Lodgement	15,800
Wages	32,000
Drawings	5,000
Cash purchase of goods	6,200
Heating cost	3,900
Cash sales	62,900

Calculation of profit

	€
Sales (€302,340 + €62,900)	365,240
Purchases (€202,140 + €6,200)	(208,340)
Gross profit	156,900
Wages	(32,000)
Heating cost	(3,900)
Net profit	121,000

In the examples so far the amount paid has been equal to the expenses incurred but, in real life, this is not always the case. Entities may incur expenses but may not have received an invoice in relation to such an expense by the reporting date, in which case an accrual will have to be recognised in the financial records. Alternatively, some payments made in the current reporting period may relate to the next reporting period, so a prepayment adjustment will have to be made to the financial records to determine the amount to be presented in the SOPL.

13.4 ACCRUALS AND PREPAYMENTS

It is important to remember that the amount paid in relation to an expense is not necessarily the amount recognised in the SOPL. The reason for this is that the expense charged to the SOPL represents the cost that relates to the reporting period whether it has been paid or not. To review the accounting for accruals and prepayment see **Chapter 4, Accruals and Prepayments**.

Example 13.6 demonstrates the situation when an invoice has not been received at the reporting date.

EXAMPLE 13.6: ACCRUAL

The company has paid €2,470 in relation to heat and light expenses during the reporting period ended 31 December 2019. Management estimates that an accrual is necessary for €380 in relation to light and heat expense at the reporting date.

Requirement:

(a) What is the charge for light and heat in the SOPL for the reporting period ended 31 December 2019?
(b) Prepare the journal entry to recognise the accrual.

Solution

(a)

	€
Amount paid during the reporting period	2,470
Accrual	380
Charge to SOPL	2,850

(b)

	Debit €	Credit €
Light and heat expense account	380	
Accruals account		380

To recognise the accrual in relation to light and heat.

Example 13.7 demonstrates the incidence where an amount has been paid in relation to an expense for the next reporting period.

EXAMPLE 13.7: PREPAYMENT

Mr A. Bolton paid rent during the year ended 31 December 2019 amounting to €13,600. Of this amount, €1,200 relates to rent for the period 1 January 2020 to 31 March 2020.

Requirement:

(a) What is the charge for rent in the income statement for the reporting period ended 31 December 2019?
(b) Prepare the journal entry to recognise the prepayment.

Solution

(a)

	€
Amount paid during the reporting period	13,600
Accrual	(1,200)
Charge to SOPL	12,400

(b)

	Debit €	Credit €
Prepayments account	1,200	
Rent expense account		1,200

To recognise the prepayment in relation to rent expense.

(Try **Review Questions 13.3** and **13.4** at the end of this chapter.)

13.5 DRAWINGS

Drawings reduce the net assets of the business. The drawings are shown as a deduction from capital. It is important to remember that drawings are not an expense of the business. Drawings may involve the withdrawal of cash or goods from the business for the owner's own personal use. The accounting entries and an explanation were included in **Chapter 2**.

Example 13.8 demonstrates the impact of drawings on the capital available within the business.

EXAMPLE 13.8: DRAWINGS

The following information has been provided to you in relation to the balances in the books of R. Hammond on 1 January 2019:

	€000
Property	500
Inventory	50
Trade receivables	40
Cash on hand	10
Cash at bank	20
Trade payables	45

Profit for the year ended 31 December 2018 is €116,000 and drawings for the period were €38,000.

Requirement:

(a) What is the amount of capital as at 1 January 2019?
(b) What is the amount of capital as at 31 December 2019?

Solution

(a)

	€000
Property	500
Inventory	50
Trade receivables	40
Cash on hand	10
Cash at bank	20
Trade payables	(45)
Capital as at 1 January 2019	575

(b)

	€000
Capital as at 1 January 2019	575
Profit for year	116
Less drawings	(38)
Capital as at 31 December 2019	653

(Try **Review Question 13.5** at the end of this chapter.)

So far the examples have dealt with individual issues that may occur in an incomplete records question. The next example will combine a number of issues and, from minimal financial information provided in the financial records, a set of financial statements will be prepared.

Example 13.9 demonstrates the preparation of financial statements of a business that only maintained cash records.

EXAMPLE 13.9: SET OF FINANCIAL STATEMENTS FROM INCOMPLETE SET OF RECORDS

You have been provided with the following information from the financial records of A. Walsh:

As at	31 December 2019 €000	31 December 2018 €000
Property as at 31 December 2018	600	600
Motor vehicles as at 31 December 2018	120	120
Inventory	80	47
Trade receivables	112	82
Trade payables	96	54
Bank (asset)		28

Additional information:

1. A number of payments were made out of the bank account during the year:

	€000
Wages	72
Heat and light	18
Insurance	29
Delivery expenses	116
Administration	35
Payment of goods	267

2. All sales and purchases are made on credit terms.
3. Selling prices are set to achieve a 100% mark-up on cost of sales.
4. The property was acquired a number of years ago for €700,000. The property is depreciated on a straight-line basis over 35 years.
5. The motor vehicles originally cost €150,000 and are depreciated on a reducing-balance basis at a rate of 20% per annum.

Requirement:
(a) What is the capital as at 31 December 2018?
(b) Prepare the trade payables ledger account.
(c) Prepare the trade receivables ledger account.
(d) Prepare the bank account.
(e) Prepare the SOPL of A. Walsh for the year ended 31 December 2019.
(f) Prepare the statement of financial position (SOFP) of A. Walsh as at 31 December 2019.

Solution

(a)

As at	31 December 2018 €000
Property as at 31 December 2018	600
Motor vehicles as at 31 December 2018	120
Inventory	47
Trade receivables	82
Bank	28
Trade payables	(54)
Capital as at 31 December 2018	823

(b)

TRADE PAYABLES ACCOUNT

Account Name	€	Account Name	€
Bank	267	Balance b/d	54
Balance c/d	96	Purchases (balancing figure)	309
	363		363
		Balance b/d	96

(c)

TRADE RECEIVABLES ACCOUNT

Date	Account Name	€	Date	Account Name	€
	Balance b/d	82		Bank	
	Sales revenue	?		Balance c/d	112

We are not provided with either the amount received from customers in relation to goods sold or the actual revenue for the period. We are, however, provided with information to assist us to calculate the revenue figure for the period.

	€000
Opening inventory	47
Purchases	309
Less closing inventory	(80)
Cost of sales	276
Mark-up on cost (100% × €276,000)	276
Sales revenue	552

Now that we know the revenue figure, we can calculate the amount received from customers during the reporting period.

TRADE RECEIVABLES ACCOUNT

Date	Account Name	€	Date	Account Name	€
	Balance b/d	82		Bank	522
	Revenue	552		Balance c/d	112
		634			634
	Balance b/d	112			

(d)

BANK ACCOUNT

Date	Account Name	€	Date	Account Name	€
	Balance b/d	28		Wages	72
	Revenue	522		Heat and Light	18
				Insurance	29
				Delivery expenses	116
				Administration	35
				Payment of goods	267
				Balance c/d	13
		550			550
	Balance b/d	13			

(e)

A. Walsh
STATEMENT OF PROFIT OR LOSS
for the year ended 31 December 2019

	€000	€000
Revenue		552
Opening inventory	47	
Purchases	309	
Less closing inventory	(80)	(276)
Gross profit		276
Wages	(72)	
Heat and light	(18)	
Insurance	(29)	
Delivery expenses	(116)	
Administration	(35)	
Depreciation:		
Property (€700,000/35)	(20)	
Motor vehicles (120 × 20%)	(24)	(314)
Loss		(38)

(f)

A. Walsh
STATEMENT OF FINANCIAL POSITION
as at 31 December 2019

	Cost €000	Accumulated Depreciation €000	Carrying Amount €000
Assets			
Non-current Assets			
Property	700	120	580
Motor vehicles	150	54	96
	850	174	676
Current Assets			
Inventory		80	
Trade receivables		112	
Bank		13	205
Total Assets			881
Equity and Liabilities			
Equity and Reserves			
Capital			823
Profit/(loss) for the period			(38)
			785
Current Liabilities			
Trade payables			96
Total Equity and Liabilities			881

Exam Tips

Read the question carefully noting whether:
- Opening capital figure has been provided – if not, it will have to be calculated.
- The revenue figure has been provided – if not, use the cash receipts information and opening and closing balances of trade receivables to calculate it.
- The purchases figure has been provided – if not, use the cash payments information and opening and closing balances of trade payables to calculate it.

13.6 CONCLUSION

An entity may only maintain cash/bank records rather than maintaining a complete set of financial records. The basis of the preparation of the financial statements is accrual accounting, therefore adjustments will have to be made to the cash/bank receipts/payments figure/(s).

Summary of Learning Objectives

After having studied this chapter, readers should be able to:

Learning Objective 1 Explain why an entity might not maintain a full set of financial records.

An entity may not maintain a full set of financial records because the owner/manager of the business does not know how to record financial transactions in accordance with the requirements of double-entry bookkeeping, or because the key focus is to ensure that the entity is liquid, that is, able to meet its obligations as they fall due.

Learning Objective 2 Explain the implications for an entity of not maintaining a full set of financial records.

The implications are that:
- the financial statements are prepared on an accrual basis, so cash receipts and payments will not always be equal to the income earned and expenses incurred; and
- some financial transactions, such as depreciation, do not involve cash so a set of financial statements prepared on a cash basis will **not** be compliant with basic accounting principles.

Learning Objective 3 Understand the key calculations required to compile a set of financial statements from cash records.

When an entity only records transactions that impact bank or cash records a number of adjustments need to be made, including:
- Sales receipts will not reflect the total sales for the period as there may be amounts due from trade receivables at the start and end of the reporting period. This means that some of the cash receipts relate to sales for the previous reporting period and some of the customers to whom goods were sold on credit may not have made payment by the reporting date. Cash sales, as well as credit sales, should be included in the revenue figure presented in the SOPL.

- Payments for goods purchased may not reflect the total purchases for the period as there may be amounts due to trade payables at the start and end of the reporting period. This means that some of the cash payments relate to purchases for the previous reporting period and some of the suppliers from whom goods were purchased on credit during the reporting period may not have been paid by the reporting date. Cash purchases, as well as credit purchases, should be included in the purchases figure presented in the SOPL.
- There are items included in the SOPL that do not impact the cash or bank accounts in the reporting period – the most common example of this is depreciation. Depreciation for each class of property, plant and equipment must be included in the calculation of the profit for the period.
- If any assets were disposed of during the period, the only entry recorded may be the cash received. To account fully for the disposal, the asset must be derecognised and a profit or loss on disposal calculated.

Learning Objective 4 Prepare a set of financial statements from an incomplete set of records.

Accounts will have to be reconstructed based on the information provided so a good knowledge of double-entry bookkeeping is necessary to be able to do this correctly.

Item	Impact on the Expenses Charged to the SOPL	Impact on the SOFP
Opening accrual	Reduce amount paid during the year by opening accrual	N/A
Opening prepayment	Increase amount paid during the year by opening prepayment	N/A
Closing accrual	Increase amount paid during the year by closing accrual	Present accrual under current liabilities
Closing prepayment	Reduce amount paid during the year by closing prepayment	Present prepayment under current assets

QUESTIONS

Review Questions

(See **Appendix A** for Solutions to Review Questions.)

Question 13.1

You have been provided with the following information for the reporting period ended 31 December 2019:

	€
Trade receivables balance:	
as at 31 December 2018	36,900
as at 31 December 2019	21,820
Discounts allowed	3,500

Discounts received	2,150
Sales returns	8,600
Bad debts	12,400
Cheques received as payment for credit sales	345,100
Cash received as payment for credit sales	51,900
Bad debts provision:	
as at 31 December 2018	4,300
as at 31 December 2019	6,800

All cheques and cash received had been lodged in full to the bank account by the reporting date.

Requirement What is the revenue figure to be presented in the statement of profit or loss for the reporting period ended 31 December 2019?

Question 13.2

You are provided with the following balances on the trade payables accounts as at:

	€
Inventory	
31 December 2018	56,250
31 December 2019	32,910
Trade Payables	
31 December 2018	65,147
31 December 2019	58,965

The cheque payments made to credit suppliers were €387,600.

Some credit suppliers were paid by cash and the amount of these cash payments was €35,050.

All purchases are on credit terms.

Requirement What is the cost of sales figure to be presented in the statement of profit or loss/income statement for the reporting period ended 31 December 2019?

Question 13.3

The following information has been extracted from the financial records of P. Jones in relation to rates expenses as at 31 December 2019:

	€
Accrual as at 1 January 2019	1,850
Paid during year ended 31 December 2019	16,480

€840 of the rates costs paid during the reporting period relate to January 2020.

Requirement What is the rates expense to be presented in the statement of profit or loss for the year ended 31 December 2019?

Question 13.4

The following information has been extracted from the financial records of B. Wicker in relation to rent expenses as at 31 December 2019:

	€
Prepayment as at 1 January 2019	2,500
Paid during year ended 31 December 2019	29,150

Management estimates the accrual in relation to rent expenses at €1,180 as at 31 December 2019.

Requirement What is the motor expense to be presented in the statement of profit or loss for the year ended 31 December 2019?

Question 13.5

The following information is available as at 31 December 2019:

	€000
Property	290
Motor vehicles	42
Inventory	28
Trade receivables	35
Bank overdraft	23
Cash	8
Trade payables	31
Prepayment	6

Requirement What is the capital balance as at 31 December 2019?

Challenging Questions

(Suggested Solutions to Challenging Questions are available through your lecturer.)

Question 13.1

Pearl, a sole trader, runs a home accessory shop. She sells all her goods at cost plus 30%. Her position at 1 January 2019 was as follows:

	€
Premises (10-year lease from 1 January 2018; original cost €100,000)	90,000
Inventories	70,500
Receivables	2,250
Cash float	500
Trade payables	59,000
Cash at bank	9,200

Pearl has kept limited records, except her cash book. The following amounts were paid by cheque during the year to 31 December 2019:

	€
Suppliers	226,450
Insurance	8,550
Wages	18,000
Rental of fittings	4,900
Drawings	21,400
Heat, light and administration	3,850

Most customers pay cash, but Pearl has a small number of trade customers who have credit accounts. Pearl banks all cash daily, but admits that she has taken approximately €3,000 from the till during the year for non-business expenses. No other expenses were paid by cash.

The following balances are available for 31 December 2019:

	€
Inventories	85,800
Receivables	1,960
Cash float	500
Trade payables	66,850
Cash at bank	8,025

Requirement:
(a) Prepare the following T accounts:
    (i)   Bank account.
    (ii) Payables account.
    (iii) Receivables account.
    (iv) Cash account.

12 Minutes

(b) Prepare Pearl's income statement for the year ended 31 December 2019 and a statement of financial position at that date.

12 Minutes

(Based on Chartered Accountants Ireland, CAP 1 Financial Accounting, Autumn 2012, Question 8)

Question 13.2

Mr Bennett, a sole trader, runs a small interior design shop. His statement of financial position as at 31 December 2018 is as follows:

STATEMENT OF FINANCIAL POSITION
as at 31 December 2018

	€	€
Assets		
Non-current Assets		
Property, plant and equipment		126,000
Accumulated depreciation		(19,600)
		106,400
Current assets		
Inventories	9,100	
Trade receivables	7,910	
Bank	2,000	
Cash	100	19,110
		125,510
Equity and liabilities		
Capital		119,000
Current Liabilities		
Trade payables	6,300	
Accruals	210	6,510
		125,510

During December 2019, while the shop was closed for the holiday season, a small fire broke out in a back store. While damage to the shop was limited, accounting records and additional merchandise held in the back store were severely damaged. You have been asked to assist in preparing the financial statements to 31 December 2019.

You have been able to ascertain the following:
1. All the cash received is banked on the day of receipt to the business bank account, after shop assistants' wages of €12,000 for the year have been paid.
2. Mr Bennett paid himself €22,000 by cheque.
3. At 1 January 2019, light and heat expenses of €210 were accrued. The accrual at 31 December 2019 was €300.
4. The premises at a cost of €90,000, which consist of a 30-year lease, are to be depreciated on a straight-line basis. Plant and equipment, at a cost of €36,000 and a carrying amount of €25,400 at 31 December 2018, are to be depreciated at 20% per annum on a reducing-balance basis, with a full year's depreciation charged in the year of acquisition and none charged in the year of disposal.

5. The balance on the business bank account at 31 December 2019 was €2,660 overdrawn.
6. Cheques paid during the year were as follows:
    (a) Rates €2,000.
    (b) Light and heat €1,500.
    (c) Payments to suppliers €56,600.
    (d) Marketing €1,350.
7. The inventory at 31 December 2019 was physically counted and valued at a cost of €11,280. Mr Bennett is of the view that he will have to sell some of this stock, which had an original cost price of €3,400, for €1,760 due to smoke damage.
8. The trade receivables at 31 December 2019 were €9,240. When these were reviewed by Mr Bennett, he considered that these included irrecoverable debts of €560, and that a general provision for doubtful debts should be made of 5%.
9. Invoices received from trade payables at 31 December 2019 that had not been paid at that date amounted to €7,980.
10. The cash float at 31 December 2019 was €100.

Requirement:
(a) Prepare T accounts for the year ended 31 December 2019 for the following:
    (i)   Bank account.
    (ii) Cash account.
    (iii) Receivables account.
    (iv) Payables account.

12 Minutes

(b) Prepare an income statement for the year ended 31 December 2019.

10 Minutes

(c) Prepare a statement of financial position for Mr Bennett as at 31 December 2019.

9 Minutes

(Based on Chartered Accountants Ireland, CAP 1 Financial Accounting, Autumn 2008, Question 3)

PART III

SPECIALISED FINANCIAL STATEMENTS

14

Financial Statements of Clubs and Societies

LEARNING OBJECTIVES

Having studied this chapter, readers should be able to:
1. prepare an income and expenditure account for a club or society;
2. calculate the subscription income to be presented in the income and expenditure account; and
3. account for life memberships.

14.1 INTRODUCTION

Income and expenditure accounts are prepared for clubs and societies. They are used in organisations that are not set up for profit but are for the benefit of their members, for example a local sports club.

The club generates its income from:
- subscriptions paid by its members; and
- fundraising activities.

At the annual general meeting, which members are entitled to attend, the officers of the club are appointed. Officers of the club are the chairperson, treasurer and secretary.

14.2 ROLE OF A CLUB TREASURER

The duties of a club treasurer are as follows:
- collection and monitoring of subscriptions from members;
- making payments on behalf of the club for its day-to-day costs;
- lodging cash and cheques to the club's bank account;
- maintaining proper records for the club to ensure that the balance on the account can be readily ascertained;
- preparing relevant financial information for club officers; and
- preparing financial information to be presented to the members at the annual general meeting.

14.3 RECEIPTS AND PAYMENTS

The club treasurer may keep a record of the receipts and payments made during the year, but such a record will be insufficient for the club's needs. The club needs to know the following information:
- the amount of subscriptions in arrears;
- the amount of subscriptions in advance;

- expenses incurred but not yet paid (i.e. accruals);
- expenses paid in relation to the next reporting period (i.e. prepayments);
- an analysis of expenditure by category;
- capital expenditure; and
- whether or not the current cash inflow is adequate to meet the club's costs.

To overcome the deficiencies of the receipts and payments approach an income and expenditure account is prepared by the club.

14.4 INCOME AND EXPENDITURE ACCOUNT

The income and expenditure account is prepared on the same basis as the statement of profit or loss, that is, the accrual basis. The income and expenditure account does not report a profit or loss for the period but instead a surplus or deficit.

A surplus in the period means that the income earned in the period exceeds the expenses incurred. A deficit in the period means that the income earned in the period is less than the expenses incurred.

The club may have income sources other than just the members' subscriptions; the most common examples of income other than subscriptions are:
- fundraising events, such as raffles; and
- bar profit – some clubs may have a clubhouse with bar facilities.

For each of the 'other income' categories, a profit or loss is calculated and included in the club's income and expenditure account.

Example 14.1 demonstrates the preparation of an income and expenditure account.

EXAMPLE 14.1: INCOME AND EXPENDITURE ACCOUNT

The following balances are available in relation to Valley Basketball Club as at 31 December 2019:

	€
Subscriptions due as at 31 December 2018	600
Subscriptions in advance as at 31 December 2018	780
Insurance prepaid as at 31 December 2018	1,200

The transactions on the bank account for the period were as follows:

BANK ACCOUNT

Account Name	€	Account Name	€
Balance b/d	5,300	Referee fees	15,800
Subscriptions	116,900	Hall rental	50,500
		Insurance	15,000
		Balance c/d	40,900
	122,200		122,200

Subscriptions due to Valley Basketball Club as at 31 December 2019 amounted to €1,050.

Note: the bank account provided above is a summary of all amounts that were paid and received during the period. Each figure is made up of a number of transactions that occurred at various dates during the reporting period. The individual dates of each transaction are not listed.

Requirement Prepare the income and expenditure account for Valley Basketball Club for the year ended 31 December 2019.

Solution

Valley Basketball Club
INCOME AND EXPENDITURE ACCOUNT
for the year ended 31 December 2019

	€	€
Income		
Subscriptions (W1)		118,130
Expenditure		
Referee fees	15,800	
Insurance (W2)	16,200	
Hall rental	50,500	(82,500)
Surplus		35,630

W1 Subscriptions

SUBSCRIPTIONS ACCOUNT

Account Name	€	Account Name	€
Subscriptions due at 31 December 2018	600	Subscriptions in advance at 31 December 2018	780
Income and expenditure	118,130	Bank	116,900
		Subscriptions due at 31 December 2019	1,050
	118,730		118,730

SUBSCRIPTIONS IN ADVANCE ACCOUNT

Account Name	€	Account Name	€
Subscriptions account	780	Balance b/d	780

SUBSCRIPTIONS DUE ACCOUNT

Account Name	€	Account Name	€
Balance b/d	600	Subscription	600
Subscription	1,050	Balance c/d	1,050
	1,650		1,650

W2 Insurance

INSURANCE ACCOUNT

Account Name	€	Account Name	€
Prepayments	1,200	Income and expenditure	16,200
Bank	15,000		
	16,200		16,200

PREPAYMENTS ACCOUNT

Account Name	€	Account Name	€
Balance b/d	1,200	Insurance account	1,200

14.5 ACCUMULATED FUND

A club's or society's accumulated fund is similar to a business's capital balance. A club's accumulated fund is equal to its net assets/liabilities. 'Net assets/liabilities' is the difference between the total assets of the club (non-current and current assets) and the liabilities of the club. When the total assets exceed the club's liabilities, the figure is referred to as 'net assets'. When the total assets are less then the club's liabilities, the figure is referred to as 'net liabilities'.

Example 14.2 demonstrates the calculation of the accumulated fund.

EXAMPLE 14.2: ACCUMULATED FUND

The following balances were extracted from the financial records of Wintergreen Golf Club as at 31 December 2019:

	€
Clubhouse	600,000
Motor vehicles	34,000
Subscriptions due	2,700
Subscriptions in advance	6,900
Expenses prepaid	700
Accruals	1,500

Requirement Calculate the accumulated fund balance as at 31 December 2019.

Solution

	€
Clubhouse	600,000
Motor vehicles	34,000
Subscriptions due	2,700
Expenses prepaid	700
	637,400
Subscriptions in advance	(6,900)
Accruals	(1,500)
	629,000

14.6 FINANCIAL STATEMENTS OF A CLUB OR SOCIETY

Clubs or societies need to be able to present to their members details about their financial performance for the reporting period and the financial position as at a particular point in time. The financial statements of a club or society are:

- The income and expenditure account, which presents details of the financial performance, showing the surplus of income over expenses (or deficit if expenses exceed income) for the period. The income and expenditure account is prepared on the accrual basis.
- The balance sheet, which presents the value of the club's or society's assets and liabilities at a particular date. The balance sheet is another name for the statement of financial position (SOFP).
- Trading account for activities undertaken by the club, such as operating a bar. The layout of the bar trading account is as follows:

	€	€
Sales		X
Opening inventory	X	
Purchases	X	
Less closing inventory	(X)	
Less cost of sales		(X)
Gross profit		X
Bar staff salaries		(X)
Net profit		X

Example 14.3 demonstrates the preparation of the income and expenditure account and the balance sheet for a club.

EXAMPLE 14.3: INCOME AND EXPENDITURE ACCOUNT AND BALANCE SHEET

As at 31 December 2018 the following assets and liabilities balances related to Redcar Rugby Club:

	€
Cash at bank	8,100
Premises	156,000
Fixtures and fittings	45,000
Subscriptions due	5,600
Subscriptions in advance for the year ended 31 December 2019	5,195
Bar stock	3,800

The following are the details from the bank account for the year ended 31 December 2019:

BANK ACCOUNT

Account Name	€	Account Name	€
Balance b/d	8,100	Insurance	30,000
Subscriptions	206,140	Bar staff salaries	23,800
Bar receipts	58,200	Bar purchases	19,600
		Cleaners' wages	15,600
		Maintenance	30,400
		Motor vehicle	30,000
		Balance c/d	123,040
	272,440		272,440

Note: the bank account provided above is a summary of all the amounts that were paid and received during the period. Each figure is made up of a number of transactions that occurred at various dates during the reporting period. The individual dates of each transaction are not listed.

You are provided with the following information:
1. Bar stock on hand as at 31 December 2019 was €1,760.
2. Depreciation is charged on premises at a rate of 2% per annum on a straight-line basis. The premises originally cost €200,000.
3. Fixtures and fittings are depreciated at a rate of 20% on a reducing-balance basis.
4. The club owes €2,480 in relation to bar purchases as at 31 December 2019.
5. Motor vehicles are depreciated at a rate of 20% on a reducing-balance basis.
6. As at 31 December 2019:

	€
Subscriptions in advance	3,820
Subscriptions due	1,240

Requirement:
(a) Calculate the accumulated fund as at 31 December 2018.
(b) Prepare the bar trading account for the year ended 31 December 2019.
(c) Prepare the income and expenditure account for the year ended 31 December 2019.
(d) Prepare the balance sheet for Redcar Rugby Club as at 31 December 2019.

A trading account is prepared to determine the profit or loss made. The profit or loss is then included as a single line item in the income and expenditure account for the club or society.

Solution

(a) Accumulated fund as at 31 December 2018

	€
Cash at bank	8,100
Premises	156,000
Fixtures and fittings	45,000
Subscriptions due	5,600
Bar stock	3,800
	218,500
Subscriptions in advance	(5,195)
	213,305

(b)

Bar Trading Account
for the year ended 31 December 2019

	€	€
Sales		58,200
Opening inventory	3,800	
Purchases (€19,600 + €2,480)	22,080	
Less closing inventory	(1,760)	
Less cost of sales		(24,120)
Gross profit		34,080
Bar staff salaries		(23,800)
Net profit		10,280

(c)

Redcar Rugby Club
Income and Expenditure Account
for the year ended 31 December 2019

	€	€
Income		
Subscriptions (W1)		203,155
Bar profit		10,280
		213,435
Expenditure		
Insurance	30,000	
Maintenance	30,400	
Cleaners' wages	15,600	
Depreciation:		
Property (€200,000 × 2%)	4,000	
Motor vehicle (€30,000 × 20%)	6,000	
Fixtures and fittings (€45,000 × 20%)	9,000	(95,000)
Surplus		118,435

W1 Subscriptions

Subscriptions Account

Account Name	€	Account Name	€
Subscriptions due	5,600	Subscriptions in advance	5,195
Subscriptions in advance	3,820	Bank	206,140
Income and expenditure	203,155	Subscription due	1,240
	212,575		212,575

Subscriptions in Advance Account

Account Name	€	Account Name	€
Subscriptions	5,195	Balance b/d	5,195
Balance c/d	3,820	Subscriptions	3,820
	9,015		9,015
		Balance b/d	3,820

SUBSCRIPTIONS DUE ACCOUNT

Account Name	€	Account Name	€
Balance b/d	5,600	Subscription	5,600
Subscription	1,240	Balance c/d	1,240
	6,840		6,840
Balance b/d	1,240		

Redcar Rugby Club
BALANCE SHEET
as at 31 December 2019

	€	€
Non-current Assets		
Property (€156,000 − €4,000)		152,000
Motor vehicles (€30,000 − €6,000)		24,000
Fixtures and fittings (€45,000 − €9,000)		36,000
		212,000
Current Assets		
Inventory	1,760	
Subscriptions due	1,240	
Bank	123,040	
		126,040
		338,040
Accumulated Fund		
At 1 January 2019		213,305
Surplus for the year ended 31 December 2019		118,435
		331,740
Current Liabilities		
Bar suppliers	2,480	
Subscriptions in advance	3,820	
		6,300
		338,040

14.7 LIFE MEMBERSHIP

Clubs may allow members, or new members, to make a once-off payment known as a 'life membership' payment. There are two possible treatments:
1. Recognise the amount received as deferred income and release an amount equivalent to the annual membership fee to the income and expenditure account; or
2. Recognise the amount received as deferred income and make an estimate of the likely period over which membership will be claimed and release the life membership fee paid over that period.

The difference between the two approaches is the amount transferred to subscription income in each reporting period. The life membership represents subscription income for a number of years – remember that the amount of income presented in the income and expenditure account is the subscription income that relates to that particular period only. The life membership that has not yet been taken to the income and expenditure account at the reporting date is referred to as 'deferred income' and is presented in the balance sheet as a liability. The balance on the deferred income account is presented under both current and non-current liabilities. The amount presented under current liabilities is the amount to be transferred to the income and expenditure account in the next reporting period. The amount presented under non-current liabilities is the amount to be transferred to the income and expenditure accounts for the reporting periods more than 12 months from the current reporting date.

When the life membership income is received, the impact is to increase the amount the club has in its bank account (an asset) and increase the deferred income. Therefore, the effect of recording this transaction is to debit the bank account (an asset) and credit the deferred income account, which is shown in the following journal entry:

	Debit €	Credit €
Bank account	X	
Deferred income account		X

To recognise receipt of life membership.

Each year an amount is transferred from the deferred income account to the subscription income account. (The subscription income account's balance is transferred to the income and expenditure account at the end of the reporting period.) The impact of this transaction is to increase the subscription income account's balance and decrease the deferred income account's balance. Therefore, the effect of the transaction is that the subscription income account is credited and the deferred income account is debited, as shown in the following journal entry:

	Debit €	Credit €
Deferred income account	X	
Subscription income account		X

To recognise part of life membership in the income and expenditure account.

Example 14.4 demonstrates the impact of the choice of method used to account for life membership on the presentation of the club's financial statements.

EXAMPLE 14.4: LIFE MEMBERSHIP

Ormond Tennis Club has introduced a life membership option for its members. The amount of the life membership is €10,000 and the annual membership fee is currently €1,000. During the reporting period ended 31 December 2019, five people paid the life membership.

The treasurer of the club has estimated that the likely period over which members will claim their membership is eight years.

Requirement For the current year, calculate the amount of subscription income to be presented in the income and expenditure account and the amount of deferred income to be presented in the balance sheet as at 31 December 2019 under each of the approaches available:
(a) Amount transferred each year is the amount of the annual membership; and
(b) Amount transferred is based on the estimated period for which the membership will be claimed.

Solution

Under both options the following journal entry will be posted to recognise the life membership received in the current year:

	Debit €	Credit €
Bank account	50,000	
Deferred income account		50,000

To recognise the life membership received.

(a) *Amount transferred each year is the amount of the annual membership*
The amount transferred is equivalent to the annual membership subscription, which is currently €1,000 per member – this means that €1,000 per member is debited to the deferred income account and credited to the subscription income account. The journal entry to recognise the portion of the life membership for the year ended 31 December 2019 in the income and expenditure account is:

	Debit €	Credit €
Deferred income account (Note 1)	5,000	
Subscription income account		5,000

To recognise the current part of life membership in the current income and expenditure account.

Note 1 There were five members in the reporting period that availed of the life membership, so the amount of subscription income is €5,000 (€1,000 × 5).

Ormond Tennis Club
INCOME AND EXPENDITURE ACCOUNT (EXTRACT)
for the year ended 31 December 2019

	€
Subscription income (Note 1)	5,000

Ormond Tennis Club
BALANCE SHEET (EXTRACT)
as at 31 December 2019

	€
Non-current Liabilities	
Life membership (Note 2)	40,000
Current Liabilities	
Life membership (Note 2)	5,000

Note 2 The deferred income is reduced by the amount of the life membership income released to the income and expenditure account. The balance on the deferred income account at 31 December 2019 is €45,000 (€50,000 − €5,000).

The amount of the life membership balance to be transferred to the income expenditure account in the next reporting period, that is the year ended 31 December 2020, is €5,000. This amount is presented in current liabilities in the balance sheet as at 31 December 2019.

The remainder of the balance on the deferred income account, €40,000 (the difference between the balance as at 31 December 2019 of €45,000 and the amount to be released to the income and expenditure account in the reporting period ended 31 December 2020 of €5,000), is presented under non-current liabilities in the balance sheet as at 31 December 2019.

(b) *Amount transferred each year is based on expected period of time that members will claim their membership*

The amount transferred is equivalent to the estimate of the period of time that members will claim membership. The amount of each life membership is €10,000 and the expected period that a member is likely to claim membership is eight years, therefore the amount of the annual transfer is €1,250 (€10,000 ÷ 8 years). This amount is debited to the deferred income account and credited to the subscription income account. The journal entry to recognise the relevant portion of the life membership in the income and expenditure account for the year ended 31 December 2019 is:

	Debit €	Credit €
Deferred income account (Note 3)	6,250	
Subscription income account		6,250

To recognise part of life membership in the income and expenditure account.

Note 3 There were five members who availed of the life membership option in the reporting period, so the amount of subscription income is €6,250 (€1,250 × 5).

Ormond Tennis Club
INCOME AND EXPENDITURE (EXTRACT)
for the year ended 31 December 2019

	€
Subscription income (Note 3)	6,250

Ormond Tennis Club
BALANCE SHEET (EXTRACT)
as at 31 December 2019

	€
Non-current Liabilities	
Life membership (Note 4)	37,500
Current Liabilities	
Life membership (Note 4)	6,250

Note 4 The deferred income is reduced by the amount of the life membership income released to the income and expenditure account. The balance on the deferred income account at 31 December 2019 is €43,750 (€50,000 − €6,250).

The amount of the life membership balance to be transferred to the income and expenditure account in the next reporting period, that is the reporting period ended 31 December 2020, is €6,250; this amount is presented in current liabilities in the balance sheet as at 31 December 2019.

The remainder of the balance on the deferred income account is €37,500 (i.e. the difference between the balance as at 31 December 2019 of €43,750 and the amount to be released to the income and expenditure account in the reporting period ended 31 December 2020 of €6,250) and is presented under non-current liabilities in the balance sheet as at 31 December 2019.

Exam Tips

- Calculate the subscription income taking into account subscription income in advance and due at the start and end of the reporting period.
- In the income and expenditure account the income will include the subscription income and a single line item for bar profit or various fundraising events.
- Check if any of the payments made during the reporting period relate to capital expenditure items. Items of capital expenditure need to be depreciated.

14.8 CONCLUSION

Clubs need to provide financial information to their members; this financial information is presented in the club's income and expenditure account and balance sheet. These financial statements are prepared on an accrual basis and show surplus or deficit for the reporting period rather than profit or loss, and accumulated funds rather than capital.

Summary of Learning Objectives

After having studied this chapter, readers should be able to:

Learning Objective 1 Prepare an income and expenditure account for a club or society.

The steps involved in the preparation of club accounts are as follows.
1. Calculate the accumulated fund as at the start of the reporting period.
2. Calculate the subscription income for the period.
3. Calculate any depreciation charge for the reporting period.
4. Adjust expenses for accruals and prepayments at the start and end of the reporting period.
5. Calculate the net proceeds from the bar or from fundraising events.
6. Prepare the income and expenditure account.
7. Prepare the balance sheet for the club.

Learning Objective 2 Calculate the subscription income to be presented in the income and expenditure account.

The subscription income figure for the income and expenditure account is calculated as follows:

	€
Amount received from club members	X
Subscription in advance at the start of the reporting period	X
Subscription due at the end of the reporting period	X
Subscription in advance at the end of the reporting period	(X)
Subscription due at the start of the reporting period	(X)
Subscription income figure for income and expenditure account	X

Learning Objective 3 Account for life memberships.

There are two accounting treatments allowed in relation to life membership as follows.
1. recognise the life membership income received as deferred income and release an amount equivalent to the annual membership to the income and expenditure account in each reporting period until the balance on the deferred account is zero; or
2. recognise the life membership income received as deferred income and make an estimate of the period over which the membership will be claimed. An amount is then released to the income and expenditure account each year.

It is important to remember that the deferred income balance is presented under both current and non-current liabilities. The amount presented under current liabilities is the amount to be released to the income and expenditure account in the next reporting period. The amount presented under non-current liabilities is the amount to be released to the income and expenditure accounts of the reporting periods more than 12 months from the current reporting date.

QUESTIONS

Review Questions

(See **Appendix A** for Solutions to Review Questions.)

Question 14.1
You have been provided with the following information in relation to Supergreen Tennis Club:

	31 December 2019 €	31 December 2018 €
Bank and cash		68,400
Bar stock	12,800	10,000
Premises (original cost €1,600,000)	1,200,000	1,200,000
Fittings (original cost €500,000)	375,000	375,000
Subscriptions due	9,200	14,600
Subscriptions in advance	15,350	8,100
Treasurer's bonus	6,000	
Amount due to bar suppliers	5,800	2,700

The following cash receipts and payments were recorded during the year ended 31 December 2019.

	€
Receipts	
Subscriptions	405,200
Bar receipts	208,500
Payments	
Bar purchases	124,000
Tennis coach	60,000
Bar staff salaries	43,000
Rates	21,000
Maintenance	168,000
Cleaning	79,500

There have been no additions to non-current assets in the period. Depreciation is charged on a straight-line basis as follows:

Property	40-year useful life
Fittings	10-year useful life

Requirement:
(a) Calculate the accumulated fund as at 31 December 2018.
(b) Prepare the bank ledger account.
(c) Prepare the bar trading account of Supergreen Tennis Club for the year ended 31 December 2019.
(d) Prepare the income and expenditure account of Supergreen Tennis Club for the year ended 31 December 2019.
(e) Prepare the balance sheet of Supergreen Tennis Club as at 31 December 2019.

Challenging Questions

(Suggested Solutions to Challenging Questions are available through your lecturer.)

Question 14.1

You are provided with the following balances for Greenwood Golf and Country Club:

	As at 31 December 2018 €	As at 31 December 2019 €
Bank	35,640	82,110
Clubhouse	760,000	760,000
Fixtures and fittings	140,000	140,000
Bar inventory	6,800	9,100
Bar payables	12,420	13,620
Subscriptions in advance	6,150	10,230
Subscriptions due	3,405	8,500
Light and heat accrual	2,400	1,530

BANK ACCOUNT

Details	€	Details	€
Balance b/d	35,640	Bar salaries	58,000
Subscriptions	316,900	Insurance	42,000
Bar	287,300	Light and heat	35,600
Raffle	15,620	Raffle prizes and costs	2,100
		Greenkeepers' salaries	72,000
		Bar purchases	114,200
		General expenses	166,550
		Green maintenance	32,900
		Bar maintenance	8,000
		Cleaning	42,000
		Balance c/d	82,110
	655,460		655,460

Additional information:
1. The clubhouse originally cost €800,000 and is depreciated on a straight-line basis over its 40-year useful life.
2. The fittings originally cost €200,000 and are depreciated at a rate of 15% per annum on a straight-line basis.
3. Costs are attributable to the bar and the golf club as follows:

	Golf Club	Bar
Bar salaries		100%
Insurance	75%	25%
Light and heat	60%	40%
Greenkeepers' salaries	100%	
Bar purchases		100%
General expenses	70%	30%
Green maintenance	100%	
Bar maintenance		100%
Cleaning	50%	50%

Requirement:
(a) Calculate the accumulated fund as at 31 December 2018.
(b) Prepare the bar trading account of Greenwood Golf and Country Club for the year ended 31 December 2019.
(c) Calculate the proceeds from the raffle.
(d) Prepare the income and expenditure account of Greenwood Golf and Country Club for the year ended 31 December 2019.
(e) Prepare the balance sheet of Greenwood Golf and Country Club as at 31 December 2019.

Question 14.2

You are provided with the following balances for Griffin Tennis Club:

	As at 31 December 2018 €	As at 31 December 2019 €
Bank	18,610	9,220
Clubhouse –	240,000	240,000
accumulated depreciation	48,000	48,000
Fixtures and fittings –	20,000	20,000
accumulated depreciation	6,000	6,000
Subscriptions in advance	3,290	5,100
Subscriptions due	4,505	1,120
Life memberships	27,000	27,000
Rent prepaid	1,500	2,400
Insurance accrual	1,230	2,350

BANK ACCOUNT

Details	€	Details	€
Balance b/d	18,610	Insurance	25,300
Subscriptions	182,900	Rent	28,150
		Light and heat	12,900
		Coach salaries	45,000
		Caretaker	38,000
		General expenses	20,840
		Maintenance	22,100
		Balance c/d	9,220
	201,510		201,510

The life membership relates to monies received in 2017 from members. The total value of the life membership was €30,000 and is being released to the income and expenditure account on a straight-line basis over 10 years. The current year's figure has not been accounted for in the above accounts.

The current year's depreciation charges are not reflected in the 2019 figures. Depreciation is charged:

Property	2% per annum on a straight-line basis
Fixtures	10% per annum on a straight-line basis

Requirement:
(a) Calculate the accumulated fund as at 31 December 2018.
(b) Prepare the income and expenditure account of Griffin Tennis Club for the year ended 31 December 2019.
(c) Prepare the balance sheet of Griffin Tennis Club as at 31 December 2019.

PART IV

PARTNERSHIPS

CHAPTERS

15

Partnerships: An Introduction

LEARNING OBJECTIVES

Having studied this chapter, readers should be able to:
1. prepare the partners' capital accounts;
2. prepare the partners' current accounts; and
3. prepare the profit or loss appropriation account.

15.1 INTRODUCTION

Up until this point in this textbook, transactions have been looked at from the point of view of a sole trader – someone who has set up a business and managed it themselves. Another form in which businesses operate is a partnership. A partnership is defined as:

> " ... the relation which subsists between persons carrying on a business in common with a view of profit."

Partnership Act 1890

People may form a partnership to obtain all the skills or financing requirements to operate the business. This chapter demonstrates the accounting techniques used to ensure that each partner's share of profits/ losses, are identified and correctly attributed to each partner.

15.2 DIFFERENCES BETWEEN A SOLE TRADER AND A PARTNERSHIP

There are a number of differences between a sole trader and a partnership:
- There is a specific Act governing the operations of partnerships – the Partnership Act, 1890. There is no such equivalent legislation in relation to a sole trader.
- The ownership and management in a sole trader is vested in a single individual whereas a partnership may have a number of partners some of whom may not be involved in the day-to-day operations of the business.
- All transactions in relation to the sole trader and the business are conducted through a single account known as the capital account. The types of transaction are: introduction of capital, share of profits and drawings. In a partnership there are two accounts maintained for each partner: a fixed capital account and a current account. The partner's current account is used for transactions such as: share of profits, drawings and interest on capital. Partners' capital and current accounts will be discussed in more detail later.
- As the partnership has more than one owner, use is made of an appropriation account to share out profits and losses.

15.3 PARTNERSHIP AGREEMENT

A group of people starting a business as a partnership would be best advised to prepare a partnership agreement in which the rules for operating as a partnership are set out. The following items would typically be included in the partnership agreement:
* name of firm;
* description of the type of business;
* statement of the duration of the business if it is for a fixed period of time;
* capital to be introduced by each partner;
* level of involvement of each partner in the day-to-day operation of the business;
* amount of salaries to be paid to each partner/mechanism for setting partners' salaries;
* how profits or losses are to be shared out between partners, known as the **profit-sharing ratio**;
* whether or not interest is to be paid on capital balances invested and, if so, the interest rate;
* whether or not penalty interest applies on drawings and, if so, the rate of interest to be applied;
* rules in relation to drawings from the business by partners;
* reasons why the partnership would be dissolved, for example, retirement or death of one of the partners;
* procedures to be followed if the partnership is being dissolved;
* dispute resolution procedures to be followed; and
* roles and responsibilities in the preparation and audit of accounts.

If the partners do not put in place a partnership agreement, the Partnership Act 1890 applies. Under the Partnership Act the following terms will apply to the operation of the partnership:
* no interest is paid on the capital balances of the partners;
* no salaries are paid to any partner acting in the business;
* profits and losses are to be shared equally between partners; and
* interest at the rate of 5% per annum is to be paid on loans made by partners to the partnership in excess of their agreed capitals.

15.4 ACCOUNTING FOR PARTNERSHIPS

As stated earlier (see **Section 15.2**) there are two accounts maintained for each partner:
* partner's fixed capital account; and
* partner's current account.

Partners' Fixed Capital Accounts

A fixed capital account is used to record the following for each partner:
* capital introduced by each partner;
* capital withdrawn by each partner; and
* the impact of the revaluation of an asset used in the business (see **Chapter 16, Partnerships: Changes in Profit-sharing Ratios**).

In the examples in this chapter, and the other chapters relating to partnerships, the transactions recorded in the various ledger accounts would have occurred on various dates throughout the year – the actual dates on which the transactions took place are not provided.

Example 15.1 demonstrates the setting-up of a partnership.

EXAMPLE 15.1: SETTING UP A PARTNERSHIP

On 1 March 2019 Bill and Ben set up a partnership and introduced the following into the business:

Partner		€
Bill	Cash	40,000
	Car	20,000
Ben	Cash	50,000
	Office equipment	10,000

Requirement:
(a) Prepare the journal entries to record the capital introduced into the partnership by each partner on 1 March 2019.
(b) Prepare the capital account for each partner.
(c) Prepare the statement of financial position (SOFP) of the partnership as at 1 March 2019.

Solution

(a) The journal entries to recognise the introduction of assets to the partnership by the partners are as follows:

	Debit €	Credit €
Cash account	40,000	
Motor vehicles account	20,000	
Partner's capital account – Bill		60,000

To recognise the introduction of capital into the partnership.

	Debit €	Credit €
Cash account	50,000	
Office equipment account	10,000	
Partner's capital account – Ben		60,000

To recognise the introduction of capital into the partnership.

(b)

CAPITAL ACCOUNT – BILL

Date	Account Name	€	Date	Account Name	€
01/03/2019	Balance c/d	60,000	01/03/2019	Cash and motor vehicles	60,000
			02/03/2019	Balance b/d	60,000

CAPITAL ACCOUNT – BEN

Date	Account Name	€	Date	Account Name	€
01/03/2019	Balance c/d	60,000	01/03/2019	Cash and office equipment	60,000
			02/03/2019	Balance b/d	60,000

(c)

Bill and Ben
STATEMENT OF FINANCIAL POSITION (EXTRACT)
as at 1 March 2019

	€
Non-current Assets	
Motor vehicles	20,000
Office equipment	10,000
Current Assets	
Cash	90,000
	120,000
Capital	
Bill	60,000
Ben	60,000
	120,000

Partners' Current Accounts

Current accounts are used to record the following for each of the partners.
• Partners' shares of profit/loss for the period.
• Interest on partners' capital account balances. Under a partnership agreement, partners may be entitled to interest at a specified rate. The impact of the interest on capital is to reduce the profit for the period to be apportioned among the partners and increase the amount due to each partner.
• Partners' salaries. Partners may be entitled to salaries; each partner's salary reduces the profit for the period to be apportioned among partners and increases the amount due to that partner. When the salary is paid out to the partner, the bank (asset) is reduced and the amount due to the partner is reduced.
• Drawings. Drawings made by partners are either in the form of cash or goods. The impact of these transactions is to reduce the amount owed to the partner and reduce the bank (asset) or purchases (expense).
• Interest on drawings. A partnership agreement may include a condition that imposes a penalty on partners withdrawing cash or goods from the business. The impact of this transaction is to increase the profit available to be apportioned among partners and reduce the amount owed to the relevant partner.

The journal entries in relation to each of the above will be dealt with in the remainder of this chapter.

Profit or Loss Appropriation Account

The profit or loss appropriation account is a **ledger account** presented after the profit or loss for the period has been determined. The profit or loss appropriation will show the following transactions with the partners:
• interest charge to partners on drawings – this will increase the profit for the period (or reduce the reported loss);

- salaries;
- interest on capital – this reduces the reported profit;
- share of profit or loss for the period. It is important to note that this is always the **final** appropriation in this account.

The transactions recorded in the appropriation account impact the partners' current accounts.

The journal entries to recognise each partner's share of profit or loss:

	Debit €	Credit €
Profit or loss appropriation account	X	
Partner's current account – share of profits		X
To recognise each partner's share of profits.		
Partner's current account – share of losses	X	
Profit or loss appropriation account		X
To recognise each partner's share of losses.		

Example 15.2 demonstrates the calculation of each partner's share of the partnership profit.

EXAMPLE 15.2: PARTNERS' PROFIT-SHARING RATIO

As at 1 January 2019 the following balances were on the capital and current accounts of Bing and Bong.

	€
Capital Accounts	
Bing	42,000 credit
Bong	55,000 credit
Current Accounts	
Bing	5,700 credit
Bong	6,310 credit

The profit for the year ended 31 December 2019 was €82,400.

Bing and Bong share profits in the ratio 3:2 respectively.

Requirement:
(a) What is each partner's share of the profit for the year ended 31 December 2019?
(b) Prepare the partners' capital and current accounts.

Solution
(a) Bing's share of profit: €82,400 × 3/5 = €49,440
Bong's share of profit: €82,400 × 2/5 = €32,960
(b)

CAPITAL ACCOUNT – BING

Date	Account Name	€	Date	Account Name	€
31/12/2019	Balance c/d	42,000	01/01/2019	Balance b/d	42,000
			01/01/2020	Balance b/d	42,000

CAPITAL ACCOUNT – BONG

Date	Account Name	€	Date	Account Name	€
31/12/2019	Balance c/d	55,000	01/01/2019	Balance b/d	55,000
			01/01/2020	Balance b/d	55,000

CURRENT ACCOUNT – BING

Date	Account Name	€	Date	Account Name	€
31/12/2019	Balance c/d	55,140	01/01/2019	Balance b/d	5,700
			31/12/2019	Share of profit	49,440
		55,140			55,140
			01/01/2020	Balance b/d	55,140

CURRENT ACCOUNT – BONG

Date	Account Name	€	Date	Account Name	€
31/12/2019	Balance c/d	39,270	01/01/2019	Balance b/d	6,310
			31/12/2019	Share of profit	32,960
		39,270			39,270
			01/01/2020	Balance b/d	39,270

To recognise drawings (of cash or goods) made by partners, the following journal entry is required:

	Debit €	Credit €
Partner's current account – drawings	X	
Cash/purchases account		X

To recognise drawings made by partner during the period.

It is important to remember that drawings are not an expense to be charged in the calculation of profit or loss for the reporting period.

To recognise interest on capital earned by the partners during the reporting period:

	Debit €	Credit €
Profit or loss appropriation account	X	
Partner's current account – interest on capital		X

To recognise interest on partner's capital balance.

Example 15.3 demonstrates the accounting for drawings and the preparation of the profit or loss appropriation account.

EXAMPLE 15.3: DRAWINGS

Eric and Ernie share profits in the proportion 30:70 respectively. The balances on their capital and current accounts as at 1 January 2019 are:

	Capital Account	Current Account
Eric	€58,000 credit	€5,100 debit
Ernie	€43,000 credit	€3,960 credit

Profit for the year ended 31 December 2019 was €120,000.

Eric and Ernie made drawings from the business of €7,000 and €12,000 respectively.

Under the terms of the partnership agreement, interest is paid on the balances on the partners' capital accounts at a rate of 5% per annum. There have been no changes in the balances on the partners' capital accounts since the start of the reporting period.

Requirement:
(a) Calculate the interest earned on the capital balances of the partners.
(b) Prepare the appropriation account.
(c) Prepare the partners' capital accounts.
(d) Prepare the partners' current accounts.

Solution
(a) Interest earned by Eric on his capital balance: €58,000 × 5% = €2,900
     Interest earned by Ernie on his capital balance: €43,000 × 5% = €2,150
(b)

Eric and Ernie
PROFIT OR LOSS APPROPRIATION ACCOUNT
for the year ended 31 December 2019

	€	€
Profit for year		120,000
Interest on Capital		
Eric	(2,900)	
Ernie	(2,150)	(5,050)
		114,950
Share of profits		
Eric (€114,950 × 30%)	(34,485)	
Ernie (€114,950 × 70%)	(80,465)	(114,950)

Note: drawings are **not** presented in the profit or loss appropriation account.

The interest on capital is deducted from profit before the apportionment of profit. The profit or loss apportionment account is a ledger account but may be presented in table format as above. The ledger presentation is as follows:

PROFIT OR LOSS APPROPRIATION ACCOUNT

Account Name	€	Account Name	€
Eric – interest	2,900	Profit for year	120,000
Eric – share of profit	34,485		
Ernie – interest	2,150		
Ernie – share of profit	80,465		
	120,000		120,000

(c)

CAPITAL ACCOUNT – ERIC

Date	Account Name	€	Date	Account Name	€
31/12/2019	Balance c/d	58,000	01/01/2019	Balance b/d	58,000
			01/01/2020	Balance b/d	58,000

CAPITAL ACCOUNT – ERNIE

Date	Account Name	€	Date	Account Name	€
31/12/2019	Balance c/d	43,000	01/01/2019	Balance b/d	43,000
			01/01/2020	Balance b/d	43,000

(d)

CURRENT ACCOUNT – ERIC

Date	Account Name	€	Date	Account Name	€
01/01/2019	Balance b/d	5,100	31/12/2019	Interest on capital	2,900
31/12/2019	Drawings	7,000	31/12/2019	Share of profit	34,485
31/12/2019	Balance c/d	25,285			
		37,385			37,385
			01/01/2020	Balance b/d	25,285

CURRENT ACCOUNT – ERNIE

Date	Account Name	€	Date	Account Name	€
31/12/2019	Drawings	12,000	01/01/2019	Balance b/d	3,960
31/12/2019	Balance c/d	74,575	31/12/2019	Interest on capital	2,150
			31/12/2019	Share of profit	80,465
		86,575			86,575
			01/01/2020	Balance b/d	74,575

(Try **Review Questions 15.1** and **15.2** at the end of this chapter.)

Interest on drawings is a charge levied on partners for withdrawing inventory, cash or other assets from the partnership. The following accounting journal entry recognises the interest on drawings charged against partners in the business accounting records.

	Debit €	Credit €
Partner's current account – interest on drawings	X	
Profit or loss appropriation account		X

To recognise the interest charged to partner on drawings.

Example 15.4 demonstrates the appropriation treatment of interest on drawings.

EXAMPLE 15.4: INTEREST ON DRAWINGS

You are provided with the following information in relation to the partners of Able, Cable and Babel as at 31 December 2018:

Partner	Able €	Cable €	Babel €
Capital account balance (all credit)	45,000	30,000	25,000
Current account balance (all credit)	6,250	4,150	3,627
Drawings	6,000	5,000	10,000

The profit-sharing ratio is 5:3:2 for Able, Cable and Babel respectively. The profit for the year ended 31 December 2019 is €115,000.

There have been no changes in the partners' capital balances during the reporting period. Interest on capital is paid at a rate of 4% per annum.

Interest has been calculated in relation to drawings as follows:

Able   €500   Cable   €450   Babel   €900

Requirement:
(a) Calculate the interest earned on the capital balances of the partners.
(b) Prepare the appropriation account.
(c) Prepare the partners' capital accounts.
(d) Prepare the partners' current accounts.

Solution
(a) Able: €45,000 × 4% = €1,800
      Cable: €30,000 × 4% = €1,200
      Babel: €25,000 × 4% = €1,000
(b)

Able, Cable and Babel
PROFIT OR LOSS APPROPRIATION ACCOUNT
for the year ended 31 December 2019

	€	€
Profit for year		115,000
Interest on Drawings		
Able	500	
Cable	450	
Babel	900	1,850
		116,850
Interest on Capital		
Able	(1,800)	
Cable	(1,200)	
Babel	(1,000)	(4,000)
		112,850
Share of profits		
Able (€112,850 × 5/10)	(56,425)	
Cable (€112,850 × 3/10)	(33,855)	
Babel (€112,850 × 2/10)	(22,570)	(112,850)

Note: drawings are **not** presented in the profit or loss appropriation account.

The interest on drawings increases the profit for the period. The profit or loss apportionment account is a ledger account but may be presented in table format as above. The ledger presentation is as follows:

PROFIT OR LOSS APPROPRIATION ACCOUNT

Account Name	€	Account Name	€
Able – interest on capital	1,800	Profit for year	115,000
Able – share of profit	56,425	Able – interest on drawings	500
Cable – interest on capital	1,200	Cable – interest on drawings	450
Cable – share of profit	33,855	Babel – interest on drawings	900
Babel – interest on capital	1,000		
Babel – share of profit	22,570		
	116,850		116,850

(c)

CAPITAL ACCOUNT – ABLE

Date	Account Name	€	Date	Account Name	€
31/12/2019	Balance c/d	45,000	01/01/2019	Balance b/d	45,000
			01/01/2020	Balance b/d	45,000

CAPITAL ACCOUNT – CABLE

Date	Account Name	€	Date	Account Name	€
31/12/2019	Balance c/d	30,000	01/01/2019	Balance b/d	30,000
			01/01/2020	Balance b/d	30,000

CAPITAL ACCOUNT – BABEL

Date	Account Name	€	Date	Account Name	€
31/12/2019	Balance c/d	25,000	01/01/2019	Balance b/d	25,000
			01/01/2020	Balance b/d	25,000

(d)

CURRENT ACCOUNT – ABLE

Date	Account Name	€	Date	Account Name	€
31/12/2019	Drawings	6,000	01/01/2019	Balance b/d	6,250
31/12/2019	Interest on drawings	500	31/12/2019	Interest on capital	1,800
31/12/2019	Balance c/d	57,975		Share of profit	56,425
		64,475			64,475
			01/01/2020	Balance b/d	57,975

CURRENT ACCOUNT – CABLE

Date	Account Name	€	Date	Account Name	€
31/12/2019	Drawings	5,000	01/01/2019	Balance b/d	4,150
31/12/2019	Interest on drawings	450	31/12/2019	Interest on capital	1,200
31/12/2019	Balance c/d	33,755	31/12/2019	Share of profit	33,855
		39,205			39,205
			01/01/2020	Balance b/d	33,755

CURRENT ACCOUNT – BABEL

Date	Account Name	€	Date	Account Name	€
31/12/2019	Drawings	10,000	01/01/2019	Balance b/d	3,627
31/12/2019	Interest on drawings	900	31/12/2019	Interest on capital	1,000
31/12/2019	Balance c/d	16,297		Share of profit	22,570
		27,197			27,197
			01/01/2020	Balance b/d	16,297

Salaries paid to partners are presented as a deduction from profit in the appropriation account.

The journal entry to recognise the salary earned by a partner:

	Debit €	Credit €
Profit or loss appropriation account	X	
Partner's current account – salaries		X

To recognise salary attributable to the partner.

If the partner has withdrawn their salary or part thereof, the journal entry required is:

	Debit €	Credit €
Partner's current account	X	
Cash/bank account		X

To recognise the withdrawal of a salary by a partner.

Example 15.5 demonstrates the accounting for partners' salaries.

EXAMPLE 15.5: PARTNERS' SALARIES

Ann and Joe have been in partnership for a number of years, sharing profits in the ratio 2:1 respectively. The balances on the partners' accounts as at 1 January 2019 are as follows:

Partner	Ann €	Joe €
Capital account balance	35,000 credit	28,000 credit
Current account balance	8,000 credit	6,200 credit

Profit for the year ended 31 December 2019 was €106,000 before partners' salaries of €20,000 (Ann) and €32,000 (Joe). Both partners have withdrawn their salary over the year in full on a monthly basis in cash.

Requirement:
(a) Prepare the profit or loss appropriation account for the partnership for the year ended 31 December 2019.
(b) Prepare the partners' capital accounts.
(c) Prepare the partners' current accounts.

Solution
(a)

Ann and Joe
PROFIT OR LOSS APPROPRIATION ACCOUNT
for the year ended 31 December 2019

	€	€
Profit for year		106,000
Salaries		
Ann	(20,000)	
Joe	(32,000)	
		(52,000)
		54,000
Share of profits		
Ann (€54,000 × 2/3)	(36,000)	
Joe (€54,000 × 1/3)	(18,000)	(54,000)

An alternative presentation of the profit or loss appropriation account:

PROFIT OR LOSS APPROPRIATION ACCOUNT

Account Name	€	Account Name	€
Salary – Ann	20,000	Profit for year	106,000
Salary – Joe	32,000		
Ann – share of profit	36,000		
Joe – share of profit	18,000		
	106,000		106,000

(c)

CAPITAL ACCOUNT – ANN

Date	Account Name	€	Date	Account Name	€
31/12/2019	Balance c/d	35,000	01/01/2019	Balance b/d	35,000
			01/01/2020	Balance b/d	35,000

CAPITAL ACCOUNT – JOE

Date	Account Name	€	Date	Account Name	€
31/12/2019	Balance c/d	28,000	01/01/2019	Balance b/d	28,000
			01/01/2020	Balance b/d	28,000

(d)

CURRENT ACCOUNT – ANN

Date	Account Name	€	Date	Account Name	€
31/12/2019	Cash	20,000	01/01/2019	Balance b/d	8,000
31/12/2019	Balance c/d	44,000	31/12/2019	Salary	20,000
			31/12/2019	Share of profit	36,000
		64,000			64,000
			01/01/2020	Balance b/d	44,000

CURRENT ACCOUNT – JOE

Date	Account Name	€	Date	Account Name	€
31/12/2019	Cash	32,000	01/01/2019	Balance b/d	6,200
31/12/2019	Balance c/d	24,200	31/12/2019	Salary	32,000
			31/12/2019	Share of profit	18,000
		56,200			56,200
			01/01/2020	Balance b/d	24,200

(Try **Review Questions 15.3** and **15.4** at the end of this chapter.)

There may be a clause in the partnership agreement that guarantees a particular partner a specified amount of profit.

Example 15.6 demonstrates the calculation of the share of profits when one partner is guaranteed a certain profit level.

EXAMPLE 15.6: GUARANTEED PROFIT

Archer and Arrow have been in partnership for many years and share profits 60:40 respectively. Under the terms of the partnership agreement, Arrow is guaranteed a minimum profit of €50,000 each year.

In the most recent reporting period, ended 31 December 2019, profit was €86,000.

Requirement Prepare the profit or loss appropriation account for the partnership for the year ended 31 December 2019.

Solution

Partner	Share of profit based on profit-sharing ratio	Guaranteed amount	Share of profit after guarantee
Archer	€51,600 [€86,000 × 60%]		€36,000 [€51,600 − €15,600]
Arrow	€34,400 [€86,000 × 40%]	€50,000	€50,000 [€34,400 + €15,600]

The shortfall of Arrow's profit is made up by Archer. Calculate the share of profit first then make the necessary adjustment to give Arrow his guaranteed amount.

Archer and Arrow
PROFIT OR LOSS APPROPRIATION ACCOUNT
for the year ended 31 December 2019

	€
Profit for year	86,000
Share of profits	
Archer	(36,000)
Arrow	(50,000)

When a partnership is loss-making the partners must also take a share of the losses in the profit/loss sharing ratio.

Example 15.7 demonstrates the apportionment of losses among partners.

EXAMPLE 15.7: LOSS-SHARING AMONG PARTNERS

Jim and Tim have been in partnership for a number of years, sharing profits and losses 40:60 respectively. The following balances were on their capital and current accounts as at 1 January 2019:

	Capital €	Current €
Jim	60,000 credit	15,600 credit
Tim	45,000 credit	9,200 credit

The partnership made a loss of €61,000 for the reporting period ended 31 December 2019.

Requirement:
(a) Prepare the profit or loss appropriation account for the year ended 31 December 2019.
(b) Prepare the partners' current accounts.

Solution
(a)

Jim and Tim
PROFIT OR LOSS APPROPRIATION ACCOUNT
for the year ended 31 December 2019

	€	€
Loss for year		(61,000)
Share of profits		
Jim (€61,000 × 40%)	24,400	
Tim (€61,000 × 60%)	36,600	61,000

(b)

Current Account – Jim

Date	Account Name	€	Date	Account Name	€
31/12/2019	Share of loss	24,400	01/01/2019	Balance b/d	15,600
			31/12/2019	Balance c/d	8,800
		24,400			24,400
01/01/2020	Balance b/d	8,800			

Current Account – Tim

Date	Account Name	€	Date	Account Name	€
31/12/2019	Share of loss	36,600	01/01/2019	Balance b/d	9,200
			31/12/2019	Balance c/d	27,400
		36,600			36,600
01/01/2020	Balance b/d	27,400			

Exam Tips

- It is important to note the profit-sharing ratio and any guaranteed profit levels for a particular partner.
- All transactions recognised in the profit or loss appropriation account are reflected in the partners' current accounts. Drawings are also recognised in the partners' current accounts.
- Partners' capital accounts show:
  - capital introduced by partners; and
  - capital removed from the partnership permanently.

15.5 CONCLUSION

A partnership maintains two accounts for each partner: a capital account and a current account. The current account is the account to which transactions are regularly posted; these transactions include partners' shares of profits or losses, drawings, interest on capitals, interest on drawings and salaries. The profit or loss appropriation account is prepared after the profit or loss account and sets out the apportionment of the profit among the partners.

Summary of Learning Objectives

After having studied this chapter, readers should be able to:

Learning Objective 1 Prepare the partners' capital accounts.

To recognise capital introduced into the partnership:

	Debit €	Credit €
Cash/asset account	X	
Partner's capital account		X

To recognise the introduction of capital to the partnership.

To recognise capital withdrawn from the partnership permanently:

	Debit €	Credit €
Partner's capital account	X	
Cash/asset account		X

To recognise the withdrawal of capital from the partnership.

Learning Objective 2 Prepare the partners' current accounts.

The most common items that impact the partners' current accounts are demonstrated in a current account as follows:

CURRENT ACCOUNT

Account Name	€	Account Name	€
Drawings	X	Balance b/d	X
Interest on drawings	X	Salaries	X
Balance c/d	X	Interest on capital	X
		Share of profit	X
	X		X

Learning Objective 3 Prepare the profit or loss appropriation account.

The profit or loss appropriation account is presented in either the ledger or the table format. The table format of the appropriation account is:

	€	€
Profit/(loss) for the year		X/(X)
Plus: Interest on drawings	X	
Less: Interest on capital	(X)	
Less: Salaries	(X)	
		X/(X)
Profit/(loss) available for appropriation		X/(X)
Share profit/(loss) among partners		(X)/X

QUESTIONS

Review Questions

(See **Appendix A** for Solutions to Review Questions.)

Question 15.1

Wind and Rain have been in partnership for a number of years. The partnership made a profit of €90,000 for the year ended 31 December 2019. The balances on the partners' accounts at the start of the year were:

Partner	Wind	Rain
Capital account	€64,000	€55,000
Current account	€13,450	€15,680

Wind and Rain share profits in the ratio 2:1 respectively.

Wind and Rain withdrew cash from the partnership during the reporting period ended 31 December 2019 of €8,000 and €14,300 respectively.

Requirement:
(a) Prepare the profit or loss appropriation account.
(b) Prepare the partners' current accounts.

Question 15.2

Harry and Barry have been in partnership for a number of years. The partnership made a profit of €110,000 for the year ended 31 December 2019. The balances on the partners' accounts at the start of the year were:

Partner	Harry	Barry
Capital account	€70,000	€60,000
Current account	€18,200	€12,100

Harry and Barry share profits in the ratio 3:1 respectively. Harry is entitled to a salary of €24,000 each year. Harry has not withdrawn any of his salary from the partnership.

Requirement:
(a) Prepare the profit or loss appropriation account.
(b) Prepare the partners' current accounts.

Question 15.3

Will and Bill have been in partnership for a number of years. The partnership made a profit of €150,000 for the year ended 31 December 2019. The balances on the partners' accounts at the start of the year were:

Partner	Will	Bill
Capital account	€62,000	€80,000
Current account	€30,400	€25,500

Will and Bill share profits in the ratio 2:3 respectively. Bill is entitled to a salary of €30,000 each year. Bill has withdrawn €2,500 per month as his salary during the reporting period.

Requirement:
(a) Prepare the profit or loss appropriation account.
(b) Prepare the partners' current accounts.

Question 15.4

You are provided with the following information in relation to the partnership:

	€
Capital account balances as at 1/1/2019	
John	31,500
Paul	35,600
Current account balance as at 1/1/2019	
John	7,220
Paul	10,300
Drawings during the reporting period ended 31/12/2019	
John	9,700
Paul	14,100

Interest on drawings

John	360
Paul	400

Salaries

John	15,000
Paul	12,000

Profit for year ended 31/12/2019	92,000

Profits are shared by John and Paul equally, with Paul guaranteed a minimum profit share of €42,000. Interest is due to be paid on partners' capital balances at a rate of 5% per annum.

Requirement:
(a) Prepare the profit or loss appropriation account.
(b) Prepare the partners' current accounts.

Challenging Questions

(Suggested Solutions to Challenging Questions are available through your lecturer.)

Question 15.1

Bridge, Fort and Getty are in partnership sharing profits 1:2:3, after interest on capital of 10%. Partners are charged 15% interest on cash drawings.

At 1 January 2019 the capital account and current account balances of the partners were as follows:

	Capital Account €	Current Account €
Bridge	18,000	3,450
Fort	36,000	(1,080)
Getty	66,000	2,850

Cash drawings, which accrue evenly throughout the year to 31 December 2019, were as follows:

	Drawings €
Bridge	24,000
Fort	28,000
Getty	30,000

The partnership has experienced cash flow problems during the year, due to the unwillingness of its bank to extend its overdraft. The partners had to introduce additional capital during the year to assist cash flow. Bridge introduced an additional €12,000 on 1 March 2019, while Fort and Getty introduced €18,000 each on 1 August 2019.

Profit for the year ended 31 December 2019 was €120,550 after adjusting for goods valued at €1,400 taken by Bridge. Getty is guaranteed a residual share of profit of €58,500.

Requirement:
(a) Prepare the profit appropriation account.
(b) Prepare the partners' capital accounts and current accounts in T account format.

26 Minutes

(Based on Chartered Accountants Ireland, CAP 1 Financial Accounting, Summer 2012, Question 8)

Question 15.2

Abbott and Costello have been in partnership for a number of years sharing profits 2:3. They receive a salary of €17,000 and €16,000 respectively. They also receive interest on capital of 5% per annum.

Extracts from the trial balance at 31 December 2019 are as follows:

	Debit €	Credit €
Capital Account		
Abbott		30,000
Costello		20,000
Current Account (1 January 2019)		
Abbott		3,250
Costello		2,470
Drawings		
Abbott	20,000	
Costello	22,000	

Profit for year ended 31 December 2019: €90,000.

Requirement Prepare Abbott's current account for the year ended 31 December 2019 in T account format.

(Based on Chartered Accountants Ireland, CAP 1 Financial Accounting, Summer 2013, Question 1.1)

16

Partnerships: Changes in Profit-sharing Ratios

Learning Objectives

Having studied this chapter, readers should be able to:
1. account for the introduction of a new partner;
2. account for the retirement/resignation of one of the partners; and
3. account for a change in the profit-sharing ratio of the partners.

16.1 INTRODUCTION

The introduction of a new partner, the retirement/resignation of a partner, and a change in the profit-sharing ratio of the partners are all scenarios that involve a change in the structure of the partnership. Each will involve the valuation of assets and liabilities, at the date of the change, to ensure that each partner receives the fair value of their investment at that date.

Fair value is "the price that would be received to sell an asset or paid to transfer a liability in an orderly transaction between market participants at the measurement date" (IFRS 13 *Fair Value Measurement*, paragraph 9).

16.2 INTRODUCTION OF A NEW PARTNER

Revaluation at the Date When a New Partner Joins a Partnership

When a new partner is introduced into a partnership, the existing partners need to be attributed with their fair share of the net assets of the business at that date and not the **historical cost** less accumulated depreciation of the net assets. The **carrying amount** of assets and liabilities in the the statement of financial position (balance sheet) may not be the same as their fair values, so an adjustment is required to reflect the difference in the partners' accounts. This section will look at how this difference is accounted for.

The change in fair values of assets and liabilities is effected through a revaluation account. The revaluation account is debited with the carrying amount of an asset and then credited with the fair value. The balance on the revaluation account is taken to the partners' capital accounts in the old profit-sharing ratio, that is, the method used to share profits and loss before the introduction of the new partner.

The journal entry to transfer the carrying amount of the asset to the revaluation account:

	Debit €	Credit €
Revaluation account	X	
Property/asset account		X

To transfer the carrying amount to the revaluation account.

The journal entry to take into account the change in value of the asset:

	Debit €	Credit €
Property/asset account	X	
Revaluation account		X

To account for the change on revaluation.

On revaluation the fair value may be higher or lower than the carrying amount of the asset at the revaluation date. (The carrying amount of an asset being its cost less the accumulated depreciation.)

If the fair value is greater than the carrying amount, the partnership has made a profit on the revaluation and the revaluation account is debited and the partners' capital accounts credited with their respective share of the revaluation profit (based on the profit-sharing ratio up to the date of the revaluation). The journal entry posted to recognise a revaluation profit is:

	Debit €	Credit €
Revalution account	X	
Partner's capital account		X

To recognise each partner's share of the profit on revaluation.

If the fair value is less than the carrying amount, the partnership has made a loss on the revaluation and the revaluation account is credited and partners' capital accounts debited with their respective shares of the revaluation loss (based on the profit-sharing ratio up to the date of the revaluation). The journal entry posted to recognise the revaluation loss is:

	Debit €	Credit €
Partner's capital account	X	
Revaluation account		X

To recognise each partner's share of the loss on revaluation.

Example 16.1 demonstrates the situation where an asset's fair value, at the date a new partner is introduced, is greater than the carrying amount of the asset.

EXAMPLE 16.1: REVALUATION OF PARTNERSHIP'S ASSETS

A and B have been in partnership for a number of years, sharing profits in the ratio 2:1 respectively. The following is the statement of financial position (SOFP) of A and B as at 31 December 2019:

	€000
Non-current Assets	
Property	500
Current assets	200
	700
Capital Accounts	
A	350
B	250
	600

Current Accounts

A	40
B	60
	700

A new partner, C, is being admitted to the partnership. C will introduce cash of €164,000: €150,000 with respect to the capital account and the balance to the current account. A, B and C will share profits 50:30:20 respectively.

At the date that C joins the partnership, the property has a fair a value of €620,000.

Requirement:
(a) Prepare the revaluation ledger account to recognise the change in value of the property.
(b) Prepare the journal entry to recognise the cash introduced into the partnership by C.
(c) Prepare the partners' capital and current accounts.
(d) Prepare the SOFP of the new partnership.

Solution
(a)

REVALUATION ACCOUNT

Account Name	€000	Account Name	€000
Property	500	Property – carrying amount	620
Partners' capital accounts			
A (€120,000 × 2/3)	80		
B (€120,000 × 1/3)	40		
	620		620

PROPERTY ACCOUNT – CARRYING AMOUNT

Account Name	€000	Account Name	€000
Balance b/d	500	Revaluation account	500
Revaluation Account	620	Balance c/d	620
	1,120		1,120

(b)

	Debit €000	Credit €000
Cash account	164	
Capital account – C		150
Current account – C		14

To account for the introduction of a new partner.

(c)

CAPITAL ACCOUNTS

Account Name	A €000	B €000	C €000	Account Name	A €000	B €000	C €000
Balance c/d	430	290	150	Balance b/d	350	250	
				Revaluation	80	40	
				Bank			150
	430	290	150		430	290	150
				Balance b/d	430	290	150

CURRENT ACCOUNTS

Account Name	A €000	B €000	C €000	Account Name	A €000	B €000	C €000
Balance c/d	40	60	14	Balance b/d	40	60	
				Bank			14
	40	60	14		40	60	14
				Balance b/d	40	60	14

(d)

A, B and C
STATEMENT OF FINANCIAL POSITION
as at 31 December 2019

	€000
Non-current Assets	
Property (€500,000 + €120,000)	620
Current assets (€200,000 + €164,000)	364
	984
Capital Accounts	
A	430
B	290
C	150
	870
Current Accounts	
A	40
B	60
C	14
	984

Goodwill

Goodwill is an intangible asset, that is, an asset without physical substance. A business may be worth more than the carrying amount of the net assets due to the fact that a potential buyer may be prepared to pay a premium for a business that is already established with a good reputation and a customer base rather than starting a business from scratch.

The partnership has two choices in relation to the treatment of goodwill:
1. recognise and maintain goodwill in the SOFP of the partnership; or
2. recognise each of the old partners' shares of goodwill but do **not** present goodwill in the SOFP of the partnership.

Option One: Goodwill Presented in the SOFP of the Partnership
The journal entry to reflect the goodwill in the SOFP is:

	Debit €	Credit €
Goodwill account	X	
Capital account of each partner in the **old** profit-sharing ratio		X

To recognise goodwill in the partnership.

Example 16.2 demonstrates the treatment of goodwill in the partnership where goodwill is to be presented in the partnership's SOFP.

EXAMPLE 16.2: GOODWILL PRESENTED IN THE PARTNERSHIP'S SOFP

Lawson and Dawson are in partnership, sharing profits in the ratio 60:40 respectively.

Lawson and Dawson
STATEMENT OF FINANCIAL POSITION
as at 31 December 2019

	€000	€000
Non-current Assets		
Property		220
Motor vehicles		45
		265
Current Assets		120
		385
Capital Accounts		
Lawson		160
Dawson		125
		285
Current Accounts		
Lawson	55	
Dawson	45	100
		385

Lawson and Dawson want to recognise goodwill in the books of the partnership – goodwill is estimated at €60,000.

Requirement:
(a) Prepare the journal entries to recognise goodwill.
(b) Prepare the capital and current accounts after goodwill has been recognised.
(c) Prepare the SOFP of Lawson and Dawson after goodwill has been recognised.

Solution
(a)

	Debit €000	Credit €000
Goodwill account	60	
Capital account – Lawson (€60,000 × 60%)		36
Capital account – Dawson (€60,000 × 40%)		24

To recognise goodwill in the partnership.

(b)

CAPITAL ACCOUNTS

Account Name	Dawson €000	Lawson €000	Account Name	Dawson €000	Lawson €000
Balance c/d	196	149	Balance b/d	160	125
			Goodwill	36	24
	196	149		196	149
			Balance b/d	196	149

CURRENT ACCOUNTS

Account Name	Dawson €	Lawson €	Account Name	Dawson €	Lawson €
Balance c/d	55	45	Balance b/d	55	45

(c)

Lawson and Dawson
STATEMENT OF FINANCIAL POSITION
as at 31 December 2019

	€000	€000
Non-current Assets		
Property		220
Motor vehicles		45
Goodwill		60
		325
Current Assets		120
		445
Capital Accounts		
Lawson		196
Dawson		149
		345
Current Accounts		
Lawson	55	
Dawson	45	100
		445

Option Two: Goodwill is Recognised and then Eliminated

Under this method goodwill is recognised, as before, in the old profit-sharing ratio and then eliminated in the new profit-sharing ratio.

The journal entry to recognise goodwill:

	Debit €	Credit €
Goodwill account	X	
Capital accounts (old profit-sharing ratio)		X

To recognise goodwill in the partnership.

The journal entry to eliminate the goodwill:

	Debit €	Credit €
Capital accounts (new profit-sharing ratio)	X	
Goodwill account		X

To eliminate goodwill from the partnership.

Example 17.3 demonstrates the treatment of goodwill in the partnership where goodwill is not to be presented in the partnership's SOFP.

EXAMPLE 17.3: GOODWILL IS NOT PRESENTED IN THE PARTNERSHIP'S SOFP

Doyle and Flynn are in partnership, sharing profits in the ratio 55:45 respectively.

Doyle and Flynn
STATEMENT OF FINANCIAL POSITION
as at 31 December 2019

	€000	€000
Non-current Assets		
Property		280
Motor vehicles		55
		335
Current Assets		90
		425
Capital Accounts		
Doyle		150
Flynn		125
		275
Current Accounts		
Doyle	90	
Flynn	60	150
		425

A new partner, Murphy, is being admitted to the partnership. Murphy will contribute €100,000, which will be split 75:25 between the capital and current accounts. The existing partners believe the goodwill of the partnership is valued at €40,000; they do not want to present goodwill in the partnership's SOFP.

The new profit-sharing ratio is 40:40:20 (Doyle : Flynn : Murphy).

Requirement:
(a) Prepare the journal entries to recognise goodwill and eliminate goodwill from the financial statements of Doyle and Flynn.
(b) Prepare the capital and current accounts after goodwill has been recognised.
(c) Prepare the SOFP of Doyle, Flynn and Murphy after goodwill has been recognised.

Solution
(a)

	Debit €000	Credit €000
Goodwill account	40	
Capital account – Doyle (€40,000 × 55%)		22
Capital account – Flynn (€40,000 × 45%)		18

To recognise goodwill in the partnership.

	Debit €000	Credit €000
Capital account – Doyle (€40,000 × 40%)	16	
Capital account – Flynn (€40,000 × 40%)	16	
Capital account – Murphy (€40,000 × 20%)	8	
Goodwill account		40

To eliminate goodwill from the partnership.

(b)

CAPITAL ACCOUNTS

Account Name	Doyle €000	Flynn €000	Murphy €000	Account Name	Doyle €000	Flynn €000	Murphy €000
Goodwill	16	16	8	Balance b/d	150	125	
Balance c/d	156	127	67	Goodwill	22	18	
				Bank			75
	172	143	75		172	143	75
				Balance b/d	156	127	67

CURRENT ACCOUNTS

Account Name	Doyle €000	Flynn €000	Murphy €000	Account Name	Doyle €000	Flynn €000	Murphy €000
Balance c/d	90	60	25	Balance b/d	90	60	
				Bank			25
	90	60	25		90	60	25

(c)

Doyle, Flynn and Murphy
STATEMENT OF FINANCIAL POSITION
as at 31 December 2019

	€000	€000
Non-current Assets		
Property		280
Motor vehicles		55
		335
Current Assets		190
		525
Capital Accounts		
Doyle		156
Flynn		127
Murphy		67
		350

	€000	€000
Current Accounts		
Doyle	90	
Flynn	60	
Murphy	25	175
		525

(Try **Review Question 16.1** at the end of this chapter.)

16.3 ACCOUNTING FOR THE RETIREMENT/RESIGNATION OF ONE OF THE PARTNERS

When a partner retires/resigns they may:
- be paid out in cash in full; or
- take an asset, such as a motor vehicle, as part-payment; and/or
- leave some of their funds in the partnership as a loan.

On retirement/resignation of a partner, the balances recognised in the partners' capital and current accounts may not reflect the fair value of the net assets of the business. Assets will have to be valued at their respective fair values and the retiring/resigning partner is entitled to a share of any goodwill in the partnership.

The following are the journal entries required on retirement/resignation of a partner:

	Debit €	Credit €
Capital account	X	
Current account	X	
Bank/cash account		X

To record the retirement of the partner from the partnership when the partner is paid in full in cash.

Example 16.4 demonstrates the retirement of a partner who chooses to withdraw their investment in full in cash.

EXAMPLE 16.4: PARTNER RETIRES TAKING THEIR INVESTMENT IN CASH FROM THE PARTNERSHIP

Ann, Bernie and Carol have been in partnership for many years, sharing profits 40:30:30 respectively.

STATEMENT OF FINANCIAL POSITION
as at 31 December 2019

	€000	€000
Non-current Assets		
Property		450
Motor vehicles		42

Current Assets

Inventory	20	
Trade receivables	30	
Bank	140	190
		682

Capital Accounts

Ann	200
Bernie	80
Carol	60
	340

Current Accounts

Ann	80	
Bernie	76	
Carol	36	192

Loan	150
	682

On 31 December 2019, Carol decided to retire from the partnership and wants to be repaid in full in cash. All assets are recognised at their fair value in the SOFP.

Requirement Prepare the statement of financial position of the partnership as at 31 December 2019 after Carol retires.

Solution

CAPITAL ACCOUNTS

Account Name	Ann €000	Bernie €000	Carol €000	Account Name	Alan €000	Bernie €000	Carol €000
Bank			60	Balance b/d	200	80	60
Balance c/d	200	80					
	200	80	60		200	80	60
				Balance b/d	200	80	

CURRENT ACCOUNTS

Account Name	Ann €000	Bernie €000	Carol €000	Account Name	Alan €000	Bernie €000	Carol €000
Bank			36	Balance b/d	80	76	36
Balances c/d	80	76					
	80	60	36		90	60	36
				Balance b/d	80	76	

BANK ACCOUNT

Account Name	€000	Account Name	€000
Balance b/d	140	Capital account – Carol	60
		Current account – Carol	36
		Balance c/d	44
	140		140
Balance b/d	44		

Alan and Bernie
STATEMENT OF FINANCIAL POSITION
as at 31 December 2019

	€000	€000
Non-current Assets		
Property		450
Motor vehicles		42
Current Assets		
Inventory	20	
Trade receivables	30	
Bank	44	94
		586
Capital Accounts		
Ann		200
Bernie		80
		280
Current Accounts		
Ann	80	
Bernie	76	156
Loan		150
		586

When a partner retires/resigns there may not be sufficient cash available within the partnership to pay them out in full. In this case the retiring/resigning partner may withdraw assets from the partnership in settlement of the amount due to them. The assets other than cash are also shown as a reduction in the amount owed to the partner on their current account. The journal entry to record the settlement of the amount due to the partner leaving the partnership is as follows:

	Debit €	Credit €
Capital account	X	
Current account	X	
Non-current asset account		X
Bank/cash account		X

To record partner's retirement from the partnership when the partner is paid in full in cash and assets.

Example 16.5 demonstrates the situation where the retiring/resigning partner withdraws both cash and other assets from the partnership.

EXAMPLE 16.5: WITHDRAWAL OF CASH AND OTHER ASSETS BY RETIRING PARTNER

Andy, Brendan and Cerys are in partnership, sharing profits 3:4:3 respectively. On 31 December 2019 Andy decides to retire; he has agreed to take a motor vehicle with a carrying amount of €25,000 and the balance in cash on retirement.

The partnership has reviewed the value of its assets and liabilities – their fair values were assessed as the following values as at 31 December 2019:

	€
Property	460,000
Goodwill	50,000

Goodwill is not to be maintained in the financial statements of the partnership.

STATEMENT OF FINANCIAL POSITION
as at 31 December 2019

	€000	€000
Non-current Assets		
Property		420
Motor vehicles		74
Current Assets		
Inventory	60	
Trade receivables	55	
Bank	110	225
		719
Capital Accounts		
Andy		180
Brendan		120
Cerys		90
		390

continued overleaf

Current Accounts

Andy	100	
Brendan	95	
Cerys	75	270
Current Liabilities		59
		719

Brendan and Cerys will share profits equally after Andy retires.

Requirement Prepare the SOFP of the partnership as at 31 December 2019 after Andy retires.

Solution

CAPITAL ACCOUNTS

Account Name	Andy €000	Brendan €000	Cerys €000	Account Name	Andy €000	Brendan €000	Cerys €000
Goodwill		25	25	Balance b/d	180	120	90
Bank	207			Revaluation	12	16	12
Balance c/d		131	92	Goodwill	15	20	15
	207	156	117		207	156	117
				Balance b/d		131	92

CURRENT ACCOUNTS

Account Name	Andy €000	Brendan €000	Cerys €000	Account Name	Andy €000	Brendan €000	Cerys €000
Motor vehicle	25			Balance b/d	100	95	75
Bank	75						
Balance c/d		95	75				
	100	95	75		100	95	75
				Balance b/d		95	75

GOODWILL ACCOUNT

Account Name	€000	Account Name	€000
Capital – Andy	15	Capital – Brendan	25
Capital – Brendan	20	Capital – Cerys	25
Capital – Cerys	15		
	50		50

PROPERTY ACCOUNT

Account Name	€000	Account Name	€000
Balance b/d	420	Revaluation account	420
Revaluation	460	Balance c/d	460
	880		880
Balance b/d	460		

REVALUATION ACCOUNT

Account Name	€000	Account Name	€000
Property	420	Property	460
Capital – Andy	12		
Capital – Brendan	16		
Capital – Cerys	12		
	460		460

Andy and Brendan
STATEMENT OF FINANCIAL POSITION
as at 31 December 2019

	€000	€000
Non-current Assets		
Property		460
Motor vehicles (€74,000 – €25,000)		49
Current Assets		
Inventory	60	
Trade receivables	55	115
		624
Capital Accounts		
Brendan		131
Cerys		92
		223
Current Accounts		
Brendan	95	
Cerys	75	170
Current liabilities (W1)		231
		624

W1 CURRENT LIABILITIES FIGURE

	€
Overdraft (€110,000 – €207,000 – €75,000)	172,000
Per question	59,000
	231,000

When a partner retires/resigns there may not be sufficient cash available within the partnership to repay them in full. In this case the retiring/resigning partner may leave some or all of the amount due to them as a loan.

Interest may be paid to the partner on the loan account balance. The interest expense incurred is presented in the statement of profit or loss (SOPL) as an expense of the business – it is not presented in the profit or loss appropriation account.

The journal entry to record the settlement of the amount due to the partner leaving the partnership is as follows:

	Debit €	Credit €
Capital account	X	
Current account	X	
Loan account		X
Bank/cash account		X

To record the retirement of the partner from the partnership when the partner is paid partly in cash and provides the balance as a loan to the partnership.

Example 16.6 demonstrates the impact on the financial statements of the partnership when a partner retires/resigns but leaves some of their investment in the partnership as a loan.

EXAMPLE 16.6: RETIRING PARTNER LEAVES FUNDS IN PARTNERSHIP AS A LOAN

Alan, Brian and Cynthia share profits in the ratio 5:3:2. On 31 December 2019 Brian decides to retire, he has agreed to withdraw €50,000 in cash from the business and the balance due to him will remain as a loan to the partnership, repayable as a loan over the next three years.

The property has a fair value of €500,000 as at 31 December 2019; this has not been reflected in the partners' SOFP.

STATEMENT OF FINANCIAL POSITION
as at 31 December 2019

	€000	€000
Non-current Assets		
Property		450
Motor vehicles		80

Current Assets

Inventory	40	
Trade receivables	70	
Bank	85	195
		725

Capital Accounts

Alan	140
Brian	90
Cynthia	100
	330

Current Accounts

Alan	160	
Brian	120	
Cynthia	115	395
		725

Requirement Prepare the SOFP of the partnership as at 31 December 2019 after Brian retires.

Solution

CAPITAL ACCOUNTS

Account Name	Alan €000	Brian €000	Cynthia €000	Account Name	Alan €000	Brian €000	Cynthia €000
Bank		50		Balance b/d	140	90	100
Loan		55		Revaluation	25	15	10
Balance c/d	165		110				
	165	105	110		165	105	110
				Balance b/d	165		110

CURRENT ACCOUNTS

Account Name	Alan €000	Brian €000	Cynthia €000	Account Name	Alan €000	Brian €000	Cynthia €000
Loan		120		Balance b/d	160	120	115
Balance c/d	160		115				
	160	120	115		160	120	115
				Balance b/d	160		115

PROPERTY ACCOUNT

Account Name	€000	Account Name	€000
Balance b/d	450	Revaluation account	450
Revaluation	500	Balance c/d	500
	950		950
Balance b/d	500		

REVALUATION ACCOUNT

Account Name	€000	Account Name	€000
Property	450	Property	500
Capital – Alan	25		
Capital – Brian	15		
Capital – Cynthia	10		
	500		500

STATEMENT OF FINANCIAL POSITION
as at 31 December 2019

	€000	€000
Non-current Assets		
Property		500
Motor vehicles		80
Current Assets		
Inventory	40	
Trade receivables	70	
Bank (€85,000 – €50,000)	35	145
		725
Capital Accounts		
Alan		165
Cynthia		110
		275
Current Accounts		
Alan	160	
Cynthia	115	275
Loan (€55,000 + €120,000)		175
		725

(Try **Review Question 16.2** at the end of this chapter.)

16.4 ACCOUNTING FOR A CHANGE IN THE PROFIT-SHARING RATIOS OF THE PARTNERS

When there is a change in the profit-sharing ratio, the assets must be fair valued and any goodwill in the partnership must be reflected in the partners' balances. In addition, if a change in the profit-sharing ratio occurs during a reporting period, it will need to be accounted for.

Example 16.7 demonstrates the impact on the profit or loss appropriation account when there is a change in the profit-sharing ratio during the reporting period.

EXAMPLE 16.7: IMPACT ON PROFIT AND LOSS APPROPRIATION
OF A CHANGE IN THE PROFIT-SHARING RATIO

Rose, Sandy and Tara have been in partnership for a number of years, sharing profits 4:4:2 respectively.

On 30 June 2019, Rose decided to take a step back from the business due to other business obligations. To reflect this reduced involvement in the partnership they have agreed a new profit-sharing ratio for Rose, Sandy and Tara as 2:5:3.

The profit for the year ended 31 December 2019 was €140,000. Profits accrue evenly over the reporting period.

Requirement Prepare the profit or loss appropriation account for the year ended 31 December 2019.

Solution

Rose, Sandy and Tara
PROFIT OR LOSS APPROPRIATION ACCOUNT
for the year ended 31 December 2019

	€000	**€000**
Profit for the year		140
Share of profit 01/01/2019–30/06/2019		
Rose (€140,000 × 6/12 × 40%)	28	
Sandy (€140,000 × 6/12 × 40%)	28	
Tara (€140,000 × 6/12 × 20%)	14	(70)
Share of profit 01/07/2019–31/12/2019		
Rose (€140,000 × 6/12 × 20%)	14	
Sandy (€140,000 × 6/12 × 50%)	35	
Tara (€140,000 × 6/12 × 30%)	21	(70)
		Nil

Example 16.8 demonstrates a change in the profit-sharing ratio during the year with assets, including goodwill, revalued.

EXAMPLE 16.8: CHANGE IN PROFIT-SHARING RATIO

On 31 December 2019 Frank has decided to retire from the partnership. David, Eamon and Frank have shared profits in the ratio 50:30:20 respectively. After Frank retires, David and Eamon will share profits 60:40 respectively.

Frank wishes to withdraw all of his funds as follows:
• motor vehicle with a carrying amount of €12,000;
• cash of €40,000; and
• balance on accounts left as a loan to the partnership.

David, Eamon and Frank
STATEMENT OF FINANCIAL POSITION
as at 31 December 2019

	€000	€000
Non-current Assets		
Property		280
Motor vehicles		48
		328
Current Assets		
Inventory	51	
Trade receivables	64	
Cash	80	195
		523
Capital		
David		210
Eamon		105
Frank		80
		395
Current		
David	45	
Eamon	50	
Frank	33	128
		523

The property has a fair value of €350,000 at 31 December 2019. Goodwill is valued at €40,000; it is not to be presented in the SOFP.

Requirement:
(a) Prepare the partners' capital accounts.
(b) Prepare the partners' current accounts.
(c) Prepare the SOFP as at 31 December 2019 of David and Eamon.

Solution

PROPERTY ACCOUNT

Account Name	€000	Account Name	€000
Balance b/d	280	Revaluation	280
Revaluation	350	Balance c/d	350
	630		630
Balance b/d	350		

REVALUATION ACCOUNT

Account Name	€000	Account Name	€000
Property	280	Revaluation	350
Capital – David	35		
Capital – Eamon	21		
Capital – Frank	14		
	350		350

GOODWILL ACCOUNT

Account Name	€000	Account Name	€000
Capital – David	20	Capital – David	24
Capital – Eamon	12	Capital – Eamon	16
Capital – Frank	8		
	40		40

CAPITAL ACCOUNTS

Account Name	David €000	Eamon €000	Frank €000	Account Name	David €000	Eamon €000	Frank €000
Goodwill	24	16		Balance b/d	210	105	80
Bank			40	Revaluation	35	21	14
Motor vehicle			12	Goodwill	20	12	8
Loan			50				
Balance c/d	241	122					
	265	138	102	Balance b/d	265	138	102
					241	122	

CURRENT ACCOUNTS

Account Name	David €000	Eamon €000	Frank €000	Account Name	David €000	Eamon €000	Frank €000
Loan			33	Balance b/d	45	50	33
Balance c/d	45	50					
	45	50	33		45	50	33
				Balance b/d	45	50	

BANK ACCOUNT

Account Name	€000	Account Name	€000
Balance b/d	80	Capital – Frank	40
		Balance c/d	40
	80		80

David and Eamon
STATEMENT OF FINANCIAL POSITION
as at 31 December 2019

	€000	€000
Non-current Assets		
Property (€280,000 + €70,000)		350
Motor vehicles (€48,000 – €12,000)		36
		386
Current Assets		
Inventory	51	
Trade receivables	64	
Bank	40	155
		541

continued overleaf

Capital		
David		241
Eamon		122
		363
Current Accounts		
David	45	
Eamon	50	95
Loan		83
		541

EXAM TIPS

- Be clear on the adjustments that impact the partners' capital accounts and those that impact the partners' current accounts.
- Note the date the change in the partnership occurred and determine any impact on profits.
- Check if goodwill is to be maintained in the books of the partnership or not and deal with it accordingly.

16.5 CONCLUSION

When a change occurs to the partnership structure, the partnership assets, including goodwill, have to be revalued. If the fair values differ from their carrying amounts, this must be reflected in the financial records of the partnership.

SUMMARY OF LEARNING OBJECTIVES

After having studied this chapter, readers should be able to:

Learning Objective 1 Account for the introduction of a new partner.

The assets and liabilities of the partnership must be recognised at fair value at the date of the admission of the new partner. Changes in fair value of assets and liabilities are accounted for through a revaluation account; the surplus (debit balance on the account) or the deficit (credit balance on the account) is taken to the partners' capital accounts in the **old** profit-sharing ratio.

The partners must decide whether they want to present goodwill in the books of the partnership or not – the usual treatment is not to present it in the SOFP of the partnership. The accounting journal entries for each of the treatments of goodwill are set out below:

Option One: Goodwill is presented in the SOFP of the partnership

The journal entry to reflect the goodwill in the SOFP is:

	Debit €	Credit €
Goodwill account	X	
Capital account of each partner in the **old** profit-sharing ratio		X

To recognise goodwill in the partnership.

Option Two: Goodwill is recognised and then eliminated

Under this method goodwill is recognised, as before, in the old profit-sharing ratio and then eliminated in the new profit sharing ratio.

The journal entry to recognise goodwill:

	Debit €	Credit €
Goodwill account	X	
Capital account (old profit-sharing ratio)		X

To recognise goodwill in the partnership.

The journal entry to eliminate goodwill:

	Debit €	Credit €
Capital account (new profit-sharing ratio)	X	
Goodwill account		X

To eliminate goodwill from the partnership.

It is important to note the date on which the partner is admitted to the partnership as the new partner is entitled to a share of the profits from that date.

Learning Objective 2 Account for the retirement/resignation of one of the partners.

The same principles apply when a partner retires as when a new partner is admitted. Take care to notice what the partner is withdrawing from the business:
- cash, and/or
- other assets.

A partner may decide to leave some funds in the partnership as a loan. The loan is presented as a liability and the interest charged on the loan is an expense calculated in arriving at the profit for the year. The interest on the loan is **not** included in the profit or loss appropriation account.

It is important to note the date the partner leaves the partnership as they are entitled to a share of the profits up to that date.

Learning Objective 3 Account for a change in the profit-sharing ratio of the partners.

Note the date of the change and, if any assets that are subject to depreciation are revalued, remember there will be an impact on the profit if the depreciation charge changes as a result of the revaluation.

QUESTIONS

Review Questions

(See **Appendix A** for Solutions to Review Questions.)

Question 16.1

Adam and Brian have been in partnership since July 2014, sharing profits 3:2 respectively. On 31 December 2019 they have agreed to admit a new partner, Charlie. The profit-sharing ratio for Adam, Brian and Charlie will be 4:4:2. As at 31 December 2019 the following information is available.
1. Property has a fair value of €380,000.
2. Goodwill is valued at €80,000 and is not to be presented in the statement of financial position of the partnership.
3. Charlie will introduce cash of €100,000 into the partnership, €20,000 of which is to be put into his current account.

Adam and Brian
TRIAL BALANCE
as at 31 December 2019

	€	€
Property – cost	280,000	
Motor vehicles – cost	50,000	
Property – accumulated depreciation		14,000
Motor vehicles – accumulated depreciation		15,000
Inventory as at 31 December 2019	25,000	
Trade receivables	37,500	
Bank	8,500	
Capital Accounts:		
Adam		190,000
Brian		110,000
Current Accounts:		
Adam		45,000
Brian		27,000
	401,000	401,000

Requirement Prepare the following:
(a) Revaluation account.
(b) Goodwill account.
(c) Capital accounts of the partners.
(d) Current accounts of the partners.
(e) Statement of financial position as at 31 December 2019 of the partnership after the introduction of the new partner.

Question 16.2

On 31 December 2019 Peter has decided to retire from the partnership. Niall, Oliver and Peter have shared profits in the ratio 30:40:30 respectively. After Peter retires, Niall and Oliver will share profits equally.

Peter wishes to withdraw all of the balance on his accounts in cash.

Niall, Oliver and Peter
STATEMENT OF FINANCIAL POSITION
as at 31 December 2019

	€000	€000
Non-current Assets		
Property		210
Motor vehicles		25
		235
Current Assets		
Inventory	36	
Trade receivables	42	
Cash	106	184
		419
Capital		
Niall		100
Oliver		80
Peter		45
		225
Current		
Niall	100	
Oliver	60	
Peter	34	194
		419

Requirement:
(a) Prepare the partners' capital accounts.
(b) Prepare the partners' current accounts.
(c) Prepare the statement of financial position as at 31 December 2019 of Niall and Oliver.

Challenging Questions

(Suggested Solutions to Challenging Questions are available through your lecturer.)

Question 16.1

Harry and Paddy have carried on business in partnership for a number of years, sharing profits in the ratio 6:4. No interest on capital was paid. The partnership accounts are prepared annually to 31 December.

On 1 April 2019, Tony was admitted as a partner, and the terms of the partnership from then were agreed as follows:
(a) Partners' annual salaries to be: Harry €2,700; Paddy €1,800; Tony €1,650.
(b) Interest on capital to be charged at 4% per annum.
(c) Profits to be shared between Harry, Paddy and Tony in the ratio 5:3:2.

On 1 April 2019 Tony paid €10,500 into the partnership bank account. Of this amount, €3,150 was in respect of the share of goodwill acquired by him. Since the partnership has never created, and does not intend to create, a goodwill account, the full amount of €10,500 was credited, for the time being, to Tony's capital account at 1 April 2019.

The profit of the partnership for the year ended 31 December 2019 was calculated to be €18,600.

Assume that this profit accrued evenly over the year.

Details of the summarised trial balance as at 31 December 2019 are as follows:

	Debit €	Credit €
Freehold premises	18,000	
Fixtures and fittings – carrying amount	7,830	
Inventories	22,500	
Bank	4,636	
Trade receivables and payables	41,200	20,596
Allowance for doubtful debts		1,030
Profit for year to 31 December 2019		18,600
Capital Accounts		
Harry		33,000
Paddy		16,500
Tony		10,500
Current Accounts		
Harry	3,300	
Paddy	1,650	
Tony	1,110	
	100,226	100,226

Requirement   Prepare the following accounts:
(a) Partners' capital accounts for the year ended 31 December 2019 to reflect the admission of Tony.

9 Minutes

(b) Profit or loss appropriation account for the year ended 31 December 2019.

9 Minutes

(c) Partners' current accounts for the year ended 31 December 2019.

9 Minutes

(Based on Chartered Accountants Ireland, CAP 1 Financial Accounting, Summer 2009, Question 7)

Question 16.2

Ken, Connor and Edward have been in partnership for a number of years, sharing profits equally. Interest on capital is paid at 10% and Ken gets a salary of €5,000 per annum.

TRIAL BALANCE
as at 31 December 2019

	Debit €	Credit €
Capital accounts		
Ken		110,000
Connor		80,000
Edward		110,000
Current accounts		
Ken		3,650
Connor	1,360	
Edward		3,360
Drawings		
Ken	8,460	
Connor	6,850	
Edward	4,690	
Profit		80,960

continued overleaf

Premises at cost	280,000	
Accumulated depreciation – premises		20,000
Plant and equipment at cost	35,000	
Accumulated depreciation – plant and equipment		9,660
Bank	26,460	
Trade receivables	28,800	
Inventory	62,000	
Trade payables		35,990
	453,620	453,620

NOTES
1. Edward is to retire on 31 December 2019.
2. The following has been agreed:
   (a) Ken and Connor will continue in partnership sharing profits 2:1.
   (b) Goodwill, which is valued at €60,000, is not to be shown in the accounts.
   (c) The valuations relating to the assets of the partnership are as follows:
       (i) Premises €250,000;
       (ii) Plant and equipment €27,000.
   (d) Edward is to be paid any balance due to him on 1 January 2020, except €150,000, which he will leave in the partnership as a loan to be repaid over five years.

Requirement:
(a) Prepare the appropriation account for the year ended 31 December 2019.

7 Minutes

(b) Prepare T accounts to 31 December 2019 for:
   (i) Partners' current accounts;
   (ii) Revaluation account;
   (iii) Partners' capital accounts;
   (iv) Bank account.

15 Minutes

(Based on Chartered Accountants Ireland, CAP 1 Financial Accounting, Summer 2010, Question 6)

Question 16.3

Apple, Pear and Orange have been in partnership sharing profits 5:3:2. The trial balance of the partnership as at 31 December 2018 is as follows:

TRIAL BALANCE
as at 31 December 2018

	Debit €	Credit €
Motor vehicles	27,000	
Fixtures and fittings	9,000	
Accumulated depreciation – motor vehicles		18,000
Accumulated depreciation – fixtures and fittings		6,300
Bank	1,020	
Receivables	40,430	
Payables		34,500
Inventory at 31 December 2018	43,500	
Provision for doubtful debts		2,050

continued overleaf

	Debit €	Credit €
Current account		
Apple		2,250
Pear		3,450
Orange		1,500
Capital account		
Apple		5,000
Pear		10,000
Orange		8,000
Drawings		
Apple	12,000	
Pear	10,000	
Orange	5,000	
Profit for the year ended 31 December 2018		56,900
	147,950	147,950

Additional information:

1. Interest on drawings for the year ended 31 December 2018 have been calculated as follows: Apple €600, Pear €500, and Orange €300.
2. Interest on capital is payable at a rate of 10%.
3. On 1 January 2019 a new partner, Banana, was admitted to the partnership. Banana introduced €20,000 in cash.
4. Goodwill, which is estimated at €15,000, is not to be shown in the financial statements for the year ended 31 December 2018.
5. Motor vehicles are to be revalued to €8,000 and fixtures to €6,000. These revaluations are to be incorporated in the financial statements for the year ended 31 December 2018.
6. The partners will share profits equally from 1 January 2019.
7. The current accounts are to be cleared to the capital accounts and any amount in excess of €15,000 is to be transferred to a loan account.

Requirement:

(a) Prepare the profit appropriation account for the year ended 31 December 2018.

5 Minutes

(b) Prepare the partners' current accounts at 31 December 2018.

7 Minutes

(c) Prepare the revaluation account and the entries for goodwill at 1 January 2019.

5 Minutes

(d) Prepare the partners' capital accounts at 1 January 2019.

7 Minutes

(e) Prepare the 'statement of financial position' of Apple, Pear, Orange and Banana at 1 January 2019.

5 Minutes

(Based on Chartered Accountants Ireland, CAP 1 Financial Accounting, Autumn 2013, Question 2)

17

Partnerships: Complex Issues

LEARNING OBJECTIVES

Having studied this chapter, readers should be able to:
1. account for the winding up of a partnership;
2. account for the conversion of a partnership into a limited company;
3. account for the merging of two partnerships into one partnerships;
4. apply the *Garner v. Murray* rule; and
5. account for a piecemeal realisation.

17.1 INTRODUCTION

Partnerships may terminate for a number of reasons, such as all partners are retiring or the business has grown and a limited company structure is more appropriate. On realisation, all of the partnership's debts will have to be repaid and its assets sold. In these scenarios a realisation account is opened. The realisation account is used as follows.

- **Assets**
  - The **carrying amount** of the assets held, with the exception of cash and bank, are debited to the realisation account and credited from the respective asset accounts.
  - When the assets are sold the proceeds are debited to bank or cash account and credited to the realisation account.
- **Liabilities**
  - When the partnership negotiates a reduction in a liability on dissolution, the discount is debited to the liability account and credited to the realisation account
- **Expenses related to the dissolution of the partnership**
  - Any expenses incurred in relation to the dissolution of the partnership are debited to the realisation account and credited to the bank/cash account.
- **Balance on the realisation account**
  - The balance on the realisation account represents either a profit or loss on dissolution. A profit or loss on the realisation of assets is shared among the partners in their profit-sharing ratio.
- **Balances on the partners' current accounts**
  - The balances on the partners' current accounts are generally transferred to the partners' capital accounts at the start of the dissolution process.

Each of the scenarios set out in the Learning Objectives for this chapter will now be dealt with separately.

17.2 ACCOUNTING FOR THE WINDING UP OF A PARTNERSHIP

The sequence of events in the winding up or dissolution of a partnership is set out in the Partnership Act 1890:

1. dispose of the assets (either externally or to partners);
2. pay all the liabilities other than amounts due to the partners;
3. pay partners their loans advanced to the business or amounts over and above their agreed capital balances;
4. partners pay any amounts that they owe to the partnership (i.e. they settle the debit balances on their capital or current accounts); and
5. pay the balances due to the partners on their capital and current accounts.

When a partnership is being dissolved the following steps should be followed:

1. Transfer each of the balances at the date of dissolution on the partners' current accounts to the partners' capital accounts. Each of the journal entries to record these transactions would be as follows:

	Debit €	Credit €
Partner's current account	X	
Partner's capital account		X

To transfer the balance on the partner's current account to their capital account.

2. Open a realisation account and transfer the balances on the partnership's asset accounts to this account. Each of the journal entries to record these transactions would be as follows:

	Debit €	Credit €
Realisation account	X	
Asset account		X

To transfer the assets of the partnership to the realisation account.

3. Recognise the proceeds from the sale of the assets. The journal entry to record this transaction would be as follows:

	Debit €	Credit €
Bank/partners' account	X	
Realisation account		X

To recognise the amount realised on disposal of assets on dissolution of the partnership.

The assets disposed of may be sold for cash or one of the partners may take possession of one (or more) of the asset(s) for an agreed sum. The agreed sum in relation to the transfer of an asset from the partnership to a particular partner reduces the amount owed to that partner on dissolution.

4. When a partnership is dissolved, any partnership liabilities must be paid before any payments are made to the partners. The journal entry to record each of these payments would be as follows:

	Debit €	Credit €
Loan/liability account	X	
Bank account		X

To recognise the repayment of liabilities on dissolution.

5. Recognise any costs associated with the dissolution of the partnership. The journal entry to record this transaction would be as follows:

	Debit €	Credit €
Realisation account	X	
Bank account		X

To recognise the costs associated with dissolution.

6. Balance the realisation account. If the total of the debit entries to the realisation account is greater than the total of the credit entries, this means that a loss has been made on the realisation. The loss on realisation must be apportioned between the partners in their profit-sharing ratio. The journal entry to record the loss on realisation is shown below:

	Debit €	Credit €
Partners' capital accounts	X	
Realisation account		X

To recognise a loss on realisation.

If the total of the debit entries on the realisation account is less than the total of the credit entries this means a profit has been made on the realisation of the partnership. The profit on realisation must be apportioned between the partners in their profit-sharing ratio. The journal entry to record the profit on realisation is shown below:

	Debit €	Credit €
Realisation account	X	
Partners' capital accounts		X

To recognise a profit on realisation.

7. Settle the amounts due to/from each partner. After the above transactions have been recorded (transfer of the current account balances to the capital accounts, the profit/loss on realisation and any assets taken over by individual partners), the total balances due to the partners as shown on their capital accounts should equal the balance on the bank account.

When a partner is owed money by the partnership on dissolution, the following journal entry will record the settlement of the amount due:

	Debit €	Credit €
Partner's capital account	X	
Bank account		X

To recognise the settlement of amounts due to a partner on dissolution of the partnership.

When a partner owes money to the partnership on dissolution, the following journal entry will record the settlement of the amount due by the partner:

	Debit €	Credit €
Bank account	X	
Partner's capital account		X

To recognise the settlement of amounts due from a partner on dissolution of the partnership.

Example 17.1 demonstrates the steps involved in the dissolution of a partnership.

EXAMPLE 17.1: DISSOLUTION OF A PARTNERSHIP

Alan and Brian have been in partnership for a number of years, sharing profits equally. On 31 December 2019 Alan and Brian decide to dissolve the partnership.

Alan and Brian
STATEMENT OF FINANCIAL POSITION
as at 31 December 2019

	€000	€000
Non-current Assets		
Property		800
Plant and equipment		240
Motor vehicles		80
		1,120
Current Assets		
Inventory	60	
Trade receivables	110	
Bank	50	220
		1,340
Capital Accounts		
Alan		400
Brian		350
		750
Current Accounts		
Alan	140	
Brian	70	210
Non-current Liability – Loan		300
Current Liability – Trade payables		80
		1,340

The following additional information is available:

1. The assets were settled at the following amounts:

	€000
Property	830
Plant and equipment	180
Motor vehicles	70
Inventory	50
Trade receivables	110

2. The liabilities were paid in full.
3. Expenses incurred in relation to the dissolution of the partnership amounted to €8,500.

Requirement To record the dissolution of the partnership, prepare the following ledger accounts:
(a) Realisation account.
(b) Partnership capital accounts.
(c) Bank account.

Solution

Step 1 Transfer the balances on the partners' current accounts to the partners' capital accounts.

PARTNERS' CURRENT ACCOUNTS

Account Name	Alan €	Brian €	Account Name	Alan €	Brian €
Capital account	140,000	70,000	Balance b/d	140,000	70,000

PARTNERS' CAPITAL ACCOUNTS

Account Name	Alan €	Brian €	Account Name	Alan €	Brian €
			Balance b/d	400,000	350,000
			Current account	140,000	70,000

Step 2 Open the realisation account and transfer the balances on the asset accounts to it.

REALISATION ACCOUNT

Account Name	€	Account Name	€
Property	800,000		
Plant and equipment	240,000		
Motor vehicles	80,000		
Inventory	60,000		
Trade receivables	110,000		

Step 3 Recognise the proceeds from the sale of the assets.

BANK ACCOUNT

Account Name	€	Account Name	€
Balance b/d	50,000		
Property	830,000		
Plant and equipment	180,000		
Motor vehicles	70,000		
Inventory	50,000		
Trade receivables	110,000		

REALISATION ACCOUNT

Account Name	€	Account Name	€
Property	800,000	Bank	830,000
Plant and equipment	240,000	Bank	180,000
Motor vehicles	80,000	Bank	70,000
Inventory	60,000	Bank	50,000
Trade receivables	110,000	Bank	110,000

Step 4 Recognise the settlement of the liabilities.

BANK ACCOUNT

Account Name	€	Account Name	€
Balance b/d	50,000	Loan	300,000
Property	830,000	Trade payables	80,000
Plant and equipment	180,000		
Motor vehicles	70,000		
Inventory	50,000		
Trade receivables	110,000		

LOAN ACCOUNT

Account Name	€	Account Name	€
Bank	300,000	Balance b/d	300,000

TRADE PAYABLES

Account Name	€	Account Name	€
Bank	80,000	Balance b/d	80,000

Step 5 Recognise the dissolution expenses.

BANK ACCOUNT

Account Name	€	Account Name	€
Balance b/d	50,000	Loan	300,000
Property	830,000	Trade payables	80,000
Plant and equipment	180,000	Realisation account	8,500
Motor vehicles	70,000		
Inventory	50,000		
Trade receivables	110,000		

REALISATION ACCOUNT

Account Name	€	Account Name	€
Property	800,000	Bank	830,000
Plant and equipment	240,000	Bank	180,000
Motor vehicles	80,000	Bank	70,000
Inventory	60,000	Bank	50,000
Trade receivables	110,000	Bank	110,000
Bank – expenses	8,500		

Step 6 Balance-off the realisation account.

The total of the debit side of the realisation account is €1,298,500, while the total of the credit side is €1,240,000. This means that the partnership has incurred a loss on dissolution. The loss on dissolution is shared between the partners in their profit-sharing ratio, that is, equally:

Alan: €58,500 × 50% = €29,250

Brian: €58,500 × 50% = €29,250

REALISATION ACCOUNT

Account Name	€	Account Name	€
Property	800,000	Bank	830,000
Plant and equipment	240,000	Bank	180,000
Motor vehicles	80,000	Bank	70,000
Inventory	60,000	Bank	50,000
Trade receivables	110,000	Bank	110,000
Bank – expenses	8,500	Alan	29,250
		Brian	29,250
	1,298,500		1,298,500

PARTNERS' CAPITAL ACCOUNTS

Account Name	Alan €	Brian €	Account Name	Alan €	Brian €
Realisation	29,250	29,250	Balance b/d	400,000	350,000
			Current account	140,000	70,000

Step 7 Settle the amounts due to the partners.

PARTNERS' CAPITAL ACCOUNTS

Account Name	Alan €	Brian €	Account Name	Alan €	Brian €
Realisation	29,250	29,250	Balance b/d	400,000	350,000
Bank	510,750	390,750	Current account	140,000	70,000
	540,000	420,000		540,000	420,000

BANK ACCOUNT

Account Name	€	Account Name	€
Balance b/d	50,000	Loan	300,000
Property	830,000	Trade payables	80,000
Plant and equipment	180,000	Realisation account	8,500
Motor vehicles	70,000	Alan	510,750
Inventory	50,000	Brian	390,750
Trade receivables	110,000		
	1,290,000		1,290,000

If everything has been accounted for correctly, the amount paid to the partners will clear the balance on the bank account to zero.

(Try **Review Question 17.1** at the end of this chapter.)

In the next section, the situation where a partnership converts to a limited company rather than continuing as a partnership is considered.

17.3 CONVERSION OF A PARTNERSHIP INTO A LIMITED COMPANY

There are advantages that a limited company structure offers over a partnership:
• gives limited liability to owners; and
• better opportunities for raising finance.

When the partnership is dissolved the assets must be transferred from the partnership to the company at their fair value. The terms of the transfer need to be read carefully, such as who will settle liabilities and the shares to be issued in the company.

When a partnership is converted to a limited company, the assets being taken over by the company must be transferred at their fair value. Fair value is defined by IFRS 13 *Fair Value Measurement* (IFRS 13) as "the price that would be received to sell an asset or paid to transfer a liability in an orderly transaction between market participants at the measurement date". 'An orderly transaction' means that you are not under pressure to sell quickly. 'Market participants' are considered to have a good understanding of the types of assets involved and their valuation in the current market.

When a partnership is converted to a limited company, the following steps should be followed.
1. Transfer the balances on the partners' current accounts to the partners' capital accounts at the date of conversion (as outlined for a partnership's dissolution above).
2. Open a realisation account and transfer the balances on the asset accounts to this account (as outlined for a partnership's dissolution above).
3. Open an account in the name of the company to whom the partnership is being transferred. The amount paid by the company for the net assets of the partnership is recognised in the books of the partnership. The journal entry to recognise the proceeds paid by the company is as follows:

	Debit €	Credit €
Account in company's name	X	
Realisation account		X

To recognise the proceeds received from the company.

The proceeds paid may be made up of shares in the company and cash. The shares issued by the company are apportioned to the partners on an agreed basis. The value of the shares issued to each partner reduces the amount owed by the partnership to each partner. The journal entry to recognise the apportionment of the shares among the partners is as follows:

	Debit €	Credit €
Partners' capital accounts	X	
Account in company's name		X

To recognise the shares attributed to each partner.

The cash portion of the proceeds is transferred from the account in the company's name to the bank account. After this transaction is recorded, the balance on the account in the company's name should be zero. The journal entry to transfer the cash proceeds is as follows:

	Debit €	Credit €
Bank account	X	
Account in company's name		X

To recognise the cash received by the company.

4. One of the partners may take possession of one (or more) of the asset(s) at an agreed valuation. This agreed sum in relation to the transfer of an asset from the partnership to a particular partner reduces the amount owed to that partner on dissolution. The journal entry to reflect this transaction is shown below:

	Debit €	Credit €
Partner's capital account	X	
Realisation account		X

To recognise an asset taken over by a partner.

5. When a partnership is converted to a limited company, any of the partnership's liabilities not taken over by the company must be paid before any payments are made to the partners. The journal entry is as outlined for a partnership's dissolution above. Alternatively, the trade payables or other liabilities may be taken over by the new company. The journal entry in this case is: debit the liability account and credit the realisation account.

6. Recognise any costs associated with the conversion of the partnership to a limited company. The journal entry is as outlined for a partnership's dissolution above.

7. Balance the realisation account. If the total of the debit entries on the realisation account is greater than the total of the credit entries, this means that a loss has been made on realisation. The loss on realisation must be apportioned between the partners in their profit-sharing ratio. The journal entry is as outlined for a partnership's dissolution above.

   If the total of the debit entries on the realisation account is less than the total of the credit entries, this means a profit has been made on realisation. The profit on realisation must be apportioned between the partners in their profit-sharing ratio. The journal entry is as outlined for a partnership's dissolution above.

8. Settle the amounts due to each partner. After the above transactions have been recorded, the total balances due to/from the partners should equal the balance on the bank account.

Example 17.2 demonstrates the situation where the consideration paid is greater than the fair value of the net assets of the partnership When the company pays an amount for the partnership that is greater than the value of the partnership's net assets (i.e. assets – liabilities) taken over by the company, this difference is known as '**goodwill**'. Goodwill is presented as a non-current asset in the statement of financial position (SOFP) of the company.

EXAMPLE 17.2: CONVERSION TO LIMITED COMPANY WHEN CONSIDERATION IS GREATER THAN VALUE OF NET ASSETS TAKEN OVER FROM THE PARTNERSHIP

You have been provided with the following financial statements for the partnership of Arthur and Bruce, who share profits and losses 60:40 respectively.

Arthur and Bruce
STATEMENT OF FINANCIAL POSITION
as at 31 December 2019

	€000	€000
Non-current Assets		
Property		500
Motor vehicles		80
		580
Current Assets		
Inventory	65	
Trade receivables	100	
Bank	105	270
		850

continued overleaf

	€000	€000
Capital Accounts		
Arthur		350
Bruce		310
		660
Non-current Liability – Loan		100
Current Liability – Trade payables		90
		850

Additional information:
1. AB Ltd will pay a total consideration of €750,000 for the partnership. The consideration is made up of 500,000 €1 ordinary shares and €250,000 cash payment. AB Ltd has taken out a loan from a local bank to make the cash payment.
2. The partnership loan will be paid off in full by the partnership.
3. The trade payables will be taken over by the company.

Requirement:
(a) Prepare the accounts in the partnership to record its dissolution.
(b) Prepare the SOFP of AB Ltd as at 31 December 2019.

Solution
(a)

REALISATION ACCOUNT

Account Name	€	Account Name	€
Premises	500,000	AB Ltd	750,000
Motor vehicles	80,000	Trade payables	90,000
Inventory	65,000		
Trade receivables	100,000		
Arthur	57,000		
Bruce	38,000		
	840,000		840,000

AB LTD'S ACCOUNT

Account Name	€	Account Name	€
Realisation	750,000	Ordinary shares – Arthur	300,000
		Ordinary shares – Bruce	200,000
		Cash	250,000
	750,000		750,000

CAPITAL ACCOUNTS

Account Name	Arthur €	Bruce €	Account Name	Arthur €	Bruce €
Ordinary shares	300,000	200,000	Balance c/d	350,000	310,000
Cash	107,000	148,000	Profit on disposal	57,000	38,000
	407,000	348,000		407,000	348,000

BANK ACCOUNT

Account Name	€	Account Name	€
Balance b/d	105,000	Loan	100,000
AB Ltd	250,000	Arthur	107,000
		Bruce	148,000
	355,000		355,000

(b)

AB Ltd
STATEMENT OF FINANCIAL POSITION
as at 31 December 2019

	€000	€000
Non-current Assets		
Property		500
Motor vehicles		80
Goodwill (€57,000 + €38,000)		95
		675
Current Assets		
Inventory	65	
Trade receivables	100	165
		840
Equity		
Ordinary share capital		500
Non-current Liability – Loan		250
Current Liabilities – Trade payables		90
		840

In **Example 17.2** the shares in the company are apportioned to the partners in their profit-sharing ratio. Apportionment is not always on this basis. **Example 17.3** demonstrates the situation where partners' entitlement to shares in the new company is not based on the profit-sharing ratio.

EXAMPLE 17.3: CONVERSION TO A LIMITED COMPANY

Adam, Bobby and Clare have been in partnership for a number of years, sharing profits and losses 3:2:1 respectively.

On 31 December the partners formed a company, Friends Ltd. It is the intention of the partners to transfer the business of the partnership to the limited company.

Adam, Bobby and Clare
STATEMENT OF FINANCIAL POSITION
as at 31 December 2019

	€000	€000
Non-current Assets		
Property		640
Equipment		120
Motor vehicles		45
		805
Current Assets		
Inventory	35	
Trade receivables	60	
Bank	50	145
		950
Capital Accounts		
Adam		310
Bobby		290
Clare		220
		820
Non-current Liability – Partner's loan (Clare)		88
Current Liabilities – Trade payables		42
		950

Additional information:
1. Friends Ltd will pay a total consideration of €880,000 for the partnership. The consideration is made up of 540,000 €1 ordinary shares and €340,000 cash payment. Friends Ltd has taken out a loan from a local bank to make the cash payment. The ordinary share capital of Friends Ltd will be apportioned equally between the partners.
2. The partner's loan provided by Clare will be paid off in full by the partnership.
3. The trade payables will be taken over by the company.

Requirement:
(a) Prepare the accounts in the partnership to record its dissolution.
(b) Prepare the SOFP of Friends Ltd as at 31 December 2019.

Solution
(a)

REALISATION ACCOUNT

Account Name	€	Account Name	€
Premises	640,000	Friends Ltd	880,000
Equipment	120,000	Trade payables	42,000
Motor vehicles	45,000		
Inventory	35,000		
Trade receivables	60,000		
Adam	11,000		
Bobby	7,333		
Clare	3,667		
	922,000		922,000

FRIENDS LTD'S ACCOUNT

Account Name	€	Account Name	€
Realisation	880,000	Ordinary shares – Adam	180,000
		Ordinary shares – Bobby	180,000
		Ordinary shares – Clare	180,000
		Bank	340,000
	880,000		880,000

CAPITAL ACCOUNTS

Account Name	Adam €	Bobby €	Clare €	Account Name	Adam €	Bobby €	Clare €
Ordinary shares	180,000	180,000	180,000	Balance c/d	310,000	290,000	220,000
Bank	141,000	117,333	43,667	Profit on disposal	11,000	7,333	3,667
	321,000	297,333	223,667		321,000	297,333	223,667

BANK ACCOUNT

Account Name	€	Account Name	€
Balance b/d	50,000	Loan – Clare	88,000
Friends Ltd	340,000	Adam	141,000
		Bobby	117,333
		Clare	43,667
	390,000		390,000

(b)

Friends Ltd
STATEMENT OF FINANCIAL POSITION
as at 31 December 2019

	€000	€000
Non-current Assets		
Property		640
Equipment		120
Motor vehicles		45
Goodwill (€11,000 + €7,333 + €3,667)		22
		827
Current Assets		
Inventory	35	
Trade receivables	60	95
		922
Equity		
Ordinary share capital		540
Non-current Liability – Loan		340
Current Liabilities – Trade payables		42
		922

17.4 MERGING OF TWO PARTNERSHIPS INTO ONE PARTNERSHIP

To account for the merging of two partnerships into one partnership, the assets and liabilities of each partnership are recognised at the fair value and any gains or losses are shared between the partners in their profit-sharing ratio. The terms of the merger will state the capital to be contributed by each of the partners.

The approach to be followed in relation to the merging of two partnerships is broadly similar to that outlined in relation to **Example 17.1**. For each partnership follow the steps outlined earlier.

Example 17.4 demonstrates the accounting for the merging of two partnerships.

EXAMPLE 17.4: MERGING OF TWO PARTNERSHIPS

The following information is provided in relation to two partnerships that operate the same type of business.

STATEMENTS OF FINANCIAL POSITION
as at 31 December 2019

	A & B €000	C & D €000
Non-current Assets		
Property	400	500
Plant and equipment	120	150
Motor vehicles	50	70
	570	720
Current Assets		
Inventory	40	50
Trade receivables	50	80
Bank	35	110
	695	960
Capital Accounts		
A	330	
B	280	
C		480
D		360
	610	840
Current Liabilities – Trade payables	85	120
	695	960

Additional information:
1. On 31 December 2019 the two partnerships are going to merge into a new partnership, ABCD. The partners have agreed the following values for their respective assets:

	A & B €000	C & D €000
Property	450	580
Plant and machinery	110	160
Motor vehicles	44	62
Inventory	40	50
Trade receivables	50	80

2. The trade payables are to be taken into the new partnership at their carrying amount.
3. The partners shared profit and losses equally in the old partnerships.
4. Each of the partners will contribute €250,000, 80% will be attributed to the partners' capital accounts and the balance to their current accounts.
5. If any partner has an amount in excess of their €250,000 required capital contribution it will be provided as a loan to the new partnership.

Requirement:
(a) Close the books of partnership of A & B.
(b) Close the books of partnership of C & D.
(c) Prepare the SOFP of the new partnership as at 31 December 2019.

Solution
(a) **Step 1** Open a realisation account and transfer the balances on the asset accounts to it.

REALISATION ACCOUNT

Account Name	€	Account Name	€
Property	400,000		
Plant and equipment	120,000		
Motor vehicles	50,000		
Inventory	40,000		
Trade receivables	50,000		

Step 2 Transfer the assets to the new partnership.

REALISATION ACCOUNT

Account Name	€	Account Name	€
Property	400,000	ABCD – property	450,000
Plant and equipment	120,000	ABCD – plant and equipment	110,000
Motor vehicles	50,000	ABCD – motor vehicles	44,000
Inventory	40,000	ABCD – inventory	40,000
Trade receivables	50,000	ABCD – trade receivables	50,000

Step 3 Balance-off the realisation account.

The total of the debit side of the realisation account is €660,000, while the total of the credit side is €694,000. This means that the partnership has made a profit on dissolution. The profit on dissolution is shared between the partners in their profit-sharing ratio, that is, equally:

A: €34,000 × 50% = €17,000
B: €34,000 × 50% = €17,000

REALISATION ACCOUNT

Account Name	€	Account Name	€
Property	400,000	ABCD – property	450,000
Plant and equipment	120,000	ABCD – plant and equipment	110,000
Motor vehicles	50,000	ABCD – motor vehicles	44,000
Inventory	40,000	ABCD – inventory	40,000
Trade receivables	50,000	ABCD – trade receivables	50,000
A	17,000		
B	17,000		
	694,000		694,000

PARTNERS' CAPITAL ACCOUNTS

Account Name	A €	B €	Account Name	A €	B €
ABCD – Capital	200,000	200,000	Balance b/d	330,000	280,000
ABCD – Current	50,000	50,000	Realisation	17,000	17,000
ABCD – Loan	97,000	47,000			
	347,000	297,000		347,000	297,000

(b) **Step 1** Open a realisation account and transfer the balances on the asset accounts to it.

REALISATION ACCOUNT

Account Name	€	Account Name	€
Property	500,000		
Plant and equipment	150,000		
Motor vehicles	70,000		
Inventory	50,000		
Trade receivables	80,000		

Step 2 Transfer the assets to the new partnership.

REALISATION ACCOUNT

Account Name	€	Account Name	€
Property	500,000	ABCD – property	580,000
Plant and equipment	150,000	ABCD – plant and equipment	160,000
Motor vehicles	70,000	ABCD – motor vehicles	62,000
Inventory	50,000	ABCD – inventory	50,000
Trade receivables	80,000	ABCD – trade receivables	80,000

Step 3 Balance off the realisation account.

The total of the debit side of the realisation account is €850,000, while the total of the credit side is €932,000. This means that the partnership has made a profit on dissolution. The profit on dissolution is shared between the partners in their profit-sharing ratio, that is, equally:

C: €82,000 × 50% = €41,000
D: €82,000 × 50% = €41,000

REALISATION ACCOUNT

Account Name	€	Account Name	€
Property	500,000	ABCD – property	580,000
Plant and equipment	150,000	ABCD – plant and equipment	160,000
Motor vehicles	70,000	ABCD – motor vehicles	62,000
Inventory	50,000	ABCD – inventory	50,000
Trade receivables	80,000	ABCD – trade receivables	80,000
C	41,000		
D	41,000		
	932,000		932,000

PARTNERS' CAPITAL ACCOUNTS

Account Name	A €	B €	Account Name	A €	B €
ABCD – Capital	200,000	200,000	Balance b/d	480,000	360,000
ABCD – Current	50,000	50,000	Realisation	41,000	41,000
ABCD – Loan	271,000	151,000			
	521,000	401,000		521,000	401,000

(c)

ABCD
STATEMENT OF FINANCIAL POSITION
as at 31 December 2019

	€000	€000
Non-current Assets		
Property (€450,000 + €580,000)		1,030
Plant and equipment (€110,000 + €160,000)		270
Motor vehicles (€44,000 + €62,000)		106
		1,406
Current Assets		
Inventory (€40,000 + €50,000)	90	
Trade receivables (€50,000 + €80,000)	130	
Bank (€35,000 + €110,000)	145	365
		1,771
Capital Accounts		
A		200
B		200
C		200
D		200
		800
Current Accounts		
A	50	
B	50	
C	50	
D	50	200

	€000	€000
Non-current Liabilities		
Partner loan – A	97	
Partner loan – B	47	
Partner loan – C	271	
Partner loan – D	151	566
Current Liabilities – Trade payables (€85,000 + €120,000)		205
		1,771

17.5 THE WINDING UP OF A PARTNERSHIP

When a partnership is wound up partners may or may not have sufficient personal funds available to make good any deficits on their partners' capital and current accounts.

When one of the partners is unable to pay any deficit on the dissolution of the partnership, case law indicates the appropriate treatment. The rule established in *Garner v. Murray* (1904) states that any deficiency on a partner's account has to be made up by the other partners in the ratio of their **last agreed capital balances** and **not** their profit-sharing ratio. The last agreed capital balances are usually the balances on their capital accounts at the last reporting date.

The only way to avoid the application of the principle established in *Garner v. Murray* is to specifically state in the Partnership Agreement the method to be used on dissolution.

Note: always read questions on dissolution carefully to ensure that *Garner v. Murray* is to be applied.

Example 17.5 demonstrates the application of the *Garner v. Murray* rule when funds are being distributed after all assets have been disposed of and liabilities settled.

EXAMPLE 17.5: *GARNER V. MURRAY* APPLIED WHEN ONLY ONE DISTRIBUTION IS MADE

Anthea, Bernie and Charlie have been in partnership for a number of years, sharing profits 40:30:30 respectively.

Anthea, Bernie and Charlie
STATEMENT OF FINANCIAL POSITION
as at 31 December 2019

	€000
Non-current Assets	
Property	320
Motor vehicles	45
	365
Current Assets	
Inventory	30
Trade receivables	25
Bank	62
	482

Capital Accounts

Anthea	60
Bernie	50
Charlie	22

Non-current Liability – Loan   280

Current Liabilities – Trade payables   70
482

Additional information:
1. The following sales proceeds were achieved in relation to assets sold:

	€
Property	267,000
Motor vehicles	28,000
Inventory	25,000

2. All liabilities were paid in full.
3. Costs of winding up the partnership amounted to €5,000.

Requirement Prepare the accounts to wind up the partnership applying the *Garner v. Murray* rule.

Solution
(a)

REALISATION ACCOUNT

Account Name	€	Account Name	€
Premises	320,000	Bank (€267,000 + €28,000 +	
Motor vehicles	45,000	€25,000 + €25,000)	345,000
Inventory	30,000	Anthea	32,000
Trade receivables	25,000	Bernie	24,000
Realisation expenses	5,000	Charlie	24,000
	425,000		425,000

CAPITAL ACCOUNTS

Account Name	Anthea €	Bernie €	Charlie €	Account Name	Anthea €	Bernie €	Charlie €
Realisation	32,000	24,000	24,000	Balance b/d	60,000	50,000	22,000
Balance c/d	28,000	26,000		Balance c/d			2,000
	60,000	50,000	24,000		60,000	50,000	24,000
Balance b/d			2,000	Balance b/d	28,000	26,000	

When the *Garner v. Murray* rule applies, any loss on a partner's account is covered by the other partners in the proportion of their last agreed capital balances.

The capital balances as at 31 December 2019 were:

	€
Anthea	60,000
Bernie	50,000
Total	110,000

Anthea's share of Charlie's deficit: €2,000 × €60,000/€110,000 = €1,090
Bernie's share of Charlie's deficit: €2,000 × €50,000/€110,000 = €910

CAPITAL ACCOUNTS

Account Name	Anthea €	Bernie €	Charlie €	Account Name	Anthea €	Bernie €	Charlie €
Balance b/d			2,000	Balance b/d	28,000	26,000	
Transfer	1,090	910		Transfer			2,000
Bank	26,910	25,090					
	28,000	26,000	2,000		28,000	26,000	2,000

BANK ACCOUNT

Account Name	€	Account Name	€
Balance b/d	62,000	Loan	280,000
Realisation account	345,000	Trade payables	70,000
		Realisation account	5,000
		Anthea	26,910
		Bernie	25,090
	407,000		407,000

Piecemeal Realisation

Earlier in this chapter it has been assumed that the partnership is wound up quickly and the proceeds distributed, but in reality it may take longer and the partners may not be prepared to wait until every asset has been realised to get their investment back. When paying money out before the winding up is complete, care must be exercised to ensure that, in the event of an overall loss being incurred, money is not paid to a partner who subsequently cannot make any contribution towards a loss. Therefore, the procedure is as follows.

1. Treat each receipt as if it is the final receipt.
2. Share any loss to date among the partners in the profit-sharing ratio.
3. If a partner has a debit balance on his account, assume he/she is unable to pay and share loss as set out in *Garner v. Murray* (unless otherwise specified).
4. Pay liabilities and costs of dissolution with the remainder being paid to partners.
5. If more money becomes available or a partner cannot pay his/her share of loss, then money has only been allocated in agreement with the legal requirements.

Example 17.6 demonstrates the application of the *Garner v. Murray* rule when funds are being distributed on a piecemeal basis.

EXAMPLE 17.6: *GARNER V. MURRAY* RULE APPLIED WHEN DISTRIBUTIONS ARE BEING MADE TO PARTNERS ON A PIECEMEAL BASIS

A & B
STATEMENT OF FINANCIAL POSITION
as at 31 December 2019

	€000	€000
Non-current Assets		
Property		240
Current Assets		
Inventory	18	
Trade receivables	34	
Bank	6	58
		298
Capital Accounts		
A		200
B		62
		262
Current Liabilities		
Trade payables		36
		298

Additional information:

1. On 31 December 2019, A and B decide to dissolve the partnership.
2. Expenses associated with dissolution amounted to €4,000.
3. On 10 January the inventory was sold for €15,000. The trade receivables paid €30,000 in full and final settlement of the amount due.
4. On 31 January the property was sold for €210,000.
5. B is unable to make up any deficit on their capital account.
6. A and B share profits equally.
7. The balance on the trade payables account is paid in full on dissolution.

Requirement:

(a)   Determine how much each partner will receive at each distribution, 10 January and 31 January.
(b)   Prepare the realisation accounts, bank accounts and capital accounts for each partner.

Solution

(a)

10 January	€	A €	B €
Capital balance		200,000	62,000
Net assets (W1)	256,000		
Net proceeds (W2)	(5,000)		
Loss	251,000	(125,500)	(125,500)
		74,500	(63,500)
B's loss		(63,500)	
First cash distribution		11,000	

WORKING 1 NET ASSETS FIGURE: €256,000 [€240,000 + €18,000 + €34,000 − €36,000]

WORKING 2 NET PROCEEDS AFTER PAYING LIABILITIES AND DISSOLUTION EXPENSES €5,000 [€15,000 + €30,000 − €4,000 − €36,000]

On 10 January, partner A will receive €11,000 and partner B will not receive any cash as the balance on their capital account is not sufficient to absorb the losses of the partnership at this time. The €11,000 being paid out to A is the sum of the net proceeds (W1) and the balance at the bank.

31 January		A	B
	€	€	€
Capital balance		200,000	62,000
Net assets as at 10 January	251,000		
Cash	(210,000)		
Loss	41,000	(20,500)	(20,500)
		179,500	(41,500)
First cash distribution		(11,000)	(Nil)
		168,500	41,500

The cash paid out to each partner is:

	€
A (€11,000 + €168,500)	179,500
B	41,500

Each partner will receive the same amount irrespective of whether a number of distributions are made or only a single payment is made when all assets have been realised and liabilities and expenses settled.

Same example – distribution only made when all assets realised.

REALISATION ACCOUNT

Account Name	€	Account Name	€
Property	240,000	Bank (Inventory)	15,000
Inventory	18,000	Bank (Trade receivables)	30,000
Trade receivables	34,000	Bank (Property)	210,000
Expenses	4,000	Loss on realisation	
		A	20,500
		B	20,500
	296,000		296,000

CAPITAL ACCOUNTS

Account Name	A €	B €	Account Name	A €	B €
Loss	20,500	20,500	Balance b/d	200,000	62,000
Bank	179,500	41,500			
	200,000	62,000		200,000	62,000

BANK ACCOUNT

Account Name	€	Account Name	€
Balance b/d	6,000	Realisation account	4,000
Inventory	15,000	Trade payable	36,000
Trade receivables	30,000	Capital A	179,500
Property	210,000	Capital B	41,500
	261,000		261,000

EXAM TIPS

- Know when to use revaluation and realisation accounts.
- On dissolution of a partnership, note whether *Garner v. Murray* is to apply.

17.6 CONCLUSION

In this chapter, a realisation account was used to record the winding up of a partnership; this should not be confused with the revaluation account dealt with in the previous chapter. If a partnership ceases to trade, its liabilities must be paid first and any remaining funds are then paid to the partners in settlement of the balances due to them.

SUMMARY OF LEARNING OBJECTIVES

After having studied this chapter, readers should be able to:

Learning Objective 1 Account for the winding up of a partnership.

On winding up of a partnership, open a realisation account:

REALISATION ACCOUNT

Account Name	€	Account Name	€
Asset carrying amount		Proceeds from sale of asset	
Dissolution expenses			

The balance on the realisation account is shared between partners in the profit-sharing ratio.

Learning Objective 2 Account for the conversion of a partnership into a limited company.

To account for the conversion to a limited company you need to do the following.
1. Treat the change in the fair value of the assets as a realisation, any profit or loss is taken to the partners' capital accounts in the profit-sharing ratio.
2. Assets taken over by an individual partner and not transferred to the company: the accounting journal entry is to debit the partner's capital account and credit the asset account.

3. Open an account in the name of the company to record the purchase consideration offered. The accounting journal entries are as follows:

	Debit	Credit
Total consideration paid by company	Account in company's name in partnership records	Realisation account
Shares issued by company	Partners' capital accounts	Account in company's name in partnership records
Cash paid by company as part of the consideration	Bank	Account in company's name in partnership records

4. Merge the partnerships into the new limited company at the agreed values.

Learning Objective 3 Account for the merging of two partnerships into one partnership.

The assets and liabilities of each partnership are recognised at the fair value; any gains or losses are shared between the partners in their profit-sharing ratio. The terms of the merger will state the capital to be contributed by each of the partners.

Learning Objective 4 Apply the *Garner v. Murray* rule.

If a partnership does not want the *Garner v. Murray* rule to apply on dissolution, this must be specifically stated in the Partnership Agreement and an alternative basis to be applied must be identified in the agreement.

Under *Garner v. Murray*, if on dissolution a partner is unable to make good a deficit on their account, the deficit must be split between the remaining partners on the basis of their last agreed capital balances.

Learning Objective 5 Account for a piecemeal realisation.

Partners may decide to wind up the partnership but do not want to wait to receive a distribution until all assets are realised and liabilities and expenses paid. In this case, each distribution to the partners is accounted for as if it is the final distribution.

QUESTIONS

Review Questions

(See **Appendix A** for Solutions to Review Questions.)

Question 17.1

Mango and Tango have been in partnership for a number of years. Mango and Tango have shared profits and losses 60:40 respectively.

On 31 December 2019 Mango and Tango decided to dissolve the partnership.

Mango and Tango
STATEMENT OF FINANCIAL POSITION
as at 31 December 2019

	€000	€000
Non-current Assets		
Property		700
Plant and equipment		180
Motor vehicles		60
		940
Current Assets		
Inventory	50	
Trade receivables	90	
Bank	45	185
		1,125
Capital Accounts		
Mango		300
Tango		250
		550
Current Accounts		
Mango	200	
Tango	105	305
Non-current Liability – Loan		200
Current Liabilities – Trade payables		70
		1,125

Additional information:
1. The assets were settled at the following amounts:

	€000
Property	810
Plant and equipment	190
Motor vehicles	50
Inventory	45
Trade receivables	85

2. The liabilities were paid in full.
3. Expenses incurred in relation to the dissolution of the partnership amounted to €12,000.

Requirement To record the dissolution of the partnership prepare the following ledger accounts:
(a) Realisation account.
(b) Partnership capital accounts.
(c) Bank account.

Challenging Questions

(Suggested Solutions to Challenging Questions are available to lecturers.)

Question 17.1

Alex, Bob and Charlie were in partnership for many years sharing profits and losses in the ratio 5:3:2 and making up their accounts to 31 December each year. Alex died on 31 December 2019, and the partnership was dissolved as from that date.

The partnership statement of financial position at 31 December 2019 was as follows:

	Cost €	Accumulated Depreciation €	Carrying Amount €
Non-current Assets			
Land and buildings	525,000	75,000	450,000
Plant and machinery	330,000	156,150	173,850
Motor vehicles	147,750	59,850	87,900
			711,750
Current Assets			
Inventories		165,900	
Trade receivables		134,100	
Cash at bank		18,900	318,900
Total Assets			1,030,650
Capital Accounts			
Alex			350,400
Bob			283,350
Charlie			159,300
			793,050
Non-current Liabilities			
Bank loan (10%)			60,000
Current Liabilities			
Trade payables			177,600
			1,030,650

In the period January to March 2019 the following transactions took place to effect the dissolution.

These were dealt with in the partnership records:
1. With regard to the non-current assets of the partnership:
    (i)   Land and buildings were sold for €570,000.
    (ii) Plant and machinery were sold for €132,000.
    (iii) Bob and Charlie took over the cars they had been using at the following agreed values:

	€
Bob	13,500
Charlie	21,000

    (iv) The remaining vehicles were sold for €57,000.
2. Inventory was taken over by Charlie at the agreed value of €180,000.
3. With regard to trade receivables, the partnership received €102,600 in cash and the remainder was taken over by Charlie at the agreed value of €30,000.
4. Trade payables were all settled for a total of €172,500.

5. The bank loan was repaid on 31 March 2019 with interest accrued since December 2018.
6. Dissolution expenses totalling €3,600 were paid by the partnership.
7. The final balances due to or from Alex, Bob and Charlie were paid/received on 31 March 2019.

Requirement Prepare the following accounts as at 31 March 2019 showing the dissolution of the partnership:
(a) Realisation account.

10 Minutes

(b) Partners' capital accounts.

7 Minutes

(c) Cash book/account.

9 Minutes

(Based on Chartered Accountants Ireland, CAP 1 Financial Accounting, Summer 2008, Question 8)

Question 17.2

Arthur, Bruce and Connie have been in partnership for many years, sharing profits and losses in the ratio of 2:2:1. They have recently agreed to convert the partnership into a limited company, Highland Ltd, with effect from 1 January 2019.

The statement of financial position of the partnership as at 31 December 2018 was as follows:

	€000	€000
Non-current Assets		
Land and buildings		9,000
Plant and equipment		6,000
Motor vehicles		1,500
		16,500
Current Assets		
Inventory	5,500	
Accounts receivables	7,000	
Bank	4,500	17,000
Total Assets		33,500
Capital		
Arthur		11,000
Bruce		9,000
Connie		5,000
		25,000
Non-current Liabilities		
Loan account – Arthur		3,500
Current Liabilities		
Accounts payable		5,000
		33,500

Additional information:
1. The company will take over all the non-current assets and the inventory of the partnership.
2. The purchase consideration of €29 million, which is to be divided between the partners in their profit-sharing ratio, consists of:
   • A cash payment of €5 million;
   • 6 million 10% preference shares of €1 at par; and
   • The balance made up of €1 ordinary shares in Highland Ltd.

3. The partnership's accounts payable were all settled by 31 December 2018 after the taking of cash discounts of €100,000.
4. The partnership's accounts receivable were collected by 31 December 2018 except for bad debts amounting to €400,000. Discounts allowed to customers amounted to €200,000.
5. Any balances on the partners' capital and loan accounts are to be settled in cash.

Requirement:
(a) Prepare the ledger accounts of the partnership required in order to close off the books as at 31 December 2018.

20 Minutes

(b) Prepare the statement of financial position of Highland Ltd on 1 January 2019, after it has taken over the partnership.

10 Minutes

(Based on Chartered Accountants Ireland, CAP 1, Financial Accounting, Autumn 2009, Question 3)

PART V

COMPANIES

18

The Regulatory and Conceptual Frameworks for Financial Reporting

LEARNING OBJECTIVES

Having studied this chapter, readers should be able to:
1. explain the regulatory framework impacting the preparation and presentation of financial statements;
2. summarise the roles and objective of the International Accounting Standards Board (IASB);
3. summarise the standard-setting process;
4. describe the principles set out in the IASB's *Conceptual Framework for Financial Reporting*;
5. identify and briefly explain the conditions under which businesses can, or must, apply one of the accounting frameworks; and
6. outline how the *Code of Ethics* guides members of Chartered Accountants Ireland in the resolution of ethical issues that may arise.

18.1 INTRODUCTION

Financial reporting is the process of producing a set of financial statements that communicate financial information about the financial performance and position of the entity. Financial reporting is part of the financial accounting process. Financial accounting is the recording, summarising and reporting of the financial transactions of the entity. An entity's purpose in issuing financial information is to communicate with the users of its financial statements. The financial statements provide information about an entity's: financial performance, financial position, changes in its owners' equity and its cash-generating capability. The directors of the entity are responsible for the periodic preparation of financial information, including:
- A set of financial statements made up of:
  - a statement of profit or loss and other comprehensive income (SPLOCI);
  - a statement of financial position (SOFP);
  - a statement of changes in equity (SOCIE); and
  - a statement of cash flows (SOCF).
- Notes to the financial statements detailing the accounting policies and accounting estimates used in the preparation of financial information. These notes normally also include descriptions or more detailed analysis of items in the financial statements, as well as other information to help the user understand the basis on which the financial information has been prepared, such as accounting policies and estimates.
- Other information, such as the chairman's and directors' reports.

Rules and guidelines have been developed to ensure that financial information prepared by entities is presented in a consistent manner from one reporting period to another and is relevant to users. This chapter deals with two particular areas that provide rules and guidelines, namely the regulatory framework and the International Accounting Standards Board's *Conceptual Framework for Financial Reporting*.

18.2 REGULATORY FRAMEWORK

The regulatory framework encompasses: company law, **accounting standards** and the regulations of relevant stock exchanges. Each of these will be discussed in more detail in turn.

Company Law

Company law is part of the regulatory framework. The legislation sets out the requirements in terms of the incorporation of entities, regulations with respect to meetings, and directors' duties. The legislation impacting the operation of companies in the Republic of Ireland and Northern Ireland are set out in **Figure 18.1** below.

FIGURE 18.1: RELEVANT LEGISLATION

Republic of Ireland	Northern Ireland
Companies Act 2014	Companies Act 2006
European Union (Companies: Group Accounts) Regulations 1992 (Republic of Ireland) S.I. No. 201 of 1992	Insolvency (NI) Order 1989
	Insolvency (NI) Order 2005
European Communities (International Financial Reporting Standards and Miscellaneous Amendments) Regulations 2005, S.I. No. 116 of 2005	
European Communities (Fair Value Accounting) Regulations 2004, S.I. No. 765 of 2004	

Accounting Standards

Adherence to the accounting standards developed by the International Accounting Standards Board (IASB) became obligatory within EU Member States in June 2002 when the EU Council of Ministers adopted the EU regulations requiring publicly quoted companies to prepare their **consolidated financial statements**[1] (also referred to as group accounts) in accordance with the requirements of **international accounting standards**. This requirement came into effect in relation to the preparation of financial statements for the reporting periods beginning on or after 1 January 2005. The term 'international accounting standards' refers to **International Financial**

---

[1] Consolidated financial statements are financial statements prepared to reflect the financial results and position of a number of companies that form a group of companies. The financial statements are combined as a result of the relationship between the companies, i.e. that of a parent and its subsidiary/ies. A subsidiary company is one in which the parent has control. Control exists when one entity has power over another entity which it can exercise and which gives them entitlement to variable returns (IFRS 3 *Business Combinations*).

Reporting Standards (IFRSs) and **International Accounting Standards (IASs)**, plus any related interpretations issued by the IASB and endorsed by the EU.

IFRSs are a numbered series of accounting standards issued by the IASB in its role as the independent standard-setter of the IFRS Foundation (see **Section 18.3**). IASs are those standards originally issued by the IASB's predecessor standards-issuing body.

IAS 1 *Presentation of Financial Statements* defines IFRSs as:
- IFRSs;
- IASs;
- interpretations of the standards by the IFRS Interpretations Committee; and
- interpretations of the standards by the Standing Interpretations Committee (SIC).

Financial statements prepared in accordance with IFRSs are required by IAS 1 to make an explicit statement in their notes to the financial statements to this effect. This statement can only be made if the financial statements comply fully with IFRSs.

The IASB's standard-setting process is dealt with in **Section 18.4**.

Companies that do **not** have to adopt international accounting standards under the EU's regulations (including companies not listed on a stock exchange) have a choice of what financial reporting framework to use. They can choose to adopt either IFRSs if they so wish, or they can choose to use the standards issued by the Financial Reporting Council (FRC), which is the standard-setting authority for the UK and Ireland. The FRC's financial reporting standards are referred to as the 'UK and Irish GAAP' and are contained in the suite of standards known as FRS 100–105.

The choice of accounting framework is dealt with in more detail in **Section 18.6**.

Stock Exchange Regulations

When a company is listed on a stock exchange it must comply with a set of rules known as the 'listing rules'. Each stock exchange will have its version of the listing rules. These listing rules include:
- conditions to be met when a company applies to be listed on the stock exchange;
- rules and procedures to be followed for a company listed on the particular stock exchange;
- disclosure requirements for a company listed on the particular stock exchange – these tend to be greater than those required under companies legislation. The reason for this greater burden in relation to disclosure is to ensure that sufficient information is provided to existing and potential shareholders; and
- details of situations that will cause the withdrawal/suspension of a company's listing on the stock exchange.

18.3 THE FUNCTION AND STRUCTURE OF THE IFRS FOUNDATION[2]

The IFRS Foundation is a "not-for-profit, public interest organisation established to develop a single set of high-quality, understandable, enforceable and globally accepted accounting standards—IFRS Standards—and to promote and facilitate adoption of the standards."

The mission statement of the IFRS Foundation is "to develop IFRS Standards that bring transparency, accountability and efficiency to financial markets around the world". It continues:

---

[2] The information and quoted material in this section can be found at www.ifrs.org/about-us/who-we-are/ accessed June 2019.

"Our work serves the public interest by fostering trust, growth and long-term financial stability in the global economy.

- IFRS Standards bring **transparency** by enhancing the international comparability and quality of financial information, enabling investors and other market participants to make informed economic decisions.
- IFRS Standards strengthen **accountability** by reducing the information gap between the providers of capital and the people to whom they have entrusted their money. Our Standards provide information needed to hold management to account. As a source of globally comparable information, IFRS Standards are also of vital importance to regulators around the world.
- IFRS Standards contribute to economic **efficiency** by helping investors to identify opportunities and risks across the world, thus improving capital allocation. Use of a single, trusted accounting language lowers the cost of capital and reduces international reporting costs for businesses."

The IFRS Foundation has a three-tier governance structure consisting of:
- the IASB – the Foundation's independent standard-setters – which is governed and overseen by
- the IFRS Foundation Trustees, who are in turn governed and overseen by
- the IFRS Foundation Monitoring Board, which ensures the public accountability of the Foundation.

Outside of this three-tier structure, the IFRS Foundation has a wide network of advisory committees and bodies. There are two formal advisory bodies – the IFRS Advisory Council and the Accounting Standards Advisory Forum (ASAF) – and a number of more specialised consultative groups.

Each of these aspects is dealt with in detail below.

The Monitoring Board

The IFRS Foundation Monitoring Board was set up in 2009 to improve the Foundation's public accountability and to provide a "formal link between the Trustees and public authorities". It consists of capital market authorities, including representatives from the European Commission, the US Securities and Exchange Commission (SEC), the Financial Services Agency of Japan and the Ministry of Finance of the People's Republic of China.

The principal responsibility of the Monitoring Board is to ensure the Trustees discharge their duties (as defined by the IFRS Foundation *Constitution*). It also approves the appointment or reappointment of Trustees. It meets with the Trustees at least once a year to perform its responsibilities.

Trustees of the IFRS Foundation

The IFRS Foundation Trustees are individuals with an understanding of the "international issues" needed to develop high-quality global accounting standards. Trustees are appointed for a renewable three-year term. There are strict rules to ensure the Trustees reflect a "diversity of geographical and professional backgrounds". Hence, six Trustees must be selected from Asia/Oceania, six from Europe, six from the Americas and one from Africa, plus three Trustees selected from any area (subject to maintaining overall geographical balance).

In general, the Trustees are responsible for the governance and oversight of the IASB as well as other bodies within the Foundation, such as the IFRS Advisory Council, the IFRS Interpretations Committee and the Accounting Standards Advisory Forum (ASAF). Specifically, this remit covers:
- the appointment of Trustees (subject to approval from the Monitoring Board);
- the appointment of members to the IASB, the Interpretations Committee, the Advisory Council and the ASAF;

- establishing and amending those bodies operating procedures and "due process";
- reviewing the Foundation's and the IASB's strategy and assessing their effectiveness; and
- financial and budgetary control of the Foundation.

In addition, the Foundation's *Constitution* requires that the Trustees review their own structure and effectiveness every five years.

As part of their responsibility to oversee the Foundation's standard-setting "due process", the Trustees have the **Due Process Oversight Committee (DPOC)** which issues the *Due Process Handbook*. The Handbook, last updated in May 2016,[3] sets out the due process requirements of the IASB and the Interpretations Committee. In paragraph 1.6 it states:

> "The due process requirements are built on the principles of transparency, full and fair consultation—considering the perspectives of those affected by IFRSs globally—and accountability."

To achieve this objective, the DPOC engages in public consultation and provides access to reports detailing conclusions, discussions and materials on the IFRS Foundation website.

The Handbook also sets out the responsibilities of the DPOC:
- regular and timely reviews of the due process activities of the standard-setting activities of the IASB;
- review of the *Due Process Handbook*, with any proposed updates to ensure best practice;
- review of the composition of the IASB's consultative groups to ensure "balance of perspectives" and the monitoring of the effectiveness of these groups;
- response to third parties about due process matters (in collaboration with the Trustees and technical staff);
- monitor the effectiveness of the Foundation's various bodies in respect to its standard-setting activities, including the Advisory Council, the IASB and the Interpretations Committee;
- make recommendations (to the Trustees) on "constitutional changes related to the composition of committees that are integral to due process".

Independent Standard-setting

The standard-setting activities of the IFRS Foundation are principally conducted by the IASB and its Interpretations Committee. The IASB is:

> "an independent group of experts with an appropriate mix of recent practical experience in setting accounting standards, in preparing, auditing, or using financial reports, and in accounting education".

The composition of the IASB is specified in the Foundation's *Constitution* and includes "broad geographical diversity". IASB members are appointed by the Trustees through an "open and rigorous process that includes advertising vacancies and consulting relevant organisations".

The IASB is responsible for:
- "development and publication of IFRS Standards"; and
- "approving interpretations of IFRS Standards as developed by the IFRS Interpretations Committee".

The standard-setting process is dealt with in detail in **Section 18.4**. To assist in the development of IFRSs, the IASB issues its *Conceptual Framework for Financial Reporting*, which is considered in detail in **Section 18.5**.

---

[3] In November 2017, the DPOC undertook a review of the Handbook. The DPOC proposed amendments and invited comment from various stakeholders until 29 July 2019.

The IFRS Interpretations Committee

The IFRS Interpretations Committee (also referred to as IFRIC) sits within the IASB and responds to stakeholders' questions about the application of standards. Its 14 members and a non-voting chairperson are appointed by the Trustees, and its composition reflects the "diversity of international business and market experience".

The process of the Interpretations Committee is designed to:
- "allow any stakeholder to submit a question; and
- be transparent—all submissions are considered at a public meeting."

In response to a question, the Interpretations Committee decides whether or not to recommend standard-setting. The decision to not recommend standard-setting (referred to as an "agenda decision") might be because to do so would be:
- unnecessary – the standard is sufficient for a company to determine its accounting; or
- unhelpful – standard-setting would cause more confusion.

Agenda decisions are published and subject to the due process. They remain open for 60 days and further comments are considered before the decision is closed. In addition, agenda decisions often include explanatory information about the applicable principles and requirements of the standard in question.

An alternative approach is a recommendation for "narrow-scope standard-setting". This can either be:
- development of an "IFRIC Interpretation of a Standard", which does not change the standard itself but adds to its requirements; or
- a narrow-scope amendment to the standard.

In more specific terms, the Foundation's *Constitution*, paragraph 42, states that the role of the Interpretations Committee is to:

> "(a) interpret the application of IFRS Standards and provide timely guidance on financial reporting issues not specifically addressed in the Standards … ;
> (b) in carrying out its work under (a) above, have regard to the Board's [the IASB's] objective of working actively with national standard-setters to bring about convergence of national accounting standards and IFRS Standards to high quality solutions".

Advisory Bodies and Consultative Groups

The IFRS Foundation refers to the development of global accounting standards as a "collaborative exercise". The due process (see above) **requires** that the perspectives of the different stakeholders are considered when standard-setting and that the standards are "developed free from undue influence". Wider consultation with many different stakeholders is therefore necessary and the Foundation seeks input from a network of advisory committees and bodies to "efficiently consult with interested parties from a range of backgrounds and geographical regions".

The Foundation has two formal advisory bodies – the IFRS Advisory Council and Accounting Standards Advisory Forum (ASAF). The Advisory Council's focus is on strategic support and advice to the Foundation, in particular to the IASB and the Trustees. Its members comprise individuals and organisations with an interest in international financial reporting.

The ASAF supports the IASB and has a narrower focus – to "constructively contribute … [to the IASB's] goal of developing globally accepted high quality accounting standards". It has three particular objectives:
- support and contribute to developing international financial reporting standards that "serve investors and other market participants in making informed resource allocations and other economic decisions";

- "formalise and streamline" the IASB's engagement with national standard-setters and regional bodies to ensure a broad range of input into standard-setting activities; and
- "facilitate effective technical discussions on standard-setting issues".

In addition to the advisory bodies, there are a number of specialised consultative groups. Some examples include:
- the Capital Markets Advisory Committee, which provides the IASB with input from the users of financial statements;
- the Emerging Economies Group, which focuses on the application and implementation of IFRSs in emerging economies; and
- the Islamic Finance Consultative Group, which addresses the development of Shariah-compliant instruments and transactions.

18.4 STANDARD-SETTING PROCESS

As noted above, the IASB is the standard-setting body of the IFRS Foundation, but in its own view the development of international standards is seen as a "collaborative exercise" and the due process requires the perspectives of stakeholders from a range of backgrounds and geographical regions to be considered. The participants in the process will include national standard-setters and regional bodies, advisory and consultative committees as well as the users of financial statements, such as business leaders, investors, accountants, financial analysts and international stock exchanges.

At this point it is worth remembering that the due process is built on the principles of **transparency, full and fair consultation and accountability** (as stated in the *Due Process Handbook* and noted above).

The IASB follows four steps in its standard-setting process:[4]
1. Agenda consultation
2. Research programme
3. Standard-setting programme
4. Maintenance programme.

1. Agenda Consultation

The IASB conducts a comprehensive review every five years to identify the international standard-setting priorities and to develop its work plan. This review involves the IFRS Trustees, the IFRS Advisory Council and Accounting Standards Advisory Forum (ASAF).

Between these consultation periods topics may be added to the work plan, usually as a result of "Post-implementation Reviews of Standards" or requests for review from the IFRS Interpretations Committee.

2. Research Programme

Most projects begin with a research phase in which issues are explored, possible solutions identified and a decision made on whether or not the standard-setting process is required. Research ideas may result in a discussion paper being issued and public comment sought. The process to issue a new standard or to amend an existing one only begins when there is evidence to support the contention that an accounting problem exists and a practical solution can be found.

---

[4] www.ifrs.org/about-us/how-we-set-standards/#agenda

3. Standard-setting Programme

When the IASB decides to amend or issue a new standard, a review is undertaken of:
- the research;
- the discussion paper with comments from the public consultation; and
- any proposal to resolve the issue identified in the other phases

Any proposals for a new or amended standard are published in an **exposure draft**, which is available for public consultation. The IASB and IFRS Foundation technical staff will consult with a broad range of stakeholders from diverse geographical locations to obtain additional evidence.

This feedback is analysed and the proposal may be refined before a new, or amended, standard is issued.

4. Maintenance Programme

Following the issue of a new or amended standard, support is provided for its implementation. If there are implementation problems or other issues, the Interpretations Committee will review and, as part of the due process, may recommend an "IFRIC Interpretation of the Standard" or a narrow-scope amendment (see **Section 18.3**).

A few years after the issue of a new or amended standard, a **post-implementation review** is undertaken by the IASB to assess if the standard is achieving its objective. If the objective has not been met, then consideration is given as to whether or not amendments are required.

18.5 THE *CONCEPTUAL FRAMEWORK FOR FINANCIAL REPORTING*

The IASB issues its *Conceptual Framework for Financial Reporting* (*Conceptual Framework*) with the aim of setting out the "objective of, and concepts for, general purpose financial reporting". Its purpose is to:

"(a) assist the … [IASB] to develop IFRS Standards that are based on consistent concepts;
(b) assist preparers to develop consistent accounting policies when no Standard applies to a particular transaction or other event, or when a Standard allows a choice of accounting policy; and
(c) assist all parties to understand and interpret the Standards." [5]

The *Conceptual Framework* is seen as contributing to the IFRS Foundation's mission statement (see **Section 18.3**) to develop IFRSs that bring "transparency, accountability and efficiency to financial markets" (paragraph SP1.5). However, it is important to appreciate that the *Conceptual Framework* is not an IFRS and that the IFRSs always take precedence over it.

The *Conceptual Framework* is set out in a number of chapters, each of which is discussed in detail below.

Chapter 1: The Objective of General Purpose Financial Reporting

The objective of general purpose financial reporting is to set out information about the financial performance and position of a reporting entity in such a way as to assist users of the financial statements. The users of financial statements are current and future users and include:
- investors,
- lenders, and
- other creditors.

---

[5] *Conceptual Framework for Financial Reporting*—March 2018, paragraph SP1.1.

The users of the financial information are concerned with decisions about the provision of resources to the entity. For example, whether or not to invest in shares in the entity; to provide credit facilities; to dispose of existing shareholdings; or to exercise their voting rights.

When considering investing in a company, potential investors will look at the company's ability to generate a dividend income for the investor or increase the value of the company, which will result in an increase in the price of the company's shares.

Providers of credit will want to know that the entity can repay the amounts advanced or has sufficient assets that can be used to settle any amounts due to its creditors.

In order to make these types of decisions, users of financial statements must assess an entity's ability to generate future cash inflows. Such an assessment will involve analysing the assets and resources available to the entity and its ability to use these both effectively and efficiently. In making these decisions, users have to rely on the information presented in the general purpose financial statements provided by the entity on an annual basis. The annual financial statements cannot provide all the information required so, in their assessment, users must consider the:
- general economic environment, i.e. whether the economy is in a recession or booming;
- outlook for the industry;
- company's expectations; and
- company's past performance relative to that of the market.

Different user groups require different information that may conflict with one another – when the IASB develops standards, its aim will be to meet the needs of the maximum number of user groups.

An entity's management is also interested in the financial statements but, unlike other users, it has access to internal reports and information. Management are entrusted to use the entity's economic resources in the most efficient and effective manner. For example, by protecting those resources from unfavourable economic factors (e.g. price and technological changes) and ensuring the necessary compliance with laws, regulations, etc. The user's understanding of how those resources have been managed in previous, as well as current, reporting periods can help them to assess the future management of those resources.

General purpose financial statements provide information with regard to:
- economic resources and claims;
- changes in economic resources and claims;
- financial performance reflected by accrual accounting;
- financial performance reflected by past cash flows; and
- changes in economic resources and claims not resulting in financial performance.

The meaning of each of these items is explained below.

Economic Resources and Claims The financial statements provide information about the resources available to the entity, such as assets used in the production of goods and balances due from credit customers. Knowing what resources an entity has available can help a user to make an assessment about the entity's strengths and weaknesses. For example, if an entity has non-current assets that are at the end of their useful lives, capital investment will need to be made in the near future. If the entity has little or no cash available, the acquisition of new non-current assets will have to be financed through borrowing funds or issuing additional ordinary shares. A review of the statement of financial position will show the entity's current lending obligations.

Changes in Economic Resources and Claims Changes in an entity's economic resources and claims arise due to:
- its financial performance; and
- other events and transactions, e.g. issuing of debt by the entity.

To be able to assess an entity's future cash inflows, users must be able to identify these changes. Financial performance information is presented in the SPLOCI, while information in relation to other events and transactions is detailed in the SOFP.

Information about financial performance helps users to understand the return that has been generated on the resources employed within the entity. The more effectively and efficiently the entity is managed, the better the return generated. While past performance does not guarantee future results, it does provide a means of assessing the past management of the entity.

In assessing financial performance of an entity it is important to understand the basis on which the information has been prepared. The accounting policies and estimates used by the entity in preparing its financial statements are detailed in the notes to the financial statements. Understanding the accounting policies and estimates helps the user to understand the financial information.

Financial Performance Reflected by Accrual Accounting Financial statements are prepared on the accrual basis, meaning that costs incurred and income earned in the reporting period (rather than costs paid and income received) are presented in the SPLOCI. This is a better basis for assessing past and future performance than cash receipts and payments made during the period. The information in the SPLOCI quantifies the change in economic resources as a result of the entity's operations rather than from any external funding, i.e from creditors or investors. It is therefore a good indication of the entity's own cash-generating ability and the management of its resources.

While an entity may be able to generate accounting profits, its generation of cash is just as important; the reporting of cash flows generated by the entity will be considered next.

Financial Performance Reflected by Past Cash Flows The information provided by the SOCF helps users to understand how and where cash is being generated and spent by the entity – through operating, investing or financing activities. This information will help users to assess an entity's **solvency** (its ability to pay its long-term liabilities) and its **liquidity** (its ability to pay its short-term liabilities).

There are a number of other influences impacting the assets and liabilities of an entity other than its financial performance – these are explained below.

Changes in Economic Resources and Claims Not Resulting from Financial Performance Changes in economic resources and claims not resulting from financial performance could be due to, for example, the entity issuing ordinary shares or debt. The provision of information about changes in resources and claims helps users to understand the impact of such changes on the entity's performance in the period. If, for example, during the most recent reporting period the entity took out a loan of €50 million at an interest rate of 10%, this would result in an increase in the entity's level of debt, a reduction in its profits (due to an additional interest expense), an increased risk for shareholders (on liquidation shareholders are paid out after all liabilities have been discharged, which means that the greater the debt level the higher the risk associated with the entity) and shareholders will require a higher return in light of this increased risk. In this scenario, the SOCIE would provide information relating to share issues and dividends.

Chapter 2: Qualitative Characteristics of Useful Financial Information

In order for a user to rely on a set of financial statements, the two fundamental qualitative characteristics they must exhibit are relevance and faithful representation.

Relevance Relevance, in the context of financial information, means that information can make a difference to the decisions being made by users of financial statements. Financial information can impact a decision if it has:

- predictive value, e.g. it can assist in estimating future performance, and/or
- confirmatory value, i.e. it confirms previous estimates or assessments.

Financial information can have both a predictive and a confirmatory value, e.g. revenue earned in the current period can be indicative of future performance and confirm past assessments of the entity's revenue-generating ability.

The omission or misstatement of **material** information can impact economic decisions made by users of financial statements. Materiality levels are specific to each entity; materiality depends on the size and/or nature of an item itself – it is not the same absolute amount for every entity. In paragraph 2.11, the IASB states that it "cannot specify a uniform quantitative threshold for materiality or predetermine what could be material in a particular situation". For example, if an entity reports a profit for a period of €80 million and an error was made that resulted in an electricity bill of €15,000 being omitted from the SPLOCI, this error is not material for this entity – the inclusion of the electricity cost would not impact any decision made by a user of these financial statements.

Faithful Representation For financial information to be a faithful representation of an entity's transactions and events it must have all of the following qualities:
- completeness – a user must be able to understand the information being provided. To achieve this there should be both descriptions and explanations and not just the amounts involved;
- neutrality – the information must not have been manipulated to present information in a more favourable or unfavourable way. Neutrality is supported by a prudent approach to decision-making where there is uncertainty; and
- error-free – this does **not** mean that the financial information is "perfectly accurate in all respects" but that there are no errors or omissions in the description of the information or in the processes used to produce the information (paragraph 2.18). For example, the use of estimates in the preparation of financial statements estimates is common and does not necessarily mean that it is not a faithful presentation of the amount involved. It will be a faithful presentation if it clearly indicates that it is an estimate, describing the nature and limitations involved in making the estimate and that no errors were made in either the selection or application of that process.

The two fundamental qualitative characteristics are "enhanced" if the financial information is also "comparable, verifiable, timely and understandable" (paragraph 2.4).

Comparability Comparability allows users to compare information from one period to the next. Items must be presented consistently from period to period to make them comparable; 'consistently' means that the same information is prepared using the same methods from period to period. Consistency in determining the figures presented in the financial statements will assist in making similar items comparable.

For example, if depreciation is a material cost in the determination of the profit or loss for an entity, and in the reporting period ended 31 December 2019 the depreciation expense is presented in the line item 'cost of sales', whereas in the following reporting period it is presented within the line item 'administration costs'. The users of these financial statements need to know that this change in presentation has occurred as well as its financial impact, so that they can understand the financial information presented.

Verifiability Verifiability assures the users of financial statements that the information provided is reflective of the events and transactions represented. Paragraph 2.30 explains verifiability as being when "different knowledgeable and independent observers could reach concensus, although not necessarily complete agreement". The verification of the financial information can be either:
- direct verification, which means the amount can be verified by direct observation, e.g. by conducting an inventory count; or

- indirect verification, which means that figures can be verified through checking inputs to models and formulae or recalculating the amounts presented in the financial statements, e.g. recalculating the depreciation charge for the reporting period.

Timeliness Timeliness ensures that information is provided to users in a prompt manner that allows them to benefit from the information and to use it in their decision-making. Older information may not have a direct impact on current decisions but can be very beneficial in assessing trends in relation to financial performance and position. A user of financial information may want to assess the performance of an entity over a number of reporting periods so that they can understand any trends – such as, where there has been growth in revenue, has it been at a steady rate over the last five years or has it been a more recent occurrence? Users will be more interested in the information contained in the most recent financial statements, but information from earlier reporting periods can help them to understand the progress made by the entity.

Understandability 'Understandability' means that financial information is prepared on the basis that users with a reasonable knowledge of business and economic activities would be able to understand it. Information is understandable when it is classified, characterised (as asset, liability, equity, income or expense) and presented both clearly and concisely. In the preparation of financial statements, financial information is classified and presented on a consistent basis – it therefore follows that changes in amounts presented from one period to the next are due to changes in the activities undertaken by the entity and not changes in presentation and classification. Changes in presentation and classification can occur but must be explained in the notes to the financial statements.

Some transactions or events are too complex to be made more understandable; however, for completeness and to avoid misleading users, they must be included in the financial information.

In preparing financial information that has the six qualitative characteristics described above, an entity must balance the additional cost of providing high-quality information with the benefit to be derived from the information. Additional information, or improved quality of the information, should only be provided when the benefit derived from the information is greater than its cost.

Chapter 3: Financial Statements and the Reporting Entity

Chapters 3–8 of the *Conceptual Framework* focus on financial statements (as opposed to general purpose financial reports in Chapters 1 and 2).

The objective and scope of financial statements is to provide financial information that allows the users of the financial statements to assess the stewardship of the entity's economic resources for the **reporting period**. The 'reporting entity' is defined as "an entity that is required, or chooses, to prepare financial statements". It is not necessarily a legal entity (paragraph 3.10). The information provided includes:
- the statement of financial position – information about the entity's recognised assets, liabilities and equity (unrecognised assets and liabilities will be included in the 'Notes' to the SOFP);
- the statement of profit or loss – information about the entity's financial performance for the reporting period by recognising income and expenses; and
- other statements and disclosure notes in relation to:
  - recognised assets, liabilities, income expense and equity, including risks arising from assets and liabilities;
  - assets and liabilities not recognised, including any risks arising;
  - cash flows;
  - contributions and distributions to equity holders; and
  - methods, assumptions and judgements used in estimating, and any changes in these.

'Comparative information' for at least one preceding reporting period is provided to give the user an understanding of the changes that have occurred. Information in relation to transactions or events that have occurred after the reporting date may be provided if it is necessary to meet the objectives of the financial statements.

Financial statements are prepared on the underlying assumption of **going concern**, i.e. on the basis that the entity will be in existence for the foreseeable future, normally the next 12 months. If there is any doubt that the entity will not continue for the foreseeable future, the basis on which the financial statements are prepared will have to be amended. For example, on the basis that the business will have to be liquidated in the foreseeable future or that there are plans to significantly curtail the entity's operations.

Chapter 4: The Elements of Financial Statements

The elements of the financial statements that relate to the entity's financial position are assets, liabilities and equity; while those that relate to financial performance are income and expenses.

Assets An asset is defined as "a present economic resource **controlled** by the entity as a result of past events" (paragraph 4.3). An economic resource is "a **right** that has the potential to produce **economic benefits**" (paragraph 4.4). The emphasis on the terms 'controlled', 'right' and 'economic benefits' has been added as they are key to understanding what an asset is.

Control An entity has control over an asset if it has the present ability to make the decisions about its use (or conversely, to prevent others from using the asset) and collect any benefits that accrue from the use of that asset.

Control can arise from legal rights, but this is not necessarily always the case. For example, if an entity has know-how in a specific field it is able to keep this information secret and so prevent anyone else from using it even if there is no registered patent protecting this knowledge.

Rights Assets may take many forms:
• physical assets, such as property, plant and equipment;
• non-physical assets, such as intangible assets (development, goodwill); and
• those that arise from a legal right, for example a trade receivable.

The *intention* of an entity to purchase or produce an asset is not in itself an asset. Expenditure is usually required in the recognition of an asset (e.g. purchase of a machine) but is not always necessary (e.g. assets can be donated to the entity).

Rights that provide the entity with the potential to obtain economic benefits may take many forms, including:
• rights that **correspond** to an obligation in another party, such as:
   ○ right to receive cash;
   ○ right to receive goods/services;
   ○ right to exchange economic resources on favourable terms; and
   ○ right to benefit from an obligation of another party to transfer an economic resource if a specified uncertain future event occurs; and
• rights that **do not correspond** to an obligation in another party, such as:
   ○ right over physical assets; and
   ○ right to use intellectual property.

Potential to Produce Economic Benefits The *potential* to produce economic benefit means that it does not have to be certain, or likely, that it will happen – it is "only necessary that the right already exists and that, in at least one circumstance, it would produce for the entity economic benefits beyond those available to all other parties" (paragraph 4.14). Therefore a right can be an economic resource, even if the probability attaching to the economic benefit occurring is low. A low probability would, however, impact decisions about the information to be provided about that asset, whether the asset is recognised and how it is measured.

An economic resource produces economic benefits in many ways, for example:
- receiving cash flows or other economic resource under a contract;
- exchanging economic resource on favourable terms with another entity;
- generating cash flows or avoiding cash outflows, e.g. leasing an economic recourse to another party;
- receiving proceeds from the sale of an economic resource; and
- transferring an economic resource to eliminate a liability.

When we think about acquiring an asset we usually think in terms of making a payment. The payment may provide evidence to support the fact that the entity has obtained a future economic benefit, but this does not necessarily mean that an asset has been obtained. An asset can be obtained without any related expenditure being incurred, for example, a government granting the entity rights free of charge.

Liability Paragraph 4.26 defines a liability as "a **present obligation** of the entity to **transfer an economic resource** as a result of **past events**". Again, the emphasis here is the key to understanding.

Three conditions must be satisfied for a liability to exist:
1. there is an obligation;
2. the obligation is to transfer economic resources; and
3. the obligation is a present one arising from past events.

Obligation An obligation is a duty that the entity cannot avoid and that is owed to another party/parties. It is not necessary to know the identity of the other party. One entity has the obligation to transfer economic resources and another entity must have a right to receive those economic resources. While one entity may recognise its obligation as a liability at a certain amount, it does not necessarily follow that the other party must recognise the asset at that same amount. For example, certain accounting standards have different recognition criteria for the liability and the asset (IAS 37 *Provisions, Contingent Liabilities and Contingent Assets*).

Obligations may arise as a result of contractual or constructive obligations. Constructive obligations arise from an entity's customary practices or published policies.

The preparation of the financial statements on a going concern basis also means, by necessity, that an entity cannot avoid an obligation that could only arise if the entity was being liquidated or was going to cease trading.

Transfer of an Economic Resource As with an asset's potential to produce economic benefits, a liability's obligation need only have the *potential* to require the entity to make the economic transfer to another party, i.e. it does not have to be certain or even likely – it is "only necessary that the obligation already exists and that, in at least one circumstance, it would require the entity to transfer an economic resource" (paragraph 4.37). Similarly, an obligation can satisfy the definition of a liability even if the probability of the transfer of the economic resource being made is low. A low probability would however impact decisions about the information to be provided about that liability, whether the liability is recognised and how it is measured.

Obligations to transfer an economic resource include:
- obligation to pay cash;
- obligation to deliver goods or to provide services;
- obligation to exchange economic resources to another party under unfavourable terms;

- obligation to transfer economic resources if unspecified uncertain future events occur; and
- obligation to issue a financial instrument if that financial instrument will oblige the entity to transfer an economic resource.

Present Obligation as a Result of Past Events A present obligation exists as a result of past events only if the following two conditions are met:
1. the entity has already obtained economic benefit (e.g. received goods or services) or taken an action (e.g. operating a business); and
2. as a consequence the entity will/may have to make a transfer of an economic resource that otherwise would not be required.

Therefore, a present obligation **does not exist** if the entity has not yet received the economic benefits or taken the action that would require the transfer of economic resources that it would not otherwise have made. An example would be an entity entering into an employment contract – the present obligation does not arise until such time as the employee provides their services.

Constructive obligations give rise to a present obligation only if the entity has to transfer an economic resource that would not otherwise have to be made.

The transfer of economic resources at a future date does not mean that a present obligation cannot exist now. For example, an entity may enter into a contract that requires it to perform work at a future date, but this still gives rise to a contractual obligation now.

Equity Equity is defined as the residual interest in the entity's assets after all of its liabilities have been recognised, i.e. they are claims on the entity other than liabilities.

Equity includes shares of various types issued by the entity and the entity's obligations to issue another equity claim. Equity claims include items such as ordinary and preference shares, holders of which may have different rights to receive some or all of the following from the entity:
- dividends, at the entity's discretion;
- proceeds from satisfying equity claims, either in full or on liquidation, or in part at other times; or
- other equity claims.

Legal, regulatory and other requirements affect one or more components of equity. For example, if an entity can only make a distribution to equity holders if it has sufficient reserves to meet the requirements for distribution, it may be appropriate to present these reserves separately. The legal and regulatory frameworks to be employed can depend on the type of entity, e.g. there are different requirements for partnerships compared to companies.

Definitions of Income and Expenses Income is an increase in equity as a result of either an increase in assets or a decrease in liabilities and not from contributions received from equity holders. A contribution made by an equity holder is, therefore, not considered as income.

Expenses are decreases in equity as a result of either a decrease in assets or an increase in liabilities, and not from distributions to equity holders. Distributions to equity holders are therefore not expenses.

Income and expenses provide information about financial performance. Transactions and events generate income and expenses with different characteristics so, to assist the user's understanding of the financial statements, this information is presented in the financial statements grouped by the same characteristics.

Chapter 5: Recognition and Derecognition
Recognition is defined in the *Conceptual Framework* as "the process of capturing for inclusion in the statement of financial position or the statement(s) of financial performance an item that meets the

definition of one of the elements of financial statements—an asset, a liability, equity, income or expenses" (paragraph 5.1).

Recognition involves identifying the item in words and at a monetary value, either alone or in aggregation with other items. The 'carrying amount' is the amount at which an asset, liability or equity is recognised in the statement of financial position.

Assets, liabilities, equity, income and expenses are presented in the financial statements in structured detail to make the information comparable and understandable.

Recognition links the elements, statement of financial position and the statement of financial performance, which is demonstrated in **Figure 18.2** as depicted in the *Conceptual Framework*, paragraph 5.4.

FIGURE 18.2: HOW RECOGNITION LINKS THE ELEMENTS OF FINANCIAL STATEMENTS

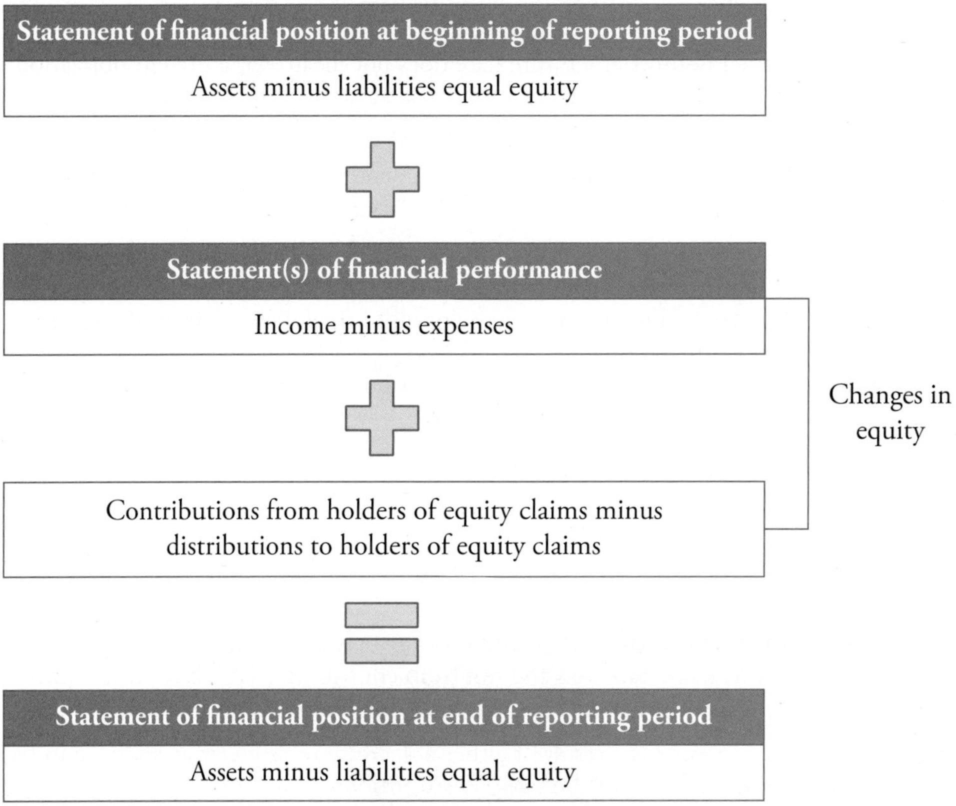

The statements are linked because the recognition/change in the carrying amount of one item requires the recognition/derecognition/change in the carrying amount of one or more items. **Figures 18.3** and **18.4** are helpful in illustrating this concept.

FIGURE 18.3: RECOGNITION OF INCOME

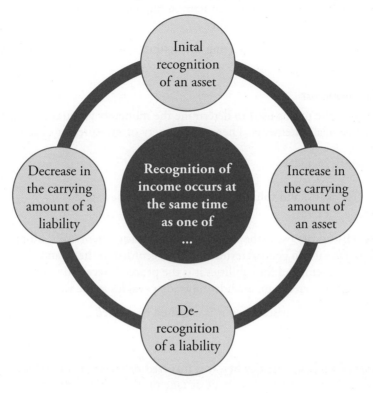

FIGURE 18.4: RECOGNITION OF EXPENSES

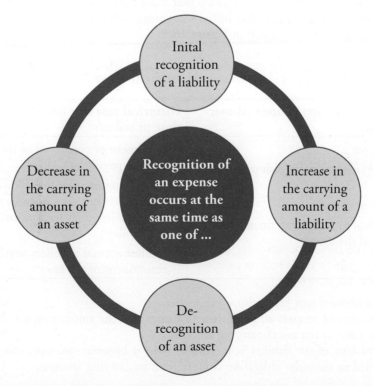

To recognise an item in the statement of financial position the definitions of an asset, liability or equity must be met. Likewise, to recognise an item in the statement(s) of financial performance, the definition of income or expenses must be met.

However, it is important to note that meeting the definition of one of the elements does not mean that the item will be recognised.

Chapter 6: Measurement

'Measurement basis' is the means used to determine the monetary amount at which an item will be recognised in the financial statements. There are a variety of measurement bases:
- historical cost;
- current value, which includes:
  - fair value;
  - value in use (for assets) and fulfillment value (for liabilities); and
  - current cost.

Historical Cost Historical cost is the most common measurement basis adopted in the preparation of financial statements. In general terms, the cost recorded in the financial statements for assets is the amount paid for them; and for liabilities it is the proceeds received in exchange for the obligation (e.g. goods bought on credit are included in trade payables at the value of the goods acquired).

The historical cost of an asset arises when it is acquired or created and is the:
- consideration price paid; **plus**
- transaction costs.

The historical cost of a liability arises when it is incurred or taken on and is the:
- value of the consideration received to incur or take on the liability; **minus**
- transaction costs.

The important point about the historical cost is that it does not take into account any price changes and it does not reflect current value after initial recognition. The historical cost of assets and liabilities are updated over time, as outlined in **Figure 18.5**.

FIGURE 18.5: UPDATES TO HISTORICAL COST OVER TIME

Historical cost of an asset is updated over time to reflect:	Historical cost of a liability is updated over time to reflect:
- Use of the asset - Payments received to extinguish part of the asset - Impairment of an asset - Interest accrual to reflect any financing component of the asset	- Fulfilment of part or all of the liability, e.g. making payments - Events that increase the value of the liability such that it becomes onerous (that is, historical costs less than the obligation to fulfil the liability) - Interest accrual to reflect any financing component of the asset

The updates to historical cost given above mean that:
1. The historical cost of an asset after adjustment means that the amount expected to be recovered is at least the same as the asset's carrying amount.
2. The historical cost of the liability is increased when it becomes onerous, this means that the amount needed to settle the obligation is more than its carrying amount.

Historical cost is relevant to users of the financial statements as it is based on information from when the transaction, i.e. the acquisition/creation of the asset or the incurring/taking on of the liability, initially took place. When an entity acquires an asset it expects to use the asset and to generate sufficient cash inflows to cover the cost of the asset.

Information about the cost of assets sold/consumed compared to the sales revenue may have a predictive value, helping users to assess the potential future margins that can be earned. Income and expenses measured at historical cost provides feedback to users confirming previous predictions about cash flows or margins.

Current Value The current value measurement basis reflects the value of the elements at a particular measurement date, and reflects changes since the previous measurement date. The current value cost, unlike historical cost, is not concerned with the cost of the transaction or event that gave rise to the asset or liability.

Current value bases include:
- fair value;
- value in use (for assets) and fulfilment value (for liabilities); and
- current cost.

Fair Value Fair value is defined as "the price that would be received to sell an asset, or paid to transfer a liability, in an **orderly transaction** between **market participants** at the **measurement date**" (paragraph 6.12).

An "orderly transaction" means normal business conditions, in other words there is no urgency to undertake the transaction due to liquidity or trading issues. If an entity is experiencing difficulties it may undertake a transaction below fair value due to pressure to generate cash flows. In an orderly transaction no such pressures exist so the entity will only accept the fair value.

"Market participants" indicates a level of knowledge about the business and an accurate assessment of the fair value given that knowledge. The measurement date is the date at which the fair value applies based on the market conditions and knowledge available. On another date these factors will be different and therefore the fair value will also be different.

Fair value can be an observable market price or it can be determined using measurement techniques that reflect all of the following factors:
- estimates of future cash flows;
- possible variations in the estimated amounts or timing of future cash flows for the asset or liability being measured, due to inherent uncertainty related to the cash flows;
- the time value of money;
- the price for bearing the uncertainty inherent in the cash flows;
- other factors, such as liquidity.

As noted previously, fair value does not reflect the transaction costs related to the asset or liability. That is, the fair value is not increased by transaction costs incurred when acquiring an asset; and not reduced by the transaction costs incurred when the liability is incurred or taken on.

As a measurement basis, fair value has both a predictive and confirmatory relevance. It has a predictive relevance as it is based on the expectations of market participants, taking into consideration information available in respect of the amount and timing of future cash flows – which are based on an assessment of uncertainties. The confirmatory relevance comes from the fact that any changes in fair value can confirm a user's previous expectations.

An asset acquired in one market but whose fair value in determined in another market (usually the market in which the asset is sold) may give rise to a difference in its fair value. If such a difference arises it is recognised as income when the fair value is first established.

Value in Use and Fulfilment Value   Value in use is used for assets and is the present value of future cash flows discounted at a discount rate. It is the sum of the present value of the net cash flows generated from the use of the asset and its ultimate disposal. The discount rate usually reflects the risk involved – the greater the risk, the higher the discount rate; the lower the risk, the lower the discount rate.

Liabilities are carried in the financial statements at their fulfilment value. Fulfilment value is the present value of the net cash flows that an entity expects to settle a liability under normal operating conditions.

Value in use and fulfilment values are based on future cash flows. Future cash flows involve using forecast information that may be subjective, reflecting their timing and any uncertainties. Neither of the values includes any transaction costs incurred in acquiring the asset or taking on a liability. They do, however, include the present value of any transaction costs related to the sale of the asset or on fulfilment of the liability.

Value in use and fulfilment value can have a predictive relevance as they require an assessment of future cash flows. Revision of values in use and fulfilment values can also have a confirmatory relevance of past assessments.

Current Cost   Current cost, like historical cost, is an entity value. It represents the market price an entity would have to pay to acquire an asset or incur a liability. While the historical cost is measured at the acquisition date of the asset or the date the liability is taken on, current cost is determined at the measurement date. The disadvantage to this is that the current cost has to be re-measured at each measurement date.

Unlike values in use and fulfilment values, the current cost is not an 'exit value'. Similarly, current costs are not discounted.

The current cost of an asset is the:
- consideration price that would be paid at the measurement date; **plus**
- transaction costs that would be incurred at that date.

The current cost of a liability is the:
- value of the consideration that would be received to incur or take on the liability; **minus**
- transaction costs that would be incurred at that date.

Current costs cannot be observed from prices in an active market. Market prices must be adjusted to reflect the age and condition of the assets owned by the entity. A change in the carrying amount of an asset/liability measured at current cost must be split between the:
- consumption of the asset or the current income from fulfilment of the liability; and
- the effect of changes in price, referred to as a "holding gain" or "holding loss".

Factors to Consider when Selecting a Measurement Basis   The choice of measurement basis will depend on the information that it is intended to provide in the financial statements and its usefulness to users. The decision on what measurement basis to use also needs to consider the costs involved in providing the information that will be of benefit to users.

As Chapter 2 of the *Conceptual Framework* notes, financial information is useful if it is **relevant** and a **faithful representation** of the transaction and events that occurred.

Relevance   The relevance of the information provided by a measurement basis is impacted by:
- the characteristics of the asset/liability; and
- how that asset/liability contributes to future cash flows.

The characteristics that affect the measurement basis include the variability in cash flows and the sensitivity of the value of the asset/liability to market factors or other risks. The influence on the choice of measurement basis of the sensitivity to market factors or other risks can include:

- Historical cost will not be the same as current value, which will not be relevant if information about changes in value is important to the users of the financial statements.
- Historical cost only reports changes in value on disposal, impairment or fulfilment. As a result users may think that the income/expenses occurred when reported and not over a number of reporting periods.
- Historical cost does not report changes in value on a timely basis, which will impact the information's predictive and confirmatory relevance.
- Fair value may not have predictive or confirmatory relevance if the asset is held solely for its contractual cash flows or to fulfil the entity's liabilities.

The nature of an entity's business activities impact how economic resources are used and how assets and liabilities generate cash flows, i.e. contribute to future cash flows. The influence of this contribution to the choice of measurement basis can include:

- Historical cost is appropriate when several economic resources are used in combination to generate cash flows from the sale of goods and services.
- Current value provides the most relevant information when assets and liabilities produce cash flows directly and an asset can be sold on its own without disrupting the business. Current value is most appropriate as the estimates made reflect the amount, timing and any uncertainties affecting cash flows.

Faithful Representation If different measurement bases are used for assets and liabilities that are related in some way this may lead to measurement inconsistency, such as an accounting mismatch. Measurement inconsistencies will not provide a faithful representation of the entity's financial performance and position. Faithful representation, as noted above, means that the financial information is free from error, but measurement bases do not have to be perfectly accurate.

When a measure cannot be obtained from observable data it must be determined based on estimates and measurement uncertainty arises. The level of measurement uncertainty impacts the ability for the financial information to provide a faithful representation of the financial position and performance. A high level of measurement uncertainty does not prevent the use of a particular measurement basis, as long as the information provided is relevant. If measurement uncertainty is so high that it cannot provide a faithful representation, an alternative measurement basis should be used.

Measurement uncertainty is not the same as outcome and existence uncertainty. Outcome uncertainty is when there is uncertainty about cash inflows/outflows resulting from an asset or liability. Existence uncertainty arises when there is uncertainty about the existence of an asset of a liability.

Enhancing Characteristics Chapter 2 of the *Conceptual Framework* refers to characteristics that enhance the fundamental requirements of relevance and faithful representation. The enhancing characteristics of comparability, verifiability and understandability may also affect the choice of measurement basis.

Consistent use of the same measurement basis can make financial statements more comparable.

The verifiability of financial information is improved where measures are observable from market data or from inputs to models that can be checked. When a measure cannot be verified:

- additional information may need to be disclosed to assist a user's understanding of the financial information; or
- an alternative measurement basis may need to be selected.

The understandability of financial information depends on:
- the number of measurement bases used; and
- whether the measurement basis change over time.

The use of more than one measurement basis can also increase the complexity of the financial information and reduce the understandability. So for example, using the same measurement basis at initial recognition and subsequent measurement will mean that the recognition of a gain/loss at the time of the first subsequent measurement will not require a change in the measurement basis.

A change in the measurement basis may impact the understandability of the financial information – but this would be justified if the information provided is more relevant, and provided that additional disclosure is given to help users understand the nature of the change.

When deciding on a measurement basis, it may be considered appropriate to use more than one basis to ensure that the information provided is relevant and a faithful representation of the financial performance and position. The most *understandable* way to provide information in this situation would be to use a single measurement basis (in the statement of financial position for assets and liabilities; and in the statement of profit or loss for the income and expenses) and to provide additional notes applying a different measurement basis. However, to provide information that is more relevant or a more faithful presentation, the current value basis should be used for the SOFP and a different basis for the related income and expenses in the SPLOCI.

Chapter 7: Presentation and Disclosure

An entity communicates financial information by presenting and disclosing the elements in the financial statements. Effective communication results in more relevant financial information that represents a faithful representation and enhances both its understandability and comparability. To ensure that financial information is communicated effectively it needs to:
- meet the presentation and disclosure objectives and principles (rather than just the rules);
- classify information so that similar items are grouped together; and
- aggregate information to avoid unnecessary detail or excessive aggregation.

It is important to consider whether the benefit to users of financial statements of presenting and disclosing information will exceed the cost of providing that information.

When developing presentation and disclosure requirements, a balance is needed between the entity's flexibility to provide relevant information that faithfully represents the elements in the financial statements and making that information comparable from one period to another as well as across entities.

In general, entity-specific information is more beneficial to users than standardised information. If information is duplicated in the financial statements it is usually unnecessary and reduces the understandability.

The elements of financial statement are classified based on their shared characteristics for presentation and disclosure purposes. These characteristics include the nature of the item, its role in the business activities and its measurement. Classification of dissimilar items together reduces the information's understandability and comparability and, as a result, its faithful representation. To enhance the usefulness of financial information it may be necessary to separate assets and liabilities into components if they have different characteristics, for example, separation of asset and liabilities into current and non-current.

Offsetting happens when an entity recognises and measures assets and liabilities separately but nets them off against one another in the SOFP. It classifies dissimilar items together and is usually not appropriate. Offsetting is not the same as treating a set of rights and obligations as a single unit of account.

It is necessary to classify components of equity separately due to specific legal, regulatory or other requirements. For example, if distributions to shareholders are allowed only when the entity has sufficient distributable reserves. The separation presentation of these reserves may provide useful information to the users of financial statements.

Income and expenses are classified and included in either:
- the entity's statement of profit or loss; or
- its other comprehensive income (the SPLOCI).

The SPLOCI is the primary source of information for users of financial statements about the entity's performance for the reporting period. When developing accounting standards, the IASB may decide that income and expenses arising from a change in current value of an asset/liability are included in other comprehensive income when it would result in the SPLOCI providing more relevant information or a more faithful representation of the entity's performance.

Chapter 8: Concepts of Capital and Capital Maintenance

The concept of 'financial capital' represents the amount of money invested in a business. Under a 'physical capital' concept the productive capacity of an entity is considered, which could be measured in terms of the number of units produced in a single day. The needs of the users of the financial statements will influence the method chosen: financial capital maintenance or physical capital maintenance.

Financial Capital Maintenance Using a financial capital maintenance approach, a change in the capital balance at the end of the reporting period compared to the balance at the start is due to: the profit earned or loss incurred for the period, distributions to the owners, and capital introduced by the owners. Under this approach profit earned/loss incurred is the increase/decrease in net assets for the period after taking into account distributions to and contributions from the owners.

Physical Capital Maintenance A profit is earned in this approach if the productive capacity has increased during the reporting period. An adjustment must be made for contributions and distributions to or from owners during the period. This method requires the adoption of the current cost measurement base.

18.6 CHOICE OF ACCOUNTING FRAMEWORK

There are two accounting frameworks that can be used in Ireland and the UK:
- international accounting standards; and
- UK and Irish GAAP, i.e. FRS 100–105.

The applicability of each accounting framework to companies is discussed below.

International Accounting Standards

All companies with securities traded on a regulated market within the EU are required to prepare their consolidated financial statements using international accounting standards (see **Section 18.2**). Under Article 5 of the International Accounting Standard Regulation (EC) No. 1606/2002, Member States are allowed to extend the use of international accounting standards to the individual accounts of publicly traded companies and the consolidated/individual accounts of companies other than publicly traded companies.

UK and Irish GAAP – FRS 100–105

If an entity is not *required* to prepare financial statements using international accounting standards (under Article 5 as noted above), it can choose to either apply IFRSs voluntarily or it must adopt the standards set by the UK and Irish standard-setting authority, the Financial Reporting Council (FRC). The FRC's standards, commonly referred to as 'UK and Irish GAAP' are contained in the suite of standards known as FRS 100–105.

The principal standard in UK and Irish GAAP is FRS 102 *The Financial Standard applicable in the UK and Republic of Ireland*. This is the default standard which must be applied if IFRSs are not adopted. There are, however, reduced reporting requirement frameworks for small and micro-entities that meet certain criteria regarding turnover, balance sheet total and the number of employees. Small entities can opt to report under Section 1A of FRS 102, while micro-entities can apply FRS 105 *The Financial Reporting Standard applicable to the Micro-entities Regime*.

18.7 ETHICS AND THE ACCOUNTANT

An accountant is a professional and, as such, must ensure that their actions are in the public interest and do not damage the reputation of the accountancy profession. Chartered Accountants Ireland has issued the *Code of Ethics* to provide its members with guidance of the ethical standards expected of them. The *Code of Ethics* sets out the fundamental principles of professional ethics and provides a framework for Chartered Accountants to ensure their behaviour meets the ethical standard required.

Fundamental Principles

The fundamental principles identified in the *Code of Ethics* are integrity, objectivity, professional competence with due care, confidentiality and professional behaviour.

'Integrity' means that the accountant, in their business role, will act with honesty and in a straightforward manner.

'Objectivity' means that the accountant does not allow anyone to exercise undue influence over them in discharging their duties. An accountant should ensure that they are not biased in their assessment or interpretation of information.

'Professional competence and due care' means that an accountant is required to maintain their professional knowledge and skill at a level required for the duties that they undertake to be performed competently and professionally. Accountants should not undertake any task that they are not competent to do.

'Confidentiality' means that accountants respect any information that they have acquired as part of their professional and business relationships. Information cannot be disclosed to third parties without the appropriate and specific authority unless there is a legal or professional right to do so. An accountant cannot use any such information that they have obtained to their own personal advantage or that of any third party.

'Professional behaviour' means that an accountant must comply with relevant laws and regulations and avoid engaging in any activity that will bring the profession into disrepute.

Safeguards and Threats

The *Code of Ethics* identifies threats that impact the ability of an accountant to comply with the fundamental principles. Safeguards created by the profession, legislation and regulation are aimed at either eliminating or reducing threats that may be encountered.

The threats to compliance with the fundamental principles include:
- Self-interest – this occurs when an accountant makes decisions that benefit them directly, e.g. concern over continued employment may create pressure to act in a way that may not be appropriate.
- Self-review – this occurs when an accountant involved in making a recommendation or advising on a course of action is also involved in the post-implementation review of that decision.
- Advocacy – when an accountant, in promoting a company, makes statements to support certain actions, such as making an investment in the company. The promotion is only an issue if the statements made by the accountant are false and/or misleading.
- Familiarity – a long-standing association with a member of the key management personnel may influence decisions being made or could lead to an accusation of bias being made against the accountant. An accountant should ensure that safeguards are put in place to minimise these risks.
- Intimidation – a dominant individual may influence the decisions made by an accountant by using threats or intimidation.

The safeguards detailed in the *Code of Ethics* that can be used to mitigate the threats that an accountant may face include:
1. obtaining advice either from within the organisation by whom the accountant is employed or from an independent professional;
2. using a formal dispute-resolution service provided by their employer; and
3. seeking legal advice.

EXAM TIPS

> Read the question carefully and answer the question asked.

18.8 CONCLUSION

The preparation and presentation of financial statements that are used by a number of user groups to make economic decisions are governed by the regulatory environment. The regulatory environment is made up of company law, accounting standards and regulations of relevant stock exchanges.

The accounting frameworks for Ireland and the UK are international accounting standards or the UK and Irish GAAP, i.e. FRS 100–105.

The IASB issues its *Conceptual Framework for Financial Reporting* (March 2018), identifying:
- objectives of financial reporting;
- characteristics of financial information;
- elements of financial statements including their recognition and measurement; and
- concepts of capital and capital maintenance.

SUMMARY OF LEARNING OBJECTIVES

After having studied this chapter, readers should be able to:

Learning Objective 1 Explain the regulatory framework impacting the preparation and presentation of financial statements.

The preparation and presentation of financial statements is governed by the regulatory framework encompassing: company law, accounting standards and regulations of relevant stock exchanges. The accounting standards followed by the entity can be:
- international accounting standards; or
- UK and Irish GAAP, i.e. FRS 100–105.

Learning Objective 2 Summarise the roles and objective of the International Accounting Standards Board (IASB).

The IASB is the independent standard-setting body of the IFRS Foundation. Its principle role is to prepare and issue IFRS Standards and following the "due process". In its standard-setting role it is responsible for approving the recommendations from the IFRS Interpretations Committee

The objective of the IASB is to develop a single set of global accounting standards.

Learning Objective 3 Summarise the standard-setting process.

The standard-setting process involves the following stages.
1. Agenda consultation – review of standard-setting priorities every five years
2. Research programme – discussion and consultation on agenda items, issuing of discussion paper and public comment sought
3. Standard-setting programme – if decided that a new standard is required or an existing standard should be amended, consultation with all relevant stakeholders and issuing of an exposure draft for public consultation before new/amended standard is issued
4. Maintenance programme – post-implementation review to assess if new/amended standard is achieving its purpose; further amendments may be considered and put forward for agenda consultation.

Learning Objective 4 Describe the principles set out in the IASB's *Conceptual Framework for Financial Reporting*.

The *Conceptual Framework* states that the objective of financial reporting is to present information in relation to the financial performance and position of the entity. The financial statements provide this information. The elements of financial statements are: income, expenses, assets, liabilities and capital/equity. To recognise an item as an element in the financial statements it must be probable that future economic benefit will flow to/from the entity and the item must be capable of being measured reliably.

Learning Objective 5 Identify and briefly explain the conditions under which businesses can, or must, apply one of the accounting frameworks.

Framework:	**Applies to:**
International accounting standards	Preparation of consolidated financial statements for entities whose securities are traded on a stock exchange.

| UK and Irish GAAP, i.e. FRS 100–105 | Individual financial statements of companies whose securities are traded on stock exchanges in the EU. |
| | Companies whose securities are not traded on stock exchanges in the EU and that do not meet the definition of a 'small company'. |

Learning Objective 6 Outline how the *Code of Ethics* guides members of Chartered Accountants Ireland in the resolution of ethical issues that may arise.

The fundamental principles identified in the *Code of Ethics* are:
- integrity;
- objectivity;
- professional competence with due care;
- confidentiality; and
- professional behaviour.

There are threats to an accountant's ability to meet the fundamental principles, which are:
- self-interest;
- self-review;
- advocacy;
- familiarity; and
- intimidation.

QUESTIONS

Review Questions

(See **Appendix A** for Solutions to Review Questions.)

Question 18.1

Requirement:
(a) Describe briefly the procedures and practices followed by the International Accounting Standards Board when developing an accounting standard.
(b) The setting of standards has both supporters and opponents. Discuss the arguments in support of standard-setting and those against standard-setting.

(Based on Chartered Accountants Ireland, CAP 1 Financial Accounting, Summer 2008, Question 4)

Question 18.2

The IASB's *Conceptual Framework* states that the objective of financial statements is to provide information about an enterprise that is useful to a wide range of users in making economic decisions.

Requirement Describe what useful information is provided by each of the following components of financial statements:
(a) statement of financial position;
(b) statement of profit or loss and other comprehensive income;
(c) statement of cash flows;
(d) statement of changes in equity; and
(e) notes and supplementary schedules.

(Based on Chartered Accountants Ireland, CAP 1 Financial Accounting, Autumn 2009, Question 4)

Question 18.3

(a) The IASB's *Conceptual Framework* highlights several principal classes of users of financial statements who rely on the information therein to help them in decision-making.

Requirement Explain why each of the following groups might rely on information contained within financial statements to help them in decision-making, and describe the type of financial information that each group would find most useful.

(i) Present and potential investors.
(ii) Employees/managers.
(iii) Lenders and other suppliers.
(iv) Government.

(b) The *Conceptual Framework* notes that financial statements cannot provide all the information that users may need to make economic decisions.

Requirement Give **two** examples of the type of information that is missing from financial statements.

(Based on Chartered Accountants Ireland, CAP 1 Financial Accounting, Autumn 2009, Question 5)

19

Presentation of Financial Statements

LEARNING OBJECTIVES

Having studied this chapter, readers should be able to:
1. prepare the statement of profit or loss and other comprehensive income;
2. prepare the statement of financial position; and
3. prepare the statement of changes in equity.

19.1 INTRODUCTION

The *Conceptual Framework* and the process involved in setting standards were dealt with in **Chapter 18, The Regulatory and Conceptual Frameworks for Financial Reporting**. IAS 1 *Presentation of Financial Statements* is an accounting standard relating to the preparation of general purpose financial statements. General purpose financial statements are defined in IAS 1 as "those intended to meet the needs of the users who are not in a position to require an entity to prepare reports tailored to their particular information needs."

The purpose of a set of financial statements is to provide details about the entity's financial position, financial performance and cash flows for the reporting period. The financial statements provide information about an entity's:
• financial position – assets, liabilities and equity;
• financial performance – income and expenses, profits and losses;
• cash flows; and
• contributions by owners and distributions to owners.

IAS 1 requires a complete set of financial statements to include:
1. a statement of financial position (SOFP) as at the reporting date;
2. a statement of profit or loss and other comprehensive income (SPLOCI) for the reporting period;
3. a statement of changes in equity (SOCIE) for the reporting period;
4. a statement of cash flows (SOCF) for the reporting period;
5. notes to the financial statements comprising significant accounting policies and other explanatory information; and
6. comparative information in respect of the preceding period.

The next section of this chapter will work through the features of a set of financial statements.

19.2 GENERAL FEATURES OF A SET OF FINANCIAL STATEMENTS

A set of financial statements should present the financial position, financial performance and cash flows of the entity fairly, that is, they should be a faithful representation of the events and transactions of the entity. An entity achieves this fair presentation by:
- selecting and applying accounting policies in a manner that complies with the requirements of IAS 8 *Accounting Policies, Changes in Accounting Estimates and Errors* (the accounting rules relating to IAS 8 are explained in **Chapter 22, Accounting Policies, Changes in Accounting Estimates and Errors**);
- presenting information so that it is relevant, reliable, comparable and understandable to the users of financial statements; and
- providing additional information in the disclosure notes, which complies with the requirements of International Financial Reporting Standards (IFRSs) and is in sufficient detail to assist users to understand the impact of transactions and events on the financial performance and position of the entity.

In the disclosure notes, the entity must state that the financial statements have been prepared in compliance with IFRS. The use of inappropriate accounting policies is **not** remedied by disclosure of accounting policies used or by the provision of explanatory notes or material.

The only situation in which an entity is allowed to depart from the requirements of IFRS is when compliance with an accounting standard would result in:
- misleading information being provided; and
- the financial statements would not be able to meet the objectives of financial statements as set out in the *Conceptual Framework* (see **Chapter 18**).

When an entity does not apply the requirements of an accounting standard it must make the following disclosures in the notes to the financial statements:
1. identify the relevant accounting standard;
2. the nature of the standard requirements that it cannot comply with and why it believes compliance would be so misleading that it cannot meet the objectives of the financial statements as set out in the *Conceptual Framework*; and
3. for each reporting period presented, the adjustment to each line item in the financial statements that management believe is necessary to achieve a fair presentation.

There are a number of accounting concepts but two of the most pervasive ones are the going concern concept and the accrual concept, which will now be explained.

Going Concern

Financial statements are presented on the basis that the entity will continue to operate for the foreseeable future; this is known as the going concern basis. If the management of the entity think that, within the next 12 months, the entity will either be liquidated or it will cease to trade, then the going concern basis cannot be applied in the preparation and presentation of the financial statements.

When the going concern basis is not applied, the management of the entity will have to disclose the uncertainties about the entity's operations and identify the basis that they have used to prepare the financial statements. In assessing an entity's ability to continue as a going concern they will look at items such as:
- the available information about the future;
- past profits earned or losses incurred;
- continuing availability of funds/potential funding; and
- debt repayment schedules.

Accrual Basis of Accounting

Financial statements are prepared on the accrual basis (this accounting concept was explained in **Chapter 1, Financial Accounting: Key Terms and Concepts**), that is:
- costs are recognised when they are incurred rather than when they are paid; and
- income is recognised when it is earned rather than when it is received.

The elements of financial statements are recognised when they meet the recognition criteria set out in the *Conceptual Framework*. To recognise an element of the financial statements both of the recognition criteria must be met. The recognition criteria are as follows:
- it is probable that any future economic benefit associated with the item will flow to or from the entity; and
- the item can be measured reliably.

Materiality

In relation to the term 'material', IAS 1 states that "omissions or misstatements of items are material if they could, individually or collectively, influence the economic decisions that users make on the basis of the financial statements. Materiality depends on the size and nature of the omission or misstatement judged in the surrounding circumstances. The size or nature of the item, or a combination of both, could be the determining factor."

Materiality will vary from entity to entity and involves the use of judgement by the management of a company. For example, if an invoice for €1,200 in relation to electricity costs was omitted from the SPLOCI for a company that has a reported profit of €5,600,000, this omission is not material in the context of this company's reported profit. It should be noted that while the omission of this item would not impact the decisions made by a user of the financial statements, it would be relevant to the management of the business because the management is responsible for making sure that proper accounting records are maintained for the business.

Each accounting standard has specific disclosure requirements but these do not need to be complied with if the amount involved is not material.

Financial statements present the results of a reporting period; similar items are aggregated together by either nature (for example, employee costs, raw materials and consumables used, depreciation, etc.) or by function (for example, cost of sales, administration, selling and distribution). If the amount attributed to a particular classification is not material, then it is not presented separately but included in another line item.

Offsetting

IAS 1 only allows offsetting of assets and liabilities or income and expenses in the following circumstances:
- offsetting allowed by a particular IFRS or IAS;
- when offsetting would reflect the substance of the transaction or event; or
- offsetting would not reduce users' ability to understand the transactions and events that occurred during the reporting period.

It is important to understand that the presentation of inventory net of obsolescence or trade receivables net of provision for bad debts is **not** offsetting. The netting off of an allowance for bad debts against the trade receivables balance will present the amount in the financial statements that management estimate is receivable.

Frequency of Reporting

A complete set of financial statements is prepared at least annually. If an entity changes its reporting date and this results in the reporting period being either longer or shorter than a one-year period, then the entity must disclose:

- the reason the reporting period is not a 12-month period; and
- the fact that the figures presented in the financial statements are not entirely comparable with those of other financial statements presented by the entity.

Consistency of Presentation and Comparative Information

Items shall be presented and classified in the same way from period to period; the exceptions to this are:

- when there has been a significant change in the nature of the entity's operations or a review of the entity's financial statements and a change in presentation would be more appropriate; or
- an IFRS requires a change in the presentation.

The change in presentation must result in more relevant and reliable information being provided to the users of the financial statements.

An entity is required to present comparative information in relation to the preceding reporting period. Comparatives must be presented for each line item in the financial statements.

If an entity changes the presentation or classification of an item, for example, in previous reporting periods the depreciation expense was presented in the cost of sales line item and from the current reporting period onwards this expense will be presented in the administration cost line item. When a change in either the presentation or classification of an item is made in the current period, the comparatives must also be restated and presented in the same manner; this is to ensure comparability of the information presented in the financial statements. When the restatement of the comparatives is not possible, this fact must be disclosed in the notes to the financial statements.

The disclosure required when there is a change in the presentation or classification of an item is set out in **Figure 19.1**.

FIGURE 19.1: DISCLOSURE REQUIRED WHEN THERE IS A CHANGE IN THE PRESENTATION OR CLASSIFICATION OF AN ITEM

Comparatives can be reclassified	**Reclassification of comparatives is impracticable**
- nature of the reclassification; - amount of each item or class of items that are reclassified; and - reason for the reclassification.	- reason for not reclassifying the amounts; and - nature of the adjustments that would have been made if the reclassification could have been made.

19.3 STRUCTURE AND CONTENT OF FINANCIAL STATEMENTS

Each of the financial statements should be clearly identified and distinguished from the other information provided in the published set of accounts. The requirements of IFRS and IAS only apply to the financial statements and not to the other information contained within the annual report.

The following information must be presented prominently and it may have to be repeated throughout the financial statements to help users' understanding:

- the name of the reporting entity and any change since the last reporting date;
- identification of whether the financial statements are for the company itself or relate to a group of entities (consolidated financial statements are beyond the scope of this textbook);
- the reporting date, that is, the end of the reporting period or the period covered by the set of financial statements;

- the presentation currency, for example, euro, dollars, sterling; and
- the level of rounding used in the presentation of financial information, for example, thousands or millions of euro.

Assets and liabilities are presented split between current and non-current. The criteria used to assist in making the decision about classifying items as either current or non-current are given below.

Assets are classified as current if **any** of the following conditions are met:
- The entity expects to realise, consume or sell the asset within its normal operating cycle. The operating cycle may cover a period greater than one year, for example, the distillation process of whiskey will take longer than 12 months but the inventory is still classified as a current asset.
- The asset is held purely for trading purposes, for example, finished goods held for sale.
- It expects to realise the asset within 12 months of the reporting date.
- The asset is a cash or cash equivalent. Cash equivalents are defined in IAS 7 *Statement of Cash Flows* to include investments that are short-term, readily convertible to cash, subject to **insignificant** risk and have a maturity date of about three months from the investment date.

If an asset does not meet any of the above conditions then it is classified as non-current. The most common current assets are inventories, trade receivables and cash.

Liabilities are classified as current liabilities if **any** of the following conditions are met:
- The entity expects to settle the liability within its normal operating cycle.
- The liability is held primarily for trading purposes.
- The liability is expected to be paid within 12 months of the reporting date.
- The entity does not have an unconditional right to defer the settlement of the liability for at least 12 months after the reporting date.

If a liability does not meet any of the conditions above then it is classified as a non-current liability.

Examples 19.1 and **19.2** deal with the classification of a loan.

EXAMPLE 19.1: ENTITY HAS THE OPTION TO ROLLOVER OR REFINANCE A LOAN

Abigail Ltd has a loan facility with the local bank for €560,000. Under the terms of the loan it is due to be repaid on 30 September 2020. The loan contract allows Abigail to refinance the loan obligation for an additional three-year period rather than the original repayment date.

Abigail expects to take the refinancing option rather than repaying the loan in 2020.

Requirement How is the loan classified in the SOFP as at 31 December 2019?

Solution

The loan is due for repayment within 12 months of the reporting date, which would generally indicate that the loan should be classified as current. However, as Abigail has **both** the intention and the choice about refinancing (or rolling over) the loan for a period after 12 months from the reporting date, then it is classified as a non-current liability.

EXAMPLE 19.2: ENTITY DOES NOT HAVE THE OPTION TO ROLLOVER OR
REFINANCE A LOAN FACILITY

Winkler Ltd has a loan facility with the local bank for €430,000. Under the terms of the loan it is due to be repaid on 31 October 2020. The loan contract does not allow Winkler to refinance the loan. Winkler wants to refinance the loan over a longer period rather than repaying the loan in 2020.

Requirement How is the loan classified in the SOFP as at 31 December 2019?

Solution

In the circumstances Winkler does not have a choice about the refinancing of the loan, therefore the loan is classified as a current liability.

Example 19.3 demonstrates the situation where an entity has breached the terms of a long-term loan facility, which means that the loan is now repayable on demand.

EXAMPLE 19.3: BREACH OF LOAN FACILITY MAKES LONG-TERM LOAN REPAYABLE

Thompson Ltd has a loan facility of €2,100,000, with a repayment date of 30 June 2023. Under the terms of the loan facility Thompson must maintain a number of key ratios or the loan will become immediately repayable.

During December 2019, Thompson breached the ratios required by the loan facility and the loan should now be repaid on demand in accordance with the terms of the loan agreement. Thompson entered into negotiations with the loan provider and on 10 January 2020 the lender confirmed that they will not demand repayment of the loan and the original repayment date of June 2023 still applies.

The financial statements are authorised for issue on 12 March 2020.

Requirement How is the loan classified in the SOFP as at 31 December 2019?

Solution

IAS 1 requires that the loan facility be classified as current at the reporting date. The reason for this is that at the reporting date Thompson does not have the right to defer the repayment of the loan.

The choice about the loan repayment is the lending provider's and not Thompson's. Even though the lender confirms that the loan does not have to be repaid before the financial statements are authorised for issue, it does not alter the situation that existed at the reporting date.

If an entity has a loan that is classified as a current liability and any of the following events occur between the reporting date and the date the financial statements are authorised for issue, the event or transaction is classified as a **non-adjusting event** in accordance with IAS 10 *Events After the Reporting Period* (see **Chapter 23, Events After the Reporting Period**):
• refinancing on a long-term basis;
• rectification of a breach of a long-term loan arrangement; and

- lender allows a period of grace for the entity to rectify a breach of one of the terms of the long-term lending agreement that ends 12 months after the reporting date.

Next in this chapter, the layout of financial statements under IAS 1 is explained.

19.4 STATEMENT OF FINANCIAL POSITION

The layout of the SOFP is set out in the Implementation Guidance section of IAS 1. For the purpose of this textbook the suggested layout is as follows:

WARREN LTD
STATEMENT OF FINANCIAL POSITION
as at 31 December 2019
(in thousands of euro) (Note 1)

	31 December 2019		31 December 2018	
	€	€	€	€
ASSETS				
Non-current Assets				
Property, plant and equipment		X		X
Intangible assets		X		X
Investment in equity instruments		X		X
		X		X
Current Assets (Note 2)				
Inventory	X		X	
Trade receivables	X		X	
Other current assets	X		X	
Cash and cash equivalents	X	X	X	X
Total Assets		X		X
EQUITY AND LIABILITIES				
Equity and Reserves				
Ordinary share capital		X		X
Share premium		X		X
Revaluation surplus		X		X
Retained earnings		X		X
		X		X
Non-current Liabilities				
Long-term loans	X		X	
Long-term provisions	X		X	
Total Non-current Liabilities		X		X
Current Liabilities				
Trade and other payables	X		X	
Short-term borrowings	X		X	
Current tax payable (Note 3)	X		X	
Short-term provisions	X		X	
Total Current Liabilities		X		X
Total Liabilities		X		X
Total Equity and Liabilities		X		X

Notes:

1. IAS 1 requires the level of rounding and the currency used in the financial statements to be clearly indicated. In this case the information has been presented in the title of the financial statement. Alternatively, this information could have been presented at the top of each column as €000.

2. The order of presentation within the financial statements is from the least liquid (the item that will take the longest to convert to cash) to the most liquid.

3. IAS 1 requires the tax liability to be presented as a separate line item and not amalgamated with any other line item. (The term 'line item' is used to refer to each item for which financial information is provided in the financial statements; in the SOFP above long-term loans and current tax payable are examples of line items.)

The entity must make the following disclosures in one of the following: the SOFP, the SOCIE, or the notes to the financial statements.

1. For each class of share capital:
   - the number of shares authorised;
   - the number of shares issued and fully paid and issued but not fully paid;
   - the par value (also known as nominal value) of the shares, or that the shares have no par value;
   - a reconciliation of the number of shares outstanding at the beginning and end of the reporting period;
   - any rights, restrictions or preferences attaching to shares. The restrictions can relate to dividend payments or the repayment of capital;
   - the entity's shares held by the entity, its associates or subsidiaries; and
   - any shares reserved for issue under share options.

2. A description of each reserve listed within equity. The description should explain the nature and purpose of each reserve.

Example 19.4 demonstrates the preparation of a SOFP in accordance with IAS 1.

EXAMPLE 19.4: STATEMENT OF FINANCIAL POSITION

You are provided with the following trial balance for Smithers Ltd as at 31 December 2019:

Smithers Ltd
TRIAL BALANCE
as at 31 December 2019

	Debit €	Credit €
Property – cost	2,500,000	
Plant and equipment – cost	1,200,000	
Motor vehicles – cost	280,000	
Accumulated Depreciation as at 31 December 2019:		
Property		250,000
Plant and equipment		600,000
Motor vehicles		100,800

Ordinary share capital €1 each		250,000
Share premium		110,000
Retained earnings as at 31 December 2019		1,934,300
Loan (repayable in 2026)		800,000
Trade receivables	65,000	
Inventory as at 31 December 2019	82,500	
Prepayments	6,600	
Cash and cash equivalents	105,000	
Trade payables		48,500
Current tax payable		145,500
	4,239,100	4,239,100

Requirement Prepare the SOFP of Smithers Ltd as at 31 December 2019.

Note: in the above trial balance the retained earnings figure and the accumulated depreciation figures are as at 31 December 2019. This means that the depreciation and profit for the year have been determined and reflected in the above figures.

Solution

Smithers Ltd
STATEMENT OF FINANCIAL POSITION
as at 31 December 2019

	€	€
ASSETS		
Non-current Assets		
Property, plant and equipment (Working 1)		3,029,200
Current Assets		
Inventory	82,500	
Trade receivables	65,000	
Prepayments	6,600	
Cash and cash equivalents	105,000	259,100
TOTAL ASSETS		3,288,300
EQUITY AND LIABILITIES		
Equity and Reserves		
Ordinary share capital €1		250,000
Share premium		110,000
Retained earnings		1,934,300
		2,294,300

	€	€
Non-current Liabilities		
Loan		800,000
Current Liabilities		
Trade payables	48,500	
Current tax payable	145,500	194,000
		3,288,300

WORKING I: PROPERTY, PLANT AND EQUIPMENT

Asset Class	Property €	Plant and Equipment €	Motor Vehicles €	Total €
Cost	2,500,000	1,200,000	280,000	3,980,000
Accumulated depreciation	(250,000)	(600,000)	(100,800)	(950,800)
Carrying amount	2,250,000	600,000	179,200	3,029,200

Each time the company issues shares to investors the transaction is recognised in the financial records of the entity. When a company issues shares it is known as the issuer and the investors are known as the holders.

Subsequent sales of those shares by holders to other investors do not impact on the accounting records of the entity. When a company issues shares to investors at a price above their nominal value, the impact of the transaction will be to increase an asset (bank) and increase the capital. The capital element of the transaction is presented in two ledger accounts, namely, ordinary share capital account and share premium account. The nominal value of the shares issued is posted in the ordinary share capital account, and the excess of the share price over the nominal value is posted to the share premium account. Therefore, the effect of recording the transaction is to debit the bank account and credit the ordinary share capital account and the share premium account, as shown in the following journal entry:

	Debit €	Credit €
Bank account	X	
Ordinary share capital account		X
Share premium account		X

To recognise an issue of ordinary share capital at a premium.

The issue of shares is presented as a reconciling line item in the SOCIE in the year that the share issue took place. The SOCIE presents a reconciliation of the movements from the opening balance at the beginning of the reporting period to the closing balance at the end of the reporting period for each of the components of the equity and reserves section of the SOFP.

Example 19.5 demonstrates the treatment of shares issued at market price and how they are accounted for.

EXAMPLE 19.5: ISSUE OF SHARES AT MARKET PRICE

The memorandum and articles of association/constitution for Windsor Plc allow for the issue of 20 million ordinary shares at a nominal value (also known as par value) of €1 per share.

As at 1 January 2019, Windsor had 10 million shares in issue; all of these shares had been issued at par value at the date of incorporation. On 15 May 2019, Windsor issued 2 million ordinary shares at the market price of €4.30 each. The proceeds from the share issue were lodged to the bank account.

Windsor prepares its financial statements to 31 December each year.

Requirement How is the share issue on 15 May 2019 accounted for?

Solution

The proceeds of the share issue were €8,600,000, i.e. 2 million shares at €4.30 each.

The nominal value of the shares issued is €2,000,000, i.e. 2 million shares at their par value of €1 per share. The nominal value of the shares is presented in the ordinary share capital line item.

The difference between the proceeds raised (€8,600,000) from the share issue and the par value (€2,000,000) is presented in the share premium line item in the SOFP.

The accounting journal entry to recognise the share issue is:

	Debit €	Credit €
Bank account	8,600,000	
Ordinary share capital account		2,000,000
Share premium account		6,600,000
To recognise the share issue.		

Windsor Plc
STATEMENT OF FINANCIAL POSITION (EXTRACTS)
as at 31 December

	2019 €	2018 €
Equity and Reserves		
Ordinary share capital €1	12,000,000	10,000,000
Share premium	6,600,000	

Windsor Plc
STATEMENT OF CHANGES IN EQUITY (EXTRACT)
for the year ended 31 December 2019

	Ordinary Share Capital €000	Share Premium €000
As at 1 January 2019	10,000	–
Share issue	2,000	6,600
As at 31 December 2019	12,000	6,600

Note: the SOCIE will be explained in further detail in **Section 19.6**.

(Try **Review Question 19.1** at the end of this chapter.)

19.5 STATEMENT OF PROFIT OR LOSS AND OTHER COMPREHENSIVE INCOME

An entity has a choice regarding the presentation of the SPLOCI: it can use a classification based on either the nature or function of the expenses. In making the choice between the two presentations the entity shall consider the following:
- industry factors;
- nature of the entity; and
- which method will provide more relevant and reliable information.

The presentation based on the nature of the expenses is as follows:

	€	€
Revenue		X
Other income		X
Changes in inventories of finished goods and work in progress	X	
Raw materials and consumables used	X	
Employee benefits expense	X	
Depreciation and amortisation expense	X	
Other expenses	X	
Total expenses		(X)
Profit before tax		X

The presentation based on the function of the expenses is as follows:

	€
Revenue	X
Cost of sales	(X)
Gross profit	X
Other income	X
Distribution costs	(X)
Administrative expenses	(X)
Other expenses	(X)
Profit before tax	X

Example 19.6 demonstrates the calculation of figures for presentation in the SPLOCI using both the nature and function methods for classifying of expenses.

EXAMPLE 19.6: NATURE OF EXPENSES AND FUNCTION OF EXPENSES

You are provided with the following information in relation to the financial statements of Moore Ltd:

Reporting date	31 December 2019 €	31 December 2018 €
Inventory:		
Raw materials	118,150	74,300
Work in progress	290,500	305,400
Finished goods	135,800	158,500
Purchase of raw materials	2,987,000	2,750,300

Requirement:

(a) For presentation in the SPLOCI using the nature of expense classification, calculate the following figures:
  (i) changes in inventory of finished goods and work in progress; and
  (ii) raw materials and consumables used.
(b) For presentation in the SPLOCI using the function of expense classification, calculate the cost of sales figure.

Solution

(a)

	€
Changes in inventory of finished goods and work in progress (W1)	37,600
Raw materials and consumables used (W2)	2,943,150
	2,980,750

W1 CHANGES IN INVENTORY OF FINISHED GOODS AND WORK IN PROGRESS

	€
Change in finished goods (€158,500 – €135,800)	22,700
Changes in work in progress (€305,400 – €290,500)	14,900
	37,600

From the above working it is worth noting that the €37,600 is an expense of the period. In this case both the value of the work in progress and the finished goods have **decreased** from the start of the reporting period (i.e. 31/12/2018) to the end of the reporting period (i.e. 31/12/2019), thereby **increasing** the expenses of the period. Conversely, if the value of the work in progress or the finished goods had **increased** from the start to the end of the reporting period, this would have **reduced** the expenses of the reporting period.

W2 RAW MATERIALS AND CONSUMABLES USED

	€
Opening inventory of raw materials	74,300
Raw materials purchases	2,987,000
Less closing inventory of raw materials	(118,150)
	2,943,150

(b)

	€
Opening inventory (€74,300 + €305,400 + €158,500)	538,200
Purchases	2,987,000
Less closing inventory (€118,150 + €290,500 + €135,800)	(544,450)
	2,980,750

When an entity chooses the function of expense classification method it will have to include additional disclosure in relation to the nature of expenses such as depreciation, amortisation and employee benefit expenses.

Material items can be presented separately in the SPLOCI. The following are examples of items that require separate presentation in the SOPL if they are material:

- write-down of inventories to net realisable value;
- write-down of property, plant and equipment to recoverable amount;
- reversals of write-downs of inventories to net realisable value;
- reversals of write-downs of property, plant and equipment to recoverable amount;
- restructuring provisions;
- reversal of restructuring provisions;
- disposals of items of property, plant and equipment;
- disposal of investments;
- discontinued operations;
- litigation settlements; and
- other reversals of provisions.

Example 19.7 demonstrates the preparation and presentation of a SPLOCI and SOFP for a company in accordance with the requirements of IAS 1.

EXAMPLE 19.7: SPLOCI AND SOFP

You have been provided with the trial balance of Creighton Ltd as at 31 December 2019:

Creighton Ltd
TRIAL BALANCE
as at 31 December 2019

	Debit €	Credit €
Property – cost	4,000,000	
Plant and equipment – cost	2,600,000	
Motor vehicles – cost	750,000	
Accumulated Depreciation as at 31 December 2018:		
Property		600,000
Plant and equipment		1,040,000
Motor vehicles		275,000
Revenue		11,250,600
Purchases	6,587,000	
Inventory as at 1 January 2019	510,000	
Administration costs	890,250	
Selling and distribution expenses	655,000	
Finance cost	65,000	
Ordinary share capital €1 each		300,000
Share premium		100,000
Retained earnings as at 31 December 2018		1,985,650
Loan (repayable in 2023)		1,200,000

Trade receivables	950,000	
Prepayments	62,500	
Cash and cash equivalents	167,000	
Trade payables		485,500
	17,236,750	17,236,750

The following additional information has been provided:

1. Inventory on hand as at 31 December 2019 was valued at €478,200.
2. Depreciation has to be charged for the year ended 31 December 2019 as follows:

Class of property, plant and equipment	Depreciation rate and method	Depreciation charged to
Property	2% straight-line	Administration costs
Plant and equipment	20% straight-line	Cost of sales
Motor vehicles	20% reducing-balance	Selling and distribution

3. The current year's tax charge has been estimated at €536,200. It has not been reflected in the above trial balance.

Requirement Prepare the SPLOCI for the year ended 31 December 2019 and the SOFP as at that date for Creighton Ltd.

Solution

Creighton Ltd
STATEMENT OF PROFIT OR LOSS AND OTHER COMPREHENSIVE INCOME
for the year ended 31 December 2019

	€
Revenue	11,250,600
Cost of sales (Working 1)	(7,138,800)
Gross profit	4,111,800
Administration costs (Working 1)	(970,250)
Selling and distribution expenses (Working 1)	(750,000)
Finance cost	(65,000)
Profit before tax	2,326,550
Income tax (Working 3)	(536,200)
PROFIT FOR YEAR	1,790,350
Other comprehensive income	Nil
TOTAL COMPREHENSIVE INCOME FOR YEAR	1,790,350

Note: there are no items in this example that have to be presented under other comprehensive income (OCI). As progress is made through the chapters dealing with various accounting standards there will be adjustments that have to be presented in the OCI section of the SOPL.

Creighton Ltd
STATEMENT OF FINANCIAL POSITION
as at 31 December 2019

	€	€
ASSETS		
Non-current assets		
Property, plant and equipment (Working 4)		4,740,000
Current assets		
Inventory	478,200	
Prepayments	62,500	
Trade receivables	950,000	
Cash and cash equivalents	167,000	1,657,700
Total assets		6,397,700
EQUITY AND LIABILITIES		
Equity and reserves		
Ordinary share capital €1		300,000
Share premium		100,000
Retained earnings (€1,985,650 + €1,790,350)		3,776,000
		4,176,000
Non-current liabilities		
Loan		1,200,000
Current liabilities		
Trade payables	485,500	
Current tax payable (Working 3)	536,200	1,021,700
Total equity and liabilities		6,397,700

WORKING 1

	Cost of Sales €	Administration Costs €	Selling and Distribution Costs €
Opening inventory	510,000		
Purchases	6,587,000		
Closing inventory	(478,200)		
Administration costs		890,250	
Selling and distribution expenses			655,000
Depreciation – Working 2:			
Buildings		80,000	
Plant and machinery	520,000		
Motor vehicles			95,000
	7,138,800	970,250	750,000

WORKING 2: DEPRECIATION CALCULATION

Asset	Cost €	Carrying Amount €	Depreciation rate	Depreciation Charge €
Buildings	4,000,000		2%	80,000
Plant and equipment	2,600,000		20%	520,000
Motor vehicles		475,000	20%	95,000

WORKING 3: TAX

	Debit €	Credit €
SPLOCI – tax	536,200	
Current tax payable account		536,200

To recognise the tax expense and liability.

WORKING 4: PROPERTY, PLANT AND EQUIPMENT

	Buildings €	Plant and Equipment €	Motor Vehicles €	TOTAL €
Cost	4,000,000	2,600,000	750,000	7,350,000
Accumulated Depreciation				
600,000 + 80,000	(680,000)			
1,040,000 + 520,000		(1,560,000)		
275,000 + 95,000			(370,000)	(2,610,000)
Carrying amount	3,320,000	1,040,000	380,000	4,740,000

(Try **Review Question 19.2** at the end of this chapter.)

19.6 STATEMENT OF CHANGES IN EQUITY

The SOCIE shows the movement in the opening balances on each of the line items listed in the equity and reserves section of the SOFP. Examples of transactions that are presented in the SOCIE are:
- profit for year;
- other comprehensive income;
- dividends accrued and paid;
- revaluations of property, plant and equipment that impact the revaluation surplus account;
- share issues; and
- impact of changes in accounting policy or errors.

Using the information from **Example 19.7** a SOCIE will be prepared taking the steps outlined below.

Step 1 Identify the column headings to be presented in the SOCIE.

Looking at the information presented in the equity and reserves section of the SOFP, a heading is required in the SOCIE for each line item presented, i.e. in this case:
- ordinary share capital;
- share premium; and
- retained earnings.

Step 2 Identify the opening balances on each of these accounts.

The opening balances as at 1 January 2019 are according to the trial balance before the SPLOCI for the period is prepared:
• ordinary share capital: €300,000;
• share premium: €100,000; and
• retained earnings: €1,985,650.

Step 3 Identify those transactions that occurred during the reporting period ended 31 December 2019 that impact the three accounts identified in Step 1.

The only transaction that occurred during the reporting period was the recognition of the profit for the period.

Step 4 Prepare the SOCIE.

Creighton Ltd
STATEMENT OF CHANGES IN EQUITY
for the year ended 31 December 2019

	Ordinary Share Capital	Share Premium	Retained Earnings	Total €
As at 01/01/2019	300,000	100,000	1,985,650	2,385,650
Profit for year			1,790,350	1,790,350
As at 31/12/2019	300,000	100,000	3,776,000	4,176,000

Example 19.8 demonstrates the relationship between the figures presented in the SOFP for the comparative period and those in the SOCIE for the current period.

EXAMPLE 19.8: STATEMENT OF CHANGES IN EQUITY

The following figures have been extracted from the SOFP of Victoria Plc:

	31 December 2019 €000	31 December 2018 €000
Equity and Reserves		
Ordinary share capital €1	600	500
Share premium	100	20
Revaluation surplus	120	50
Retained earnings	2,350	1,980
	3,170	2,550

Additional information has been provided in relation to transactions that occurred during the year:
1. Victoria issued 100,000 ordinary shares at a fair value of €1.80 per share on 3 March 2019.
2. Dividends were proposed by the directors at a rate of 4 cent per share. The dividend was approved by the shareholders at the annual general meeting on 12 December 2019. The dividend was paid on 15 January 2020.
3. The following is an extract from the SPLOCI:

	31 December 2019 €000	31 December 2018 €000
Profit before tax	504	360
Income tax	(110)	(80)
Profit for year	394	280
Other comprehensive income		
Gain on revaluation	70	
Total comprehensive income	464	280

Requirement Prepare the SOCIE of Victoria Plc for the year ended 31 December 2019.

Solution

Victoria Plc
STATEMENT OF CHANGES IN EQUITY
for the year ended 31 December 2019

	Ordinary Share Capital €000	Share Premium €000	Revaluation Surplus €000	Retained Earnings €000	Total €000
As at 01/01/2019	500	20	50	1,980	2,550
Share issue	100	80			180
Total comprehensive income			70	394	464
Dividend				(24)	(24)
As at 31/12/2019	600	100	120	2,350	3,170

Dividend figure: even though the dividend has not been paid during the reporting period it is presented in the SOCIE when the obligation has been created, that is, when the dividend payment has been approved by shareholders at the annual general meeting (AGM). The amount of the dividend is calculated as follows:

Number of shares in issue at the date the dividend is proposed	600,000
Dividend per share	4c
Total dividend (600,000 shares × €0.04)	€24,000

To recognise the dividend payable after the approval by shareholders at the AGM:

	Debit €	Credit €
Retained earnings – SOCIE	24,000	
Dividend payable account		24,000

To recognise the dividend payable during the reporting period 31 December 2019.

When the dividend is paid in 2014 the accounting entry is:

	Debit €	Credit €
Dividend payable account	24,000	
Bank account		24,000

To recognise the payment of the dividend in January 2020.

It is very important to remember that ordinary dividends are **never** presented in the SPLOCI.

It is important to understand what constitutes an **accounting policy** and the circumstances in which a change in accounting policy is allowed; these areas are covered in **Chapter 22**. **Example 19.9** demonstrates the presentation of the impact of a change in accounting policy when applied retrospectively in the financial statements.

EXAMPLE 19.9: CHANGE IN ACCOUNTING POLICY

The following figures have been extracted from the SOFP of Sandwich Plc:

	31 December 2019 €000	31 December 2018 €000
Equity and Reserves		
Ordinary share capital €1	250	250
Share premium	100	100
Retained earnings	1,930	1,490
	2,280	1,840

Sandwich made a change to one of its accounting policies to ensure that the information presented is more relevant and reliable to the users of the financial statements.

The change in accounting policy is a change to the measurement base for inventory from weighted average to the first in first out (FIFO) basis. If inventory had been valued using the FIFO method previously, the opening retained earnings at the start of the year (i.e. 1 January 2019) would be €45,000 higher than stated above for 2018 (see **Chapter 21, Section 21.2** for greater detail on the measurement of inventory).

The reported profit for 2019 of €470,000 has been prepared on the basis of valuing inventory using the FIFO method. Dividends paid during the year were €30,000.

Requirement Prepare the SOCIE of Sandwich Plc for the year ended 31 December 2019.

Solution

Sandwich Plc
STATEMENT OF CHANGES IN EQUITY
for the year ended 31 December 2019

	Ordinary Share Capital €000	Share Premium €000	Retained Earnings €000	Total €000
As at 01/01/2019	250	100	1,490	1,840
Change in accounting policy			45	45
Restated	250	100	1,535	1,885
Profit for year			470	470
Dividend			(30)	(30)
As at 31/12/2019	250	100	1,975	2,325

(Try **Review Question 19.3** at the end of this chapter.)

19.7 DISCLOSURE

The entity must disclose the significant accounting policies used in the preparation of the financial statements. In deciding whether to make disclosures about accounting policies, it must be considered whether the information would assist the users' understanding.

Entities must disclose information about assumptions they have made in relation to the future and major sources of uncertainty. Examples of the disclosures required are:
* the nature of the assumptions made and the uncertainty;
* the sensitivity of the amounts presented to any changes in methods used and assumptions used in the calculation; and
* an explanation of the changes to assumptions made in the past or if the uncertainty has been resolved.

Other disclosures to be made are as follows:
* disclosure is required when there is a change in the presentation of items;
* disclosure of the fact that the financial statements have been prepared in compliance with international financial reporting standards;
* disclosure of the amount of any dividend proposed before the financial statements were authorised for issue but not recognised in the financial statements;
* disclosure of the amount of any cumulative preference dividends not recognised; and
* the following should be disclosed in the notes to the financial statements if they have not been disclosed elsewhere in the published annual report:
  * domicile of the entity;
  * legal form of the entity;
  * country of the entity's incorporation;
  * address of the entity's registered office;
  * description of the entity's principal operations and activities;
  * name of the entity's parent and the ultimate parent of the group;
  * if the entity has a limited life, the length of its life.

Example 19.10 demonstrates the disclosure requirements in relation to compliance with IFRS.

EXAMPLE 19.10: DISCLOSURE NOTE TO FINANCIAL STATEMENTS

Statement of Compliance

Company financial statements have been prepared in accordance with the International Financial Reporting Standards (IFRS) as adopted by the EU and as applied in accordance with the Companies Acts 2014 (in the ROI) or Companies Act 2006 (in the UK).

The IFRS applied in the financial statements were those effective for reporting periods ending on 31 December 2019.

19.8 IAS 1 COMPARED WITH FRS 102

Under both IFRS and FRS 102 *The Financial Reporting Standard applicable in the UK and Republic of Ireland*, the income statement may be presented with the statement of comprehensive income as a single statement referred to as the 'statement of profit or loss and other comprehensive income'.

Under IFRS the SOCIE is presented as a separate financial statement, while under FRS 102, if certain conditions are met, the SOCIE may be combined with the statement of comprehensive income and referred to as the 'statement of income and retained earnings'.

If the financial statements are prepared in accordance with FRS 102, rather than IFRS, in the disclosure notes there must be a clear statement that the financial statements are prepared in compliance with FRS 102.

Under FRS 102 an entity does not have to disclose the number of authorised shares for each class of shares, as required under IAS 1.

There are some differences in relation to the layout of the SOFP and the terminology used under IFRS and FRS 102. The terms 'debtors' and 'creditors' are used under FRS 102 rather than 'trade receivables' and 'trade payables', which are used under IFRS.

Exam Tips

1. Know the correct layout for each financial statement.
2. Dividends on ordinary shares are presented in the SOCIE not the SPLOCI.
3. Dividends are only accrued at the reporting date if they were approved by shareholders at the AGM before the reporting date.
4. Make sure of depreciation policies for each class of property, plant and equipment – straight-line or reducing-balance.
5. Check if depreciation is time apportioned in the years of purchase and sale.
6. Present the current tax payable as a separate line item in the current liabilities section of the SOFP.

   Make sure you know the layout of the SPLOCI and what is presented in the other comprehensive section of the statement. The most common item to be presented in the other comprehensive income section from an exam point of view would be in relation to the revaluation of an item of property, plant and equipment (see **Chapter 25, Property, Plant and Equipment**).

7. Make sure you classify expenses correctly:

Line item in the SPLOCI	Costs included unless specific information to the contrary
Cost of sales	Opening inventory
	Purchases
	Carriage inwards
	Manufacturing wages
	Manufacturing costs
	Depreciation on production machinery, such as plant and equipment
	The following items reduce the cost of sales figure:
	Closing inventory
	Purchase returns

Administration costs	Administration cost
	Administration salaries
	Auditor's fee
	Directors' remuneration
	Depreciation on administration buildings
Selling and distribution costs	Depreciation on motor vehicles
	Carriage outwards
	Bad debts
	Increase/decrease in allowance for bad debts

8. Remember, a material item should be presented as a separate line item, for example if an item of property, plant and equipment is sold at a loss, it should be presented as follows in the SPLOCI:
   - Loss on disposal is material – present as a separate line item;
   - Loss on disposal is not material – present in the same line item as the depreciation expense for the related class of asset, that is, if the item sold was a piece of equipment and the depreciation charged is presented in cost of sales figure in the SPLOCI, then the loss on disposal would also be included in the calculation of cost of sale.

19.9 CONCLUSION

In this chapter the layout of published financial statements prepared in accordance with IFRS was set out. The concepts of aggregation, materiality, offsetting, comparatives, and consistency of presentation were explained.

SUMMARY OF LEARNING OBJECTIVES

After having studied this chapter, readers should be able to:

Learning Objective 1 Prepare the statement of profit or loss and other comprehensive income.

The SPLOCI provides users of financial statements with information about the financial performance of the entity for a particular period of time. This financial statement is prepared on an accrual basis.

The format of this financial statement is either on a basis that reflects the nature of the expenses incurred or the functions to which the expenses relate. The presentation chosen should be appropriate to the relevant entity and result in the information provided being relevant and reliable to users of the financial statements.

Learning Objective 2 Prepare the statement of financial position.

The SOFP presents the balances on asset, liability and capital accounts at the reporting date. The layout requires assets and liabilities to be presented as either current or non-current.

Learning Objective 3 Prepare the statement of changes in equity.

The SOCIE shows the movement in each line item presented in the equity and reserves section of the SOFP. It shows the transactions that reconcile the opening and closing balance for each line item in equity and reserves. The items most commonly presented in the SOCIE are:
- profit for year;
- other comprehensive income;
- dividends accrued and paid;
- revaluation of property, plant and equipment;
- share issues; and
- impact of changes in accounting policy or errors.

QUESTIONS

Review Questions

(See **Appendix A** for Solutions to Review Questions.)

Question 19.1

You have been provided with the following information in relation to the ordinary share capital of Tent Plc:

Authorised ordinary share capital	5,000,000 shares
Par value of each share (also known as nominal value)	50c each
Issue share capital as at 1 January 2019:	
Ordinary shares (all issued at par value on the date of incorporation)	€1,800,000

On 30 April 2019, Tent issued 1,000,000 ordinary shares at the market price of €2.80 per share.

Requirement Prepare the journal entry to recognise the share issue and the extract from the statement of financial position as at 31 December 2019 (with comparatives).

Question 19.2

Warwick Plc
TRIAL BALANCE
as at 31 December 2019

	Debit €	Credit €
Buildings – cost	2,800,000	
Machinery – cost	1,500,000	
Motor vehicles – cost	620,000	
Accumulated Depreciation as at 31 December 2018:		
Buildings		224,000
Machinery		450,000
Motor vehicles		186,000
Revenue		6,105,800
Purchases	3,160,400	
Inventory as at 1 January 2019	280,100	
Purchases returns		135,000
Sales returns	198,000	
Manufacturing wages	435,000	

Administration costs	285,900	
Administration wages	306,200	
Auditor's fee	15,000	
Directors' fees	189,000	
Motor expenses	220,000	
Bad debts	10,500	
Allowance for bad debts		6,500
Finance cost	14,000	
Ordinary share capital €1 each		500,000
Share premium		450,000
Retained earnings as at 31 December 2018		1,364,100
7% loan (repayable in 2022)		900,000
Trade receivables	518,000	
Bank	168,700	
Trade payables		399,400
	10,720,800	10,720,800

Additional information is available:
1. The inventory on hand as at 31 December 2019 is valued at €346,200.
2. The estimate of the tax charge for the year ended 31 December 2019 is €294,280.
3. Management feels an allowance for bad debts is required at a level of 3% of trade receivables.
4. The loan was taken out on 1 January 2019.
5. Depreciation is to be charged as follows:
   Buildings – 2% on a straight-line basis charged to administration costs.
   Machinery – 10% on a straight-line basis charged to cost of sales.
   Motor vehicles – 15% on a straight-line basis charged to selling and distribution expenses.

Requirement:
(a) Prepare the statement of profit or loss and other comprehensive income of Warwick Plc for the year ended 31 December 2019.
(b) Prepare the statement of financial position of Warwick Plc as at 31 December 2019.

Question 19.3

You are provided with the following information in relation to the equity and reserves of Walker Ltd as at 31 December 2018:

	€
Ordinary share capital €0.20 each	500,000
Share premium	260,000
Retained earnings	1,910,000

1. Profit for the year ended 31 December 2019 was reported as €302,500.
2. Dividends of €40,000 were proposed by the directors on 1 December 2019, the shareholders' AGM is scheduled for 14 January 2020.
3. 200,000 ordinary shares were issued on 1 October 2019 at €2.80 per share.
4. Management has made a change to an accounting policy in order to provide more relevant and reliable information to the users of the financial statements. The impact of the change in accounting policy is that the reported retained earnings as at 31 December 2018 were overstated by €65,000.

Requirement Prepare the statement of changes in equity of Walker Ltd for the year ended 31 December 2019.

Challenging Questions

(Suggested Solutions to Challenging Questions are available through your lecturer.)

Question 19.1

The trial balance extracted from Acorn Ltd as at 31 December 2019 was as follows:

	€	€
Share capital		150,000
Retained earnings at 1 January 2019		170,572
Freehold property at cost	271,000	
Plant and equipment at cost	84,000	
Accumulated depreciation at 1 January 2019:		
Freehold property		54,000
Plant and Equipment		21,000
Purchases	66,347	
Sales		180,400
General administrative expenses	1,852	
Wages and salaries	37,975	
Rent and rates	6,100	
Heat and light	4,800	
Delivery costs	2,565	
Selling and advertising costs	3,180	
Interest costs	621	
Allowance for doubtful debts at 1 January 2019		398
Accounts receivable	12,430	
Accounts payable		15,595
Inventory at 1 January 2019	10,573	
Bank	40,522	
Dividends	10,000	
Investments	40,000	
	591,965	591,965

You have been provided with the following additional information:

1. Inventory at 31 December 2019 is €9,500. Included within this balance are inventory items valued at a cost of €1,672. These items would normally be marked up by 25% before sale. However, they were damaged in a fire on 10 December 2019 and will need to be marked down and sold for 50% of their original selling price.

2. Depreciation is to be provided as follows:
    Property – 2% per annum on cost
    Plant and equipment – 20% per annum on reducing balances

    Depreciation is to be allocated as follows:
    Property 80% to cost of sales and 20% to administrative expenses
    Plant and equipment – 100% to cost of sales.

3. The rent and rates expense included in the trial balance relates to both office accommodation and factory space for production.

    Rent and rates is to be allocated as follows:
    80% to cost of sales and 20% to administrative expenses.

    This is the first year that the company has required additional space. In August 2019 the company paid €2,100 for rent in respect of the year ending 31 August 2020. This full amount is included within rent and rates in the trial balance above.

4. Wages and salaries included within wages and salaries are €33,715 of production wages and €4,260 of administration wages. At 31 December 2019, €2,865 of production wages and €310 of administration wages were still owed by Acorn.
5. Heat and light, €1,020, is due for the three months to 31 January 2019. This has not been included in the figure above.

   Heat and light is to be allocated as follows:
       70% to cost of sales and 30% to administrative expenses.

Requirement:
(a) Prepare Acorn's statement of profit or loss and other comprehensive income for the year ended 31 December 2019 in accordance with IAS 1 *Presentation of Financial Statements*.

12 Marks

(b) Prepare Acorn's statement of changes in equity for the year ended 31 December 2019.

3 Marks

(Based on Chartered Accountants Ireland, CAP 1 Financial Accounting, Summer 2011, Question 2)

Question 19.2

The following trial balance has been extracted from the records of Aubin Ltd at 31 December 2019:

TRIAL BALANCE
as at 31 December 2019

	Debit €000	Credit €000
Land and buildings at cost	11,250	
Provision for depreciation on buildings		750
Motor vehicles at cost	4,530	
Provision for depreciation on motor vehicles		2,620
Purchases	8,700	
Revenue		15,787
Inventory at 1 January 2019	1,477	
Trade receivables	1,650	
Distribution costs	1,342	
Trade payables		1,200
Administrative expenses	1,822	
Interim ordinary dividend	210	
Bank overdraft		833
Bank and cash	61	
Interim preference dividend	150	
Taxation	35	
Loan stock interest	40	
Allowance for bad debts		83
Share premium account		1,125
5% loan stock		1,500
Retained earnings		1,369
10% preference shares of €1 each		3,000
Ordinary share capital account		3,000
	31,267	31,267

Additional information:

1. Closing inventory at 31 December 2019 is valued at a cost of €2,025,000.
2. The financial statements were approved by the board of directors on 5 March 2020.
3. The directors propose a final ordinary dividend of 12 cent/pence per share, which was approved on 5 March 2020.
4. On 20 February 2020 Aubin issued 10 million €1 shares at €1.50 each.
5. On 28 February 2020 Aubin agreed to purchase a major competitor, which had gone into liquidation, for €10,000,000.
6. Due to continuing poor economic conditions, Aubin has estimated that 5% of the outstanding receivables balance may not be recovered. Bad debts and movements in allowance for bad debts are treated as distribution costs.
7. Depreciation is to be provided as follows:
   (i)   land (at a cost of €4,000,000) is not depreciated;
   (ii) buildings are depreciated at 2% per annum on a straight-line basis (treated as administrative expense);
   (iii) motor vehicles are depreciated at 20% per annum on a reducing-balance basis (treated as a distribution cost).
8. The tax charge in the trial balance relates to an under-provision for the year ended 31 December 2018. Taxation for the year ended 31 December 2019 is estimated to be €450,000.
9. Administrative expenses of €8,000 were outstanding at 31 December 2019.
10. Preference dividends are to be accrued at 31 December 2019. No adjustments have been made to the draft accounts for any of the items 1.−10. listed above.

Requirement:

(a) Prepare the statement of profit or loss and other comprehensive income for Aubin for the year ended 31 December 2019 in accordance with IAS 1 *Presentation of Financial Statements.*

12 Minutes

(b) Prepare the statement of financial position for Aubin at 31 December 2019 in accordance with IAS 1 *Presentation of Financial Statements.*

12 Minutes

(c) Prepare the statement of changes in equity for Aubin for the year ended 31 December 2019 in accordance with IAS 1 *Presentation of Financial Statements.*

5 Minutes

(d) Prepare the disclosure note for events after the reporting period for inclusion in the annual report of Aubin for the year ended 31 December 2019.

10 Minutes

(Based on Chartered Accountants Ireland, CAP 1 Financial Accounting, Autumn 2013, Question 3)

20

Statement of Cash Flows

LEARNING OBJECTIVES

Having studied this chapter, readers should be able to:
1. prepare the reconciliation of profit before tax to net cash flow from operating activities; and
2. prepare a statement of cash flows.

20.1 INTRODUCTION

To successfully operate a business an entity needs to generate cash flows. The statement of profit or loss and other comprehensive income (SPLOCI) presents the profit or loss for the period based on the accrual concept, but both entities and users of the financial statements need to know where cash is being generated and spent.

Preparation of the statement of cash flows (SOCF) is covered by IAS 7 *Statement of Cash Flows*. The SOCF looks at inflows and outflows under three different headings:
- operating activities,
- investing activities, and
- financing activities.

The SOCF shows the increase or decrease in **cash and cash equivalents** since the start of the reporting period.
- 'Cash' is made up of cash on hand and demand deposits.
- 'Cash equivalents' are short-term **highly liquid** investments that have very little risk associated with them, in other words, the date of maturity of the investment is no more than three months after the investment date and the entity is more or less guaranteed to be repaid in full at the maturity date of the investment.

Example 20.1 demonstrates when investments may be classified as cash and cash equivalents.

EXAMPLE 20.1: CASH AND CASH EQUIVALENTS

Which of the following investments would be considered to be a cash and cash equivalent? You can assume that the investments are subject to insignificant risk.

	Investment 1	Investment 2
Reporting date	31 December 2018	31 March 2019
Investment date	1 July 2018	1 March 2019
Maturity date	31 January 2019	30 April 2019

Solution

Investment 1 is not a cash equivalent because the duration of the investment is seven months. IAS 7 indicates a maturity date of around three months from the date of the investment to qualify as a cash equivalent.

Investment 2 is included in cash and cash equivalents because the duration of the investment is for less than three months and the risks associated with the investment are insignificant.

20.2 OPERATING ACTIVITIES

In determining the profit or loss for a period, a number of items are included that do not involve either a cash payment or receipt. Examples of such items are:
- depreciation (see **Chapter 6, Section 6.3**);
- profit on disposal of items of property, plant and equipment (see **Chapter 6, Section 6.4**);
- loss on disposal of items of property, plant and equipment (see **Chapter 6, Section 6.4**);
- amortisation of intangibles; and
- amortisation of grants.

To calculate the net cash flow from operating activities the profit or loss for the period must be adjusted for:
- non-cash items included in the SPLOCI, such as depreciation;
- movements in working capital, that is, inventory, trade receivables and trade payables; and
- items included in the statements of profit or loss that do not relate to operating activities.

Changes in working capital have an impact on the cash levels within the entity; this impact is summarised in **Figure 20.1**.

FIGURE 20.1: IMPACT OF CHANGES IN WORKING CAPITAL ON CASH

Working Capital Element	Change	Impact on Cash and Cash Equivalents
Inventory	Inventory balance at the end of the reporting date is higher than the balance at the start of the year.	Reduces the cash available.
Inventory	Inventory balance at the end of the reporting date is lower than the balance at the start of the year.	Increases the cash available.
Trade receivables	Amount due from credit customers is higher at the end of the year compared to the balance at the start of the year.	Reduces the cash available.
Trade receivables	Amount due from credit customers is lower at the end of the year compared to the balance at the start of the year.	Increases the cash available.
Trade payables	The amount owed to suppliers is higher at the end of the reporting period than at the start of the period.	Increases the cash of the entity.
Trade payables	The amount owed to suppliers is lower at the end of the reporting period than at the start of the period.	Reduces the cash available to the entity.

Sometimes expenses are charged to the SPLOCI that do not relate to the normal day-to-day operations of the business. For example, a supermarket chain buys goods from producers then sells them to consumers; if the supermarket raises funds through the stock market and incurs expenses related to the share issue, these costs, if presented in the SPLOCI, should be added back to the reported profit or loss for the period. The share issue expenses are not an operating cost of the business but a financing cost.

There are two methods used to determine the cash generated from operations:
• direct method, and
• indirect method.

The indirect method is most commonly used in Ireland but both methods are allowed under IAS 7 and readers should familiarise themselves with both.

Direct Method

The approach under the direct method focuses on the following key figures:

	€
Cash received from customers	X
Cash paid to suppliers	(X)
Cash paid for other expenses	(X)
Cash generated from operations	X/(X)

It is important to remember that any non-cash items, such as depreciation, should not be included in any of the above figures.

Example 20.2 demonstrates how these figures would be calculated.

EXAMPLE 20.2: DIRECT METHOD

Ogilvy Ltd has provided you with the following information:

STATEMENT OF PROFIT OR LOSS AND OTHER COMPREHENSIVE INCOME
for the year ended 31 December 2019

	€
Revenue	2,145,600
Cost of sales	(1,263,200)
Gross profit	882,400
Operating expenses	(268,000)
Profit before tax	614,400
Income tax expense	(185,000)
Profit for year	429,400

Depreciation of €86,000 was charged in the period and is included in operating expenses.

The following has been extracted from the statement of financial position (SOFP) as at 31 December 2019:

	2019 €	2018 €
Current Assets		
Inventory	134,200	148,500
Trade receivables	215,500	189,000
Cash and cash equivalents	81,700	42,900
Current Liabilities		
Trade payables	152,900	141,250

Requirement Prepare the calculation of cash generated from operations using the direct method.

Solution

In this example dates are not included in the ledger accounts; as the transactions occurred throughout the year, the specific dates for the transactions are not provided. The opening and closing balances on the trade receivables account and the sales revenue for the period are known. As there are amounts due from customers at both the start and end of the period, it follows that the amount received from customers is not the same as the revenue recognised in the SPLOCI.

Step 1 Calculate the amount of cash receipts from customers.

TRADE RECEIVABLES ACCOUNT

Account Name	€	Account Name	€
Balance b/d	189,000	Bank	?
Revenue	2,145,600	Balance c/d	215,500
	2,334,600		2,334,600

The trade receivables account has been completed, as far as possible, with the information available. The total of the debit side is €2,334,600, but the credit side of the account only has the balance carried down figure of €215,500. The difference between the two sides of the account is a credit entry which represents the cash received from customers during the reporting period: €2,119,100 [€2,334,600 – €215,500].

The balancing of the trade receivables account is now demonstrated.

TRADE RECEIVABLES ACCOUNT

Account Name	€	Account Name	€
Balance b/d	189,000	Bank	2,119,100
Revenue	2,145,600	Balance c/d	215,500
	2,334,600		2,334,600

The figure of €2,119,100 is presented as 'cash received from customers' in the SOCF prepared under the direct method.

To calculate the amount paid to suppliers, first work out the value of the purchases for the period. The purchases figure is not presented separately in the SPLOCI but is included in the calculation of cost of sales.

Cost of sales is made up of (at a minimum):

	€
Opening inventory	X
Purchases	X
	X
Less closing inventory	(X)
Cost of sales	X

Step 2 Calculate the purchase expense for the period and the amount paid in relation to purchases.

Using the information provided, the value of the purchases can be calculated.

	Fill in the figures that are known	Work back to determine the total for opening inventory and purchases	Calculate the figure for purchases
Opening inventory	148,500	148,500	148,500[2]
Purchases			1,248,900
		1,397,400[1]	1,397,400
Less closing inventory	(134,200)	(134,200)	(134,200)
Cost of sales	1,263,200	1,263,200	1,263,200

[1] €1,397,400 = €1,263,200 + €134,200.
[2] €1,248,900 = €1,397,400 − €148,500.

As there are balances outstanding in relation to trade payables, it follows that the amount paid to suppliers in the period in not the same as the purchases figure in the SPLOCI. Using the information provided in the example, the amount paid can be calculated.

TRADE PAYABLES ACCOUNT

Account Name	€	Account Name	€
Bank	?	Balance b/d	141,250
Balance c/d	152,900	Purchases	1,248,900
	1,390,150		1,390,150

The trade payables account has been completed, as far as possible, with the information available. The total of the credit side is €1,390,150, but the debit side of the account only has the balance carried down figure of €152,900. The difference between the two sides of the account is a debit entry that represents the cash paid to suppliers during the reporting period: €1,237,250 (€1,390,150 − €152,900).

Trade Payables Account

Account Name	€	Account Name	€
Bank	1,237,250	Balance b/d	141,250
Balance c/d	152,900	Purchases	1,248,900
	1,390,150		1,390,150

The figure of €1,237,250 is presented as 'cash paid to suppliers' in the SOCF prepared under the direct method.

Step 3 Calculate the cash payments in relation to other costs.

The question states that depreciation costs are presented within the operating expenses line. Depreciation does not involve any cash payment as the operating costs must be reduced by the amount of the depreciation charge for the period. There are no liabilities outstanding in relation to other payables, so the figure included in the SOCF is €182,000 (€268,000 − €86,000).

The following will be presented in the SOCF under operating activities:

	€
Cash received from customers	2,119,100
Cash paid to suppliers	(1,237,250)
Cash paid for other expenses	(182,000)
Cash generated from operations	699,850

The presentation of tax paid and refunds of tax is explained in **Section 20.7** of this chapter.

Indirect Method

Under the indirect method the following approach is taken:
- start with the profit before tax;
- add back/deduct any items included in the SPLOCI that do not involve cash;
- add back/deduct any items included in the SPLOCI that do not relate to operating activities; and
- make adjustments for changes in working capital.

Example 20.3 demonstrates how these figures would be calculated.

EXAMPLE 20.3: INDIRECT METHOD

Using the information provided in the previous example the calculation of the cash generated from operations would appear as follows under the indirect method:

	€
Profit before tax	614,400
Depreciation	86,000
	700,400

Changes in working capital	
Decrease in inventory	14,300
Increase in trade receivables	(26,500)
Increase in trade payables	11,650
Cash generated from operations	699,850

The decrease in inventory of €14,300 (it reduced from €148,500 at the start of the year to €134,200 at the end of the year) has increased the cash available as the company has less funds tied up in its investment in inventories.

The increase in trade receivables of €26,500 (they increased from €189,000 at the start of the year to €215,500 at the end of the year) has reduced the cash available as the company has to finance a higher amount.

The increase in trade payables of €11,650 (they increased from €141,250 at the start of the year to €152,900 at the end of the year) has increased the cash available as the company has been able to avail of additional credit facilities from suppliers.

The two methods differ in the way the cash generated from operations figure is calculated, but in all other respects the presentation of the SOCF is the same under both methods.

(Try **Review Question 20.1** at the end of this chapter.)

The next section will present the layout of the SOCF and explanations of the calculations in relation to the most frequently occurring items.

20.3 LAYOUT OF STATEMENT OF CASH FLOWS

The layout of the SOCF per IAS 7 is set out below:

	€	€
Cash flows from operating activities		
Cash generated from operations (see **Section 20.1**)		X/(X)
Interest paid	(X)	
Income taxes paid	(X)	X/(X)
Net cash from operating activities		X/(X)
Cash flows from investing activities		
Purchase of property, plant and equipment	(X)	
Proceeds from sale of property, plant and equipment	X	
Interest received	X	
Dividends received	X	
Net cash from investing activities		X/(X)
Cash flows from financing activities		
Loan repayments	(X)	
Proceeds from issue of share capital	X	
Proceeds from long-term borrowing	X	
Dividends paid	(X)	
Net cash from financing activities		X/(X)

continued overleaf

	€	€
Increase/(decrease) in cash and cash equivalents		X/(X)
Cash and cash equivalents at the beginning of the period		X/(X)
Cash and cash equivalents at the end of the period		X/(X)

The above layout does not include an exhaustive list of items that can be presented under investing and financing activities. An explanation of the types of items presented under investing activities will be dealt with in the next section.

20.4 INVESTING ACTIVITIES

The investing activities section of the SOCF identifies the cash flows paid and received in relation to the purchase or disposal of items of property, plant and equipment and those investments that do **not** meet the definition of cash and cash equivalents. Examples of investing activities include:
• proceeds from sale of property, plant and equipment;
• purchase cost paid for property, plant and equipment; and
• proceeds received in relation to government grants related to capital expenditure.

Example 20.4 illustrates the calculation of the cost of purchasing an item of property, plant and equipment when this is the only transaction affecting non-current assets in the reporting period.

EXAMPLE 20.4: PURCHASE OF PROPERTY, PLANT AND EQUIPMENT FOR CASH

Alley Ltd has provided you with the following information in relation to the cost of its property, plant and equipment at its reporting date and at its comparative reporting date:

	€
As at 31 December 2019	855,000
As at 31 December 2018	730,000

The only transaction in relation to property, plant and equipment that occurred during the reporting period ended 31 December 2019 was the purchase of assets for cash.

Solution

In the SOCF the purchase of the property, plant and equipment is presented under investing activities as an outflow of €125,000 (€855,000 – €730,000).

The two most frequently occurring line items presented under the 'investing activities' heading relate to the purchase and disposal of items of property, plant and equipment. The calculation of these figures is explained in the examples below.

20.5 PROPERTY, PLANT AND EQUIPMENT

The most common items presented in the SOCF in relation to property, plant and equipment would be:
• adding back the depreciation charge for the period to determine the cash generated from operations;
• cash paid to purchase property, plant and equipment; and
• cash received from the sale of property, plant and equipment.

When calculating the cash paid to purchase property, plant and equipment, care must be taken not to include items that do not involve cash, such as:
- property, plant and equipment purchased by loans or leases; and
- increases in the **carrying amount** of assets as a result of a revaluation of assets.

Example 20.5 demonstrates the calculation of the amount paid to acquire new items of property, plant and equipment.

EXAMPLE 20.5: PURCHASE OF PROPERTY, PLANT AND EQUIPMENT

You have been provided with the following information extracted from the financial statements of Wagner Ltd:

STATEMENT OF FINANCIAL POSITION
as at 31 December 2019

	2019 €	2018 €
Non-current Assets		
Cost	2,140,000	1,960,000
Accumulated depreciation	(812,000)	(695,000)
Carrying amount	1,328,000	1,265,000

The following are included in the SPLOCI for the year ended 31 December 2019:

	€
Depreciation	228,000
Profit on disposal	24,000

The asset disposed of had originally cost €120,000.

Requirement Calculate the figures to be included in investing activities in relation to the purchase and disposal of property, plant and equipment.

Solution

In this example dates are not included in the ledger accounts; as the transactions occurred throughout the year, the specific dates for the transactions are not provided. The actual proceeds received from the sale of the asset and the amount spent on the acquisition of new assets needs to be calculated. Despite the sale of the asset, the total cost of all property, plant and equipment has increased; without the full details of the SOFP it would be assumed that the increase is due to the purchase of additional assets.

To determine the amount received in relation to the sale of the asset the carrying amount of the asset at the date of disposal needs to be determined. The carrying amount of the asset is the difference between the cost of the asset, €120,000, and the accumulated depreciation charged on the asset since it was purchased. The accumulated depreciation on the asset sold needs to be calculated, which is done as follows:

ACCUMULATED DEPRECIATION ACCOUNT

Account Name	€	Account Name	€
Disposal	?	Balance b/d	695,000
Balance c/d	812,000	SPLOCI – depreciation	228,000
	923,000		923,000

It can be seen from the above ledger account that the accumulated depreciation account does not balance. The difference between the debit and credit sides is due to the disposal of the asset. On derecognition, the accumulated depreciation in relation to the asset that has been disposed of is transferred to the disposal account. The accumulated depreciation on the asset that has been disposed of is €111,000 (€923,000 − €812,000).

ACCUMULATED DEPRECIATION ACCOUNT

Account Name	€	Account Name	€
Disposal	111,000	Balance b/d	695,000
Balance c/d	812,000	SPLOCI – depreciation	228,000
	923,000		923,000

At the date of disposal, the carrying amount of the asset is €9,000 [€120,000 − €111,000].

To calculate the proceeds from the disposal of the asset:
Proceeds from the disposal of the asset = Carrying amount + Profit on disposal or − Loss on disposal
$$= €9,000 + €24,000$$
$$= €33,000$$

The second figure that needs to be calculated is the amount paid to acquire property, plant and equipment. The cost information is used in this calculation.

PROPERTY, PLANT AND EQUIPMENT – COST ACCOUNT

Account Name	€	Account Name	€
Balance b/d	1,960,000	Disposal	120,000
Bank	?	Balance c/d	2,140,000
	2,260,000		2,260,000

The account does not balance and it can assumed, in the absence of any other information, that the missing figure relates to the cash (or cheque) purchase of property, plant and equipment.

PROPERTY, PLANT AND EQUIPMENT – COST ACCOUNT

Account Name	€	Account Name	€
Balance b/d	1,960,000	Disposal	120,000
Bank	300,000	Balance c/d	2,140,000
	2,260,000		2,260,000

In the 'investing activities' section of the SOCF, the following will be presented:

	€	€
Investing activities		
Proceeds from sale of property, plant and equipment	33,000	
Purchase of property, plant and equipment	(300,000)	
Net cash flow from investing activities		(267,000)

Note: remember, the depreciation charge is added back to the profit before tax in the operating section of the SOCF.

The carrying amount of property, plant and equipment may be impacted by transactions involving cash (e.g. purchases or sales of items) and transactions not involving cash (e.g. revaluations, see **Chapter 25, Property, Plant and Equipment**). An asset revaluation may result in either an increase or a decrease in the carrying amount of the asset. A revaluation does not involve a cash/bank element in the transaction so it is not presented in the SOCF.

Example 20.6 demonstrates the impact of a revaluation of property, plant and equipment on the SOCF.

EXAMPLE 20.6: REVALUATION AND PURCHASE OF PROPERTY, PLANT AND EQUIPMENT

You are provided with the following information in relation to property, plant and equipment:

STATEMENT OF FINANCIAL POSITION (EXTRACT)
as at 31 December

	2019 €	2018 €
Property, plant and equipment – cost	830,000	550,000
Revaluation surplus	160,000	100,000

There were no disposals of property, plant and equipment during the reporting period ended 31 December 2019. All assets acquired during 2019 were paid for by cheque.

Requirement Calculate the figure to be included in the SOCF in relation to the purchase of property, plant and equipment.

Solution

In this example dates are not included in the ledger accounts; as the transactions occurred throughout the year, the specific dates for the transactions are not provided. The movement in the cost of the property, plant and equipment is due to both the purchase of new assets and the revaluation of assets. The revaluation of assets does not involve any cash movement so it is not included in the SOCF.

PROPERTY, PLANT AND EQUIPMENT – COST ACCOUNT

Account Name	€	Account Name	€
Balance b/d	550,000	Balance c/d	830,000
Revaluation surplus	60,000		
Additions	?		
	830,000		830,000

The total of the debit side of the account is only €610,000 (€550,000 + €60,000), whereas the total of the credit side is €830,000; the difference is due to the assets purchased for cash during the reporting period of €220,000 (€830,000 − €610,000).

PROPERTY, PLANT AND EQUIPMENT – COST ACCOUNT

Account Name	€	Account Name	€
Balance b/d	550,000	Balance c/d	830,000
Revaluation surplus	60,000		
Additions	220,000		
	830,000		830,000

	€
Cash flows from investing activities	
Purchase of Property, Plant and Equipment	(220,000)
Net cash flow from investing activities	(220,000)

An entity may finance a purchase of property, plant and equipment by taking out a loan or a lease. Such a financing transaction does not have an impact on the cash or bank balances of the entity so it is not presented in the SOCF.

Example 20.7 demonstrates the situation where assets are financed by loans or leases.

EXAMPLE 20.7: PURCHASE OF PROPERTY, PLANT AND EQUIPMENT
FINANCED BY A TERM LOAN

You are provided with the following information in relation to property, plant and equipment:

STATEMENT OF FINANCIAL POSITION (EXTRACT)
as at 31 December

	2019 €	2018 €
Property, plant and equipment – cost	4,500,000	3,680,000
Revaluation surplus	230,000	230,000

There were no disposals of property, plant and equipment during the reporting period ended 31 December 2019. Assets acquired for €500,000 during 2019 under a lease.

Requirement Calculate the figure to be included in the SOCF in relation to the purchase of property, plant and equipment.

Solution

In this example dates are not included in the ledger accounts; as the transactions occurred throughout the year, the specific dates for the transactions are not provided. The movement in the cost of the property, plant and equipment is due to both the purchase of new assets for cash and by way of a lease. The assets acquired through borrowed funds do not involve a cash payment so they are not included in the SOCF.

PROPERTY, PLANT AND EQUIPMENT – COST ACCOUNT

Account Name	€	Account Name	€
Balance b/d	3,680,000	Balance c/d	4,500,000
Lease	500,000		
Bank	?		
	4,500,000		4,500,000

The total of the debit side of the account is only €4,180,000 (€3,680,000 + €500,000) and the total of the credit side is €4,500,000; the difference is due to the assets purchased for cash during the reporting period of €320,000 (€4,500,000 − €4,180,000).

PROPERTY, PLANT AND EQUIPMENT – COST ACCOUNT

Account Name	€	Account Name	€
Balance b/d	3,680,000	Balance c/d	4,500,000
Lease	500,000		
Bank	320,000		
	4,500,000		4,500,000

	€
Cash flows from investing activities	
Purchase of Property, Plant and Equipment	(320,000)
Net cash flow from investing activities	(320,000)

Information may not always be provided about the cost and accumulated depreciation in relation to property, plant and equipment. The next example will look at the calculation of the relevant figures for the SOCF when the carrying amount of property, plant and equipment is provided at the beginning and end of the reporting period.

Example 20.8 demonstrates the calculation of figures for a SOCF when only the carrying amount of asset is provided, rather than both the cost and the accumulated depreciation.

EXAMPLE 20.8: NON-CURRENT ASSETS

The following is an extract from a SOFP:

	2019 €	2018 €
Property, plant and equipment – carrying amount	2,820,000	2,390,000
Revaluation surplus	400,000	230,000

The following events occurred during the reporting period ended 31 December 2019:
1. Depreciation was charged of €180,000.
2. An asset with a carrying amount of €120,000 was sold at a loss of €35,000.

Requirement Calculate the figures to be included in investing activities in relation to the purchase and disposal of property, plant and equipment.

Solution

In this example dates are not included in the ledger accounts; as the transactions occurred throughout the year, the specific dates for the transactions are not provided.

PROPERTY, PLANT AND EQUIPMENT – CARRYING AMOUNT ACCOUNT

Account Name	€	Account Name	€
Balance b/d	2,390,000	Depreciation	180,000
Revaluation (€400,000 − €230,000)	170,000	Disposal	120,000
Bank/cash (balancing figure)	?	Balance c/d	2,820,000
	3,120,000		3,120,000

The carrying amount of the property, plant and equipment is increased (debit to the account) by the purchase of new assets or the upward revaluation of existing assets.

The carrying amount of the property, plant and equipment is decreased (credit to the account) by the depreciation charge for the year and disposal of items of property, plant and equipment or a downward revaluation of existing assets.

The account is not balanced; the difference on the account is €560,000 (€3,120,000 − €2,560,000). This difference is due to the purchase of more items of property, plant and equipment.

In the 'investing activities' section of the SOCF the following will be presented:

	€	€
Investing Activities		
Proceeds from sale of property, plant and equipment	85,000	
Purchase of property, plant and equipment	(560,000)	
Net cash flow from investing activities		(475,000)

To calculate the proceeds from the disposal of the asset:

Proceeds from the disposal of the asset = Carrying amount + profit on disposal or − Loss on disposal
$$= €120,000 - €35,000$$
$$= €85,000$$

(Try **Review Questions 20.2** and **20.3** at the end of this chapter.)

The third section of the SOCF deals with the the entity's financing activities. Examples of items commonly presented in this section are identified in the next section.

20.6 FINANCING ACTIVITIES

The financing activities section of the SOCF identifies the cash paid and received in relation to changes in loans made to the company and its share capital. Examples of financing activities include:
• cash proceeds from the issue of shares;
• cash payments to redeem the entity's shares;
• cash proceeds from the issue of loans;
• cash repayments on loans or borrowings; and
• capital repayments on leases.

The issue of ordinary shares by an entity may have an impact on the cash/bank balance of the entity. An issue of ordinary shares may be at an amount over and above the shares' nominal value. The accounting entries in relation to shares issued above their nominal value was dealt with in **Chapter 19, Presentation of Financial Statements**.

Example 20.9 demonstrates how an issue of ordinary shares is presented in the SOCF.

EXAMPLE 20.9: ISSUE OF ORDINARY SHARES

The following information has been extracted from the financial statements of Thompson Plc.

Thompson Plc
STATEMENT OF FINANCIAL POSITION (EXTRACT)
as at 31 December

	2019	2018
	€000	**€000**
Equity and Reserves		
Ordinary shares €1	450	400
Share premium	80	10
Retained earnings	905	940

The only transaction that impacted the ordinary share capital during the reporting period was the issue of ordinary shares for cash.

Requirement How is the issue of ordinary shares presented in the SOCF of Thompson Plc for the year ended 31 December 2019?

Solution

The cash impact of the issue of ordinary shares during the period is presented under financing activities in the SOCF for the year ended 31 December 2019.

Thompson Plc
STATEMENT OF CASH FLOWS (EXTRACT)
for year ended 31 December 2019

	€000
Cash Flows from Financing Activities	
Issue of ordinary shares (€450,000 + €80,000) − (€400,000 + €10,000)	120
Net cash flows from financing activities	120

20.7 TAX PAID/REFUNDED

Tax paid is generally presented under operating activities; the only exception to this is when the tax relates to non-operating activities. An example of a tax charge that does not relate to operating activities is capital gains tax (CGT) on the disposal of property; in this case the tax related to the sale of the asset is presented under investing activities along with the proceeds from the disposal. The tax and proceeds from the sale of the asset in this situation would be presented as a separate line item.

Example 20.10 demonstrates the calculation of the amount of tax paid.

EXAMPLE 20.10: CALCULATION OF TAX PAID

Zenith Ltd prepares its financial statements to 31 December 2019 and the following figures have been extracted from them:

STATEMENT OF PROFIT OR LOSS AND OTHER COMPREHENSIVE INCOME (EXTRACT)

	€
Profit before tax	364,000
Income tax expense	(108,000)
Profit for year	256,000

STATEMENT OF FINANCIAL POSITION (EXTRACT)

	2019	2018
	€	€
Current Liabilities		
Current tax payables	10,800	15,600

Requirement Calculate the amount of tax paid in the year ended 31 December 2019.

Solution

In this example dates are not included in the ledger accounts; as the transactions occurred throughout the year, the specific dates for the transactions are not provided.

TAX LIABILITY ACCOUNT

Account Name	€	Account Name	€
Bank	?	Balance b/d	15,600
Balance c/d	10,800	SPLOCI – tax charge	108,000
	123,600		123,600

The total of the credit side of the tax liability account is €123,600, but the debit side is only €10,800; the balancing figure represents, in this situation, the tax paid in the reporting period. The tax paid is €112,800 (€123,600 − €10,800).

TAX LIABILITY ACCOUNT

Account Name	€	Account Name	€
Bank	112,800	Balance b/d	15,600
Balance c/d	10,800	SPLOCI – tax charge	108,000
	123,600		123,600

Example 20.11 demonstrates the situation where the tax paid in the period relates to both operating and investing activities.

EXAMPLE 20.11: PRESENTATION OF TAX PAID

Hopper Ltd included in its SPLOCI a tax expense of €245,000, which includes €95,000 in relation to capital gains tax related to the sale of an item of property, plant and equipment. The asset was sold for €890,000.

In the SOFP the following balances were outstanding in relation to the corporation tax liability at the most recent reporting date and the comparative period.

	€
As at 31 December 2019	18,200
As at 31 December 2018	14,100

The capital gains tax was paid in full during the year ended 31 December 2019.

Requirement Calculate the tax paid and identify where it will be presented in the SOCF for the year ended 31 December 2019.

Solution

In this example dates are not included in the ledger accounts; as the transactions occurred throughout the year, the specific dates for the transactions are not provided. For the reporting period ended 31 December 2019 the tax charge is made up of:
- an amount relating to tax on operating activities, and
- an amount relating to the capital gains tax incurred on the disposal of the property, plant and equipment.

Step 1 Calculate the tax on operating profit.

	€
Tax charge per SPLOCI	245,000
Capital gains tax	(95,000)
Tax on operating activities	150,000

Step 2 Calculate the amount of tax paid in relation to operating activities.

TAX LIABILITY ACCOUNT

Account Name	€	Account Name	€
Bank	?	Balance b/d	14,100
Balance c/d	18,200	SPLOCI – tax charge	150,000
	164,100		164,100

The total of the credit side of the tax liability account is €164,100 but the debit side is only €18,200; the balancing figure represents, in this situation, the tax paid in the reporting period. The tax paid is €145,900 (€164,100 – €18,200).

TAX LIABILITY ACCOUNT

Account Name	€	Account Name	€
Bank	145,900	Balance b/d	14,100
Balance c/d	18,200	SPLOCI – tax charge	150,000
	164,100		164,100

The amount of €145,900 is presented in the operating activities section as a deduction in arriving at the net cash from operating activities.

In the investing activities section of the SOCF the following items will be listed:

	€
Cash flows from investing activities	
Proceeds from sale of property, plant and equipment	890,000
Tax paid on disposal of property, plant and equipment	(95,000)
Net cash flow from investing activities	795,000

(Try **Review Question 20.4** at the end of this chapter.)

20.8 FINANCE EXPENSE AND INCOME

The total finance cost paid for the period is either expensed to the SPLOCI or it is capitalised (i.e. included in the cost of the asset).

Finance expense and finance income are presented as separate line items; they are **never** netted off against one another. IAS 7 allows finance cost paid and finance income received to be presented in any of the three sections of the SOCF (operating, investing or financing) but they must be presented consistently from one reporting period to the next.

The only exception to the presentation rule is in relation to finance costs paid and finance income received by lending institutions, such as banks. In this case they should be presented as separate line items under operating activities.

(Try **Review Question 20.5** at the end of this chapter.)

20.9 DIVIDENDS

Dividends received and paid should not be netted off against one another but should be presented as separate line items. IAS 7 allows the entity to choose which activity's heading it presents these lines items under: operating, investing or financing activities. However, they must be presented consistently over reporting periods.

In considering where to present dividends paid the entity should consider the following:
- It may be considered appropriate to present dividends paid under financing activities as they are a cost associated with the financing of the entity.
- If the dividend paid is presented under operating activities it allows users of the financial statements to determine the ability of the entity to make dividend payments out of operating cash flows.

Example 20.12 demonstrates how to calculate a dividend accrued in a reporting period.

EXAMPLE 20.12: CALCULATION OF DIVIDEND ACCRUED

You have been provided with the following information in relation to Flaherty Ltd:

	€
Profit for year ended 31 December 2019	740,000
Retained earnings as at 1 January 2019	2,225,000
Retained earnings as at 31 December 2019	2,830,000

Requirement Calculate the dividend accrued in the reporting period ended 31 December 2019.

Solution

	€
Retained earnings as at 1 January 2019	2,225,000
Profit for year	740,000
	2,965,000
Retained earnings as at 31 December 2019	(2,830,000)
Dividend	135,000

The profit for the year increases the retained earnings at the start of the year, dividend accrued and paid reduces the retained earnings balance.

The SOCF presents information about cash paid and received in the reporting period. It is important, in calculating the amount paid in relation to dividends, to take into account any dividend liability at the start and/or end of the reporting period.

Example 20.13 demonstrates the calculation of the dividend paid when there is an outstanding liability at the reporting date.

EXAMPLE 20.13: CALCULATION OF DIVIDEND PAID

You have been provided with the following information in relation to Zebra Ltd:

Profit for year ended 31 December 2019	€850,000
Retained earnings as at 1 January 2019	€2,190,000
Retained earnings as at 31 December 2019	€2,790,000

There is a liability in the SOFP in relation to dividends at each reporting date as follows:

As at 31 December 2019	€40,000
As at 31 December 2018	€25,000

Requirement Calculate the dividend paid during the reporting period ended 31 December 2019.

Solution

In this example dates are not included in the ledger accounts; as the transactions occurred throughout the year, the specific dates for the transactions are not provided.

	€
Retained earnings as at 1 January 2019	2,190,000
Profit for year	850,000
	3,040,000
Retained earnings as at 31 December 2019	(2,790,000)
Dividend	250,000

The dividend figure represents the amount declared and approved for payment by the shareholders at the AGM. Always check the current liabilities section of the SOFP to see if there are any amounts outstanding in relation to dividends. If there is a balance due in relation to dividends, the actual dividend paid during the reporting period would need to be calculated.

DIVIDEND LIABILITY ACCOUNT

Account Name	€	Account Name	€
Bank	?	Balance b/d	25,000
Balance c/d	40,000	SOCIE – dividend*	250,000
	275,000		275,000

* The dividend accrued figure is presented in the statement of changes in equity (SOCIE) and **not** in the SPLOCI.

The dividend liability account is not balanced – there is a difference of €235,000 (€275,000 – €40,000), which represents the amount paid out in relation to dividends in the period.

DIVIDEND LIABILITY ACCOUNT

Account Name	€	Account Name	€
Bank	235,000	Balance b/d	25,000
Balance c/d	40,000	SOCIE – dividend	250,000
	275,000		275,000

	€
Cash flows from financing activities	
Dividend paid	(235,000)
Net cash flow from financing activities	(235,000)

(Try **Review Question 20.6** at the end of this chapter.)

20.10 GRANT RELATED TO PROPERTY, PLANT AND EQUIPMENT

A grant is recognised in the SOCF of the entity in the period that it is received as a cash inflow under investing activities.

Example 20.14 demonstrates the impact of a grant received in relation to an item of property, plant and equipment.

EXAMPLE 20.14: CAPITAL GRANT RECEIVED DURING THE PERIOD

You are provided with the following information with respect to the purchase of assets during the reporting period ended 31 December 2019:

	€000
Cost of assets acquired for cash during the year	270
Government grant received in relation to property, plant and equipment purchased	50

Requirement Identify the figures to be presented in the SOCF for the year ended 31 December 2019.

Solution

STATEMENT OF CASH FLOWS
for the year ended 31 December 2019

	€000	€000
Cash flow from investing activities		
Proceeds from government grant	50,000	
Purchase of property, plant and equipment	(270,000)	
Net cash flow from investing activities		(220,000)

IAS 20 *Accounting for Government Grants and Disclosure of Government Assistance* allows for two different treatments of capital grants received (see **Chapter 28, Accounting for Government**

Grants and Disclosure of Government Assistance), the impact on the SOCF for each of these methods will be dealt with below.

Method 1: Reduce the Cost of the Asset by the Amount of the Grant Received

If the cost of the asset is reduced by the amount of the grant received, the result is a reduced depreciation charge in the SPLOCI each year. In the reporting periods after the grant was received there are no figures or adjustments made in relation to the grant.

Example 20.15 demonstrates the impact of a capital grant received in the reporting period where the entity has chosen to reduce the cost of the asset by the amount of the grant received.

EXAMPLE 20.15: CAPITAL GRANT TREATED AS A REDUCTION
IN THE COST OF AN ASSET

The following has been extracted from the financial statements of Star Ltd:

	2019 €	2018 €
Property, plant and equipment – cost	925,000	830,000
Accumulated depreciation	(174,600)	(152,000)
	750,400	678,000

A government grant of €40,000 was received during the year in relation to the purchase of the asset. Company policy is to net off the grants received in relation to capital assets against the cost of the asset. Depreciation charge during the reporting period ended 31 December 2019 was €46,800.

An asset was disposed of during the year for €28,600; the asset had originally cost €60,000 and had accumulated depreciation of €24,200.

Requirement Prepare the relevant extracts from the SOCF of Star Ltd for the year ended 31 December 2019.

Solution

In this example dates are not included in the ledger accounts; as the transactions occurred throughout the year, the specific dates for the transactions are not provided.

Star Ltd
STATEMENT OF CASH FLOWS
for the year ended 31 December 2019

	€	€
Profit before tax		X
Depreciation		46,800
Loss on disposal (W1)		7,200
Cash flows from investing activities		
Proceeds from the sale of property, plant and equipment	28,600	
Proceeds from capital grant	40,000	
Purchase of property, plant and equipment	(195,000)	
Net cash flow from investing activities		(126,400)

W₁ Loss on Disposal

	€
Cost of asset	60,000
Accumulated depreciation	(24,200)
Carrying amount at the date of disposal	35,800
Proceeds from disposal	(28,600)
Loss on disposal	7,200

PROPERTY, PLANT AND EQUIPMENT – COST ACCOUNT

Account Name	€	Account Name	€
Balance b/d	830,000	Disposal	60,000
Additions	195,000	Grant received – bank	40,000
		Balance c/d	925,000
	1,025,000		1,025,000
Balance b/d	925,000		

Method 2: Grant Amortised Over Useful Life of Asset

A grant recognised as deferred income would be presented in the SOFP with the balance split between current and non-current liabilities. Each year an amount in relation to the grant (deferred income) will be released to the SPLOCI; this amount is known as amortisation (see **Chapter 28**). This figure is deducted from the profit before tax in the calculation of the cash generated from operations.

Example 20.16 demonstrates the impact of a capital grant received in an earlier reporting period where the entity has chosen to treat the grant received as deferred income.

EXAMPLE 20.16: AMORTISATION OF CAPITAL GRANT

The following information has been extracted from the SOFP of Planet Ltd:

	2019 €000	2018 €000
Non-current Assets		
Cost	3,142	2,863
Accumulated depreciation	(730)	(624)
	2,412	2,239
Non-current Liabilities		
Deferred income	40	60
Current Liabilities		
Deferred income	20	20

The depreciation charge during 2019 was €106,000. A government grant of €100,000 was received in 2018.

Requirement Prepare the relevant extracts from the SOCF of Planet Ltd for the year ended 31 December 2019.

Solution

In this example dates are not included in the ledger accounts; as the transactions occurred throughout the year, the specific dates for the transactions are not provided.

Planet Ltd
STATEMENT OF CASH FLOWS
for the year ended 31 December 2019

	€000	€000
Profit before tax		X
Depreciation		106,000
Amortisation		(20,000)

DEFERRED INCOME ACCOUNT

Account Name	€000	Account Name	€000
SPLOCI − amortisation	20,000	Balance b/d (€60,000 + €20,000)	80,000
Balance c/d (€40,000 + €20,000)	60,000		
	80,000		80,000

Note: in the year that the grant was received, i.e. the reporting period ended 31 December 2018, the amount received in relation to the grant would have been presented as an inflow under the investing section of the SOCF.

Disclosures

Disclosures may include:
- the amount of undrawn borrowing facilities, as well as any restrictions on the use of such facilities;
- the aggregate amount of cash flows that represent increases in operating capacity separately from those to maintain operating capacity; and
- the amount of cash flows for each activity for each reporting segment (reporting segments are outside the scope of this textbook).

20.11 IAS 7 COMPARED WITH FRS 102

The treatment outlined in FRS 102 *The Financial Reporting Standard applicable in the UK and Republic of Ireland* for statements of cash flows is largely the same as that in IAS 7.

Under FRS 102 the entity is not required to present a reconciliation of the amounts included in the SOCF to the equivalent items presented in the SOFP if the amounts presented in both financial statements are identical.

The entity is not required under FRS 102 to make the following disclosures encouraged under IAS 7:
- the amount of undrawn borrowing facilities that may be available for operating activities;
- the aggregate amount of cash flows that represent increased operating capacity separately from those required to maintain operating capacity; and
- the amount of cash flows arising from operating, investing and financing activities of each reportable segment.

EXAM TIPS

- Always remember that the figures presented in the SOCF involve either cash paid or received during the reporting period.
- Know the layout of the SOCF.
- When calculating the additions for property, plant and equipment:
  - revaluation increases do not involve cash so are not included in the statement of cash flows, and
  - assets acquired by using loan facilities are not included in the statement of cash flows.
- When ordinary shares are issued at a premium the transaction is recognised in ordinary share capital and share premium. The issue of ordinary shares is presented in a single line item in the SOCF under financing activities, which reflects the movement in the ordinary share capital and share premium accounts.

20.12 CONCLUSION

Statements of cash flows are not part of the double-entry system; they show the cash inflows and outflows for the reporting period. A SOCF explains the movement in cash and cash equivalents in the reporting period. Cash flows are analysed into three activities: operating, investing and financing.

SUMMARY OF LEARNING OBJECTIVES

After having studied this chapter, readers should be able to:

Learning Objective 1 Prepare the reconciliation of profit before tax to net cash flow from operating activities.

To calculate the net cash flow from operating activities, the profit or loss for the period must be adjusted for:
- non-cash items included in the SPLOCI;
- movements in working capital, that is, inventory, trade receivables and trade payables; and
- items included in the statements of profit or loss that do not relate to operating activities.

Learning Objective 2 Prepare a statement of cash flows.

There are two methods of preparing the cash generated from operations:
- the indirect method (referred to in **Learning Objective 1**); and
- the direct method.

Examples of investing activities are:
1. the proceeds from the sale of property, plant and equipment;
2. the total amount paid for property, plant and equipment; and
3. the proceeds received in relation to government grants related to capital expenditure.

Examples of financing activities are:
1. cash proceeds from the issue of shares;
2. cash payments to redeem the entity's shares;
3. cash proceeds from taking out loans;
4. cash repayments on loans or borrowings; and
5. capital repayments on leases.

QUESTIONS

Review Questions

(See **Appendix A** for Solutions to Review Questions.)

Question 20.1

Walter Ltd
STATEMENT OF PROFIT OR LOSS
for the year ended 31 December 2019

	€
Revenue	1,830,000
Cost of sales	(695,000)
Gross profit	1,135,000
Operating expenses	(716,000)
Profit before tax	419,000
Tax expense	(108,000)
Profit for year	307,000

The following figures have been extracted from the statement of financial position as at 31 December:

	2019 €	2018 €
Inventory	35,600	52,900
Trade receivables	120,100	96,200
Trade payables	20,250	27,800

Depreciation of €32,500 is included in the operating expense line in the statement of profit or loss.

Requirement Calculate the cash generated from operations under both the direct and indirect methods.

Question 20.2

The following information is provided from the financial statements of Circus Ltd:

	2019 €000	2018 €000
STATEMENT OF FINANCIAL POSITION		
Property, plant and equipment – cost	940	750
Accumulated depreciation	280	230
Equity and Reserves		
Revaluation surplus	100	0

STATEMENT OF PROFIT OR LOSS (EXTRACT)
for the year ended 31 December 2019

	€
Depreciation	80,000
Loss on disposal	9,500

The asset sold during the year had originally cost €65,000.

Requirement Calculate the figures to be included in the 'investing activities' section of the statement of cash flows for Circus Ltd for the year ended 31 December 2019.

Question 20.3

The following is an extract from the statement of financial position of Millicent Ltd:

	2019 €000	2018 €000
Property, plant and equipment – cost	1,420	1,305
Accumulated depreciation	316	280

The depreciation charge for the year was €59,200. An asset that originally cost €85,000 was sold during the year for €48,000.

Requirement Calculate the figures to be included in the 'operating activities' and 'investing activities' sections of the statement of cash flows for Millicent Ltd for the year ended 31 December 2019.

Question 20.4

The following figures have been extracted from the financial statements of Terry Ltd.

STATEMENT OF PROFIT OR LOSS (EXTRACT)
for the year ended 31 December

	2019 €	2018 €
Profit before tax	816,400	726,500
Tax	(163,200)	(145,300)
Profit for year	653,200	581,200

STATEMENT OF FINANCIAL POSITION (EXTRACT)
as at 31 December

	2019 €	2018 €
Current Liability		
Current tax	89,100	164,200

Requirement Calculate the amount of tax paid to be presented in the statement of cash flows of Terry Ltd for the year ended 31 December 2019.

Question 20.5

Freeman Ltd
STATEMENT OF PROFIT OR LOSS
for the year ended 31 December 2019

	€
Gross profit	192,700
Operating expenses	(64,300)
Finance cost	(10,400)
Profit before tax	118,000
Tax	(32,000)
Profit for year	86,000

There was no liability in relation to finance cost at either the start or end of the reporting period.

Requirement Identify how the finance costs are treated in the statement of cash flows for the year ended 31 December 2019.

Question 20.6

Shaw Ltd
STATEMENT OF CHANGES IN EQUITY
for the year ended 31 December 2019

	Ordinary Share Capital €	Retained Earnings €	Total €
As at 1 January 2019	180,000	644,200	824,200
Profit for the year		184,300	184,300
Dividend		(30,000)	(30,000)
As at 31 December 2019	180,000	798,500	978,500

Shaw Ltd
STATEMENT OF FINANCIAL POSITION (EXTRACT)
as at 31 December

	2019 €	2018 €
Current Liabilities		
Dividend payable	18,000	6,500

Requirement Calculate the figure for the equity dividend paid to be presented in the statement of cash flows during the reporting period ended 31 December 2019.

Challenging Questions

(Suggested Solutions to Challenging Questions are available through your lecturer.)

Question 20.1

Cecil Ltd
STATEMENT OF PROFIT OR LOSS
for the period ended 31 December 2019

	€000
Operating profit	23,595
Finance costs – interest payable	(1,095)
Profit on ordinary activities before tax	22,500
Tax charge for the year	(6,525)
Profit for the year	15,975

Cecil Ltd
STATEMENT OF FINANCIAL POSITION
as at 31 December

	2019 €000	2019 €000	2018 €000	2018 €000
Assets				
Non-current assets		66,390		39,830
Plant, equipment, vehicles (Note 1)				
Current assets				
Inventory	5,340		14,450	
Receivables	9,610		6,810	
Cash in hand	840	15,790	1,595	22,855
		82,180		62,685
Equity and Liabilities				
Capital and reserves				
Ordinary share capital		24,000		22,500
Preference share capital		5,050		3,750
Retained earnings		23,445		9,700
		52,495		35,950
Non-current liabilities				
9% loan stock		12,000		15,500
Current liabilities				
Trade payables	11,160		6,400	
Bank overdraft	1,815		545	
Tax payable	4,530		4,140	
Accruals	180	17,865	150	11,235
		82,180		62,685

Additional information
1. The carrying amount of the non-current assets is made up as follows:

	Cost	Accumulated Depreciation	Carrying amount at 31 December 2019
	€000	€000	€000
Balance b/d	49,800	9,970	39,830
Additions	36,510		36,510
Disposals	(4,450)	(1,490)	(2,960)
Depreciation charge		6,990	6,990
Balance c/d	81,860	15,470	66,390

2. Non-current asset disposals realised €4,040,000.
3. Dividends totalling €2,230,000 were paid during the year ended 31 December 2019.
4. The accrual listed under current liabilities relates to interest outstanding on the loan stock for both years.

Requirement Prepare a statement of cash flows for Cecil Ltd in accordance with IAS 7 *Statement of Cash Flows* for the year ended 31 December 2019.

(Based on Chartered Accountants Ireland, CAP 1 Financial Accounting, Summer 2009, Question 2)

Question 20.2

A potential investor is considering the acquisition of Bangor Ltd and has been told that a review of the business's statement of cash flows will provide useful information in the analysis of the health of the business.

He has provided you with the statement of profit or loss and other comprehensive income and the statement of cash flows for the year ended 31 December 2019.

He is also concerned that last year's statement of cash flows showed a negative cash flow from operations and that this must surely signal that the business was unprofitable in 2019.

Bangor Ltd
STATEMENT OF PROFIT OR LOSS AND OTHER COMPREHENSIVE INCOME
for the year ended 31 December 2019

	€000
Revenue	1,728
Cost of sales	(921)
Gross profit	807
Distribution expenses	(195)
Administrative expenses	(78)
	534
Other operating income	63
Operating profit	597
Interest receivable	51
	648
Finance cost	(69)
Profit before taxation	579
Taxation	(138)
Profit for the year	441

Bangor Ltd
STATEMENT OF CASH FLOWS
for the year ended 31 December 2019

	€000	€000
Cash flows from operating activities		
Net profit before interest and tax		597
Adjustment for:		
Depreciation		237
		834
Changes in working capital		
Increase in trade receivables	(54)	

continued overleaf

	€000	€000
Decrease in trade payables	(3)	
Decrease in inventories	9	(48)
Cash generated from operations		786
Interest paid	(69)	
Tax paid	(117)	
Dividend paid	(150)	(336)
Net cash from operating activities		450
Cash flows from investing activities		
Payments to acquire tangible non-current assets	(285)	
Interest received	51	
Net cash used in investing activities		(234)
Cash flows from financing activities		
Proceeds from issue of share capital	270	
Repayment of loan notes	(450)	
Net cash used in financing activities		(180)
Increase in cash and cash equivalents		36
Cash and cash equivalents at 1 January 2019		(204)
Cash and cash equivalents at 31 December 2019		(168)

Analysis of cash and cash equivalents during the year ended 31 December 2019:

	€000
Overdraft balance at 1 January 2019	(204)
Net cash inflow	36
Overdraft balance at 31 December 2019	(168)

Requirement Draft a memorandum to the potential investor to include the following.

(a) A summary of the key points that can be derived from the statement of cash flows for the year ended 31 December 2019.

(b) Any reasons to support the claim that a statement of cash flows is better than a statement of profit or loss and other comprehensive income when assessing the performance of a business.

(c) An alternative reason that may explain the negative cash flow from operations in the previous year ended 31 December 2019.

(Based on Chartered Accountants Ireland, CAP 1 Financial Accounting, Summer 2010, Question 8)

21

Inventories

LEARNING OBJECTIVES

Having studied this chapter, readers should be able to:
1. identify the components of inventory;
2. calculate the value of inventory to be presented in the financial statements;
3. apply FIFO and weighted average cost of inventory valuation methods; and
4. prepare the appropriate disclosure notes for inventory.

21.1 INTRODUCTION

IAS 2 *Inventories* sets out the accounting rules in relation to inventories. The basic accounting entries in relation to inventory are explained in **Chapter 3, Inventory and Cost of Sales**.

Entities hold different categories of inventory, such as:
- raw materials, which are goods that have been acquired for use in the production process. During the production process raw materials will be converted to finished goods;
- work in progress refers to goods that are in the process of being converted from raw materials to finished goods; and
- finished goods are those that have been converted from raw materials to finished goods.

21.2 VALUATION OF INVENTORIES

Inventories, in accordance with IAS 2, are to be measured at the **lower** of:
- cost, and
- net realisable value.

Cost

Cost of inventory includes all costs incurred in relation to the purchase and conversion of goods. IAS 2 defines cost as "all costs of purchase, costs of conversion and other costs incurred in bringing the inventories to their present location and condition."

Purchase Cost
The cost of purchase includes the following items:
- purchase price,
- import duties,
- other taxes that are not recoverable,
- transport costs,
- any costs directly attributable to purchases, e.g. handling costs.

The purchase cost can be reduced by trade discounts, rebates and any other item that can be deducted to determine the purchase cost.

Example 21.1 demonstrates the costs that can be included in the cost of an item of inventory and considers the impact of discounts on the cost of inventory recognised.

EXAMPLE 21.1: COST OF INVENTORY

You are provided with the following information in relation to the purchase of an item of inventory:

	€
Purchase price per published price list	3,200
Trade discount	10%
Transport costs	150

Requirement What is the cost of the item of inventory?

Solution

	€
Purchase price per published price list	3,200
Less trade discount (€3,200 × 10%)	(320)
	2,880
Plus transport costs	150
Cost	3,030

Conversion Costs

The cost of inventory may include the cost involved in converting the raw material to finished goods. These conversion costs relate to the production process. Direct production costs are included in the valuation of inventory because they can be directly allocated to the inventory. Indirect production costs, also known as production overheads, are allocated to inventory on the basis of **normal** capacity. Indirect production costs include depreciation of production machinery, production supervisors' salaries and machine maintenance. Non-production overheads are charged as an expense to the statement of profit or loss and other comprehensive income (SPLOCI) in the period that the cost is incurred and are **not** included in the valuation of inventory.

Example 21.2 demonstrates the inclusion of fixed production overhead costs in the valuation of inventory.

EXAMPLE 21.2: PRODUCTION OVERHEAD COSTS

The following information is available in relation to the costs incurred in relation to product AB15:

Direct material	€10.00 per unit
Direct labour	€6.00 per unit
Budgeted production overhead	€1,200,000
Expected production volume	200,000 units
Actual production volume	120,000 units

Budgeted production was expected to be 200,000 units in the reporting period but due to a strike by employees, production volumes were much lower than expected.

Requirement What cost is the inventory recognised at?

Solution

	€ per unit
Direct material	10.00
Direct labour	6.00
Production overhead (€1,200,000 ÷ 200,000 units)	6.00
	22.00

Production overhead is included on the basis of normal or expected activity levels. It may only be based on actual production levels if this approximates normal capacity. Normal capacity is the activity level that would be expected to be achieved over a period of time under normal operating circumstances.

(Try **Review Question 21.1** at the end of this chapter.)

Other Costs

Any other costs are only included in the valuation of inventory if they are necessarily incurred in "bringing the inventories to their present location and condition."[1] The general rule is that non-production costs are not included in the valuation of inventory. The only exception to this would be costs incurred that specifically relate to the item of inventory; an example of this would be cost of designing a product for a specific customer may be included in the cost of inventories.

IAS 2 specifically **excludes** the following items from being included in the cost of inventories:
(a) abnormal amounts of waste materials, labour or other production costs;
(b) storage costs other than those that are necessary as part of the production process before a further production stage;
(c) administration overhead; and
(d) selling costs.

Net Realisable Value (NRV)

Net realisable value (NRV) is selling price less costs that have to be incurred to achieve the selling price. NRV is used when:
• inventory is damaged,
• goods have become obsolete, or
• selling prices have deteriorated.

Items of inventory are usually written down to NRV on an item-by-item basis, however, it may be appropriate to group similar or related items together. Items that can be grouped together are those relating to the same product line that have similar purposes or end uses, are produced and marketed in the same geographical area and, practicably, cannot be evaluated separately from other items in that product line.

---

[1] IAS 2 *Inventories*, paragraph 10.

Example 21.3 demonstrates the valuation of inventory by comparing the lower of cost and NRV.

EXAMPLE 21.3: VALUATION OF INVENTORY – LOWER OF COST OR NRV

You are provided with the following information in relation to the production of product CT90:

	€ per unit
Direct material	12.00
Direct labour	6.00
Production overhead	5.00
Selling price	35.00
Selling costs per unit	2.50

Requirement What is the value of the item of inventory?

Solution

Cost of producing one unit of inventory:

	€ per unit
	12.00
Direct material	6.00
Direct labour	5.00
Production overhead	23.00

Net realisable value of one unit of inventory:

	€ per unit
Selling price	35.00
Less selling costs per unit	(2.50)
	32.50

Inventory is valued at the lower of:

Cost	€23.00 or
Net realisable value	€32.50

Inventory is valued at €23.00.

Example 21.4 demonstrates the situation where an item of inventory is damaged and has to be repaired before it can be sold.

EXAMPLE 21.4: VALUATION OF INVENTORY – DAMAGED ITEMS

An item of inventory which cost €4,000 to produce was damaged when a water pipe burst. The item can now be sold for €4,500 if repair work is undertaken at a cost of €1,000.

Requirement What is the value of the item of inventory?

Solution

	€
Cost of inventory item	4,000
Net realisable value [€4,500 – €1,000]	3,500

Item is valued at the lower of cost or net realisable value, i.e. €3,500.

As stated earlier, the valuation rule is generally applied on an item-by-item basis; however, it can be also applied on a group basis when the entity has a number of similar items. **Example 21.5** demonstrates the valuation of inventory on an item-by-item basis or by grouping similar items together.

EXAMPLE 21.5: VALUATION OF INVENTORY – ITEM-BY-ITEM OR GROUPED

The following items of inventory were on hand at the most recent reporting date:

Inventory Item	Purchase Cost	Conversion Cost	Selling Price	Selling and Distribution Costs
	€	€	€	€
AG23	250	110	500	25
AH12	280	70	360	15
AK39	210	60	300	20
AL47	190	30	250	10

Requirement What is the inventory value if:
(a) Inventory is valued on an item-by-item basis.
(b) Inventory items are similar in nature and can be grouped together for valuation purposes.

Solution
(a) Inventory items are valued at lower of cost or net realisable value:

Inventory Item	Purchase Cost (1)	Conversion Cost (2)	Total Cost (3) [(1) + (2)]	Selling Price (4)	Selling and Distribution Costs (5)	Net Realisable Value (6) [(4) – (5)]	Value [lower of (3) or (6)]
	€	€	€	€	€	€	€
AG23	250	110	360	500	25	475	360
AH12	280	70	350	360	15	345	345
AK39	210	60	270	300	20	280	270
AL47	190	30	220	250	10	240	220
							1,195

(b) Inventory items are grouped together and valued at lower of cost or net realisable value:

Inventory Item	Purchase Cost	Conversion Cost	Total Cost	Selling Price	Selling and Distribution Costs	Net Realisable Value
	€	€	€	€	€	€
AG23	250	110	360	500	25	475
AH12	280	70	350	360	15	345
AK39	210	60	270	300	20	280
AL47	190	30	220	250	10	240
			1,200			1,340

The total cost and total net realisable value are compared and the inventory is valued at the lower of the two figures:

	€
Total cost	1,200
Net realisable value	1,340

Inventory is valued at the lower of cost or net realisable value, i.e. €1,200.

(Try **Review Questions 21.2** and **21.3** at the end of this chapter.)

Exception to Write-down to Lower of Cost or Net Realisable Value

When an item of inventory is held for use in the production of finished goods, the item of raw material is not written down to net realisable value if the finished product that it will ultimately be included in will be sold at a profit.

Cost Formulas

IAS 2 allows cost to be assigned to inventory using either the first in first out method (FIFO) or the weighted average cost method. The last in first out method (LIFO) is not allowed under IAS 2 to value inventories.

Under the FIFO method inventory is valued on the basis that the items of inventory that are sold or used first are those that have been on hand the longest and is demonstrated in **Example 21.6**.

EXAMPLE 21.6: COST OF INVENTORY – FIFO METHOD

Allen Ltd has the following purchases of inventory in January 2019:

Date Items Received	Number of Units Received	Cost Per Unit €	Total Cost €
1 January 2019	200	10.00	2,000
4 January 2019	300	11.00	3,300
10 January 2019	250	10.50	2,625
20 January 2019	100	12.00	1,200
			9,125

Requirement:
(a) On 30 January 2019 Allen sold 400 units of inventory. Using FIFO, how much are they valued at?
(b) What is the value of the inventory on hand at 30 January 2019?

Solution
(a) The inventory units sold are valued as follows:

	€	
200 units × €10.00	2,000	Items received on 1 January 2019
200 units × €11.00	2,200	Items received on 4 January 2019
	4,200	

Under FIFO, the inventory issues are valued at the oldest items of inventory on hand.
(b)

	€
Total purchases	9,125
Value of goods sold	(4,200)
Value of inventory on hand	4,925

Items on hand:

	€
100 units × €11.00	1,100
250 units × €10.50	2,625
100 units × €12.00	1,200
	4,925

Under the weighted average cost method an average cost is calculated when goods are received. This average is calculated by taking the total value of goods on hand divided by the number of units on hand and is demonstrated in **Example 21.7**.

EXAMPLE 21.7: COST OF INVENTORY – WEIGHTED AVERAGE COST METHOD

Balfe Ltd has the following items of inventory on hand at its reporting date:

Date Items Received	Number of Units Received	Cost Per Unit €	Total Cost €
1 March 2019	40	20.00	800
6 March 2019	60	22.00	1,320
9 March 2019	30	25.00	750
18 March 2019	50	24.00	1,200
			4,070

Requirement:
(a) On 31 March 2019 Balfe Ltd sold 110 units of inventory. Using the weighted average cost method, how much are they valued at?
(b) What is the value of inventory on hand at 31 March 2019?

Solution
(a)

Total cost (€800 + €1,320 + €750 + €1,200)	€4,070
Total units (40 + 60 + 30 +50)	180 units
Weighted average cost per unit (€4,070 ÷ 180 units)	€22.61
Value of units issue (110 units × €22.61)	€2,487

(b) Value of inventory on hand is €1,583 [70 units at €22.61 per unit].

(Try **Review Question 21.4** at the end of this chapter.)

21.3 REVERSAL OF WRITE-DOWN TO NET REALISABLE VALUE

If an item of inventory has been written down to net realisable value in one reporting period and is still on hand at a later date and the selling price has improved, the previous write-down can be reversed. The amount of the reversal is limited to the amount of the original write-down – the item cannot be carried at an amount greater than its original cost.

Example 21.8 demonstrates the write-down of an item of inventory and the subsequent reversal of the write-down.

EXAMPLE 21.8: REVERSAL OF WRITE-DOWN TO NET REALISABLE VALUE

As at 31 December 2018, Waterloo Ltd had an item of inventory that originally cost €2,300; the economic conditions had deteriorated and the selling price was €1,840 at that date. €50 transport costs are involved in the delivery of the item.

On 31 December 2019, the item of inventory is still on hand and demand for the product has improved significantly. The selling price now being achieved is €2,800 before the transport costs of €50.

Requirement:
(a) What is the value of inventory as at 31 December 2018? Prepare the journal entry.
(b) What is the value of inventory as at 31 December 2019? Prepare the journal entry.

Solution
(a)

	€
Cost	2,300
Net realisable value (€1,840 – €50)	1,790
Value inventory at the lower of cost or net realisable value as at 31 December 2018	1,790

	Debit €	Credit €
SPLOCI – write-down of inventory	510	
Inventory account (SOFP)		510

To recognise the write-down of inventory to net realisable value.

(b)

	€
Cost	2,300
Net realisable value (€2,800 – €50)	2,750
Value inventory at the lower of cost and net realisable value as at 31 December 2019	2,300

	Debit €	Credit €
Inventory account (SOFP)	510	
SPLOCI – write-down of inventory reversed		510

To recognise the reversal of the write-down of inventory to net realisable value.

(Try **Review Question 21.5** at the end of this chapter.)

21.4 DISCLOSURE

The following shall be disclosed in the financial statements:
• accounting policies used to measure inventory, including any cost formulae used;
• total carrying value of inventory and the **carrying amount** for each class – different classes will apply to different industries, for example, a supermarket would not have raw materials;
• carrying amount of inventories carried at fair value less costs to sell;
• amount of inventories recognised as an expense during the period;
• amount of any write-downs of inventories recognised as an expense in the period;
• amount of any reversal of write-downs of inventories recognised in the period;
• circumstances that led to the reversal of the write-down; and
• carrying amount of inventories pledged as security for liabilities.

Example 21.9 sets out the disclosure note in relation to inventory.

EXAMPLE 21.9: INVENTORY DISCLOSURE NOTE

The following is an extract from the statement of financial position (SOFP) of Ant Plc:

	31/12/2019 €	31/12/2018 €
Current Assets		
Inventory	298,700	289,450

The cost of inventory for the reporting periods is assigned on a FIFO basis. An analysis of the above inventory amounts is set out below:

	31/12/2019 €	31/12/2018 €
Raw materials	45,000	38,500
Work in progress	80,000	96,800
Finished goods	173,700	154,150

Requirement Prepare the disclosure note based on the information available.

Solution
Accounting Policy

Inventories are stated at the lower of cost or net realisable value. Cost is based on the FIFO principle and includes all expenditure incurred in acquiring the inventories and bringing them to their present location and condition. Raw materials are valued on the basis of purchase cost on a FIFO basis. In the case of finished goods and work in progress, cost includes direct materials, direct labour and attributable overheads based on normal operating capacity and excludes borrowing costs. Net realisable value is the estimated proceeds of sale less all further costs to completion and less all costs to be incurred in marketing, selling and distribution.

Other Disclosures: Inventory

	2019 €	2018 €
Raw materials	45,000	38,500
Work in progress	80,000	96,800
Finished goods	173,700	154,150
	298,700	289,450

21.5 IAS 2 COMPARED WITH FRS 102

The treatment outlined in FRS 102 *The Financial Reporting Standard applicable in the UK and Republic of Ireland* in relation to inventory is the same as that in IAS 2.

There is no requirement under FRS 102 to disclose the carrying amount of inventories carried at fair value less costs to sell; it is required under IAS 2.

EXAM TIPS

Inventory adjustments are very common in published accounts. The key rules to remember are:
- Inventory is valued at the lower of cost and net realisable value.
- Inventory issues are valued using either the FIFO or weighted average cost methods.
- Reversal of write-downs to net realisable value is limited to the amount of the original write-down.

21.6 CONCLUSION

Inventory is valued at the lower of cost and net realisable value. Cost includes production overheads based on the normal capacity and not the actual activity for the period. This valuation rule is applied on an item-by-item basis unless there is a group of similar items, in which case the rule is applied to each group of similar items.

Summary of Learning Objectives

After having studied this chapter, readers should be able to:

Learning Objective 1 Identify the components of inventory.

The components of inventory include:
- raw materials;
- work in progress;
- finished goods; and
- goods purchased for resale.

Learning Objective 2 Calculate the value of inventory to be presented in the financial statements.

Inventory on hand at the start of a reporting period is an expense included in the cost of sales calculation. Inventory on hand at the end of the reporting period reduces the cost of sales for the period and is presented in the SOFP under current assets. The cost of sales represents the costs incurred in relation to the goods sold during the reporting period – if goods are still on hand at the reporting date, the cost of these goods is deferred until the next reporting period when the items of inventory are sold.

Inventory is valued at the lower of cost and net realisable value. 'Cost' can be summarised as any costs incurred in bringing the item of inventory to its present location and condition; this is made up of the cost to purchase the raw materials and the production costs to convert them to finished goods.

The 'lower of cost and net realisable value' rule is applied on an item-by-item basis unless there is a group of similar items. The only exception to this rule is in relation to raw materials where they will be included in the production of a finished product that will make a profit for the entity; in such a case the item of raw material is not written down to its net realisable value.

Learning Objective 3 Apply FIFO and weighted average cost of inventory valuation methods.

There are three methods for valuing issues and inventories of goods – FIFO, LIFO and weighted average cost. LIFO is not allowed under IAS 2.

The application of the FIFO valuation method means that issues of goods are valued at the oldest price of the goods first – inventories on hand at the end of a reporting period would be valued at the most recent purchase prices.

The application of the weighted average cost valuation method means that each time goods are received, a weighted average cost valuation is calculated by taking the total cost of goods on hand

and dividing by the number of goods on hand. This unit valuation is used to value issues of goods until the next receipt of goods.

Learning Objective 4 Prepare the appropriate disclosure notes for inventory.

The accounting policy must be disclosed and a breakdown given of the inventory into the various classifications, such as raw materials, work in progress, finished goods and consumables.

QUESTIONS

Review Questions

(See **Appendix A** for Solutions to Review Questions.)

Question 21.1

You are provided with the following information in relation to an inventory item:

	€
Direct materials – per unit	8.00
Direct labour – per unit	7.00
Direct expenses – per unit	5.00
Production overhead – annual	300,000
Selling overhead – annual	120,000

Normal production is 100,000 units, but due to a strike only 60,000 units were actually produced during the year.

Requirement What is the value of one unit of inventory?

Question 21.2

Neeson Ltd has two lines of inventory (stock) at 31 December 2019, detailed below:

Product	A €	B €
Cost	7,600	5,000
Estimated selling price	7,900	5,500
Additional costs to be incurred in selling	400	450

What amount should be included in inventories at 31 December 2019 in respect of these items?

(Based on Chartered Accountants Ireland, CAP 1 Financial Accounting, Summer 2008, Question 1.1)

Question 21.3

At 31 December 2019 Leigh's business is suffering serious cash flow problems and its future is in doubt. At that date Leigh has an inventory of goods in hand that had originally cost €5,800. It is estimated that the goods could be sold to the trade through an agent for €6,100. The agent would charge a fee of €400.

Requirement:
(a) At what value should these goods be included in Leigh's financial statements at 31 December 2019?
(b) Give a reason for your answer.

(Based on Chartered Accountants Ireland, CAP 1 Financial Accounting, Autumn 2008, Question 1.1)

Question 21.4

As at 1 January 2019 Smith Ltd had 300 units on hand, which had cost €15.00 per unit. The following receipts of inventory were recorded during January 2019:

Date	Units Received	Cost Per Unit
3 January 2019	400	€14.50
12 January 2019	500	€15.00
20 January 2019	350	€16.00
25 January 2019	750	€18.00

2,000 units were issued on 31 January 2019.

Requirement:
(a) What is the value of the inventory on hand as at 31 January 2019 using the first in first out method?
(b) What is the value of the inventory on hand as at 31 January 2019 using the weighted average cost method?

Question 21.5

As at 31 December 2018 an item of inventory, which had originally cost €1,900, was selling for €1,850 before selling and distribution costs of €70.

Due to poor demand for the product for most of 2019, the item is still on hand at 31 December 2019. The market for the product has improved considerably and is now selling for €2,100 after selling and distribution costs of €75.

Requirement What is the value of inventory as at 31 December 2019?

Challenging Questions

(Suggested Solutions to Challenging Questions are available through your lecturer.)

Question 21.1

Two companies, Bill Ltd and Ben Ltd, have identical opening and closing inventories and purchases for the year ended 31 December 2019, as follows.

	Units	Values €
Opening inventory	100	990
Purchases		
March	40	520
June	220	1,870
September	60	580
December	160	1,550
Closing inventory	240	

Bill Ltd chooses to determine the value of its closing inventory by the FIFO method; Ben Ltd does so by the weighted average cost method.

Requirement What figures should be included for inventory in the respective company statements of financial position as at 31 December 2019?
(a) Bill €1,680 and Ben €2,280.
(b) Bill €2,300 and Ben €2,180.

(c) Bill €2,300 and Ben €2,280.
(d) Bill €2,325 and Ben €2,325.
(Based on Chartered Accountants Ireland, Prof II Financial Accounting, Summer 2003, Question 2.9)

Question 21.2

Mr Baker had closing inventory of goods for resale of €10,000. This does not include some goods that have been damaged in his store. These goods originally cost €1,200. It is estimated that these goods could be sold for €1,600 if €350 was spent on repairing the damage to them.

Requirement The total value of closing inventory in Mr Baker's final accounts will be:
(a) €10,000;
(b) €11,200;
(c) €11,250;
(d) €11,300.
(Based on Chartered Accountants Ireland, Prof II Financial Accounting, Autumn 2005, Question 2.10)

Question 21.3

Requirement Write a memorandum to the managing director of a newly established manufacturing company explaining IAS 2.

Your memorandum should include the following:
(a) The definition of 'inventories' and a description of how inventories should be measured in the financial statements.

5 Minutes

(b) A discussion of the costs that should be included in inventories in financial statements.

5 Minutes

(c) A brief description of LIFO, FIFO and average cost, stating which methods are in accordance with IAS 2.

5 Minutes
(Based on Chartered Accountants Ireland, Prof II Financial Accounting, Summer 2006, Question 6)

Question 21.4

Candle Ltd prepares its financial statements to 31 December each year. The inventory was counted on 31 December 2019 and valued at cost price. The total value of inventory was €131,418. The following information has come to light since the year end.
1. Due to lack of space in the warehouse some inventory was stored in a secure yard. This inventory was valued at cost of €855. However, due to bad weather before Christmas, the inventory has deteriorated. It could be sold for €1,300 if €270 was spent to make it suitable for sale.
2. Inventories costing €3,015 sent to customers on a sale or return basis have been included in inventory valuation at their selling price of €3,769.
3. A fire broke out in one of the company's warehouses, on 2 January 2020, destroying inventory valued at cost of €10,250.

Requirement State the amount that should be included in the financial statements of Candle Ltd for inventories as at 31 December 2019. Give reasons for your answer.

9 Minutes
(Based on Chartered Accountants Ireland, Prof II Financial Accounting, Summer 2006, Question 6)

Question 21.5

Mr Banks trades in one product for the Christmas market. He uses the FIFO method to value his inventories. He had the following transactions during December 2019.

	Purchases			Sales	
Date	Units	Price €	Date	Units	Price €
1	1,000	1.15	2	800	1.80
6	600	1.20	7	600	2.00
10	1,100	1.30	12	1,100	2.20
14	800	1.35	15	900	2.50
20	700	1.40	23	400	2.25

At 31 December the selling price of these goods had fallen due to the nature of the product. Remaining inventories could be sold to a discount house for €600, with Mr Banks paying transport costs of €50.

Requirement:
(a) Calculate the cost of inventories at 31 December 2019.

5 Minutes

(b) Calculate the net realisable value at 31 December 2019.

2 Minutes

(c) State the amount that should be included in the financial statements of Mr Banks at 31 December 2019 for inventories.

2 Minutes

(Based on Chartered Accountants Ireland, Prof II Financial Accounting, Summer 2006, Question 6)

Question 21.6

Harris Ltd has the following balances:

	€
Opening inventory – 1 January 2019	1,800,000
Closing inventory – 31 December 2019	2,050,000
Purchases	6,680,000
Purchases returns	300,000
Carriage inwards	60,000

Included in inventory at 31 December 2019 was slow-moving inventory that had originally cost €600,000. This is expected to realise €400,000 at a discount warehouse. Commission costs of 3% will be incurred.

Requirement What is its cost of sales?

(Based on Chartered Accountants Ireland, CAP 1 Financial Accounting, Summer 2009, Question 1.1)

22

Accounting Policies, Changes in Accounting Estimates and Errors

LEARNING OBJECTIVES

Having studied this chapter, readers should be able to:
1. identify an accounting estimate;
2. explain the appropriate accounting treatment of a change in an accounting estimate;
3. prepare the disclosure note in relation to a change in an accounting estimate;
4. identify an accounting policy;
5. explain the appropriate accounting treatment for a change in accounting policy;
6. prepare the disclosure note in relation to accounting policies;
7. explain the accounting treatment of the correction of an error made in an earlier reporting period; and
8. prepare the disclosure note in relation to the correction of an error.

22.1 INTRODUCTION

In this chapter the difference between accounting policies and **accounting estimates** is explained. How entities account for changes in accounting policies, changes in accounting estimates and how errors in financial statements are dealt with are all demonstrated. The relevant accounting standard is IAS 8 *Accounting Policies, Changes in Accounting Estimates and Errors*.

22.2 TERMINOLOGY

Accounting Estimates

When an entity prepares its financial statements it may not have complete information so it has to make estimates. These estimates are based on:
- management's past experience;
- judgement; and
- economic environment in which the entity operates.

For example, a lot of businesses sell goods on credit and would expect that some of these customers will not pay the amounts they owe in full. The entity will make an allowance (also referred to as a 'provision') for bad debts based on management's knowledge of:
- the business and the environment in which it operates;
- the customer base; and
- changes in the payment patterns of its customers.

The management of the business cannot know with certainty how much of the amounts due from the credit customers will not be paid in the future, so it makes an estimate.

Accounting Policy

IAS 8 defines accounting policies as "the specific principles, bases, conventions, rules and practices applied by an entity in preparing and presenting financial statements". Management selects the accounting policy that it considers to be the most appropriate to the entity.

22.3 ACCOUNTING ESTIMATES

A large number of accounting estimates are used in the preparation of a set of financial statements. Examples of accounting estimates include:
- useful lives of property, plant and equipment,
- residual values of property, plant and equipment,
- depreciation method used (straight line or reducing balance), and
- provision for bad debts.

Financial statements are prepared on the basis of accounting estimates and there is an element of judgement involved in these estimates. Estimates depend on the information available and the situation that exists at a particular point in time. As time passes more information may become available so estimates are reviewed annually to ensure that they are still appropriate. If the review finds that the estimate should be amended, then the change is made in the period that the new information became available and in future periods. No change is made to the figures brought forward from previous reporting periods and comparative figures are **not** restated. This is known as applying the change in accounting estimate **prospectively**.

Example 22.1 demonstrates how a change in accounting estimate is dealt with in the financial statements.

EXAMPLE 22.1: CHANGE IN AN ACCOUNTING ESTIMATE

Sewell Ltd purchased an item of machinery on 1 January 2017 for €140,000. At the purchase date Sewell estimated the useful life of the machine at 10 years. Sewell reviewed the useful lives of all property, plant and equipment on 1 January 2019. The review found that the remaining useful life of the machine is five years.

Requirement Explain how to account for the change in useful life.

Solution

The first step is to determine the carrying amount of the asset at the start of the reporting period in which the review has taken place, i.e. 1 January 2019. The second step is to apply the new information about the remaining useful life to the opening carrying amount.

Step 1 Determine the carrying amount at the start of the reporting period.

	€
Cost of Machine as at 1 January 2017	140,000
Depreciation year ended 31 December 2017	(14,000)
Depreciation year ended 31 December 2018	(14,000)
Carrying Amount as at 31 December 2018	112,000

Step 2 Apply the new accounting estimate.

	€
Depreciation charge for the year ended 31 December 2019 (€112,000 ÷ 5 years)	22,400

The useful life of the machine is an accounting estimate. When new information becomes available the depreciation charge is amended in the current year and for future reporting periods. No change is made to the financial statements of previous periods.

(Try **Review Question 22.1** at the end of this chapter.)

Disclosure in Relation to Changes in Accounting Estimates

When an entity changes its accounting estimates it must disclose the nature and amount of the change in the current period or expected in future periods. If the entity cannot make an estimate of the effect on future periods, it must state that it cannot do so.

Example 22.2 demonstrates the disclosure requirement in relation to a change in an accounting estimate.

EXAMPLE 22.2: DISCLOSURE NOTE IN RELATION TO A CHANGE IN AN ACCOUNTING
ESTIMATE

Bowler Ltd has carried out its annual review of all accounting estimates used in preparation of its financial statements.

The review identified that the residual value of production machinery is now estimated at €10,000 as a result of technological advances made in the past five years since the assets were originally purchased. The depreciation charged in previous reporting periods was based on an estimated useful life of 20 years and a residual value of €400,000 and amounted to €80,000 per annum. The carrying amount of the asset at the start of the current reporting period was €1,600,000. The remaining useful life is unchanged as a result of the review at 15 years.

Requirement Prepare the disclosure note in relation to this change in the accounting estimate to be presented in the financial statements for the year ended 31 December 2019.

Carrying amount	1,600,000
Revised residual value	(10,000)
Revised depreciable amount	1,590,000
Remaining useful life	15 years
Depreciation charge	106,000

Solution

DISCLOSURE NOTE

Management has undertaken its annual review of accounting estimates in relation to property, plant and equipment. As a result it now considers a residual value of €10,000 more appropriate than the original estimate of €400,000. The change in estimate is due to the technological advances made in the past five years that have affected the expected residual value.

The depreciation charge that will apply to the current and future reporting periods is €106,000 (€80,000 in previous reporting period).

22.4 ACCOUNTING POLICY

An accounting policy is set when the particular transaction or event takes place for the first time and is then applied consistently to all subsequent transactions. For example, when an entity purchases its first building it must decide whether to apply the cost model or the revaluation model (see **Chapter 25, Property, Plant and Equipment**). If the entity chooses the cost model, any other properties purchased will also use the cost model.

An entity can only change its accounting policy if one of the following conditions is met:
• it is required by international financial reporting standards; or
• the change is necessary to provide more relevant and reliable information.

A change in an accounting policy must be applied retrospectively, that is, from the first day that the original accounting policy was applied. IAS 8 allows for one exception to this rule, that is, when an entity changes from the cost model to the revaluation model under IAS 16 *Property, Plant and Equipment*, this initial change in fair value is treated as a revaluation and not a change in accounting policy.

Example 22.3 shows how a change in accounting policy is treated in the financial statements.

EXAMPLE 22.3: CHANGE IN AN ACCOUNTING POLICY

Bloom Ltd purchased a property for its ability to generate rental income. The investment property cost €2,000,000 on 1 January 2017.

Bloom decided to adopt the cost model for measuring investment property. The estimated useful life of the investment property at the purchase date was 40 years. The following information is available in relation to the fair value of the property as at:

Reporting Date	Fair Value €
31 December 2017	2,020,000
31 December 2018	2,050,000
31 December 2019	2,060,000

The retained earnings balance as at 31 December 2018 was €2,810,500 and the profit for the reporting period ended 31 December 2019 was €286,700 (based on the use of the cost model).

During the year ended 31 December 2019 the management of Bloom decided that the fair value model would be a more appropriate base to use for the measurement of the investment property and the change would result in the provision of more relevant and reliable information to users of the financial statements.

Requirement Prepare the retained earnings extract from the statement of changes in equity (SOCIE) for the year ended 31 December 2019.

Solution

STATEMENT OF CHANGES IN EQUITY (RETAINED EARNINGS EXTRACT)
for the year ended 31 December 2019

	€
As at 1 January 2019	2,810,500
Change in accounting policy (W1)	150,000
Restated	2,960,500
Profit for year (W2)	346,700
As at 31 December 2019	3,307,200

W1 CHANGE IN ACCOUNTING POLICY

	€	€
Cost of Property	2,000,000	
Depreciation year ended 31 December 2017	(50,000)	
Depreciation year ended 31 December 2018	(50,000)	
Carrying amount as at 31 December 2018		1,900,000
Fair value as at 31 December 2018		2,050,000
Difference in carrying amount		150,000

W2 PROFIT FOR YEAR

	€
Profit for year ended 31 December 2019	286,700
Fair value adjustment for year ended 31 December 2019	10,000
Add back depreciation charge	50,000
	346,700

(Try **Review Question 22.2** at the end of this chapter.)

Change in an Accounting Policy – Disclosure Requirements

When there is a change in an accounting policy during the reporting periods the following disclosures must be made:
- the title of the international financial reporting standard;
- where the change is the result of changes in an existing accounting standard or the introduction of a new standard, this must be stated;
- the nature of the change in the accounting policy;
- where applicable, a description of the transitional provisions contained in the accounting standard;

- where applicable, the transitional provisions that might have an effect on future periods;
- for the current and each period presented, the amount of each adjustment for each statement line affected;
- the amount of the adjustment relating to periods before those presented to the extent that this is practicable; and
- if retrospective application is not practicable for a particular prior period, then a description of how and from when the change in accounting policy has been applied.

Example 22.4 demonstrates the disclosure note in relation to a change in accounting policy during the reporting period.

EXAMPLE 22.4: DISCLOSURE NOTE – CHANGE IN AN ACCOUNTING POLICY

Abbott Ltd has one investment property that it purchased on 1 January 2018 for €1,200,000. At the purchase date Abbott decided to adopt the cost model to measure the investment property. Using the cost model, the useful life was estimated at 40 years. Depreciation is charged in the line item 'administration costs'.

Abbott is now preparing its financial statements for the reporting date 31 December 2019 and has reviewed all of its accounting policies and has decided that the fair value model would be a more appropriate basis of measurement for the investment property. The change will provide more relevant and reliable information to users of the financial statements.

Date	Fair Value Assessment €
31 December 2018	1,220,000
31 December 2019	1,250,000

Requirement Prepare the disclosure note in relation to this change in accounting policy.

Solution

DISCLOSURE NOTE – INVESTMENT PROPERTY

Following a review of the accounting policies it has been decided that the measurement method used for investment properties is to be changed from the cost model to the fair value model. This change is to ensure that the information provided in the financial statements is both more relevant and reliable to the users.

Prior to the change, depreciation was charged in relation to the investment property amounting to €30,000 and presented under the administration expense line. The impact of the change on prior years' results is that profit has been understated by €50,000, which consists of the depreciation charge of €30,000 and the fair value adjustment of €20,000 as at 31 December 2018.

22.5 ERRORS

When an error is discovered, management must make the correction in the first set of financial statements prepared after the error is discovered. Depending on the nature and timing of the error, the figures brought forward may need to be amended.

If the amount of the error is not material, an adjustment is made in the current year's statement of profit or loss and other comprehensive income (SPLOCI). If the amount of the error is material, an adjustment is made in the current year's SOCIE by restating the opening retained earnings figure.

Example 22.5 demonstrates the accounting treatment of a prior-period error.

EXAMPLE 22.5: PRIOR-PERIOD ERROR IN FINANCIAL STATEMENTS

Leopold Ltd has discovered that capital expenditure of €420,000 on new machinery was expensed in the financial statements for the year ended 31 December 2018. When the error was discovered, management estimated the residual value of the machine at €20,000 and the useful life at five years. Leopold charges a full year's depreciation in the year of purchase and none in the year of sale.

The retained earnings balance as at 31 December 2018 was €4,288,400 and the profit for the reporting period ended 31 December 2019 was €895,200.

Tax is charged at a rate of 20%.

Requirement Prepare the retained earnings extract from the SOCIE for the year ended 31 December 2019.

Solution

STATEMENT OF CHANGES IN EQUITY (RETAINED EARNINGS EXTRACT)
for the year ended 31 December 2019

	€
As at 1 January 2019	4,288,400
Error (W1)	272,000
Restated	4,560,400
Profit for year (W2)	831,200
As at 31 December 2019	5,391,600

W1

	€
Cost of asset expensed in error	420,000
Should have charged depreciation (€420,000 − €20,000) ÷ 5 years	(80,000)
Difference	340,000
Tax (€340,000 × 20%)	(68,000)
Net impact	272,000

W2

	€
Depreciation charge (€420,000 − €20,000) ÷ 5 years	80,000
Tax saving	16,000
Net impact	64,000

continued overleaf

Profit reported for the year	895,200
Depreciation net of tax	(64,000)
Revised profit for the year	831,200

(Try **Review Questions 22.3** and **22.4** at the end of this chapter.)

Disclosure Note – Correction of Errors

The following disclosures should be made in relation to prior period errors in the period that they are discovered:
- the nature of the prior period error;
- for each prior period presented, where practicable, the amount of the correction for each financial statement line affected;
- the amount of the correction at the beginning of the earliest prior period presented; and
- if retrospective application is not practicable for a particular prior period, then a description of how, and from when, the error correction has been applied.

Example 22.6 demonstrates how to prepare the disclosure note required when an error is corrected.

EXAMPLE 22.6: DISCLOSURE NOTE – CORRECTION OF ERRORS

It is 31 December 2019 and Crawford Ltd has just been informed that some of its purchases for the month of November 2018 were omitted in error from its financial statements for the reporting period ended 31 December 2018. The amount of the error is €180,000 before tax.

Tax is charged at a rate of 20% on all operating profits.

Requirement Prepare the disclosure note in relation to this change in accounting policy for the financial statements for the reporting period ended 31 December 2019.

Solution

An error has been discovered in relation to the prior period's financial statements. The error arose as a result of the omission from the financial statements of a number of purchase transactions amounting to €180,000. The after-tax impact of this error, when adjusted, will be to reduce profits by €144,000.

The error relates only to the reporting period ended 31 December 2018.

22.6 IAS 8 COMPARED WITH FRS 102

In relation to the disclosure of changes in accounting estimates, if the entity cannot make an estimate of the impact of the change on one or more future periods, it is not required to make a statement to that effect under FRS 102, as required by IAS 8.

EXAM TIPS

- Be clear on the difference between an accounting policy and an accounting estimate.
- Know the only circumstances in which a change in accounting policy is allowed.
- Read the question carefully and be prepared to draft disclosure note if required.

22.7 CONCLUSION

Accounting estimates are based on information available and are reviewed annually. A change in an accounting estimate is applied prospectively.

A change can only be made to an accounting policy if it is required by an accounting standard or where it will provide more relevant and reliable information. The change is applied retrospectively, quantified and presented in the SOCIE in the period in which the change in accounting policy is made.

When an error made in a previous reporting period is discovered in the current period, it must be corrected in the financial statements.

SUMMARY OF LEARNING OBJECTIVES

After having studied this chapter, readers should be able to:

Learning Objective 1 Identify an accounting estimate.

In preparing the financial statements management must make estimates. These estimates are based on management's knowledge of the business and its past experience. Estimates are used when the entity does not have certain knowledge about events. Examples of accounting estimates are bad debts provisions and useful lives of property, plant and equipment.

Learning Objective 2 Explain the appropriate accounting treatment of a change in accounting estimate.

Estimates are reviewed annually. Changes in accounting estimate are applied in the current year with no retrospective application.

Learning Objective 3 Prepare the disclosure note in relation to a change in an accounting estimate.

The disclosure note in relation to a change in an accounting estimate must provide the following information:
- the nature of the change in the accounting estimate;
- the amount of the change in the accounting estimate in the current period or in future periods; and
- if the entity cannot make an estimate of the effect on future periods, it must state that it cannot make the estimate.

Learning Objective 4 Identify an accounting policy.

An accounting policy is chosen by the entity and applied consistently: from period to period and for the same type of transactions and events.

An accounting policy is defined as "the specific principles, bases, conventions, rules and practices applied by an entity in preparing and presenting financial statements" (IAS 8, paragraph 5).

Learning Objective 5 Explain the appropriate accounting treatment of a change in accounting policy.

A change in accounting policy is only allowed if required by an international financial reporting standard or if it will provide more relevant and reliable information.

Changes in accounting policy and the impact of the change are presented in the SOCIE in the reporting period in which the change in accounting policy is made.

Learning Objective 6 Prepare the disclosure note in relation to accounting policies.

The disclosure note should identify the following:
- the title of the international financial reporting standard;
- where the change is the result of changes in an existing accounting standard or the introduction of a new standard, this must be stated;
- the nature of the change in the accounting policy;
- where applicable, a description of the transitional provisions contained in the accounting standard;
- where applicable, the transitional provisions that might have an effect on future periods;
- for the current and each period presented, the amount of each adjustment for each statement line affected;
- the amount of the adjustment relating to periods before those presented to the extent that this is practicable; and
- if retrospective application is not practicable for a particular prior period, then a description of how and from when the change in accounting policy has been applied.

Learning Objective 7 Explain the accounting treatment of the correction of an error made in an earlier reporting period.

When an error is detected, amendments must be made in the period the error is discovered. If the error was made in a prior period, the comparative financial statements must be amended and the cumulative impact from previous reporting periods presented in the SOCIE.

Learning Objective 8 Prepare the disclosure note in relation to the correction of an error.

The disclosure note in relation to the correction of an error should contain the following information:
- the nature of the prior period error;
- for each prior period presented, where practicable, the amount of the correction for each financial statement line affected;
- the amount of the correction at the beginning of the earliest prior period presented; and
- if retrospective application is not practicable for a particular prior period, then a description of how, and from when, the error correction has been applied.

QUESTIONS

Review Questions

(See **Appendix A** for Solutions to Review Questions.)

Question 22.1

Stout Ltd purchased an asset on 1 January 2016 for €160,000; at that date the management of the company made the following estimates regarding the asset:

Useful life	10 years
Residual value	€10,000
Depreciation method	Straight-line

During 2019, as part of the annual management review of accounting estimates used in the preparation of its financial statements, management revised the useful life of the asset to eight years in total and the residual value to €2,500.

Requirement Calculate the depreciation charge for the reporting period ended 31 December 2019.

Question 22.2

Alvin Ltd commenced business on 1 January 2018 and adopted an accounting policy of measuring inventories using the first in first out method (FIFO). During a review of its financial operations it has realised that the weighted average cost method of measuring inventories is more appropriate to its business as it will provide more relevant and reliable information to the users of financial statements.

You are provided with the following information in relation to the valuation of inventory for the past two years.

Valuation Method	FIFO €	Weighted Average €
Inventory as at 1 January 2018	Nil	Nil
Inventory as at 31 December 2018	85,600	96,300
Inventory as at 31 December 2019	105,250	104,620

Alvin applied the FIFO method for both reporting periods and calculated its profits for each year as:

Reporting period ended 31 December 2018	€286,900
Reporting period ended 31 December 2019	€299,100

Requirement Calculate the impact on profits of the change in accounting policy.

Question 22.3

Morrissey Ltd has discovered an error made in its previous year's financial statements: wages costs of €400,000 were omitted from the statement of profit or loss for the year ended 31 December 2018. The wages cost is an allowable deduction in the calculation of taxable profit; the tax rate on profits is 20%.

STATEMENT OF PROFIT OR LOSS (EXTRACTS)
for the years ended

	31 December 2019	31 December 2018
Gross profit	4,150,000	3,860,000
Wages cost	(1,840,000)	(1,320,000)
Distribution costs	(960,000)	(925,000)
Profit before tax	1,350,000	1,615,000
Income tax expense	(270,000)	(323,000)
Profit for the year	1,080,000	1,292,000

The retained earnings as at 31 December 2018 were reported as €4,825,650.

Requirement Redraft the statement of profit or loss for the years ended 31 December 2018 and 2019. Prepare the retained earnings extract from the statement of changes in equity for Morrissey Ltd for the year ended 31 December 2019.

Question 22.4

During 2018, Mr Tarrant noticed that the company Donnelly had failed to charge amortisation of €250,000 relating to an intangible asset in the previous year. Extracts from the statement of profit or loss for the current and prior years before correction of this error are shown below:

	2019 €	2018 €
Gross profit	500,000	650,000
General and admin. expenses	(410,000)	(181,000)
Profit before tax	90,000	469,000
Tax	(27,000)	(140,700)
Profit for year	63,000	328,300

Retained earnings before correction of the error:

	2019 €	2018 €
As at 1 January	1,200,000	871,700
As at 31 December	1,263,000	1,200,000

Requirement Set out for Donnelly the extract of the statement of profit or loss, after correction of the error, together with the statement of changes in equity (retained earnings only) and the appropriate disclosure note. Assume a tax rate of 30%, with amortisation being fully deductible for tax purposes.

(Based on Chartered Accountants Ireland, FAE Financial Reporting, May 2010)

Challenging Questions

(Suggested Solutions to Challenging Questions are available through your lecturer.)

Question 22.1

Hilary has reviewed the useful life of her office equipment and has decided to change the depreciation from a 35% reducing-balance to a 25% straight-line basis.

Requirement:
(a) How would you describe this change according to IAS 8 *Accounting Policies, Changes in Accounting Estimates and Errors*?
(b) Should the change described be accounted for retrospectively or prospectively?
(Based on Chartered Accountants Ireland, CAP 1 Financial Accounting, Summer 2011, Questions 1.5 and 1.6)

Question 22.2

Requirement How is a prior period error corrected in accordance with IAS 8?
(Based on Chartered Accountants Ireland, CAP 1 Financial Accounting, Autumn 2011, Question 1.4)

Events After the Reporting Period

LEARNING OBJECTIVES

Having studied this chapter, readers should be able to:
1. identify non-adjusting events and explain the appropriate accounting treatment;
2. identify adjusting events and explain the appropriate accounting treatment;
3. account for dividends; and
4. understand the implications for an entity when the going concern basis of preparation of the financial statements is not appropriate.

23.1 INTRODUCTION

The purpose of this chapter is to set out the accounting treatment of events that occur in the period between the reporting date and the date the financial statements are approved for issue by the board of directors.

Transactions that occur between the reporting date and the date the financial statements are approved for issue are subject to accounting rules set out in IAS 10 *Events after the Reporting Period*.

23.2 TERMINOLOGY

The reporting date is the date to which the financial statements are prepared. The reporting date is contained in the title of each financial statement, for example:

ABC Ltd
STATEMENT OF PROFIT OR LOSS AND OTHER COMPREHENSIVE INCOME
for the year ended 31 December 2019

ABC Ltd
STATEMENT OF FINANCIAL POSITION
as at 31 December 2019

The reporting date for these financial statements is 31 December 2019. The statement of profit or loss and other comprehensive income (SPLOCI) presents the income earned and expenses incurred for the year ended 31 December 2019, that is, the period 1 January 2019–31 December 2019.

The statement of financial position (SOFP) presents the amount attributed to assets, liabilities, equity and reserves as at a particular date, in this example, 31 December 2019.

The annual financial statements are approved by the Board of Directors and this date is shown in the directors' report.

Example 23.1 is concerned with identifying whether or not a transaction is subject to the accounting rules set out in IAS 10.

EXAMPLE 23.1: PERIOD COVERED BY IAS 10

	Reporting Date	**Date Financial Statements Approved by Board of Directors**	**Transaction Date**
Scenario 1	31 December 2018	4 April 2019	10 May 2019
Scenario 2	30 June 2018	3 September 2018	8 August 2018

Requirement For each of the above scenarios, indicate whether the transactions are within the scope of IAS 10 or not.

Solution

Scenario 1 This transaction is not within the scope of IAS 10 as the transaction occurred on 10 May 2019, which is after the financial statements were approved for issue by the board of directors (4 April 2019).

Scenario 2 This transaction is within the scope of IAS 10 as the transaction occurred on 8 August 2018, which is between the reporting date and the date the financial statements were approved for issue by the board of directors.

There are two types of events identified under IAS 10 – adjusting and non-adjusting events. The accounting treatment in relation to adjusting events will be explained next.

23.3 ADJUSTING EVENTS

An **adjusting event** is one that provides further evidence of a situation that existed at the reporting date.

Examples of adjusting events include:
- the sale of goods at a price below that estimated at the reporting date where the reduction in selling price is **not** due to events that have occurred after the reporting date that resulted in damage to the items;
- the bankruptcy of a customer who owed money to the company at the reporting date; and
- the settlement of an insurance claim that was in negotiation at the reporting date.

Accounting Treatment

The impact of an adjusting event is reflected in the financial statements at the reporting date. A journal entry is posted to the financial statements to reflect this additional information.

Example 23.2 will explain the accounting treatment for an adjusting event.

Example 23.2: Adjusting Event

Anton Ltd prepared its financial statements to the year ended 31 December 2019. At the reporting date Anton is owed €20,000 by a customer, Flipper Ltd. The financial statements were approved for issue on 25 February 2020.

On 10 January 2020 Flipper Ltd is declared bankrupt and it is expected that it will only be able to pay 15c in the €.

Requirement Explain the appropriate accounting treatment for the year ended 31 December 2019.

Solution

Anton Ltd found out about the bankruptcy of Flipper Ltd on 10 January 2020. This is within the period covered by IAS 10. The bankruptcy provides additional information about the trade receivables balance due to Anton Ltd at the reporting date. It is therefore an adjusting event.

The bankruptcy of Flipper Ltd means that Anton Ltd will not receive the full amount of the balance due to it from Flipper Ltd. The balance on trade receivables needs to be reduced to the amount expected to be received. The journal entries to reflect this are:

	Debit €	Credit €
Bad debts expense account	17,000	
Trade receivables account		17,000
To write off bad debt in relation to Flipper Ltd.		

	Debit €	Credit €
SPLOCI – bad debts expense	17,000	
Bad debts expense account		17,000
To recognise the bad debt expense in the SPLOCI.		

Calculation of amount to be written off:

	€
Balance on trade receivables account of Flipper	20,000
Amount expected to be received (€20,000 × 15%)	(3,000)
Amount to be written off	17,000

It is important to note the date that the transaction has occurred as not all transactions that occur after the reporting date are subject to the accounting treatment outlined under IAS 10.

Example 23.3 demonstrates the accounting treatment of an event outside the scope of IAS 10.

Example 23.3: Event Outside the Scope of IAS 10

Bilton Ltd prepared its financial statements to the year ended 31 August 2019. At the reporting date Bilton Ltd has inventory recognised at a cost of €32,000. The financial statements were approved for issue on 28 October 2019.

On 12 November 2019 the inventory was sold for €26,300.

Requirement Explain the appropriate accounting treatment for the year ended 31 December 2019.

Solution

The sale of inventories after the reporting date can be an adjusting event, however, in the circumstances outlined in this example, the sale of the inventories took place after the financial statements were approved for issue by the board of directors and is therefore outside the scope of IAS 10 and cannot be classed as an adjusting event, so no adjustment is made to the financial statements.

23.4 NON-ADJUSTING EVENTS

Non-adjusting events are events/transactions that occurred after the reporting date and before the financial statements were approved for issue by the board of directors. The occurrence of these events is completely unrelated to any conditions in existence at the reporting date.

Examples of non-adjusting events include:
• issue of shares,
• fire, and
• theft.

Accounting Treatment

As non-adjusting transactions/events are independent of conditions in existence at the reporting date, no adjustment is made to the financial statements in relation to these items. Disclosure is required in relation to **material** non-adjusting transactions/events. The disclosure to be made is in relation to:
• the nature of the event, and
• the amount of the transaction.

If disclosure is not made of material non-adjusting events, this would mean that the users of the financial statements may not have full information when making decisions. 'Material' relates to both the size and significance of the transaction.

Example 23.4 demonstrates the accounting treatment of a non-adjusting event where the amount involved is not material.

EXAMPLE 23.4: NON-ADJUSTING EVENT

Walker Ltd prepares its financial statements to 31 March each year. The financial statements were approved for issue on 10 June 2019.

On 18 May 2019 a hurricane damaged a number of motor vehicles that will cost €20,000 to repair or replace.

The profit reported for the year ended 31 March 2019 was €1,200,000.

Requirement Explain the appropriate accounting treatment for the year ended 31 March 2019.

Solution

The occurrence of the hurricane is unrelated to the conditions that existed at the reporting date. It does not provide evidence of a situation that existed at the reporting date. It is therefore a non-adjusting event.

No adjustment is required to the financial statements for non-adjusting events, but disclosure is required for material events. Based on the profit for the year, the damage caused by the hurricane is not material, so no disclosure is required in the financial statements of Walker.

(Try **Review Questions 23.1** and **23.2** at the end of this chapter.)

23.5 ORDINARY DIVIDENDS

Ordinary dividends are the payments made to the ordinary shareholders of a company. There is no automatic entitlement to dividends on ordinary shares; ordinary dividends are at the discretion of the entity. Dividends are only accrued for in the financial statements if they are proposed by the board of directors **and** approved by the shareholders at the AGM before the reporting date.

Dividends proposed but not approved by shareholders before the reporting date are not accrued for but are still disclosed in the notes to the financial statements as required by IAS 1 *Presentation of Financial Statements*.

Example 23.5 demonstrates when it is appropriate to accrue for dividends and when it is not appropriate.

EXAMPLE 23.5: WHEN TO ACCRUE FOR ORDINARY DIVIDENDS

You are provided with the following details in relation to a number of scenarios:

Scenario	Date Dividend Proposed by Directors	Date of AGM at which Dividend Approved	Reporting Date	Date Dividend Payment Made
1	12 November 2019	7 December 2019	31 December 2019	10 January 2020
2	12 December 2019	24 January 2020	31 December 2019	1 February 2020
3	15 January 2020	23 January 2020	31 December 2019	10 February 2020

Requirement For each of the scenarios, outline the appropriate accounting treatment.

Solution

Scenario 1 The dividends were both proposed by the board of directors and approved by the shareholders before the reporting date. The dividend amount should be accrued in the financial statements for the year ended 31 December 2019.

The dividend will be presented in the statement of changes in equity (SOCIE) as a reduction in retained earnings and disclosed in the notes to the financial statements.

Scenario 2 The dividend was proposed by the board of directors before the reporting date but was not approved by the shareholders until after the reporting date. The dividend amount should not be accrued in the financial statements for the year ended 31 December 2019.

The dividend will be disclosed in the notes to the financial statements. No entry will be made in the SOCIE.

Scenario 3 The dividends were both proposed by the board of directors and approved by the shareholders after the reporting date.

The dividend amount should not be accrued in the financial statements for the year ended 31 December 2019.

The dividend will not be presented in the SOCIE and will not be disclosed in the notes to the financial statements.

Example 23.6 deals with the situation where the dividend has been proposed by the board of directors and accrued in the accounting records but the dividend payment has not been approved by the shareholders at an AGM by the reporting date.

EXAMPLE 23.6: REVERSAL OF DIVIDEND ACCRUAL

Harbour Ltd prepared its financial statements to 31 December 2019. The retained earnings as at 31 December 2019 were €2,165,000. The directors proposed a dividend of 1.5c per share on 10 December 2019 and have made an accrual for it in the financial statements. The AGM is scheduled for 5 January 2020 and management are confident that the dividend payment will be approved.

There were 200,000 ordinary shares in issue for the entire reporting period.

Requirement Is the accounting treatment of the dividend appropriate?

Solution

Harbour Ltd has made an accrual for the dividend in the financial statements for the year ended 31 December 2019. Dividends are only accrued when the dividend has been approved by shareholders at the AGM before the reporting date.

In the circumstances outlined, the dividend should not have been accrued at the reporting date. The journal entry required to reverse the dividend accrual is:

	Debit €	Credit €
Dividend liability account	3,000	
Retained earnings account		3,000
To reverse the dividend accrual.		

Calculation of the amount of the dividend accrued:	
Number of ordinary shares	200,000
Dividend per share	1.5c
Total dividend	€3,000

23.6 GOING CONCERN

Financial statements are presented on the basis that the entity is a going concern, that is, the entity will continue in operation for the next 12 months. If there is evidence available at the reporting date that suggests the entity will not continue in operation for the next 12 months the going concern basis should not be applied to the preparation of the financial statements.

The going concern basis is not appropriate if there has been a significant deterioration in the operating results and the financial position of the entity after the reporting date. The change to the entity's going concern status will require a fundamental change in the basis of accounting used in the preparation of financial statements.

23.7 DISCLOSURE

The date the financial statements were authorised for issue and who authorised their issue must be disclosed in the financial statements.

For each **material** non-adjusting event disclosure is required in the notes to the financial statements. The disclosure that must be provided for each material category of non-adjusting event is:
• a description of the nature of the event; and
• an estimate of the financial impact of the event or a statement to say why an estimate of the financial impact cannot be made.

Examples 23.7 and **23.8** demonstrate the disclosure requirements for non-adjusting events.

EXAMPLE 23.7: DISCLOSURE OF NON-ADJUSTING EVENTS

Arnold Ltd prepared its financial statements to 31 December each year. The profit reported for the reporting period ended 31 December 2019 was €2,158,200.

An item of inventory was destroyed by fire on 10 January 2020; the item had originally cost €260 and at the reporting date was expected to sell for €500 before selling and distribution costs of €25. As a result of the fire the item is completely destroyed and has no sales value; the item was not insured.

The financial statements were approved for issue on 13 March 2020.

Requirement Explain the appropriate accounting treatment of this event.

Solution

The fire that destroyed the item of inventory occurred between the reporting date and the date the financial statements were approved for issue, 31 December 2019 and 13 March 2020 respectively; this is within the period covered by IAS 10.

The destruction of the inventory by fire is a non-adjusting event as it does not provide any information about the situation that existed at the reporting date. The value of the inventory is €260; this is not material in terms of the reported profit for the period so no disclosure is required in the notes to the financial statements in relation to this event.

EXAMPLE 23.8: DISCLOSURE OF NON-ADJUSTING EVENTS

Maisy Ltd prepared its financial statements to 31 December each year. The profit reported for the reporting period ended 31 December 2019 was €1,245,800.

On 20 January 2020 a customer visiting the trading premises of Maisy Ltd was seriously injured when a shelving unit collapsed on them. Notice of legal proceedings was received on 12 February 2020. Legal opinion is that Maisy will lose the case; past settlements in relation to these types of claims have resulted in damages being awarded of €600,000.

The financial statements were approved for issue on 30 March 2020.

Requirement Explain the appropriate accounting treatment of these events.

Solution

The accident suffered by the customer occurred between the reporting date, 31 December 2019, and the date the financial statements were approved for issue, 30 March 2020; this is within the period covered by IAS 10.

As the accident occurred after the reporting date it does not provide additional information in relation to the situation that existed at the reporting date; it is, therefore, classified as a non-adjusting event. The amount being claimed as damages is material in the context of the reported profit, therefore a disclosure note must be included in the notes to the financial statements in relation to this issue.

DISCLOSURE NOTE

On 20 January 2020 a customer was injured when a shelving unit collapsed on them in our trading premises. On 12 February 2020 notice of legal proceedings was received by the company in relation to the accident. Legal opinion is that the claim will probably result in damages being awarded against the company. An estimate of damages is €600,000, based on similar cases.

23.8 IAS 10 COMPARED WITH FRS 102

The treatment outlined in FRS 102 *The Financial Reporting Standard applicable in the UK and Republic of Ireland* in relation to events after reporting date is the same as that in IAS 10.

EXAM TIPS

- Always note the reporting date and the date the financial statements are approved for issue. This is the key time period for adjusting and non-adjusting events. Outside of this time period the rules set out in IAS 10 do not apply.

- Be clear as to what makes a transaction/event material.
- Only accrue dividends that have been proposed by directors and approved by shareholders at the AGM before the reporting date.
- Know how to reverse a dividend that has been accrued in error.

23.9 CONCLUSION

IAS 10 outlines the accounting treatment in relation to adjusting and non-adjusting events that occur between the reporting date and the date the financial statements are approved for issue.

The financial statements are amended for the effects of adjusting events while disclosure in the notes to the financial statements is only required for material non-adjusting events.

Dividends are only accrued in the financial statements when the dividend has been approved by the shareholders at an AGM held before the reporting date.

SUMMARY OF LEARNING OBJECTIVES

After having studied this chapter, readers should be able to:

Learning Objective 1 Identify non-adjusting events and explain the appropriate accounting treatment.

Does the transaction/event provide additional information about a situation that existed at the reporting date? If the answer is 'no', then it is a non-adjusting event and no adjustment should be made to the financial statements.

Is the amount of the transaction/event material (due to either its size or significance)? If 'yes', then disclosure is required in the notes to the financial statements in relation to the transaction/event. The disclosure note will provide a description of the event and the amount involved. If an estimate cannot be made, that fact must be disclosed.

Learning Objective 2 Identify adjusting events and explain the appropriate accounting treatment.

Does the transaction/event provide additional information about a situation that existed at the reporting date? If the answer is 'yes', then it is an adjusting event and should be reflected in the financial statements.

Learning Objective 3 Account for dividends.

It is important to note that a dividend only becomes an obligation for the company when the shareholders approve the dividend. If the dividend was approved before the reporting date, it is accrued; if not, it is not accrued.

Learning Objective 4 Understand the implications for an entity when the going concern basis of preparation of the financial statements is not appropriate.

The basis on which the financial statements have been prepared must be amended to reflect that the going concern basis is no longer appropriate.

QUESTIONS

Review Questions

(See **Appendix A** for Solutions to Review Questions.)

Question 23.1

Stewart Ltd prepares its financial statements to 31 December each year. A number of events have taken place between the reporting date, 31 December 2019, and the date the financial statements were approved for issue.

Requirement Which of the following events would **not** qualify as an adjusting event in relation to the financial statements for the year ended 31 December 2019?
(a) On 1 January 2020 Stewart Ltd agreed very favourable terms for the acquisition of Snowy Ltd on 1 February 2020.
(b) An insurance claim pending at 31 December 2019 in respect of a building that burnt down in December 2019 was settled for €1,500,000 on 10 February 2020.
(c) A customer who owed €154,000 went into liquidation.

(Based on Chartered Accountants Ireland, Prof III Financial Reporting)

Question 23.2

The directors of Misfortune Ltd are to meet at the end of the week to approve its financial statements for the year ended 31 December 2019. Since that date a number of significant events have occurred.
(i)   The company's main retailing premises were destroyed in a hurricane.
(ii) The company's main supplier has declared bankruptcy.
(iii) Inventory valued at year at €345,000 was subsequently sold for €210,000.

Which of the above should be included in the financial statements of Misfortune Ltd for the year ended 31 December 2019 as adjusting events after the reporting date?
(a) (i) and (iii)
(b) (ii) and (iii)
(c) (iii)

(Based on Chartered Accountants Ireland, Prof III Financial Reporting)

Challenging Questions

(Suggested Solutions to Challenging Questions are available through your lecturer.)

Question 23.1

Bookworm Ltd prepared accounts for the year ended 31 December 2019. The directors have planned a meeting for 1 April 2020 at which these accounts will be approved, and you have been provided with the following information:
• On 2 February 2020 the company had a fire, which resulted in inventory costing €8,000 being destroyed. This inventory had been purchased before Christmas and had a selling price of €10,000.
• Trend Ltd, a trade receivable that owed Bookworm Ltd €2,500 at 31 December 2019, went into liquidation on 2 January 2020. The directors do not expect to recover any of this debt.
• A new factory costing €100,000 was purchased in February 2020.

The directors believe all these events are material.

According to IAS 10 *Events after the Reporting Period*, which of the following adjustments are required in the accounts of Bookworm Ltd for the year ended 31 December 2019?
(a) Inventory reduced by €8,000; trade receivables reduced by €2,500; property increased by €100,000.
(b) Inventory reduced by €10,000; trade receivables remain the same; property increased by €100,000.
(c) Inventory reduced by €8,000; trade receivables reduced by €2,500; property remains the same.
(d) Inventory remains the same; trade receivables reduced by €2,500; property remains the same.
 (Based on Chartered Accountants Ireland, Prof II Financial Accounting, Autumn 2003, Question 2.4)

Question 23.2

Varsity Ltd manufactures school uniforms. The company's draft accounts for the year ended 31 December 2019 indicated a retained earnings figure of €34,500. During the course of the audit the following information was made available:
• In January 2020 the directors proposed a final dividend for the year ended 31 December 2019 of €5,500.
• Machinery costing €10,000 was destroyed in a fire in February 2020. The carrying amount of this machinery at 31 December 2019 was €6,000.
• Inventory originally costing €12,000 was discovered to have a net realisable value of €10,000 as at 31 December 2019. No entries have been made in the company's draft accounts for the year ended 31 December 2019 in respect of the above items.

After adjusting (where necessary) for the above items, the company's retained profit for the year ended 31 December 2019 will be:
(a) €21,000
(b) €27,000
(c) €28,500
(d) €32,500.
 (Based on Chartered Accountants Ireland, Prof II Financial Accounting, Summer 2004, Question 2.8)

Question 23.3

Superstar Plc is finalising its financial statements for the year ended 31 December 2019. The following events occurred after the reporting date but before the financial statements were authorised for issue.
1. The value of the US Dollar fell and this resulted in a material foreign exchange loss on the company's US Dollar account.
2. The shares in a listed company in which the company has a holding fell in value and are now worth significantly less than at 31 December 2019.
3. The company declared dividends.
4. A court case has been settled that has confirmed that the company owes an employee a significant sum of money. At 31 December 2019 no provision was included in the financial statements as it was not considered probable that a liability would materialise.

Requirement Write a memorandum to the directors advising them on how each of the above items should be dealt with in accordance with IAS 10 *Events after the Reporting Period*, stating in each case whether an event is an adjusting or a non-adjusting event.
20 Minutes
 (Based on Chartered Accountants Ireland, Prof II Financial Accounting, Summer 2006, Question 5)

Question 23.4

IAS 10 *Events after the Reporting Period* relates to a period of time after the reporting date.

Requirement What is that time period?
 (Based on Chartered Accountants Ireland, CAP 1 Financial Accounting, Summer 2008, Question 1.7)

Income Taxes

Having studied this chapter, readers should be able to:
1. account for the current reporting period's tax charge.

24.1 INTRODUCTION

Companies are liable to corporation tax on their profits and they must recognise the tax expense or refund in the period to which it relates.

IAS 12 *Income Taxes* sets out the accounting rules in relation to income tax charges. When the financial statements are being prepared an estimate is made of the current year's tax charge/refund. Estimates are based on the information available.

24.2 ACCOUNTING FOR CURRENT TAX CHARGE

An estimate is made at the reporting date for the corporation tax charge for the period. The tax charge must be recognised in the financial statements in the period to which it relates. The tax charge will not have been paid at the reporting date so it is a liability in the statement of financial position (SOFP). IAS 12 *Income Taxes* sets out the accounting rules in relation to both current year's tax charge and deferred tax. (Deferred tax is beyond the scope of this textbook.)

It is important to note that the tax liability should be presented as a separate line item in the current liabilities section of the SOFP; it should **not** be combined with any other items.

Example 24.1 deals with the journal entries in relation to the income tax expense and the presentation in the financial statements.

EXAMPLE 24.1: PRESENTATION OF CURRENT TAX

Power Ltd estimates its tax charge for the reporting period ended 31 December 2019 at €185,000. Power made profit before tax of €1,134,500 in the period.

Requirement Prepare the journal entries to recognise the tax expense and the extracts from the financial statements.

Solution

	Debit €	Credit €
Income tax expense	185,000	
Tax liability account		185,000

To recognise the tax liability at the reporting date.

	Debit €	Credit €
SPLOCI – income tax expense	185,000	
Income tax expense account		185,000

To charge the tax expense to the SPLOCI.

STATEMENT OF PROFIT OR LOSS AND OTHER COMPREHENSIVE INCOME (EXTRACT)
for the year ended 31 December 2019

	€
Profit before tax	1,134,500
Income tax expense	(185,000)
Profit for year	949,500

STATEMENT OF FINANCIAL POSITION (EXTRACT)
as at 31 December 2019

	€
Current Liabilities	
Income tax	185,000

An entity estimates its tax charge for the year when it prepares its financial statements for the reporting period. If the amount subsequently paid to the taxation authorities is different from the amount charged to the statement of profit or loss (SPLOCI), then this results in an under- or over-provision that must be corrected in the next reporting period. As a result, the income tax expense in the SPLOCI is made up of:

current year's tax charge
plus under-provision from previous reporting period
or
less (over-) provision from previous reporting period.

Example 24.2 demonstrates the accounting implications for the current reporting period of an under-provision of tax in the previous reporting period.

EXAMPLE 24.2: UNDER-PROVISION OF TAX IN PREVIOUS REPORTING PERIOD

Argent Ltd began trading on 1 January 2018. At the reporting date, 31 December 2018, management estimates its tax liability at €58,000.

On 30 September 2019 Argent paid its tax bill for 2018, which was finalised as €64,200.

As at 31 December 2019 management estimates its tax liability at €101,150.

Requirement:
(a) Prepare the journal entry to recognise the tax charge for the year ended 31 December 2018.
(b) What is the tax charge in the SPLOCI for the year ended 31 December 2018?
(c) What is the tax charge in the SPLOCI for the year ended 31 December 2019?
(d) Prepare the journal entry to recognise the tax charge for the year ended 31 December 2019.
(e) Prepare the tax liability and tax expense accounts for the years ended 31 December 2018 and 2019.

Solution
(a)

	Debit €	Credit €
Income tax expense account	58,000	
Tax liability account		58,000

To recognise the tax liability at the reporting date, 31 December 2018.

SPLOCI – income tax expense	58,000	
Income tax expense account		58,000

To recognise the tax expense in the SPLOCI.

(b) Income tax charge in the SPLOCI for the year ended 31 December 2018 is €58,000.
(c) Income tax charge in the SPLOCI for the year ended 31 December 2019 is €107,350.

The tax charge to the SPLOCI is made up of the current year's charge and the under-provision for last year's charge.

	€
Current year's tax charge (2019)	101,150
Under-provision from 2018 (€64,200 – €58,000)	6,200
	107,350

The estimate made in relation to the tax expense was incorrect. The difference between the estimate and the actual amount is taken into the tax charge in the reporting period that the difference was discovered. As with any change in an accounting estimate, the change is accounted for prospectively.

(d)

	Debit €	Credit €
Income tax expense account	107,350	
Tax liability account		107,350

To recognise the tax liability at the reporting date – 31 December 2019.

SPLOCI – income tax expense	107,350	
Income tax expense account		107,350

To recognise the tax expense in the SPLOCI.

(e)

TAX LIABILITY ACCOUNT

Date	Account Name	€	Date	Account Name	€
31/12/2018	Balance c/d	58,000	31/12/2018	Tax expense	58,000
30/09/2019	Bank	64,200	01/01/2019	Balance b/d	58,000
31/12/2019	Balance c/d	101,150	31/12/2019	Tax expense	107,350
		165,350			165,350
			01/01/2020	Balance b/d	101,150

TAX EXPENSE ACCOUNT

Date	Account Name	€	Date	Account Name	€
31/12/2018	Tax liability	58,000	31/12/2018	SPLOCI – tax expense	58,000
31/12/2019	Tax liability	107,350	31/12/2019	SPLOCI – tax expense	107,350

(Try **Review Questions 24.1** and **24.2** at the end of this chapter.)

24.3 DISCLOSURE

The major components of the tax charge are disclosed separately. Deferred tax is not considered in this textbook so, disregarding deferred tax, the components of the tax charge that would need to be disclosed separately are:
• the current year's tax charge, and
• any under-/over-provision for the previous year.

Example 24.3 deals with the disclosure note in relation to current tax.

EXAMPLE 24.3: DISCLOSURE NOTE

Winston Ltd has charged €389,550 to its SPLOCI for the year ended 31 December 2019. Winston Ltd had under-provided for its tax charge by €15,200 in the year ended 31 December 2018.

Requirement Prepare the disclosure note in relation to the financial statements for the year ended 31 December 2019.

Solution

The tax charge is made up of:

	€
Current year's tax charge	374,350
Under-provision for the year ended 31 December 2018	15,200
	389,550

24.4 IAS 12 COMPARED WITH FRS 102

The treatment outlined in FRS 102 *The Financial Reporting Standard applicable in the UK and Republic of Ireland* in relation to current taxes is the same as that in IAS 12.

24.5 CONCLUSION

The income tax expense in the SPLOCI is made up of the current year's estimate and the under-/over-provision in relation to the previous reporting period.

The tax liability is presented under current liabilities as a separate line item.

SUMMARY OF LEARNING OBJECTIVES

After having studied this chapter, readers should be able to:

Learning Objective 1 Account for the current reporting period's tax charge.

In the trial balance, before the tax charge in the current year is accounted for, a debit balance on the tax liability account means that there was an under-provision for tax in the previous reporting period.

In the trial balance, before the tax charge in the current year is accounted for, a credit balance on the tax liability account means that there was an over-provision for tax in the previous reporting period.

The income tax charge is made up of the current year's tax charge plus/minus the under-/over-provision from the previous reporting period.

The tax liability is presented as a separate line item in the current liabilities section of the SOFP.

QUESTIONS

Review Questions

(See **Appendix A** for Solutions to Review Questions.)

Question 24.1
Bumble Ltd began trading on 1 July 2019 and prepares its financial statements to 30 June. For the year ended 30 June 2020 the management of Bumble estimates its tax liability at €21,300.

Requirement Prepare the journal entry and ledger account in relation to tax for the year-end 30 June 2020.

Question 24.2
Drizzle Ltd began trading on 1 January 2019 and prepares its financial statements to 31 December. For the year ended 31 December 2019 the management of Drizzle estimates its tax liability at €82,450.

On 30 September 2020 Drizzle paid its tax liability in full; the amount paid was €91,500.

Requirement Prepare the journal entries and ledger account using the information above.

25

Property, Plant and Equipment

LEARNING OBJECTIVES

Having studied this chapter, readers should be able to:
1. determine the cost of an item of property, plant and equipment;
2. explain the relevant measurement models available to an entity, i.e. the cost model and the revaluation model;
3. calculate the depreciation charge;
4. account for the revaluation of an asset;
5. account for the profit/gain or loss on disposal of an asset; and
6. prepare disclosure notes in relation to property, plant and equipment.

25.1 INTRODUCTION

Items of property, plant and equipment are classified as non-current assets in the statement of financial position (SOFP) because they are intended for use in the business for more than one reporting period (see **Chapter 6, Property, Plant and Equipment, and Depreciation**). Examples of property, plant and equipment include buildings and motor vehicles. IAS 16 *Property, Plant and Equipment* sets out the accounting rules in relation to such non-current assets. Intangible assets (e.g. goodwill and capitalised development costs) and investments, although presented under the non-current assets section of the SOFP, are not covered by IAS 16.

A fundamental principle of accounting is matching the revenue earned with costs incurred to generate revenue in the same reporting period. This chapter explains how to account for items of property, plant and equipment from initial recognition at the date of purchase to derecognition on the disposal or retirement of an asset.

25.2 CLASSES OF PROPERTY, PLANT AND EQUIPMENT

There are many different classes of property, plant and equipment, including:
• buildings;
• machinery;
• plant and equipment; and
• motor vehicles.

It is important to note that the same accounting treatment must be applied for all of the assets in a particular class. For example, an entity cannot use one accounting treatment for one building and another accounting treatment for another building.

25.3 TERMINOLOGY

A number of accounting estimates are used in relation to property, plant and equipment. In **Chapter 22, Accounting Policies, Changes in Accounting Estimates and Errors** the concept of an accounting estimate is explained. An accounting estimate is based on the information available at the date that the estimate is made; estimates should be reviewed annually. Changes in accounting estimates are applied to the period in which the change is made and future reporting periods, i.e. applied prospectively.

The **useful life** of an asset is defined by IAS 16, paragraph 6, as "(a) the period over which an asset is expected to be available for use by an entity; or (b) the number of production or similar units expected to be obtained from the asset by the entity". The assessment of an asset's useful life is based on the information available at a particular date. Factors considered in determining this accounting estimate include:
- intended usage of the asset. The usage of the asset will be based on the capacity of the asset as indicated by the manufacturer's or the entity's past experience of the same or similar assets;
- wear and tear of the assets considering the usage of the asset and the maintenance programme followed by the entity;
- obsolescence due to either technical or commercial changes; and
- legal or similar limits on the use of the asset.

Residual value is an accounting estimate; it is the amount for which the entity expects to be able to sell the item of property, plant and equipment at the end of its useful life.

Depreciable amount is the total amount of depreciation that should be charged over the useful life of the asset. Depreciable amount is the difference between the cost of the asset and its residual value. It is appropriate that the total amount of depreciation charged over the useful life should be the depreciable amount of the asset as this is the cost of the asset to the entity.

Depreciation is defined by IAS 16 as "the systematic allocation of the depreciable amount of an asset over its useful life." The depreciation methods and calculations are explained in **Chapter 6**. Land is generally not depreciated because the value of land tends to increase over time.

25.4 INITIAL RECOGNITION

When an entity purchases an item of property, plant and equipment it must recognise the asset in the financial statements. Assets are always initially recognised at cost.

There are a number of costs that are incurred when an item of property, plant and equipment is purchased. Examples of these costs are the purchase price, transport costs, installation costs, and legal or professional costs. In deciding whether a cost should be capitalised (included in the cost of the asset and recognised in the SOFP) or expensed to the statement of profit or loss and other comprehensive income (SPLOCI), consider whether the cost is '**directly attributable**' to bringing the asset to the location and condition necessary for it to be capable of operating in the manner intended by management. 'Directly attributable' means that the cost relates specifically to the purchase of the asset – if the asset had not been purchased, the cost would not have been incurred.

Figure 25.1 provides examples of costs that can and cannot be included in the cost of an asset.

FIGURE 25.1: MEASUREMENT OF THE INITIAL COST OF AN ASSET

Costs that can be included	Costs that cannot be included
• Purchase price • Import duties • Non-refundable purchase taxes • Initial estimate of dismantling the asset at the end of its useful life • Employee costs in relation to the construction or acquisition of the asset • Cost of site preparation • Initial delivery and handling costs • Installation and assembly costs • Professional fees • Costs of testing that the asset is operating properly	• Cost of opening a new facility • Costs of introducing a new product or service • Costs of conducting business in a new location or with a new customer • Administration costs • Other general overheads • Costs incurred while an asset is capable of being operated in the manner intended but has not yet been brought into use or is not operating at full capacity • Initial operating losses • Costs of relocating/reorganising part of the entity's operations

The initial cost is reduced by any trade discounts or rebates received.

When an item of property, plant and equipment is purchased, the costs associated with its acquisition are capitalised and the asset is recognised and presented in the entity's SOFP. To recognise the item of property, plant and equipment at the date of purchase, the journal entry posted in the accounting records of the entity is:

	Debit €	Credit €
Property, plant and equipment – cost account	X	
Bank/other payables/loan account		X

To initially recognise property, plant and equipment.

Examples 25.1 and **25.2** demonstrate the cost at which property, plant and equipment is recognised in the financial statements.

EXAMPLE 25.1: INITIAL RECOGNITION OF AN ASSET

Brighton Ltd purchased a machine for use in the production process on 1 January 2019. The list price of the machine was €500,000 and the supplier offered a trade discount of 5%. The machine needs to be installed by a specialist engineer and the fee for this work is €10,000.

Requirement Prepare the journal entry to recognise the asset in the accounting records of Brighton Ltd as at 1 January 2019.

Solution

	Debit €	Credit €
Property, plant and equipment – cost account	485,000	
Other payables account		485,000

To recognise the building at cost on 1 January 2019.

WORKING

	€
Cost of asset	500,000
Less: trade discount 5%	(25,000)
Plus: installation costs	10,000
	485,000

EXAMPLE 25.2: INITIAL RECOGNITION OF ASSET

Drumm Ltd has incurred the following costs in relation to the construction of its new warehouse distribution building:

	€
Site cost	540,000
Preparing site for building work	120,000
Construction costs	1,350,000
Share of general administration costs	60,000

Requirement Prepare the journal entry to recognise the asset in the accounting records of Drumm Ltd.

Solution

	Debit €	Credit €
Property, plant and equipment – cost account	2,010,000	
Other payables account		2,010,000

To recognise the warehouse at cost (€540,000 + €120,000 + €1,350,000).

The costs representing the "share of general administration costs" are not capitalised as they appear to be an allocation of existing costs incurred as a result of the construction of the warehouse.

(Try **Review Question 25.1** at the end of this chapter.)

25.5 DEPRECIATION

Depreciation is used to charge the depreciable amount of the item of property, plant and equipment to SPLOCI over the period that the entity will be able to generate benefits from the use of the asset. The depreciation method chosen reflects the pattern of the entity's usage of the asset over its useful life. The two most widely used methods are:
- straight-line method, and
- reducing-balance method.

Straight-line Method

If the benefit from the use of the item of property, plant and equipment is expected to occur evenly over its useful life, then the straight-line method is appropriate. For example, the benefit from the use of a building would be expected to be constant over its useful life so the straight-line method of depreciation would be used.

Reducing-balance Method

The reducing-balance method is most frequently used to depreciate motor vehicles. The reason for this is that motor vehicles tend to reduce in value by higher amounts in the early years of ownership than in later periods.

To calculate the depreciation charge under the reducing-balance method, the **carrying amount** of the asset is multiplied by the depreciation rate.

It is important to note that assets may be purchased or sold at anytime during the reporting period. When an asset is not owned for the full reporting period, the entity must make a choice as to how to account for depreciation in the periods that the asset was purchased or sold. There are two options available:
- time apportion the depreciation charge in both the year of acquisition and the year the asset is sold; or
- charge a full year's depreciation in relation to the asset in the year it is purchased and none in the year it is sold.

The accounting for and calculation of depreciation were explained in detail in **Section 6.3** of **Chapter 6**.

(Try **Review Question 25.2** at the end of this chapter.)

25.6 CHANGES IN ACCOUNTING ESTIMATES

The accounting rules in relation to changes in accounting estimates are set out in IAS 8 *Changes in Accounting Policy, Accounting Estimates and Errors*, see **Chapter 22**.

An estimate is an entity's best guess at a particular point in time. The estimate is based on the entity's past experience and knowledge of the business. As additional information becomes available the entity might decide that earlier estimates are no longer appropriate and need to be amended to reflect this new information. To reflect this change in estimate, simply apply the new information in the period that the new information becomes available and future periods; IAS 8 uses the term "**apply prospectively**".

The estimates used in the accounting for property, plant and equipment include:
• setting useful lives of assets;
• determining the residual value of the asset at the end of its useful life; and
• depreciation method that best matches the pattern that benefits are generated from the use of the asset, i.e. straight-line or reducing-balance method.

Example 25.7 demonstrates the calculations involved in accounting for a change in an accounting estimate when there is change in the useful life of the asset.

EXAMPLE 25.7: CHANGE IN USEFUL LIFE

Williams Ltd acquired a machine on 1 January 2016 for €800,000 and its useful life was estimated at 20 years.

On 1 January 2019 a review was undertaken of useful lives, residual values and depreciation methods used in relation to property, plant and equipment. The review found that this machine had a remaining useful life of 10 years.

Requirement Calculate the depreciation charge for the year ended 31 December 2019.

Solution

Step 1 Calculate the carrying amount of the machine at the start of the reporting period in which the change in estimate took place.

	€
Cost as at 1 January 2016	800,000
Depreciation for the year ended 31/12/2016	(40,000)
Depreciation for the year ended 31/12/2017	(40,000)
Depreciation for the year ended 31/12/2018	(40,000)
Carrying amount at 31/12/2018	680,000

Step 2 Calculate the revised depreciation charge.

Revised remaining useful life	10 years
Depreciation charge based on new information	= €680,000 ÷ 10 years
	= €68,000

	Debit €	Credit €
SPLOCI – depreciation expense	68,000	
Accumulated depreciation account		68,000

To record the depreciation charge for the year ended 31 December 2019.

A change in residual value is a change in an accounting estimate. A change in residual value will impact the depreciable amount and a revised depreciation charge will have to be calculated for the current and future reporting periods.

Example 25.8 deals with accounting for a change in the residual value of an asset.

EXAMPLE 25.8: CHANGE IN RESIDUAL VALUE

Topple Ltd acquired a piece of equipment on 1 January 2017 for €25,000 and estimates the asset has a useful life of eight years and a residual value of €5,000. Depreciation is charged on a straight-line basis over the useful life of the asset.

On 1 January 2019 the residual value was reviewed and a more appropriate estimate was considered to be €1,200.

Requirement Calculate the depreciation charge for the year ended 31 December 2019.

Solution

Annual depreciation charge = depreciable amount ÷ expected useful life in years

$$= \frac{€25,000 - €5,000}{8 \text{ years}}$$

= €2,500 per annum

	€
Cost as at 1 January 2017	25,000
Depreciation year ended 31/12/2017	(2,500)
Depreciation year ended 31/12/2018	(2,500)
Carrying Amount 31/12/2018	20,000
Carrying amount as at 1 January 2019	20,000
Residual value (revised)	(1,200)
Depreciable amount	18,800
Remaining useful life (8 years – 2 years)	6 years
Revised depreciation charge (€18,800/6 years)	3,133

	Debit €	Credit €
SPLOCI – depreciation expense	3,133	
Accumulated depreciation account		3,133

To record the depreciation charge for the year ended 31 December 2019.

(Try **Review Questions 25.3** and **25.4** at the end of this chapter.)

25.7 SUBSEQUENT MEASUREMENT

After the item of property, plant and equipment is recognised, the entity has a choice to measure each class of property, plant and equipment using either the cost model or the revaluation model. The model chosen must be used in relation to all items of property, plant and equipment in that particular class. Property tends to increase in value over time, so the revaluation model may be more appropriate to use for assets that have long useful lives. The cost model tends to be used for assets such as motor vehicles and plant and equipment because their values decrease over time and with use.

Cost Model

Under the **cost model** items of property, plant and equipment are recognised at cost and depreciated over their useful lives. They are recognised in the SOFP at their **carrying amount**, i.e. cost less accumulated depreciation and any impairment loss. (Impairment loss is beyond the scope of this textbook.)

Revaluation Model

Under the **revaluation model** items of property, plant and equipment are regularly revalued and recognised at their fair value less any accumulated depreciation and impairment losses. (Impairment losses are beyond the scope of this textbook.) Fair value is the amount that an unrelated party would be prepared to pay for the asset under normal market conditions.

IAS 16 allows an entity to choose between two approaches to revaluations. Either:
1. proportionately restate the asset relative to the difference between the current carrying amount and the revalued figure. For example, if the revalued amount was twice that of the carrying amount, the balances on the cost account and the accumulated depreciation account would be doubled to reflect the change in the value as a result of the revaluation; or
2. the accumulated depreciation at the revaluation date is eliminated against the gross carrying amount (cost) of the asset and then the change in valuation effected.

A revaluation can result in either an increase or a decrease in the carrying amount of an asset. IAS 16 sets out specific rules in relation to the presentation of revaluation gains and losses under four different scenarios. Each scenario is explained below, with **Figures 25.2–25.5** summarising the accounting implications (based on the application of the second of the approaches identified above as this is the more commonly used approach).

Scenario 1 deals with a situation where an asset is revalued for the first time and the fair value is greater than the carrying amount of the asset. The treatment set out here also applies to an asset for which only revaluation increases have ever been recorded.

FIGURE 25.2: IMPACT OF REVALUATION INCREASE (ASSET REVALUED FOR THE FIRST TIME)

Event	Asset revalued and the fair value is greater than the carrying amount
Journal adjustment	Debit (Dr) Asset – cost account / Credit (Cr) Asset – cost account Dr Accumulated depreciation account Cr Revaluation surplus account (OCI gain) (Note 1)
Presentation in SPLOCI	Increase is presented as a revaluation gain in OCI
Impact on SOFP	Carrying amount now equal to revalued amount Balance on the revaluation surplus account is increased by the amount of the revaluation increase

Note 1 In these circumstances the gain on revaluation is presented under 'other comprehensive income' (OCI) in the SPLOCI (see **Chapter 19, Presentation of Financial Statements**). The asset cost account is debited when the amount of the revaluation increase is greater than the accumulated depreciation relating to the asset at the revaluation date. The asset cost account is credited when the amount of the revaluation increase is less than the accumulated depreciation relating to the asset at the revaluation date.

Example 25.9 demonstrates the revaluation of an item of property, plant and equipment using both of the approaches allowed under IAS 16.

EXAMPLE 25.9: REVALUATION APPROACHES

Winger Ltd purchased a building on 1 January 2018 for €1,400,000 and depreciated it at a rate of 2% per annum on a straight-line basis. On 31 December 2019 the asset was revalued to €1,680,000.

Requirement How will Winger account for the revaluation if it:
(a) Proportionately restates the carrying amount of the asset?
(b) Eliminates the accumulated depreciation against the gross carrying amount of the asset?

Solution
(a)

	€
Cost as at 1 January 2018	1,400,000
Depreciation year ended 31 December 2018	(28,000)
Depreciation year ended 31 December 2019	(28,000)
Carrying amount as at 31 December 2019	1,344,000
Revalued to	1,680,000
Revaluation increase	336,000

Revalued to €1,680,000, which is 125% of the current carrying amount
(€1,680,000 ÷ €1,344,000 = 125%)

	Before Revaluation €	After Revaluation €
Cost	1,400,000	1,750,000 (Note 1)
Accumulated depreciation	(56,000)	(70,000) (Note 2)
Carrying amount	1,344,000	1,680,000

Note 1 Cost after revaluation (€1,400,000 × 125%)

Note 2 Accumulated depreciation after revaluation (€56,000 × 125%).

The journal entries to effect these changes in the accounting records, and therefore in the financial statements, are as follows:

	Debit €	Credit €
Buildings – cost account	350,000	
Accumulated depreciation account		14,000
SOPL–OCI – revaluation surplus		336,000

To reflect increase in value.

(b)

The journal entry to reflect this increase in value is:

	Debit €	Credit €
Accumulated depreciation account	56,000	
Buildings – cost account	280,000	
SOPL–OCI – revaluation surplus		336,000

After an asset is revalued the depreciation charge has to be recalculated.

	€
Revalued amount	1,680,000

Remaining useful life
Irrespective of the method used to account for the revaluation, the depreciation charge must be recalculated based on the revalued amount.

Original estimate of useful life (Note 1)	50 years
Depreciated already	2 years
Remaining useful life	48 years
Depreciation charge (€1,680,000 ÷ 48 years)	35,000

Note 1 The asset is depreciated at a rate of 2% per annum, which is equivalent to a 50-year useful life.

Scenario 2 deals with the situation when an asset is revalued for the first time and the fair value is less than the carrying amount of the asset. The treatment set out here also applies to an asset for which only a revaluation decrease has ever been recorded. **Figure 25.3** summarises the accounting implications.

FIGURE 25.3: IMPACT OF REVALUATION DECREASE (ASSET REVALUED FOR THE FIRST TIME)

Event	Asset revalued and fair value is less than carrying amount
Journal adjustment	Dr SPLOCI – P/L (loss on revaluation) Dr Accumulated depreciation account Cr Asset – cost account
Presentation in SPLOCI	Decrease presented as a revaluation loss in the profit or loss section
Impact on SOFP	Carrying amount now equal to revalued amount

Example 25.10 demonstrates the accounting entries in relation to a revaluation of an asset where the fair value is less than the carrying amount.

EXAMPLE 25.10: IMPACT OF REVALUATION DECREASE

Bill Ltd purchased a property for €150,000 on 1 January 2016. Depreciation is charged at a rate of 5% per annum using the straight-line method. The carrying amount as at 31 December 2019 was €120,000.

The asset was revalued for the first time as at 31 December 2019 when it had a fair value of €100,000.

Requirement Prepare the journal entries to reflect the revaluation as at 31 December 2019.

Solution

	€
Carrying amount	120,000
Revalued to	(100,000)
Decrease in value	20,000

	Debit €	Credit €
SPLOCI–P/L – loss on revaluation	20,000	
Accumulated depreciation account	30,000	
Property – cost account		50,000
To recognise the revaluation decrease.		

As can be seen from the above, the revaluation decrease is taken to the SPLOCI as an expense when there is no balance in the revaluation surplus account in relation to the revalued asset.

Scenario 3 deals with the situation where an asset, which had previously been revalued upwards, is subsequently revalued again resulting in a revaluation decrease, i.e. the fair value of the asset is less than its carrying amount. The asset was previously revalued and there is a balance on the revaluation surplus account in relation to this asset. **Figure 25.4** summarises the accounting implications.

FIGURE 25.4: IMPACT OF REVALUATION DECREASE WHEN ASSET PREVIOUSLY REVALUED UPWARDS

Event	Decrease on current revaluation is less than previous revaluation increases	Decrease on current revaluation is greater than previous revaluation increases
	Asset is revalued and its fair value is less than its carrying amount	Asset is revalued and its fair value is less than its carrying amount
Journal adjustment	Dr Revaluation surplus account (OCI loss) Dr Accumulated depreciation account Cr Asset – cost account	Dr SPLOCI–P/L – revaluation loss Dr Revaluation surplus account (OCI loss) Dr Accumulated depreciation account Cr Asset – cost account
Presentation in SPLOCI	Decrease presented as a revaluation loss in the OCI section	Decrease presented as a revaluation loss in **both** the profit or loss and the OCI section
Impact on SOFP	Carrying amount is now equal to the revalued amount Revaluation surplus is reduced by the amount of the revaluation decrease	Carrying amount is now equal to the revalued amount Revaluation surplus is eliminated

Note 1 The amount taken to the profit or loss section of the SPLOCI is the excess of the revaluation decrease over the balance in the revaluation surplus that relates to the revalued asset.

Example 25.11 demonstrates the accounting treatment of the revaluation of an asset that was previously revalued upwards and now its fair value is less than its carrying amount at the previous revaluation date.

EXAMPLE 25.11: ASSET SUBSEQUENTLY REVALUED DOWNWARDS (BALANCE ON REVALUATION SURPLUS RELATES TO THIS ASSET)

Rose Ltd purchased a property for €750,000 on 1 January 2017. The property has a useful life of 40 years and no residual value. The depreciation method is the straight-line method. The property is revalued annually and depreciation is calculated on the opening carrying amount.

The valuations were as follows:

	€
31 December 2018	904,400 (remaining useful life 38 years)
31 December 2019	601,250 (remaining useful life 37 years)

Requirement Prepare the journal entries to reflect the revaluation as at 31 December 2018 and 2019.

Solution
Calculation of change to carrying amount as at 31 December 2018:

	€
Cost as at 1 January 2017	750,000
Depreciation year ended 31 December 2017 (€750,000 ÷ 40 years)	(18,750)
Depreciation year ended 31 December 2018	(18,750)
Carrying amount as at 31 December 2018	712,500
Revalued as at 31 December 2018	904,400
Increase of	191,900

	Debit €	Credit €
Accumulated depreciation account	37,500	
Property – cost account	154,400	
SPLOCI–OCI – revaluation gain		191,900

To recognise the revaluation increase.

Annual depreciation charge after the revaluation at 31 December 2018 = €904,400 ÷ 38 years
= €23,800

Calculation of change to carrying amount as at 31 December 2019:

	€
Revalued as at 31 December 2018	904,400
Depreciation year ended 31 December 2019	(23,800)
Carrying amount as at 31 December 2019	880,600
Revalued as at 31 December 2019	601,250
Decrease of	279,350

The amount of the revaluation decrease on 31 December 2019 is €279,350, which is greater than the revaluation gain that occurred on 31 December 2018. The revaluation loss incurred on 31 December 2019 is presented in both the P/L section and the OCI section. The amount presented in the OCI is the balance on the revaluation surplus account; the amount presented in the P/L is the excess of the revaluation decrease that occurred on 31 December 2019 over the balance on the revaluation surplus account.

	Debit €	Credit €
Accumulated depreciation account	23,800	
SPLOCI – P/L – loss on revaluation	87,450	

SPLOCI–OCI – revaluation loss	191,900
Property – cost account	303,150
To recognise the revaluation decrease.	

Annual depreciation charge after the revaluation at 31 December 2019 = €601,250 ÷ 37 years
= €16,250

As illustrated in **Example 25.11**, a revaluation decrease is generally taken as an expense to the SPLOCI. However, where there is a balance in the revaluation surplus account that relates to the asset that is the subject of the revaluation decrease, then the balance on the revaluation surplus account is first eliminated and any additional write-down is taken to the SPLOCI.

Scenario 4 deals with the situation where an asset, which was previously revalued downwards, is subsequently revalued resulting in a revaluation increase, i.e. the fair value of the asset is higher than its carrying amount. When the asset was previously revalued downwards, a loss was recognised in profit or loss. **Figure 25.5** summarises the accounting implications.

FIGURE 25.5: IMPACT OF REVALUATION INCREASE WHEN ASSET PREVIOUSLY REVALUED DOWNWARDS

Event	Increase on current revaluation is less than previous revaluation decreases	Increase on current revaluation is greater than previous revaluation decreases
	Asset revalued and its fair value is greater than its carrying amount	Asset revalued and its fair value is greater than its carrying amount
Journal adjustment	Dr Accumulated depreciation account Dr/Cr Asset – cost account Cr SPLOCI–P/L (gain on revaluation)	Dr Accumulated depreciation account Dr/Cr Asset – cost account Cr SPLOCI–P/L (gain on revaluation) Cr SPLOCI–OCI – revaluation gain
Presentation in SPLOCI	Increase is presented as a revaluation gain in the profit or loss section	Increase is presented as a revaluation gain in **both** the profit or loss and OCI sections
Impact on SOFP	Carrying amount is now equal to the revalued amount	Carrying amount is now equal to the revalued amount Revaluation surplus is increased by the excess of the current revaluation increase over the previous revaluation decreases

Example 25.12 demonstrates the accounting treatment of the revaluation of an asset that was previously revalued downwards and now its fair value is greater than its carrying amount at the previous revaluation date.

EXAMPLE 25.12: ASSET SUBSEQUENTLY REVALUED UPWARDS

Tulip Ltd purchased a property for €800,000 on 1 January 2017. The property has a useful life of 40 years and no residual value. The depreciation method used is the straight-line method. The property is revalued annually and depreciation is calculated on the opening carrying amount.

The valuations were as follows:

	€
31 December 2018	570,000 (remaining useful life 38 years)
31 December 2019	925,000 (remaining useful life 37 years)

Requirement Prepare the journal entries to reflect the revaluations as at 31 December 2018 and 2019.

Solution

Calculation of change to carrying amount as at 31 December 2018:

	€
Cost as at 1 January 2017	800,000
Depreciation year ended 31 December 2017 (€800,000 ÷ 40 years)	(20,000)
Depreciation year ended 31 December 2018	(20,000)
Carrying amount as at 31 December 2018	760,000
Revalued as at 31 December 2018	570,000
Decrease of	190,000

	Debit €	Credit €
Accumulated depreciation account	40,000	
SPLOCI–P/L – loss on revaluation	190,000	
Property – cost account		230,000
To recognise the revaluation decrease.		

Annual depreciation charge after the revaluation at 31 December 2018 = €570,000 ÷ 38 years
= €15,000

Calculation of change to carrying amount as at 31 December 2019:

	€
Revalued as at 31 December 2018	570,000
Depreciation year ended 31 December 2019	(15,000)
Carrying amount as at 31 December 2019	555,000
Revalued as at 31 December 2019	925,000
Increase of	370,000

	Debit €	Credit €
Accumulated depreciation account	15,000	
Property – cost account	355,000	
SPLOCI–P/L – revaluation gain		190,000
SPLOCI–OCI – revaluation gain		180,000
To recognise revaluation increase.		

Annual depreciation charge after the revaluation at 31 December 2019 = €925,000 ÷ 37 years
= €25,000

As illustrated in **Example 25.12**, a revaluation increase is generally taken to the revaluation surplus account unless the revalued asset was previously reduced in value on an earlier revaluation in which case only the excess over the previous revaluation decrease(s) is then taken to the revaluation surplus account.

Transfers from the Revaluation Surplus Account

IAS 16 allows the entity two options in relation to the balance on the revaluation surplus account. Entities can either:

1. leave the balance on the revaluation surplus account until the asset is sold and then transfer it to retained earnings; or
2. transfer an amount each year from the revaluation surplus to offset against the higher depreciation charge on the revalued asset. The amount that can be transferred is limited to the difference between:
   (a) the depreciation charge based on the revalued amount; and
   (b) the original depreciation charge.

The transfer out of revaluation surplus is presented in the statement of changes in equity (SOCIE) and is accounted for as follows:

	Debit €	Credit €
Revaluation surplus account	X	
Retained earnings account		X

(Try **Review Questions 25.5** and **25.6** at the end of this chapter.)

25.8 DISPOSAL OF AN ITEM OF PROPERTY, PLANT AND EQUIPMENT

When an asset is sold it needs to be 'derecognised', i.e. the asset is no longer presented in the financial statements. Over the period of ownership, the entity has estimated the benefit it has derived from the use of the asset; this estimate of the use of the asset is recognised in the accumulated depreciation account. When the asset is sold it may achieve a selling price larger or smaller than its carrying amount; this difference is accounted for as follows:

- When the asset is sold for an amount greater than its carrying amount at its disposal date, then a profit on disposal is recognised.
- When the asset is sold for an amount less than its carrying amount at its disposal date, then a loss on disposal is recognised.

When an asset is disposed of, a disposal account is opened. The following amounts are transferred to this account:

- cost/revalued amount of asset (Dr disposal account and Cr property, plant and equipment – cost/revalued amount);
- accumulated depreciation in relation to the asset (Dr accumulated depreciation and Cr disposal account);
- proceeds received on disposal (Dr bank/other receivables account and Cr disposal account); and
- the balance on the disposal account is either the profit/gain or the loss on disposal (Dr disposal account and Cr SPLOCI – profit on disposal of non-current asset or Dr SPLOCI – loss on disposal of non-current asset and Cr disposal account).

Example 25.13 demonstrates the accounting entries to record the disposal of an asset in the financial statements.

EXAMPLE 25.13: DISPOSAL OF AN ITEM OF PROPERTY, PLANT AND EQUIPMENT

A machine was sold for €23,800. At the disposal date the accumulated depreciation in relation to this machine was €32,000. The asset originally cost €50,000.

Requirement Prepare the ledger accounts and journal entries to record the disposal of the machine.

This example is focused on the accounting entries only. The dates of the transactions have not been provided so the date column has been left out of the ledger accounts.

Solution

Ledger accounts

MACHINE – COST ACCOUNT

Account Name	€	Account Name	€
Balance b/d	50,000	Disposal account	50,000

MACHINE – ACCUMULATED DEPRECIATION ACCOUNT

Account Name	€	Account Name	€
Disposal account	32,000	Balance b/d	32,000

DISPOSAL ACCOUNT

Account Name	€	Account Name	€
Machine – cost	50,000	Accumulated depreciation	32,000
SPLOCI – profit on disposal	5,800	Bank/other receivables	23,800
	55,800		55,800

Journal entries

	Debit €	Credit €
Disposal account	50,000	
Machine – cost account		50,000
To derecognise cost of non-current asset on disposal.		
Accumulated depreciation account	32,000	
Disposal account		32,000
To eliminate the accumulated depreciation on the non-current asset sold.		
Bank/other receivables account	23,800	
Disposal account		23,800
To recognise the proceeds from the disposal of a non-current asset.		
Disposal account	5,800	
SPLOCI – profit on disposal		5,800
To recognise profit on disposal of non-current asset.		

(Try **Review Questions 25.7** and **25.8** at the end of this chapter.)

25.9 DISCLOSURE

The disclosure required by IAS 16 is to help the users of financial statements to understand the figures presented in relation to the property, plant and equipment. In the published financial statements a single figure is presented in the SOFP for 'property, plant and equipment'. This single figure is at too high a level, i.e. it does not provide enough detail, to enable users to understand the assumptions used by management in arriving at this total figure. Users of financial statements need to be able to understand the figures presented and how they are arrived at so they can compare these figures over time for the entity and with other entities operating in the same industry.

The disclosure requirements for property, plant and equipment in the financial statements are as follows:
- the useful life of each class,
- the residual value,
- the depreciation method used for each class,
- whether the cost model or revalulation model is used for each class,
- any changes in accounting estimates,
- a reconciliation to show the transactions that resulted in the difference between the opening and closing carrying amounts. These transactions are typically:
  - purchase of new property, plant and equipment,
  - disposal of property, plant and equipment,
  - revaluation of property, plant and equipment,
  - depreciation charge on property, plant and equipment, and
  - impairment of property, plant and equipment.

The purpose of **Example 25.14** is to show how the information from the financial records is presented in the disclosure notes.

EXAMPLE 25.14: DISCLOSURE

You are provided with the following ledger accounts for the year ended 31 December 2019:

MACHINE – COST ACCOUNT

Date	Account Name	€	Date	Account Name	€
01/01/2019	Balance b/d	2,100,000	15/09/2019	Disposal	500,000
10/03/2019	Bank (Additions)	300,000	31/12/2019	Balance c/d	1,900,000
		2,400,000			2,400,000
01/01/2020	Balance b/d	1,900,000			

MACHINE – ACCUMULATED DEPRECIATION ACCOUNT

Date	Account Name	€	Date	Account Name	€
15/09/2019	Disposal	230,000	01/01/2019	Balance b/d	420,000
31/12/2019	Balance c/d	380,000	31/12/2019	Depreciation	190,000
		610,000			610,000
			01/01/2020	Balance b/d	380,000

Requirement Prepare the reconciliation of the opening carrying amount to the closing carrying amount for machines as it would appear in the disclosure note to the financial statements.

Solution

	€
Cost	
As at 1 January 2019	2,100,000
Additions	300,000
Disposals	(500,000)
As at 31 December 2019	1,900,000
Accumulated Depreciation	
As at 1 January 2019	420,000
Charge for year	190,000
Disposal	(230,000)
As at 31 December 2019	380,000
Carrying amount as at 31 December 2019	1,520,000
Carrying amount as at 31 December 2018	1,680,000

Note: in the SOFP the following would be presented in relation to property, plant and equipment.

	2019 €	2018 €
Property, plant and machinery	1,520,000	1,680,000

(Try **Review Questions 25.9** and **25.10** at the end of this chapter.)

25.10 IAS 16 COMPARED WITH FRS 102

The treatment outlined in FRS 102 in relation to property, plant and equipment is broadly the same as that in IAS 16. Section 17 of FRS 102 does not outline the approach to deal with revaluations in the same detail as IAS 16, which identifies two methods:
- eliminate accumulated depreciation against the gross carrying amount of the asset and then effect the revaluation adjustment; or
- proportionately restate the cost and accumulated depreciation to reflect the revalued amount.

Under FRS 102 an entity is not required to make the following disclosures:
- the amount of expenditures recognised in the carrying amount of an item of property, plant and equipment in the course of its construction (IAS 16, paragraph 74 (b));
- if it is not disclosed separately in the statement of comprehensive income, the amount of compensation from third parties for items of property, plant and equipment that were impaired, lost or given up that is included in profit or loss (IAS 16, paragraph 74 (d)); and
- the revaluation surplus, indicating the change for the period and any restrictions on the distribution of the balance to shareholders (IAS 16, paragraph 77 (f)).

FRS 102 requires the methods and significant assumptions used in estimating fair value to be disclosed; there is no such requirement under IAS 16.

EXAM TIPS

- The main areas where students lose marks in questions related to IAS 16 are:
  - Not picking up whether the company time apportions depreciation charges in the year of purchase and sale **or** charges a full year's depreciation in the year of purchase and none in the year that the asset is sold.
  - When calculating annual depreciation charge, not dealing correctly with the residual value.
  - When calculating the profit or loss on sale of an asset, not calculating the depreciation for the correct number of years to determine the **carrying amount** of the asset.
  - Using the straight-line method instead of the reducing-balance method and vice versa.
- When instructed where to present depreciation charge in the SPLOCI, follow the guidance provided in the question. If no guidance is given, the following approach should be followed in relation to the presentation of the depreciation expense in SPLOCI:
  - property, plant and equipment should be made to cost of sales;
  - motor vehicles should be made to selling and distribution costs; and
  - office buildings should be made to administration expenses.
- For revaluations, always check if the remaining life of the asset has been affected by the revaluation or remains the same as the original expectation.
- Always remember to recalculate the new depreciation charge after a revaluation.
- When there is a change in accounting estimate (change in depreciation method, useful life or residual value), always apply the change prospectively.
- You need to be able to prepare the journal entries to derecognise the asset disposed of during the reporting period

25.11 CONCLUSION

This chapter describes the rules in relation to accounting for property, plant and equipment. On initial recognition, an item of property, plant and equipment is recorded at cost. 'Cost' includes any expenses directly attributable to bringing an asset to its present location and condition.

The entity must make a number of choices and decisions in relation to accounting for the cost of the asset, including:
- choosing between the accounting policies of the cost model and the revaluation model;
- making an estimate of the useful life of the asset;
- making an estimate of the expected residual value at the end of the asset's useful life; and
- choosing a depreciation method (straight-line or reducing-balance) that best reflects the manner in which benefits will be derived from the use of the asset over its life.

An annual review must be undertaken of the estimates (e.g. depreciation method, useful life and residual value) used in relation to property, plant and equipment. If a change is required in relation to the estimates used by the entity, the change is made in the current and future periods to reflect the new information that is available.

When an asset is disposed of the proceeds of the disposal are compared with the carrying amount of the asset at the disposal date and a profit or loss is recognised in the SPLOCI.

SUMMARY OF LEARNING OBJECTIVES

After having studied this chapter, readers should be able to:

Learning Objective 1 Determine the cost of an item of property, plant and equipment.

The cost of property, plant and equipment includes costs **directly attributable** to the purchase of the asset.

Learning Objective 2 Explain the measurement models available to an entity, i.e. the cost model and the revaluation model.

The entity has an accounting policy choice between the cost and revaluation models; the model chosen must be applied to all assets of a particular class.

Under the cost model an estimate of the useful life and residual value is made and the asset is depreciated over its useful life. The total depreciation charged over the useful life equates to the depreciable amount.

Under the revaluation model the asset is restated at its market value on a regular basis. After each revaluation the depreciation charge on the asset has to be recalculated.

Learning Objective 3 Calculate the depreciation charge.

Depreciation is a measure of the use of the asset and the method selected depends on the pattern of usage of the asset. Useful lives, residual values and depreciation methods are accounting estimates. Estimates have to be reviewed annually and any changes applied in the current period and future periods.

Learning Objective 4 Account for the revaluation of an asset.

You need to be able to account for revaluation increases and decreases and remember to recalculate the depreciation charge after each revaluation. **Figure 25.6** shows where the revaluation gain or loss is presented in the SPLOCI – in the profit or loss section or the other comprehensive income section.

FIGURE 25.6: REVALUATION SURPLUS

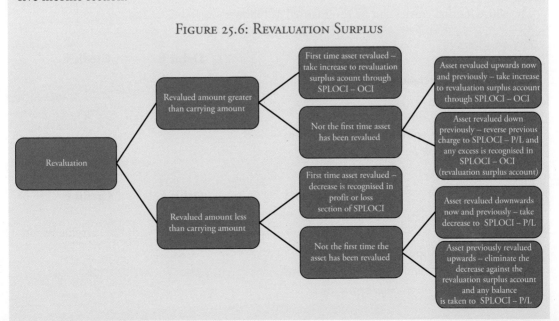

Learning Objective 5 Account for the profit or loss on disposal of an asset.

	Debit €	Credit €
Disposal account	X	
Property, plant and equipment – cost account		X

To derecognise the asset disposed of.

	Debit €	Credit €
Accumulated depreciation account	X	
Disposal account		X

To derecognise accumulated depreciation on the asset disposed of.

	Debit €	Credit €
Bank account	X	
Disposal account		X

To recognise the proceeds from the disposal of the asset.

If the proceeds from the sale of the asset are greater than the carrying amount, then there is a profit on disposal:

	Debit €	Credit €
Disposal account	X	
SPLOCI (profit on disposal)		X

To recognise the profit on the disposal of the asset.

If the proceeds from the sale of the asset are less than the carrying amount, then there is a loss on disposal:

	Debit €	Credit €
SPLOCI (loss on disposal)	X	
Disposal account		X

To recognise the loss on disposal of the asset.

The above journal entries can be summarised as follows:

Profit:

	Debit €	Credit €
Accumulated depreciation account	X	
Bank account	X	
SPLOCI (profit on disposal)		X
Property, plant and equipment – cost account		X

To recognise the profit on disposal of the asset.

Loss:

	Debit €	Credit €
Accumulated depreciation account	X	
Bank account	X	
SPLOCI (loss on disposal)	X	
Property, plant and equipment – cost account		X

To recognise the loss on disposal of the asset.

The profit/loss on disposal is recognised in the SPLOCI in the period that the asset was disposed of.

Learning Objective 6 Prepare disclosure notes in relation to property, plant and equipment.

An entity will need to disclose:
- the components of the cost of items of property, plant and equipment;
- accounting policies used;
- accounting estimates, e.g. depreciation methods and useful lives; and
- a reconciliation of the opening carrying amount to the closing carrying amount.

QUESTIONS

Review Questions

(See **Appendix A** for Solutions to Review Questions.)

Question 25.1

Hamley Ltd purchased a piece of machinery on credit for €250,000 on 10 March 2019. The supplier has agreed a trade discount of 1.5% and offers an early settlement discount of 2% for payment within 30 days. Hanley paid for the equipment on 20 March 2019.

Requirement What are the journal entries to record the purchase and payment of the asset?

Question 25.2

Bloom Ltd bought a piece of equipment on 1 April 2018 for €25,000. Bloom time apportions depreciation in the years of purchase and disposal. Bloom depreciates equipment on a reducing-balance basis at a rate of 20% per annum.

Requirement:
(a) What is the depreciation charge in the year ended 30 June 2018?
(b) What is the depreciation charge in the year ended 30 June 2019?

Question 25.3

An item of plant costing €200,000 on 1 July 2018 was depreciated over a five-year useful life using the straight-line method. On 1 January 2019 the directors revised the remaining useful life of the asset to nine years. The company believes the change provides a fairer reflection of the use of the asset.

The company time apportions depreciation in the years of purchase and disposal.

Requirement:
(a) Calculate the depreciation charge for year ended 31 December 2018.
(b) Calculate the depreciation charge for year ended 31 December 2019.

Question 25.4

Polton Ltd purchased a piece of equipment for €80,000 on 1 October 2017. At the purchase date the useful life was estimated at 10 years and residual value estimated at €5,000. Depreciation is charged on a straight-line basis.

During the review of accounting estimates relating to property, plant and equipment, on 1 January 2019 a more appropriate value for residual value was estimated as €1,500. All other estimates remain the same.

Polton time apportions depreciation for the years of purchase and disposal.

Requirement:
(a) What is the depreciation charge for the year ended 31 December 2017?
(b) What is the depreciation charge for the year ended 31 December 2018?
(c) What is the depreciation charge for the year ended 31 December 2019?

Question 25.5

Moore Ltd purchased a property on 1 January 2018 for €1,500,000. Moore uses the revaluation model to measure properties. Moore estimates the useful life of the property as 40 years.

On 31 December 2019 the property had a fair value of €1,650,000 and the useful life is estimated at 40 years as at the revaluation date.

Requirement:
(a) What is the depreciation charge in relation to the property for the years ended 31 December 2018 and 2019?
(b) What are the accounting entries to record the revaluation as at 31 December 2019?
(c) What is the depreciation charge for the year ended 31 December 2020?

Question 25.6

Newton Ltd purchased a property on 1 January 2018 for €1,200,000. Newton uses the revaluation model to measure properties. Moore estimates the useful life of the property as 50 years.

On 31 December 2018 the property had a fair value of €1,020,000 and the useful life is estimated at 40 years as at the revaluation date.

Requirement:
(a) What is the depreciation charge in relation to the property for the year ended 31 December 2018?
(b) What are the accounting entries to record the revaluation as at 31 December 2018?
(c) What is the depreciation charge for the year ended 31 December 2019?

Question 25.7

Frampton Ltd purchased a machine for €260,000 on 1 January 2016. The useful life is estimated at 10 years and depreciation is charged on a straight-line basis.

Frampton sold the machine for €180,000 on 31 December 2019.

Frampton prepares its financial statements for 31 December. Frampton time apportions the depreciation charge in the year of purchase and the year of disposal.

Requirement:
(a) What is the profit or loss on disposal?
(b) Prepare the ledger accounts in relation to the machine.
(c) Prepare the journal entries to record the disposal of the machine.

Question 25.8

Waldon Ltd purchased a machine for €300,000 on 1 May 2017. The useful life is estimated at five years and depreciation is charged on a straight-line basis.

Waldon sold the machine for €100,000 on 30 September 2019.

Waldon prepares its financial statements for 31 December. Waldon time apportions depreciation in the year of purchase and the year of disposal.

Requirement:
(a) What is the profit or loss on disposal?
(b) Prepare the ledger accounts in relation to the machine.
(c) Prepare the journal entry/(ies) to record the disposal of the machine.

Question 25.9

The following is an extract from the financial statements of Antler Ltd as at 31 December 2019:

	€
Cost of equipment as at 1 January 2019	800,000
Accumulated depreciation as at 1 January 2019	120,000
Equipment purchased during year ended 31 December 2019	130,000
Depreciation charge for year	95,000
Cost of equipment disposed of during the year	75,000
Accumulated depreciation in relation to equipment disposed of during the year	35,000

Requirement Prepare the reconciliation of the carry amount at the beginning and end of the period for inclusion in the disclosure notes to the published financial statements.

Question 25.10

Walter Ltd has provided you with the following extract from the financial statements as at 31 December 2019:

	€
Cost of property as at 1 January 2019	3,900,000
Accumulated depreciation as at 1 January 2019	780,000
Depreciation charge for year	78,000

One of the properties was revalued to €1,280,000 on 31 December 2019. At that date the property had accumulated depreciation of €110,000 and had originally cost €1,100,000. The revaluation has not yet been reflected in the financial statements.

Requirement Prepare the reconciliation of the carry amount at the beginning and end of the period for inclusion in the disclosure notes to the published financial statements.

Challenging Questions

(Suggested Solutions to Challenging Questions are available through your lecturer.)

Question 25.1

McBride Ltd is a transport company. It owns a fleet of trucks which it depreciates at 20% on cost, with depreciation charged on a proportionate basis on additions and disposals made during the year.

At 31 December 2018 it had the following trucks:

Truck	Date of Purchase	Cost €
1	1 January 2016	70,000
2	1 April 2017	80,000
3	1 August 2017	60,000
4	1 March 2018	100,000

On 31 March 2019 McBride disposed of Truck 1 for €10,000.

At 31 December 2019, in light of the small proceeds on disposal and the increased mileage covered by the trucks, it was decided to decrease the useful economic lives of the trucks from five to four years for the year ended 31 December 2019 and thereafter. Trucks are to continue to be depreciated on a straight-line basis.

Requirement:
(a) Calculate the depreciation to be charged to the statement of profit or loss and other comprehensive income for the year ended 31 December 2019.

10 Minutes

(b) Prepare the journal entries to account for trucks and depreciation for the year ended 31 December 2019.

9 Minutes

(c) Give a reason for your treatment of the change in useful economic life from five years to four years.

3 Minutes

(Based on Chartered Accountants Ireland, CAP 1 Autumn 2008, Question 6)

Question 25.2

Part (a)

Cable Ltd has a policy of carrying its property in the financial statements at their revalued amounts. In June 2018, the company purchased a property for €1.9 million. The property had a useful life of 20 years and no residual value. The company charges depreciation on a straight-line basis. A full year's depreciation is charged in the year of acquisition.

At 31 December 2018, the property was valued and the market price had remained at €1.9 million.

At 31 December 2019, the property was again valued and the market price had fallen to €1.5 million.

Requirement:

For each of the years ended 31 December 2018 and 2019, calculate the following:

(i) Depreciation to be charged to the statement of profit or loss and other comprehensive income.

(ii) Revaluation gains/losses to be charged to the Revaluation Surplus and statement of profit or loss and other comprehensive income – profit or loss, or statement of profit or loss and other comprehensive income – other comprehensive income, respectively.

(iii) Carrying amount of the property at the year-end.

10 Minutes

Part (b)

Cable Ltd purchased a machine on 1 January 2011 for €200,000. On acquisition, management determined a useful life of 10 years and a residual value of €20,000 for this particular machine. Cable Ltd charges depreciation using the straight-line method, with a full year's depreciation being charged in the year of acquisition.

On 1 January 2019, the directors reviewed the estimated life and residual value of the asset and determined that the useful life should be extended from 10 to 12 years. As a result, the residual value is expected to reduce to €10,000.

Requirement Calculate the depreciation to be charged in respect of the machine for the year ended 31 December 2019 and determine the carrying amount as at 31 December 2019.

7 Minutes

Part (c)

Describe three possible factors which may have contributed to the increased useful life of the machine in **Part (b)**.

5 Minutes

Part (d)

When a revalued item of property is derecognised (e.g. on disposal of the property), how is the corresponding balance on the revaluation surplus treated in the financial statements?

3 Minutes

(Based on Chartered Accountants Ireland, CAP 1 Autumn 2011, Question 6)

Question 25.3

Freshco Ltd operates a major chain of supermarkets in Ireland under the 'Fresh' brand. During 2019 it acquired a store in Newry to take advantage of the flow of customers into Northern Ireland. It also renovated one of its stores in Dublin.

Newly acquired store – Newry

Before acquiring the supermarket in Newry, Freshco reviewed a number of existing supermarket stores in various border towns. After a comprehensive review, the company decided to acquire the store in Newry. The store required significant renovation expenditure before it could be operated under the 'Fresh' brand. The renovations lasted three months, during which time the store was closed.

The following costs have been incurred in relation to the Newry store:

	€000
Professional fees – survey of various stores prior to decision to acquire Newry store	400
Purchase price of Newry store (including cost of site)	3,500
Legal fees and taxes associated with purchase of store	150
Renovation costs – labour and materials	1,640
New signage erected outside and inside the store	620
Advertising costs to promote store prior to opening	180
In-store promotions during opening week	74
New staff uniforms	28

Renovated store – Dublin

During 2019, Freshco carried out extensive renovation work on one of its larger stores in Dublin. The store now has considerably more available space for in-store promotions and incorporates a restaurant. Freshco's managers are confident that the renovations will attract more customers to the store and, to date, sales have seen a significant increase. The cost of the renovations totalled €280,000. While the renovations were carried out, Freshco also repainted the interior of the store to match the new company brand colours and replaced most of the shelving. The painting cost totalled €9,000 and the shelving totalled €18,000.

Requirement:
(a) Outline the criteria that must be met before Freshco can capitalise any of the expenditure detailed above as property plant and equipment.

5 Minutes

(b) In relation to the newly acquired Newry store, determine the total amount that will be capitalised in 2019.

9 Minutes

(c) In relation to the renovated Dublin store, determine the total amount that will be capitalised in 2009.

7 Minutes

(d) Explain how the company will determine the depreciation charges for 2019 in respect of the amounts capitalised.

5 Minutes

(Based on Chartered Accountants Ireland, CAP 1 Autumn 2010, Question 8)

26

Accounting for Leases

Learning Objectives

Having studied this chapter, readers should be able to:
1. account for short-term and low-value leases from the lessee's perspective;
2. calculate the interest rate implicit in a lease;
3. account for right-of-use assets;
4. prepare the journal entries in relation to leases; and
5. prepare the disclosure notes in relation to leases.

26.1 INTRODUCTION

Leases are a widely used source of finance in businesses today. As of 1 January 2019, IFRS 16 *Leases* became the international accounting standard for leases, replacing IAS 17 Leases. The main impact of the introduction of IFRS 16 is the recognition of more leases in the statement of financial position (SOFP) than previously required by IAS 17. There are two parties to a lease agreement – the lessee and the lessor. In this chapter accounting for leases is considered only from the point of view of the lessee, i.e. the entity making the payments under a lease.

IFRS 16 applies to annual reporting periods beginning on or after 1 January 2019. It sets the accounting rules in relation to the recognition and measurement of leases for both parties to the lease, the lessor and the lessee. The **lessor** is the party that provides the asset and collects the lease payments. The **lessee** is the party that has the use of the asset over the lease term and makes the lease payments.

Implementation of IFRS 16 will result in many organisations recognising most leases in their SOFP. Consequently, these entities will have an increase in the lease liabilities recognised in their SOFPs. There are two exemptions from this recognition – low-value assets and short-term leases.

26.2 DEFINITION OF A LEASE

When an entity becomes a party to a contract, it must determine whether the contract gives rise to a lease obligation. For a contract to give rise to a lease obligation it must provide the lessee with the ability to direct the use of an identified asset for a period of time in exchange for a consideration. In order to direct the use of the asset the lessee must have control of the asset. Control of the asset allows the lessee to:
1. determine how the asset should be used; and
2. obtain substantially all of the benefits from the use of the asset.

The terms of the contract should be reviewed and each of the following questions considered in this order:
1. Is there an identifiable asset?
2. Does the lessee decide how the asset is to be used?
3. Does the lessee receive substantially all the economic benefits from the use of the asset?

If the answer to each of the questions is 'Yes', then the contract is, or contains, a lease. The entity must then capitalise the asset and recognise the lease liability **unless**:

(a) the lease is short term , that is less than 12 months' duration and there is no repurchase option; or
(b) the asset value is low when new.

If the answer to any of the three questions above is 'No', then the contract does not provide evidence of the existence of a lease. In this situation, neither the asset nor a lease obligation are recognised in the financial statements and the rental made under the contract is treated as expenses in the SOPL in the period that they are incurred.

26.3 ACCOUNTING BY LESSEES

Under IFRS 16, once a lessee has the right to direct the use of the asset at the inception of the lease and makes payments over the lease term then an asset and a financing obligation is recognised in the financial statements. An asset held under a lease is subject to depreciation in the same way as other non-current assets.

Under IAS 17, leases were classified as either operating leases or finance leases. The implementation of IFRS 16 means this classification no longer applies.

IFRS 16 allows entities two exclusions from the requirements to recognise an asset and a lease obligation:
1. when the lease term is for 12 months or less and there is no purchase option within the contract; and
2. when the asset is low value, e.g. a computer.

IFRS 16 allows the entity to either:
- recognise the expense on a straight-line or other systematic basis to allow the lease cost to be taken to the statement of profit or loss (SOPL) in a manner that ensures the 'matching principle' is applied. The timing of payments under the lease contract, and their recognition as an expense in the SOPL, may result in either an accrual or a prepayment; or
- recognise the leased asset and related obligation in the SOFP.

Example 26.1 illustrates the accounting treatment for a lease of a low-value asset.

EXAMPLE 26.1: LOW-VALUE ASSET LEASE

On 1 February 2020, Pear Plc leased a laptop for one of its sales team. The laptop has a cost of €2,000. Under the terms of the lease agreement:

Quarterly payments	€240 commencing on 1 February 2020
Interest rate implicit in the lease	8%
Term of the lease	2 years

All payments were made on time.

Pear Plc has elected to account for the lease as an expense.

Requirement Prepare the journal to recognise the lease expense in the financial statements for the year ended 31 December 2020.

Solution

The following payments were made in relation to the lease during the reporting period ended 31 December 2020:

1 February 2020	€240
1 May 2020	€240
1 August 2020	€240
1 November 2020	€240

The payment made on 1 November 2020 relates to the period 1 November 2020 to 31 January 2021. Part of the payment relates to the next reporting period and constitutes a prepayment.

The journal entry to reflect the lease transaction in the financial records is:

	Debit €	Credit €
SOPL–P/L – Lease expense	880	
Prepayment	80	
Bank		960

To record the lease expense for the period.

When discussing leases, reference is often made to payments being 'in advance' or 'in arrears'. This simply refers to the timing of payments under the lease contract. For example, if a lease is taken out on 1 January 2019 and requires annual payments to be made in advance, the first payment will be made on 1 January 2019 and annually thereafter. If a lease is taken out on 1 January 2019 and requires annual payments to be made in arrears, the first payment will be made on 31 December 2019 and annually thereafter.

Under lease agreements, payments can be made at any stage over the lease term. The finance (or interest) expense is recognised in the SOPL over the lease term at the **interest rate implicit in the lease**. The interest rate is the rate at which if the payments were discounted under the lease, the sum of those discounted payments would equal the asset cost at the start of the lease. Discounting means re-stating the future leases payments at their present value. Only future payments are discounted, any payment made when the lease is initially taken out is not subject to discounting.

The calculation of the interest rate implicit in the lease when the same annual lease payments are made under the lease agreement involves the use of cumulative discount factors and annuity tables. The cumulative discount factor is calculated as:

$$\frac{\text{Asset cost}}{\text{Annual lease payment}}$$

and provides an estimate figure of the annuity factor. This estimated figure can then be used to ascertain the actual discounted interest rate by reference to an annuity table. An extract of an annuity table is shown in **Figure 26.1** below and is used in **Example 26.2** to demonstrate how to determine the interest rate implicit in a lease when payments are in arrears.

FIGURE 26.1: ANNUITY TABLE (EXTRACT)

Periods (n)	Discount rates (r)									
	1%	**2%**	**3%**	**4%**	**5%**	**6%**	**7%**	**8%**	**9%**	**10%**
1	0.990	0.980	0.971	0.962	0.952	0.943	0.935	0.926	0.917	0.909
2	1.970	1.942	1.913	1.886	1.859	1.833	1.808	1.783	1.759	1.736
3	2.941	2.884	2.829	2.775	2.723	2.673	2.624	2.577	2.531	2.487
4	3.902	3.808	3.717	3.630	3.546	3.465	3.387	3.312	3.240	3.170
5	0.951	0.906	0.863	0.822	0.784	0.747	0.713	0.681	0.650	0.621

EXAMPLE 26.2: IMPLICIT INTEREST RATE – LEASE IN ARREARS

Adam Plc has leased an asset for a period of four years. The annual lease payments are €16,000, made in arrears. The asset cost is €52,000.

Requirement What is the interest rate implicit in the lease?

Solution

Under the terms of the lease each of the four annual payments are made in arrears, meaning that all of the payments are at future dates and must be discounted.

To calculate the cumulative discount factor:

$$\frac{\text{Asset cost}}{\text{Annual lease payment}} = \frac{€52,000}{€16,000} = 3.25$$

The lease has four payments to be made at future dates after the lease is taken out; therefore, using the annuity table in **Figure 26.1** above, the period (n) is 4 and the relevant extract is.

Periods (n)	Discount rates (r)									
	1%	**2%**	**3%**	**4%**	**5%**	**6%**	**7%**	**8%**	**9%**	**10%**
4	3.902	3.808	3.717	3.630	3.546	3.465	3.387	3.312	**3.240**	3.170

In the annuity table we look for the annuity factor that is closest to our estimated cumulative discount factor, i.e. 3.25. The closest figure is 3.24 with a discount rate of 9%. The annuity figure is not an exact match for the figure we calculated, meaning that the interest rate implicit in the lease is close to 9%.

You will notice from the annuity table that as the interest rate increases the annuity factor decreases. At the discount rate of 8%, the annuity factor is 3.312. Our calculated figure is between 3.312 and 3.240, so the interest rate is between 8% and 9% – but 3.25 is closer to 3.240 so we know the actual rate will be closer to 9%.

To arrive at a more accurate interest rate we must carry out the following calculations:

1. Calculate the difference between the cumulative discount factor at the two rates either side of our calculated figure of 3.25:

$$\text{Annuity factor at } 8\% - \text{Annuity factor at } 9\%$$

$$3.312 - 3.240 = 0.072$$

2. Calculate the difference between the annuity factor at the lower rate and the cumulative figure calculated:

$$3.312 - 3.250 = 0.062$$

3. Extrapolate the interest rate by:

$$\text{Figure calculated in Step 2} \div \text{Figure calculated in Step 1}$$

$$0.062 \div 0.072 = 0.8611$$

The interest rate implicit in the lease is therefore 8.86%.

Example 26.3 demonstrates how to determine the interest rate implicit in a lease when the payments are in advance.

EXAMPLE 26.3: IMPLICIT INTEREST RATE – LEASE IN ADVANCE

Adam Plc has a leased an asset for a period of four years. The annual lease payments are €15,000, made in advance. The asset cost is €52,000.

Requirement What is the interest rate implicit in the lease?

Solution

Under the terms of the lease each of the four annual payments are made in advance. This means that not all of the payments are at future dates. The first payment made on the date the lease is taken out is not discounted, but all of the other lease payments will be.

To calculate the cumulative discount factor:

$$\frac{\text{Asset cost} - \text{First lease payment}}{\text{Annual lease payment}} = \frac{€52,000 - €15,000}{€15,000} = 2.4666$$

Again, using a set of annuity tables, identify the cumulative discount factor closest to 2.4666. As the lease is in advance and the first payment has been deducted, only three of the payments in the lease are discounted, so the period is 3 and not 4.

Periods (n)	Discount rates (r)									
	10%	**11%**	**13%**	**14%**	**15%**	**16%**	**17%**	**18%**	**19%**	**20%**
3	2.487	**2.444**	2.361	2.322	2.283	2.246	2.210	2.174	2.140	2.106

The annuity factor closest to 2.4666 calculated above is 2.444 (11%). The interest rate is between 10% and 11%, but closer to 10%. Following the process used in the previous example we will calculate the interest rate more accurately.

1. Difference between the cumulative discount factor at the two rates either side of our calculated figure of 2.4666:

$$\text{Annuity factor at } 10\% - \text{Annuity factor at } 11\%$$

$$2.487 - 2.444 = 0.043$$

2. Difference between the annuity factor at the lower rate and the cumulative figure calculated:

$$2.487 - 2.4666 = 0.0204$$

3. Extrapolate the interest rate by:

$$\text{Figure calculated in Step 2} \div \text{Figure calculated in Step 1}$$

$$0.0204 \div 0.043 = 0.4744$$

The interest rate implicit in the lease is therefore 10.47%.

26.4 INITIAL RECOGNITION

If a contract gives rise to a lease and does not meet the low-value or short-term exclusions, there must be an initial recognition of the asset that the entity has the right to use and of the lease liability in the financial statements. The asset and related lease obligation are initially recognised at cost, consistent with other tangible assets (see **Chapter 25, Property, Plant and Equipment**) and intangible assets (which are beyond the scope of this textbook).

Figure 26.2 sets out the amount at which the right-of-use asset and the lease liability are initially recognised.

FIGURE 26.2: INITIAL RECOGNITION OF A LEASE

Initial recognition of the lease liability	Initial recognition of the leased asset
Present value of the lease payments over the term of the lease	Amount at which the lease liability is recognised at initial recognition
PLUS	**PLUS**
Present value of any lease payments expected at the end of the lease	Initial direct costs incurred
	PLUS
	Present value of any estimated costs related to the dismantling, restoration or removal of the asset at the end of its use (beyond the scope of this textbook)
	LESS
	Any lease incentives received

The journal entries to record the above costs are set out below.

	Debit €	Credit €
Asset – cost	X	
Lease obligation		X

Initial recognition of the leased asset and liability.

	Debit €	Credit €
Asset – cost	X	
Bank/other payables		X

To recognise costs associated with the acquisition of the leased asset. *

* See **Chapter 25, Figure 25.1** for examples of costs allowed to be capitalised under IAS 16 *Property, Plant and Equipment.*

The balance on the lease liability is affected by each of the following transactions:
- increased by interest charges on the lease;
- reduced by payments made under the lease; and
- re-measured when there is a reassessment or a lease modification (this is beyond the scope of this textbook).

The journal entry for recording a payment under a lease obligation would be:

	Debit €	Credit €
Lease obligation	X	
Bank		X

To record payment made under the lease contract.

Like all assets used by a business, leased assets are also subject to depreciation. The journal entry to record the depreciation would be:

	Debit €	Credit €
SOPL – depreciation expense	X	
Accumulated depreciation		X

To recognise the depreciation charge on the leased asset.

How to account and present leased assets and the related lease obligation, along with worked examples, will be covered in the next section.

26.5 LEASE TERM

The lease term is the period over which the lessee has the right to use the asset, plus any periods covered by an option to extend or terminate the lease if there is an economic incentive to do so.

Example 26.4 looks at the lease term of a contract where there is an option to extend the contract.

EXAMPLE 26.4: LEASE TERM

Beta Plc has entered into a four-year lease for an item of equipment, the contract for which includes an option to extend the lease for a further period of two years.

The item of equipment has an estimated 10-year useful life. The nature of the equipment leased under the contract is expected to be updated and improved over the initial four-year lease term, which will mean that at the end of the lease term more efficient and technologically advanced equipment will be available to Beta.

At commencement of the lease, Beta's management feel it is unlikely that it will exercise the option to extend the lease term by a further two years.

Requirement What is the lease term for this lease?

Solution

As management believe that it is unlikely that they will extend the lease contract by two years due to the technological advancements expected within the four years of the lease contract, the lease will be accounted for over the four-year lease term and not for the extended period.

26.6 SUBSEQUENT MEASUREMENT

The asset that the entity has obtained a right to use will be accounted for in line with IAS 16 *Property Plant and Equipment* (see **Chapter 25**) or IAS 40 *Investment Property* (see **Chapter 31**).

IFRS 16 states that the entity should measure the leased asset using the **cost model** unless the asset belongs to a class of property, plant and equipment that the entity measures using the **revaluation model**. When the leased asset belongs to a class that is measured using the revaluation model, the entity may choose to use the revaluation model for the leased asset also.

Example 26.5 demonstrates the treatment of a right-of-use lease when the payments are made in arrears.

EXAMPLE 26.5: LEASE IN ARREARS

Bounce Ltd leased an asset on 1 January 2019. The present value of the lease payments payable over the term of the lease on 1 January 2019 is €86,590. The interest rate implicit in the lease is 5%. Lease payments are €20,000 made annually in arrears. The term of the lease and the useful life of the asset are both five years.

Requirement:

(a) Prepare the journal entries in relation to the financial statements for the year ended 31 December 2019.
(b) Prepare the extracts from the financial statements for each year ended 31 December 2019 to 31 December 2023.

Solution

(a) On 1 January 2019 the right-to-use asset and the lease obligation are recognised:

	Debit €	Credit €
Cost – right-of-use asset	86,590	
Lease obligation		86,590

Initial recognition of the leased asset and liability.

In the SOPL, two figures are presented: depreciation and the finance cost. The depreciation charge is €17,318 (€86,590/5 years); the journal to recognise the depreciation charge is:

	Debit €	Credit €
SOPL – P/L – depreciation expense	17,318	
Accumulated depreciation		17,318

To recognise the depreciation charge on the leased asset.

The finance charge is calculated as follows:

Year ended	Opening balance	Finance cost @ 5% of opening balance	Payment	Capital repaid (payment – finance cost)	Closing balance
	€	€	€	€	€
31 December 2019	86,590	4,330	(20,000)	15,670	70,920
31 December 2020	70,920	3,546	(20,000)	16,454	54,466
31 December 2021	54,466	2,723	(20,000)	17,277	37,189
31 December 2022	37,189	1,859	(20,000)	18,141	19,048
31 December 2023	19,048	952	(20,000)	19,048	Nil

The journal entry for the finance charge is:

	Debit €	Credit €
SOPL – P/L – finance cost	4,330	
Lease obligation		4,330

To recognise the finance cost for the year ended 31 December 2019.

(b) The extracts from the financial statements for the years ended 2019–2023 would be:

STATEMENT OF PROFIT OR LOSS (EXTRACT)
for the years ended 31 December

	2019	2020	2021	2022	2023
	€	€	€	€	€
Depreciation	(17,318)	(17,318)	(17,318)	(17,318)	(17,318)
Finance cost	(4,330)	(3,546)	(2,723)	(1,859)	(952)

STATEMENT OF FINANCIAL POSITION (EXTRACT)
for the years ended 31 December

	2019	2020	2021	2022	2023
	€	€	€	€	€
Non-current Assets					
Right-of-use asset	69,272	51,954	34,636	17,318	–
Non-current Liabilities					
Lease liability	54,666	37,189	19,048	–	–
Current Liabilities					
Lease liability	16,454	17,277	18,141	19,048	–

Example 26.6 demonstrates the treatment of a right-of-use lease when the payments are made in advance.

EXAMPLE 26.6: LEASE IN ADVANCE

Tumble Ltd leased an asset on 1 January 2019. The present value of the lease payments payable over the term of the lease on 1 January 2019 is €84,480. The interest rate implicit in the lease is 6%. Lease payments are €23,000 made annually in advance. The term of the lease and the useful life of the asset are both four years.

Requirement:

(a) Prepare the journal entries in relation to the financial statements for the year ended 31 December 2019.
(b) Prepare the extracts from the financial statements for the years ended 31 December 2019 to 31 December 2022.

Solution

(a) On 1 January 2019 the right-to-use asset and the lease obligation are recognised:

	Debit €	Credit €
Cost – right-of-use asset	84,480	
Lease obligation		84,480

Initial recognition of the leased asset and liability.

In the SOPL, two figures are presented: depreciation and the finance cost. The depreciation charge is €21,120 (€84,480/4 years); the journal to recognise this is:

	Debit €	Credit €
SOPL – P/L – depreciation expense	21,120	
Accumulated depreciation		21,120

To recognise the depreciation charge on the leased asset.

The finance charge is calculated as follows:

Year end	Opening balance	Payment	Adjusted balance	Finance cost @ 6% of adjusted balance	Closing balance
	€	€	€	€	€
31 December 2019	84,480	(23,000)	61,480	3,689	65,169
31 December 2020	65,169	(23,000)	42,169	2,530	44,699
31 December 2021	44,699	(23,000)	21,699	1,301	23,000
31 December 2022	23,000	(23,000)	Nil		

The journal entry for the finance charge is:

	Debit €	Credit €
SOPL – P/L – finance cost	3,689	
Accrual		3,689

To recognise the finance cost for the year ended 31 December 2019.

(b) The extracts from the financial statements for the years ended 2019–2022 would be:

STATEMENT OF PROFIT OR LOSS (EXTRACT)
for the years ended 31 December

	2019 €	2020 €	2021 €	2022 €
Depreciation	(21,120)	(21,120)	(21,120)	(21,120)
Finance cost	(3,689)	(2,530)	(1,301)	–

STATEMENT OF FINANCIAL POSITION (EXTRACT)
for the years ended 31 December

	2019 €	2020 €	2021 €	2022 €
Non-current Assets				
Right-of-use asset	63,360	42,240	21,120	–
Non-current Liabilities				
Lease liability	42,169	21,699	–	–
Current Liabilities				
Lease liability	19,311	20,470	21,699	–
Accrual	3,689	2,530	1,301	–

26.7 DISCLOSURE

The purpose of the disclosure requirements is to provide information to the users of the financial statements to assist them in assessing the effect of the leases on the lessee's statements of profit or loss, financial position and cash flows.

IFRS 16 requires disclosures to be made and presented in a tabular format unless another format is more appropriate. Both quantitative and qualitative information must be disclosed as detailed in **Figure 26.3**.

FIGURE 26.3: LEASES – QUANTITATIVE AND QUALITATIVE DISCLOSURE REQUIREMENTS

Quantitative Disclosure Requirements		
SOFP	**SOPL**	**SOCF**
• Additions to right-of-use assets • Carrying value of right-of-use assets at the end of the reporting period by each class of asset • Maturity analysis of lease liabilities separately from other liabilities based on IFRS 7 requirements	• Depreciation for assets by each class • Finance (or interest) expense on lease liabilities • Short-term leases expensed to SOPL • Low-value leases expensed to SOPL • Variable lease payments expensed • Income from subleasing • Gains or losses arising from sale-and-leaseback transactions (beyond the scope of this text book)	• Total cash outflow for leases
Qualitative Disclosure Requirements		

• Summary of the nature of the entity's leasing activities
• Potential cash outflows the entity is exposed to that are not included in the lease liability, including:
   ○ variable lease payments
   ○ extension options and termination options
   ○ residual value guarantees
   ○ leases not yet commenced to which the lessee is committed
   ○ Restrictions or covenants imposed by leases
   ○ Information about sale-and-leaseback transactions (beyond the scope of the textbook).		

If the right-of-use asset is accounted for as an investment property under IAS 40 *Investment Property*, the entity does not have to disclose some of the above information (depreciation charge, income from sub-letting, total cash outflow and the carrying amount of the asset at the reporting date).

Under IFRS 16, the lessee is allowed to measure property, plant and equipment using the revaluation model. In these circumstances, disclosure requirements relating to the revaluation model set out in IAS 16 *Property, Plant and Equipment* must also be met.

A maturity analysis of lease liabilities must be provided in line with paragraph 39 of IFRS 7 *Financial Instruments: Disclosure*. This analysis must be separate to the disclosure for other financial liabilities. The entity must choose the appropriate time bands for the maturity analysis, but IFRS 7 provides the following examples:
• not later than one month;
• later than one month but not later than three months;
• later than three months but not later than one year; or
• later than one year but not later than five years.

Other information to help users assess the impact of the leases on the lessee's statements of profit or loss, financial position and cash flow include:
• the nature of the entities leasing activities;
• predicted future cash outflows to which the lessee is potentially exposed but which are not reflected in the measurement of financial liabilities;
• any restrictions or covenants imposed by leases; and
• sale and leaseback transactions.

Example 26.7 demonstrates the disclosure note in relation to leases.

EXAMPLE 26.7: DISCLOSURE NOTE

Wonder Ltd leased an item of machinery on 1 January 2019. The present value of the lease payments payable over the term of the lease on 1 January 2019 is €86,905. The interest rate implicit in the lease is 9%. Lease payments are €24,610 made annually in advance. The term of the lease and the useful life of the asset are both four years.

Requirement Prepare the disclosure note in relation to the lease for the year ended 31 December 2019.

Solution

Step 1 Calculate the depreciation charge for the year ended 31 December 2019.

Depreciation charge: €86,905/4 years = €21,726

Step 2 Calculate the finance cost for the year ended 31 December 2019.

Year ended	Opening balance	Payment	Adjusted balance	Finance cost @ 9% of adjusted balance	Closing balance
	€	€	€	€	€
31 December 2019	86,905	(24,610)	62,295	5,607	67,902
31 December 2020	67,902	(24,610)	43,292	3,896	47,188
31 December 2021	47,188	(24,610)	22,578	2,032	24,610
31 December 2022	24,610	(24,610)	Nil		

Step 3 Prepare the disclosure note.

Right-of-use Asset

	Machinery €
As at 1 January 2019	0
Additions	86,905
Depreciation	(21,726)
As at 31 December 2019	65,179

Lease Liabilities

	€
Maturity analysis – contractual undiscounted cash flows	
Less than one year	–
One to five years (€24,610 × 3 payments)	73,830
More than five years	–
As at 31 December 2019	73,830

Lease liabilities in the SOFP as at 31 December 2019	67,902
Current liabilities	24,610
Non-current liabilities	43,292
Amounts recognised in profit or loss	
Interest expense	5,607
Amounts recognised in statement of cash flows	
Operating activities	0
Financing activities – total cash outflows for leases	24,610

The principal of €24,610 is recorded in financing activities and interest (€0 in this case) can be recorded in either operating or financing activities.

The interest cost is £0 in the first year of the lease as the payment was made in advance and represents capital only. In the year ended 31 December 2020 the capital repayment would be €19,003 (€24,610 – €5,607) and the interest payment €5,607.

26.8 IFRS 16 COMPARED WITH FRS 102

With the introduction of IFRS 16 there are now significant differences between the accounting treatment of leases by the lessee when compared to FRS 102. The accounting treatment under FRS 102 is very similar to that under IAS 17 *Leases* (which was replaced by IFRS 16 from 1 January 2019) and categorises leases, from the lessees perspective, as either finance leases or operating leases.

When compared to FRS 102, under IFRS 16 a greater number of lease obligations will be recognised in the SOFP using the right-of-use classification, with the option to avoid this only in the case of low-value or short-term assets.

There are also greater disclosure requirements under IFRS 16 than under FRS 102, such as:
• qualitative disclosure (listed in **Figure 26.3**);
• expenses relating to variable lease payments not included in the measurement of liabilities; and
• expenses in relation short-term leases and leases in relation low-value assets.

Exam Tips

• It is important to identify whether a contract is, or contains, a lease obligation.
• Identify whether the entity is electing to use the exemption, i.e. the lease is low-value or short-term.

26.9 CONCLUSION

When an entity enters into a contract it must ask the following questions:

1. Is there an identifiable asset?
2. Does the lessee decide how the asset is to be used?
3. Does the lessee receive substantially all of the economic benefits from the use of the asset?

If the answer to any of these questions is "No" then there is no lease and neither the asset nor a lease obligation are recognised in the financial statements and the payments made are treated as an expense in the SOPL in the period that they are incurred.

If the answer to all of the above questions is "Yes", then the contract contains a lease and the entity has a right-of-use asset. Unless the lease is short term (less than 12months' duration) or low value, the entity must capitalise the leased asset and recognise the lease liability in the SOFP. The right-of-use asset is depreciated over the shorter of the lease term and the asset's useful life. In the SPLOCI, the only costs recognised in relation to the lease are depreciation and finance cost.

SUMMARY OF LEARNING OBJECTIVES

After having studied this chapter, readers should be able to:

Learning Objective 1 Account for short-term and low-value leases from the lessee's perspective.

The lease payments can be recognised as an expense in the SPLOCI in the period to which each lease payment relates (optional).

Learning Objective 2 Calculate the interest rate implicit in a lease.

The interest rate implicit in a lease is calculated by estimating the cumulative discount factor (asset cost ÷ annual lease payment) and using annuity tables to extrapolate the interest rate.

Finance (interest) expenses are recognised in the SOPL.

Learning Objective 3 Account for right-of-use assets.

Right-of-use assets are recognised in the financial statements along with the related lease obligation.

Finance (interest) cost and depreciation charges are recognised in the SOPL. In the SOFP, the right-of-use asset is presented at its carrying amount. The lease obligation balance is presented split between current and non-current liabilities.

Learning Objective 4 Prepare the journal entries in relation to leases.

Short-term or low-value asset (optional)			Right-of-use asset		
	DR	**CR**		**DR**	**CR**
SOPL – P/L – Lease expense	X		Right-of-use asset	X	
Bank		X	Lease obligation		X
To recognise the lease expense paid during the period.			*Initial recognition of right-of-use leased asset.*		
			Lease obligation	X	
			Bank		X
			To recognise the lease payment made.		

SOPL – P/L – depreciation expense	X	
Accumulated depreciation		X
To recognise depreciation expense.		
SOPL – P/L – finance cost	X	
Lease obligation		X
To recognise the finance cost.		

Learning Objective 5 Prepare the disclosure notes in relation to leases.

The user of the financial statements must be provided with information to assist them in understanding the financial information presented. The disclosure requirements relate to both quantitative and qualitative information.

QUESTIONS

Review Questions

(See **Appendix A** for Solutions to Review Questions.)

Question 26.1

Jubilee Ltd leased a photocopier for a period of 12 months on 1 May 2019. The lease contract requires quarterly payments of €600, the first of which is due to be paid on 1 May 2019.

Jubilee Ltd's management have elected to avail of the exemption under IFRS 16 and expense lease payments to the SOPL.

Requirement Prepare the journal entries in relation to the lease for the reporting period ended 31 December 2019.

Question 26.2

Wrinkle Ltd leased a computer server for a period of 12 months on 1 March 2019. The lease contract requires quarterly payments of €1,000, the first of which is due to be paid on 31 May 2019.

Wrinkle Ltd's management have elected to avail of the exemption under IFRS 16 and expense lease payments to the SOPL.

Requirement Prepare the journal entries in relation to the lease for the reporting period ended 31 December 2019.

Question 26.3

Coronation Ltd entered into a lease agreement on 1 January 2019 for a piece of machinery to be used in the production process. The following are the terms set out in the lease agreement:

Cost of asset	€120,000
Lease term	5 years
Useful life of the asset	5 years
Lease payments	€30,000 per annum, in arrears
Lease payments begin on	31 December 2019

Requirement:

(a) Calculate the interest rate applicable to the lease (using the annuity table extract in **Figure 26.1**).
(b) Prepare the extracts from the financial statements in relation to the lease for the reporting period ended 31 December 2019.

Question 26.4

You are provided with the following information from the lease contract taken out by Sally Ltd on 1 January 2019:

Annual lease payment	€25,370
First lease payment due on	1 January 2019
Interest rate implicit in the lease	10%
Term of the lease	3 years
Useful life of the asset	3 years

Requirement Prepare the journal entries and the extracts from the financial statements in relation to the lease for the reporting period ended 31 December 2019.

Challenging Questions

(Suggested Solutions to Challenging Questions are available through your lecturer.)

Question 26.1

Oates Ltd requires a new machine. It has researched various options and is considering purchasing a machine for a cash price of €110,000. The machine has a seven-year useful life and a residual value of €12,000.

Oates Ltd has decided to lease the machine under a five-year lease with annual payments of €26,380 on 1 January, the first being due on 1 January 2019. The effective interest rate on the lease is 10% per annum.

It is not expected that management will extend the contract after the five-year term.

Requirement:

(a) Calculate the finance charge that should be shown in the company's financial statements for each of the years to 31 December 2019 and 31 December 2020.
(b) Calculate Oates Ltd's liability in relation to the lease at the end of 31 December 2019 and 31 December 2020, and show how this liability should be presented in the SOFP.

(Based on Chartered Accountants Ireland, CAP 1 Financial Accounting, Summer 2011, Question 8)

Question 26.2

The trial balance extracted from Beech Ltd as at 31 December 2019 was as follows:

	€000	€000
Share capital		180,000
Retained profits at 1 January 2019		85,217
Freehold premises at cost	325,000	
Machinery at cost	100,800	
Accumulated depreciation at 1 January 2019		
Freehold premises		64,800
Machinery		25,200
Purchases	79,610	
Sales		216,480

General administrative expenses	2,222	
Wages and salaries	45,570	
Rent and rates	7,320	
Heat and light	5,760	
Delivery costs	3,080	
Selling and advertising costs	3,820	
Overdraft interest	745	
Allowance for doubtful debts at 1 January 2019		478
Accounts receivable	14,920	
Accounts payable		18,720
Inventory at 1 January 2019	12,688	
Bank overdraft		10,640
	601,535	601,535

You have been provided with the following additional information:

1. **Inventory**
   Inventory at 31 December 2019 is €11,400,000.

2. **Wages and salaries**
   Included within wages and salaries are €40,450,000 of production wages and €5,120,000 of administration wages. Additionally, at 31 December 2019, €1,250,000 of production wages and €180,000 of administration wages were still owed by Beech Ltd.

3. **General administrative expenses**
   Specialist Machine Payment of €37,664 was made on 31 December 2019 and correctly recorded in the financial records, with subsequent payments made annually in arrears. The fair value of the machine at the date of the lease agreement on 1 January 2019 was €140,000. The machine has an expected useful life of five years. The lease term is four years, with four annual payments of €37,664. Except for the lease payment made on 31 December 2019, no other entries were made in respect of this lease. The effective interest rate is 3%.

4. **Depreciation**
   Depreciation is to be provided as follows:
   Freehold premises – 2% per annum on cost;
   Machinery – 20% per annum on reducing balances.
   Depreciation is to be allocated as follows:
   Freehold premises – 80% to cost of sales and 20% to administrative expenses;
   Machinery – 100% to cost of sales.

5. **Rent and rates**
   Rent and rates are to be allocated as follows: 75% to cost of sales and 25% to general administrative expenses.

6. **Heat and light**
   Heat and light is to be allocated as follows: 75% to cost of sales and 25% to general administrative expenses.

Requirement:

(a) Prepare Beech Ltd's statement of profit or loss and other comprehensive income for the year ended 31 December 2019 in accordance with IAS 1 *Presentation of Financial Statements*.

20 Minutes

(b) Prepare Beech Ltd's statement of financial position as at 31 December 2019.

15 Minutes

(Based on Chartered Accountants Ireland, CAP 1 Financial Accounting, Autumn 2012, Question 3)

27

Borrowing Costs

LEARNING OBJECTIVES

Having studied this chapter, readers should be able to:
1. explain what 'capitalisation of borrowing costs' means;
2. identify what costs are classified as borrowing costs;
3. identify what is a qualifying asset;
4. calculate the amount of borrowing costs that can be capitalised; and
5. prepare the disclosure note in relation to borrowing costs.

27.1 INTRODUCTION

IAS 23 *Borrowing Costs* sets out the accounting rules in relation to capitalisation of **borrowing costs**. Up to this point in this textbook when costs were incurred in a reporting period they were charged (or expensed) to the profit or loss section of the statement of profit or loss and other comprehensive income (SPLOCI) for that reporting period; however, borrowing costs, in certain situations, are not expensed to the profit or loss section of the SPLOCI but are capitalised instead. 'Capitalising' a cost means that the cost incurred is added to the cost of an asset rather than being expensed to profit or loss. The impact of capitalisation is that the profit for the period is not impacted by the cost incurred – instead the figure for assets in the statement of financial position (SOFP) is increased. The journal entry to capitalise the cost is:

	Debit €	Credit €
Asset – cost account	X	
Bank/accrual account		X

To capitalise borrowing costs.

27.2 WHAT COSTS ARE INCLUDED IN BORROWING COSTS?

Borrowing costs include both interest costs and other costs that are incurred in relation to loans obtained by an entity. These costs include:
- interest cost using effective interest rate;
- finance costs on leases; and
- exchange differences arising on foreign currency borrowings.

The borrowing costs must be directly attributable to the acquisition, construction or production of a qualifying asset. A 'directly attributable cost' is one that would not have been incurred if the asset had not been acquired, constructed or produced.

27.3 ACCOUNTING POLICY IN RELATION TO BORROWING COSTS

IAS 23 sets out the accounting rules in relation to borrowing costs. The accounting policy is that qualifying borrowing costs must be capitalised when the asset is a qualifying asset and the capitalisation rules are met.

Assets that qualify for capitalisation of borrowing costs include:
- inventories;
- manufacturing plant;
- power-generation facilities;
- intangible assets; and
- investment properties.

Assets that do **not** qualify for capitalisation of borrowing costs are:
- financial assets;
- inventories manufactured or produced over a short period of time; and
- assets that are ready for their intended use or for sale when purchased.

IAS 23 sets out rules in relation to the capitalisation of borrowing costs; these rules relate to three areas:
- when capitalisation of borrowing costs can begin;
- when capitalisation of borrowing costs ends;
- when capitalisation of borrowing costs is suspended.

Commencement of Capitalisation

An entity can begin to capitalise borrowing costs when **all** of the following conditions are met:
- expenditure on the asset has been/is being incurred;
- borrowing costs have been incurred; and
- activities necessary to prepare the asset for its intended use or sale are underway.

Example 27.1 demonstrates the accounting for capitalisation of borrowing costs.

EXAMPLE 27.1: COMMENCEMENT OF CAPITALISATION

Swing Ltd has borrowed €3 million to fund the construction of a new property. The funds were drawn down from the financial institution on 1 March 2019 and the rate of interest on the loan was 5%.

Construction of the asset began on 1 April 2019 and was completed on 31 December 2019. The loan was repaid in full on 31 December 2019.

All borrowing costs were paid in full at 31 December 2019.

Requirement:
(a) Prepare the journal entry in relation to the capitalisation of the borrowing costs.
(b) Prepare the journal entry in relation to the borrowing costs that are not capitalised.

Solution

The total interest cost on the loan for the period that funds were borrowed (1 March 2019 to 31 December 2019, 10 months) is €125,000.

(a)
Borrowing costs can be capitalised from 1 April to 31 December 2019 – the period in which expenditure is being incurred, borrowing costs incurred and work being undertaken in relation to the preparation of the asset for use.

Capitalise: €3m × 5% × 9/12 = €112,500.

	Debit €	Credit €
Property – cost account (SOFP)	112,500	
Bank account		112,500
To capitalise borrowing costs.		

(b)
The loan is taken out on 1 March 2019 but work on the construction of the asset does not begin until 1 April 2019 so the borrowing costs incurred during March 2019 cannot be capitalised, they must be expensed to profit or loss.

Borrowing costs that do not meet the capitalisation are €12,500 (€3m × 5% × 1/12)

	Debit €	Credit €
SPLOCI – finance cost	12,500	
Bank account		12,500
To expense borrowing costs to profit or loss.		

Cessation of Capitalisation

An entity can no longer capitalise borrowing costs when all activities necessary to prepare the qualifying asset for its intended use have been completed.

Example 27.2 demonstrates the application of the cessation rules in relation to the capitalisation of borrowing costs.

EXAMPLE 27.2: CESSATION OF CAPITALISATION

Ping Ltd has borrowed €6 million to fund the construction of a new property. The funds were drawn down on 1 February 2019 and the rate of interest on the loan was 4%.

Construction on the asset began on 1 March 2019 and was completed on 30 November 2019. The loan was repaid in full on 31 December 2019.

All borrowing costs were paid in full at 31 December 2019.

Requirement:
(a) Prepare the journal entry in relation to the capitalisation of the borrowing costs.
(b) Prepare the journal entry in relation to the borrowing costs that are not capitalised.

Solution

The total interest cost on the loan for the period that funds were borrowed (1 February 2019 to 31 December 2019, 11 months) is €220,000.

(a)
Borrowing costs can be capitalised from 1 March to 30 November 2019 – the period in which expenditure is being incurred, borrowing costs are being incurred and work is being undertaken in relation to the preparation of the asset for use.

Capitalise: €6m × 4% × 9/12 = €180,000.

	Debit €	Credit €
Property – cost account (SOFP)	180,000	
Bank account		180,000

To capitalise borrowing costs.

(b)
The loan is taken out on 1 February 2019 but work on the construction of the asset does not begin until 1 March 2019, so the borrowing costs incurred during March 2019 cannot be capitalised.

Work on the construction of the asset ends on 30 November 2019 but the loan is not repaid until 31 December 2019 – the borrowing costs incurred during December 2019 cannot be capitalised as the work on the asset has been completed.

Borrowing costs that do not meet the capitalisation are €40,000 (€6m × 4% × 2/12 (February and December 2019)).

	Debit €	Credit €
SPLOCI – finance cost	40,000	
Bank account		40,000

To expense borrowing costs to profit or loss.

(Try **Review Question 27.1** at the end of this chapter.)

Suspension of Capitalisation

An entity cannot capitalise borrowing costs when all the activities necessary to prepare the qualifying asset for its intended use are not being undertaken. Work on the construction of an asset can be suspended for a number of different reasons, such as: a strike by workers, and a court order to suspend work due to planning issues.

If work on the asset is suspended, the borrowing costs in this period cannot be capitalised but must be expensed to the SPLOCI.

Example 27.3 demonstrates the application of the suspension rules in relation to the capitalisation of borrowing costs.

Example 27.3: Suspension of Capitalisation

You are provided with the following information in relation to the construction of an asset:

Loan amount	€4,000,000
Rate of interest on loan	6%
Date loan taken out	1 January 2019
Date work on construction of asset began	1 January 2019
Date work on asset was completed	31 December 2019
Date loan repaid	31 December 2019

During March 2019, there was a strike by workers involved in the construction of the asset. No work was undertaken in relation to the asset in March 2019. All borrowing costs were paid in full at 31 December 2019.

Requirement Prepare the journal entries in relation to the borrowing costs for the year ended 31 December 2019.

Solution

The total interest cost on the loan for the period that funds were borrowed (1 January 2019 to 31 December 2019, i.e. 12 months) is €240,000.

Borrowing costs can be capitalised from 1 January to 29 February 2019 and 1 April 2019 to 31 December 2019 – the period in which expenditure is being incurred, borrowing costs are being incurred and work being undertaken in relation to the preparation of the asset for use.

Capitalise: €4m × 6% × 11/12 = €220,000.

Borrowing costs cannot be capitalised during March when work on the asset was suspended.

Expense to profit or loss: €4m × 6% × 1/12 = €20,000.

	Debit €	Credit €
Property – cost account (SOFP)	220,000	
SPLOCI – finance cost	20,000	
Bank account		240,000
To account for borrowing costs incurred during 2019.		

(Try **Review Question 27.2** at the end of this chapter.)

In the examples so far, loans were taken out for the specific expenditure being incurred. In the next section the situation where the purchase or construction of a qualifying asset is financed from more than one loan facility is looked at.

27.4 INTEREST RATE TO BE USED FOR CAPITALISATION

When borrowings have been taken out specifically in relation to funding the production, construction or acquisition of a qualifying asset, then that rate shall be used to capitalise any borrowing costs. In the above examples, the borrowings have been taken out specifically for the qualifying asset and the interest rate of those borrowings was used for the capitalisation of the borrowing costs.

If borrowings have been raised generally, then a weighted average rate shall be calculated and used for the capitalisation of borrowing costs.

Example 27.4 demonstrates the calculation of a weighted borrowing cost and its use in the capitalisation of borrowing costs.

EXAMPLE 27.4: WEIGHTED AVERAGE BORROWING COSTS

Miles Ltd has incurred €2.5 million of costs in the construction of a production asset during the year ended 31 December 2019. The qualifying asset was not funded with a loan specifically taken out in relation to it, but instead has been funded through general borrowings agreed with the company's bankers at the start of the financial year.

Miles has the following borrowings in place for the year ended 31 December 2019:

5% loan	€6,000,000
2.5% loan	€4,000,000

The loan facilities were taken out on 1 January 2019 and were still in place at the reporting date, 31 December 2019. All borrowing costs were paid in full at the reporting date.

The work on the construction of the qualifying asset began on 1 March 2019 and was fully completed on 31 August 2019. The asset was brought into use on 1 November 2019.

Requirement Prepare the journal entries in relation to the borrowing costs for the year ended 31 December 2019.

Solution

Step 1 Calculate the weighted average cost of borrowing.

Loan Amount €	% of total borrowings	Interest Rate on Loan	Weighting
6,000,000	60	5.0%	3.0%
4,000,000	40	2.5%	1.0%
10,000,000			4.0%

Step 2 Calculate the total borrowing cost.

	€
€6,000,000 × 5%	300,000
€4,000,000 × 2.5%	100,000
Total borrowing cost	400,000

Step 3 Determine the period for which borrowing costs can be capitalised.

Borrowing costs can be capitalised from 1 March to 31 August 2019, i.e. the period in which expenditure is being incurred, borrowing costs are being incurred and work is being undertaken in relation to the preparation of the asset for use.

Capitalise: €2,500,000 × 4% × 6/12 = €50,000.

Step 4 Prepare the accounting journal entry in relation to borrowing costs.

	Debit €	Credit €
Production assets – cost account (SOFP)	50,000	
SPLOCI – finance cost	350,000	
Bank account		400,000

To account for borrowing costs incurred during 2019.

(Try **Review Question 27.3** at the end of this chapter.)

Interest Earned

A loan to fund the construction of an asset may be drawn down by the entity in full at the start of the construction phase, however payments under the construction contract will probably be made over the period of construction and not in one lump sum at the start of the project. In the period of time between the funds being drawn down on the loan and actual payments being made in relation to the construction costs the funds may be invested, attracting interest income. Interest earned on these funds reduces the amount of borrowing costs that can be capitalised.

Any interest income earned when borrowing costs do not qualify for capitalisation (for example, when commencement conditions are not met or work on the construction is suspended) is recognised as income in the SOPL and does not reduce the amount of the borrowing costs capitalised.

Example 27.5 demonstrates the treatment of interest earned from surplus funds invested.

EXAMPLE 27.5: INTEREST EARNED

You are provided with the following information in relation to the construction of an asset during the current reporting period:

Loan amount	€2,800,000
Rate of interest on loan	5%
Date loan taken out	1 January 2019
Date work on construction of asset began	1 January 2019
Date work on asset was completed	31 December 2019
Date loan repaid	31 December 2019

Surplus funds were invested during the reporting period and earned interest income of €2,900. Interest on the loan was paid in full on 31 December 2019, interest earned was received.

Requirement Prepare the accounting journal entry in relation to the borrowing costs and interest income earned during the reporting period ended 31 December 2019.

Solution

	€
Capitalise interest cost: €2,800,000 × 5%	140,000
Less: interest earned	(2,900)
Capitalise	137,100

	Debit €	Credit €
Property – cost account (SOFP)	137,100	
Bank account		137,100

To capitalise the net borrowing costs.

27.5 DISCLOSURE

The following shall be disclosed in the financial statements in relation to the capitalisation of borrowing costs:
- the amount of borrowing costs capitalised during the year; and
- the capitalisation rate used to determine the amount to be capitalised.

Example 27.6 will demonstrate the disclosure note in relation to IAS 23.

EXAMPLE 27.6: BORROWING COSTS DISCLOSURE NOTE

A property was constructed at a cost of €2,940,000 during the year ended 31 December 2019. The cost of the asset includes €80,000 in relation to borrowing costs specifically related to the construction of the property.

The cost of the property construction was funded out of general loans made up as follows:

8% loan	€10,000,000
4% three-year loan	€15,000,000

Requirement Prepare the disclosure note in relation to the above.

Solution

DISCLOSURE NOTE

Borrowing costs in relation to construction, acquisition or production of an asset are capitalised. The borrowing costs capitalised during the reporting period amounted to €80,000. The capitalisation rate applied was 5.6%, which was calculated as a weighted average of the interest costs on borrowings (W1).

WORKING 1: CALCULATION OF WEIGHTED AVERAGE RATE
$(8\% \times €10m \div €25m) + (4\% \times €15m \div €25m) = 3.2\% + 2.4\% = 5.6\%$.

27.6 IAS 23 COMPARED WITH FRS 102

Under IAS 23 borrowing costs must be capitalised; whereas under FRS 102 there is a choice between capitalising or expensing costs to the profit or loss section of the SPLOCI in the period that they are incurred. The accounting policy chosen must be applied consistently from one reporting period to the next.

EXAM TIPS

- The most important point is to be careful about the calculation of the number of months for which borrowing costs are capitalised.
- Note whether the interest rate is specific to the asset; if not, a weighted cost would have to be calculated.

27.7 CONCLUSION

IAS 23 sets out the rules in relation to the capitalisation of borrowing costs incurred in relation to qualifying assets. 'Capitalisation of borrowing costs' means the borrowing costs increase the cost of the asset and are not expensed to the profit or loss section of the SPLOCI when they are incurred. Capitalisation can only begin when costs are being incurred and work has commenced. Capitalisation is not allowed when work is suspended or the construction phase has ended. The amount capitalised is reduced by any interest earned when surplus funds are invested.

SUMMARY OF LEARNING OBJECTIVES

After having studied this chapter, readers should be able to:

Learning Objective 1 Explain what 'capitalisation of borrowing costs' means.

Capitalisation means that borrowing costs increase the cost of an asset rather than being expensed to the profit or loss section of the SPLOCI in the period that they are incurred. The accounting policy is that borrowing costs on qualifying assets must be capitalised.

Learning Objective 2 Identify what costs are classified as borrowing costs.

Borrowing costs must be directly attributable to the acquisition, construction or production of a qualifying asset and include:
- interest cost using effective interest rate;
- finance costs on leases; and
- exchange differences arising on foreign currency borrowings.

Learning Objective 3 Identify what is a qualifying asset.

Assets that qualify for capitalisation of borrowing costs are:
- inventories;
- manufacturing plant;
- power-generation facilities;
- intangible assets; and
- investment properties.

Assets that do **not** qualify for capitalisation of borrowing costs are:
- financial assets;
- inventories manufactured or produced over a short period of time; and
- assets that are ready for their intended use or for sale when purchased.

Learning Objective 4 Calculate the amount of borrowing costs that can be capitalised.

Borrowing costs can be capitalised when: expenditure is being incurred, borrowing costs are being incurred and work is being undertaken in relation to the preparation of the asset for use.

While work is suspended on the construction, production or acquisition of an asset, interest cannot be capitalised and must be expensed to the SPLOCI in the period in which the borrowing costs are incurred.

The amount capitalised is reduced by any interest earned on any surplus funds invested during the period involved in the construction, acquisition and production of the asset.

Learning Objective 5 Prepare the disclosure note in relation to borrowing costs.

The following shall be disclosed in the financial statements:
- the amount of borrowing costs capitalised during the year; and
- the capitalisation rate used to determine the amount to be capitalised.

QUESTIONS

Review Questions

(See **Appendix A** for Solutions to Review Questions.)

Question 27.1
Strong Ltd has borrowed €3.5 million to fund the construction of a new property. The funds were drawn down from the financial institution on 1 February 2018 and the rate of interest on the loan was 6% per annum.

Construction on the asset began on 1 April 2018 and was completed on 30 June 2019. The loan was repaid in full on 31 August 2019.

Requirement Prepare the accounting journal entries in relation to the borrowing for the reporting periods ended 31 December 2018 and 2019.

Question 27.2
You are provided with the following information in relation to the construction of an asset:

Loan amount	€4,200,000
Rate of interest on loan	6%
Date loan taken out	1 January 2018
Date work on construction of asset began	1 April 2018
Date work on asset was completed	31 October 2019
Date loan repaid	31 December 2019

During September 2018, there was a strike by workers involved in the construction of the asset. No work was undertaken in relation to the asset in September 2018. All borrowing costs were paid in full.

Requirement Prepare the accounting journal entries in relation to the borrowing for the reporting periods ended 31 December 2018 and 2019.

Question 27.3

Triple Ltd has incurred €1.5 million of costs in the construction of an asset during the year ended 31 December 2019. A single loan was **not** taken out specifically in relation to the qualifying asset; instead it has been funded through general borrowings agreed with its bankers at the start of the financial year.

Triple has the following borrowings in place for the year ended 31 December 2019:

	€
6% loan	4,000,000
4.5% loan	2,800,000
7% loan	1,200,000

The loan facilities were taken out on 1 January 2019 and were still in place at the reporting date, 31 December 2019. All borrowing costs were paid in full at the reporting date.

Requirement What interest rate is used for capitalising borrowing costs during the reporting period ended 31 December 2019?

Challenging Questions

(Solutions to Challenging Questions are available through your lecturer.)

Question 27.1

On 1 January 2018, Duggan entered into a contract with a property developer to have a manufacturing facility built at a cost of €15 million.

In order to finance the cost of the contract, Duggan entered into a loan agreement with a bank to borrow €15 million from 1 January 2018 at an interest rate of 6% per annum. The borrowings were drawn down in full on 1 January 2018.

The facility was expected to be completed by 31 March 2019, but delays were incurred as a result of a strike by workers during the period 1 November 2018 to 28 February 2019. During the period of the strike, no work was undertaken on-site.

Duggan invested available funds from 1 November 2018 to 28 February 2019 and earned interest income amounting to €24,000.

The manufacturing facility was completed on 31 May 2018 and the loan was repaid on 30 June 2019.

Requirement Calculate the amount that would be capitalised as a non-current asset.

28

Accounting for Government Grants and Disclosure of Government Assistance

LEARNING OBJECTIVES

Having studied this chapter, readers should be able to:
1. account for grants provided in relation to capital expenditure;
2. account for grants provided in relation to current expenditure;
3. account for repayment of grants received in relation to capital expenditure; and
4. account for repayment of grants received in relation to current expenditure.

28.1 INTRODUCTION

Governments offer a variety of incentives to businesses to encourage and/or support economic activity. The accounting rules in relation to the treatment of government grants are set out in IAS 20 *Accounting for Government Grants and Disclosure of Government Assistance*.

A grant is recognised when the entity complies with all of the conditions associated with the grant and they are reasonably certain that the grant will be received.

Grants may be provided in relation to items of either capital or revenue expenditure. Capital expenditure relates to costs incurred in relation to the purchases or improvement in the performance of items of property, plant and equipment. Current expenditure relates to costs that are incurred that are normally expensed to the profit or loss section of the SPLOCI in the period they are incurred; such costs include training and recruitment of staff. The accounting treatment in relation to items of capital and current expenditure are explained in this chapter.

28.2 GRANTS IN RELATION TO CAPITAL EXPENDITURE

Some government grants are provided to entities to offset the cost of property, plant and equipment. As the grant relates to an asset that will provide benefits to the entity over its useful life, it is important that the grant is released to the statement of profit or loss and other comprehensive income (SPLOCI) on the same basis as the depreciation on the relevant asset is charged to the SPLOCI.

There are two methods of accounting for capital grants:
• reduce the cost of the asset by the amount of the grant received; or
• treat the grant as deferred income.

Reduce the Cost of the Asset by the Amount of the Grant Received

Under this method, the cost of the asset is reduced by the grant received, which reduces the depreciable amount. The depreciable amount is the total amount of depreciation that can be charged in relation to an asset over its useful life.

Example 28.1 shows the journal entries required in relation to a grant when the entity chooses this policy.

EXAMPLE 28.1: CAPITAL GRANT

Cotton Ltd purchased a machine for €520,000 on 1 January 2019. Cotton received a grant of €120,000 on 1 January 2019. At the purchase date, the useful life is estimated at 10 years and residual value is zero.

Cotton's accounting policy is to treat grants related to property, plant and equipment as a reduction in the cost of the asset.

Requirement:
(a) Prepare the journal entries in relation to the grant and the machine as at 1 January 2019.
(b) Calculate the depreciation charge and prepare the journal entries for the year ended 31 December 2019.

Solution
(a)

	Debit €	Credit €
Machine – cost account	520,000	
Bank account		520,000
To recognise cost of the machine purchased.		
Bank account	120,000	
Grant account		120,000
To recognise the grant received.		
Grant account	120,000	
Machine – cost account		120,000
To reduce cost of the machine by the amount of the grant received.		

(b)

	€
Cost of machine	520,000
Less: grant	(120,000)
	400,000
Useful life	10 years
Depreciation charge (€400,000 ÷ 10 years)	40,000

	Debit €	Credit €
Depreciation expense account	40,000	
Accumulated depreciation account		40,000
To recognise the depreciation expense for the year ended 31 December 2019.		
SPLOCI – depreciation expense account	40,000	
Depreciation expense account		40,000
To recognise the depreciation expense in the SPLOCI.		

Deferred Income Approach

Under the deferred income method the grant received in relation to an item of capital expenditure is treated as deferred income. An amount of the grant is released to the profit or loss section of the SPLOCI over the useful life of the asset in a manner that reflects the pattern in which benefit is derived from the use of the asset. The release of the grant is known as amortisation of the grant. The amortisation amount is presented in the SPLOCI either as 'other income' or as a reduction to the related expense.

The deferred income is presented in the statement of financial position (SOFP) in the liabilities section. The amount of the deferred income to be amortised in the next financial reporting period is presented under current liabilities and the amount to be released more than one year after the reporting date is presented under non-current liabilities.

Example 28.2 demonstrates the journal entries required in relation to a grant when the entity chooses this policy.

EXAMPLE 28.2: CAPITAL GRANT – DEFERRED INCOME

Linen Ltd purchased a machine for €650,000 for cash on 1 January 2019. Linen received a grant of €100,000 on 1 January 2019. At the purchase date the useful life is estimated at five years and residual value is zero.

Linen's accounting policy is to treat grants related to property, plant and equipment as deferred income.

Requirement:
(a) Prepare the journal entries in relation to the grant and the machine as at 1 January 2019.
(b) Calculate the depreciation charge and prepare the journal entries for the year ended 31 December 2019.
(c) Prepare the extract from the SOFP as at 31 December 2019.

Solution
(a)

	Debit €	Credit €
Machine – cost account	650,000	
Cash account		650,000
To recognise cost of the machine purchased.		

	Debit €	Credit €
Bank account	100,000	
Deferred income account – grant		100,000

To recognise the grant received.

(b)

	€
Cost of machine	650,000
Useful life	5 years
Depreciation charge (€650,000 ÷ 5 years)	130,000

	€
Grant	100,000
Useful life	5 years
Amortisation (€100,000 ÷ 5 years)	20,000

	Debit €	Credit €
Depreciation expense account	130,000	
Accumulated depreciation account		130,000

To recognise the depreciation expense for the year ended 31 December 2019.

SPLOCI – depreciation expense	130,000	
Depreciation expense account		130,000

To recognise the depreciation expense in the SPLOCI.

Deferred income account – grant	20,000	
Other income account		20,000

To recognise the amortisation of the grant.

Other income account	20,000	
SPLOCI – other income		20,000

To recognise the amortisation of the grant in the SPLOCI.

(c)

STATEMENT OF FINANCIAL POSITION (EXTRACT)
as at 31 December 2019

	€
Non-current Assets	
Machine (€650,000 – €130,000)	520,000
Non-current Liabilities	
Deferred income (W1)	60,000
Current Liabilities	
Deferred income (W2)	20,000

W1 Deferred Income – Non-current Liabilities

	€
Amount of grant received	100,000
Amount amortised year ended 31 December 2019	(20,000)
Current liability – amount to be amortised year ended 31 December 2020	(20,000)
Balance of deferred income under non-current liabilities	60,000

W2 Deferred Income – Current Liabilities

The amount to be amortised in the year ended 31 December 2020:
$$€100,000 \div 5 \text{ years}$$
$$= €20,000.$$

(Try **Review Question 28.1** at the end of this chapter.)

So far in this chapter the accounting entries in relation to the recognition of grants has been considered. Normally grants have a number of conditions attached to them and if the entity fails to comply with any of the conditions, the grant may have to be repaid in full. In the next section the accounting entries in relation to the repayment of grants are explained.

Repayment of Capital Grants

An entity may have to repay a grant if it fails to comply with the conditions attaching to a grant. Repayment of a grant is accounted for as a change in accounting estimate under IAS 8 *Accounting Policies, Changes in Accounting Estimates and Errors* (see **Chapter 22**). Changes in accounting estimate are applied prospectively.

Example 28.3 demonstrates the journal entries required in relation to the repayment of a grant when the entity chooses the policy to reduce the cost of the asset by the grant.

EXAMPLE 28.3: REPAYMENT OF CAPITAL GRANT WHERE THE
COST OF THE ASSET IS REDUCED BY THE GRANT

Silk Ltd purchased an item of equipment on 1 January 2018 for cash – €320,000. A grant was received in relation to the piece of equipment on 1 January 2018 that amounted to €80,000. The asset is depreciated on a straight-line basis over eight years.

Silk Ltd's policy is to reduce the cost of the asset by the amount of the grant.

Requirement:
(a) Prepare the journal entries for the year ended 31 December 2018 in relation to the asset and the grant.
(b) Prepare the extract from the SOFP as at 31 December 2018.
(c) On 31 December 2019 Silk realised that it had not met all of the conditions relating to the grant and will now have to repay it in full. The amortisation charge has not been recorded for the year ended 31 December 2019. Prepare the journal entries to recognise the repayment of the grant.

Solution
(a)

	Debit €	Credit €
Machine – cost account	320,000	
Cash account		320,000

To recognise cost of the machine purchased.

	Debit €	Credit €
Bank account	80,000	
Grant account		80,000

To recognise the grant received.

	Debit €	Credit €
Grant account	80,000	
Machine – cost account		80,000

To reduce the machine account by the amount of the grant received.

	€
Cost of machine	320,000
Less: grant	(80,000)
	240,000
Useful life	8 years
Depreciation charge (€240,000 ÷ 8 years)	30,000

	Debit €	Credit €
Depreciation expense account	30,000	
Accumulated depreciation account		30,000

To recognise the depreciation expense for the year ended 31 December 2018.

	Debit €	Credit €
SPLOCI – depreciation expense	30,000	
Depreciation expense account		30,000

To recognise the depreciation expense in the SPLOCI.

(b)

STATEMENT OF FINANCIAL POSITION (EXTRACT)
as at 31 December 2018

	€
Non-current Assets	
Machine	210,000

(c)

	If Grant had not been Received €	Grant Received €
Cost/net of grant	320,000	240,000
Depreciation – year ended 31/12/2019	(80,000)	(60,000)
Carrying amount	240,000	180,000

The asset needs to be restated to the carrying amount as if the grant had not been received.

	Debit €	Credit €
Machine – cost account	80,000	
Grant repayment liability account		80,000
To restate the cost of the asset to its original cost.		
SPLOCI – grant repayment	20,000	
Accumulated depreciation account		20,000
To recognise the liability in relation to the grant.		

Example 28.4 demonstrates the journal entries required in relation to the repayment of a grant when the entity chooses the policy of deferring income in relation to the grant.

EXAMPLE 28.4: REPAYMENT OF CAPITAL GRANT (DEFERRED INCOME APPROACH)

Velvet Ltd purchased an item of equipment on 1 January 2018 for €480,000. A grant was received in relation to the piece of equipment on 1 January 2018 that amounted to €60,000. The asset is depreciated on a straight-line basis over five years.

Velvet Ltd policy is to treat the grant as deferred income and amortise over the useful life.

Requirement:
(a) Prepare the journal entries for the year ended 31 December 2018 in relation to the asset and the grant.
(b) Prepare the extract from the SOFP as at 31 December 2018.
(c) On 31 December 2019 Velvet realised that it had not met all of the conditions relating to the grant and will now have to repay in full. The amortisation charge has not been recorded for the year ended 31 December 2019. Prepare the journal entries to recognise the repayment of the grant.

Solution
(a)

	Debit €	Credit €
Machine – cost account	480,000	
Bank account		480,000
To recognise cost of the machine purchased.		

	Debit €	Credit €
Bank account	60,000	
Deferred income account – grant		60,000
To recognise the grant received as deferred income.		

	€
Cost of machine	480,000
Useful life	5 years
Depreciation charge (€480,000 ÷ 5 years)	96,000
Grant received	60,000
Useful life	5 years
Amortisation (€60,000 ÷ 5 years)	12,000

	Debit €	Credit €
Depreciation expense account	96,000	
Accumulated depreciation account		96,000
To recognise the depreciation expense for the year ended 31 December 2018.		
SPLOCI – depreciation expense	96,000	
Depreciation expense account		96,000
To recognise the depreciation expense in the SPLOCI.		
Deferred income account – grant	12,000	
Other income account		12,000
To recognise the amortisation of the grant.		
Other income account	12,000	
SPLOCI – other income		12,000
To recognise the amortisation of the grant in the SPLOCI.		

(b)

STATEMENT OF FINANCIAL POSITION (EXTRACT)
as at 31 December 2018

	€
Non-current Assets	
Machine (€480,000 – €96,000)	384,000
Non-current Liabilities	
Deferred income (W1)	36,000
Current Liabilities	
Deferred income (W2)	12,000

W1 Deferred Income – Non-current Liabilities

	€
Amount of grant received	60,000
Amount amortised year ended 31 December 2018	(12,000)
Amount amortised in the year ended 31 December 2019	(12,000)
Balance on deferred income	36,000

W2 Deferred Income – Current Liabilities

The amount to be amortised in the year ended 31 December 2019 is:

$$€60,000 \div 5 \text{ years}$$
$$= €12,000$$

(c)

	Debit €	Credit €
Deferred income account	48,000	
SPLOCI – grant repayment	12,000	
Grant repayment liability account		60,000

To recognise the liability in relation to the grant.

(Try **Review Question 28.2** at the end of this chapter.)

28.3 ACCOUNTING TREATMENT OF GRANTS RECEIVED IN RELATION TO CURRENT EXPENDITURE

Government agencies may provide grants to offset the costs incurred. They relate to costs incurred in the period, such as wages and training. The grant is recognised in the reporting period in which it becomes receivable.

The grant income can be presented as either 'other income' or it can reduce the related expense in the SPLOCI.

Example 28.5 demonstrates the presentation alternatives in relation to grants received in respect of current expenditure.

EXAMPLE 28.5: GRANT RELATED TO CURRENT EXPENDITURE

Cashmere Ltd received a grant in relation to training costs incurred in the reporting period ended 31 December 2019. The total training costs for the period were €265,000 and the grant received was €35,000.

Requirement Prepare the extract from the SPLOCI for the year ended 31 December 2019.

Solution

Option 1 Present as 'other income'

	€
Gross profit	X
Other income	35,000
Training costs	(265,000)

Option 2 Reduce the related expense by the amount of the grant

	€
Gross profit	X
Training costs (€265,000 – €35,000)	(230,000)

(Try **Review Question 28.3** at the end of this chapter.)

28.4 OTHER ASSISTANCE

Government agencies may provide non-cash assistance to companies, such as technical or marketing advice. It may not be reasonable to place a value on such assistance provided. "The significance of the benefit ... may be such that disclosure of the nature, extent and duration of the assistance is necessary in order that the financial statements may not be misleading" (IAS 20, paragraph 36).

28.5 DISCLOSURE

In the notes to the financial statements the following disclosures should be made:
- The accounting policy adopted for government grants.
- The nature and extent of government grants recognised in the financial statements and an indication of other forms of government assistance from which the entity has directly benefited.
- Any unfulfilled conditions relating to the grants.

28.6 IAS 20 COMPARED WITH FRS 102

FRS 102, unlike IAS 20, allows the entity an accounting choice in relation to the treatment of grants:
- recognise the grant income in profit or loss when the performance-related conditions have been met, this is known as the performance model; or
- recognise the grant income in the SPLOCI when the related expense is recognised.

FRS 102 requires the entity to provide an indication of other forms of government assistance from which the entity has directly benefited.

A performance-related condition is defined in FRS 102, Appendix I, as "a condition that requires the performance of a particular level of service or units of output to be delivered, with payment of, or entitlement to, the resources conditional on that performance."

EXAM TIPS

- Check to see whether you have been provided with details of the accounting policy adopted by the entity.
- Identify whether the grant relates to capital or current expenditure.
- Make sure you identify the date the grant was received and the reporting date of the financial statements.

28.7 CONCLUSION

IAS 20 deals with the accounting treatment of government grants. Grants received in relation to current expenditure (e.g. training costs) are either presented in the SPLOCI as 'other income' or are deducted from the costs with which they are associated. Grants received in relation to the purchase of assets (known as capital grants) are treated in one of two ways: they either reduce the cost of the related asset or they are treated as deferred income. The net impact on the reported profit is the same irrespective of the method chosen to present the grant.

SUMMARY OF LEARNING OBJECTIVES

After having studied this chapter, readers should be able to:

Learning Objective 1 Account for grants provided in relation to capital expenditure.

Grants received in relation to capital expenditure can be treated in either of the following ways:
- reduce the cost of the asset by the grant amount – this results in a lower depreciable amount and as a result the depreciation charge is reduced; or
- treat the grant as deferred income and amortise it over the useful life of the asset in a manner that reflects the benefit derived from the use of the asset. Deferred income is presented in the SOFP split between current and non-current liabilities.

Learning Objective 2 Account for grants provided in relation to current expenditure.

Grants received in relation to current expenditure can be treated in either of the following ways:
- present them as 'other income' in the SPLOCI in the period in which the related cost is recognised in the SPLOCI; or
- reduce the relevant cost by the amount of the grant in the SPLOCI.

Learning Objective 3 Account for the repayment of grants received in relation to capital expenditure.

Repayment of a grant is treated as a change in accounting estimate in accordance with IAS 8.

The journal entries to recognise a repayment when the grant reduced the cost of the asset can be summarised as follows:

	Debit €	Credit €
Property, plant and equipment – cost account	X	
Accumulated depreciation account		X

	Debit €	Credit €
SPLOCI – repayment of grant	X	
Bank/liability account		X

To record the repayment of a grant that reduced the cost of an asset.

The journal entries to recognise a repayment when the grant is treated as deferred income can be summarised as follows:

	Debit €	Credit €
Deferred income account	X	
SPLOCI – repayment of grant	X	
Bank/liability account		X

To record the repayment of a grant that is treated as deferred income.

Learning Objective 4 Account for repayment of grants received in relation to current expenditure.

Repayment of the grant is treated as a change in accounting estimate in accordance with IAS 8.

The grant has been recognised in the SPLOCI in an earlier reporting period:

	Debit €	Credit €
SPLOCI – repayment of grant	X	
Bank/liability account		X

To record the repayment of a grant that had been recognised in an earlier period.

If the grant was recognised in the current reporting period, then reverse the initial journal entries.

QUESTIONS

Review Questions

(See **Appendix A** for Solutions to Review Questions.)

Question 28.1

The following transactions took place during the reporting period ended 31 December 2019:

Date	Transaction	Amount €
1 May 2019	Purchased a machine by cheque	280,000
10 May 2019	Received a grant payment in relation to the purchase of the asset	30,000

No entries have been posted in relation to any of the above. The company treats grants in relation to capital expenditure as deferred income.

Depreciation is charged on machinery on a straight-line basis over the estimated useful life of six years.

A full year's depreciation charge is made in the year of purchase and none in the year of sale. The machine has an estimated residual value of €40,000.

Requirement Prepare the journal entries in relation to the above transactions and the extract from the financial statements as at 31 December 2019.

Question 28.2

Punch Ltd purchased an asset on 1 January 2017 for €360,000. It received a government grant of €60,000 in relation to the purchase of the asset, which it netted off against the cost of the asset.

Punch Ltd depreciated the asset on a straight-line basis over six years, charging a full year's depreciation in the year of purchase and none in the year of disposal.

Towards the end of 2019, it was discovered that Punch had not complied with the full conditions of the grant and now has to repay it in full. A cheque was issued on 12 January 2020 to repay the grant in full.

Requirement Prepare the journal entries in relation to the reporting period ended 31 December 2019.

Question 28.3

During 2019, Wingding Ltd embarked on a significant expansion programme that involved the employment of an additional 40 staff. The government is providing grants towards the cost of employing additional staff at a rate of €5,000 for each new employee in the year that the employment commences.

The total labour cost for the reporting period ended was €4,256,000.

Requirement Prepare the extracts from the financial statements in relation to the current grant received in 2019.

Challenging Questions

(Solutions to Challenging Questions are available through your lecturer.)

Question 28.1

What are the requirements of IAS 20 *Accounting for Government Grants and Disclosure of Government Assistance* concerning:
(a) Grants relating to assets?

5 Minutes

(b) Grants relating to income?

2 Minutes

(c) Non-monetary grants?

2 Minutes

(Based on Chartered Accountants Ireland, Prof II Financial Accounting, Summer 2006, Question 4)

Financial Instruments

Having studied this chapter, readers should be able to:
1. understand what constitutes a financial instrument;
2. understand the different accounting treatments and presentations of debt and equity instruments; and
3. understand when an effective interest rate is used.

29.1 INTRODUCTION

'**Financial instrument**' is a term used to cover a wide range of items in the financial statements: from the most basic of financial instruments, such as trade receivables, to more complicated items, such as derivatives. The aim of this chapter is to provide an introduction to financial instruments and some of the key concepts.

There are a number of accounting standards that deal with the treatment of financial instruments:
- IAS 32 *Financial Instruments: Presentation*;
- IFRS 7 *Financial Instruments: Disclosures*; and
- IFRS 9 *Financial Instruments*.

29.2 PRESENTATION OF FINANCIAL INSTRUMENTS

IAS 32 defines a financial instrument as "any contract that gives rise to a financial asset of one entity and a financial liability or equity instrument of another entity."

An equity instrument is a contract that evidences a residual interest. A residual interest means that the holder of the equity instruments, or ordinary shares (that is, the person who purchased the shares), is entitled to a share of any excess of assets over all of its liabilities if, and when, the company winds up.

The purpose of the next two examples is to provide details of common transactions that create a financial instrument. Sometimes when people hear the words 'financial instrument' they think they are dealing with very difficult and complex transactions, but they are often very simple and frequently occurring transactions.

Example 29.1 demonstrates the recognition of a financial asset and liability by the parties to a transaction.

EXAMPLE 29.1: RECOGNITION OF FINANCIAL INSTRUMENTS

Anthony Ltd sold goods on credit to Cleopatra Ltd for €50,000 on 1 June 2019.

Requirement Explain this transaction in terms of the recognition of financial instruments by each party to the transaction.

Solution

There is a contractual obligation between Anthony Ltd and Cleopatra Ltd:
- in the financial statements of Anthony Ltd, a trade receivable (financial asset) would be recognised of €50,000; and
- in the financial statements of Cleopatra Ltd, a trade payable (financial liability) would be recognised of €50,000.

This transaction creates a financial instrument for both Anthony Ltd and Cleopatra Ltd.

Anthony's financial records
The journal entry to recognise the sale on credit is:

	Debit €	Credit €
Trade receivables account (SOFP)	50,000	
SPLOCI – revenue account		50,000

To recognise the credit sale to Cleopatra Ltd.

Cleopatra's financial records
The journal entry to recognise the purchase on credit is:

	Debit €	Credit €
SPLOCI – purchases account	50,000	
Trade payables account (SOFP)		50,000

To recognise the credit purchases from Anthony Ltd.

In **Example 29.1** the situation resulted in the creation of a financial asset in one entity and a financial liability in another entity. The other situation that could arise is where a transaction gives rise to a financial asset in one entity and equity in another entity.

Example 29.2 demonstrates the recognition of a financial asset in the financial statements of one party to a transaction and equity in the financial statements of the other party to the transaction.

EXAMPLE 29.2: ORDINARY SHARES – ISSUER AND HOLDER

Caesar Ltd issued ordinary shares on 1 March 2019; 10,000 of the €1 ordinary shares issued were purchased by Brutus Ltd for €5.20 per share. Before this share issue Caesar Ltd had 2,000,000 ordinary shares in issue.

Solution

The transaction gives rise to:
- a financial asset in Brutus – the investment in Caesar Ltd's equity; and
- an equity instrument in Caesar Ltd.

Brutus Ltd's financial records
The journal entry to recognise the share purchase is:

	Debit €	Credit €
Investment in Caesar Ltd account	52,000	
Bank account		52,000

To recognise the investment in Caesar Ltd.

Caesar Ltd's financial records
The journal entry to recognise the share issue:

	Debit €	Credit €
Bank account	52,000	
Ordinary share capital account		10,000
Share premium account		42,000

To recognise the ordinary shares issued.

(Try **Review Questions 29.1** and **29.2** at the end of this chapter.)

So far in this chapter the recognition of financial assets and liabilities has been dealt with at a high level, but the accounting standards require that these items are classified on initial recognition. The initial recognition of an item as either a financial liability or as equity will now be explained.

29.3 DEBT VERSUS EQUITY

When an entity takes out a loan it is contractually obliged to repay the loan and interest attached to the loan. The interest cost is presented as a finance cost in the statement of profit or loss and other comprehensive income (SPLOCI) as a reduction in retained earnings. The loan is presented under liabilities in the statement of financial position (SOFP).

When an entity issues ordinary shares there is no contractual obligation on the company to pay the shareholder a dividend or to repay the investment. Any dividend must be proposed by the board of directors and approved by the shareholders at the AGM. The dividend is presented in the statement of changes in equity (SOCIE) as a reduction in retained earnings and **not** in the SPLOCI. The ordinary shares are presented under the 'equity and reserves' section of the SOFP.

An item is classified as equity if the following conditions are met:
1. there is no contractual obligation; and
2. it will be settled by the issue of a fixed number of shares in exchange for a fixed amount of cash or another financial asset.

In the following examples the classification of a transaction as either debt or equity will be considered.

Example 29.3 demonstrates the accounting treatment for preference shares when they are classified as a liability.

EXAMPLE 29.3: PREFERENCE SHARES CLASSIFIED AS DEBT

The following is an extract from the trial balance of Walker Ltd as at 31 December 2019:

8% Redeemable preference shares   €2,000,000

The preference shares were issued on 1 June 2013 and will be redeemed in full on 31 December 2021.

Requirement Explain the accounting treatment for the reporting period ended 31 December 2019.

Solution

Walker's contractual obligation to the preference shareholders is to:
- pay an annual dividend of €160,000 [€2,000,000 × 8%]; and
- repay the nominal value (i.e. €2 million) of the preference shares on 31 December 2021.

The existence of the contractual obligation means that the preference shares will be presented as a liability in the SOFP. As the preference shares will not be repaid within 12 months of the reporting date, they will be presented within non-current liabilities.

The preference dividend will be presented as a finance cost in the SPLOCI. The amount charged to finance cost for the reporting period ended 31 December 2019 is €160,000.

In **Example 29.3** there was a contractual obligation to repay the principal (i.e. the amount borrowed) and the dividend on the preference shares, therefore the preference shares were classified as a liability.

Example 29.4 demonstrates the accounting treatment for preference shares when they are classified as equity.

EXAMPLE 29.4: PREFERENCE SHARES CLASSIFIED AS EQUITY

The following is an extract from the trial balance of Winter Ltd as at 31 December 2019:

	€
Non-redeemable preference shares	1,800,000
Retained earnings as at 31 December 2018	5,235,000

The preference shares were issued by Winter Ltd on 1 January 2017 and there is no redemption date. Preference dividends are at the discretion of the board of directors and subject to the approval of the shareholders at the AGM. A preference dividend of 6% was approved on 15 December 2019.

The profit for the year ended 31 December 2019 was €812,500.

Requirement Explain the accounting treatment for the reporting period ended 31 December 2019.

Solution

Winter Ltd does not have a contractual obligation to either repay the nominal value of the preference shares or to pay preference dividends so they are classified as equity in the SOFP. The dividend on preference shares is presented in the SOCIE in the period that the dividend is approved for payment.

Winter Ltd
STATEMENT OF CHANGES IN EQUITY (EXTRACT)
for the year ended 31 December 2019

	Retained Earnings €
As at 1 January 2019	5,235,000
Profit for year	812,500
Preference dividend	(108,000)
As at 31 December 2019	5,939,500

(Try **Review Questions 29.3** and **29.4** at the end of this chapter.)

29.4 FINANCIAL ASSETS

At initial recognition, i.e. the day the entity becomes a party to the transaction, a financial asset is recognised in the financial statements. IFRS 9 *Financial Instruments* allows financial assets to be classified and measured using one of the following options:
1. fair value through profit or loss (FVTPL);
2. fair value through other comprehensive income (FVTOCI); or
3. financial assets at amortised cost.

Each of the above will be explained in more detail below.

Financial Assets Measured at FVTPL

Financial assets classified and measured at FVTPL are:
- equity instruments held for trading and purchased with the intention of making short-term gains;
- derivatives other than hedging instruments; and
- debt instruments not classified and measured at fair value through other comprehensive income or amortised cost.

A financial asset is classified as FVTPL unless another classification has been chosen. Transaction costs associated with the acquisition of a financial asset measured in this category are expensed to the statement of profit or loss when incurred.

Example 29.5 illustrates the recognition of a financial asset using FVTPL.

EXAMPLE 29.5: INITIAL RECOGNITION OF A FINANCIAL ASSET
MEASURED AT FVTPL

Armada Plc made an investment, which at initial recognition, it has chosen to measure at fair value through profit or loss. The financial asset cost €1,500,000, with transactions costs of €40,000.

Requirement Prepare the journal(s) to recognise the financial asset.

Solution

	Debit €	Credit €
Financial asset account	1,500,000	
Bank account		1,500,000
Initial recognition of financial asset.		
SOPL–P/L – transaction costs	40,000	
Bank account		40,000
To recognise transaction cost in SOPL.		

After their initial recognition, financial assets measured at FVTPL are subsequently measured at fair value, with any changes in fair value recognised in the profit or loss section of the SPLOCI.

Example 29.6 demonstrates how to record a change in fair value for a FVTPL financial asset.

EXAMPLE 29.6: ACCOUNTING FOR CHANGES IN THE FAIR VALUE
OF A FVTPL FINANCIAL ASSET

Weldon Ltd acquired a financial asset on 10 April 2019 that it classified as FVTPL. Its fair value at that date was €140,000.

Weldon prepares its financial statements to 31 December each year. The fair value of the financial asset as at 31 December 2019 was €155,000.

Requirement Prepare the journal entries to recognise the financial asset in the financial reporting period ended 31 December 2019.

Solution

	Debit €	Credit €
Financial asset at FVTPL account	140,000	
Bank		140,000
To recognise the financial asset at 10 April 2019.		
Financial asset at FVTPL account	15,000	
SPLOCI – gain on financial asset		15,000
To recognise the change in fair value at the reporting date.		

Financial Assets Measured at FVTOCI

The classification of financial assets measured at FVTOCI is designated at initial recognition and cannot be changed. As a result, changes in fair value are presented in the other comprehensive income section of the SPLOCI.

Transaction costs incurred in relation to the acquisition of a financial asset are included in the cost of the asset at initial recognition.

Example 29.7 demonstrates the recording of a financial asset at initial recognition.

EXAMPLE 29.7: INITIAL RECOGNITION OF A FINANCIAL ASSET MEASURED AT FVTOCI

Nevada Plc made an investment which it has chosen to measure at initial recognition at fair value through other comprehensive income. The financial asset cost €1,250,000 with associated transactions costs of €30,000.

Requirement Prepare the journal(s) to recognise the financial asset.

Solution

	Debit €	Credit €
Financial asset account	1,280,000	
Bank account		1,280,000
Initial recognition of financial asset.		

Example 29.8 demonstrates how to record a change in fair value when the financial asset is measured at FVTOCI.

EXAMPLE 29.8: ACCOUNTING FOR CHANGES IN THE FAIR VALUE OF A FVTOCI FINANCIAL ASSET

Scully Ltd acquired a financial asset on 5 July 2019 that it classified as FVTOCI. Its fair value at that date was €160,000.

Weldon prepares its financial statements to 31 December each year. The fair value of the financial asset as at 31 December 2019 was €154,000.

Requirement Prepare the journal entries to recognise the financial asset in the financial reporting period ended 31 December 2019.

Solution

	Debit €	Credit €
Financial asset at FVTOCI account	160,000	
Bank		160,000
To recognise the financial asset at 5 July 2019.		

	Debit €	Credit €
SPLOCI – loss on financial asset	6,000	
Financial asset at FVTOCI account		6,000
To recognise the change in fair value at the reporting date.		

Financial Assets Measured at Amortised Cost

A financial asset may have costs or income other than just interest income associated with it. In these circumstances an 'effective interest' is used to recognise the income in the statement of profit or loss in a constant manner over the term of the asset's life. The effective interest rate is the interest rate that discounts future cash flows to zero. (The calculation of the effective interest rate is beyond the scope of this textbook, we are merely interested in its use.)

Unless an entity has chosen to measure a financial asset at FVTPL, a debt instrument that meets the following two tests must be designated at amortised cost:
1. **Business Model Test** – where the financial asset is held for the purpose of collecting contractual cash flows relating to the asset rather than for short-term trading.
2. **Contractual Cash Flow Characteristic Test** – where the cash flows only relate to the collection of principal and interest.

Example 29.9 demonstrates the use of effective interest rates in relation to financial assets measured at amortised cost.

EXAMPLE 29.9: FINANCIAL ASSET MEASURED AT AMORTISED COST

On 1 January 2019, Armstrong Plc made an investment in a debt instrument in the amount of €2,500,000. Under the terms of the debt instrument, Armstrong is entitled to earn annual interest at a rate of 5%. The term of the investment in the debt instrument is five years.

Transaction costs related to the issue of the debt instrument amounted to €90,000. The effective interest rate has been determined to be 4.1871%.

Interest income is received annually in arrears with the investment repaid in full at the end of the term.

Requirement:

(a) Prepare the journal to recognise the investment at initial recognition on 1 January 2019.
(b) Prepare the journal to recognise the interest income for the year ended 31 December 2019 and 2020.

Solution

(a)

	Debit €	Credit €
Financial asset account	2,590,000	
Bank account		2,590,000
Initial recognition of financial asset.		

(b) To calculate the interest income in the SOPL the effective interest rate is used. The calculation of the entire term of the investment is set out below:

Year end	Opening balance	SOPL interest income @ 4.1871%	Received @ nominal rate	Closing balance
	€	€	€	€
31 December 2019	2,590,000	108,446	125,000	2,573,446
31 December 2020	2,573,446	107,752	125,000	2,556,198
31 December 2021	2,556,198	107,030	125,000	2,538,228
31 December 2022	2,538,228	106,278	125,000	2,519,506
31 December 2023	2,519,506	105,494	125,000	2,500,000

The journal entries would be:

	Debit €	Credit €
Bank account	125,000	
SOPL – finance income		108,446
Financial asset account		16,554

To recognise finance income at the effective interest rate for year ended 31 December 2019.

	Debit €	Credit €
Bank account	125,000	
SOPL – finance income		107,752
Financial asset account		17,248

To recognise finance income at the effective interest rate for year ended 31 December 2020.

29.5 FINANCIAL LIABILITIES

There are two categories of financial liability:
- financial liability at fair value through profit and loss; and
- financial liabilities measured at amortised cost.

Classification is made at the initial recognition date.

Financial Liabilities Measured at FVTPL

A financial liability is measured at FVTPL if:
- it reduces or eliminates the accounting mismatch that would arise from measuring assets and liabilities on different bases; or
- the liability is part of a group of financial liabilities (or a group of financial assets and liabilities) whose performance is measured and managed on a fair value basis. The management of such a group should be documented in terms of management's risk management and investment strategy and the information provided to key management personnel.

Changes in fair value are recognised in the SPLOCI in the period that the change in fair value occurred.

Financial Liabilities Measured at Amortised Cost

Loans can have several costs, such as interest, issue costs and premiums on redemption. A bank charges issue costs in relation to the arrangement of a loan facility. Loans can be structured so that minimum interest is paid over the term of the loan and a large payment made at the end of the loan term (i.e. premium on redemption).

When there are costs other than just the interest cost, an effective interest rate is used to charge the total cost associated with the loan facility over the term of the loan. The use of an effective interest rate means that the total cost is charged over the term of the loan rather than when the costs are incurred – for example, at the start of the loan period when the issue costs are incurred, or at the end of the loan when the premium on redemption is paid. (The calculation of the effective interest rate is beyond the scope of this textbook, we are merely interested in its use.)

Example 29.10 demonstrates the treatment of a loan where the only cost associated with the loan is the interest cost.

EXAMPLE 29.10: DEBT RECOGNITION – INTEREST COST ONLY ASSOCIATED WITH THE DEBT

On 1 January 2019, Weldon Ltd borrowed €500,000 from its local bank. The rate of interest on the loan is 6%, interest is paid in arrears and no capital is repaid until the end of the loan period – 31 December 2023.

Requirement Explain the accounting treatment and prepare the journal entries for the reporting period ended 31 December 2019.

Solution

The loan is recognised in the financial statements on 1 January 2019. The journal entry posted is:

	Debit €	Credit €
Bank account	500,000	
Loan liability account		500,000

To recognise the loan liability on 1 January 2019.

There is a finance cost associated with the loan and this is paid annually in arrears. The journal entry to recognise the finance cost in the financial statements is:

	Debit €	Credit €
SPLOCI – finance cost	30,000	
Bank account		30,000

To recognise finance cost on loan (6% × €500,000).

The loan is a financial liability in the financial statements of Weldon as there is a contractual obligation to repay the amount borrowed and the interest cost. The finance cost is recognised each year over the term of the loan.

In **Example 29.10** above, the only borrowing costs associated with the loan facility are the interest costs. In this situation, the interest cost is charged to the profit or loss section of the SPLOCI based on the nominal interest rate attaching to the loan. When there are other costs associated with the loan, an effective rate must be calculated and used to charge a portion of the total borrowing costs to each reporting period over the term of the loan. The effective interest rate is higher than the nominal rate attached to the loan.

Example 29.11 demonstrates the accounting for the costs associated with a loan if the loan involves issue costs as well as the interest cost.

EXAMPLE 29.11: EFFECTIVE INTEREST RATE

On 1 January 2019, Trident Ltd borrowed €800,000 from its local bank. The rate of interest on the loan is 5%, interest is paid in arrears and no capital is repaid until the end of the loan period – 31 December 2021. The bank has charged issue costs in relation to the loan of €10,000.

The effective interest rate on the loan is 5.463%.

Requirement Explain the accounting treatment and the journal entries for the reporting period ended 31 December 2019.

Solution

An effective interest rate is a necessary piece of information in this situation as there are issue costs relating to the loan in addition to the usual interest cost. The loan is recognised on the date it was made net of the issue costs. The journal entry is:

	Debit €	Credit €
Bank account	790,000	
Loan liability account		790,000

To recognise the loan liability, net of issue costs of €10,000.

The total costs associated with the loan are:

	€
Issue costs	10,000
Finance cost (€800,000 × 5% × 3 years)	120,000
Total cost	130,000

Under the matching concept, the total cost of the loan facility must be spread over the period of the loan rather than the issue costs being charged to the SPLOCI in the period that the cost was incurred. The effective interest rate is the rate used to apportion the total cost over the term of the loan.

The finance cost for the reporting date 31 December 2019 is based on the opening balance on the loan (net of the issue costs) and the effective interest rate:

$$€790,000 \times 5.463\%$$
$$= €43,158$$

The journal entry to recognise the finance cost is:

	Debit €	Credit €
SPLOCI – finance cost	43,158	
Loan liability account		43,158

To charge finance cost to SPLOCI based on the effective interest rate for the period ended 31 December 2019.

When the interest charge is paid, it is based on the nominal value of the loan and the interest rate attaching to the loan:

$$€800,000 \times 5\%$$
$$= €40,000$$

	Debit €	Credit €
Loan liability account	40,000	
Bank account		40,000

To recognise the payment of the interest charge at 31 December 2019.

At the end of the reporting period the balance on the loan is €793,158:

Reporting Date	Opening Balance €	SPLOCI – Finance Cost @ 5.463% €	Interest Paid €	Closing Balance €
31 December 2019	790,000	43,158	(40,000)	793,158

At the end of each reporting period the balance on the loan account will increase until the end of the term when the full balance of €800,000 is reached.

Reporting Date	Opening Balance €	SPLOCI – Finance Cost @ 5.463% €	Interest Paid €	Closing Balance €
31 December 2019	790,000	43,158	(40,000)	793,158
31 December 2020	793,157	43,330	(40,000)	796,488
31 December 2021	796,488	43,512	(40,000)	800,000

In the reporting period ended 31 December 2020, the following accounting journal entries will be posted:

	Debit €	Credit €
SPLOCI – finance cost	43,330	
Loan liability account		43,330

To charge finance cost to SPLOCI based on the effective interest rate for the period ended 31 December 2020.

Loan liability account	40,000	
Bank account		40,000

To recognise the payment of the interest charge at 31 December 2020.

continued overleaf

In the reporting period ended 31 December 2021 the following accounting journal entries will be posted:

	Debit €	Credit €
SPLOCI – finance cost	43,512	
Loan liability account		43,512

To charge finance cost to SPLOCI, based on the effective interest rate, for the period ended 31 December 2021.

	Debit €	Credit €
Loan liability account	40,000	
Bank account		40,000

To recognise the payment of the interest charge at 31 December 2021.

	Debit €	Credit €
Loan liability account	800,000	
Bank account		800,000

To recognise the repayment of the loan on 31 December 2021.

(Try **Review Question 29.6** at the end of this chapter.)

29.6 IFRS 7 COMPARED WITH FRS 102

Under FRS 102, financial instruments are either measured at amortised cost or fair value through profit or loss depending on their characteristics. The disclosure requirements are greater under IFRS than under FRS 102.

Exam Tip

It is important to look at each item and identify whether it should be presented as either a liability or as an equity.

29.7 CONCLUSION

In this chapter the concepts of debt and equity were explained and the implications of this classification to the presentation and preparation of financial statements. Financial assets and liabilities are classified on initial recognition and this classification determines how the asset or liability is accounted for.

SUMMARY OF LEARNING OBJECTIVES

After having studied this chapter, readers should be able to:

Learning Objective 1 Understand what constitutes a financial instrument.

A financial instrument is a contractual obligation that gives rise to a financial asset in one entity and either a financial liability or an equity instrument in another.

Learning Objective 2 Understand the different accounting treatments and presentations of debt and equity instruments.

In order to be presented as equity, there must be no contractual obligation to make a dividend payment or to repay the investment and no agreement to issue a fixed number of shares in exchange for a fixed monetary amount.

Learning Objective 3 Understand when an effective interest rate is used.

An effective interest rate is used to spread the total costs over the term of the loan. The finance income/charge to the SPLOCI is based on the effective rate being applied to the opening balance.

QUESTIONS

Review Questions

(See **Appendix A** for Solutions to Review Questions.)

Question 29.1

Andrew Ltd purchased 20,000 ordinary shares in Smyth Ltd on 1 May 2019 for €80,000. How will the transaction be classified in the respective entities' financial statements?

	Andrew Ltd	**Smyth Ltd**
(a)	Equity	Financial asset
(b)	Financial asset	Equity
(c)	Financial asset	Liability

Question 29.2

Walker Ltd purchased goods worth €90,000 on credit from Swamp Ltd. Which company has the financial asset and which has the financial liability?

	Walker Ltd	**Swamp Ltd**
(a)	Financial asset	Financial liability
(b)	Financial liability	Financial asset

Question 29.3

Parker Ltd issued 200,000 preference shares on 1 October 2019. The shares do not have a redemption date and a dividend is only paid at the discretion of the board of directors with the approval of the ordinary shareholders at the AGM.

Requirement Are the preference shares classified as debt or equity in the financial statements of Parker Ltd?

Question 29.4

Prince Ltd issued 100,000 preference shares on 1 November 2019. The shares do not have a redemption date and there is a mandatory annual dividend of 5% payable.

Requirement Are the preference shares classified as debt or equity in the financial statements of Prince Ltd?

Question 29.5

Sutton Ltd has a financial asset that it has classified as fair value through profit or loss. The asset has a carrying amount of €240,000.

At the reporting date, 31 December 2019, the fair value of the financial asset is €226,000.

Requirement What is the journal entry to recognise the fair value adjustment?

Question 29.6

Tumble Ltd took out a loan from a financial institution of €500,000 on 1 January 2019. The interest rate, according to the loan agreement, is 6%. The loan has arrangement fees of €15,000. The term of the loan is five years.

The effective interest rate has been calculated as 6.73%.

Requirement Prepare the extracts from the financial statements in relation to the loan at the reporting date 31 December 2019.

Provisions, Contingent Liabilities and Contingent Assets

LEARNING OBJECTIVES

Having studied this chapter, readers should be able to:
1. identify and account for provisions;
2. identify and account for contingent liabilities;
3. identify and account for contingent assets;
4. identify and account for onerous contracts;
5. identify and account for restructuring costs;
6. identify and account for reimbursement of provisions; and
7. prepare relevant disclosure notes.

30.1 INTRODUCTION

IAS 37 *Provisions, Contingent Liabilities and Contingent Assets* sets out the accounting rules in relation to **provisions, contingent liabilities** and **contingent assets**. Each of these items will be dealt with in terms of the specific accounting rules and journal entries.

30.2 PROVISIONS

A provision is defined by IAS 37 as "a liability of uncertain timing and amount". It is known that payment will probably have to be made, but it is not known exactly when the payment will be made or how much will be involved, for example, a company is being sued by a former employee for unfair dismissal and legal advice is that the company will lose the case. It is expected that the case will be in the courts within the next 12 months and similar cases have resulted in damages being awarded of €80,000. The entity does not know exactly when the case will be settled or how much will have to be ultimately paid in damages, but it can make an estimate based on what has happened in the past in similar situations.

In order to raise a provision, IAS 37 requires that all of the following conditions are met:
• there is an obligating event;
• it is probable there will be an outflow of economic benefit; and
• a reliable estimate of the amount can be made.

A provision can only be used in relation to expenditure for which it was originally set up. A provision cannot be 'repurposed', that is, if a provision is set up for one purpose, it cannot be used for a different one. For example, a provision set up in relation to a legal case cannot be used for the dismantling cost of an asset at the end of its useful life.

Each of the conditions to be met to raise a provision is dealt with in turn below.

Obligating Event

An obligating event can be the result of either a legal or a constructive obligation.

A legal obligation means that the entity must act in a certain way due to the existence of legislation or a legal requirement.

A constructive obligation arises because there is an expectation that the company will act in a certain way as a result of their past actions or published views. For example, a company operates in a country where there is no legislation in place in relation to the environment but the company has a well-publicised policy of minimising damage to the environment; the policy creates an obligating event for the entity.

Outflow of Economic Benefit

'Outflow of economic benefit' simply means that the entity will have to make a payment or transfer an asset to satisfy the provision at a future date.

Reliable Estimate can be made

An estimate can be made based on past experience in relation to similar transactions/events. A provision may be required for a large number of items (such as warranty claims) or a single item (such as a legal case); estimates used in each scenario will be slightly different.

Example 30.1 shows how to determine the amount to be provided for when there is a large number of items.

EXAMPLE 30.1: PROVISION AMOUNT BASED ON EXPECTED VALUE

A company manufactures a product for which it offers a one-year warranty to fix any defects. Based on the entity's past experience, 8% of all products will require a minor repair and 1% will require a major repair.

The estimated costs of these repairs are:

Minor	€15 per unit
Major	€80 per unit

In the reporting period ended 31 December 2019, 500,000 units of the product were produced and sold.

Requirement At what amount should the provision be recognised as at 31 December 2019?

Solution

Based on guidance provided in IAS 37, in order to determine the amount of the provision the expected value technique should be used.

The expected costs of repairs are estimated as follows:

% of Total Units Produced and Sold	No. of Units	Cost of Repair Per Unit €	Total Cost €
8%	40,000	15	600,000
1%	5,000	80	400,000
			1,000,000

A provision is raised in the financial statements for €1,000,000.

Example 30.2 shows how to determine the amount to be provided for when there is a single item with a number of possible outcomes.

EXAMPLE 30.2: PROVISION AMOUNT FOR A SINGLE ITEM WITH A NUMBER OF POSSIBLE OUTCOMES

When a provision is required for a single item, the estimate is based on the most likely cost.

Arbour Ltd is being sued by a customer over the supply of faulty goods. There is a range of possible payments for damages and the likelihood of each possible payment has been assessed as follows:

Damages Amount €	Probability
20,000	0.25
150,000	0.70
240,000	0.05

Requirement At what amount should the provision be recognised?

Solution

The provision will be included in the financial statements at the 'most likely' amount, that is, the one with the highest probability. In this case the amount of the provision will be €150,000.

The purpose of **Example 30.3** is to demonstrate the accounting treatment arising from a legal obligation.

EXAMPLE 30.3: PROVISION – LEGAL OBLIGATION

A customer visiting Arnold Ltd's showrooms on 15 December 2019 fell on a wet floor and broke his left arm. On 23 December 2019, Arnold Ltd received notice that legal proceedings had been issued against it by the customer for the amount of €80,000, which is similar to amounts awarded in similar cases.

Legal opinion is that the customer is highly likely to win the case. There is a delay in the courts and the case is not expected to be heard until June 2021.

Requirement Explain the accounting treatment and prepare any journal entries required for the reporting period ended 31 December 2019.

Solution

IAS 37 requires three conditions to be met in order to raise a provision. The conditions are:
- There must have been an obligating event. In this case an accident occurred in the company's showroom and a customer was injured.
- It must be possible for a reliable estimate to be made. The customer's legal action claiming damages of €80,000 provides a reliable estimate for the financial statements.
- An outflow of economic benefit must be probable. If the company loses the case it will have to pay damages and the legal opinion is that this is highly likely.

All three conditions have been met so a provision should be raised in the financial statements of Arnold in the reporting period ended 31 December 2019.

The journal entry required is:

	Debit €	Credit €
SPLOCI – provision for legal case	80,000	
Non-current liabilities account – provision		80,000

To recognise a provision in relation to a legal case due before the courts in 2021.

As the case will not be heard until 2021, and the reporting date is 31 December 2019, the provision will be presented within non-current liabilities.

Example 30.4 demonstrates the creation of a provision as a result of a constructive obligation.

EXAMPLE 30.4: PROVISION – CONSTRUCTIVE OBLIGATION

Under consumer legislation in Merryville, companies only have to provide refunds to customers if the goods they sold are faulty. Everhopefull Ltd has a much publicised customer care policy in which it includes reference to its policy of providing refunds not just for faulty goods but also if a customer changes their mind about the purchase.

In previous reporting periods, the amount of refunds to customers due to a change of mind were negligible, but in the current year the amount has increased quite significantly and Everhopefull's auditors are advising them to raise a provision in relation to future refunds as this trend is expected to continue. The auditors estimate a provision is required in the amount of €20,000. All claims for refunds are expected to be made within 12 months of the reporting date.

The company has a provision policy in relation to refunds for faulty goods.

Requirement Explain the accounting treatment for refunds.

Solution

Everhopefull Ltd has two obligating events.
1. A legal obligation to refund customers for faulty goods sold. The company has a provision policy in relation to this issue.
2. A constructive obligation to refund customers if they change their minds about their purchases and return the goods. There is no legal obligation for the company to make a refund

in these circumstances but, based on its past practice and publicised policy, it has created an obligation.

A reliable estimate can be made. For a number of years the company has provided a negligible amount of refunds to customers who simply changed their mind about their purchases. The pattern of claims has changed and the amount claimed in the current year was significant. The auditors have assessed the amount of the provision required at €20,000. The factors that they would have considered include:
- sales patterns and changes in these over the period as well as expectations for the future;
- customer profile and possible changes;
- quality of products sold;
- change in pattern of refunds claimed; and
- economic conditions.

There is a probable outflow of economic benefit as refunds have had to be made to customers in the past and are expected to be made in the future as the company's policy has not been amended.

The journal entry required is:

	Debit €	Credit €
SPLOCI – provision for refunds	20,000	
Current liabilities account – provision		20,000
To recognise a provision in relation to customer refunds.		

(Try **Review Questions 30.1** and **30.2** at the end of this chapter.)

30.3 CONTINGENT LIABILITY

The main difference between a provision and a contingent liability relates to the level of certainty: a provision involves a probable outflow but a contingent liability only involves a **possible** outflow.

In accordance with IAS 37, no adjustment is made in the financial statements in relation to a contingent liability but disclosure must be made in the notes to the financial statements. The disclosure of the contingent liability should include:
- an estimate of its financial effect;
- an identification of any uncertainties in relation to the timing or the amount involved;
- an assessment of the possibility of any **reimbursement**.

Example 30.5 demonstrates a contingent liability and explains the accounting treatment.

EXAMPLE 30.5: CONTINGENT LIABILITY

Bobcat Ltd dismissed one of its employees on 20 November 2019. The employee had been through a number of performance meetings and had been informed that their performance was below the acceptable standard.

A performance improvement plan was agreed between the employee, their line manager and a representative from human resources. The plan set out a number of targets to be achieved by the employee and the support that would be provided by the line manager to assist them. The employee failed to achieve any of the targets set and was dismissed.

On 5 December 2019, the former employee initiated legal proceedings against the company for unfair dismissal. The company received notice of these legal proceedings on 10 December 2019.

In past legal cases the settlement has been equivalent of two years' annual salary. In this case the employee's annual salary was €60,000 at the date of their dismissal. Legal advice is that the company has followed best practice and complied with all relevant legal obligations, and it estimates the former employee has a 25% chance of winning the case.

Requirement Explain the accounting treatment for the reporting period ended 31 December 2019.

Solution

The company has an obligating event: it dismissed an employee who has initiated legal proceedings on the grounds of unfair dismissal. An estimate of the amount that could be payable can reliably be made based on past cases: two years' annual salary which, based on the information provided, would amount to €120,000. The likelihood that the company will lose the case and have to make a payment to the former employee is only 'possible', as legal opinion is that the employee only has a 25% chance of winning the case.

A provision cannot be raised as the likelihood that a payment will have to be made is only at the level of 'possible'. The payout due to the legal case is a contingent liability so no adjustment is made to the financial statements in relation to the item, but a disclosure note will have to be included in the notes to the financial statements.

(Try **Review Question 30.3** at the end of this chapter.)

30.4 CONTINGENT ASSET

A contingent asset arises when the entity is expecting a future **inflow** of economic benefit and the level of certainty that the amount will be received is only probable. Contingent assets are not recognised in the financial statements – if entities recognised contingent assets, it would mean that income would be recognised that may not ultimately be received. Accounting is based on the concept of prudence, under which costs are recognised as soon as they are incurred and income or gains only when virtually certain to be received.

The disclosures required in relation to contingent assets are as follows:
- a brief description of the nature of the contingent asset; and
- an estimate of the financial effect.

Example 30.6 demonstrates a contingent asset and explains the accounting treatment.

EXAMPLE 30.6: CONTINGENT ASSET

Meredith Ltd entered into a contract with SuperMaintenance Ltd to manage the electrical, plumbing and heating systems of its office building. The contract set out agreed response times to failures in the electrical, heating and plumbing systems and the penalties for failure to meet these targets were specified clearly in the contract.

SuperMaintenance Ltd failed to deliver the minimum performance levels, which meant that Meredith Ltd had to engage other contractors to repair a number of faults that occurred.

Meredith Ltd issued legal proceedings on 8 November 2019 to recover the costs it had incurred in relation to the contractors that they had to employ to correct faults not dealt with by SuperMaintenance Ltd and a portion of the fees paid under the contract. The total of these costs and the fees refund claimed amounts to €92,000.

Requirement Explain the accounting treatment.

Solution

The company in this situation has instigated legal proceedings against a service provider for failure to meet the terms of the contract. If the company wins the case, it will be the recipient of an amount of money, which means the event is a contingent asset.

No adjustment is made in the financial statements in relation to the contingent asset at this time as the case is still outstanding and no decision has been made. However, a disclosure note will be have to be included in the financial statements, providing a brief description of the court case and the amount involved.

The amount claimed would only be recognised in the financial statements when the receipt is virtually certain.

(Try **Review Question 30.4** at the end of this chapter.)

30.5 ONEROUS CONTRACTS

An **onerous contract** is one in which the costs associated with the contract are greater than the benefits derived from that contract. The costs under the onerous contract are recognised in the financial statements.

Example 30.7 demonstrates an onerous contract and the accounting journal entries required.

EXAMPLE 30.7: ONEROUS CONTRACT

Brighton Ltd entered into a contract to supply goods to a customer for a period of five years at a fixed selling price per unit. It is now in the fourth year of the contract and the cost of producing the goods exceeds the selling price. Brighton Ltd does not have any choice but to continue the contract as the terms cannot be amended at this time.

The loss expected on the contract for the current year is estimated at €10,000 and for next year at €32,000.

Requirement Explain the accounting treatment and prepare the journal entries for the current year.

Solution

When the cost of a contract exceeds the revenue it is referred to as an onerous contract. The accounting treatment for such a contract is to recognise the expected loss on the remaining period of the contract in full.

The journal entry required to reflect the onerous contract in the financial statements of Brighton is:

	Debit €	Credit €
SPLOCI – onerous contract	32,000	
Current liabilities account – onerous contract		32,000
To recognise a provision in relation to the onerous contract.		

30.6 REIMBURSEMENT

When the entity can claim some of the costs under a provision from another party, this is known as reimbursement.

The rules set out in IAS 37 in relation to reimbursement are as follows:
- do not recognise the reimbursement amount unless it is **virtually certain** to be received;
- the reimbursement is recognised as an asset separately – it is not netted off against the provision in the statement of financial position (SOFP); and
- the reimbursement and the provision may be netted off against one another in the statement of profit or loss and other comprehensive income (SPLOCI).

Example 30.8 demonstrates the situation where a reimbursement is due to the company. The journal entries and extracts from the financial statements are provided to assist your understanding.

EXAMPLE 30.8: REIMBURSEMENT

Constructo Ltd is involved in the construction industry. A year ago it sold a building to Wilfred Ltd for use as its head office. Wilfred Ltd is suing Constructo Ltd in relation to faulty electrical work – the damages claimed in its law suit amount to €240,000. Legal advice is that Wilfred Ltd will win the case.

Constructo Ltd subcontracted the electrical work to Electro Ltd; under the terms of the contract Electro Ltd is liable for 75% of all damages that may be paid in relation to any faulty work it had undertaken.

As at 31 December 2018, the notice of the legal proceedings issued by Wilfred Ltd had been received by Constructo Ltd and Electro Ltd was aware of the potential amounts due.

As at 31 December 2019, the legal case has been concluded and damages were awarded to Wilfred Ltd in the amount of €250,000. Electro Ltd has confirmed that it will pay its share of the damages and payment of €187,500 was received from it on 4 January 2020.

Constructo Ltd prepares its financial statements to 31 December each year.

The financial statements of Constructo for the reporting period 31 December 2019 were approved for issue on 3 March 2020.

Requirement Explain the accounting treatment and prepare the journal entries, where appropriate, for the reporting periods ended 31 December 2018 and 2019.

Solution

Reporting period ended 31 December 2018

Constructo raises a provision in its financial statements for the amount of €240,000 as all of the IAS 37 conditions have been met as follows:
- Constructo has an obligating event as it sold the building;
- the company will probably have to make a payment to settle the case as the legal advice is that Wilfred will probably win; and
- an estimate can be made based on the amount being claimed by Wilfred.

Constructo can claim 75% of the total cost of the case from Electro, the company to which it sub-contracted the electrical work. As at the reporting date, the reimbursement by Electro is not virtually certain so it is not recognised in the financial statements.

	Debit €	Credit €
SPLOCI – provision	240,000	
Current liabilities account – provision		240,000

To recognise a provision.

STATEMENT OF PROFIT OR LOSS AND OTHER COMPREHENSIVE INCOME (EXTRACT)
for the year ended 31 December 2018

	€
Provision	(240,000)

STATEMENT OF FINANCIAL POSITION (EXTRACT)
as at 31 December 2018

	€
Current Liabilities	
Provision	240,000

Reporting period ended 31 December 2019

A decision was made in relation to the legal proceedings and the case was won by Wilfred, which was awarded €250,000. Constructo is liable for 25% of this amount, i.e. €62,500. The sub-contractor is liable for 75%, i.e. €187,500.

As at the reporting date, Constructo cannot recognise the amount to be reimbursed by Electro as it is still not virtually certain that the amount will be received. However, within the period after the reporting date covered by IAS 10 *Events After the Reporting Period* (see **Chapter 23**), the amount received from Electro is an adjusting event as the payment relates to a situation that existed at the reporting date. The reimbursement is presented separately in the SOFP, but can be netted off against the related provision in the SPLOCI.

Note: there is a greater level of certainty required for the recognition of the reimbursement than for the provision, which may result in the provision cost being recognised in an earlier reporting period than the reimbursement.

	Debit €	Credit €
SPLOCI – provision	10,000	
Current liabilities account – legal case liability		10,000

To recognise the liability in relation to the settled case, 31 December 2019.

	Debit €	Credit €
Reimbursement due account	187,500	
SPLOCI – reimbursement		187,500

To recognise the reimbursement due in relation to the settled case, 4 January 2020.

	Debit €	Credit €
Bank account	187,500	
Reimbursement due account		187,500

To recognise the receipt, 4 January 2020.

STATEMENT OF PROFIT OR LOSS AND OTHER COMPREHENSIVE INCOME (EXTRACT)
for the year ended 31 December 2019

	€
Legal case (€187,500 – €10,000)	177,500

STATEMENT OF FINANCIAL POSITION (EXTRACT)
as at 31 December 2019

	€
Current Assets	
Reimbursement – Electro Ltd	187,500
Current Liabilities	
Amount due on settlement of legal case	250,000

Note: the reimbursement is presented in the SOFP as due because it was not received until after the reporting date.

30.7 RESTRUCTURING

The following are examples of events that involve restructuring of organisations:
• sale of a business;
• termination of a business;
• closure of certain business locations in countries or regions;
• relocation of certain business locations from one country or region to another; and
• changes in the management structure of the organisation, for example, elimination of a management layer.

A provision for restructuring can only be recognised when the entity has an obligation. The obligation arises when the entity has a detailed formal plan in place and has raised a valid expectation among those affected by the restructuring. An entity can create a valid expectation by either informing those affected by the planned restructuring or commencing the implementation of the restructuring before the reporting date.

The detailed formal restructuring plan should identify the following:
- the business or part of the business affected by the restructuring;
- the principal locations affected;
- the costs involved in the restructuring;
- when the plan will be implemented; and
- the employees affected – their location, function and the approximate number of staff.

To raise a provision in the current reporting period in relation to restructuring, the decision must have been made before the reporting date and the company has either:
1. begun implementation of the restructuring plan; or
2. announced the major features of the plan to those affected by the restructuring so that they are aware that it will be undertaken.

If the restructuring begins, or is only announced, after the reporting date but before the financial statements are approved for issue, it will constitute a non-adjusting event under IAS 10. Disclosure in relation to the restructuring is only required if the amount involved is material, see **Chapter 23**.

Restructuring costs are those directly arising from the restructuring of the organisation and not with the ongoing activity of the entity. Costs specifically excluded from a restructuring provision are:
- retraining of continuing staff;
- relocation costs of continuing staff;
- marketing; and
- investment in new systems and distribution networks.

Example 30.9 demonstrates the accounting for restructuring in the financial statements.

EXAMPLE 30.9: ACCOUNTING FOR RESTRUCTURING

During the reporting period ended 31 December 2019, the company experienced a deterioration in its financial performance and, as a result, has decided to review its operations and product offerings. Following the findings of the review, management decided to restructure its operations, which will involve the closure of one of its divisions. Management has drawn up a plan detailing the area to be closed, how the planned closure would be achieved and the costs involved.

The costs involved in the restructuring are as follows:

	€
Redundancy cost	810,000
Retraining costs	40,000

The restructuring plan was implemented in November 2019 and is expected to be completed by August 2020.

Requirement Explain the accounting treatment for the reporting period ended 31 December 2019.

Solution

The company has met the conditions necessary to raise a provision in relation to restructuring as it has prepared a detailed formal plan and begun implementation before the reporting date. The provision can be raised for the amount of €810,000. The retraining costs cannot be included in the provision.

The accounting journal entry required is:

	Debit €	Credit €
SPLOCI – restructuring provision	810,000	
Restructuring provision account		810,000

To recognise the restructuring provision.

The training costs should be expensed to the profit or loss section of the SPLOCI when incurred.

30.8 DISCLOSURE

For each class of provision the entity will reconcile the opening and closing balance on the provision, including some or all of the following, as appropriate:
- the opening amount;
- additional provisions made in the period, including increases to existing provisions;
- amounts used during the period;
- unused amounts reversed during the period; and
- any increase in the discounted amount due to the passage of time or changes in the discount rate.

Example 30.10 provides a sample of a disclosure note in relation to the movement in a provision.

EXAMPLE 30.10: DISCLOSURE NOTE

As at 31 December 2018, Bowler Ltd had a balance on its provision in relation to WEE recycling of €36,400.

During the year, Bowler used €12,600 of the provision balance in relation to items recycled during the reporting period. The balance required on the provision account as at 31 December 2019 was €43,900.

Requirement Prepare the reconciliation of the balance on the provision that would be used in the disclosure note.

Solution

	€
Balance at 1 January 2019	36,400
Used during the year	(12,600)
Additional provision	20,100
Balance at 31 December 2019	43,900

For each class of provision the entity will have to disclose:
- a brief description of the provision and the expected timing of the outflow of economic benefits;
- a statement of any uncertainties about the amount or timing of those outflows; and
- the amount of any expected reimbursements, stating the amount of any asset that is recognised for the expected reimbursement.

Example 30.11 demonstrates the requirements for a disclosure note relating to a provision.

EXAMPLE 30.11: DISCLOSURE NOTE

During the reporting period ended 31 December 2019, Topple Ltd is sued by a customer as a result of goods sold that the customer alleges are faulty. Similar cases have awarded damages to the customer of €20,000. Topple Ltd has insurance that will reimburse 20% of the damages if it loses the case. The insurance company has confirmed in writing that the insurance cover applies to the circumstances of the case.

Legal advice is that Topple Ltd will probably lose the case.

Requirement Prepare the disclosure note in relation to the provision to be included in the financial statements for the reporting date 31 December 2019.

Solution

DISCLOSURE NOTE

Topple Ltd is being sued by a customer for supply of faulty goods. Legal advice is that it will lose the case and have to pay an estimated €20,000 in damages. Topple has insurance in relation to such claims and can claim reimbursement from its insurance provider of 20% of the damages award, which we estimate at €4,000.

30.9 IAS 37 COMPARED WITH FRS 102

The treatment outlined in FRS 102 in relation to provisions, contingent liabilities and contingent assets is the same as that in IAS 37.

EXAM TIPS

- Read the question carefully and when the question asks you to advise on the appropriate accounting treatment, the following approach is a good one to follow:
  1. identify the accounting standard;
  2. identify the accounting rule being tested and apply the rule to the situation presented; and
  3. prepare journal entries, if required, remembering that a journal entry identifies the accounts being debited and credited and includes a brief narrative explaining the nature of the transaction.
- When asked to draft a disclosure note you must not simply list the items to be included – you must prepare the note in a format suitable for inclusion in the notes to the financial statements.
- You should be able to differentiate between a provision and a contingent liability.
- You should be able to provide examples of restructuring and identify a restructuring situation.

30.10 CONCLUSION

It is important to understand the conditions that must be fulfilled in order to recognise a provision in the financial statements. A provision is recognised in the financial statements because the likelihood of an outflow of resources is highly probable, while a contingent liability is less likely to occur (its occurrence is only a possibility), therefore only disclosure, not recognition, of a contingent liability is required.

SUMMARY OF LEARNING OBJECTIVES

After having studied this chapter, readers should be able to:

Learning Objective 1 Identify and account for provisions.

The conditions that must be satisfied before a provision can be raised in the financial statements are that:
* there is an obligating event;
* it is probable there will be an outflow of economic benefit; and
* a reliable estimate of the amount can be made.

Learning Objective 2 Identify and account for contingent liabilities.

A contingent liability only involves a possible outflow rather than a probable outflow. No accounting entry is made in the financial statements in relation to a contingent liability but disclosure is required.

Learning Objective 3 Identify and account for contingent assets.

No accounting adjustments are made for contingent assets but disclosure of the following is required:
* a brief description of the nature of the contingent asset; and
* an estimate of the financial effect.

Learning Objective 4 Identify and account for onerous contracts.

An onerous contract is one where the costs exceed the benefit. The **full** amounts under the onerous contract are recognised in full when the contract becomes onerous.

Learning Objective 5 Identify and account for restructuring costs.

To raise a restructuring provision the following conditions have to be met:
* the entity has to have prepared a detailed formal restructuring plan before the reporting date; and
* the entity must have created a valid expectation, that is, the entity has either begun implementation of the restructuring plan or has informed those that will be affected by the restructuring, before the reporting date.

Only costs that relate specifically to the restructuring can be included in the provision; costs related to the ongoing business cannot be included.

Learning Objective 6 Identify and account for reimbursement of provisions.

Reimbursement is only recognised when the receipt is virtually certain. The reimbursement and the related provision can be offset against each other in the SPLOCI, but cannot be offset in the SOFP.

Learning Objective 7 Prepare relevant disclosure notes.

You should be able to prepare the following disclosure notes for each class of provision and contingent liability:
- Reconciliation of opening to closing balances,
- Brief description, an indication of any uncertainties and amount of any expected reimbursement.

For contingent assets the entity must provide a brief description of the nature of the contingent asset and an estimate of the financial effect.

QUESTIONS

Review Questions

(See **Appendix A** for Solutions to Review Questions.)

Question 30.1

Warrington Ltd is being sued by a customer over goods that it supplied; the customer claims the goods were faulty as a result of which their machinery has been damaged.

The goods were sold on 20 September 2019. Legal opinion is that Warrington has a 70% chance of losing the case and having to pay €310,000 with respect to damages and legal costs. A backlog in the courts means that the case will not be heard until February 2021.

Requirement Explain the appropriate accounting treatment of this issue for the reporting period ended 31 December 2019.

Question 30.2

A customer visiting Mayfair Ltd's restaurant on 10 December 2019 has issued legal proceedings claiming that they were injured after falling on a wet floor in the restrooms. The customer claims that warning signs were not visibly displayed, indicating the danger, as required.

Management of Mayfair has reviewed video footage of the area and can clearly see the customer and a companion pouring water on the floor prior to the accident.

Similar claims for damages where the business was at fault have resulted in payments being made to claimants of €40,000.

Legal opinion is that the restaurant will not lose the case. The case is scheduled for court in May 2020.

Financial statements are prepared to 31 December annually.

Requirement Explain the appropriate accounting treatment of this issue for the reporting period ended 31 December 2019.

Question 30.3

Winston Ltd has issued legal proceedings against a supplier for damages of €150,000. The legal case arises as a result of faulty goods supplied by Wigan Ltd. The goods were used in the production process and, due to their inferior quality, caused significant damage to the production machinery.

Estimates have been made in relation to the cost to repair the machinery at €40,000 and loss of earnings due to the disruption of supply at €110,000.

Legal opinion is that it is highly likely that Winston will win the case.

Requirement Explain the appropriate accounting treatment of this issue in the financial statements of Winston Ltd.

Question 30.4

Sweet Ltd leased premises for a period of five years. The lease was taken out on 1 April 2015 when the business was initially set up. Since then the business has grown significantly and needs bigger premises. It moved to new premises on 1 November 2018. The old premises are empty and are not used as part of Sweet's operations.

The original premises required quarterly lease payments of €2,400, which began on 1 April 2015. Under the terms of the lease Sweet cannot sublet the premises or cancel the lease agreement.

Sweet prepares its financial statements to 30 June each year.

Requirement Outline the accounting treatment for the original lease in the reporting period ended 30 June 2019.

Challenging Questions

(Solutions to Challenging Questions are available through your lecturer.)

Question 30.1

(a) In accordance with IAS 37 *Provisions, Contingent Liabilities and Contingent Assets,* define a provision and explain briefly when a provision should be recognised in the financial statements.
(b) Jeans and Jumpers Plc is a well-known, high-street retail outlet with branches all over Ireland. The year end of the company is 31 December 2019. The following information is available:
  • As part of its customer service, the company has a policy of refunding purchases to dissatisfied customers, even though there is no legal obligation to do so. In the past, approximately 10% of goods sold were returned and refunds given.
  • During November 2019, a decision was taken, in principle, to close the company's Cork branch. However, no formalised plan in connection with the closure has been devised; the decision had not been communicated to the employees of the company at the reporting date and no other steps had been taken to implement this decision at that date.
  • The company is famous for its in-store tea rooms, where tired shoppers can avail of light refreshments. During the year ended 31 December 2019, 200 people became ill after eating the Jeans and Jumpers "special super deluxe gateau". Ten of these people died. Legal proceedings have been started against the company for compensation. However, the company denies liability, stating that at the time of the food poisoning outbreak, the local council was working on the water mains to fix burst pipes, and it firmly believes that the water became contaminated during the repair process. The company's lawyers indicated, up to the date of approval of the financial statements, that the company would probably be found not liable.
  • The company had a lease on an old warehouse in Galway. As part of the centralisation programme, all merchandise is now being stored in Dublin warehouses. Jeans and Jumpers Plc has tried to cancel the Galway lease, which still has three years to run. However, due to the terms of the lease contract, it has been unable to do so.

Requirement (b) In respect of the financial statement of Jeans and Jumpers Plc for the year ended 31 December 2019, outline each of the following in accordance with IAS 37 *Provisions, Contingent Liabilities and Contingent Assets*:
  (i) The accounting treatment for each of the above items.
  (ii) Where appropriate, the disclosure requirements for each of the items.

(Based on Chartered Accountants Ireland, Prof II Financial Accounting, Summer 2000, Question 4)

Question 30.2

(a)

    (i) Explain briefly the term 'contingent liability'.

    (ii) Describe briefly the **three** circumstances under which a provision should be recognised.

(b) You are the auditor of Panel Ltd, a manufacturer of wooden flooring. The following information is available for the year ended 31 December 2019.

    (i) Under new health and safety legislation, Panel Ltd is required to install a new air-conditioning system at a cost of €100,000 to disperse fumes from the production process. The final deadline for installation was 31 August 2019. Non-compliance will result in a fine of €60,000. The air conditioning system had not been installed by the reporting date.

    (ii) Panel Ltd's main supplier is Laminate Ltd. An agreement between the companies entitles Panel Ltd to a 5% rebate on purchases over €250,000 from Laminate Ltd. In the year ended 31 December 2019, Panel Ltd purchased €360,000 of material from Laminate Ltd. Panel Ltd has had an excellent relationship with Laminate Ltd over a period of years, and the rebate has been paid in full in the past.

    (iii) Flooring installed by Panel Ltd in a church hall became warped during the warm summer. The church's committee has instigated legal proceedings against Panel, which disputes liability. At 31 December 2019 Panel Ltd's solicitors advised the company that they were unsure as to whether or not the outcome of the court action would find in the company's favour.

Requirement (b) Draft a **letter** to the financial controller of Panel Ltd, advising on how each of the above items should be dealt with in the financial statements for the reporting period ended 31 December 2019.

(Based on Chartered Accountants Ireland, Prof II Financial Accounting, Autumn 2001, Question 5)

31

Investment Property

LEARNING OBJECTIVES

Having studied this chapter, readers should be able to:
1. identify an investment property;
2. account for investment property under the cost model; and
3. account for investment property under the fair value model.

31.1 INTRODUCTION

An **investment property** is held for its ability to generate rental income and/or capital appreciation rather than for use within the business. The accounting rules are set out in IAS 40 *Investment Property*. Examples of investment properties are:
- land held for long-term capital appreciation rather than short-term sale in the ordinary course of business;
- land held for a currently undetermined future use;
- building owned under a finance lease and leased out under one or more operating leases;
- vacant building held to be leased out under one or more operating leases; and
- property that is under construction, or being developed, for future use as an investment property.

The following are **not** classified as investment properties:
- properties intended for sale in the ordinary course of business;
- properties currently under construction or development and intended for sale;
- properties being constructed or developed for third parties;
- owner-occupied properties; and
- property that is leased to another party under a finance lease.

31.2 INITIAL RECOGNITION

Investment property is recognised at cost. Cost is the amount of cash and cash equivalents paid, or the fair value of the consideration given, to purchase the asset.

An investment property is recognised in the financial statements when the following conditions are met:
1. the cost of the investment property can be measured reliably; and
2. it is probable that the entity will receive benefits from owning the investment property.

Cost of Investment Property

The costs that can be included in the cost of the investment property are:
- the purchase price of the property; and
- directly attributable expenditure, such as:
  - o professional fees for legal services,
  - o property transfer taxes, and
  - o transaction costs.

The following costs cannot be included in the cost of the investment property:
- start-up costs – the only exception to this are costs that relate to bringing the property into the condition necessary to make it capable of operating in the manner intended;
- operating losses incurred before the investment property achieves the planned occupancy level; and
- abnormal levels of waste materials, labour and other resources incurred in the construction or development of the property.

Example 31.1 demonstrates the costs that can be included in the initial recognition of an investment property.

EXAMPLE 31.1: INITIAL RECOGNITION

Blake Ltd purchased a property that it intends to rent out to third parties. The costs incurred as part of the property purchase are as follows:

	€
Purchase price	1,450,000
Legal costs	25,000
Non-refundable taxes	35,000
Renovation costs	180,000

The renovation costs include costs of €10,000 relating to materials that were damaged while in storage and could not be used in the renovations; the goods were not covered by insurance.

Requirement Prepare the journal entry to recognise the investment property in the financial records of Blake Ltd.

Solution

	Debit €	Credit €
Investment property account	1,680,000	
Bank/cash/loan account		1,680,000
To recognise the investment property on acquisition.		

The cost is made up of: €1,450,000 + €25,000 + €35,000 + €170,000
          = €1,680,000

The abnormal waste of material is not included in the cost of the investment property but expensed to the statement of profit or loss and other comprehensive income (SPLOCI) when the cost was incurred.

	Debit €	Credit €
SPLOCI – abnormal material wastage	10,000	
Bank/cash account		10,000
To expense the abnormal waste materials.		

(Try **Review Question 31.1** at the end of this chapter.)

An entity may occupy part of the property rented out or may provide additional services, such as security or maintenance. The impact of owner occupation and the provision of ancillary services will be discussed next.

Portion of Investment Property is for Own Use

If a part of the investment is used in the production or supply of goods and services or for administration purposes and can be sold or leased out under a finance lease separately, then only the portion held to earn rental income or capital appreciation shall be accounted for as an investment property.

If the portion used as an investment property or for any other purpose cannot be sold or leased out separately, then the asset can only be accounted for as an investment property if the portion not used as an investment property is insignificant.

(Try **Review Question 31.2** at the end of this chapter.)

Ancillary Services Provided

An entity may also provide ancillary services, such as security or maintenance, as part of the rental agreement. The investment is treated as an investment property if the ancillary services are **insignificant**. Judgement is required to determine whether the amount of ancillary services is significant or not and the criteria used to determine the level must be applied consistently.

The amount attributable to the investment property and the conditions to be met to satisfy the classification as an investment property have been discussed so far. In the next section the choice of accounting policies that are available after initial recognition of the investment property by the entity will be explained.

31.3 MEASUREMENT AFTER INITIAL RECOGNITION

Management of the entity must choose its accounting policy in relation to investment property. The choice allowed under IAS 40 is between the cost model and the fair value model.

It is important to remember that a change from the cost model to the fair value model or vice versa is a change in accounting policy and is only allowed under IAS 8 *Accounting Policies, Changes in Accounting Estimates and Errors* if it is required by an accounting standard or if it will provide more relevant and reliable information. It is pointed out in IAS 40 that it is highly unlikely that a change from the fair value model to the cost model will result in more relevant presentation.

Cost Model

If the cost model is chosen then it must be applied to all of the entity's investment properties. The cost model under IAS 40 is the same as the cost model under IAS 16 *Property, Plant and Equipment.* Under the cost model the investment property will be depreciated over its estimated useful life.

Management will have to make estimates about:
• residual value,
• useful life of the property, and
• depreciation method.

The entity will have to disclose the fair value of the investment property in the notes to the financial statements.

Example 31.2 demonstrates the accounting entries involved and the presentation in the application of the cost model for an investment property.

EXAMPLE 31.2: COST MODEL

Holden Ltd decided at a board meeting to purchase a property for the sole purpose of generating rental income.

On 4 March 2019, the property was purchased for €3 million and at that date management estimated the useful life at 30 years and the residual value at €1.2 million. Management has decided to adopt the cost model to measure its investment property.

Holden's policy is to charge a full year's depreciation in the year of purchase and none in the year of sale.

Requirement Prepare the journal entries in relation to the investment property for the reporting period ended 31 December 2019.

Solution

On 4 March 2019, the following journal entry is posted in the accounting records of Holden:

	Debit €	Credit €
Investment property account	3,000,000	
Bank/cash/loan account		3,000,000

To recognise the investment property on acquisition.

The investment property is presented under non-current assets in the statement of financial position (SOFP).

	€
Cost of property	3,000,000
Residual value	(1,200,000)
Depreciable amount	1,800,000
Useful life	30 years
Depreciation charge per annum	€60,000

The journal entry to recognise the depreciation charge for the reporting period ended 31 December 2019 is:

	Debit €	Credit €
SPLOCI – depreciation expense	60,000	
Accumulated depreciation account		60,000

To recognise the investment property on acquisition.

The depreciation charge is not time apportioned as the company's policy is to charge a full year's depreciation in the year of purchase.

STATEMENT OF FINANCIAL POSITION (EXTRACT)
as at 31 December 2019

	€
Non-current Assets	
Property, plant and equipment	X
Investment property	2,940,000

The investment property is presented at its carrying amount, i.e. cost less the accumulated depreciation (€3,000,000 − €60,000).

Fair Value Model

It is important to understand that the fair value model is **not** the same as the revaluation model under IAS 16. The change in fair value impacts retained earnings; it does not impact the revaluation surplus.

Changes in the fair value of the property are taken to the SPLOCI (in the profit and loss section). The change is taken to retained earnings in the profit and loss section of the SPLOCI and **not** to the revaluation surplus account through other comprehensive income.

Depreciation is not charged on the investment property under the fair value model.

Example 31.3 demonstrates the accounting entries involved and the presentation in the application of the fair value model for an investment property.

EXAMPLE 31.3: FAIR VALUE MODEL

On 12 July 2019, the board of directors approved the purchase of an investment property for €2,000,000. Management has decided to adopt the fair value model to measure its investment property.

As at the reporting date, 31 December 2019, the property had a fair value of €2,080,000.

Requirement Prepare the journal entries in relation to the investment property for the reporting period ended 31 December 2019.

Solution

On 12 July 2019 the following journal entry is posted in the accounting records:

	Debit €	Credit €
Investment property account	2,000,000	
Bank/cash/loan account		2,000,000

To recognise the investment property on acquisition.

The investment property is presented under non-current assets in the SOFP. Under the fair value model the asset is **not** depreciated.

The change in fair value is taken to the profit and loss section of the SPLOCI.

	€000
Fair value as at 31 December 2019	2,080
Cost	(2,000)
Fair value adjustment	80

The journal entry to recognise the depreciation charge for the reporting period ended 31 December 2019 is:

	Debit €	Credit €
Investment property account	80,000	
SPLOCI – gain on investment property		80,000

To recognise the fair value adjustment on the investment property.

STATEMENT OF FINANCIAL POSITION (EXTRACT)
as at 31 December 2019

	€000
Non-current Assets	
Property, plant and equipment	X
Investment property	2,080

(Try **Review Questions 31.3** and **31.4** at the end of this chapter.)

31.4 TRANSFER TO/FROM INVESTMENT PROPERTY

IAS 40 sets out rules on the valuation of properties when there is a change in use, for example, from owner-occupied to investment property. The intention to change the use of a property is not enough, there must also be **evidence** of a change in use. These rules are summarised in the table below.

Previously classified as	Changing to	At date of change, measure at
Investment property (fair value model)	Owner occupied (IAS 16 now applies)	Fair value at the date of change
Investment property (cost model)	Owner occupied (IAS 16 now applies)	No change in the carrying amount of the property
Investment property (fair value model)	Inventory (IAS 2 now applies)	Fair value at the date of change
Investment property (Cost model)	Inventory (IAS 2 now applies)	No change in the carrying amount of the property
Owner occupied (IAS 16) or Completion of the construction/ development of a self-constructed investment property	Investment property (cost model)	No change in the carrying amount of the property
Owner-occupied (IAS 16)	Investment property (fair value model)	Fair value at the date of change. Any difference between the carrying amount and the fair value is treated as a revaluation under IAS 16.

continued overleaf

Previously classified as	Changing to	At date of change, measure at
Inventory	Investment property (fair value model)	Fair value at the date of change. Any difference between the fair value and the previous carrying amount is recognised in profit or loss.
Completion of the construction/ development of a self-constructed investment property	Investment property (fair value model)	Fair value at the date of change. Any difference between the fair value and the previous carrying amount is recognised in profit or loss.

Example 31.4 demonstrates the accounting entries required when there is a change in the use of an investment property measured under the cost model.

Example 31.4: Change in Use of Investment Property Measured Using Cost Model

Hermon Ltd has a property that is leased out to another company until 31 March 2019. When the lease term ended management of Hermon decided that rather than lease the property again it would use it as its new sales headquarters. On 15 April renovation work began on the property.

Hermon had used the cost model to measure the investment property. At 31 March 2019 the carrying amount of the property was €1,650,000, i.e. cost of €1,820,000 less accumulated depreciation of €170,000. On 15 April 2019 the fair value of the property is estimated at €1,680,000.

Requirement Explain the accounting treatment of the change in use of the property.

Solution

The property is treated as an investment property up to the date the change in use takes place. In this case the commencement of the renovation works is the date of the change in use. As the cost model is used to measure the investment property, the owner-occupied property is recognised at the carrying amount; no adjustment is made to fair value at this time.

The accounting entry to reflect the change in use is as follows:

	Debit €	Credit €
Property, plant and equipment – cost account	1,820,000	
Investment property – cost account		1,820,000
To recognise change in use of property.		
Accumulated depreciation account – investment property	170,000	
Accumulated depreciation account – property, plant and equipment		170,000
To recognise change in use of property.		

Example 31.5 demonstrates the accounting entries required when there is a change in the use of an investment property measured under the fair value model.

EXAMPLE 31.5: CHANGE IN USE OF INVESTMENT PROPERTY
MEASURED USING FAIR VALUE MODEL

Hendon Ltd has a property that is leased out to another company until 30 June 2019. When the lease term ended, management of Hendon decided that, rather than lease the property again, it would redevelop the site with a view to selling it at the end of the conversion works. On 1 August renovations works began on the property.

Hendon had used the fair value model to measure the investment property; at 30 June 2019 the carrying amount of the property was €1,520,000 and its fair value is estimated at €1,600,000.

Requirement Explain the accounting treatment of the change in use of the property.

Solution

The property is treated as an investment property up to the date the change in use takes place. In this case the commencement of the renovation works is the date of the change in use. As the fair value model is used to measure the investment property and it is subsequently reclassified as inventory, then the fair value adjustment is reflected at the date of the change in use.

The accounting entry to reflect the change in use is as follows:

	Debit €	**Credit €**
Inventory account	1,600,000	
SPLOCI – gain on fair value adjustment		80,000
Investment property – cost account		1,520,000
To recognise change in use of property.		

31.5 DISPOSALS

When an investment property is sold it is removed from the SOFP. The profit or loss on disposal is calculated by comparing the difference between the disposal proceeds and the **carrying amount** of the asset. The gain or loss is recognised in the SPLOCI in the period that the asset is sold.

Example 31.6 demonstrates the disposal of an investment property measured using the cost model.

EXAMPLE 31.6: DISPOSAL OF INVESTMENT PROPERTY
MEASURED USING THE COST MODEL

On 30 June 2019 Dresden Ltd sold its investment property for €1,980,000. The asset had originally cost €2,150,000 and at the disposal date had accumulated depreciation in its financial statements of €215,000.

Requirement Prepare the journal entries and ledger accounts to record the disposal of the investment property.

Solution

The journal entries to recognise the disposal of the investment property are as follows:

	Debit €	Credit €
Disposal account	2,150,000	
Investment property – cost account		2,150,000

To recognise the disposal of the investment property.

	Debit €	Credit €
Accumulated depreciation account	215,000	
Disposal account		215,000

To recognise the disposal of the investment property.

	Debit €	Credit €
Bank account	1,980,000	
Disposal account		1,980,000

To recognise the disposal of the investment property.

	Debit €	Credit €
Disposal account	45,000	
SPLOCI – profit on disposal		45,000

To recognise the profit on disposal of the investment property.

The above journal entries can be combined into a single journal entry as follows:

	Debit €	Credit €
Accumulated depreciation account	215,000	
Bank account	1,980,000	
Investment property – cost account		2,150,000
SPLOCI – profit on disposal		45,000

To recognise the profit on disposal of the investment property.

The ledger accounts are as follows:

INVESTMENT PROPERTY – COST ACCOUNT

Date	Account Name	€	Date	Account Name	€
30/06/2019	Balance b/d	2,150,000	30/06/2019	Disposal	2,150,000

INVESTMENT PROPERTY – ACCUMULATED DEPRECIATION ACCOUNT

Date	Account Name	€	Date	Account Name	€
30/06/2019	Disposal	215,000	30/06/2019	Balance b/d	215,000

DISPOSAL ACCOUNT

Date	Account Name	€	Date	Account Name	€
30/06/2019	Investment property – cost	2,150,000	30/06/2019	Investment property – accumulated depreciation	215,000
30/06/2019	SPLOCI – profit	45,000	30/06/2019	Bank	1,980,000
		2,195,000			2,195,000

Example **31.7** demonstrates the disposal of an investment property measured using the fair value model.

EXAMPLE 31.7: DISPOSAL OF INVESTMENT PROPERTY
MEASURED USING THE FAIR VALUE MODEL

On 31 December 2019 White Ltd sold its investment property for €2,430,000. The asset had originally cost €2,250,000 on 1 January 2018. White uses the fair value method to measure the investment property and the fair value at 31 December 2018 was €2,360,000.

Requirement Prepare the journal entries and ledger accounts to record the disposal of the investment property.

Solution

The journal entries to recognise the disposal of the investment property are as follows:

	Debit €	Credit €
Disposal account	2,360,000	
Investment property – cost account		2,360,000
To recognise the disposal of the investment property.		
Bank account	2,430,000	
Disposal account		2,430,000
To recognise the disposal of the investment property.		
Disposal account	70,000	
SPLOCI – profit on disposal		70,000
To recognise the profit on disposal of the investment property.		

The above journal entries can be combined into a single journal entry as follows:

	Debit €	Credit €
Bank account	2,430,000	
Investment property – cost account		2,360,000
SPLOCI – profit on disposal		70,000
To recognise the profit on disposal of the investment property.		

The ledger accounts are as follows:

INVESTMENT PROPERTY – COST ACCOUNT

Date	Account Name	€	Date	Account Name	€
31/12/2019	Balance b/d	2,360,000	31/12/2019	Disposal Account	2,360,000

DISPOSAL ACCOUNT

Date	Account Name	€	Date	Account Name	€
31/12/2019	Investment property – cost	2,360,000	31/12/2019	Bank	2,430,000
31/12/2019	SPLOCI – profit	70,000			
		2,430,000			2,430,000

(Try **Review Questions 31.5** and **31.6** at the end of this chapter.)

31.6 PROPERTY LEASED TO PARENT/SUBSIDIARY

A **subsidiary** is an entity that is controlled by another entity. Control is usually demonstrated by ownership of the majority of the ordinary share capital.

Parent Leases Property to Subsidiary

Parent owns a property that it rents out at the market rates to a subsidiary company. In the separate financial statements of the parent the property is recognised as an investment property. In the consolidated financial statements the property occupied by the subsidiary is treated as owner-occupied and accounted for under IAS 16 and not as an investment property under IAS 40.

Subsidiary Leases Property to Parent

Subsidiary owns a property that it rents out at the market rates to its parent company. In the separate financial statements of the subsidiary the property is recognised as an investment property. In the consolidated financial statements the property occupied by the parent is treated as owner-occupied and accounted for under IAS 16 and not as an investment property under IAS 40.

31.7 DISCLOSURE

The entity is required to make the following disclosures in relation to investment properties.

Disclosure for both the cost model and fair value model:
- a statement of whether the entity applies the cost model or the fair value model;
- if it is difficult to distinguish between owner-occupied and investment property, the entity must identify the criteria it uses to distinguish between owner-occupied and investment property;
- amounts recognised in profit or loss:
  - rental income,
  - direct operating expenses arising from investment property that generated rental income during the period,
  - direct operating expenses arising from investment property that did not generate rental income during the period,
  - cumulative change in fair value recognised in profit or loss on a sale of investment property,
- restrictions on the investment property's ability to be realised or the remittance of income and proceeds from disposal;
- any contractual obligations to purchase, construct or develop investment property or for repairs, maintenance or enhancement.

Additional disclosures for fair value model:
- the entity must prepare a reconciliation of the carrying amounts at the start and end of the reporting periods showing:
  - additions through acquisition of an asset alone and subsequent expenditure on that asset,
  - additions as part of a business acquisition,
  - assets classified as held for sale,
  - gains or losses through fair value adjustments,
  - net exchange differences arising on the translation of the financial statements,

    o transfers to and from inventories and owner-occupied categories,

    o other changes.

- identify if any investment properties are held under operating leases;
- whether or not the fair value has been determined by an independent valuer with recognised qualifications and experience. If no valuation has been received this should be disclosed;
- if the fair value of an investment property cannot be measured reliably then the following must be disclosed:

    o description of the investment property,

    o explanation of why fair value cannot be measured reliably,

    o if possible, a range of possible estimates within which fair value is highly likely to lie,

    o on disposal, the fact that the property was not carried at fair value, the carrying amount at the date of sale and the profit or loss recognised.

Additional disclosures for cost model:

- depreciation methods used;
- useful lives and depreciation rates used;
- gross carrying amount and accumulated depreciation at both the beginning and end of the period – any accumulated impairment losses should be included in the accumulated depreciation figure;
- reconciliation of the carrying amount at the beginning and end of the period showing:

    o additions and subsequent expenditure,

    o additions through business acquisitions,

    o assets classified as held for sale,

    o depreciation,

    o amount of impairment losses recognised,

    o amount of impairment losses reversed,

    o net exchange differences arising on the translation of the financial statements,

    o transfers to and from inventories and owner-occupied,

    o other changes;

- if the fair value of the investment property cannot be measured reliably then the following must be disclosed:

    o description of the investment property,

    o explanation of why the fair value cannot be measured reliably, and

    o if possible, a range of estimates within which the fair value is likely to lie.

31.8 IAS 40 COMPARED WITH FRS 102

Under FRS 102, investment properties are measured at fair value through profit or loss provided this can be done reliably, without undue effort and cost, on an ongoing basis. Otherwise they are accounted for as property, plant and equipment. In contrast, under IAS 40 there is an accounting policy choice between the cost model and the fair value model.

Under FRS 102 there is no disclosure requirement in relation to the amounts recognised in profit or loss as is the case under IAS 40. Under IAS 40 the entity must disclose:

- rental income from investment property;
- direct operating expenses relating to investment properties that generated rental income during the period;
- direct operating expenses relating to investment properties that did not generate rental income during the period;

• the cumulative change in fair value recognised on a sale of investment property from a pool of assets in which the cost model is used into a pool in which the fair value model is used.

In addition there is no requirement under FRS 102 to detail the criteria used between investment properties and other types of property, such as owner-occupied and property held for sale in the ordinary course of business.

Exam Tips

• You need to identify, from the information given, the method used by the reporting entity to measure investment properties.
• Remember, the fair value model under IAS 40 *Investment Property* is **not** the same as the revaluation model under IAS 16 *Property, Plant and Equipment.*
• When the cost model is used, always check the entity's depreciation policy to see whether depreciation is time apportioned in the years of purchase and sale or a full year's depreciation is charged in the year of purchase and none in the year of sale.

31.9 CONCLUSION

Under IAS 40 an entity has an accounting policy choice in relation to measurement of investment properties under either the cost model or the fair value model. The fair value model under IAS 40 is **not** the same as the revaluation model under IAS 16.

IAS 40 sets out specific rules in relation to the value to be assigned when there is a change in use either to or from the asset category 'investment properties'.

Summary of Learning Objectives

After having studied this chapter, readers should be able to:

Learning Objective 1 Identify an investment property.

An investment property is not used in the ordinary course of business but is held for its ability to generate rental income and/or capital appreciation.

Learning Objective 2 Account for investment property under the cost model.

The choice of the cost model over the fair value model is an accounting policy. A change from the cost model to the fair value model is a change in accounting policy and must be applied retrospectively in accordance with IAS 8 *Accounting Policies, Changes in Accounting Estimates and Errors.*

An investment property measured using the cost model is recognised at its carrying amount in the SOFP, i.e. at cost less accumulated depreciation. Depreciation is charged to the SPLOCI.

At the purchase date estimates are made of the:
• useful life of the investment property;
• residual value of the property; and
• depreciation method to be used.

The above are all examples of accounting estimates and should be reviewed annually. If there is a change in an accounting estimate, it should be applied prospectively in accordance with IAS 8 *Accounting Policies, Changes in Accounting Estimates and Errors.*

Learning Objective 3 Account for investment property under the fair value model.

The choice of the cost model over the fair value model is an accounting policy. A change from the cost model to the fair value model is a change in accounting policy and must be applied retrospectively in accordance with IAS 8 *Accounting Policies, Changes in Accounting Estimates and Errors.* A change in accounting policy is only allowed when it will either provide more relevant and reliable information to the users or it is required by the accounting standard. IAS 40 states that it would be "highly unlikely that a change from the fair value model to the cost model will result in a more relevant presentation".

The fair value model, under IAS 40, is not the same as the revaluation model under IAS 16. If there is a change in the fair value of an investment property under the fair value model:
- the change in fair value is **always** taken to the profit and loss section of the SPLOCI;
- the investment property is carried at the fair value in the SOFP; and
- there is never a revaluation surplus account in relation to an investment property.

QUESTIONS

Review Questions

(See **Appendix A** for Solutions to Review Questions.)

Question 31.1
Magenta Ltd purchased a property on 1 January 2019. The details of the cost involved are as follows:

	€
Purchase price	2,000,000
Legal costs associated with purchase of property	20,000
Property taxes	25,000
Start-up costs	120,000

The start-up costs were incurred prior to the first letting of the property; the costs were in relation to bringing the property to an appropriate condition for its intended use as a rental property. €20,000 of the start-up costs relates to operating losses before the target occupancy levels were achieved.

Requirement What is the cost of the investment property on initial recognition?

Question 31.2
Smithy Ltd purchased a property for €1,800,000 on 20 August 2019.

Eighty per cent of the property will be let out to tenants under a finance lease. The remainder of the property will be used by Smithy Ltd for administration purposes.

Requirement Explain how the property should be accounted for.

Question 31.3
Alison Ltd purchased a property for €1,500,000 on 1 January 2019. The property is seen as a good investment of surplus funds given its excellent location, ability to generate rental income and its potential for capital appreciation.

Management of Alison has decided to use the cost model to measure its investment property. It estimated the useful life of the property at 30 years with zero residual value.

Alison prepares its financial statements to 31 December each year.

Requirement Prepare the journal entries for the reporting period ended 31 December 2019.

Question 31.4

On 1 January 2018 Mortar Ltd purchased a property for €2 million. Mortar uses the fair value model to measure its investment properties.

	€000
Fair value as at:	
31 December 2018	2,100
31 December 2019	1,920

Requirement Prepare journal entries to reflect the change in fair values and the relevant extract from the statement of financial position as at:
(a) 31 December 2018 and
(b) 31 December 2019.

Question 31.5

An investment property was sold for €2,175,000 cash on 10 September 2019. The property had originally cost €3,000,000 and had accumulated depreciation at the disposal date of €640,000.

Requirement Prepare the journal entries to recognise the disposal of the investment property.

Question 31.6

An investment measured using the fair value model was sold for cash on 20 October 2019 for €2,260,000. The property had originally cost €2,300,000 and was measured at fair value on 31 December 2018 at €2,320,000.

Requirement Prepare the journal entries to recognise the disposal of the investment property.

Challenging Questions

(Suggested Solutions to Challenging Questions are available through your lecturer.)

Question 31.1

Irishlink acquired a retail complex near Dublin in July 2019 for €20,000,000, obtaining a 10-year bank loan to fund the acquisition at a fixed rate of 5% per annum. Irishlink is currently renting the complex to a well-known home furnishings chain at an annual rent of €1,000,000. The directors of Irishlink believe that the value of the complex at 31 December 2019 was €23,000,000.

Requirement Explain how the following should be treated in the financial statements of Irishlink for the year ended 31 December 2019:
(a) retail complex
(b) bank loan and interest
(c) rental income

(Based on Chartered Accountants Ireland, Prof III Financial Reporting, Autumn 2007, Question 6)

PART VI

INTERPRETATION OF FINANCIAL STATEMENTS

32

Interpretation of Financial Statements

LEARNING OBJECTIVES

Having studied this chapter, readers should be able to:
1. use ratios in relation to profitability to comment on the performance of an entity;
2. use ratios in relation to liquidity to comment on an entity's ability to pay its debts as they fall due;
3. use ratios to understand how efficiently an entity has used the resources available to it;
4. use ratios to assess the level of debt in an entity; and
5. use ratios to assess the performance of an entity in terms of the return generated for its shareholders.

32.1 INTRODUCTION

Ratio analysis is used to interpret the financial performance of the entity and determine how the financial position has changed over a period of time. Ratios do not provide definitive answers but highlight areas of change in the financial performance and position of the entity.

The advantages of ratio analysis include:
- ratios provide a basis for the comparison of performance from one period to the next;
- ratios highlight areas of change in either the financial performance or position where attention may be needed;
- ratios help compare the performance of companies of differing sizes operating in the same industry; and
- ratios may be easier for non-accountants to understand than the financial statements themselves.

The disadvantages of ratio analysis include:
- ratios based on the statement of financial position (SOFP) reflect the situation at a single point in time. In a business subject to seasonal fluctuations, there may be a significant difference in the ratios calculated at one date compared to another date; and
- different accounting policies in relation to measurement of assets and revaluation may have an impact on ratios calculated when comparing different companies.

Ratios can be looked at in terms of specific areas, such as:
- profitability;
- liquidity;
- efficiency;
- gearing; and
- investment.

It is important to remember that ratios are only beneficial if the figures on which they are based are accurate and the ratios themselves have been calculated correctly. Ratios can be compared to:
- company ratios relating to past periods;
- company actual results compared to budgets and/or forecast; and
- ratios relating to other companies operating in the same industry.

32.2 PROFITABILITY RATIOS

Profit is the difference between the revenue earned and the costs incurred by the entity for the period. There are two key profitability ratios: gross margin and net margin.

$$\text{Gross margin} = \frac{\text{Gross profit}}{\text{Revenue}} \times 100$$

$$\text{Net margin} = \frac{\text{Profit before interest and tax}}{\text{Revenue}} \times 100$$

Gross margin expresses the profit as a percentage of sales revenue. The only costs taken into account in this calculation are those associated with purchasing and producing goods sold. This ratio would be expected to remain similar over time; any change in the ratio could be due to one or more of the following:
- change in selling price of the goods, for example, a decrease in selling price may be as a result of competitive pressures in the market or a conscious decision by the entity in an attempt to increase market share;
- change in purchase cost of raw materials; and
- change in production costs involved in the conversion of raw materials to finished goods. Production costs include labour and production overhead.

Margins should be compared with those of other companies in the same industry as margins can vary greatly from one industry to the next. Low margins can indicate inefficiencies, such as:
- failure to obtain the best price for goods purchased;
- inefficient production processes; and
- high levels of wastage.

Industries that generate high margins attract new entrants to the market, as new entrants are attracted by the potential to generate high returns.

Net margin shows the percentage profit after all costs other than interest (also referred to as finance cost) and tax have been charged to the statement of profit or loss and other comprehensive income (SPLOCI).

Example 32.1 demonstrates the basic calculation of gross and net margins.

EXAMPLE 32.1: GROSS AND NET MARGINS

You have been provided with the following information in relation to Morrow's performance over the most recent reporting periods:

STATEMENT OF PROFIT OR LOSS AND OTHER COMPREHENSIVE INCOME
for the year ended 31 December 2019

	2019 €000	2018 €000
Revenue	8,200	7,600
Cost of sales	(5,950)	(5,720)
Gross profit	2,250	1,880

Selling and distribution	(950)	(920)
Administration costs	(1,010)	(800)
Profit before interest and tax	290	160

Requirement Calculate the gross and net margins.

Solution

$$\text{Gross margin} = \frac{\text{Gross profit}}{\text{Revenue}} \times 100$$

2019: (€2,250 ÷ €8,200) × 100 = 27.44%

2018: (€1,880 ÷ €7,600) × 100 = 24.74%

$$\text{Net margin} = \frac{\text{Profit before interest and tax}}{\text{Revenue}} \times 100$$

2019: (€290 ÷ €8,200) × 100 = 3.54%

2018: (€160 ÷ €7,600) × 100 = 2.11%

(Try **Review Question 32.1** at the end of this chapter.)

32.3 LIQUIDITY RATIOS

The SPLOCI provides the users of financial statements with information about the financial performance of an entity. While an entity may be generating profits, it is important that it is liquid, that is, that it can make payments in relation to its obligations as they fall due. The first liquidity ratios to look at are the current ratio and the quick ratio:

Current ratio = Current assets : Current liabilities

Quick ratio (also known as acid test ratio) = (Current assets – Inventory) : Current liabilities

It is important to focus on the change in the liquidity ratios over time rather than the absolute figures as these will vary greatly from industry to industry.

The **current ratio** provides an indication of the entity's ability to meet its short-term obligations using its short-term assets. In the past, a current ratio of 2:1 or higher (that is, the value of current assets is twice that of current liabilities, or more) was considered appropriate. However, in the modern operating environment 1.5:1 is considered more normal. These figures are only indications and could vary greatly from industry to industry; it is important, when analysing financial statements, to comment on the change in the ratios and whether they have improved or deteriorated over the period.

The ratio should be interpreted in light of the industry in which the entity operates; the following are examples of factors to be considered:
1. nature of inventory – special storage conditions, risk of obsolescence;
2. credit period allowed to customers compared to days credit taken;
3. seasonal nature of the business – in a seasonal business, financing levels will vary depending on whether or not the business is at the peak of its operating conditions or not; and
4. availability of funds.

The **quick ratio** or **acid test ratio** excludes inventory from the calculation. The normal range for this ratio is between 1:1 and 0.7:1.

Example 32.2 demonstrates the calculation of the current and quick ratios for a business.

EXAMPLE 32.2: CURRENT AND QUICK RATIOS

You have been provided with the following information in relation to Cooper Ltd:

	€
Current Assets as at 31 December	
Inventory	300,000
Trade receivables	280,000
Cash and cash equivalents	185,000
Current Liabilities as at 31 December	360,000

Requirement Calculate the current ratio and quick ratio for Cooper Ltd.

Solution

Current ratio = Current assets : Current liabilities
= (€300,000 + €280,000 + €185,000) : €360,000
= €765,000 : €360,000
= 2.125 : 1

Quick ratio (also known as acid test)   = (Current Assets – Inventory) : Current Liabilities
= (€765,000 – €300,000) : €360,000
= €465,000 : €360,000
= 1.292 : 1

(Try **Review Questions 32.2** and **32.3** at the end of this chapter.)

The **receivable days ratio** expresses the balance on the trade receivables in terms of the number of days' credit sales. The ratio is:

$$\text{Trade receivables days} = \frac{\text{Trade receivables}}{\text{Credit sales}} \times 365$$

The trade receivables figure used in the calculation may be either the year-end figure or the average for the year. Whenever possible, use the credit sales figure, but if this is not available total sales may be used; it is important that calculation is consistent from one period to the next.

When the trade receivables days ratio is high, it may be necessary to review an aged debtors listing. The aged debtors listing analyses receivables balance by the number of days overdue. A deterioration in the receivables days may be due to inefficient management of trade receivables.

An efficient debt management system will have:
1. a credit approval system for new customers;
2. established credit limits for credit customers;
3. procedures to be followed when a customer is in arrears;
4. refusal of additional credit for customers in arrears or when the transaction would put the balance on their account in excess of their credit limit; and
5. regular issue of statements to customers.

Example 32.3 demonstrates the calculation of the receivables days for a company.

EXAMPLE 32.3: RECEIVABLES DAYS

The trade receivables figure from the SOFP as at 31 December was €265,000. The sales figure presented in the SPLOCI for the year ended 31 December was €3,280,000. All sales are on credit.

Requirement Calculate the trade receivables days as at 31 December.

Solution

Trade receivables days: $\dfrac{\text{Trade receivables}}{\text{Credit sales}} \times 365$

$$= \dfrac{\text{€265,000}}{\text{€3,280,000}} \times 365$$

$$= 29.49 \text{ days}$$

The **payables days ratio** expresses the balance on the trade payables in terms of number of days' credit purchases. The ratio is:

Trade payables days: $\dfrac{\text{Trade payables}}{\text{Credit purchases of raw materials}} \times 365$

In a growing entity or seasonal market the average trade payables figure should be used rather than the reporting date figure. When the purchases figure is not known, cost of sales may be used in the calculation.

A high payables days ratio may indicate possible future problems with credit being provided by suppliers or liquidity problems. When an entity takes longer to pay than the credit period provided by the supplier, credit facilities may be withdrawn.

Example 32.4 demonstrates the calculation of the payables days for a company.

EXAMPLE 32.4: PAYABLES DAYS

The trade payables figure from the SOFP as at 31 December was €184,500. The following information has been extracted from the SPLOCI for the year ended 31 December:

	€
Opening inventory	135,000
Purchases	1,476,000
Less: closing inventory	(148,900)
Cost of sales	1,462,100

All of the purchases related to raw materials and were on credit terms.

Requirement Calculate the trade payables days for the year ended 31 December.

Solution

$$\text{Trade payables days:} \quad \frac{\text{Trade payables}}{\text{Credit purchases of raw materials}} \times 365$$

$$= \frac{€184,500}{€1,476,000} \times 365$$

$$= 45.63 \text{ days}$$

(Try **Review Question 32.4** at the end of this chapter.)

32.4 EFFICIENCY RATIOS

Efficiency ratios provide information about how the entity has managed its assets. The efficiency ratios are:
* return on capital employed;
* revenue to non-current assets;
* revenue to net current assets;
* inventory turnover; and
* non-current assets to total assets.

Return on capital employed is used to assess the return generated by the business from the assets available rather than looking at the absolute profit figure for the period. A change in the assets employed by the entity should result in a change in the profit generated.

The formula for return on capital employed is:

$$\frac{\text{Profit}}{\text{Capital employed}} \times 100$$

The main issue for students is what profit figure and what capital employed figure to use. Consistency between the profit figure and the capital employed figure used in the calculation needs to be ensured. The following table matches the profit figure with the appropriate capital employed figure.

Profit	Capital Employed	When to Use
Profit before interest and tax	Gross assets = Non-current assets + Current assets	To assess the overall profitability of the entity.
Profit before interest and tax	Net assets = Gross assets – Current liabilities	To assess the overall profitability of the entity.
Profit after tax	Shareholders' capital = Equity + Reserves	Useful for existing or prospective shareholders to assess performance
Profit after tax and preference dividends	Shareholders' equity capital = Ordinary share capital + Reserves	Useful for existing or prospective shareholders to assess performance

Example 32.5 demonstrates the calculations involved in the return on capital employed ratio.

EXAMPLE 32.5: RETURN ON CAPITAL EMPLOYED

STATEMENT OF PROFIT OR LOSS AND OTHER COMPREHENSIVE INCOME (EXTRACT)
for the year ended 31 December 2013

	€000
Operating profit	520
Finance cost	(45)
Profit before tax	475
Income tax	(115)
Profit for year	360

STATEMENT OF FINANCIAL POSITION (EXTRACT)
as at 31 December 2013

	€000	€000
Non-current Assets		
Property, plant and equipment		2,860
Current Assets		
Inventory	340	
Trade receivables	245	
Cash	98	683
Total Assets		3,543

Requirement Calculate the return on capital employed.

Solution

$$\text{Return on capital employed} = \frac{\text{Profit before interest and tax}}{\text{Total assets}}$$

$$= €520 \div €3{,}543$$

$$= 14.68\%$$

The return on capital employed simply indicates the performance of the entity for a particular period of time but not any of the reasons for any change. To help explain any change, the return on capital employed is analysed between:
- profit ÷ revenue; and
- revenue ÷ capital employed.

Profit ÷ Revenue is expressed as a percentage and indicates the profit generated on the sales achieved. A change in profit percentage could be due to changes in selling prices, product mix or changes in costs.

Revenue ÷ Capital employed indicates the level of revenue generated by the assets employed during the period. In order to interpret this ratio appropriately, the basis for the calculation of the capital employed (such as depreciation policies and estimates used) needs to be considered.

Example 32.6 demonstrates the calculation and interpretation of return on capital employed and its additional ratios.

EXAMPLE 32.6: RETURN ON CAPITAL EMPLOYED

STATEMENT OF PROFIT OR LOSS AND OTHER COMPREHENSIVE INCOME (EXTRACT)
for the year ended 31 December 2019

	€000
Revenue	4,150
Operating profit	550
Finance cost	(65)
Profit before tax	485
Income tax	(145)
Profit for year	340

STATEMENT OF FINANCIAL POSITION (EXTRACT)
as at 31 December 2019

	€000	€000
Non-current Assets		
Property, plant and equipment		2,710
Current Assets		
Inventory	210	
Trade receivables	232	
Cash	168	610
Total Assets		3,320
Current Liabilities		480

Requirement Calculate the return on capital employed and its constituent ratios. Use net assets as capital employed.

Solution

$$\text{Return on capital employed} = \frac{\text{Profit before interest and tax}}{\text{Net assets}}$$

$$= 550 \div (€3{,}320 - €480)$$
$$= 550 \div €2{,}840$$
$$= 19.37\%$$

The return and capital employed can be broken down between:
- Profit ÷ Revenue; and
- Revenue ÷ Capital employed.

Profit ÷ Revenue = €550 ÷ €4,150
$$= 13.25\%$$

Revenue ÷ Capital employed = €4,150 ÷ €2,840
$$= 1.46 \text{ times}$$

(Try **Review Question 32.5** at the end of this chapter.)

The formula for **revenue to non-current assets ratio** is:

$$\frac{\text{Revenue}}{\text{Tangible non-current assets}}$$

Tangible non-current assets are those with a physical substance; excluded are such items as development costs.

A high ratio is indicative of efficient use of the assets available. A low ratio indicates that a review may be necessary of the assets owned and consideration given to disposal of some of the assets. Like all ratios, there may be variations from one industry to another.

Factors that would need to be considered when undertaking an intercompany comparison:
- depreciation policy, for example, useful lives;
- age of assets; and
- frequency of revaluations.

Example 32.7 demonstrates the revenue to non-current assets ratio for two different companies.

EXAMPLE 32.7: REVENUE TO NON-CURRENT ASSETS

You are provided with the following information in relation to two companies operating in the same industry.

	Albert Ltd €	Rodney Ltd €
Non-current Assets		
Cost	2,400,000	2,400,000
Accumulated depreciation	480,000	1,600,000
Revenue	4,250,000	3,195,000

Requirement Calculate revenue to non-current asset ratio for both of the companies.

Solution

Formula: $\dfrac{\text{Revenue}}{\text{Tangible non-current assets}}$

Albert Ltd: €4,250,000 ÷ (€2,400,000 – €480,0000) = 2.21

Rodney Ltd: €3,195,000 ÷ (€2,400,000 – €1,600,000) = 3.99

Rodney has a much higher ratio than Albert, but this is due to the fact that Rodney's assets are older, being two-thirds of the way through their useful lives compared to Albert's assets, which are only 20% depreciated. Care should be taken when interpreting this ratio.

The formula for the **revenue to net current assets ratio** is:

$$\frac{\text{Revenue}}{\text{Net current assets}} \times 100$$

The ratio is expressed as a percentage and the higher the figures the more efficient the operations of the entity. This ratio should be interpreted in light of the liquidity ratios.

The formula for the **inventory turnover ratio** is:

$$\frac{\text{Cost of sales}}{\text{Inventory}}$$

The above ratio indicates the number of times inventory is turned over each year.

The higher the inventory turnover figure, the more efficient is the management of inventory. Inventory turnover needs to be interpreted in light of the type of inventory: inventory with a short shelf-life or subject to a high level of obsolescence will typically be turned over many times each year.

If the inventory turnover decreases, this could be an indication of:
1. a fall in demand for the goods;
2. poor inventory control, goods being bought and produced for which there is less demand;
3. higher inventory levels, which can result in an increased likelihood of damage and obsolescence;
4. the company having taken advantage of bulk discounts offered by suppliers; and
5. concerns about future shortages of supply.

Example 32.8 demonstrates the calculation of inventory turnover figure using the reporting date and average inventory figures.

EXAMPLE 32.8: INVENTORY TURNOVER

The following information has been extracted from the SPLOCI of Cruncher Ltd for the year ended 31 December 2019:

	€	€
Revenue		2,980,000
Less: cost of sales		
Opening inventory	180,000	
Purchases	2,180,000	
Less: closing inventory	(210,000)	(2,150,000)
Gross profit		830,000

Requirement Calculate the inventory turnover ratio using the closing figure and the average inventory for the period.

Solution

$$\frac{\text{Cost of sales}}{\text{Inventory}}$$

Using the closing inventory figure the ratio is:

$$\frac{€2,150,000}{€210,000} = 10.24 \text{ times}$$

Using the average inventory figure the ratio is:

$$\frac{€2,150,000}{€195,000} = 11.03 \text{ times}$$

Average inventory is (€180,000 + €210,000) ÷ 2 = €195,000.

Note: this can also be presented as inventory days, which is calculated as inventory ÷ cost of sales × 365.

Using the closing inventory figure, inventory days are:

€210,000 ÷ €2,150,000 × 365 = 35.65 days

(Try **Review Question 32.6** at the end of this chapter.)

The formula for the **non-current assets to total assets ratio** is:

$$\frac{\text{Non-current assets}}{\text{Total assets}}$$

Example 32.9 below demonstrates the calculation of non-current assets to total assets.

EXAMPLE 32.9: NON-CURRENT ASSETS TO TOTAL ASSETS

The following information has been extracted from the SOFP of Wilbur Ltd as at 31 December:

	€	€
Non-current Assets		
Property, plant and equipment		1,985,000
Current Assets		
Inventory	235,000	
Trade receivables	212,000	
Cash and cash equivalents	58,000	505,000
Total Assets		2,490,000

Requirement Calculate the non-current assets to total assets ratio.

Solution

$$\frac{\text{Non-current assets}}{\text{Total assets}} = \frac{1,985,000}{2,490,000} = 0.797$$

32.5 GEARING RATIOS

Gearing indicates the level of debt compared to the equity in the entity. The formula for the **gearing ratio** is:

$$\frac{\text{Total debt}}{\text{Ordinary shareholders' funds}} \times 100$$

The gearing ratio is expressed as a percentage.

Alternatively, 'total capital employed' could be used in the above formula instead of 'ordinary shareholders' funds'. 'Total capital employed' is the total of equity and non-current liabilities.

Total debt is made up of loans, short-term debt and preference shares. The higher the gearing level, the greater the financial risk associated with the company. Shareholders will require a higher return in a company with a higher level of debt.

Companies may opt for debt in their capital structure rather than equity for a number of reasons:
1. finance cost is an allowable deduction in the calculation of taxable profit; and
2. issue of debt does not affect the control of the company.

Example 32.10 demonstrates the calculation of the gearing ratio for a company.

EXAMPLE 32.10: GEARING RATIO

Wilson Ltd
STATEMENT OF FINANCIAL POSITION
as at 31 December 2019

	€	€
Non-current Assets		
Property, plant and equipment		3,140,000
Current Assets		
Inventory	125,000	
Trade receivables	168,000	
Cash and cash equivalents	42,000	335,000
Total Assets		3,475,000
Equity and Reserves		
Ordinary share capital		500,000
Retained earnings		1,955,000
		2,455,000
Non-current Liabilities		
Long-term loans		650,000
Current Liabilities		
Trade payables	154,000	
Overdraft	216,000	370,000
Total Equity and Liabilities		3,475,000

Requirement Calculate the gearing ratio.

Solution

$$\frac{\text{Total debt}}{\text{Ordinary shareholders' funds}} \times 100$$

(€650,000 + €216,000) ÷ €2,455,000 × 100 = 35.27%

The formula for the **debt ratio** is:

$$\frac{\text{Total debt}}{\text{Total assets}}$$

Total debt in this ratio usually refers to loans plus redeemable preference shares.

Example 32.11 demonstrates the calculation of the debt ratio.

EXAMPLE 32.11: DEBT RATIO

Requirement Using the information provided in **Example 32.9**, calculate the debt ratio.

Solution

$$\frac{\text{Total debt}}{\text{Total assets}} = \frac{€650,000}{€3,475,000} \times 100 = 18.71\%$$

The formula for the **interest cover ratio** is:

$$\frac{\text{Profit before interest and tax}}{\text{Loan interest paid and payable}}$$

This ratio provides an indication of the margin by which profits can fall before interest will not be covered.

Example 32.12 demonstrates the calculation of interest cover.

EXAMPLE 32.12: INTEREST COVER

The following information has been extracted from the SPLOCI of Thompson Ltd:

	31 December 2019 €	31 December 2018 €
Operating profit	350,000	315,000
Finance cost	(28,000)	(40,000)
Profit before tax	322,000	275,000
Income tax	(64,000)	(55,000)
Profit for year	258,000	220,000

Requirement Calculate the interest cover for each of the reporting periods.

Solution

$$\frac{\text{Profit before interest and tax}}{\text{Loan interest paid and payable}}$$

As at 31 December 2019: €350,000 ÷ €28,000 = 12.5 times

As at 31 December 2018: €315,000 ÷ €40,000 = 7.87 times

32.6 INVESTMENT RATIOS

There are a number of investment ratios:
- earnings per share;
- earnings yield;
- dividend yield;
- dividend cover; and
- price earnings ratio.

The formula for the **earnings per share ratio** is:

$$\frac{\text{Earnings for period}}{\text{Average number of ordinary shares in issue}}$$

The calculation of earnings per share is governed by IAS 33 *Earnings per Share*. Earnings per share is a ratio widely used by investors. It is the comparison over time that provides the most meaningful information.

Example 32.13 demonstrates the calculation of earnings per share for a company.

EXAMPLE 32.13: EARNINGS PER SHARE

Sherbert Ltd has earnings of €295,000 for the reporting period ended 31 December. The average number of ordinary shares in issue for the period was 1,200,000.

Requirement Calculate the earnings per share figure for the reporting period ended 31 December.

Solution

$$\text{Earnings per share} = \frac{\text{Earnings for period}}{\text{Average number of ordinary shares in issue}}$$

$$= €295,000 \div 1,200,000$$
$$= 24.58c$$

The formula for the **earnings yield ratio** is:

$$\frac{\text{Earnings per share}}{\text{Market price per share}} \times 100$$

The earnings yield provides a measure of the return on an investment in ordinary shares. It can be compared with returns on other investments, such as bank deposits.

Example 32.14 demonstrates the calculation of the earnings yield ratio.

EXAMPLE 32.14: EARNINGS YIELD

Sorbet Ltd has earnings of €322,500 for the reporting period ended 31 December. The average number of ordinary shares in issue for the period was 1,500,000.

The ordinary shares of Sorbet Ltd are quoted at €3.48 as at 31 December.

Requirement Calculate the following ratios as at 31 December:
(a) Earnings per share.
(b) Earnings yield.

Solution

$$\text{(a) Earnings per share} = \frac{\text{Earnings for period}}{\text{Average number of ordinary shares in issue}}$$

$$= €322,500 \div 1,500,000$$
$$= 21.5c$$

(b) Earnings yield $= \dfrac{\text{Earnings per share}}{\text{Market price per share}} \times 100$

$= (21.5c \div 348c) \times 100$

$= 6.18\%$

The formula for the **dividend yield ratio** is:

$$\frac{\text{Gross dividend per share}}{\text{Market price per share}} \times 100$$

Investors in ordinary share capital do so for one of the following reasons:
1. dividend income;
2. capital appreciation on share price;
3. combination of 1 and 2.

Dividends are at the discretion of the company. An investor looking for regular income from an investment in ordinary share capital would look at the dividend yield of the company when making their assessment.

The formula for the **dividend cover ratio** is:

$$\frac{\text{Profit after taxation and preference dividend}}{\text{Ordinary dividend}}$$

The higher the dividend cover figure, the more certain an investor will be that the dividend will be paid in the future unless there is a fundamental change in the performance of the company.

Example 32.15 demonstrates the calculation of the dividend yield and dividend cover on ordinary shares.

EXAMPLE 32.15: DIVIDEND YIELD AND COVER

You are provided with the following information in relation to the most recent reporting period:

Profit after tax	€810,000
Preference dividend paid	€80,000
Ordinary dividend paid per share	10c
Market price per share at reporting date	€4.50
Number of ordinary shares in issue	2,000,000

The preference shares were classified as equity in the financial statements.

Requirement Calculate the following investor ratios:
(a) Dividend yield.
(b) Dividend cover.

Solution

(a) Dividend yield $= \dfrac{\text{Gross dividend per share}}{\text{Market price per share}} \times 100$

$= (10c \div 450c) \times 100 = 2.22\%$

(b) Dividend cover = $\dfrac{\text{Profit after taxation and preference dividend}}{\text{Ordinary dividend}}$

$$= (\text{€}810{,}000 - \text{€}80{,}000) \div \text{€}200{,}000$$
$$= \text{€}730{,}000 \div \text{€}200{,}000$$
$$= 3.65 \text{ times}$$

Ordinary dividend is 2,000,000 ordinary shares $\times$ 10c per share = €200,000

The formula for the **price earnings ratio** is:

$$\dfrac{\text{Market price per share}}{\text{Earnings per share}}$$

A high price earnings ratio means that investors are prepared to pay a high multiple of earnings for shares in the company. Investors would be prepared to pay a high multiple if the expectation is that the company will experience high levels of growth. Expectations about a company's future performance are based on a number of factors, such as: the risk profile of the company, demand for its shares, its debt levels and its dividend policy.

32.7 GROWTH

In order to assess the growth levels of the company, compare the change in such items as:
- revenue;
- profit before tax; and
- non-current assets.

Changes in any of the above items need to be interpreted in light of other changes in the financial statements, for example, a doubling of revenue should result in comparable changes in profits and working capital (working capital is inventory plus trade receivables less trade payables).

When commenting on the financial performance and financial position of an entity, look at the changes in the level of investment in non-current assets, borrowing facilities and working capital compared to growth levels.

EXAM TIPS

- The best approach to ratio questions is to review the financial statements first and note changes in the performance and the position of the entity.
- Most students spend a significant amount of their exam time calculating ratios and insufficient time planning their answer. As a rough guide it is recommended that one-third of the time be spent on calculating ratios and two-thirds on the commentary.
- Ratios should be presented in an appendix and a commentary should be written that refers to these calculations, rather than calculating ratios throughout the commentary.

32.8 CONCLUSION

Ratios are a tool to assess the financial performance and position of an entity; they highlight areas of change. It is important to be able to provide a commentary on the significance of the ratios calculated.

SUMMARY OF LEARNING OBJECTIVES

After having studied this chapter, readers should be able to:

Learning Objective 1 Use ratios in relation to profitability to comment on the performance of an entity.

Ratio	Formula
Gross margin	Gross profit ÷ Revenue × 100
Net margin	Net profit ÷ Revenue × 100

Learning Objective 2 Use ratios in relation to liquidity to comment on an entity's ability to pay its debts as they fall due.

Ratio	Formula
Current ratio	Current assets : Current liabilities
Quick ratio	(Current assets − Inventory) : Current liabilities
Receivables days	Trade receivables ÷ Credit sales × 365
Payables days	Trade payables ÷ Credit purchases of raw materials × 365

Learning Objective 3 Use ratios to understand how efficiently an entity has used the resources available to it.

Ratio	Formula
Return on capital employed	Profit ÷ Capital employed
Revenue to non-current assets	Revenue ÷ Non-current assets
Revenue to net current assets	Revenue ÷ Net current assets
Inventory turnover	Cost of sales ÷ Inventory
Non-current assets to total assets	Non-current assets ÷ Total assets

Learning Objective 4 Use ratios to assess the level of debt in an entity.

Ratio	Formula
Gearing	$\dfrac{\text{Total debt}}{\text{Ordinary shareholders' funds}} \times 100$
Debt equity	Total debt ÷ Total assets
Interest cover	Profit before interest and tax ÷ Loan interest paid and payable

Learning Objective 5 Use ratios to assess the performance of an entity in terms of the return generated for its shareholders.

Ratio	Formula
Earnings per share	Earnings ÷ Average number of shares in issue
Earnings yield	Earnings per share ÷ Market price per share
Dividend yield	Dividend ÷ Market price per share
Dividend cover	Profit after taxation and preference dividend ÷ Ordinary dividend
Price earnings ratio	Market price per share ÷ Earnings per share

QUESTIONS

Review Questions

(See **Appendix A** for Solutions to Review Questions.)

Question 32.1

Warrington Ltd
STATEMENT OF PROFIT OR LOSS
for the year ended

	31 December 2019	31 December 2018
	€	€
Revenue	8,350,000	7,980,000
Cost of sales	(4,690,000)	(4,510,000)
Gross profit	3,660,000	3,470,000
Other income	50,000	20,000
Selling and distribution costs	(1,115,000)	(1,065,000)
Administration expenses	(895,000)	(818,000)
Finance cost	(45,000)	(35,000)
Profit before tax	1,655,000	1,572,000
Taxation	(410,000)	(396,000)
Profit for year	1,245,000	1,176,000

Requirement Calculate the gross and net margins for each reporting period.

Question 32.2

As at 31 December 2019 the assets and liabilities of Analysis Ltd are as follows:

	€000
Inventory	150
Trade payables	175
Cash at bank	75
Accruals	85
Trade receivables	125
Provisions for liabilities and charges	105
Prepayments	50

Requirement What is the acid test ratio for Analysis Ltd as at 31 December 2019?
(a) 0.68:1
(b) 0.96:1
(c) 1.09:1
(d) 1.54:1

(Based on Chartered Accountants Ireland, Prof II Financial Reporting, Autumn 2004, Question 2.5)

Question 32.3

Taz Ltd has the following net current assets at 31 December:

STATEMENT OF FINANCIAL POSITION (EXTRACT)

	31 December 2018 €	31st December 2019 €
Current Assets		
Investment in 30-day Government bonds	18,000	0
Inventory	65,000	58,000
Receivables	1,500	1,300
Bank	9,800	10,600
Cash	1,000	1,000
Current Liabilities		
Trade payables	59,000	60,600
Bank overdraft	500	0

Requirement
(a) Calculate the current ratio for Taz Ltd as at 31 December 2018 and 31 December 2019.
(b) What is the movement in cash and cash equivalents during 2019?

(Based on Chartered Accountants Ireland, CAP 1 Financial Accounting, Autumn 2012, Question 1.2)

Question 32.4

Red Ltd prepares its accounts to 31 December each year. The following information relates to Red Ltd's first year of trading.

Current assets at 31 December 2019:

Inventory	€250,000
Trade receivables	€125,000
Other current assets	€875,000
Current liabilities at 31 December 2019	€625,000
Rate of stock turnover during 2019	7
Average stock during 2019	€250,000
Sales for 2019 (all credit)	€2,100,000

Requirement What was the average period of credit given to customers during 2019?
(a) 12 days
(b) 17 days
(c) 22 days
(d) 26 days

(Based on Chartered Accountants Ireland, Prof III Financial Reporting, 2000, Question 1)

Question 32.5

The statement of financial position of Blue Ltd as at 31 December showed the following:

	€000
Non-current assets	800
Current assets	300
Current liabilities	100
Long-term liabilities	300
Share capital and reserves	700

Profit before interest and tax and retained profits were €240,000 and €120,000 respectively for the year ended 31 December.

Requirement What is Blue Ltd's return on capital employed?
(a) 12%
(b) 17.1%
(c) 24%
(d) 34.3%

(Based on Chartered Accountants Ireland, Prof III Financial Reporting, 2001, Question 1)

Question 32.6

Lowry Ltd has extracted the following information from its SPLOCI for the year ended 31 December 2019:

	€
Revenue	134,000
Opening inventory at 1 January 2019	16,150
Purchases	91,400
Closing inventory at 31 December 2019	17,950

Lowry's revenue accrues evenly throughout the year.

Requirement How many days worth of sales does Lowry have in inventory at 31 December 2019?
(Based on Chartered Accountants Ireland, CAP 1 Financial Accounting, Summer 2008, Question 1.4)

Question 32.7

Which of the following formulae would give a valid calculation of a company's gearing ratio?

(a)
$$\frac{\text{Ordinary share capital}}{\text{Ordinary share capital} + \text{loan capital}} \times 100$$

(b)
$$\frac{\text{Loan capital}}{\text{Ordinary share capital}} \times 100$$

(c)
$$\frac{\text{Ordinary share capital} + \text{reserves}}{\text{Loan capital} + \text{ordinary share capital} + \text{reserves}} \times 100$$

(d)
$$\frac{\text{Loan capital} + \text{preference share capital}}{\text{Ordinary share capital} + \text{reserves} + \text{loan capital} + \text{preference share capital}} \times 100$$

(Based on Chartered Accountants Ireland, Prof II Financial Reporting, Summer 2006, Question 1.4)

Challenging Questions

(Suggested Solutions to Challenging Questions are available through your lecturer.)

Question 32.1

Two supermarkets, Supersave Ltd and Quickshop Ltd have outlets throughout the country. The financial statements for both retailers have been reproduced below.

STATEMENTS OF FINANCIAL POSITION
as at 31 December 2019

	Supersave €000	Quickshop €000
Assets		
Non-current Assets		
Property, plant and equipment	13,750	22,500
Current Assets		
Inventories	2,000	2,250
Trade receivables	125	150
Bank	825	1,800
Total assets	16,700	26,700
Equity and Liabilites		
Equity and Reserves		
Ordinary share capital	7,500	5,000
Retained earnings	5,075	6,750
	12,575	11,750
Non-current Liabilities		
Loans	2,000	12,500
Current Liabilities	2,125	2,450
Total equity and liabilities	16,700	26,700

STATEMENTS OF PROFIT OR LOSS
for the year ended 31 December 2019

	Supersave €000	Quickshop €000
Revenue	33,400	40,050
Cost of sales	(21,710)	(25,225)
Gross profit	11,690	14,825
Distribution costs	(5,750)	(7,175)
Administration expenses	(3,440)	(4,175)
Operating profit	2,500	3,475
Finance cost	(162)	(1,000)
Net profit	2,338	2,475

STATEMENTS OF CHANGES IN EQUITY (EXTRACTS)
for the year ended 31 December 2019

	Supersave €000	Quickshop €000
Net profit	2,338	2,475
Dividends paid	(750)	(1,000)
Retained profit for the year	1,588	1,475

Requirement:
(a) For each company, calculate **two** suitable ratios in the following areas:
- (i) liquidity
- (ii) gearing
- (iii) profitability and performance

15 Minutes

(b) Draft a memorandum to a prospective investor and, using the ratios calculated above, summarise the overall financial strengths and weaknesses of Supersave when compared to Quickshop.

9 Minutes

(Based on Chartered Accountants Ireland, CAP 1 Financial Accounting, Autumn 2008, Question 7)

Question 32.2

ABC Ltd has had the following results for the last two years of trading.

STATEMENT OF FINANCIAL POSITION
as at

	31 December 2019 €000	31 December 2018 €000
Assets		
Non-current Assets		
Property, plant and equipment	14,000	8,750
Current Assets		
Inventories	7,000	4,500
Trade receivables	5,600	7,000
Bank	2,870	8,400
Total assets	29,470	28,650
Equity and Liabilities		
Equity and Reserves		
Ordinary share capital	8,400	8,400
Retained earnings	11,620	5,950
	20,020	14,350
Non-current Liabilities		
Loans – 10%	–	9,100
Current Liabilities – payables	9,450	5,200
Total equity and liabilities	29,470	28,650

STATEMENT OF PROFIT OR LOSS
for the year ended

	31 December 2019 €000	31 December 2018 €000
Revenue	59,500	50,400
Cost of sales	(44,100)	(41,300)
Gross profit	15,400	9,100
Expenses	(7,000)	(4,200)
Net profit	8,400	4,900

Note: dividends were €2,730,000 in 2019 and €1,820,000 in 2018.

Requirement:
(a) Calculate three profitability ratios for each year and comment on each.

10 Minutes

(b) Prepare a memo to ABC Ltd's bankers comparing your analysis of profitability with the decrease in bank balances and discussing possible reasons for this decrease.

14 Minutes

(Based on Chartered Accountants Ireland, CAP 1 Financial Accounting, Summer 2009, Question 8)

Question 32.3

Grainger Plc
STATEMENT OF CASH FLOWS
for the year ended 31 December 2019

	€000	€000
Cash flows from operating activities		
Profit before interest and taxation		1,620
Adjustments for:		
Depreciation		186
Loss on disposal of a non-current asset		90
Changes in working capital:		
Movement in inventories		(36)
Movement in trade receivables		(54)
Movement in trade payables		30
Cash generated from operations		1,836
Interest paid	(120)	
Tax paid	(105)	
Dividend paid	(60)	(285)
Net cash flow from operating activities		1,551
Cash flows from investing activities		
Acquisition of non-current assets	(1,020)	
Proceeds from sales of non-current assets	120	
Acquisition of investments	(150)	
Net cash outflow from investing activities		(1,050)
Cash flows from financing activities		
Proceeds from issue of share capital	330	
Proceeds from issue of 6% loan notes	300	
Repayment of 12% loan notes	(1,200)	
Net cash outflow from financing activities		(570)
Net decrease in cash and cash equivalents		(69)
Cash and cash equivalents at start of year		30
Cash and cash equivalents at end of year		(39)

Grainger Plc reports a bank overdraft of €39,000 as at 31 December 2019 whereas, a year prior to that date, it reported a favourable bank balance of €30,000. The directors of the company are concerned about the cash position of the company and are unable to appreciate fully the information contained in the statement of cash flows presented to them by the Financial Accountant.

Requirement:
(a) Explain why 'depreciation' and 'loss on disposal of a non-current asset' have been included in the statement of cash flows.

5 Minutes

(b) Provide three possible reasons for the movements in inventories and trade receivables.

5 Minutes

(c) Comment on whether the liquidity of the company has become worse in the year, taking into consideration the cash outflow of €69,000 and the bank overdraft at the year-end. Your answer should focus on each of the three types of business activities, i.e. operating, investing and financing.

15 Minutes

(Based on Chartered Accountants Ireland, CAP 1 Financial Accounting, Summer 2012, Question 7)

Question 32.4

Glitter Ltd and Sparkle Ltd are both retailers of fashion clothes. Glitter aims at the more expensive end of the market, while Sparkle targets the cheaper end. The financial statements of both companies are shown below.

STATEMENTS OF PROFIT OR LOSS AND OTHER COMPREHENSIVE INCOME
for the year ended 31 December 2019

	Glitter €000	**Sparkle €000**
Revenue	8,520	55,380
Cost of sales	(5,964)	(50,136)
Gross profit	2,556	5,244
Distribution costs	(552)	(648)
Administration expenses	(1,287)	(1,278)
Operating profit	717	3,318
Finance cost	(120)	Nil
Profit before tax	597	3,318
Taxation	(117)	(660)
Profit after tax	480	2,658

STATEMENTS OF FINANCIAL POSITION
as at 31 December 2019

	Glitter €000	**Sparkle €000**
Non-current assets	7,656	4,068
Current Assets		
Inventory	1,644	1,242
Trade receivables	1,038	84
Cash and bank	102	36
Total Assets	10,440	5,430
Equity And Liabilities		
Ordinary share capital of €1	6,000	2,700
Retained earnings	2,007	1,062
	8,007	3,762
Non-current Liabilities		
8% loan notes	1,500	Nil
Current Liabilities		
Trade payables	798	984
Taxation	135	684
	10,440	5,430

Additional Information

STATEMENTS OF COMPREHENSIVE INCOME (EXTRACTS)
for the year ended 31 December 2018

	Glitter €000	Sparkle €000
Revenue	6,420	51,600
Purchases	5,040	44,700
Depreciation	366	234
Operating profit	654	2,982

STATEMENTS OF FINANCIAL POSITION (EXTRACTS)
as at 31 December 2018

	Glitter €000	Sparkle €000
Inventories	1,416	984
Trade receivables	894	96
Cash and bank	156	117
Trade payables	651	882
Taxation	114	594

Requirement Discuss the liquidity of both companies, with specific reference to intercompany comparisons and comparisons across time. Your discussion should be supported by each of the following relevant accounting ratios:
(a) current ratio,
(b) liquidity ratio,
(c) inventory days,
(d) receivables days,
(e) payables days.

26 Minutes

(Based on Chartered Accountants Ireland, CAP 1 Financial Accounting, Summer 2013, Question 6)

Appendix A
Solutions to Review Questions

Question 1.1

(a) €150,000 − €120,000 = €30,000 Capital

(b) €80,000 − Liabilities = €25,000
   €80,000 − €25,000 = €55,000 Liabilities

(c) Assets − €90,000 = €45,000
   Assets = €45,000 + €90,000 = €135,000

Question 1.2

	€
Capital as at 01/01/2019	45,000
Profit for year	25,600
Less: drawings	(4,500)
Capital as at 31/12/2019	66,100

Question 1.3

	€
Capital as at 01/01/2019	63,000
Profit for year	48,900
Less: drawings (€26,500 + €1,200)	(27,700)
Capital as at 31/12/2019	84,200

Question 2.1

Accounts Affected by the Transaction	Account Type	Increase/Decrease the Account Balance	Debit/Credit Account
Sales	Income	Increase	Credit
Trade receivables	Asset	Increase	Debit

	Debit €	Credit €
Trade receivables account	8,000	
Sales account		8,000

To recognise the sale of goods on credit.

TRADE RECEIVABLES ACCOUNT

Debit Side of Account			Credit Side of Account		
Date	**Account Name**	**€**	**Date**	**Account Name**	**€**
12/07/2019	Sales	8,000			

SALES ACCOUNT

Debit Side of Account			Credit Side of Account		
Date	**Account Name**	**€**	**Date**	**Account Name**	**€**
			12/07/2019	Trade receivables	8,000

Question 2.2

Accounts Affected by the Transaction	Account Type	Increase/Decrease the Account Balance	Debit/Credit Account
Cash	Asset	Increase	Debit
Sales	Income	Increase	Credit

	Debit €	Credit €
Cash account	2,500	
Sales account		2,500
To recognise cash sales.		

CASH ACCOUNT

	Debit Side of Account				Credit Side of Account	
Date	**Account Name**	**€**		**Date**	**Account Name**	**€**
03/01/2019	Sales	2,500				

SALES ACCOUNT

	Debit Side of Account				Credit Side of Account	
Date	**Account Name**	**€**		**Date**	**Account Name**	**€**
				03/01/2019	Cash	2,500

Question 2.3

Sale of goods on credit:

Accounts Affected by the Transaction	Account Type	Increase/Decrease the Account Balance	Debit/Credit Account
Trade receivables account	Asset	Increase	Debit
Sales account	Income	Increase	Credit

	Debit €	Credit €
Trade receivables account	6,150	
Sales account		6,150
To recognise the sale of goods on credit.		

Payment received from customer for goods sold on credit:

Accounts Affected by the Transaction	Account Type	Increase/Decrease the Account Balance	Debit/Credit Account
Bank	Asset	Increase	Debit
Trade receivables	Asset	Decrease	Credit

	Debit €	Credit €
Bank account	6,150	
Trade receivables account		6,150
To recognise the cheque payment received from customer.		

Trade Receivables Account

	Debit Side of Account			Credit Side of Account	
Date	**Account Name**	**€**	**Date**	**Account Name**	**€**
10/01/2019	Sales	6,150	08/02/2019	Bank	6,150

Sales Account

	Debit Side of Account			Credit Side of Account	
Date	**Account Name**	**€**	**Date**	**Account Name**	**€**
			10/01/2019	Trade receivables	6,150

Bank Account

	Debit Side of Account			Credit Side of Account	
Date	**Account Name**	**€**	**Date**	**Account Name**	**€**
08/02/2019	Trade receivables	6,150			

Question 2.4

Accounts Affected by the Transaction	Account Type	Increase/Decrease the Account Balance	Debit/Credit ccount
Purchases	Expense	Increase	Debit
Trade payables	Liability	Increase	Credit

	Debit €	Credit €
Purchases account	11,000	
Trade payables account		11,000

To recognise the purchase of goods on credit.

Purchases Account

	Debit Side of Account			Credit Side of Account	
Date	**Account Name**	**€**	**Date**	**Account Name**	**€**
20/06/2019	Trade payables	11,000			

Trade Payables Account

	Debit Side of Account			Credit Side of Account	
Date	**Account Name**	**€**	**Date**	**Account Name**	**€**
			20/06/2019	Purchases	11,000

Question 2.5

Accounts Affected by the Transaction	Account Type	Increase/Decrease the Account Balance	Debit/Credit Account
Purchases	Expense	Increase	Debit
Cash	Asset	Decrease	Credit

	Debit €	Credit €
Purchases account	3,750	
Cash account		3,750

To recognise the cash purchases.

Purchases Account

Debit Side of Account			Credit Side of Account		
Date	**Account Name**	**€**	**Date**	**Account Name**	**€**
05/03/2019	Cash	3,750			

Cash Account

Debit Side of Account			Credit Side of Account		
Date	**Account Name**	**€**	**Date**	**Account Name**	**€**
			05/03/2019	Purchases	3,750

Question 2.6

Purchase of goods on credit:

Accounts Affected by the Transaction	Account Type	Increase/Decrease the Account Balance	Debit/Credit Account
Purchases	Expense	Increase	Debit
Trade payables	Liability	Increase	Credit

	Debit €	Credit €
Purchases account	10,300	
Trade payables account		10,300

To recognise the purchase of goods on credit.

Payment made to supplier by cheque:

Accounts Affected by the Transaction	Account Type	Increase/Decrease the Account Balance	Debit/Credit Account
Trade payables	Liability	Decrease	Debit
Bank	Asset	Decrease	Credit

	Debit €	Credit €
Trade payables account	10,300	
Bank account		10,300

To recognise the payment to supplier.

Purchases Account

Debit Side of Account			Credit Side of Account		
Date	**Account Name**	**€**	**Date**	**Account Name**	**€**
08/08/2019	Trade payables	10,300			

Trade Payables Account

Debit Side of Account			Credit Side of Account		
Date	**Account Name**	**€**	**Date**	**Account Name**	**€**
25/08/2019	Bank	10,300	08/08/2019	Purchases	10,300

Bank Account

Debit Side of Account			Credit Side of Account		
Date	**Account Name**	**€**	**Date**	**Account Name**	**€**
			25/08/2019	Trade payables	10,300

Question 2.7

Accounts Affected by the Transaction	Account Type	Increase/Decrease the Account Balance	Debit/Credit Account
Insurance	Expense	Increase	Debit
Bank	Asset	Decrease	Credit

	Debit €	Credit €
Insurance expense account	1,200	
Bank account		1,200

To recognise the payment of insurance expense by cheque.

INSURANCE EXPENSE ACCOUNT

	Debit Side of Account			Credit Side of Account	
Date	Account Name	€	Date	Account Name	€
13/11/2019	Bank	1,200			

BANK ACCOUNT

	Debit Side of Account			Credit Side of Account	
Date	Account Name	€	Date	Account Name	€
			13/11/2019	Insurance	1,200

Question 2.8

Invoice received in relation to electricity:

Accounts Affected by the Transaction	Account Type	Increase/Decrease the Account Balance	Debit/Credit Account
Electricity expense	Expense	Increase	Debit
Other payables	Liability	Increase	Credit

	Debit €	Credit €
Electricity account	1,209	
Other payables account		1,209

To recognise the electricity expense.

Payment made to supplier by cheque:

Accounts Affected by the Transaction	Account Type	Increase/Decrease the Account Balance	Debit/Credit Account
Other payables	Liability	Decrease	Debit
Bank	Asset	Decrease	Credit

	Debit €	Credit €
Other payables account	1,209	
Bank account		1,209

To recognise the payment to supplier.

ELECTRICITY EXPENSE ACCOUNT

	Debit Side of Account			Credit Side of Account	
Date	Account Name	€	Date	Account Name	€
10/11/2019	Other payables	1,209			

OTHER PAYABLES ACCOUNT

Debit Side of Account			Credit Side of Account		
Date	**Account Name**	**€**	**Date**	**Account Name**	**€**
30/11/2019	Bank	1,209	10/11/2019	Electricity	1,209

BANK ACCOUNT

Debit Side of Account			Credit Side of Account		
Date	**Account Name**	**€**	**Date**	**Account Name**	**€**
			30/11/2019	Other payables	1,209

Question 2.9

Invoice received in relation to insurance:

Accounts Affected by the Transaction	Account Type	Increase/Decrease the Account Balance	Debit/Credit Account
Insurance expense	Expense	Increase	Debit
Other payables	Liability	Increase	Credit

	Debit €	Credit €
Insurance expense account	1,098	
Other payables account		1,098
To recognise the insurance expense.		

Payment made to supplier by direct debit:

Accounts Affected by the Transaction	Account Type	Increase/Decrease the Account Balance	Debit/Credit Account
Other payables	Liability	Decrease	Debit
Bank	Asset	Decrease	Credit

	Debit €	Credit €
Other payables account	1,098	
Bank account		1,098
To recognise the payment to supplier.		

INSURANCE EXPENSE ACCOUNT

Debit Side of Account			Credit Side of Account		
Date	**Account Name**	**€**	**Date**	**Account Name**	**€**
04/09/2019	Other payables	1,098			

OTHER PAYABLES ACCOUNT

Debit Side of Account			Credit Side of Account		
Date	**Account Name**	**€**	**Date**	**Account Name**	**€**
25/09/2019	Bank	1,098	04/09/2019	Insurance	1,098

BANK ACCOUNT

Debit Side of Account			Credit Side of Account		
Date	**Account Name**	**€**	**Date**	**Account Name**	**€**
			25/09/2019	Other payables	1,098

Question 2.10

Accounts Affected by the Transaction	Account Type	Increase/Decrease the Account Balance	Debit/Credit Account
Motor vehicles	Asset	Increase	Debit
Loan	Liability	Increase	Credit

	Debit €	Credit €
Motor vehicles – cost account	54,000	
Loan account		54,000

To recognise the purchase of motor vehicles.

MOTOR VEHICLES – COST ACCOUNT

	Debit Side of Account			Credit Side of Account	
Date	**Account Name**	**€**	**Date**	**Account Name**	**€**
15/07/2019	Loan	54,000			

LOAN ACCOUNT

	Debit Side of Account			Credit Side of Account	
Date	**Account Name**	**€**	**Date**	**Account Name**	**€**
			15/07/2019	Motor vehicles	54,000

Question 2.11

Accounts Affected by the Transaction	Account Type	Increase/Decrease the Account Balance	Debit/Credit Account
Rent Expense	Expense	Increase	Debit
Bank	Asset	Decrease	Credit

	Debit €	Credit €
Rent expense account	7,500	
Bank account		7,500

To recognise the rent expense.

RENT EXPENSE ACCOUNT

	Debit Side of Account			Credit Side of Account	
Date	**Account Name**	**€**	**Date**	**Account Name**	**€**
31/10/2019	Bank	7,500			

BANK ACCOUNT

	Debit Side of Account			Credit Side of Account	
Date	**Account Name**	**€**	**Date**	**Account Name**	**€**
			31/10/2019	Rent	7,500

Question 2.12

Accounts Affected by the Transaction	Account Type	Increase/Decrease the Account Balance	Debit/Credit Account
Cash	Asset	Increase	Debit
Capital	Capital	Increase	Credit

	Debit €	Credit €
Cash account	40,000	
Capital account		40,000

To recognise the capital introduced to the business.

CASH ACCOUNT

Debit Side of Account			Credit Side of Account		
Date	**Account Name**	**€**	**Date**	**Account Name**	**€**
01/04/2019	Capital	40,000			

CAPITAL ACCOUNT

Debit Side of Account			Credit Side of Account		
Date	**Account Name**	**€**	**Date**	**Account Name**	**€**
			01/04/2019	Cash	40,000

Question 2.13

Accounts Affected by the Transaction	Account Type	Increase/Decrease the Account Balance	Debit/Credit Account
Drawings	Capital	Decrease	Debit
Cash	Asset	Decrease	Credit

	Debit €	Credit €
Drawings account	2,300	
Cash account		2,300

To recognise the cash withdrawn from the business for personal use.

DRAWINGS ACCOUNT

Debit Side of Account			Credit Side of Account		
Date	**Account Name**	**€**	**Date**	**Account Name**	**€**
10/04/2019	Cash	2,300			

CASH ACCOUNT

Debit Side of Account			Credit Side of Account		
Date	**Account Name**	**€**	**Date**	**Account Name**	**€**
			10/04/2019	Drawings	2,300

Question 2.14

Accounts Affected by the Transaction	Account Type	Increase/Decrease the Account Balance	Debit/Credit Account
Drawings	Capital	Decrease	Debit
Purchases	Expense	Decrease	Credit

	Debit €	Credit €
Drawings account	1,500	
Purchases account		1,500

To recognise the goods withdrawn from the business for personal use.

DRAWINGS ACCOUNT

	Debit Side of Account			Credit Side of Account	
Date	Account Name	€	Date	Account Name	€
20/05/2019	Purchases	1,500			

PURCHASES ACCOUNT

	Debit Side of Account			Credit Side of Account	
Date	Account Name	€	Date	Account Name	€
			20/05/2019	Drawings	1,500

Question 2.15

Accounts Affected by the Transaction	Account Type	Increase/Decrease the Account Balance	Debit/Credit Account
Drawings	Capital	Decrease	Debit
Bank	Asset	Decrease	Credit

	Debit €	Credit €
Drawings account	230	
Bank account		230

To recognise personal expense paid out of the business bank account.

DRAWINGS ACCOUNT

	Debit Side of Account			Credit Side of Account	
Date	Account Name	€	Date	Account Name	€
12/12/2019	Bank	230			

BANK ACCOUNT

	Debit Side of Account			Credit Side of Account	
Date	Account Name	€	Date	Account Name	€
			12/12/2019	Drawings	230

Question 2.16

	Debit €	Credit €
Trade receivables account	7,200	
Sales account		7,200

To recognise the sale of goods on credit.

Sales returns account	500	
Trade receivables account		500

To recognise goods returns inwards.

Cash account	6,700	
Trade receivables account		6,700

To recognise the cash received from a credit customer.

TRADE RECEIVABLES ACCOUNT

	Debit Side of Account			Credit Side of Account	
Date	**Account Name**	**€**	**Date**	**Account Name**	**€**
03/03/2019	Sales	7,200	10/03/2019	Sales returns	500
			20/03/2019	Cash	6,700

SALES ACCOUNT

	Debit Side of Account			Credit Side of Account	
Date	**Account Name**	**€**	**Date**	**Account Name**	**€**
			03/03/2019	Trade receivables	7,200

CASH ACCOUNT

	Debit Side of Account			Credit Side of Account	
Date	**Account Name**	**€**	**Date**	**Account Name**	**€**
20/03/2019	Trade receivables	6,700			

SALES RETURNS ACCOUNT

	Debit Side of Account			Credit Side of Account	
Date	**Account Name**	**€**	**Date**	**Account Name**	**€**
10/03/2019	Trade receivables	500			

Question 2.17

	Debit €	Credit €
Trade receivables account	5,000	
Sales account		5,000
To recognise the sale of goods on credit.		

	Debit €	Credit €
Discounts allowed account	100	
Trade receivables account		100
To recognise discount allowed.		

	Debit €	Credit €
Bank account	4,900	
Trade receivables account		4,900
To recognise the cheque received from a credit customer.		

The above two journal entries can be combined and presented as follows:

	Debit €	Credit €
Bank account	4,900	
Discounts allowed account	100	
Trade receivables account		5,000
To recognise the payment received from a credit customer.		

TRADE RECEIVABLES ACCOUNT

	Debit Side of Account			Credit Side of Account	
Date	**Account Name**	**€**	**Date**	**Account Name**	**€**
08/01/2019	Sales	5,000	30/01/2019	Discounts allowed	100
			30/01/2019	Bank	4,900

SALES ACCOUNT

Debit Side of Account			Credit Side of Account		
Date	Account Name	€	Date	Account Name	€
			08/01/2019	Trade receivables	5,000

BANK ACCOUNT

Debit Side of Account			Credit Side of Account		
Date	Account Name	€	Date	Account Name	€
30/01/2019	Trade receivables	4,900			

DISCOUNTS ALLOWED ACCOUNT

Debit Side of Account			Credit Side of Account		
Date	Account Name	€	Date	Account Name	€
30/01/2019	Trade receivables	100			

Question 2.18

	Debit €	Credit €
Trade receivables account	6,800	
Sales account		6,800

To recognise the sale of goods on credit.

Sales returns account	1,000	
Trade receivables account		1,000

To recognise goods returns inwards.

	Debit €	Credit €
Discounts allowed account	174	
Trade receivables account		174

To recognise goods discount allowed.

Cash account	5,626	
Trade receivables account		5,626

To recognise the cheque received from a credit customer.

The above two journal entries can be combined and presented as follows:

	Debit €	Credit €
Cash account	5,626	
Discounts allowed account	174	
Trade receivables account		5,800

To recognise the payment received from a credit customer.

TRADE RECEIVABLES ACCOUNT

Debit Side of Account			Credit Side of Account		
Date	Account Name	€	Date	Account Name	€
03/04/2019	Sales	6,800	06/04/2019	Returns	1,000
			30/04/2019	Discounts allowed	174
			30/04/2019	Cash	5,626

Sales Account

Debit Side of Account			Credit Side of Account		
Date	Account Name	€	Date	Account Name	€
			03/04/2019	Trade receivables	6,800

Cash Account

Debit Side of Account			Credit Side of Account		
Date	Account Name	€	Date	Account Name	€
30/04/2019	Trade receivables	5,626			

Discounts Allowed Account

Debit Side of Account			Credit Side of Account		
Date	Account Name	€	Date	Account Name	€
30/04/2019	Trade receivables	174			

Sales Returns Account

Debit Side of Account			Credit Side of Account		
Date	Account Name	€	Date	Account Name	€
06/04/2019	Trade receivables	1,000			

Question 2.19

	Debit €	Credit €
Purchases account	6,100	
Trade payables account		6,100

To recognise the purchase of goods on credit.

	Debit €	Credit €
Trade payables account	800	
Purchases returns account		800

To recognise goods returns inwards.

Trade payables account	5,300	
Cash account		5,300

To recognise the cash paid to a credit supplier.

Trade Payables Account

Debit Side of Account			Credit Side of Account		
Date	Account Name	€	Date	Account Name	€
15/05/2019	Purchases returns	800	12/05/2019	Purchases	6,100
20/05/2019	Cash	5,300			

Purchases Account

Debit Side of Account			Credit Side of Account		
Date	Account Name	€	Date	Account Name	€
12/05/2019	Trade payables	6,100			

Cash Account

Date	Debit Side of Account — Account Name	€	Date	Credit Side of Account — Account Name	€
			20/05/2019	Trade payables	5,300

Purchases Returns Account

Date	Debit Side of Account — Account Name	€	Date	Credit Side of Account — Account Name	€
			15/05/2019	Trade payables	800

Question 2.20

	Debit €	Credit €
Purchases account	6,300	
Trade payables account		6,300

To recognise the purchase of goods on credit.

	Debit €	Credit €
Trade payables account	126	
Discounts received account		126

To recognise discount received on early settlement.

	Debit €	Credit €
Trade payables account	6,174	
Bank account		6,174

To recognise the cheque payment to a credit supplier.

The above two journal entries can be combined as follows:

	Debit €	Credit €
Trade payables account	6,300	
Discounts received account		126
Bank account		6,174

To recognise the cheque payment to a credit supplier.

Trade Payables Account

Date	Debit Side of Account — Account Name	€	Date	Credit Side of Account — Account Name	€
20/09/2019	Discounts received	126	02/09/2019	Purchases	6,300
20/09/2019	Bank	6,174			

Purchases Account

Date	Debit Side of Account — Account Name	€	Date	Credit Side of Account — Account Name	€
02/09/2019	Trade payables	6,300			

Bank Account

Date	Debit Side of Account — Account Name	€	Date	Credit Side of Account — Account Name	€
			20/09/2019	Trade payables	6,174

DISCOUNTS RECEIVED ACCOUNT

	Debit Side of Account			Credit Side of Account	
Date	**Account Name**	**€**	**Date**	**Account Name**	**€**
			20/09/2019	Trade payables	126

Question 2.21

	Debit €	Credit €
Purchases account	9,500	
Trade payables account		9,500
To recognise the purchase of goods on credit.		

	Debit €	Credit €
Trade payables account	2,000	
Purchases returns account		2,000
To recognise goods returns inwards.		

	Debit €	Credit €
Trade payables account	150	
Discounts received account		150
To recognise discount received on early settlement.		

	Debit €	Credit €
Trade payables account	7,350	
Cash account		7,350
To recognise the cash payment to a credit supplier.		

The above two journal entries can be combined as follows:

	Debit €	Credit €
Trade payables account	7,500	
Discounts received account		150
Cash account		7,350
To recognise the cash payment to a credit supplier.		

TRADE PAYABLES ACCOUNT

	Debit Side of Account			Credit Side of Account	
Date	**Account Name**	**€**	**Date**	**Account Name**	**€**
11/06/2019	Returns	2,000	09/06/2019	Purchases	9,500
26/06/2019	Discounts received	150			
26/06/2019	Cash	7,350			

PURCHASES ACCOUNT

	Debit Side of Account			Credit Side of Account	
Date	**Account Name**	**€**	**Date**	**Account Name**	**€**
09/06/2019	Trade payables	9,500			

PURCHASES RETURNS ACCOUNT

	Debit Side of Account			Credit Side of Account	
Date	**Account Name**	**€**	**Date**	**Account Name**	**€**
			11/06/2019	Trade payables	2,000

CASH ACCOUNT

	Debit Side of Account			Credit Side of Account	
Date	**Account Name**	**€**	**Date**	**Account Name**	**€**
			26/06/2019	Trade payables	7,350

DISCOUNTS RECEIVED ACCOUNT

Debit Side of Account			Credit Side of Account		
Date	**Account Name**	**€**	**Date**	**Account Name**	**€**
			26/06/2019	Trade payables	150

Question 2.22

CASH ACCOUNT

Debit Side of Account			Credit Side of Account		
Date	**Account Name**	**€**	**Date**	**Account Name**	**€**
01/01/2019	Capital	20,000	02/01/2019	Purchases	3,400
25/01/2019	Sales	6,300	05/01/2019	Motor vehicle	5,000
			08/01/2019	Rent	1,000
			20/01/2019	Drawings	900
			31/01/2019	Balance c/d	16,000
		26,300			26,300
01/02/2019	Balance b/d	16,000			

CAPITAL ACCOUNT

Debit Side of Account			Credit Side of Account		
Date	**Account Name**	**€**	**Date**	**Account Name**	**€**
31/01/2019	Balance c/d	20,000	01/01/2019	Cash	20,000
			01/02/2019	Balance b/d	20,000

PURCHASES ACCOUNT

Debit Side of Account			Credit Side of Account		
Date	**Account Name**	**€**	**Date**	**Account Name**	**€**
02/01/2019	Cash	3,400	31/01/2019	Balance c/d	3,400
01/02/2019	Balance b/d	3,400			

MOTOR VEHICLE ACCOUNT

Debit Side of Account			Credit Side of Account		
Date	**Account Name**	**€**	**Date**	**Account Name**	**€**
05/01/2019	Cash	5,000	31/01/2019	Balance c/d	5,000
01/02/2019	Balance b/d	5,000			

RENT EXPENSE ACCOUNT

Debit Side of Account			Credit Side of Account		
Date	**Account Name**	**€**	**Date**	**Account Name**	**€**
08/01/2019	Cash	1,000	31/01/2019	Balance c/d	1,000
01/02/2019	Balance b/d	1,000			

DRAWINGS ACCOUNT

Debit Side of Account			Credit Side of Account		
Date	**Account Name**	**€**	**Date**	**Account Name**	**€**
20/01/2019	Cash	900	31/01/2019	Balance c/d	900
01/02/2019	Balance b/d	900			

SALES ACCOUNT

Debit Side of Account			Credit Side of Account		
Date	**Account Name**	**€**	**Date**	**Account Name**	**€**
31/01/2019	Balance c/d	6,300	25/01/2019	Cash	6,300
			01/02/2019	Balance b/d	6,300

Adam
TRIAL BALANCE
as at 31 January 2019

	Debit €	Credit €
Capital		20,000
Cash	16,000	
Purchases	3,400	
Motor vehicles	5,000	
Rent	1,000	
Drawings	900	
Sales		6,300
	26,300	26,300

Question 2.23

CASH ACCOUNT

Debit Side of Account			Credit Side of Account		
Date	**Account Name**	**€**	**Date**	**Account Name**	**€**
01/01/2019	Capital	24,000	03/01/2019	Purchases	4,900
25/01/2019	Sales	6,600	07/01/2019	Motor vehicle	4,500
			08/01/2019	Rent	1,200
			10/01/2019	Drawings	1,100
			15/01/2019	Balance c/d	18,900
		30,600			30,600
01/02/2019	Balance b/d	18,900			

CAPITAL ACCOUNT

Debit Side of Account			Credit Side of Account		
Date	**Account Name**	**€**	**Date**	**Account Name**	**€**
31/01/2019	Balance c/d	24,000	01/01/2019	Cash	24,000
			01/02/2019	Balance b/d	24,000

PURCHASES ACCOUNT

Debit Side of Account			Credit Side of Account		
Date	**Account Name**	**€**	**Date**	**Account Name**	**€**
03/01/2019	Cash	4,900	31/01/2019	Balance c/d	4,900
01/02/2019	Balance b/d	4,900			

MOTOR VEHICLE ACCOUNT

Debit Side of Account			Credit Side of Account		
Date	**Account Name**	**€**	**Date**	**Account Name**	**€**
07/01/2019	Cash	4,500	31/01/2019	Balance c/d	4,500
01/02/2019	Balance b/d	4,500			

RENT EXPENSE ACCOUNT

Debit Side of Account			Credit Side of Account		
Date	**Account Name**	**€**	**Date**	**Account Name**	**€**
08/01/2019	Cash	1,200	31/01/2019	Balance c/d	1,200
01/02/2019	Balance b/d	1,200			

Drawings Account

	Debit Side of Account			Credit Side of Account	
Date	**Account Name**	**€**	**Date**	**Account Name**	**€**
10/01/2019	Cash	1,100	31/01/2019	Balance c/d	1,100
01/02/2019	Balance b/d	1,100			

Sales Account

	Debit Side of Account			Credit Side of Account	
Date	**Account Name**	**€**	**Date**	**Account Name**	**€**
31/01/2019	Balance c/d	6,600	15/01/2019	Cash	6,600
			01/02/2019	Balance b/d	6,600

Joyce
TRIAL BALANCE
as at 31 January 2019

	Debit €	Credit €
Capital		24,000
Cash	18,900	
Purchases	4,900	
Motor vehicles	4,500	
Rent	1,200	
Drawings	1,100	
Sales		6,600
	30,600	30,600

Question 3.1

	Debit €	Credit €
Inventory account	14,600	
SOPL – cost of sales		14,600

To recognise the closing inventory in the financial statements.

Question 3.2

	Debit €	Credit €
SOPL – cost of sales	35,100	
Inventory account		35,100

To transfer the cost of opening inventory to SOPL.

	Debit €	Credit €
SOPL – cost of sales	289,700	
Purchases account		289,700

To transfer the expense to SOPL.

	Debit €	Credit €
Inventory account	44,900	
SOPL – cost of sales		44,900

To recognise the closing inventory in the financial statements.

These journal entries can be combined in a single journal entry as follows:

	Debit €	Credit €
Inventory account	9,800	
Purchases account		289,700
SOPL – cost of sales	279,900	

To recognise the cost of sales expense in the financial statements.

Question 3.3

	Debit €	Credit €
SOPL – cost of sales	34,200	
Inventory account		34,200

To transfer the opening inventory cost to SOPL.

	Debit €	Credit €
SOPL – cost of sales	512,500	
Purchases account		512,500

To transfer the expense to SOPL.

	Debit €	Credit €
Inventory account	38,700	
SOPL – cost of sales		38,700

To recognise the closing inventory in the financial statements.

	Debit €	Credit €
Purchases returns account	10,500	
SOPL – cost of sales		10,500

To recognise the purchases returns in the financial statements.

These journal entries can be combined in a single journal entry as follows:

	Debit €	Credit €
Inventory account	4,500	
Purchases returns account	10,500	
SOPL – cost of sales	497,500	
Purchases account		512,500

To recognise the cost of sales expense in the financial statements.

Question 3.4

	Debit €	Credit €
SOPL – cost of sales	1,608,840	
Purchases returns account	33,670	
Inventory account		16,110
Purchases account		1,238,100
Carriage inwards account		25,900
Manufacturing wages account		362,400

To recognise the cost of sales expense in the financial statements.

Question 4.1

	Debit €	Credit €
Electricity expense account	830	
Accruals account		830
To recognise the accrual of electricity expense.		

Question 4.2

Journal Entries

	Debit €	Credit €
Heat and lighting expense account	13,600	
Bank account		13,600
To recognise the heat and light expense.		
Heat and lighting expense account	1,150	
Accruals account		1,150
To recognise the accrual of heat and light expense.		
SOPL – heat and lighting	14,750	
Heat and lighting expense account		14,750
To recognise the heat and light expense in SOPL.		

Ledger Accounts

HEAT AND LIGHT ACCOUNT

Date	Account Name	€	Date	Account Name	€
31/12/2019	Bank	13,600	31/12/2019	SOPL – heat and light	
31/12/2019	Accruals	1,150			14,750
		14,750			14,750

ACCRUALS ACCOUNT

Date	Account Name	€	Date	Account Name	€
31/12/2019	Balance c/d	1,150	31/12/2019	Heat and light	1,150
			01/01/2020	Balance b/d	1,150

Question 4.3

Journal Entries

	Debit €	Credit €
Accruals account	450	
Rates expense account		450
To transfer the accrual to rates expense.		
Rates expense account	2,120	
Bank account		2,120
To recognise the rates expense.		
SOPL – rates	1,670	
Rates expense account		1,670
To recognise the rates expense for the current year in SOPL.		

Ledger Accounts

RATES EXPENSE ACCOUNT

Date	Account Name	€	Date	Account Name	€
02/02/2019	Bank	2,120	01/01/2019	Accruals	450
			31/12/2019	SOPL – rates expense	1,670
		2,120			2,120

ACCRUALS ACCOUNT

Date	Account Name	€	Date	Account Name	€
01/01/2019	Rates expense	450	01/01/2019	Balance b/d	450

Question 4.4

	Debit €	Credit €
Light and heating expense account	420	
Accruals account		420
To recognise the light and heating accrual as at 31/12/2019.		

	Debit €	Credit €
Accruals account	420	
Light and heating expense account		420
To transfer the accrual to light and heating expense on 01/01/2020.		

Question 4.5

Journal Entries

	Debit €	Credit €
Rent expense account	400	
Accruals account		400
To recognise the rent accrual as at 31/12/2019.		

	Debit €	Credit €
SOPL – rent	400	
Rent expense account		400
To recognise the rent expense for the current year in SOPL.		

Ledger Accounts

RENT EXPENSE ACCOUNT

Date	Account Name	€	Date	Account Name	€
31/12/2019	Accruals	400	31/12/2019	SOPL – rent expense	400

ACCRUALS ACCOUNT

Date	Account Name	€	Date	Account Name	€
31/12/2019	Balance c/d	400	31/12/2019	Rent	400
			01/01/2020	Balance b/d	400

Question 4.6

	Debit €	Credit €
Accruals account	230	
Electricity expense account		230
To transfer the accrual to electricity expense on 01/01/2019.		
Electricity expense account	870	
Bank account		870
To recognise the electricity bill paid 05/04/2019.		
Electricity expense account	810	
Bank account		810
To recognise the electricity bill paid 06/08/2019.		
Electricity expense account	780	
Bank account		780
To recognise the electricity bill paid 01/12/2019.		
Electricity expense account	290	
Accruals account		290
To recognise the electricity accrual at 31/12/2019.		

ELECTRICITY EXPENSE ACCOUNT

Date	Account Name	€	Date	Account Name	€
05/04/2019	Bank	870	01/01/2019	Accruals	230
06/08/2019	Bank	810	31/12/2019	SOPL – electricity	2,520
01/12/2019	Bank	780			
31/12/2019	Accruals	290			
		2,750			2,750

ACCRUALS ACCOUNT

Date	Account Name	€	Date	Account Name	€
01/01/2019	Electricity	230	01/01/2019	Balance b/d	230
31/12/2019	Balance c/d	290	31/12/2019	Electricity	290
		520			520
			01/01/2020	Balance b/d	290

Question 4.7

There is an opening accrual as at 1 January 2018 of €930 [€1,240 × 9 ÷ 12]:

	Debit €	Credit €
Accruals account	930	
Rent expense account		930
To transfer the accrual to rates expense on 01/01/2018.		
Rates expense account	1,240	
Bank account		1,240
To recognise the rates paid.		
Rates expense account	990	
Accruals account		990
To recognise the rates accrual (€1,320 × 9 ÷ 12 = €990).		

SOPL – rates expense	1,300
Rates expense account		1,300

To recognise the rates expense in SOPL.

RATES EXPENSE ACCOUNT

Date	Account Name	€	Date	Account Name	€
30/04/2018	Bank	1,240	01/01/2018	Accruals	930
31/12/2018	Accruals	990	31/12/2018	SOPL – rates expense	1,300
		2,230			2,230

ACCRUALS ACCOUNT

Date	Account Name	€	Date	Account Name	€
01/01/2018	Rates	930	01/01/2018	Balance b/d	930
31/12/2018	Balance c/d	990	31/12/2018	Rent	990
		1,920			1,920
			01/01/2019	Balance b/d	990

Question 4.8

	Debit €	Credit €
Insurance expense account	3,300	
Bank account		3,300

To recognise the insurance expense.

	Debit €	Credit €
Prepayments account	1,650	
Insurance expense account		1,650

To recognise the prepayment in relation to the insurance expense.

	Debit €	Credit €
SOPL – insurance expense	1,650	
Insurance expense account		1,650

To recognise the insurance expense in SOPL.

INSURANCE EXPENSE ACCOUNT

Date	Account Name	€	Date	Account Name	€
01/07/2019	Bank	3,300	31/12/2019	Prepayments	1,650
			31/12/2019	SOPL – insurance expense	1,650
		3,300			3,300

PREPAYMENTS ACCOUNT

Date	Account Name	€	Date	Account Name	€
31/12/2019	Insurance	1,650	31/12/2019	Balance c/d	1,650
01/01/2020	Balance b/d	1,650			

Question 4.9

The following journal entry is posted when rent is paid on 1 May, 1 August and 1 November:

	Debit €	Credit €
Rent expense account	2,700	
Bank account		2,700

To recognise the rent expense.

		Debit €	Credit €
Prepayments account		900	
Rent expense account			900
To recognise the prepayment in relation to the rent expense.			
SOPL – rent expense		7,200	
Rent expense account			7,200
To recognise the rent expense in SOPL.			

RENT EXPENSE ACCOUNT

Date	Account Name	€	Date	Account Name	€
01/05/2019	Bank	2,700	31/12/2019	Prepayments	900
01/08/2019	Bank	2,700	31/12/2019	SOPL – rent expense	7,200
01/11/2019	Bank	2,700			
		8,100			8,100

PREPAYMENTS ACCOUNT

Date	Account Name	€	Date	Account Name	€
31/12/2019	Rent	900	31/12/2019	Balance c/d	900
01/01/2020	Balance b/d	900			

Question 4.10

		Debit €	Credit €
Electricity account		440	
Prepayments account			440
To recognise the electricity charges paid in the previous reporting period.			
Electricity account		2,300	
Bank account			2,300
To recognise the electricity charges paid during 2019.			
SOPL – electricity		2,740	
Electricity account			2,740
To recognise the electricity charges in SOPL.			

ELECTRICITY CHARGES ACCOUNT

Date	Account Name	€	Date	Account Name	€
01/01/2019	Prepayments	440	31/12/2019	SOPL – electricity expense	2,740
	Bank	2,300			
		2,740			2,740

PREPAYMENTS ACCOUNT

Date	Account Name	€	Date	Account Name	€
01/01/2019	Balance b/d	440	01/01/2019	Prepayments	440

Question 4.11

	Debit €	Credit €
Heating account	480	
Prepayments account		480
To recognise the heating charges paid in the previous reporting period.		
Heating account	2,520	
Bank account		2,520
To recognise the heating charges paid during 2019.		
Prepayments account	425	
Heating account		425
To recognise the heating charges prepaid.		
SOPL – heating	2,575	
Heating account		2,575
To recognise the heating charges in profit or loss.		

HEATING EXPENSE ACCOUNT

Date	Account Name	€	Date	Account Name	€
01/01/2019	Prepayments	480	31/12/2019	Prepayments	425
	Bank	2,520	31/12/2019	SOPL – heating expense	2,575
		3,000			3,000

PREPAYMENTS ACCOUNT

Date	Account Name	€	Date	Account Name	€
01/01/2019	Balance b/d	480	01/01/2019	Heating expense	480
31/12/2019	Heating	425	31/12/2019	Balance c/d	425
		905			905
01/01/2020	Balance b/d	425			

Question 4.12

	Debit €	Credit €
Bank account	8,400	
Rental income account		8,400
To recognise rental income received 31 October 2019.		
Income due account	5,600	
Rental income account		5,600
To recognise income due at the reporting date.		
Rental income account	14,000	
SOPL – rental income		14,000
To recognise rental income in the SOPL.		

RENTAL INCOME ACCOUNT

Date	Account Name	€	Date	Account Name	€
31/12/2019	SOPL – income	14,000	04/11/2019	Bank	8,400
			31/12/2019	Income Due	5,600
		14,000			14,000

INCOME DUE ACCOUNT

Date	Account Name	€	Date	Account Name	€
31/12/2019	Rental Income	5,600	31/12/2019	Balance c/d	5,600
01/01/2020	Balance b/d	5,600			

The amount of the income due is €5,600. (Quarterly payment of €8,400 × 2 ÷ 3, i.e. November and December.)

The income due is presented under current assets in the SOFP.

Question 4.13

	Debit €	Credit €
Revenue account	3,000	
Income due account		3,000

To transfer income due at the end of the last reporting period to revenue.

When the revenue is received the following journal entry is posted on each date – 1 February, 1 May, 1 August and 1 November:

Bank account	4,500	
Revenue account		4,500

To recognise revenue received.

Income due account	3,120	
Revenue account		3,120

To recognise income due at the reporting date (€18,720 × 2 ÷ 12).

Revenue account	18,120	
SOPL – revenue		18,120

To recognise revenue in the SOPL.

REVENUE ACCOUNT

Date	Account Name	€	Date	Account Name	€
01/01/2019	Income due	3,000	01/02/2019	Bank	4,500
31/12/2019	SOPL – revenue	18,120	01/05/2019	Bank	4,500
			01/08/2019	Bank	4,500
			01/11/2019	Bank	4,500
			31/12/2019	Income due	3,120
		21,120			21,120

INCOME DUE ACCOUNT

Date	Account Name	€	Date	Account Name	€
01/01/2019	Balance b/d	3,000	01/01/2019	Revenue	3,000
31/12/2019	Revenue	3,120	31/12/2019	Balance c/d	3,120
		6,120			6,120
01/01/2020	Balance b/d	3,120			

The amount of the income due is €3,120. (Annual fee of €18,720 × 2 ÷ 12, i.e. for November and December.)

The income due is presented under current assets in the SOFP.

Question 4.14

When rental income was received the following journal entry was posted on 1 June, 1 September and 1 December:

	Debit €	Credit €
Bank account	5,250	
Rental income account		5,250
To recognise rental income received.		
Rental income account	3,500	
Rental in advance account		3,500
To recognise rental income received in advance 1 December 2019 (January and February 2020).		
Rental income account	12,250	
SOPL – revenue		12,250
To recognise rental income in the SOPL.		

RENTAL INCOME ACCOUNT

Date	Account Name	€	Date	Account Name	€
31/12/2019	Income in advance	3,500	01/06/2019	Bank	5,250
31/12/2019	SOPL – rental income	12,250	01/09/2019	Bank	5,250
			01/12/2019	Bank	5,250
		15,750			15,750

INCOME IN ADVANCE ACCOUNT

Date	Account Name	€	Date	Account Name	€
31/12/2019	Balance c/d	3,500	31/12/2019	Income in advance	3,500
			01/01/2020	Balance b/d	3,500

Income in advance is presented in the SOFP under current liabilities.

Question 5.1

	Debit €	Credit €
Bad debts expense account	1,440	
Trade receivables account		1,440
To recognise the write-off of amounts due from credit customers.		
SOPL – bad debts	1,440	
Bad debts expense account		1,440
To transfer the bad debt expense to the SOPL.		

Question 5.2

Journal Entries

	Debit €	Credit €
Bad debts expense account	950	
Trade receivables account		950
To recognise the write-off of amounts due from credit customers.		

	Debit €	Credit €
SOPL – bad debts	950	
Bad debts expense account		950

To transfer the bad debt expense to the SOPL.

Ledger Accounts

TRADE RECEIVABLES ACCOUNT

Date	Account Name	€	Date	Account Name	€
31/12/2019	Balance b/d	105,200	31/12/2019	Bad debts expense	950
			31/12/2019	Balance c/d	104,250
		105,200			105,200
01/01/2020	Balance b/d	104,250			

BAD DEBTS EXPENSE ACCOUNT

Date	Account Name	€	Date	Account Name	€
31/12/2019	Trade receivables	950	31/12/2019	SOPL – bad debts expense	950

STATEMENT OF PROFIT OR LOSS (EXTRACT)

	€
Bad debts expense	(950)

STATEMENT OF FINANCIAL POSITION (EXTRACT)

	€
Current Assets	
Trade receivables	104,250

Question 5.3

Trade receivables balance	€94,500
Provision required (€94,500 × 2%)	€1,890

	Debit €	Credit €
Bad debts expense account	1,890	
Provision for bad debts account		1,890

To recognise the provision for bad debts.

	Debit €	Credit €
SOPL – bad debts	1,890	
Bad debts expense account		1,890

To transfer the bad debt expense to the SOPL.

TRADE RECEIVABLES ACCOUNT

Date	Account Name	€	Date	Account Name	€
31/12/2019	Balance b/d	94,500	31/12/2019	Balance c/d	94,500
01/01/2020	Balance b/d	94,500			

BAD DEBTS EXPENSE ACCOUNT

Date	Account Name	€	Date	Account Name	€
31/12/2019	Provision for bad debts	1,890	31/12/2019	SOPL – bad debts expense	1,890

PROVISION FOR BAD DEBTS ACCOUNT

Date	Account Name	€	Date	Account Name	€
31/12/2019	Balance c/d	1,890	31/12/2019	Bad debts expense	1,890

Question 5.4

	€
Trade receivables balance	75,280
Provision required (€75,280 × 2.5%)	1,882
Current provision	1,220
Change in provision	662

	Debit €	Credit €
Bad debts expense account	662	
Provision for bad debts account		662

To recognise the provision for bad debts.

SOPL – bad debts	662	
Bad debts expense account		662

To transfer the bad debt expense to the SOPL.

TRADE RECEIVABLES ACCOUNT

Date	Account Name	€	Date	Account Name	€
31/12/2019	Balance b/d	75,280	31/12/2019	Balance c/d	75,280
01/01/2020	Balance b/d	75,280			

BAD DEBTS EXPENSE ACCOUNT

Date	Account Name	€	Date	Account Name	€
31/12/2019	Provision for bad debts	662	31/12/2019	SOPL – bad debts expense	662

PROVISION FOR BAD DEBTS ACCOUNT

Date	Account Name	€	Date	Account Name	€
31/12/2019	Balance c/d	1,882	01/01/2019	Balance b/d	1,220
			31/12/2019	Bad debts expense	662
		1,882			1,882
			01/01/2020	Balance b/d	1,882

Question 5.5

	Debit €	Credit €
Bank account	700	
Trade receivables account		700

To recognise payment from customer.

Bad debts expense account	2,100	
Trade receivables account		2,100

To recognise the write-off of amounts due from credit customers.

	€
Trade receivables balance (€123,600 − €2,800)	120,800
Provision required (€120,800 × 2%)	2,416
Current provision	3,260
Change in provision	(844)

	Debit €	Credit €
Provision for bad debts account	844	
Bad debts expense account		844

To recognise the provision for bad debts.

	Debit €	Credit €
SOPL – bad debts	1,256	
Bad debts expense account		1,256

To transfer the bad debt expense to the SOPL (€2,100 – €844).

TRADE RECEIVABLES ACCOUNT

Date	Account Name	€	Date	Account Name	€
31/12/2019	Balance b/d	123,600	31/12/2019	Bad debts expense	2,100
			31/12/2019	Bank	700
			31/12/2019	Balance c/d	120,800
		123,600			123,600
01/01/2020	Balance b/d	120,800			

BAD DEBTS EXPENSE ACCOUNT

Date	Account Name	€	Date	Account Name	€
31/12/2019	Bad debts expense	2,100	31/12/2019	Provision for bad debts	844
			31/12/2019	SOPL – bad debts expense	1,256
		2,100			2,100

PROVISION FOR BAD DEBTS ACCOUNT

Date	Account Name	€	Date	Account Name	€
31/12/2019	Bad debts expense	844	31/12/2019	Balance b/d	3,260
31/12/2019	Balance c/d	2,416			
		3,260			3,260
			01/01/2020	Balance b/d	2,430

Question 5.6

	Debit €	Credit €
Bad debts expense account	6,580	
Specific provision for bad debts account		6,580

To recognise the provision for bad debts.

	Debit €	Credit €
SOPL – bad debts	6,580	
Bad debts expense account		6,580

To transfer the bad debt expense to the SOPL.

BAD DEBTS EXPENSE ACCOUNT

Date	Account Name	€	Date	Account Name	€
31/12/2019	Specific provision	6,580	31/12/2019	SOPL – bad debts expense	6,580

SPECIFIC PROVISION FOR BAD DEBTS ACCOUNT

Date	Account Name	€	Date	Account Name	€
31/12/2019	Balance c/d	6,580	31/12/2019	Bad debts expense	6,580
			01/01/2020	Balance b/d	6,580

Question 6.1

	Debit €	Credit €
Machine – cost account	800,000	
Bank account		800,000

To recognise the asset at cost when it is purchased.

Question 6.2

(a) **Step 1** Calculate the depreciable amount.

Cost – Residual value = Depreciable amount

€60,000 − €5,000 = €55,000

Step 2 Calculate the depreciation charge.

Depreciation charge per annum = Depreciable amount ÷ Useful life

€55,000 ÷ 10 years = €5,500 per annum

(b) As at 31 December 2018 and 2019:

	Debit €	Credit €
Depreciation expense account	5,500	
Accumulated depreciation account		5,500

To recognise the depreciation expense.

	Debit €	Credit €
SOPL – cost of sales	5,500	
Depreciation expense account		5,500

To transfer the depreciation expense to the SOPL.

The depreciation charge is presented in the cost of sales line of the SOPL as the asset is used in the production of the finished goods and is therefore a production cost.

(c) Carrying amount of the asset:

	€
As at 31 December 2018 (€60,000 − €5,500)	54,500
As at 31 December 2019 (€60,000 − €11,000)	49,000

Question 6.3

(a) **Step 1** Calculate the depreciable amount.

Cost – Residual value = Depreciable amount

€2,000,000 − €0 = €2,000,000

Step 2 Calculate the depreciation charge.

Depreciation charge per annum = Depreciable amount ÷ Useful life

€2,000,000 ÷ 40 years = €50,000 per annum

Depreciation charge 2018: €50,000 × 4 ÷ 12 = €16,667

Depreciation charge 2019: €50,000

(b) As at 31 December 2018:

	Debit €	Credit €
Depreciation expense account	16,667	
Accumulated depreciation account		16,667

To recognise the depreciation expense 2018.

	Debit €	Credit €
SOPL – administration expenses	16,667	
Depreciation expense account		16,667

To transfer the depreciation expense to the SOPL.

As at 31 December 2019:

	Debit €	Credit €
Depreciation expense account	50,000	
Accumulated depreciation account		50,000
To recognise the depreciation expense.		
SOPL – administration expenses	50,000	
Depreciation expense account		50,000
To transfer the depreciation expense to the SOPL.		

The depreciation charge is presented in the administration expense line of the SOPL as the asset is used as an administrative office.

(c) Carrying amount of the asset:

	€
As at 31 December 2018 (€2,000,000 − €16,667)	1,983,333
As at 31 December 2019 (€2,000,000 − €66,667)	1,933,333

Question 6.4

2018: Cost × Depreciation rate = €85,000 × 15% = €12,750.
Carrying amount as at 31 October 2018: €85,000 − €12,750 = €72,250.
2019: Carrying amount × Depreciation rate = €72,250 × 15% = €10,837.50.

Question 6.5

2018: Cost × Depreciation rate = €32,000 × 20% = €6,400.
Time apportion 30 April to 31 October: €6,400 × 6/12 = €3,200.
Carrying amount as at 31 October 2018: €32,000 − €3,200 = €28,800.
2019: Carrying amount × Depreciation rate = €28,800 × 20% = €5,760.

As at 31 October 2018:

	Debit €	Credit €
Depreciation expense account	3,200	
Accumulated depreciation account		3,200
To recognise the depreciation expense 2018.		
SOPL – selling and distribution expenses	3,200	
Depreciation expense account		3,200
To transfer the depreciation expense to the SOPL.		

As at 31 October 2019:

	Debit €	Credit €
Depreciation expense account	5,760	
Accumulated depreciation account		5,760
To recognise the depreciation expense.		
SOPL – selling and distribution expenses	5,760	
Depreciation expense account		5,760
To transfer the depreciation expense to the statement of profit or loss.		

Question 6.6

	€
Proceeds	2,085,000
Carrying amount as at 31 December 2019 (€2,400,000 − €410,000)	(1,990,000)
Profit/(loss) on disposal	95,000

	Debit €	Credit €
Disposal account	2,400,000	
Property – cost account		2,400,000

To transfer the cost of the asset to the disposal account on derecognition.

Property – accumulated depreciation account	410,000	
Disposal account		410,000

To transfer the accumulated depreciation of the asset to the disposal account on derecognition.

Bank account	2,085,000	
Disposal account		2,085,000

To recognise the proceeds on disposal of the asset.

Disposal account	95,000	
SOPL – gain on disposal		95,000

To recognise the gain on disposal of the asset.

DISPOSAL ACCOUNT

Date	Account Name	€	Date	Account Name	€
31/12/2019	Property	2,400,000	31/12/2019	Accumulated depreciation	410,000
31/12/2019	SOPL – gain on disposal	95,000	31/12/2019	Bank	2,085,000
		2,495,000			2,495,000

The individual journal entries above can be summarised as follows:

	Debit €	Credit €
Bank account	2,085,000	
Accumulated depreciation account	410,000	
Property – cost account		2,400,000
SOPL – gain on disposal		95,000

Question 6.7

	€
Cost 1 April 2017	680,000
Depreciation year ended 31 December 2017 (€680,000 × 10%)	(68,000)
Carrying amount as at 31 December 2017	612,000
Depreciation year ended 31 December 2018 (€612,000 × 10%)	(61,200)
Carrying amount as at date of disposal	550,800

	€
Proceeds	525,000
Carrying amount as at 31 December 2019	(550,800)
Loss on disposal	(25,800)

	Debit €	Credit €
Disposal account	680,000	
Machine – cost account		680,000

To transfer the cost of the asset to the disposal account on derecognition.

	Debit €	Credit €
Machine – accumulated depreciation account	129,200	
Disposal account		129,200

To transfer the accumulated depreciation of the asset to the disposal account on derecognition.

	Debit €	Credit €
Bank account	525,000	
Disposal account		525,000

To recognise the proceeds on disposal of the asset.

	Debit €	Credit €
SOPL – loss on disposal	25,800	
Disposal account		25,800

To recognise the loss on disposal of the asset.

DISPOSAL ACCOUNT

Date	Account Name	€	Date	Account Name	€
31/12/2019	Machine	680,000	31/12/2019	Accumulated depreciation	129,200
			31/12/2019	Bank	525,000
			31/12/2019	SOPL – loss	25,800
		680,000			680,000

The individual journal entries above can be summarised as follows:

	Debit €	Credit €
Bank account	525,000	
Accumulated depreciation account	129,200	
SOPL – loss on disposal	25,800	
Property – cost account		680,000

Question 7.1

	Debit €	Credit €
Purchases account	12,100	
Trade payables account		12,100

To recognise the purchase of goods on credit.

Question 7.2

	Debit €	Credit €
Cash account	3,146	
VAT account		546
Revenue account		2,600

To recognise sale of goods for cash.

Question 7.3

	Debit €	Credit €
Cash account	30,250	
VAT account		5,250
Revenue account		25,000

To recognise sale of goods for cash.

Question 7.4

	Debit €	Credit €
Purchases account	5,100	
VAT account	1,071	
Cash account		6,171

To recognise purchase of goods for cash.

Question 7.5

	Debit €	Credit €
Purchases account	14,600	
VAT account	3,066	
Trade payables account		17,666

To recognise purchase of goods on credit.

Question 7.6

VAT ACCOUNT

Date	Account Name	€	Date	Account Name	€
08 Jan	Purchases	5,880	10 Jan	Sales	2,961
			15 Jan	Sales	468
			20 Jan	Sales	1,953
			31 Jan	Balance c/d	498
		5,880			5,880
01 Feb	Balance b/d	498			

Question 8.1

	€
Gross pay	110,240.00
Employer's PRSI 8%	8,819.20
Total wages cost	119,059.20

Question 8.2

	€
Net pay	82,105
PAYE	38,903
PRSI deductions	15,570
Gross wages	136,578

Question 9.1

(a) The trade receivables control account is impacted by the totalling error of the sales day book.

Question 9.2

Items (i) and (iii) affect the trade receivables accounts and need to be amended.

Item (ii) means the balance on an individual ledger account does not reflect the discounts allowed and needs to be reduced. You are told that the discounts have been reflected in the trade receivables control account so no adjustment is required.

TRADE RECEIVABLES CONTROL ACCOUNT

Date	Account Name	€	Date	Account Name	€
31/12/2019	Balance b/d	45,600	31/12/2019	Sales day book overcasting	40
31/12/2019	Sales returns day book overcast	100	31/12/2019	Balance c/d	45,660
		45,700			45,700
01/01/2020	Balance b/d	45,660			

Reconciliation of ledger listing with balance on trade receivables control account at the reporting date.

	€
Balance per ledger listing	45,750
Discounts allowed	(90)
Balance on trade receivables control account	45,660

Question 9.3

(a)

TRADE PAYABLES CONTROL ACCOUNT

Account Name	€	Account Name	€
Returns	55	Balance b/d	98,600
Balance c/d	98,705	Purchases day book error	160
	98,760		98,760
		Balance b/d	98,705

(b)

	Debit €	Credit €
Trade payables control account	55	
Purchases returns account		55

To correct undercasting error in purchases returns day book.

Purchases account	160	
Trade payables control account		160

To correct undercasting error on purchases day book.

Question 9.4

TRADE PAYABLES CONTROL ACCOUNT

Date	Account Name	€	Date	Account Name	€
31/12/2019	Balance c/d	59,935	31/12/2019	Balance b/d	59,720
			31/12/2019	Purchases day book error	120
					95
		59,935			59,935
			01/01/2020	Balance b/d	59,935

	€
Balance per ledger listing	60,055
Discounts received	(120)
	59,935

Question 10.1

BANK RECONCILIATION
as at 31 January 2019

	€
Balance per bank statement	16,365
Unpresented cheques:	
Cheque no. 109	(499)
Cheque no. 111	(1,745)
Balance per bank account	14,121

The bank figure presented in the SOFP as at 31 January 2019 will be €14,121.

Question 10.2

BANK RECONCILIATION
as at 31 January 2019

	€
Balance per bank statement	7,782
Unpresented cheques:	
Cheque no. 704	(911)
Cheque no. 706	(1,970)
Plus lodgements	
31 January	10,940
Balance per bank account	15,841

BANK ACCOUNT

Date	Account Name	€	Date	Account Name	€
01/02/2019	Balance b/d	15,936	01/02/2019	Fees and charges	95
			01/02/2019	Balance c/d	15,841
		15,936			15,841
02/02/2019	Balance b/d	15,841			15,936

The bank figure presented in the SOFP as at 31 January 2019 will be €15,841.

Question 10.3

BANK RECONCILIATION
as at 31 April 2019

	€
Balance per bank statement	22,284.50
Unpresented cheques:	
Cheque no. 246	(2,546.00)
Cheque no. 248	(2,812.00)
Balance per bank account	16,926.50

BANK ACCOUNT

Date	Account Name	€	Date	Account Name	€
02/04/2019	Balance b/d	17,574.00	02/04/2019	Fees and charges	87.50
			02/04/2019	Electricity	560.00
			01/04/2019	Balance c/d	16,926.50
		17,574.00			17,574.00
03/04/2019	Balance b/d	16,926.50			

The bank figure presented in the SOFP as at 31 January 2019 will be €16,926.50.

Question 11.1

Step 1 How should the journal entry have been recorded?

	Debit €	Credit €
Machine – cost account	80,000	
Loan account		80,000

To record the purchase of machinery financed by a loan.

Step 2 How was the journal entry recorded?

The journal entry was not balanced as the debit side totalled €160,000 and the credit side totalled €0; as a result the computer system would automatically credit the suspense account with €160,000.

	Debit €	Credit €
Machine – cost account	80,000	
Loan account	80,000	
Suspense account (automatically generated by computer system)		160,000

To record the purchase of machinery financed by a loan.

Step 3 The correcting journal entry.

	Debit €	Credit €
Suspense account	160,000	
Loan account		160,000

To correct the purchase of machinery financed by a loan.

The machine cost account has been correctly debited but the loan was debited instead of credited; to correct the error a journal entry for double the amount needs to be posted.

Question 11.2

The journal entry, while incorrect, is balanced so there is no impact on the suspense account.

Step 1 How should the journal entry have been recorded?

	Debit €	Credit €
Loan account	5,000	
Bank account		5,000

To record the capital repayment of a loan.

Step 2 How was the journal entry recorded?

	Debit €	Credit €
Bank account	5,000	
Loan account		5,000

To record the capital repayment of a loan.

Step 3 The correcting journal entry.

The journal entry processed resulted in:
• The bank account being debited when it should have been credited; to correct the error double the original transaction amount needs to be credited.
• The loan account was credited when it should have been debited; to correct the error the loan account needs to be debited for double the amount of the original transaction amount.

	Debit €	Credit €
Loan account	10,000	
Cash account		10,000

To correct the purchase of machinery financed by a loan.

Question 11.3

Step 1 How should the journal entry have been recorded?

	Debit €	Credit €
Trade payables account	230	
Discounts received account		230
To record the discount received from a credit supplier.		

Step 2 How was the journal entry recorded?

	Debit €	Credit €
Trade payables account	230	
Discounts allowed account	230	
Suspense account (automatically generated by the computer system)		460
To record discount received from a credit supplier.		

Step 3 The correcting journal entry.

	Debit €	Credit €
Suspense account	460	
Discounts allowed account		230
Discounts received account		230
To correct the journal entry processed in relation to discount received.		

Question 11.4

Step 1 How should the journal entry have been recorded?

	Debit €	Credit €
Cash account	830	
Sales account		830
To record the cash sales.		

Step 2 How was the journal entry recorded?

	Debit €	Credit €
Trade receivables account	830	
Sales account		830
Transaction processed in error as a credit sale.		

Step 3 The correcting journal entry.

	Debit €	Credit €
Cash account	830	
Trade receivables account		830
To correct the journal entry processed in error in relation to a cash sale treated as a credit sale.		

Question 11.5

Step 1 Detail the journal entry that should have been processed.

	Debit €	Credit €
Motor vehicle – cost account	35,000	
Bank account		35,000
To recognise the purchase of motor vehicles.		

Step 2 How was the transaction processed?

	Debit €	Credit €
SOPL – motor expenses account	35,000	
Bank account		35,000
To recognise the motor expenses incurred.		

Step 3 Correct the error.
There is no impact on the suspense account as the debit side of the transaction is equal to the credit side of the transaction.

	Debit €	Credit €
Motor vehicle – cost account	35,000	
SOPL – motor expenses account		35,000
To correct a journal entry processed incorrectly.		

The original transaction resulted in an item of capital expenditure (the purchase of a computer asset) being treated as an expense. When the correcting journal entry is posted, this will impact the reported profit – the reversal of the computer expense will result in the reported profit increasing by €35,000.

From **Chapter 6, Property, Plant and Equipment, and Depreciation** it is known that assets used over more than one reporting period are depreciated over their estimated useful lives. The correcting journal entry will result in an item of property, plant and equipment being recognised, so a depreciation charge will have to be included in the financial statements. The depreciation charge is €7,000 [€35,000 × 20%]. The journal entry to recognise the depreciation charge is:

	Debit €	Credit €
Depreciation expense account	7,000	
Accumulated depreciation account		7,000
To recognise the depreciation charge on the motor vehicle.		

The reported profit will be reduced by the depreciation charge of €7,000.

	€
Reported profit	185,240
Motor expenses reversal	35,000
Depreciation on motor vehicles	(7,000)
	213,240

Question 12.1

R. Wilson
INCOME STATEMENT
for the year ended 31 December 2019

	€	€	€
Revenue			1,570,000
Less: sales returns			(15,000)
Less: cost of sales			1,555,000
Opening inventory		78,200	
Purchases (€1,152,600 − €2,500)	1,150,100		
Less: purchases returns	(12,500)	1,137,600	
Less: closing inventory		(96,500)	(1,119,300)
Gross profit			435,700
Administration salaries		(95,800)	
Rent and rates		(25,500)	
Insurance (W2)		(17,825)	

Bad debts	(2,800)	
Loan interest (W3)	(12,000)	
Depreciation (W1):		
Property	(21,000)	
Motor vehicles	(7,040)	(181,965)
Net profit		253,735

R. Wilson
STATEMENT OF FINANCIAL POSITION
as at 31 December 2019

Assets	Cost €	Accumulated Depreciation €	Carrying Amount €
Non-current Assets			
Property	1,050,000	147,000	903,000
Motor vehicles	55,000	26,840	28,160
	1,105,000	173,840	931,160
Current Assets			
Inventory		96,500	
Trade receivables		150,000	
Prepayments		1,575	
Cash		48,600	296,675
Total Assets			1,227,835
Capital			259,100
Net profit			253,735
			512,835
Less: drawings			(18,500)
			494,335
Non-current Liabilities			
4% loan			600,000
Current Liabilities			
Trade payables		121,500	
Accruals		12,000	133,500
			1,227,835

W1 DEPRECIATION CHARGE
Property: 2% × €1,050,000 = €21,000.
Motor vehicles: (€55,000 − €19,800) × 20% = €7,040.

W2 INSURANCE

PREPAYMENTS ACCOUNT

Date	Account Name	€	Date	Account Name	€
01/01/2019	Balance b/d	500	01/01/2019	Insurance	500
31/12/2019	Insurance	1,575	31/12/2019	Balance c/d	1,575
		2,075			2,075
01/01/2020	Balance b/d	1,575			

INSURANCE ACCOUNT

Date	Account Name	€	Date	Account Name	€
31/12/2019	Bank	18,900	31/12/2019	Prepayments (€18,800 /12)	1,575
01/01/2019	Prepayments	500	31/12/2019	SOPL – insurance expense	17,825
		19,400			19,300

W3 LOAN INTEREST

	€
Loan amount	600,000
Interest rate	4%
Interest charge per annum	24,000
Interest charge for 2019 (01/07/2019 to 31/12/2019)	12,000 [€24,000 × 6 ÷12]

Question 13.1

TRADE RECEIVABLES ACCOUNT

Date	Account Name	€	Date	Account Name	€
01/01/2019	Balance b/d	36,900	31/12/2019	Discounts allowed	3,500
31/12/2019	Revenue	406,420	31/12/2019	Returns	8,600
			31/12/2019	Cash	51,900
			31/12/2019	Bank	345,100
			31/12/2019	Bad debts	12,400
			31/12/2019	Balance c/d	21,820
		443,320			443,320
01/01/2020	Balance b/d	21,820			

Question 13.2

TRADE PAYABLES ACCOUNT

Date	Account Name	€	Date	Account Name	€
31/12/2019	Bank	387,600	01/01/2019	Balance b/d	65,147
31/12/2019	Cash	35,050	31/12/2019	Purchases	416,468
31/12/2019	Balance c/d	58,965			
		481,615			481,615
			01/01/2020	Balance b/d	58,965

The cost of sales figure is €439,808 [€56,250 + €416,468 − €32,910].

Question 13.3

RATES ACCOUNT

Date	Account Name	€	Date	Account Name	€
31/12/2019	Bank	16,480	01/01/2019	Accruals	1,850
			31/12/2019	Prepayments	840
			31/12/2019	SOPL – rates	13,790
		16,480			16,480

ACCRUALS ACCOUNT

Date	Account Name	€	Date	Account Name	€
01/01/2019	Rates	1,850	01/01/2019	Balance b/d	1,850

PREPAYMENTS ACCOUNT

Date	Account Name	€	Date	Account Name	€
31/12/2019	Rates	840	01/01/2019	Balance c/d	840
01/01/2020	Balance b/d	840			

Question 13.4

RENT EXPENSES ACCOUNT

Date	Account Name	€	Date	Account Name	€
01/01/2019	Prepayments	2,500	31/12/2019	SOPL – rent	32,830
31/12/2019	Bank	29,150			
31/12/2019	Accruals	1,180			
		32,830			32,830

ACCRUALS ACCOUNT

Date	Account Name	€	Date	Account Name	€
31/12/2019	Balance c/d	1,180	31/12/2019	Rent expense	1,180
			01/01/2020	Balance b/d	1,180

PREPAYMENTS ACCOUNT

Date	Account Name	€	Date	Account Name	€
01/01/2019	Balance b/d	2,500	01/01/2019	Rent expense	2,500

Question 13.5

	€000
Property	290
Motor vehicles	42
Inventory	28
Trade receivables	35
Prepayment	6
Cash	8
Bank overdraft	(23)
Trade payables	(31)
Capital as at 31 December 2019	355

Question 14.1
(a) Accumulated Fund as at 31 December 2018:

	€
Bank and cash	68,400
Bar stock	10,000
Premises (original cost €1,600,000)	1,200,000
Fittings (original cost €500,000)	375,000
Subscriptions due	14,600
	1,668,000
Subscriptions in advance	(8,100)
Amount due to bar suppliers	(2,700)
Accumulated fund as at 31 December 2018	1,657,200

(b)

BANK (LEDGER) ACCOUNT

Account Name	€	Account Name	€
Balance b/d	68,400	Bar suppliers	124,000
Subscriptions	405,200	Tennis coach	60,000
Bar receipts	208,500	Bar-staff salaries	43,000
		Rates	21,000
		Maintenance	168,000
		Cleaning	79,500
		Balance	186,600
	682,100		682,100

(c)

Supergreen Tennis Club
BAR TRADING ACCOUNT
for the year ended 31 December 2019

	€	€
Sales		208,500
Opening stock	10,000	
Purchases	127,100	
Less: closing stock	(12,800)	
Bar-staff salaries	43,000	(167,300)
		41,200

BAR SUPPLIERS ACCOUNT

Account Name	€	Account Name	€
Bank	124,000	Balance b/d	2,700
Balance c/d	5,800	Purchases (balancing figure)	127,100
	129,800		129,800

(d)

Supergreen Tennis Club
INCOME AND EXPENDITURE ACCOUNT
for the year ended 31 December 2019

	€	€
Income		392,550
Subscriptions		41,200
Bar profit		433,750
Expenses		
Tennis coach	60,000	
Rates	21,000	
Maintenance	168,000	
Cleaning	79,500	
Treasurer's bonus	6,000	
Depreciation		
Premises	40,000	
Fittings	50,000	(424,500)
Surplus		9,250

SUBSCRIPTIONS DUE ACCOUNT

Account Name	€	Account Name	€
Balance b/d	14,600	Subscriptions	14,600
Subscriptions	9,200	Balance c/d	9,200
	23,800		23,800

SUBSCRIPTIONS IN ADVANCE ACCOUNT

Account Name	€	Account Name	€
Subscriptions	8,100	Balance b/d	8,100
Balance c/d	15,350	Subscriptions	15,350
	23,450		23,450

SUBSCRIPTIONS ACCOUNT

Account Name	€	Account Name	€
Subscriptions due	14,600	Subscriptions in advance	8,100
Subscriptions in advance	15,350	Bank	405,200
Income and expenditure	392,550	Subscriptions due	9,200
	422,500		422,500

(e)

Supergreen Tennis Club
STATEMENT OF FINANCIAL POSITION
as at 31 December 2019

	€	€
Non-current Assets		
Property		1,160,000
Fittings		325,000
		1,485,000
Current Assets		
Bar stock	12,800	
Subscriptions due	9,200	
Bank	186,600	208,600
		1,693,600
Accumulated fund as at 31/12/2012		1,657,200
Surplus		9,250
		1,666,450
Current Liabilities		
Bar suppliers	5,800	
Subscriptions in advance	15,350	27,150
Treasurer's bonus	6,000	1,693,600

Question 15.1
(a)

Wind and Rain
PROFIT OR LOSS APPROPRIATION ACCOUNT
for the year ended 31 December 2019

	€	€
Profit for year		90,000
Share of profits		
Wind (€90,000 × 2 ÷ 3)	(60,000)	
Rain (€90,000 × 1 ÷ 3)	(30,000)	(90,000)

(b)

CURRENT ACCOUNTS

Date	Account Name	Wind €	Rain €	Date	Account Name	Wind €	Rain €
31/12/2019	Drawings	8,000	14,300	01/01/2019	Balance b/d	13,450	15,680
31/12/2019	Balance c/d	65,450	31,380	31/12/2019	Share of profit	60,000	30,000
		73,450	45,680			73,450	45,680
				01/01/2020	Balance b/d	65,450	31,380

Question 15.2
(a)

Harry and Barry
PROFIT OR LOSS APPROPRIATION ACCOUNT
for the year ended 31 December 2019

	€	€
Profit for year		110,000
Salary		
Harry		(24,000)
Share of profits		86,000
Harry (€86,000 × 3 ÷ 4)	(64,500)	
Barry (€86,000 × 1 ÷ 4)	(21,500)	(86,000)

(b)

CURRENT ACCOUNTS

Date	Account Name	Harry €	Barry €	Date	Account Name	Harry €	Barry €
31/12/2019	Balance c/d	106,700	33,600	01/01/2019	Balance b/d	18,200	12,100
				31/12/2019	Salary	24,000	
				31/12/2019	Share of profit	64,500	21,500
		106,700	33,600			106,700	33,600
				01/01/2020	Balance b/d	106,700	33,600

Question 15.3
(a)

Will and Bill
PROFIT OR LOSS APPROPRIATION ACCOUNT
for the year ended 31 December 2019

	€	€
Profit for year		150,000
Salary		
Bill		(30,000)
		120,000
Share of profits		
Will (€120,000 × 2 ÷ 5)	(48,000)	
Bill (€120,000 × 3 ÷ 5)	(72,000)	(120,000)

(b)

CURRENT ACCOUNTS

Date	Account Name	Will €	Bill €	Date	Account Name	Will €	Bill €
31/12/2019	Bank (salary)		30,000	01/01/2019	Balance b/d	30,400	25,500
31/12/2019	Balance c/d	78,400	97,500	31/12/2019	Salary		30,000
					Share of profit	48,000	72,000
		78,400	127,500			78,400	127,500
				01/01/2020	Balance b/d	78,400	97,500

Question 15.4

(a)

John and Paul
PROFIT OR LOSS APPROPRIATION ACCOUNT
for the year ended 31 December 2019

	€	€
Profit for year		92,000
Interest on drawings		
John	360	
Paul	400	760
		92,760
Salary		
John	(15,000)	
Paul	(12,000)	(27,000)
Interest on capital		
John (€31,500 × 5%)	(1,575)	
Paul (€35,600 × 5%)	(1,780)	(3,355)
		62,405
Share of profits		
John	(20,405)	
Paul	(42,000)	(62,405)

Partner	Share of Profit Based on Profit-sharing Ratio €	Guaranteed Amount €	Share of Profit after Guarantee €
John	31,202.50		20,405
	[62,405 × 50%]		[31,202.50 − 10,797.50]
Paul	31,202.50	42,000	42,000
	[62,405 × 50%]		[31,202.50 + 10,797.50]

(b)

CURRENT ACCOUNTS

Date	Account Name	John €	Paul €	Date	Account Name	John €	Paul €
31/12/2019	Drawings	9,700	14,100	01/01/2019	Balance b/d	7,220	10,300
31/12/2019	Interest on drawings	360	400	31/12/2019	Salary	15,000	12,000
31/12/2019	Balance c/d	34,140	51,580	31/12/2019	Interest on capital	1,575	1,780
				31/12/2019	Share of profit	20,405	42,000
		44,200	66,080			44,200	66,080
				01/01/2020	Balance b/d	34,140	51,580

Question 16.1

Old profit-sharing ratio	3:2
New profit-sharing ratio	4:4:2

(a)

PROPERTY ACCOUNT

Date	Account Name	€000	Date	Account Name	€000
01/01/2019	Balance b/d	280	31/12/2019	Accumulated depreciation	14
31/12/2019	Revaluation	380	31/12/2019	Revaluation	266
			31/12/2019	Balance c/d	380
		660			660
01/01/2020	Balance b/d	380			

REVALUATION ACCOUNT

Account Name	€000	Account Name	€000
Property	266.0	Property	380.0
Capital – Adam	68.4		
Capital – Brian	45.6		
	380.0		380.0

(b)

GOODWILL ACCOUNT

Account Name	€000	Account Name	€000
Capital – Adam	48	Capital – Adam	32
Capital – Brian	32	Capital – Brian	32
		Capital – Charlie	16
	80		80

(c)

CAPITAL ACCOUNTS

Account Name	Adam €000	Brian €000	Charlie €000	Account Name	Adam €000	Brian €000	Charlie €000
Goodwill	32.0	32.0	16.0	Balance b/d	190.0	110.0	
Balance c/d	274.4	155.6	64.0	Revaluation	68.4	45.6	
				Goodwill	48.0	32.0	
				Bank			80.0
	306.4	187.6	80.0		306.4	187.6	80.0
				Balance b/d	274.4	155.6	64.0

(d)

CURRENT ACCOUNTS

Account Name	Adam €000	Brian €000	Charlie €000	Account Name	Adam €000	Brian €000	Charlie €000
Balance c/d	45.0	27.0	20.0	Balance b/d	45.0	27.0	
				Bank			20.0
	45.0	27.0	20.0		45.0	27.0	20.0
				Balance b/d	45.0	27.0	20.0

(e)

Adam, Brian and Charlie
STATEMENT OF FINANCIAL POSITION
as at 31 December 2019

	€000	€000
Non-current Assets		
Property		380.0
Motor vehicle (€50,000 – €15,000)		35.0
		415.0
Current Assets		
Inventory	25.0	
Trade receivables	37.5	
Bank (€8,500 + €100,000)	108.5	171.0
		586.0

continued overleaf

Capital Accounts

Adam		274.4
Brian		155.6
Charlie		64.0
		494.0

Current Accounts

Adam	45.0	
Brian	27.0	
Charlie	20.0	92.0
		586.0

Question 16.2

CAPITAL ACCOUNTS

Date	Account Name	Niall €000	Oliver €000	Peter €000	Date	Account Name	Niall €000	Oliver €000	Peter €000
31/12/2019	Cash			45	31/12/2019	Balance b/d	100	80	45
31/12/2019	Balance c/d	100	80						
		100	80	45			100	80	45
					01/01/2020	Balance b/d	100	80	

CURRENT ACCOUNTS

Date	Account Name	Niall €000	Oliver €000	Peter €000	Date	Account Name	Niall €000	Oliver €000	Peter €000
31/12/2019	Cash			34	31/12/2019	Balance b/d	100	60	34
31/12/2019	Balance c/d	100	60						
		100	60	34			100	60	34
					01/01/2020	Balance b/d	100	60	

BANK ACCOUNT

Date	Account Name	€000	Date	Account Name	€000
31/12/2019	Balance b/d	106	31/12/2019	Capital – Peter	45
			31/12/2019	Current – Peter	34
			31/12/2019	Balance c/d	27
		106			106
01/01/2020	Balance b/d	27			

Niall and Oliver
STATEMENT OF FINANCIAL POSITION
as at 31 December 2019

	€000	€000
Non-current Assets		
Property		210
Motor vehicles		25
		235
Current Assets		
Inventory	36	
Trade receivables	42	
Bank (€106,000 – €45,000 – €34,000)	27	105
		340

continued overleaf

Capital

Niall	100
Oliver	80
	180

Current Accounts

Niall	100	
Oliver	60	
		160
		340

Question 17.1

PARTNERS' CURRENT ACCOUNTS

Account Name	Mango €	Tango €	Account Name	Mango €	Tango €
Capital account	200,000	105,000	Balance b/d	200,000	105,000

PARTNERS' CAPITAL ACCOUNTS

Account Name	Mango €	Tango €	Account Name	Mango €	Tango €
Bank	552,800	390,200	Balance b/d	300,000	250,000
			Current account	200,000	105,000
			Realisation	52,800	35,200
	552,800	390,200		552,800	390,200

REALISATION ACCOUNT

Account Name	€	Account Name	€
Property	700,000	Bank	810,000
Plant and equipment	180,000	Bank	190,000
Motor vehicles	60,000	Bank	50,000
Inventory	50,000	Bank	45,000
Trade receivables	90,000	Bank	85,000
Expenses	12,000		
Mango	52,800		
Tango	35,200		
	1,180,000		1,180,000

BANK ACCOUNT

Account Name	€	Account Name	€
Balance	45,000	Realisation expenses	12,000
Property	810,000	Loan	200,000
Plant and equipment	190,000	Trade payables	70,000
Motor vehicles	50,000	Mango	552,800
Inventory	45,000	Tango	390,200
Trade receivables	85,000		
	1,225,000		1,225,000

LOAN ACCOUNT

Account Name	€	Account Name	€
Bank	200,000	Balance	200,000

TRADE PAYABLES ACCOUNT

Account Name	€	Account Name	€
Bank	70,000	Balance	70,000

Question 18.1

(a)   The IASB's standard-setting process comprises six stages.

1. Setting the Agenda – the IASB evaluates the merits of adding a potential item to its agenda with specific reference to the needs of investors.
2. Project Planning – the IASB may decide to conduct specific projects alone or in conjunction with other standard-setters. The Director of Technical Activities and the Director of Research assemble a project team. The project manager develops a project plan.
3. Development and Publication of a Discussion Paper – the IASB normally publishes a discussion paper as a vehicle to explain the issue and to solicit comment from interested parties.
4. Development and Publication of an Exposure Draft (ED) – this is a mandatory stage in the process. The ED sets out a specific proposal in the form of a proposed standard. The ED contains an invitation to comment and typically respondents have 120 days to do so.
5. Development and Publication of an IFRS – in response to the submissions made on the ED, an IFRS is developed. If the issue has proven controversial there may be a need for a further round of consultation. If IASB is satisfied that it has reached a conclusion on the issues, a pre-ballot draft is normally sent to IFRIC for review.
6. Procedure After an IFRS is Issued – regular meetings are held with interested parties to help understand any unanticipated issues related to the practical implementation and potential impact of the standard.

(b)   Arguments in support of standard-setting and those against standard-setting:

Arguments in support of standard-setting

The arguments used to support the standard-setting process are summarised under the following headings:

- Comparability – financial statements should allow a user to make comparisons with other companies. In order to make valid intercompany comparisons of performance and trends, investment decision-makers must be supplied with relevant and reliable data that have been standardised. Such comparisons would be distorted and valueless if companies were permitted to select accounting policies at random or, even worse, with the intention of disguising changes in performance and trends.
- Credibility – the accountancy profession would lose all credibility if it permitted companies experiencing similar events to produce financial reports that disclosed markedly different results simply because they could select different accounting policies. Uniformity is essential if financial reports are to disclose a true and fair view.
- Influence – the process of formulating standards has encouraged a constructive appraisal of the policies being proposed for individual reporting problems and has stimulated the development of a conceptual framework. It promotes the continual development of improved practice.
- Discipline – companies left to their own devices without the need to observe standards will eventually be disciplined by the financial market. Mandatory standards will impose systematic ongoing regulation, which should prevent serious loss to the entity and those who rely on the annual accounts when making credit, loan and investment decisions. A lack of discipline in financial reporting can lead to damaged confidence in the standard of reporting by companies.
- Departures – a benefit of producing standards is that departures from established accounting practice are highlighted.
- Confidence – promotes user confidence in financial statements.
- Consistency – responds to emerging business issues in a uniform manner.

Arguments against standard-setting

- Adverse allocative effects – the introduction of a standard could have adverse economic consequences for those companies implementing the standard, e.g. cost of implementation, and sub-optimal managerial decisions based on the impact of a standard on the financial statements.
- Consensus-seeking – the issuing of standards may be over-influenced by those with the easiest access to the standard-setters, particularly as the subject matter becomes more complex, as with e.g. capital instruments.
- Overload – this may be in a number of forms:
  - too many/too few standards;
  - standards are too detailed/not sufficiently detailed;
  - standards are general purpose and fail to recognise the differences between large and small entities and interim and final accounts; and
  - too many standard-setters with differing requirements, e.g. ASB27/07/2015, IASB, FASB, Stock Exchange.
- Not feasible to develop generally accepted or consistent framework – either imposed or abandoned.
- Costs are not justified in terms of the benefits.
- Will not lead to improvements in financial reporting.
- Standardisation leads to uniformity, which creates rigidity, a lack of flexibility, and thus less innovation.
- Standardisation results in consistency but does not enhance comparability. Different companies have different circumstances that necessitate selecting the most appropriate accounting policies.

Question 18.2

(a) **Statement of Financial Position** The SOFP details the financial position of an enterprise at a particular point in time. In particular, it details the economic resources under the control of the entity, its financial structure, its liquidity and solvency, and its capacity to adapt to changes in the environment in which it operates. In the current environment users might focus particularly on the financial structure of the business, particularly the level of gearing. Users might also concentrate on issues impacting upon working capital and evidence of liquidity problems, including high levels of inventory, receivables and payables. Users might also focus on the adequacy of shareholders' funds.

(b) **Statement of Profit or Loss and Other Comprehensive Income** A SPLOCI represents a statement of performance and includes a number of specific metrics that users tend to focus on. The SPLOCI details measures of profitability and may be used in conjunction with the SOCF in gauging the future prospects of a business. Users might look specifically at the gross profit margin in their efforts to comprehend the basic viability of the business. EBITDA, operating profit, profit before tax and profit after tax provide further measures of performance. Users might also concentrate on the significant expense headings of the business, e.g. 40% of an airline's expenses might be accounted for by fuel expenses.

(c) **Statement of Cash Flows** Cash is regarded as the lifeblood of a business. For many users their primary focus is the SOCF. The SOCF details overall net inflows/outflows of cash under three readily understood headings: operating activities, investing activities, and financing activities. While a business can sustain losses over a number of years, a sustained deterioration in cash flows could point up a serious threat to the application of the going concern concept to the business. Profitable businesses might be shown up by a SOCF as being exposed to a liquidity problem. Alternatively, loss-making entities might disclose sufficient cash to sustain their continued existence.

(d) **Statement of Changes in Equity** The SOCIE provides a detailed breakdown of the shareholders' interest in the business and the movements in that figure over the course of the year. Each individual element of shareholders' funds from share capital and share premium to retained earnings and other reserves is analysed. The SOCIE will outline increases in capital through share issues or rights issues, movements within capital, such as bonus issues of shares, and decreases in capital, such as share buyback arrangements. Dividend payouts are also included in the SOCIE.

(e) **Notes and Supplementary Schedules** The primary financial statements typically contain summary information that may suffice for certain users. However, those seeking greater levels of detail or the breakout of specific figures can obtain this information from the notes. The figure for property, plant and equipment in the SOFP can be examined in minute detail in the additional notes supporting the financial statements. Such notes and disclosures will also explain items in the SOFP and SPLOCI, disclose the risks and uncertainties affecting the enterprise, and explain any resources and obligations not recognised in the SOFP.

Question 18.3

(a) (i) **Present and Potential Investors** The decisions made by these users include whether to buy, retain or sell shares and when the best time may be for the purchase or sale of those shares. The interest of these parties in financial statement information lies in the fact that it is their money that is invested in the entity. They would like to ensure that they are getting a good return on their investment. This is assessed by how much profit the entity is making and whether their investment is increasing in value. For shareholders in companies, this means they will receive good dividend payouts and the market value of their shares will increase and they can make capital gains if these were sold.

Prospective investors are interested in an entity's profitability and potential for growth. They rely on financial statements for information in making their investment decisions.

(ii) **Employees/Managers** Employees have several motivations. They have a vested interest in the continued and profitable operations of their entity. Financial statements are an important source of information about current and potential future profitability and solvency. They may also need them to monitor the viability of their pension plans and the potential for bonuses and salary increases.

Managers are responsible to the owners/shareholders in carrying out policies and directives, and in running the business efficiently and effectively. Managers utilise financial statement information in many of their financing, investment and/or operating decisions.

The financial statements of other entities can also be used in management decisions. For instance, when deciding where to redirect the resources of an entity, the financial statement of other entities can show areas where high profit margins are currently being earned.

(iii) **Lenders and Other Suppliers** Banks and other lenders are interested not only in the entity's profitability but also in its ability to repay loans and appropriate levels of security to support loan applications.

In the initial loan-granting stage by a lender, financial statements typically are an important item. Many banks have standard evaluation procedures that stipulate that information relating to liquidity, leverage and profitability be considered when determining the amount of the loan, interest rate and the security to be requested.

Many bank loans include covenants that, if violated, can result in the bank restructuring the existing loan agreement.

Suppliers usually extend credit to the firm for goods supplied and they want to be assured of timely payments of accounts due.

(iv) **Government** Financial statements provide data that may be used in the compilation of economic statistics, including GDP, export figures and sectoral employment statistics. Financial statements are typically the starting-point in the calculations of taxable profit. The Revenue Commissioners/Inland Revenue may use financial data in compiling databases on specific industries.

The government may also want to ensure that the entity complies with legislation and regulations, for example, health and safety, equality and employee rights.

(b)   Financial statements concentrate on the financial effects of past events and transactions, whereas the decisions that most users of financial statements have to make relate to the future.
Examples of the types of information missing would include:
1. The pipeline of new products and/or the state of the order book.
2. Information as to how the business might be viewed by employees, customers, suppliers and banks.

Question 19.1

Number of shares issued during the year	1,000,000
Market price of one share	€2.80
Par value of one share	€0.50
	€
Total proceeds	2,800,000
Ordinary share capital (1m shares × €0.50)	500,000
Share premium [1m shares × (€2.80 – €0.50)]	2,300,000

	Debit €	Credit €
Bank account (1,800,000 × €2.80)	2,800,000	
Ordinary share capital account		500,000
Share premium account		2,300,000

To recognise the issue of ordinary shares.

Tent Plc
STATEMENT OF FINANCIAL POSITION (EXTRACT)
as at 31 December 2019

	2019 €	2018 €
Equity and Reserves		
Ordinary share capital	2,300,000	1,800,000
Share premium	2,300,000	

Question 19.2

Warwick Ltd
STATEMENT OF PROFIT OR LOSS AND OTHER COMPREHENSIVE INCOME
for the year ended 31 December 2019

	€
Revenue	5,907,800
Cost of sales (Working 1)	(3,544,300)
Gross profit	2,363,500

continued overleaf

Administration costs (Working 1)	(852,100)
Selling and distribution expenses (Working 1)	(332,540)
Finance cost	(63,000)
Profit before tax	1,115,860
Income tax	(294,280)
Profit for year	821,580
Other comprehensive income	Nil
Total Comprehensive Income	821,580

Warwick Ltd
STATEMENT OF FINANCIAL POSITION
as at 31 December 2019

	€	€
Assets		
Non-current Assets		
Property, plant and equipment		3,761,000
Current Assets		
Inventory	346,200	
Trade receivables	502,460	
Cash and cash equivalents	168,700	1,017,360
Total Assets		4,778,360
Equity and Liabilities		
Equity and Reserves		
Ordinary share capital €1		500,000
Share premium		450,000
Retained earnings		2,185,680
		3,135,680
Non-current Liabilities		
Loan		900,000
Current Liabilities		
Trade payables	399,400	
Accrual (€63,000 – €14,000)	49,000	
Current tax payable	294,280	742,680
		4,778,360

WORKING 1

	Cost of Sales	Administration Costs	Selling and Distribution Expenses
	€	€	€
Opening inventory	280,100		
Purchases	3,160,400		
Purchases returns	(135,000)		

continued overleaf

Closing inventory	(346,200)		
Manufacturing wages	435,000		
Administration costs		285,900	
Administration wages		306,200	
Auditor's fee		15,000	
Directors' fees		189,000	
Motor expenses			220,000
Bad debts			10,500
Depreciation:			
Property		56,000	
Machinery	150,000		
Motor vehicles			93,000
Change in provision (Working 3)			9,040
	3,544,300	852,100	332,540

WORKING 2

	Buildings €	Machinery €	Motor Vehicles €	Total €
Cost	2,800,000	1,500,000	620,000	4,920,000
Accumulated depreciation as at 31/12/2018	(224,000)	(450,000)	(186,000)	(860,000)
Depreciation for 2019				
€2,800,000 × 2%	(56,000)			
€1,500,000 × 10%		(150,000)		
€620,000 × 15%			(93,000)	(299,000)
Carrying amount as at 31 December 2019	2,520,000	900,000	341,000	3,761,000

WORKING 3

	€
Trade receivables balance	518,000
Provision required (€518,000 × 3%)	15,040
Current provision	(6,500)
Change in provision	9,040

Question 19.3

Walker Ltd
STATEMENT OF CHANGES IN EQUITY
for the year ended 31 December 2019

	Ordinary Share Capital €	Share Premium €	Retained Earnings €	Total €
As at 1 January 2019	500,000	260,000	1,910,000	2,670,000
Change in accounting policy	–	–	(65,000)	(65,000)
As restated	500,000	260,000	1,845,000	2,605,000
Share issue	40,000	520,000		560,000
Profit for year			302,500	302,500
As at 31 December 2019	540,000	780,000	2,147,500	3,467,500

Share issue
Ordinary share capital: 200,000 shares × €0.20 = €40,000.
Share premium: 200,000 shares × (€2.80 − 0.20) = €520,000.

The dividend is not accrued as there is no obligation to pay it at the reporting date. A dividend only becomes an obligation when the dividend is approved by shareholders at the annual general meeting.

Question 20.1

Indirect method

	€
Profit before tax	419,000
Depreciation	32,500
	451,500
(Increase)/decrease in inventory (€52,900 − €35,600)	17,300
(Increase)/decrease in trade receivables (€96,200 − €120,100)	(23,900)
Increase/(decrease) in trade payables (€20,250 − €27,800)	(7,550)
Cash generated from operations	437,350

Direct Method

	€
Cash received from customers (W1)	1,806,100
Cash paid to suppliers (W2)	(685,250)
Cash paid for expenses (W3)	(683,500)
Cash generated from operations	437,350

W1 CASH RECEIVED FROM CUSTOMERS

TRADE RECEIVABLES ACCOUNT

Account Name	€	Account Name	€
Balance b/d	96,200	Bank (balancing figure)	1,806,100
Sales	1,830,000	Balance c/d	120,100
	1,926,200		1,926,200
Balance b/d	120,100		

W2 CASH PAID TO SUPPLIERS

	€
Opening inventory (given in question) **Step 1**	52,900
Purchases (€730,600 − €52,900) **Step 5**	677,700
(€695,000 + €35,600) **Step 4**	730,600
Less: closing inventory (given in question) **Step 2**	(35,600)
Cost of sales (given in question) **Step 3**	695,000

TRADE PAYABLES ACCOUNT

Account Name	€	Account Name	€
Bank	685,250	Balance b/d	27,800
Balance c/d	20,250	Purchases	677,700
	705,500		705,500
		Balance b/d	20,250

W3 CASH PAID FOR OTHER EXPENSES

	€
Operating expenses	716,000
Less: depreciation	(32,500)
Cash paid for expenses	683,500

Question 20.2

PROPERTY, PLANT AND EQUIPMENT – COST ACCOUNT

Account Name	€	Account Name	€
Balance b/d	750,000	Disposal	65,000
Revaluation	100,000	Balance c/d	940,000
Additions	155,000		1,005,000
	1,005,000		
Balance b/d	940,000		

ACCUMULATED DEPRECIATION ACCOUNT

Account Name	€	Account Name	€
Disposal	30,000	Balance b/d	230,000
Balance c/d	280,000	Depreciation	80,000
	310,000		310,000

	€
Cost of asset	65,000
Accumulated depreciation	(30,000)
Carrying amount at the date of disposal	35,000
Loss on sale of asset	(9,500)
Proceeds from disposal	25,500

Circus Ltd
STATEMENT OF CASH FLOWS (EXTRACT)
for the year ended 31 December 2019

	€000	€000
Cash flow from investing activities		
Proceeds from the sale of property, plant and equipment	25,500	
Purchase of property, plant and equipment	(155,000)	
Net cash flow from investing activities		(129,500)

Question 20.3

PROPERTY, PLANT AND EQUIPMENT – COST ACCOUNT

Account Name	€	Account Name	€
Balance b/d	1,305,000	Disposal	85,000
Additions	200,000	Balance c/d	1,420,000
	1,505,000		1,505,000
Balance b/d	1,420,000		

ACCUMULATED DEPRECIATION ACCOUNT

Account Name	€	Account Name	€
Disposal	23,200	Balance b/d	280,000
Balance c/d	316,000	Depreciation	59,200
	339,200		339,200

	€
Cost of asset	85,000
Accumulated depreciation	(23,200)
Carrying amount at the date of disposal	61,800
Proceeds from disposal	(48,000)
Loss on disposal	13,800

Millicent Ltd
STATEMENT OF CASH FLOWS (EXTRACT)
for the year ended 31 December 2019

	€000	€000
Profit before Tax		X
Depreciation		59,200
Loss on disposal		13,800
Cash flow from investing activities		
Proceeds from the sale of property, plant and equipment	48,000	
Purchase of property, plant and equipment	(200,000)	
Net cash flow from investing activities		(152,000)

Question 20.4

TAX LIABILITY ACCOUNT

Account Name	€	Account Name	€
Bank	238,300	Balance b/d	164,200
Balance c/d	89,100	SPLOCI – taxation	163,200
	327,400		327,400
		Balance b/d	89,100

The figure to be presented in the SOCF in relation to taxation paid is €238,300.

Question 20.5

Indirect Method

The finance cost listed in the SPLOCI is added back to the profit before tax. The actual finance cost paid in the reporting period is presented in the SOCF as a separate line item in any of the three sections: operating, investing or financing. The entity must choose where the finance cost is presented and do so consistently from period to period.

STATEMENT OF CASH FLOWS (EXTRACT)
for the year ended 31 December 2019

	€
Profit before tax	118,000
Finance cost	10,400
Depreciation	X
Financing Activities	
Finance cost paid	(10,400)

Direct Method

The actual finance cost paid in the reporting period is presented in the SOCF as a separate line item in any of the three sections: operating, investing or financing. The entity must choose where the finance cost is presented and do so consistently from period to period.

STATEMENT OF CASH FLOWS (EXTRACT)
for the year ended 31 December 2019

	€
Financing Activities	
Finance cost paid	(10,400)

The amount of the finance paid in this example is the same as the charge in the SPLOCI as there are no outstanding liabilities in relation to the finance cost at either the start or end of the reporting period. In this question we have chosen to present the finance cost paid under financing activities.

Question 20.6

DIVIDEND PAYABLE ACCOUNT

Account Name	€	Account Name	€
Bank	18,500	Balance b/d	6,500
Balance c/d	18,000	SPLOCI – finance	30,000
	36,500		36,500
		Balance b/d	18,000

The dividend paid during the period that will be presented in the SOCF will be €18,500.

Question 21.1

	€
Direct materials	8.00
Direct labour	7.00
Direct expenses	5.00
Production overhead (€300,000 ÷ 100,000 units)	3.00
	23.00

Selling costs are not included in the value of inventory as they are not incurred in bringing the inventory to its present location and condition.

Production overhead is included in inventory based on normal capacity and not the actual capacity.

Question 21.2

Product	Cost €	Net Realisable Value €	Valued at €
A	7,600	7,500	7,500
		[7,900 – 400]	
B	5,000	5,050	5,000
		[5,500 – 450]	

Inventory is valued at the lower of cost and net realisable value on an item-by-item basis. The only exception to this rule is if there is a group of similar items these can be grouped together and total cost compared to the total net realisable value of all the items of that group.

Question 21.3

(a)

Cost	€5,800
Net realisable value (€6,100 – €400)	€5,700

Inventory is valued at €5,700.

(b) IAS 2 *Inventories* states that inventory should be valued at the lower of cost and net realisable value.

Question 21.4

(a) FIFO

	Receipts		Issues		On Hand	
Date	Units	Value €	Units	Value €	Units	Value €
01/01/2019					300	4,500
03/01/2019	400	5,800			700	10,300
12/01/2019	500	7,500			1,200	17,800
20/01/2019	350	5,600			1,550	23,400
25/01/2019	750	13,500			2,300	36,900
31/01/2019			2,000	31,500	300	5,400

The units on hand are the ones acquired most recently, that is on 25 January 2019: 300 units × €18.00 = €5,400. Alternatively, you could calculate the value of the units issued:

Units	Unit Cost €	Value €
300	15.00	4,500
400	14.50	5,800
500	15.00	7,500
350	16.00	5,600
450	18.00	8,100
		31,500

(b) Weighted Average

Date	Receipts Units	Receipts Value €	Issues Units	Issues Value €	On Hand Units	On Hand Average Cost €	On Hand Value €
01/01/2019					300	15.00	4,500
03/01/2019	400	5,800			700	14.71	10,300
12/01/2019	500	7,500			1,200	14.83	17,800
20/01/2019	350	5,600			1,550	15.10	23,400
25/01/2019	750	13,500			2,300	16.04	36,900
31/01/2019			2,000	32,080	300		4,820

Each time goods are received the average cost is calculated. Inventory issues are valued at the most recent average cost of €16.04. Issues are valued at €32,080 [€16.04 × 2,000 units].

3 January 2019: €10,300 ÷ 700 units = €14.71
12 January 2019: €17,800 ÷ 1,200 units = €14.83
20 January 2019: €23,400 ÷ 1,550 units = €15.10
25 January 2019: €36,900 ÷ 2,300 units = €16.04

Question 21.5

As at 31 December 2018 the inventory is valued at €1,780.

Cost	€1,900
Net realisable value (€1,850 − €70)	€1,780

As at 31 December 2019 the inventory is valued at €1,780.

Cost	€1,900
Net realisable value	€2,100 (Note 1)

Note 1 Selling and distribution costs have already been deducted.

The write-down to net realisable value can be reversed, however the reversal is limited to the amount of the original write-down of €120. The inventory is valued at €1,900 as at 31 December 2019.

Question 22.1

Step 1 Carrying amount at the start of the year.

	€
Cost	160,000
Depreciation year ended 31 December 2016	(15,000)
Depreciation year ended 31 December 2017	(15,000)
Depreciation year ended 31 December 2018	(15,000)
Carrying amount as at 1 January 2019	115,000

Step 2 Apply the change in accounting estimate.

	€
Carrying amount as at 1 January 2019	115,000
	(2,500)
Revised residual value	112,500
Remaining useful life (8 years – 3 years)	5 years
Depreciation charge per annum	22,500

Question 22.2

Profit for 2018 restated:

	€
Profit for 2018 as reported	286,900
Change in closing inventory (€96,300 – €85,600)	10,700
	297,600

Profit for 2019 restated:

	€
Profit for 2019 as reported	299,100
Change in opening inventory (€96,300 – €85,600)	(10,700)
Change in closing inventory (€105,250 – €104,620)	(630)
	287,770

Alvin
STATEMENT OF CHANGES IN EQUITY
for year ended 31 December 2019

	€
Retained earnings as at 1 January 2019	286,900
Changes in accounting policy	10,700
Retained earnings restated	297,600
Profit for year ended 31 December 2019	287,770
Retained earnings as at 31 December 2019	585,370

Question 22.3

Morrissey Ltd
STATEMENT OF PROFIT OR LOSS AND OTHER COMPREHENSIVE INCOME (EXTRACT)
for the year ended

	31 December 2019 €	31 December 2018 €
Gross profit	4,150,000	3,860,000
Wages cost	(1,840,000)	(1,720,000)
Distribution costs	(960,000)	(925,000)
Profit before tax	1,350,000	1,215,000
Income tax expense	(270,000)	(243,000)
Profit for the year	1,080,000	972,000

Morrissey
STATEMENT OF CHANGES IN EQUITY (EXTRACT)
for the year ended 31 December 2019

	Retained Earnings €
As at 1 January 2019	4,825,650
Error	(320,000)
Retained earnings restated	4,505,650
Profit for year	1,080,000
As at 31 December 2019	5,585,650

Question 22.4

During 2018, Donnelly Plc failed to charge amortisation of €250,000 relating to an intangible asset. In view of the fact that the reported net profit for that period was €328,300, this represents a material error. IAS 8 *Accounting Policies, Changes in Accounting Estimates and Errors* requires that material errors be corrected retrospectively in the first set of financial statements authorised for issue after their discovery. This amendment requires the restatement of the amortisation charge for 2018. Calculation of the reduction in after-tax profit for 2018: €250,000 × 70% = €175,000.

STATEMENT OF PROFIT OR LOSS AND OTHER COMPREHENSIVE INCOME (EXTRACT)
for the year ended 31 December 2019

	2019 €	2018 (restated) €
Gross profit	500,000	650,000
General and admin expenses	(410,000)	(431,000)
Profit before tax	90,000	219,000
Tax	(27,000)	(65,700)
Profit for year	63,000	153,300

STATEMENT OF CHANGES IN EQUITY (EXTRACT)
for the year ended 31 December 2019

	Retained Earnings €
Balance 1 January 2018	871,700
Profit for year ended 31 December 2018	153,300
Balance as at 31 December 2018	1,025,000
Profit for year ended 31 December 2019	63,000
Balance as at 31 December 2019	1,088,000

DISCLOSURE NOTE

The prior period adjustment relates to the correction of a material error that arose in 2018. The error arose as a result of a failure to charge amortisation of €250,000 on an intangible asset, the net effect of which was to overstate profits by €175,000 in that year.

Question 23.1

(a)

Question 23.2

(c)

Question 24.1

	Debit €	Credit €
Income tax expense account	21,300	
Tax liability account		21,300
To recognise the tax liability at the reporting date, 30 June 2019.		
SPLOCI – income tax expense	21,300	
Income tax expense account		21,300
To recognise the tax expense in the SPLOCI.		

Question 24.2

	Debit €	Credit €
Income tax expense account	82,450	
Tax liability account		82,450
To recognise the tax liability at the reporting date, 31 December 2019.		

	Debit €	Credit €
SPLOCI – income tax expense	82,450	
Income tax expense account		82,450

To recognise the tax expense in the SPLOCI.

	Debit €	Credit €
Tax liability account	91,500	
Bank account		91,500

To recognise the payment of the tax liability for the reporting date, 31 December 2019.

TAX LIABILITY ACCOUNT

Date	Account Name	€	Date	Account Name	€
31/12/2019	Balance c/d	82,450	31/12/2019	Tax expense	82,450
30/9/2020	Bank	91,500	01/01/2020	Balance b/d	82,450
			30/09/2020	Balance c/d	9,050
		91,500			91,500
01/10/2020	Balance b/d	9,050			

The balance on the tax liability account represents an under-provision in relation to the charge for the reporting period ended 31 December 2019. The tax charge for the reporting period ended 31 December 2020 will be increased by the under-provision for 2019.

Question 25.1

	€
Cost of machinery	250,000
Trade discount (1.5%)	(3,750)
Net cost	246,250

	Debit €	Credit €
Machinery – cost account	246,250	
Other payables account		246,250

To record the equipment at initial recognition.

	€
Net cost of machinery	246,250
Early settlement discount (2%)	(4,925)
Net cost	241,325

	Debit €	Credit €
Other payables account	246,250	
Discounts received account		4,925
Bank account		241,325

To record the payment and the discount received for equipment.

Question 25.2

(a)

	€
Cost as at 1 April 2018	25,000
Depreciation charge year ended 30 June 2018 (€25,000 × 20% × 3/12)	(1,250)
Carrying amount as at 30 June 2018	23,750

(b)

	€
Carrying amount as at 30 June 2018	23,750
Depreciation charge year ended 30 June 2019 (€23,750 × 20%)	(4,750)
Carrying amount as at 30 June 2019	19,000

Question 25.3

(a)

	€
Cost as at 1 July 2018	200,000
Depreciation charge year ended 31 December 2018 (€200,000 × 20% × 6 ÷ 12)	(20,000)
Carrying amount as at 31 December 2018	180,000

(b)

Carrying amount as at 31 December 2018	€180,000
Remaining useful life	9 years
Depreciation charge year ended 31 December 2019 (€180,000 ÷ 9 years)	€20,000

Question 25.4

(a)

	€
Cost as at 1 October 2017	80,000
Depreciation charge year ended 31 December 2017 (Note 1)	(1,875)
Carrying amount as at 31 December 2017	78,125

Note 1 DEPRECIATION CHARGE

	€
Cost of asset	80,000
Residual value	(5,000)
Depreciable amount	75,000

Depreciation charge p.a. = €7,500 [€75,000 ÷ 10 years]
Depreciation charge for year ended 31 December 2017 = €1,875 [€7,500 × 3 ÷ 12]

(b)

	€
Carrying amount as at 1 January 2018	78,125
Depreciation charge year ended 31 December 2018	(7,500)
Carrying amount as at 31 December 2018	70,625

(c)

	€
Carrying amount as at 1 January 2019	70,625
Depreciation charge year ended 31 December 2019 (Note 1A)	(7,900)
Carrying amount as at 31 December 2019	62,725

Note 1A DEPRECIATION CHARGE

	€
Carrying amount of asset	70,625
Revised residual value	(1,500)
Depreciable amount	69,125

Depreciation charge p.a. = €7,900 [€69,125 ÷ 8.75 years]

Question 25.5

(a)

	€
Cost as at 1 January 2018	1,500,000
Depreciation charge year ended 31 December 2018 (€1,500,000 ÷ 40 years)	(37,500)
Carrying amount as at 31 December 2018	1,462,500
Depreciation charge year ended 31 December 2019 (€1,500,000 ÷ 40 years)	(37,500)
Carrying amount as at 31 December 2019	1,425,000

(b)

	€
Fair Value as at 31 December 2019	1,650,000
Carrying amount as at 31 December 2019	(1,425,000)
Increase	225,000

Journal entries to record the fair value adjustment:

	Debit €	Credit €
Accumulated depreciation account	75,000	
Property – cost account		75,000
To eliminate the accumulated depreciation against the gross carrying amount.		
Property – cost account	225,000	
Revaluation surplus account		225,000
To recognise the fair value adjustment.		

Note: the revaluation in this case is presented in the SPLOCI under 'other comprehensive income'.

(c)

Revalued amount	€1,650,000
Remaining useful life	40 years
Depreciation (1,650,000/40 years)	€41,250

Question 25.6

(a)

	€
Cost as at 1 January 2018	1,200,000
Depreciation charge year ended 31 December 2018 (€1,200,000 ÷ 50 years)	(24,000)
Carrying amount as at 31 December 2018	1,176,000

(b)

	€
Fair value as at 31 December 2018	1,020,000
Carrying amount as at 31 December 2018	(1,176,000)
Decrease	(156,000)

Journal entries to record the fair value adjustment:

	Debit €	Credit €
Accumulated depreciation account	24,000	
Property – cost account		24,000
To eliminate the accumulated depreciation against the gross carrying amount.		

SPLOCI – loss on revaluation	156,000
Property – cost account		156,000

To recognise the fair value adjustment.

Note: the revaluation in this case is presented in the SPLOCI in the profit and loss section rather than 'other comprehensive income'. There are two situations in which revaluation loss is taken to profit and loss section of the SPLOCI:

- When the asset is revalued for the first time and the fair value is less than the carrying amount, or
- When the asset is revalued downwards and the amount in the revaluation surplus in relation to that specific asset is less than the decrease in value of the asset.

(c)

Revalued amount	€1,020,000
Remaining useful life	40 years
Depreciation (1,020,000/40 years)	€25,500

Question 25.7

(a)

	€
Cost 1 January 2016	260,000
Depreciation year ended 31 December 2016	(26,000)
Depreciation year ended 31 December 2017	(26,000)
Depreciation year ended 31 December 2018	(26,000)
Depreciation year ended 31 December 2019	(26,000)
Carrying amount as at 31 December 2019	156,000
Proceeds	180,000
Profit on disposal	24,000

(b)

MACHINE – COST ACCOUNT

Date	Account Name	€	Date	Account Name	€
01/01/2019	Balance b/d	260,000	31/12/2019	Disposal	260,000

ACCUMULATED DEPRECIATION ACCOUNT – MACHINE

Date	Account Name	€	Date	Account Name	€
31/12/2016	Balance c/d	26,000	31/12/2016	Depreciation	26,000
31/12/2017	Balance c/d	52,000	01/01/2017	Balance b/d	26,000
			31/12/2017	Depreciation	26,000
		52,000			52,000
31/12/2018	Balance c/d	78,000	01/01/2018	Balance b/d	52,000
			31/12/2018	Depreciation	26,000
		78,000			78,000
31/12/2019	Disposal Account	104,000	01/01/2019	Balance b/d	78,000
			31/12/2019	Depreciation	26,000
		104,000			104,000

DEPRECIATION ACCOUNT

Date	Account Name	€	Date	Account Name	€
31/12/2016	Accumulated depreciation	26,000	31/12/2016	SPLOCI – depreciation expense	26,000
31/12/2017	Accumulated depreciation	26,000	31/12/2017	SPLOCI – depreciation expense	26,000
31/12/2018	Accumulated depreciation	26,000	31/12/2018	SPLOCI – depreciation expense	26,000
31/12/2019	Accumulated depreciation	26,000	31/12/2019	SPLOCI – depreciation expense	26,000

DISPOSAL ACCOUNT

Date	Account Name	€	Date	Account Name	€
31/12/2019	Machinery – cost	260,000	31/12/2019	Accumulated depreciation	104,000
31/12/2019	SPLOCI – profit on disposal	24,000	31/12/2019	Bank	180,000
		284,000			284,000

(c)

	Debit €	Credit €
Disposal account	260,000	
Machine – cost account		260,000
To derecognise the machine.		
Accumulated depreciation account	104,000	
Disposal account		104,000
To remove accumulated depreciation on asset sold.		
Bank account	180,000	
Disposal account		180,000
To recognise proceeds from sale of machine.		
Disposal account	24,000	
SPLOCI – profit on disposal		24,000
To recognise the profit on disposal of machine.		

Note: if the profit/loss on disposal is material, it can be presented as a separate line item in the SPLOCI. If the profit/loss on disposal is not material, then include the profit/loss in the same line item as depreciation for that specific class of property, plant and equipment. If depreciation is included in cost of sales, then the profit/loss is also included in cost of sales.

Question 25.8

(a)

	€
Cost 1 May 2017	300,000
Depreciation year ended 31 December 2017 (€300,000 ÷ 5 years × 8/12)	(40,000)
Depreciation year ended 31 December 2018 (€300,000 ÷ 5 years)	(60,000)
Depreciation year ended 31 December 2019 (€300,000 ÷ 5 years × 9/12)	(45,000)
Carrying amount as at 30 September 2019	155,000
Proceeds	100,000
Loss on disposal	55,000

(b)

MACHINE – COST ACCOUNT

Date	Account Name	€	Date	Account Name	€
01/01/2019	Balance b/d	300,000	30/09/2019	Disposal	300,000

ACCUMULATED DEPRECIATION ACCOUNT – MACHINE

Date	Account Name	€	Date	Account Name	€
31/12/2017	Balance c/d	40,000	31/12/2017	Depreciation	40,000
31/12/2018	Balance c/d	100,000	01/01/2018	Balance b/d	40,000
			31/12/2018	Depreciation	60,000
		100,000			100,000
31/12/2019	Disposal	145,000	01/01/2019	Balance b/d	100,000
			30/09/2019	Depreciation	45,000
		145,000			145,000

DEPRECIATION ACCOUNT

Date	Account Name	€	Date	Account Name	€
31/12/2017	Accumulated depreciation	40,000	31/12/2017	SPLOCI – depreciation expense	40,000
31/12/2018	Accumulated depreciation	60,000	31/12/2018	SPLOCI – depreciation expense	60,000
31/12/2019	Accumulated depreciation	45,000	31/12/2019	SPLOCI – depreciation expense	45,000

DISPOSAL ACCOUNT

Date	Account	€	Date	Account	€
30/09/2019	Cost	300,000	30/09/2019	Accumulated depreciation	145,000
				Bank	100,000
			30/09/2019	Loss on disposal	55,000
		300,000			300,000

(c)

	Debit €	Credit €
Disposal account	300,000	
Machine – cost account		300,000
To derecognise the machine.		
Accumulated depreciation account	145,000	
Disposal account		145,000
To remove accumulated depreciation on asset sold.		
Bank account	100,000	
Disposal account		100,000
To recognise proceeds from sale of machine.		

	Debit €	Credit €
SPLOCI – loss on disposal	55,000	
Disposal account		55,000
To recognise the loss on disposal of machine.		

Question 25.9

	€
Cost	
As at 1 January 2019	800,000
Additions	130,000
Disposals	(75,000)
As at 31 December 2019	855,000
Accumulated depreciation	
As at 1 January 2019	120,000
Charge for year	95,000
Disposal	(35,000)
As at 31 December 2019	180,000
Carrying amount as at 31 December 2018	680,000
Carrying amount as at 31 December 2019	675,000

Question 25.10

	€
Cost	
As at 1 January 2019	3,900,000
Revaluation	180,000
As at 31 December 2019	4,080,000
Accumulated Depreciation	
As at 1 January 2019	780,000
Charge for year	78,000
Revaluation	(110,000)
As at 31 December 2019	748,000
Carrying amount as at 31 December 2018	3,120,000
Carrying amount as at 31 December 2019	3,332,000
Cost	1,100,000
Accumulated depreciation	(110,000)
Carrying amount as at 31 December 2019	990,000
Revalued to	1,280,000
Increase in value	290,000

	Debit €	Credit €
Accumulated depreciation account	110,000	
Property – cost account		110,000
To eliminate the accumulated depreciation on a revalued asset.		
Property – cost account	290,000	
Revaluation surplus account		290,000
To record revaluation increase.		

Question 26.1

Lease payments were made as follows:

1 May 2019 – relates to period 1 May 2019 to 31 July 2019.
1 August 2019 – relates to period 1 August 2019 to 31 October 2019.
1 November 2019 – relates to period 1 November 2019 to 31 January 2020.

The journal entries to record the payments are:

	Debit €	Credit €
Lease expense	600	
Bank		600
To recognise the lease expense paid 1 May 2019.		
Lease expense	600	
Bank		600
To recognise the lease expense paid 1 August 2019.		
Lease expense	600	
Bank		600
To recognise the lease expense paid 1 November 2019.		

SOPL – P/L – lease expense	1,600	
Prepayment	200	
Lease expense		1,800

To recognise the lease expense paid to year ended 31 December 2019.

Question 26.2

Lease payments were made as follows:

31 May 2019 – relates to period 1 March 2019 to 31 May 2019.
31 August 2019 – relates to period 1 June 2019 to 31 August 2019.
30 November 2019 – relates to period 1 September 2019 to 30 November 2019.

The journal entries to record the payments are:

	Debit €	Credit €
Lease expense	1,000	
Bank		1,000

To recognise the lease expense paid 31 May 2019.

Lease expense	1,000	
Bank		1,000

To recognise the lease expense paid 31 August 2019.

Lease expense	1,000	
Bank		1,000

To recognise the lease expense paid 30 November 2019.

Lease expense	333	
Accrual		333

To recognise the accrual lease expense.

SOPL – lease expense	3,333	
Lease expense		3,333

To recognise the lease expense paid to year ended 31 December 2019.

Question 26.3

(a)

Asset cost ÷ lease payments = €120,000 ÷ €30,000 = 4.00

Looking at the annuity table row 5:

$\quad$ 7% = 4.100

$\quad$ 8% = 3.993

Step 1– calculate the difference between the annuity factors

$\quad$ 4.100 – 3.993 = 0.107

Step 2 – calculate the difference between the figure calculated in Step 1 and the annuity factor at the lower of the two rates

$\quad$ 4.100 – 4.000 = 0.100

Step 3 – calculate the interest rate

$\quad$ 7% + 0.100 / 0.107 = 7% + 0.934579% = 7.93%

(b)

Year end	Opening balance €	Finance cost @ 7.93% €	Paid €	Capital repaid €	Closing balance €
31/12/2019	120,000	9,516	(30,000)	20,484	99,516
31/12/2020	99,516	7,892	(30,000)	22,108	77,418
31/12/2021	77,418	6,138	(30,000)	23,861	53,557
31/12/2022	53,557	4,247	(30,000)	25,753	27,804
31/12/2023	27,804	2,205	(30,000)	27,795	9

STATEMENT OF PROFIT OR LOSS AND OTHER COMPREHENSIVE INCOME (EXTRACT)
for the year ended 31 December 2019

	€
Depreciation expense (€120,000 / 5 years)	24,000
Finance cost	9,516

STATEMENT OF FINANCIAL POSITION (EXTRACT)
as at 31 December 2019

	€
Non-current Assets	
Machinery	96,000
Non-current Liability	
Lease obligation	77,418
Current Liability	
Lease obligation	22,108

Question 26.4

Step 1 Calculate the present value of the minimum lease payments.

Payment Date	€	Discount Factor	Present Value €
1 January 2019	25,370	1.000	25,370
1 January 2020	25,370	0.909	23,061
1 January 2021	25,370	0.826	20,955
			69,386

The journal entry at date the lease is taken out:

	Debit €	Credit €
Property, plant and equipment – cost account	69,386	
Lease liability account		69,386

To recognise the machine and related lease liability.

Reporting Date	Opening Balance €	Payment €	Adjusted Balance €	Finance Cost € (@ 10%)	Closing Balance €
31 December 2019	69,386	25,370	44,016	4,401	48,417
31 December 2020	48,417	25,370	23,047		

STATEMENT OF PROFIT OR LOSS AND OTHER COMPREHENSIVE INCOME (EXTRACT)
for the year ended 31 December 2019

	€
Depreciation (€69,386/3 years)	23,128
Finance cost	4,401

STATEMENT OF FINANCIAL POSITION (EXTRACT)
as at 31 December 2019

	€
Non-current Asset	
Machinery (€69,386 – €23,128)	46,258
Non-current Liabilities	
Lease liability	23,047
Current Liability	
Lease liability (€25,370 – €4,401)	20,969
Finance accrual	4,401

Journal entries:

	Debit €	Credit €
Lease account	25,370	
Bank account		25,370
To recognise the lease payment made during the reporting period.		
Finance cost account	4,401	
Lease account		4,401
To recognise the finance cost for 2019.		
Depreciation expense account	23,128	
Accumulated depreciation account		23,128
To recognise the depreciation expense for 2019.		
SPLOCI – depreciation expense	23,128	
Depreciation expense account		23,128
To recognise the depreciation expense in profit or loss.		
SPLOCI – finance cost	4,401	
Finance cost account		4,401
To recognise the finance cost in profit or loss.		

Question 27.1

The total interest cost on the loan for the period that funds were borrowed (1 February 2018 to 31 August 2019, 19 months) is €332,500 [€3,500,000 × 6% × 19 ÷ 12].

Borrowing costs can be capitalised from 1 April 2018 to 30 June 2019, the period in which expenditure is being incurred, borrowing costs are being incurred and work is being undertaken in relation to the preparation of the asset for use.

	€
Capitalise €3.5m × 6% × 15 ÷ 12	262,500
Capitalised during the reporting period ended 31 December 2018 (9 months)	157,500
Capitalised during the reporting period ended 31 December 2019 (6 months)	105,000
Expensed to SPLOCI	70,000
Expensed during the reporting period ended 31 December 2018 (2 months)	35,000
Expensed during the reporting period ended 31 December 2019 (2 months)	35,000

	Debit €	Credit €
Property – cost account	157,500	
SPLOCI – finance costs	35,000	
Bank account		192,500
To account for borrowing costs during reporting period ended 31 December 2018.		

Property – cost account	105,000	
SPLOCI – finance costs	35,000	
Bank account		140,000

To account for borrowing costs during reporting period ended 31 December 2019.

Question 27.2

The total interest cost on the loan for the period that funds were borrowed (1 January 2018 to 31 December 2019, 24 months) is €504,000 [€4,200,000 × 6% × 24 ÷ 12].

Borrowing costs can be capitalised from 1 April 2018 to 31 August 2018, and 1 October 2018 to 31 October 2019 (18 months in total), the period in which expenditure is being incurred, borrowing costs are being incurred and work is being undertaken in relation to the preparation of the asset for use.

	€
Capitalise €4.2m × 6% × 18/12	378,000
Capitalised during the reporting period ended 31 December 2018 (8 months)	168,000
Capitalised during the reporting period ended 31 December 2019 (10 months)	210,000
Expensed to SPLOCI	126,000
Expensed during the reporting period ended 31 December 2018 (4 months)	84,000
Expensed during the reporting period ended 31 December 2019 (2 months)	42,000

	Debit €	Credit €
Property – cost account	168,000	
SPLOCI – finance costs	84,000	
Bank account		252,000

To account for borrowing costs during reporting period ended 31 December 2018.

	Debit €	Credit €
Property – cost account	210,000	
SPLOCI – finance costs	42,000	
Bank account		252,000

To account for borrowing costs during reporting period ended 31 December 2019.

Question 27.3

Loan Amount	% of Total Borrowings	Interest Rate on loan	Weighting
€4,000,000	50	6.0%	3.000%
€2,800,000	35	4.5%	1.575%
€1,200,000	15	7.0%	1.050%
€8,000,000			5.625%

Question 28.1

	Debit €	Credit €
Machine – cost account	280,000	
Bank account		280,000

To recognise the machine purchased.

Bank account	30,000	
Deferred income account – grant		30,000

To recognise the grant received.

Summary journal entry:

	Debit €	Credit €
SPLOCI – depreciation	40,000	
Accumulated depreciation account		40,000

To recognise the depreciation charge in the SPLOCI.

The depreciation charge is calculated as follows:

	€
Cost of the asset	280,000
Less: residual value	(40,000)
Depreciable amount	240,000
Useful life	6 years
Depreciation charge per annum	40,000

In some exams you are required to net off journal entries rather than showing both the debit and credit figures. The depreciation journal entry is the netted-off version of the following two journal entries:

	Debit €	Credit €
Depreciation expense account	40,000	
Accumulated depreciation account		40,000

To recognise the depreciation charge.

SPLOCI – cost of sales	40,000	
Depreciation expense account		40,000

To recognise the depreciation charge in the SPLOCI.

In the two journal entries above there is a debit and a credit amount posted to the depreciation expense account. In the summary journal entry above the depreciation expense account is not shown as the debit and credit amounts cancel each other out.

The amortisation of the grant:

Summary journal entry:

	Debit €	Credit €
Deferred income account (€30,000 ÷ 6 years)	5,000	
SPLOCI – amortisation		5,000

To recognise the amortisation of the grant in the SPLOCI.

Alternatively, the journal entries in relation to the grant can be presented as follows:

	Debit €	Credit €
Deferred income account	5,000	
Amortisation account		5,000

To recognise the amortisation of the grant.

Amortisation account	5,000	
SPLOCI – amortisation		5,000

To recognise the amortisation of the grant in the SPLOCI.

STATEMENT OF FINANCIAL POSITION (EXTRACT)
as at 31 December 2019

	€
Non-current Assets	
Machinery (€280,000 – €40,000)	240,000
Non-current Liabilities	
Deferred income	20,000
Current Liabilities	
Deferred income	5,000

STATEMENT OF PROFIT OR LOSS AND OTHER COMPREHENSIVE INCOME (EXTRACT)
for the year ended 31 December 2019

	€
Gross profit	X
Amortisation	5,000
Depreciation	(40,000)

Question 28.2

Depreciation charge based on cost net of grant (€360,000 – €60,000) ÷ 6 years	€50,000
Depreciation charge based on original cost of asset (€360,000 ÷ 6 years)	€60,000

The asset has been depreciated for three years, 2017 to 2019.

	If grant had not been received €	Net of grant received €
Cost	360,000	300,000
Accumulated depreciation		
60,000 × 3 years	(180,000)	
50,000 × 3 years		(150,000)
Carrying amount	180,000	150,000

The full amount of the grant has to be repaid. The payment is not made until 2020, so the liability is recognised in 2019.

	Debit €	Credit €
Property, plant and equipment – cost account	60,000	
SPLOCI – grant repayment	30,000	
Accumulated depreciation account		30,000
Grant payable account		60,000
To recognise the grant repayment.		

Question 28.3

A current grant may be presented as "other income" or it may be netted off against the related cost.

Grant presented as "other income"

STATEMENT OF PROFIT OR LOSS AND OTHER COMPREHENSIVE INCOME (EXTRACT)
for the year ended 31 December 2019

	€
Gross profit	X
Other income (40 staff × €5,000)	200,000
Wages cost	(4,256,000)

Grant presented as reduction in the wages cost

STATEMENT OF PROFIT OR LOSS AND OTHER COMPREHENSIVE INCOME (EXTRACT)
for the year ended 31 December 2019

	€
Gross profit	X
Wages cost (€4,256,000 – €200,000)	(4,056,000)

Question 29.1
(b)

Question 29.2

(b)

Question 29.3
The difference between debt and equity is the existence of a contractual obligation between the issuer and the holder. In this case the holder of the preference shares is not entitled to:

- a dividend each year, or
- repayment of the investment.

This means that there is no contractual obligation so the preference shares are classified as equity. The preference shares will be presented in the SOFP under the equity and reserves section and any dividend will be presented in the SOCIE.

Question 29.4
The difference between debt and equity is the existence of a contractual obligation between the issuer and the holder. In this case the holder of the preference shares is not entitled to:

- a dividend each year, or
- repayment of the investment.

There is a contractual obligation to pay a dividend so the preference shares are classified as debt. The preference shares will be presented in the SOFP as a liability and any dividend will be included in finance cost in the SPLOCI.

Question 29.5

	Debit €	Credit €
SPLOCI – loss on financial asset	14,000	
Financial asset at FVTPL account		14,000

To recognise the decrease in fair value of financial asset held at FVTPL.

Question 29.6

	Debit €	Credit €
Bank account	485,000	
Loan liability account		485,000

To recognise the loan liability, net of issue costs of €15,000.

The journal entry to recognise the finance cost is:

	Debit €	Credit €
SPLOCI – finance cost (€485,000 × 6.73% = €32,640)	32,640	
Loan liability account		32,640

To charge finance cost to SPLOCI based on the effective interest rate, 31 December 2019.

When the interest charge is paid, it is based on the nominal value of the loan and the interest rate attaching to the loan:

	Debit €	Credit €
Loan liability account €500,000 × 6% = €30,000	30,000	
Bank account		30,000

To recognise the payment of the interest charge at end of the year, 31 December 2019.

At the end of the reporting period the balance on the loan is €487,640:

Reporting Date	Opening Balance €	SPLOCI – Finance Cost (@ 6.73%) €	Interest Paid €	Closing Balance €
31 December 2019	485,000	32,640	(30,000)	487,640

Question 30.1

In order to raise a provision IAS 37 *Provisions, Contingent Liabilities and Contingent Assets* requires that all of the following conditions are met:
- there must be an obligating event;
- there will probably be an outflow of economic benefit; and
- a reliable estimate can be made.

Obligating event – the obligating event is the sale of goods by Warrington during the reporting period. The customer who has issued legal proceedings is claiming that the goods sold were faulty and caused damage to their machinery.

Probable outflow – the likelihood that Warrington will lose the case is estimated at 70%, therefore to settle the case Warrington will probably have to pay damages.

Reliable estimate – based on past cases, legal opinion is that the amount that will have to be paid in damages would be €310,000.

Conclusion

A provision should be raised in relation to the legal case for the amount of €310,000, the provision will be presented in the SOFP in non-current liabilities as the case is not due before the courts until 2021, which is more than 12 months after the reporting date.

	Debit €	Credit €
SPLOCI – provision	310,000	
Non-current liabilities – provision account		310,000
To recognise the provision.		

Question 30.2

In order to raise a provision IAS 37 *Provisions, Contingent Liabilities and Contingent Assets* requires that all of the following conditions are met:
- There must be an obligating event;
- There will probably be an outflow of economic benefit; and
- A reliable estimate can be made.

Obligating Event – the obligating event is the accident that occurred on the Mayfair restaurant premises in December 2013. The customer sustained an injury and has issued legal proceedings.

Probable Outflow – the likelihood that Mayfair will lose the case is low, therefore there will not be a probable outflow of economic benefit.

Reliable Estimate – based on past cases, legal opinion is that the amount that will have to be paid in damages would be €40,000.

Conclusion

A provision will not be raised in relation to the legal case as all of the conditions have not been met.

Question 30.3

Winston is suing its supplier, Wigan Ltd, in relation to the supply of faulty goods. If Winston wins its case, the likely damages that it will receive are estimated at €150,000 [€110,000 + €40,000]. The legal action is treated as a contingent asset under IAS 37 *Provisions, Contingent Liabilities and Contingent Assets.*

A contingent asset is not recognised in the financial statements until it is virtually certain. Based on the information provided in the question, this level of certainty has not been reached so no accounting entry is made in relation to the legal case, but a disclosure note is required. The disclosure note will provide the following information:
- A brief description of the nature of the contingent asset, and
- An estimate of the financial effect.

Question 30.4

The cost of the lease from 1 July 2018 to 1 November 2018 is expensed as normal because the property is being used by the business.

From 1 November the property is vacant and does not provide any benefit to the business, the lease contract is referred to as an onerous contract. An onerous contract under IAS 37 *Provisions, Contingent Liabilities and Contingent Assets* is one in which the cost associated with the contract exceeds the benefits derived from the contract. The costs associated with an onerous contract are recognised immediately. In this situation the lease costs from 1 November 2018 to the termination of the lease agreement on 31 March 2020 are treated as costs under an onerous contract. The journal entry to recognise the onerous contract in the reporting period ended 30 June 2019 is:

	Debit €	Credit €
SPLOCI – onerous contract	13,600	
Onerous contract account		13,600

To recognise the onerous contract (17 payments × €800 = €13,600).

As lease payments are made under the lease contract the following accounting journal entry is posted to the financial statements:

	Debit €	Credit €
Onerous contract account	6,400	
Bank account		6,400

To recognise the onerous contract.

At the reporting date, 30 June 2019, the balance on the onerous contract will be €7,200.

Question 31.1

The cost of the investment property is €2,1450,000, which is made up as follows:

	€
Purchase price	2,000,000
Legal costs associated with purchase of property	20,000
Property taxes	25,000
Start-up costs (€120,000 – €20,000)	100,000
	2,145,000

The purchase price, legal costs and property taxes are all allowed to be included in the cost of the investment property.

The start-up costs are only allowed to be included in the cost of the investment property to the extent that they were necessary to bring the property to a condition necessary to enable it to operate in the manner intended. The operating losses prior to the planned level of occupancy being achieved are not allowed to be included in the cost of the investment property per IAS 40 *Investment Property*.

Question 31.2

Parts of the property can be sublet so the leased part can be classified as an investment property. The section used by Smithy is dealt with under IAS 16 *Property, Plant and Equipment*.

Question 31.3

	Debit €	Credit €
Investment property account	1,500,000	
Bank account		1,500,000

To recognise the investment property.

	Debit €	Credit €
Depreciation expense account	50,000	
Accumulated depreciation account		50,000

To recognise the depreciation expense.

	Debit €	Credit €
SPLOCI – depreciation expense	50,000	
Depreciation expense account		50,000

To recognise the depreciation expense in the SPLOCI.

Question 31.4

(a)

	Debit €	Credit €
Investment property account	100,000	
SPLOCI – fair value increase		100,000

To recognise the change in fair value.

MORTAR LTD
STATEMENT OF FINANCIAL POSITION (EXTRACT)
as at 31 December 2018

Non-current Assets

Investment property	€2,100,000

(b)

	Debit €	Credit €
SPLOCI – fair value decrease	180,000	
Investment property account		180,000

To recognise the change in fair value.

MORTAR LTD
STATEMENT OF FINANCIAL POSITION
as at 31 December 2019

Non-current Assets

Investment property	€1,920,000

Question 31.5

	€
Carrying amount of the asset (€3,000,000 − €640,000)	2,360,000
Proceeds	2,175,000
Loss on disposal	185,000

	Debit €	Credit €
Bank account	2,175,000	
Accumulated depreciation account	640,000	
SPLOCI – loss on disposal	185,000	
Investment property account		3,000,000

To recognise the disposal of the investment property.

Question 31.6

	€
Carrying amount of the asset	2,320,000
Proceeds	2,260,000
Loss on disposal	60,000

	Debit €	Credit €
Bank account	2,260,000	
SPLOCI – loss on disposal	60,000	
Investment property account		2,320,000

To recognise the disposal of the investment property.

Question 32.1

Year-end	31 December 2013	31 December 2012
Gross margin	43.83%	43.48%
	€3,660,000 ÷ €8,350,000	€3,470,000 ÷ €7,980,000
Net margin	20.36%	20.14%
	€1,700,000* ÷ €8,350,000	€1,607,000** ÷ €7,980,000

*€1,700,000 = €1,655,000 + €45,000
**€1,607,000 = €1,582,000 + €35,000

Question 32.2

Acid test – (current assets – inventory): current liabilities
(400 – 150): 365 = 0.68 : 1.00 Answer (a)

	€000
Inventory	150
Trade receivables	125
Prepayments	50
Cash at bank	75
	400
Trade payables	175
Accruals	85
Provisions for liabilities and charges	105
	365

Question 32.3

Taz Ltd has the following net current Assets at 31 December:

STATEMENT OF FINANCIAL POSITION (EXTRACTS)

	31 December 2012 €	31 December 2013 €
Current assets		
Investment in 30-day Government bonds	18,000	0
Inventory	65,000	58,000
Receivables	1,500	1,300
Bank	9,800	10,600
Cash	1,000	1,000
Current liabilities		
Trade payables	59,000	60,600
Bank overdraft	500	0

Requirement:
(a) Calculate the current ratio for Taz Ltd at 31 December 2012 and 31 December 2013.

2013: €95,300 : €59,500 = 1.6 : 1.0.

2012: €70,900 : €60,600 = 1.17 : 1.0.

(b)

	2013 €	2012 €
Investment	18,000	
Bank	9,800	10,600
Cash	1,000	1,000
Overdraft	(500)	
	28,300	11,600

Answer = €16,700 [€28,300 − €1,600].

Question 32.4

€125,000/€2,100,000 × 365 = 21.72 days = 22 days Answer (c).

Question 32.5

Answer (c) 240,000/1,000,000 = 24%.

Question 32.6

73 days calculated as
Closing inventory ÷ Cost of sales × 365 [€17,950 ÷ €89,600 × 365]
€16,150 + €91,400 − €17,950 = €89,600.

Question 32.7

(d)

Glossary of Terms and Definitions

Accounting Cycle The series of steps involved in recording a transaction from undertaking the transaction to its impact on the financial statements. It involves the preparation of a journal entry, the posting of the journal entry to the respective ledger accounts, the preparation of the trial balance and then, finally, the preparation of financial statements (including the SOPL/SPLOCI and the SOFP).

Accounting Estimate In the preparation of financial statements, a number of accounting estimates are used where information is not known with certainty. Accounting estimates are prepared on the basis of past experience and knowledge of the business. Accounting estimates are reviewed annually and when changes are required to estimates they are applied prospectively, that is in the period that the change in accounting estimate occurs and in future reporting periods.

Accounting Policy An accounting policy is defined in IAS 8, paragraph 5, as "specific principles, bases, conventions, rules and practices applied by an entity in preparing and presenting financial statements."

Accrual Basis The application of the accrual basis of accounting means that expenses incurred and income earned by the entity are presented in the SOPL/SPLOCI.

Adjusting Event A transaction or event that occurs between the reporting date and the date the financial statements are authorised for issue. It provides evidence of a situation that existed at the reporting date and an adjustment is made to the financial statements to reflect such a transaction/event.

Asset A resource from which the entity expects to generate future economic benefit.

Bad Debts Expense The write off of an amount due from a customer because the entity has reason to believe, or has specific information, that the customer will not be able to pay the amount on their account.

Bad Debts Recovered Occurs when a customer, whose balance on their account was written off at an earlier date, makes a payment in relation to the amount due.

Books of Prime Entry Books of prime entry are used to record similar types of transactions, e.g. sales, purchases, sales returns, and purchases returns. The entries in the books of prime entry are totalled periodically and posted to the ledger accounts.

Borrowing Costs Interest and other costs incurred by an entity in connection with the borrowing of funds. Examples include:
- interest on bank overdrafts and other short-term and long-term borrowings;
- amortisation of discounts on issues of borrowings and premiums on redemptions of borrowings;
- finance charges in respect of finance leases; and
- exchange differences arising from foreign currency borrowings when they cause adjustments to interest costs.

Business Entity Concept For accounting purposes, a business is separate and distinct from its owners.

Capital Represents the owner's(s') residual interest in the assets of an entity after deducting all the entity's liabilities – it is the net investment contributed by the owner(s) of the business; it is also referred to as 'equity'.

Carriage Inwards The transportation cost associated with the purchase of goods for resale; it is included in the cost of sales figure in the SOPL/SPLOCI.

Carriage Outwards The cost associated with the delivery of goods to customers and is included in the SOPL/SPLOCI after the determination of gross profit.

Carrying Amount The balance on the asset cost account less the balance on the accumulated depreciation account.

Cash and Cash Equivalents This term relates to cash, bank and some investments; the investments must be subject to insignificant risk, and must be short-term in nature, i.e. maturity within three months of the investment date.

Closing Inventory The value of goods on hand at the reporting date.

Comparability When financial information is comparable it allows users to compare information from one period to the next. In order to be comparable it must be consistently prepared and presented.

Contingent Asset A contingent asset is defined in IAS 37, paragraph 20, as "a possible asset that arises from past events and whose existence will only be confirmed by the occurrence or non-occurrence of one or more uncertain future events not wholly within the control of the entity."

Contingent Liability A contingent liability is: a possible liability that will arise from past events by the occurrence or not of future events, or a present obligation with only a possible outflow of economic benefit, or a present obligation that cannot be reliably measured.

Control Accounts When a business's volume of transactions has grown to a point where it is not practicable to process each transaction individually, control accounts will be used to provide the information required for the preparation and presentation of financial information in the financial statements. The most common control accounts are the trade receivables control account and the trade payables control account. These control accounts do not contain information about individual customers or suppliers.

Conversion Costs Costs incurred in the conversion of raw materials into finished goods. These costs include prime costs (direct material expenses, direct labour expenses and direct expenses) and production overheads.

Cost Model An accounting policy choice under IAS 16 *Property, Plant and Equipment*. Under the cost model, the asset is depreciated each year and recognised in the statement of financial position at its historical cost net of accumulated depreciation and any accumulated impairment loss. See also **revaluation model**.

Cost of Sales The total of all the costs incurred in relation to the purchase and manufacture of goods for sale in a reporting period. At its most basic it includes the value of inventory on hand at the start of the reporting period plus purchase cost of goods less closing value of inventory on hand at the reporting date. Depending on the type of business, additional costs are included in this calculation, e.g. in a manufacturing entity production costs would be included.

Credit Note A credit note is issued by the seller of goods when the amount for which a customer has been invoiced needs to be reduced, e.g. because the goods have been returned by the customer.

Depreciable Amount An asset's depreciable amount is its cost reduced by its residual value.

Depreciation A measure of the use of an asset and a charge is made to the SOPL/SPLOCI in each reporting period over the asset's useful life.

Derecognition The removal of an asset or liability from the SOFP.

Discount Allowed A reduction in the amount owed by the customer to the entity. It is an expense to the entity. It most commonly arises when a customer avails of an early settlement discount offered by the entity.

Discount Received A reduction in the amount to be paid by the entity to a supplier. It is income to the entity. It most commonly arises when an entity avails of an early settlement discount offered by its supplier.

Dividend A distribution to the owners of a company's share capital that is made at the company's discretion. Dividends are recognised in the financial records of the company when the obligation to pay the shareholders is created. The obligation is created when the dividend is approved by the shareholders at the annual general meeting.

Double-entry Bookkeeping The term used to describe the recording of financial transactions. The basic idea behind double-entry bookkeeping is that there are two sides to each transaction: one (or more) account(s) are debited and one (or more) account(s) are credited.

Drawings Withdrawals of cash or goods by the owner(s) of a business. Drawings are made in sole trader or partnership businesses.

Error of Commission This type of error occurs when a transaction is recorded in the wrong account but the correct type of account, e.g. an expense transaction recorded in the incorrect expense account.

Error of Omission This type of error occurs when a transaction is not recorded in the financial records of the entity at all.

Error of Original Entry This type of error occurs when the correct accounts are debited and credited but the amount at which the transaction is recorded is incorrect.

Error of Principle This type of error occurs when a transaction is recorded not only in the wrong account but also in the wrong type of account, e.g. an expense transaction recorded in an asset account.

Expenses Incurred Costs that relate to the current reporting period and include:
- costs of goods or services consumed during the reporting period for which an invoice has been received and the provider of the goods/services was paid in full during the reporting period;

- costs of goods or services consumed during the reporting period for which an invoice has been received but the supplier has not been paid by the reporting date;
- costs of goods or services consumed during the reporting period but for which an invoice has not been received from the supplier by the reporting date; and
- expenses paid in an earlier reporting period but incurred in the current period.

Faithful Representation For financial information to be a faithful representation of an entity's transactions and events it must be complete and free from bias.

Finance Lease A lease for substantially all of the useful life of an asset under which the risks and rewards of ownership are transferred to the lessee. The lessee is the entity making repayments under the lease contract.

Financial Instrument A transaction that gives rise to a financial asset in one entity and either a financial liability or equity in another.

Financial Transaction Any event that impacts the profitability and/or financial position of an entity.

Financing Activities (cash flows from) The cash inflows and outflows from financing activities are set out in the SOCF and include repayments of loans and issues of ordinary share capital.

General Ledger Also known as the nominal ledger, it contains the ledger accounts that form part of the double-entry bookkeeping system.

General Provision (for bad debts) A general provision for bad debts is raised by the management of an entity based on past experience. The general provision does not relate to any particular customers' balances.

Going Concern Financial statements are prepared on the basis that the entity will continue in existence for at least the next 12 months. (If the entity is expected to go into liquidation within 12 months of the reporting date, the going concern basis cannot be applied to the preparation and presentation of financial statements – the basis must instead reflect the fact that future cash flows will not be from the business operations but from the liquidation of the business.)

Gross Pay The salary of an employee before any deductions are made. Usual deductions are PAYE, PRSI/NIC and USC (USC applies to ROI only).

Historical Cost When historical cost is the measurement method used for determining the amount at which items are recognised in the financial statements, assets acquired are recorded in the financial statements at the amount paid for them or the fair value of the consideration given for them. Similarly, liabilities are recognised at the amount of the proceeds received in exchange for the obligation.

Income Earned The amount of income earned in the reporting period is presented in the SOPL/SPLOCI. It includes:

- amounts invoiced to customers for goods or services provided during the reporting period for which payment has been received in full from the customer;
- amounts invoiced to customers for goods or services provided during the reporting period for which payment has not been received from the customer by the reporting date;
- income earned during the reporting period for which an invoice has not been issued to the customer by the reporting date; and
- income received in an earlier reporting period but earned in the current period.

Inventory Also known as 'stock', includes raw materials for use in production, goods purchased for resale, and finished goods.

Investing Activities (cash flows from) The cash inflows and outflows from investing activities are set out in the SOCF and include amounts paid in relation to the purchase of items of property, plant and equipment and amounts received from the sale of items of property, plant and equipment.

Investment Property A property held for its ability to generate rental income and/or capital appreciation rather than for use within the business.

Invoice An invoice is issued to a customer when goods are sold or services provided. It provides such information as a description of the transaction, date, amount, and credit terms.

Journal Entry A journal entry is prepared to make a note of a transaction within the accounting system. When the information contained in the journal entry is input to the accounting system it is said to have been 'posted' to the relevant ledger accounts.

Ledger Accounts Ledger accounts are used to record similar transactions, e.g. a sales account would be set up in the accounting system to record the value of all sales transactions for a particular period of time, rather than an account being opened for each sales transaction.

Liabilities An amount owed by an entity – both the amount due and the timing of the required payment are known with certainty.

Limited Liability This normally applies to a company and means that the owners' (shareholders') liability is limited to the extent of any unpaid share capital on liquidation.

Material In relation to the term 'material', IAS 1, paragraph 7, states "omissions or misstatements of items are material if they could, individually or collectively, influence the economic decisions that users make on the basis of the financial statements. Materiality depends on the size and nature of the omission or misstatement judged in the surrounding circumstances. The size or nature of the item, or a combination of both, could be the determining factor." Materiality is not a specified amount but varies from entity to entity.

Net Pay An employee's net pay is their gross pay after deductions. Usual deductions are PAYE, PRSI/NIC and USC (USC applies to ROI only).

Net Realisable Value The net realisable value of an item is its selling price reduced by any costs necessarily incurred to achieve that selling price. These costs include selling and distribution costs, and costs to complete or repair the item.

Nominal Ledger See **General Ledger**.

Nominal Value (of a share) The nominal value of a share is its value as set out in the incorporation documents of the company.

Non-adjusting Event A transaction or event that occurs between the reporting date and the date the financial statements are authorised for issue. It does not provide evidence of a situation that existed at the reporting date and no adjustment is made to the financial statements to reflect such an event/transaction but, if it is material, details of the transaction must be disclosed in the notes to the financial statements.

Onerous Contract An onerous contract is one under which the costs associated with the contract exceed its benefits.

Opening Inventory The value of goods on hand at the end of the previous reporting period.

Operating Activities (cash flows from) The cash inflows and outflows from operating activities are set out in the SOCF and can be calculated using either the direct or indirect method. The indirect method is the one most commonly used in Ireland and starts with the figure for profit or loss before tax. Adjustments are made for non-cash items that were included in the determination of the profit or loss for the reporting period, and changes in working capital since the last reporting date. Net cash flows from operating activities is the net cash utilised for, and generated from, the day-to-day business operations.

Operating Lease An operating lease is one that does not meet the definition of a finance lease, in other words, the lease is not for significantly all of the useful life of the asset and the risks and rewards associated with ownership are not transferred to the lessee.

Other Payables These are amounts owed for goods and services other than goods purchased for resale, e.g. amount owed for electricity supplied.

Overcasting Overcasting occurs when a group of figures is totalled incorrectly and the incorrect total is greater than the correct total.

Partnership A business owned by a number of people and operated to generate a profit. Partners may or may not be involved in the day-to-day operations of the business.

Posted A journal entry is said to have been 'posted' when it has been reflected in the relevant ledger accounts.

Prepayment An asset of the entity that arises when a payment is made in relation to an expense that will only be incurred in the next reporting period.

Present Value The present value of a future sum of money is its current worth. Present value is the discounted value of a future amount.

Prime Cost The total of costs directly attributable to the production of a particular product, i.e. the cost of direct materials, direct labour, and direct expenses.

Profit-sharing Ratio Partners in an entity agree the basis under which profit and losses will be shared amongst themselves – this is known as the profit-sharing ratio.

Provision A liability of uncertain timing and amount. A provision is recognised in the financial statements when an obligating event has occurred the amount of which can be measured reliably and will probably involve an outflow of economic benefit.

Recognition The elements of financial statements are recognised when they can be measured reliably and it is probable that any future economic benefit associated with them will flow either to or from the entity.

Reducing-balance Method A method of depreciation used when the value of the asset derived in the earlier periods of ownership is greater than in later periods. This method allocates progressively smaller amounts of the depreciable amount to the SOPL/SPLOCI in each reporting period. The depreciation rate used under this method results in the carrying amount of the asset equalling its residual value at the end of its useful life.

Reimbursement When an entity can claim some of the costs under a provision from another party this is known as 'reimbursement', e.g. where the entity is being sued by a supplier and some of the money to be paid in settlement of the claim can be recovered from the entity's insurer.

Reporting Date The last day of the reporting period, i.e. the date at which the SOFP is prepared, which is clearly identified in the title of the SOFP.

Reporting Period The period of time to which the SOPL/SPLOCI and the SOCF relate, which is clearly identified in the title of the financial statement and is usually one year.

Residual Value The amount an asset is expected to be worth at the end of its useful life.

Retained Earnings The accumulated profits/losses made by an entity after distributions have been made.

Returns Inwards Goods returned by customers to the entity for any of a number of reasons, e.g. faulty goods.

Returns Outwards Goods returned by the entity to a supplier for any of a number of reasons, e.g. faulty goods.

Revaluation Model An accounting policy choice under IAS 16 *Property, Plant and Equipment*. Under the revaluation model assets are fair-valued regularly to ensure that the valuation is kept up to date. The asset is depreciated annually and presented is the statement of financial position at its revalued amount net of the accumulated depreciation and any accumulated impairment loss. See also **cost model**.

Shareholders Owners of shares in a company.

Sole Trader A business owned by a single individual and operated to generate a profit. The business is run by the owner, and the owner is liable for the debts of the business.

Specific Provision (for bad debts) A specific provision for bad debts is created when an entity is concerned that a particular customer may be unable to pay the balance due on their account in full.

Statement of Cash Flows The SOCF details the cash inflows and the cash outflows from operating, investing and financing activities. The SOCF is prepared on the cash basis.

Statement of Financial Position The SOFP details the balances on the asset, liability, and equity accounts of an entity at a particular point in time.

Statement of Profit or Loss The SOPL presents the profit or loss for the reporting period. The profit or loss is based on the difference between the income earned and the expenses incurred for the reporting period.

Straight-line Method A method of depreciation used when the value of the asset derived is similar from one reporting period to the next. This method allocates a portion of the depreciable amount to the SOPL/SPLOCI on an equal basis over time. The depreciation rate used under this method results in the carrying amount of the asset equalling its residual value at the end of its useful life.

Supplier A provider of goods or services.

Suspense Account A suspense account is used when a journal entry is posted that does not balance, or if the appropriate accounts to be posted with a journal entry are not known.

Total Wages (expense/cost) The total wages expense/cost is the gross pay of employees plus the employer's PRSI contributions/NIC.

Trade Discount A reduction in price provided to some customers based on the type of businesses they operate.

Trade Payables (amount owed to) The amount owed to all suppliers from whom goods or services were purchased on credit.

Trade Receivables (amount owed by) The amount owed by all customers to whom goods or services were provided on credit.

Undercasting Occurs when a group of figures is totalled incorrectly and the incorrect total is less than the correct total.

Unpresented Cheques Cheques issued by an entity (recorded in its financial records) that have not yet been presented for payment at the bank.

Useful Life The useful life of an item of property, plant and equipment is the period of time over which the entity expects to use the asset.

Index